Principles of auditing

FIRST CANADIAN EDITION

Principles of auditing

WALTER B. MEIGS, Ph.D., C.P.A.

Professor of Accounting
University of Southern California

E. JOHN LARSEN, D.B.A., C.P.A.

Associate Professor of Accounting
University of Southern California

ROBERT F. MEIGS, D.B.A.

Associate Professor of Accounting
San Diego State University

WAI P. LAM, Ph.D., C.A.

Professor of Accounting
University of Windsor

 1978
Irwin-Dorsey Limited
Georgetown, Ontario   L7G 4B3

ISBN 0-256-02092-2

Printed in the United States of America

3 4 5 6 7 8 9 0 A 5 4 3 2 1 0

Preface

This first Canadian edition of *Principles of Auditing* reflects the current environment in which the profession of public accounting operates. It incorporates the most recent legal and professional requirements that affect independent auditors, including provisions of the Canada Business Corporations Act and pronouncements of the Auditing Standards Committee of the Canadian Institute of Chartered Accountants. In addition, developments in the United States that are relevant to the Canadian auditing environment are presented.

The goal of this book is to emphasize concepts which enable the student to understand the philosophy and environment of auditing. Thus, the first ten chapters provide a sweeping overview of the public accounting profession, with special attention to auditing standards, professional ethics, the legal responsibility and liability inherent in the attest function, the study and evaluation of internal control, the nature of evidence, the growing use of statistical sampling, the impact of electronic data processing, and the basic approach to planning an audit.

In addition to this conceptual approach to the work of the auditor, this edition presents auditing practices and techniques in an organized and understandable manner.

At the end of each chapter is a list of key terms introduced in that chapter, with concise definitions for these terms. The objective is to enable students to use auditing terminology with judgment and precision.

Questions, problems, and case studies

The questions, problems, and case materials at the end of each chapter are divided as follows: Group I—Review questions; Group II—Questions requiring analysis; Group III—Problems; Group IV—Case studies in auditing.

In addition, a comprehensive case, which covers a number of issues in auditing, is included at the end of this text.

The review questions are closely related to the material in the chapter and provide a convenient means of determining whether the student has grasped the major ideas and implications contained in that chapter.

The questions requiring analysis call for a thoughtful appraisal of realistic auditing situations and the application of generally accepted auditing standards. Many of these Group II questions are taken from CA and CPA examinations, others from actual audit engagements. These thought-provoking questions requiring analysis differ from the Group III problems in that they are generally shorter and tend to stress value judgments and conflicting opinions.

Most of the Group III problems have been drawn from CA and CPA examinations. In the selection of these problems consideration was given to all auditing problems which have appeared in the CA and CPA examinations for the past 10 to 15 years, with more emphasis on the most recent examinations. Other problems reflect actual audit situations experienced by practicing accountants.

There are eight case studies in the text. The first seven appear at the end of the following chapters: Chapter 9, Audit working papers, quality control for audits; Chapter 11, Cash; Chapter 13, Accounts and notes receivable and sales transactions; Chapter 14, Inventories and cost of goods sold; Chapter 17, Interest-bearing debt and interest expense; Chapter 18, Owners' equity; and Chapter 19, Further verification of revenue and expenses. These seven cases present specific issues covered in these chapters and they also place these issues in proper perspective in relation to the entire examination and to the issuance of an audit report. The eighth case, included at the end of the text, is a comprehensive case adapted from a CICA Uniform Final Examination. This comprehensive case covers accounting as well as auditing issues and requires the student to exercise professional judgment in the appropriate application of generally accepted accounting principles and auditing standards in a realistic situation.

Case studies in auditing

The use of the case studies at strategic intervals and at the end of this text is usually one of the highlights of an auditing course. The case studies in auditing are a means of viewing audit engagements through the eyes of a partner in a public accounting firm and also from the viewpoint of the client. Students enjoy the cases thoroughly because of the lively class discussions they produce and the arguments of opposing views. In preparing and discussing these cases the student must identify the important issues, weigh the opposing arguments, and then reach a logical conclusion. Class discussions in which each student evaluates the arguments of others and participates in reaching a common ground of agreement can bring an auditing course closer to the realities of the professional practice of the public accountant.

References to authoritative sources

Numerous references are made to the pronouncements and other published materials of the Canadian Institute of Chartered Accountants, the Institute of Chartered Accountants of Ontario, the American Institute of Certified Public Accountants, the Financial Accounting Standards Board, and the United States Securities and Exchange Commission. The cooperation of the Canadian Institute of Chartered Accountants, the Institute of Chartered Accountants of Ontario, and the American Institute of Certified Public Accountants in permitting the use of their published materials and of the questions from the CICA Uniform Final Examinations and the Uniform CPA Examinations brings to this text an element of authority not otherwise available.

ACKNOWLEDGEMENTS

I am indebted to a number of my colleagues who have contributed to the successful completion of this edition. Special thanks are due to David T. Carter of the University of Windsor and John A. Edds of Brock University for their able and thorough reviews of this edition. In addition, I would like to express my sincere appreciation to D. Ross Johnston, University of Windsor, and Don J. Johnston, McMaster University, for their advice and encouragement at the early stage of this endeavour.

February 1978   Wai P. Lam

Contents

Financial reporting—an essential in achieving social and economic goals. The attest function. Credibility—the contribution of the independent auditor to financial reporting. What is an audit? Unaudited financial statements—the credibility gap. Auditing—then and now. Determining fairness of financial statements—a major auditing objective. The growing problem of management fraud. The demand for more disclosure. Development of sampling techniques. Internal control as a basis for testing and sampling. The advent of electronic data processing. Major auditing developments of the 20th century. The accounting profession. Public accountancy. The Canadian Institute of Chartered Accountants and provincial Institutes of Chartered Accountants. The chartered accountant—professional requirements and career opportunities. The *CICA Handbook*. Provincial securities acts and securities commissions. Public accountancy and the certified public accountant in the United States. American Institute of Certified Public Accountants. Financial Accounting Standards Board. U.S. Securities and Exchange Commission. The audit report. The long-form report. Importance of the auditors' report. Auditors' reports and clients' financial statements. Auditing standards. Application of auditing standards. Training and proficiency. An objective state of mind or independence—the most important consideration. Auditing standards contrasted with auditing procedures. Audit procedures not determined by the client. The opinion paragraph of the auditors' report. The financial statements "present fairly . . . ." Adequate informative disclosure. Materiality. Generally accepted accounting principles. Consistency. Other types of auditors' reports. Extensions of the auditors' attest function. Key terms introduced or emphasized in Chapter 1.

by the auditors upon internal control. Scope of the auditors' investigation of internal control. Review and description of internal control. Compliance tests of internal control. Evaluation of internal control. Preparation of an "internal control letter." Electronic data processing—effect upon internal control. Internal control in the small company.

Nature of an electronic data processing system. Internal control in the electronic data processing system. Organizational controls in an electronic data processing system. Documentation. Equipment controls. Security for files and equipment. Controls over input. Control over processing. Controls over output. Internal auditing and EDP. Impact of EDP on the audit trail. Implications of online, real-time systems. The auditors' study and evaluation of internal control in an EDP system. Review of internal control. Tests of compliance. Evaluation of internal control. Computer service centres. Time-sharing systems. Auditing EDP systems—a look at the future.

Auditors' opinion on evidence. Auditing procedures—a means of gathering evidence. Evidence needed for material items. Sufficient appropriate audit evidence. Types of audit evidence. The cost of obtaining evidence. Relative risk. Evidence provided by subsequent events. Footnote disclosure of subsequent events. The auditors' responsibility for subsequent events. The auditors' subsequent discovery of facts existing at the date of their report. Evidence for related party transactions.

Comparison of statistical with judgmental sampling. Random selection. Random number tables. Random number generators. Systematic selection. Cluster selection. Judgment block samples. Statistical measurement. Occurrence rate. Precision. Confidence level (reliability). Sample size. Estimation sampling for attributes. Illustration of estimation sampling for attributes. Discovery sampling. Sampling for variables. Estimation sampling for variables. Theory of estimation sampling for variables. Determination of sample size. Illustration of estimation sampling for variables. Ratio and difference estimation. Illustration of ratio and difference estimation. Stratification. Measurement of the auditor's risk. Key terms introduced or emphasized in Chapter 8.

AUDIT WORKING PAPERS: Definition of working papers. Confidential nature of working papers. Purposes of audit working papers. Working papers and auditing standards. Working papers and accountants' liability. Essentials of good working papers. Types of working papers. Adjusting

tests. OTHER INVESTMENTS: Balance sheet preparation of other investments. Key terms introduced or emphasized in Chapter 12.

and the computer. Audit working papers for accounts payable. AUDIT PROGRAM FOR ACCOUNTS PAYABLE: A. Study and evaluation of internal control for accounts payable. B. Substantive tests of accounts payable transactions and balances. A. Study and evaluation. B. Substantive tests. OTHER LIABILITIES: Amounts withheld from employees' pay. Sales taxes payable. Unclaimed wages. Customers' deposits. Liabilities for fines or other penalties. Accrued liabilities. Pension plan accruals. Balance sheet presentation. Time of examination. Key terms introduced or emphasized in Chapter 16.

The auditors' objectives in examination of interest-bearing debt. Internal control over interest-bearing debt. Audit working papers for interest-bearing debt. AUDIT PROGRAM FOR INTEREST-BEARING DEBT: Time of examination. DISCLOSURE OF CONTINGENCIES: Commitments. General risk contingencies. General audit procedures. Liability representations. Financial statement presentation. Key terms introduced or emphasized in Chapter 17.

The auditors' objectives in examination of owners' equity. Internal control for owners' equity. Control of capital stock transactions by board of directors. Independent registrar and stock transfer agent. The stock certificate book. The shareholders' ledger. Internal control over contributed surplus and retained earnings. Internal control over dividends. Audit working papers for owners' equity. AUDIT PROGRAM—CAPITAL STOCK: Audit procedures—contributed surplus. AUDIT PROGRAM—RETAINED EARNINGS AND DIVIDENDS: Donated capital. Time of examination. FINANCIAL STATEMENT PRESENTATION: Capital stock. Treasury stock. Retained earnings. AUDIT OF SOLE PROPRIETORSHIPS AND PARTNERSHIPS. Key terms introduced or emphasized in Chapter 18.

The auditors' approach to verification of income. Audit by comparison. Conservatism in the measurement of income. Time of examination. REVENUE: Audit objectives. Relationship of revenue to balance sheet accounts. Miscellaneous revenue. EXPENSES: Audit objectives. Relationship of expenses to balance sheet accounts. The forecast—a vital element in controlling costs and expenses. Payrolls. Internal control. Methods of achieving internal control. The employment function. Timekeeping. Payroll records and payroll preparation. Distributing paycheques or cash to employees. Description of internal control for payroll. AUDIT PROGRAM FOR PAYROLLS. AUDIT PROGRAM FOR SELLING, GENERAL, AND ADMINISTRATIVE EXPENSES. INCOME STATEMENT PRESENTATION: How much detail in the income statement? Extraordinary items. Cumulative effects of changes in accounting principle. Reporting earnings per share. Reporting by diversified companies. Key terms introduced or emphasized in Chapter 19.

20. Audit reports   753

Financial statements. Notes to financial statements. The standard audit report. Restatement of basic points concern'ng the standard report. Expression of an opinion by the auditors. Negative assurances clause in audit report. Piecemeal opinions. Comparative financial statements in audit reports. Dating the audit report; dual dating. Auditors' responsibility for other data in the annual report. Long-form audit reports. Reports to the SEC in the United States. Reporting on audits of unincorporated businesses. Reporting on audits of personal financial statements. OTHER REPORTS BY AUDITORS: Disclaimers on unaudited financial statements. Reports on unaudited quarterly financial data in the United States. Reports governed by accounting and auditing guidelines. Comfort letters to securities commissions and underwriters. Reports to regulatory agencies on internal control. Special reports. Reports on cash basis statements. Reports on not-for-profit organizations. Key terms introduced or emphasized in Chapter 20.

D Enterprises Limited: Comprehensive case   809

Nature of engagement. APPENDIX I: Description of companies. APPENDIX II: Purchase and Sale Agreement. APPENDIX III: Report of Purchinvest & Co. APPENDIX IV: Former business practices and transactions. APPENDIX V: Review by CA's staff. APPENDIX VI. APPENDIX VII.

Index   825

1

The role of the auditor
in the economy

Financial reporting—an essential in achieving social and economic goals

In our complex, highly industrialized society, the communication of financial and other economic data is vitally important. Our economy is characterized by large corporate organizations which have gathered capital from millions of investors and which control economic resources spread throughout the country or even throughout the world. Top management in the corporate headquarters is remote from the operations of company plants and branches and must rely on financial reports and other communications of economic data to control its far-flung resources. The millions of individuals who have entrusted their savings to corporations by investing in securities rely upon annual and quarterly financial statements for assurance that their invested funds are being used honestly and efficiently.

Although millions of individuals invest directly in corporate securities, even greater numbers of people entrust their savings to banks, insurance companies, and pension funds. These financial institutions, in turn, invest the money in corporate securities. Thus, directly or indirectly, almost everyone has a financial stake in corporate enterprise, and the public interest demands prompt, *dependable* financial reporting on the operations and financial health of publicly owned corporations.

The need for honest, candid public disclosure exists for federal, provincial, and city governments as well as for business entities. The federal government expends an increasing share of the gross national product and, in so doing, relies upon the communication of financial data to assure

1

that the costs it incurs are reasonable, regardless of whether the project involves energy exploration, a mass transit system, or foreign aid. The financial problems in large city governments in recent years are a further reminder that all large organizations must be held accountable for proper management of resources entrusted to them if they are to carry out the responsibilities with which they are charged.

The importance of dependable financial reporting applies to the revenue of federal, provincial, and local governments as well as to their expenditures. The revenue of federal and provincial governments is derived in large part from income taxes based on the reported incomes of individuals and corporations. Thus the financial support of the government rests on the measurement and communication of information concerning taxable income.

Sound accounting and financial reporting aid society in allocating its resources in the most efficient manner. The goal is to allocate our limited capital resources to the production of those goods and services for which demand is greatest. Economic resources tend to be attracted to the industries, areas, and organizational entities which are shown by accounting measurements to be capable of using more resources to the best advantage. Inadequate accounting and inaccurate reporting, on the other hand, conceal waste and inefficiency and thereby prevent our economic resources from being allocated in a rational manner.

Finally, most of our national policies, such as developing energy sources, controlling inflation, combating pollution, increasing employment, and maintaining a satisfactory balance of payments, rely directly on quantitative measurement of economic activity and the communication of these data. Appropriate accounting standards and reliable financial reporting are key factors in the pursuit of our economic and social goals.

What we have said thus far clearly indicates the importance of sound financial reporting to the very existence of our society. Implicit in this line of reasoning is recognition of the social need for independent auditors —individuals of professional competence and integrity who can tell us whether the financial reports being provided to the public by corporations and by governmental units constitute a fair and complete picture of what actually occurs.

The attest function

The principal reason for the existence of a public accounting profession is to perform the attest function. To *attest* to financial statements means to assume responsibility for their fairness and dependability. The attest function includes two distinct steps or stages. First, the independent public accountants must carry out an examination (or audit); this examination provides the objective evidence that enables the auditors to express an informed opinion on the financial statements. The second stage of the attest function is the issuance of the auditors' report which conveys to users of the financial statements the auditors' opinion (and reservations, if any) as to the fairness and dependability of the financial statements.

It may be helpful to pose the question: Who is qualified to perform the attest function? As a brief answer, we can say that the persons who attest to financial statements must be both technically competent to conduct an audit and independent of the company being audited, so that the public will have confidence in their credibility, objectivity, and impartiality. One reason for retaining a firm of independent public accountants to attest to financial statements is the conflict of interest which may exist between the company preparing the financial statements and those persons who use them. The users of financial statements whose interests may conflict with those of the reporting entity include bankers, creditors, shareholders, and government agencies.

In performing the attest function, the independent auditors examine the financial statements prepared by the management of the client company to determine whether these statements have been prepared in conformity with generally accepted accounting principles. In the process of studying the system of internal control for processing the information contained in the financial statements and examining the underlying transactions, the auditors must work in accordance with established professional standards.

Regular audits by independent public accountants offer the most important kind of protection to the public. Although every investment involves some degree of risk, investors will incur unnecessary risks if they invest in companies which do not have regular audits of their financial statements by independent public accountants.

Recognition of the responsibility of independent accountants to third parties led to the organization in Scotland and England more than a century ago of Institutes of Chartered Accountants. The technical competence of persons desiring to become chartered accountants was tested by examinations. Independence, integrity, and professional responsibility were recognized as qualities quite as important in chartered accountants as technical skill. Through the Institutes of Chartered Accountants, ethical principles were evolved to encourage auditors to follow professional standards in performing the attest function of auditing. In Canada, the Canadian and provincial Institutes of Chartered Accountants have played a similar role in establishing professional standards for its members.

Credibility—the contribution of the independent auditor to financial reporting

The contribution of the independent auditor is to give credibility to financial statements. Credibility, in this usage, means that the financial statements can be believed; that is, they can be relied upon by outsiders, such as creditors, shareholders, government, and other interested third parties.

Both the day-to-day operation of our economy and its long-run success are highly dependent on communication of financial data. How then do we gain assurance that the data being reported are properly measured and fairly presented? A major share of the answer lies in the audits performed by independent public accountants. *Audited* financial statements are now the accepted means by which business corporations report to their shareholders, to bankers, to creditors, and to government. In fact, many corporations are required by law to have their financial statements audited by an independent qualified party. The word "audited" when applied to financial statements means that the balance sheet, statements of income and retained earnings, and statement of changes in financial position are accompanied by an audit report prepared by independent public accountants, expressing their professional opinion as to the fairness of the company's financial statements.

What is an audit?

An audit is an examination of a company's financial statements by a firm of independent public accountants. The audit consists of a searching investigation of the accounting records and other evidence supporting those financial statements. Through the study and evaluation of the company's system of internal control, and by inspection of documents, observation of assets, making of enquiries within and outside the company, and by other auditing procedures, the auditors will gather the evidence necessary to determine whether the financial statements provide a fair and reasonably complete picture of the company's financial position and its activities during the period being audited.

The following definition of an audit appears in *Terminology for Accountants:*

> In connection with financial statements, [an audit is] an examination of the accounting records and other supporting evidence of an organization for the purpose of expressing an opinion as to whether financial statements of the organization present fairly its position as at a given date and the results of its operations for the period ended on that date in accordance with generally accepted accounting principles.[1]

The examination conducted by the independent auditors provides the basis for the audit report. *Never do auditors express an opinion on the fairness of financial statements without first performing an audit.* Personal experience with the business, audits made in prior years, belief in

---

[1] The Canadian Institute of Chartered Accountants, *Terminology for Accountants,* rev. ed. (Toronto, 1976), p. 10.

the integrity of the owners and managers—none of these factors is sufficient to warrant an expression of opinion on the financial statements by the independent public accountants. Either they make an audit of the current year's financial statements or they do not. If they do not perform an audit, they do not express an opinion on the fairness of the financial statements.

The evidence gathered by the auditors during an examination will prove that the assets listed in the balance sheet actually exist, that the company has title to these assets, and that the valuations assigned to these assets have been established in conformity with generally accepted accounting principles. Evidence will be gathered to show that the balance sheet contains *all the liabilities* of the company; otherwise the balance sheet might be grossly misleading because certain important liabilities had been deliberately or accidentally omitted. Similarly, the auditors will gather evidence about the income statement. They will demand proof that the reported sales actually occurred, the goods were actually shipped to customers, the recorded costs and expenses are applicable to the current period, and all expenses have been recognized.

The audit procedures comprising an examination vary considerably from one engagement to the next. Many of the procedures appropriate to the audit of a small retail store would not be appropriate for the audit of a giant manufacturing corporation. Auditors make examinations of all types of business enterprise, and of not-for-profit organizations as well. Banks and breweries, factories and stores, colleges and churches, air lines and labour unions—all of these are regularly visited by auditors. The selection of the audit procedures best suited to each engagement requires the exercise of professional skill and judgment.

Unaudited financial statements—the credibility gap

Financial statements prepared by management and transmitted to outsiders without first being audited by independent accountants leave a credibility gap. In reporting on its own administration of the business, management can hardly be expected to be entirely impartial and unbiased, any more than a football coach could be expected to serve as both coach and official referee in the same game.

Unaudited financial statements are not acceptable to absentee owners or other outsiders for several reasons. The financial statements may have been honestly but carelessly prepared. Liabilities may have been overlooked and omitted from the balance sheet. Assets may have been overstated as a result of arithmetical errors or through violation of generally accepted accounting principles. Net income may have been exaggerated because revenue expenditures were capitalized or because sales transactions were recorded in advance of delivery dates.

Finally, there is the possibility that unaudited financial statements have been deliberately falsified in order to conceal theft and fraud, or as a means of inducing the reader to invest in the business or to extend credit. Although deliberate falsification in financial statements is not common, it has occurred and has caused disastrous losses to persons who relied upon such misleading statements.

For all these reasons (accidental errors, deviation from accounting principles, unintentional bias, and deliberate falsification) unaudited annual financial statements are not acceptable in the business community.

Auditing—then and now

Although the objectives and concepts which guide present-day audits were almost unknown in the early years of the 20th century, audits of one type or another have been made throughout the recorded history of commerce and of government finance. The original meaning of the word "auditor" was "one who hears," and was appropriate to the era when governmental accounting records were approved only after a public hearing in which the accounts were read aloud. From medieval times through the Industrial Revolution, audits were made to determine whether persons in positions of fiscal responsibility in government and commerce were acting and reporting in an honest manner. During the Industrial Revolution, as manufacturing concerns grew in size, their owners began to use the services of hired managers. With this separation of the ownership and management groups, the absentee owners turned increasingly to auditors to protect themselves against the danger of fraud by both managers and employees. Prior to 1900 auditing was concerned principally with the detection of fraud. In the first half of the 20th century the direction of audit work generally tended to move away from fraud detection toward the new goal of determining whether financial statements give a fair picture of financial position, operating results, and changes in financial position. This shift in emphasis was a response to the needs of the millions of new investors in corporate securities.

In the last ten years or so, however, the detection of large-scale management fraud has assumed a larger role in audit philosophy. This latest shift in emphasis is a result of the dramatic increase in the number of lawsuits charging that management fraud has gone undetected by independent auditors. This issue is considered more fully later in this chapter.

Determining fairness of financial statements— a major auditing objective

In 1900 auditing work was concentrated on the balance sheet; in fact most companies at that time regarded the income statement as confidential information not to be made available to outsiders. The principal distribution of audited financial data outside the company was to bankers from whom loans were being requested. These bankers were interested in the balance sheet rather than the income statement, and they were strongly in favour of a conservative valuation of assets. In brief, they wanted assurance of debt-paying ability before they granted a loan. The independent public accountants of this era were much influenced by the attitudes of bankers who were the major users of audited financial statements. Today, corporate income statements audited by independent public accountants are eagerly awaited by the public and by government as a most significant measure of business trends. The income statement has become the dominant financial statement.

After 1900 the auditor's role as a detective was gradually pushed into the background. The principal objective of auditing changed from fraud detection to determining the *fairness* with which the financial statements presented financial position and operating results. The advent of federal income taxes added another dimension to the auditor's work; it involved not only the preparation of tax returns but also a new emphasis upon the government's interest in the fairness of reported income.

The growing problem of management fraud

We have stressed that the purpose of most audits is the expression of an expert opinion on the fairness of financial statements. The normal audit is not designed to detect small scattered instances of theft, embezzlement, or other dishonest acts. Such small localized cases of fraud will not have a material effect on the overall fairness of the financial statements. In recent years, however, investors have been deceived by a few gigantic frauds including falsified financial statements, as in the widely publicized *Atlantic Acceptance* case in Canada and *Equity Funding* case in the United States. In considering the responsibility of auditors for detection of fraud, it is helpful to distinguish non-management fraud from management fraud. Non-management fraud consists of dishonest actions that occur within a company despite management's efforts to prevent such actions. Protection against non-management fraud is provided by a strong system of internal control, as discussed in Chapter 5. The independent auditors' contribution in preventing non-management fraud is to study and evaluate the system of internal control and to make recommendations for improvement in internal control.

Management fraud occurs only when the top executives of a company deliberately deceive shareholders, creditors, and independent auditors. The purpose of management fraud is generally to issue misleading financial statements which exaggerate corporate earnings and financial strength. Such overstatements of operating results and financial position may enable the management of the company to obtain increased salaries and bonuses, or to benefit from stock options and from higher market prices for their holdings of the company's securities. The theft of assets may also be involved.

Management fraud cases such as **Atlantic Acceptance** and **Equity Funding** have appeared in newspaper headlines for months at a time and perhaps have led some persons to believe that every spectacular business failure involves fraud. Business failures may be caused by depressed economic conditions, inflation, labour strife, errors in judgment by management, and by many other causes not involving fraud. Audits by independent public accountants cannot prevent all business failures or protect investors against all risk of loss.

The independent auditors should be alert for any clues which suggest the existence of management fraud. When a business organization is dominated by one person or by very few persons, when the accounting group lacks sufficient competent people and falls behind in its work, when internal controls are weak, when important transactions occur between the company and its officers, and when the board of directors is not active and involved, the danger of management fraud is greatly increased. In these situations the independent auditors should recognize that an environment conducive to fraud exists, and they should be particularly alert. More extensive audit work than normally required may be advisable.

If management fraud is so material as to make the financial statements misleading, the independent auditors cannot avoid responsibility. Although the normal audit is not designed to detect fraud, the auditors do accept responsibility for the fairness of audited financial statements. Before issuing an audit report the auditors should do everything necessary to be reasonably satisfied that the financial statements are not materially in error for *any reason*, including possible management fraud.

The demand for more disclosure

Corporations which offer their securities for sale to the public are obligated to make public all material information about their financial affairs. The disclosure system which has evolved in Canada is intended to develop an efficient market by making available promptly to all investors all material information concerning companies whose shares are publicly bought and sold.

Prompt disclosure is necessary for both favourable and unfavourable developments. Any failure to make disclosure in a timely, complete, and accurate manner makes possible the abuse of information by insiders and lessens the efficiency of the market place. Occasionally, a corporation may be placed at a business disadvantage by making disclosure. However, it may be argued that such disadvantage is a necessary consequence of the decision to become a publicly owned company.

The question of whether or not disclosure should be made of confidential information which could be quite harmful to a company, its employees, and shareholders is presently receiving a great deal of study. Current demands for more and more disclosure of corporate actions appear to call upon independent auditors to disclose any business actions which may violate moral standards. If such trends prevail, the public accounting profession will face a difficult new challenge in defining its responsibilities. The disclosure issue has been particularly critical when auditors have discovered that some multinational companies have made political contributions or paid bribes in other countries in which such payments were considered customary practice. Also, disclosure of unfavourable news may in some cases force a company into insolvency.

Development of sampling techniques

In the early days of the auditing profession, a normal audit was one which included a *complete review of all transactions.* However, about 1900, as large-scale business enterprise developed, auditors adopted a *sampling technique.* This new auditing technique transformed the audit process from one of verifying all transactions to making tests of selected transactions. Auditors and business managers gradually came to accept the proposition that careful examination of relatively few transactions selected at random would give a reliable indication of the accuracy of other similar transactions.

Internal control as a basis for testing and sampling

As auditors gained experience with the technique of sampling, they became aware of the importance of the system of internal control. The meaning of internal control and the methods by which auditors evaluate the system of internal control are thoroughly explored in Chapter 5 and illustrated throughout this book. At this point a concise definition will serve to explain why good internal control makes it possible for auditors to rely greatly upon sampling techniques. A system of internal control consists of all measures used by a business for the purposes of (1) safeguarding its resources against waste, fraud, and inefficiency; (2) promoting accuracy and reliability in accounting and operating data; (3) encouraging and measuring compliance with company policy; and (4) judging the efficiency of operations in all divisions of the business.

One example of internal control is an organization plan which separates the custody of assets from the function of record keeping. Thus, a person handling cash should not also maintain accounting records. Another example is the subdivision of duties so that no one person handles a transaction in its entirety, and the work of one employee serves to prove the accuracy of the work of another.

Evaluation of internal control became recognized as a prerequisite to successful use of sampling techniques. Auditors found that by studying the client's accounting system, and by considering the flow of accounting work and the methods provided for automatic proof of recorded data, they could determine the extent and direction of the tests needed for a satisfactory audit of the financial statements. *The stronger the system of internal control, the less testing required by the auditors.* For any section of the accounts or any phase of financial operations in which controls were weak, the auditors learned that they must expand the scope and intensity of their tests.

The advent of electronic data processing

As more and more business concerns have developed electronic data processing systems, dramatic changes have taken place in the form and nature of accounting records and in the "information system" as a whole. One of the challenging tasks confronting auditors in recent years has been to modify auditing procedures to fit the computer age. The accounting data which auditors wish to verify may, for example, be stored on magnetic tape rather than in loose-leaf ledgers. The auditors must, therefore, be familiar with electronic data processing systems and their impact upon internal controls and the information system; they must also be competent to use the computer as a tool for performing audit functions.

Major auditing developments of the 20th century

Many of the ideas mentioned in this brief historical sketch of the development of auditing will be analyzed in detail in later sections of this book. Our purpose at this point is merely to orient ourselves with a quick overall look at some of the major auditing developments of the 20th century:

1. A shift in emphasis to the determination of fairness in financial statements.
2. Increased responsibility of the auditor to "third parties," such as governmental agencies, stock exchanges, and an investing public.
3. The change of auditing method from detailed examination of individual transactions to use of sampling techniques, including statistical sampling.
4. Recognition of the need to evaluate the system of internal control as a guide to the direction and amount of testing and sampling to be performed.
5. Development of new auditing procedures applicable to electronic data processing systems, and use of the computer as an auditing tool.
6. Recognition of the need for auditors to find means of protecting

themselves from the current wave of litigation and to cope with the increase in management fraud.

7. An increased demand for prompt disclosure of both favourable and unfavourable information concerning any publicly owned company.

The accounting profession

There are a number of professional accounting organizations in Canada which provide education and training leading to a certificate in accountancy. Notably, these are the provincial Institutes of Chartered Accountants,[2] Societies of Management Accountants (formerly, the Societies of Industrial Accountants), and Certified General Accountants' Associations. The national organizations of these three accounting bodies are the Canadian Institute of Chartered Accountants, the Society of Management Accountants of Canada, and the Canadian Certified General Accountants' Association. Members of these organizations receive their respective professional designations as chartered accountants (CAs), registered industrial accountants (RIAs), and certified general accountants (CGAs). The education, training, and examination requirements vary considerably among the three professional organizations. Also, the Institutes of Chartered Accountants place more emphasis on public accountancy, the Societies of Management Accountants are primarily interested in management accounting, and the Certified General Accountants' Associations may be considered as interested in management accounting as well as public accountancy.

Public accountancy

The right to practise public accountancy is governed by the various provincial Public Accountancy Acts. Only those persons who have met the acts' requirements are granted a license to practise public accountancy. While the specific requirements of the various acts differ from province to province, all give chartered accountants the automatic privilege to practise public accountancy. Of course, not all chartered accountants are engaged in public accountancy, but about half of them are. In addition, many certified general accountants are engaged in public accountancy, and the province of British Columbia gives them the same privilege as chartered accountants.

Why should the provinces license public accountants? The various

---

[2] The provincial organization of chartered accountants in Quebec is called "Order of Chartered Accountants of Quebec." For the sake of simplicity, the term "Institute" is used to include the Quebec organization. Also, the term "provincial institutes" is used to include the Bermuda Institute and the recently created Yukon Territory Institute.

governments assume that the public interest will be protected by an official identification of competent professional accountants who offer their services to the public. It is the opinion of an independent public accountant concerning the fairness of financial statements that causes them to be generally accepted by bankers, investors, government agencies, and the general public. To sustain such confidence, the independent public accountant must be a professional person of the highest integrity.

The Canadian Institute of Chartered Accountants and provincial Institutes of Chartered Accountants

The history of the accounting profession in Canada stems from Scottish and English practices. In the early 1880s, two accounting organizations were formally established—the Association of Accountants in Montreal in 1880 and the Institute of Chartered Accountants of Ontario in 1883. As other provincial accounting organizations were formed, there was a need to coordinate activities, strengthen relationships, and promote common standards of education, training, and admission qualifications. Consequently, a national organization, the Dominion Association of Chartered Accountants, was formed in 1902; and in 1949 its name was changed to The Canadian Institute of Chartered Accountants (CICA).

The CICA is governed by a 23-member board of governors, and its affairs are administered by the executive officers elected by the board. Its organization reflects the federalism of Canada. Thus, members of the various provincial institutes automatically become members of the national Institute. While its primary objective is to promote and maintain high professional standards, the CICA "serves not only the accounting profession at the national and international level, but provides significant input to the public and private sectors throughout Canada in respect to business practices and government legislation."[3]

Through its *Handbook,* research studies, various publications, and its concern and involvement with national standards of education, recruitment, and business practices, the CICA performs a wide range of activities and carries out a variety of functions. All of these are designed to assist its members to better serve their clients or employers and to secure and enhance a uniform high level of competence throughout the profession. Moreover, a *Uniform Code of Ethics* has been adopted by the CICA for the guidance of its members and students in their professional work and activities. In addition, each provincial institute has its own *Code of Ethics* or *Rules of Professional Conduct.*

The provincial institutes are responsible for the educational, training,

---

[3] The Canadian Institute of Chartered Accountants, *CICA Handbook* (Toronto), p. 3.

and examination requirements for their students as well as the maintenance of high standards of performance for members as set forth in their *Codes of Ethics* or *Rules of Professional Conduct,* which are similar to the CICA *Uniform Code of Ethics.* The affairs of each provincial institute are managed and conducted by a council, whose members are elected annually by the members of the institute.

Although the profession of public accountancy is not quite a century old in Canada, it is one of the fastest growing. Membership in the CICA has more than doubled in the past decade and is now more than 26,000. Despite this tremendous growth, the demand for the services of CAs appears to be growing even faster.

The chartered accountant—professional requirements and career opportunities

Specific requirements as to education and public accounting experience differ somewhat among the provinces. Generally, a university degree, a minimum of one to two years' practical training in public accounting, and certain additional education and examination requirements at the provincial level are required before a student is eligible to write the national uniform final examination.[4] A candidate for a CA certificate usually must have a minimum of two years of public accounting experience and pass the national uniform final examination. This latter consists of four papers, each about four hours in duration. The examination is given once a year and covers a wide range of topics in the areas of accounting, finance, taxation, and auditing, with a significant emphasis on the current literature in all these areas.

Although a majority of students-in-accounts hold business degrees, usually with a major in accounting, a significant number of students hold degrees in other disciplines, such as the arts, science, mathematics, and engineering. At present, more than 6,000 students in Canada are pursuing their certification as chartered accountants.

Once a student is admitted to the membership of a provincial institute and thus the CICA, a variety of rewarding opportunities are available. He or she may choose a career in public accounting, industry, management consulting, government, or teaching. Of course, a CA in public accounting is not limited to the performance of audits; he or she may do a substantial amount of professional work in the fields of taxation and management advisory services. Tax work includes advising clients on business policies which will hold the burden of taxation to a minimum as well as the

---

[4] For example, the province of Ontario requires all students-in-accounts to attend a four-week School of Accountancy; pass the school's examinations in accounting, auditing, and taxation; and have at least one year of public accounting experience in order to be eligible for the national uniform final examination.

actual preparation of income and other tax returns. Management advisory services include a wide range of activities, such as the design and installation of accounting systems, budgeting, and financial forecasting.

The CICA Handbook

Since its inception, the CICA has been concerned with the development of accounting and auditing practices for the enhancement of more reliable and informative financial reporting. Presently, two groups, the Accounting Research Committee and the Auditing Standards Committee, are authorized by the Institute's Board of Governors to issue recommendations in the *Handbook*. The Accounting Research Committee is responsible for the development and promulgation of accounting principles, and its recommendations are contained in the "Accounting Recommendations" section of the *Handbook*. Similarly, the Auditing Standards Committee is responsible for topics in the auditing areas, and its recommendations appear in the "Auditing Recommendations" section. These recommendations are considered as generally accepted accounting principles and auditing standards of the profession. A departure from these recommendations by any member must be justified on valid ground, and the responsibility for justification rests with the individual member. The *Handbook* states that "where the accounting treatment or statement presentation does not follow the recommendations in this Handbook, the practice used should be explained in notes to the financial statements with an indication of reasons why the recommendation concerned was not followed."[5]

The issuance of a recommendation by either committee is generally preceded by a thorough research on its conceptual validity and practicality. An exposure draft on the recommendation is then published to solicit comments and suggestions from Institute members and other interested parties. All comments and suggestions are then given serious consideration. Only after due deliberation and with the approval of at least two-thirds of the committee members will a recommendation be incorporated into the *Handbook*.

The Accounting Research Committee comprises 22 persons, with terms of office ranging from one to three years. Although committee membership includes a cross section of individuals with various backgrounds and occupations, some of whom may not be chartered accountants, at least two-thirds must be members of the Institute. The Auditing Standards Committee is smaller, having only 16 members, all of whom are Institute members and at least 10 of whom are in public accounting. The terms of office also range from one to three years. Since the subject matter of the two committees is interrelated to a large extent, their activities are coordinated by the Joint Research Steering Committee.

---

[5] CICA, *CICA Handbook*, p. 202.

Provincial securities acts and securities commissions

Although the securities acts vary somewhat from province to province, their primary objective is to ensure proper protection of the investing public and adequate financial statement disclosure. A provincial securities commission generally is charged with administering and enforcing the requirements and regulations set forth in the province's act. For example, the Securities Act of Ontario empowers its securities commission to over-see "administration, audits, investigations and appeals, registration proce-dures, prospecting syndicates, trading in securities generally, take-over bids, proxies and proxy solicitation, and insider trading."[6] The various securities acts and commissions appear to depend largely on the account-ing profession for the development of sound financial reporting. While national policy statements representing the views of the administrators of provincial securities commissions are issued from time to time, those related to financial reporting and accounting principles are primarily based on the *CICA Handbook* recommendations. For example, *National Policy Statement No. 27*, issued in December 1972 states:

> Where the term "generally accepted accounting principles" is used, either in Securities Legislations, Regulations, and Company Legislations and regulations, the Securities Administrators will regard pronouncements by the Accounting and Auditing Research Committee [subsequently changed to the Accounting Research Committee and the Auditing Standards Com-mittee] of the Canadian Institute of Chartered Accountants to the extent set out in the research recommendations in the "CICA Handbook" as "generally accepted accounting principles."

Public accountancy and the certified public accountant in the United States

The requirements for a license to practise public accountancy in the United States vary considerably from state to state. Licensing require-ments as to education and accounting experience are in general less rigorous than those needed to qualify as a certified public accountant (CPA). Some states restrict only the use of the CPA title and permit any-one to practise as a public accountant. In other states, laws have been adopted with the intent of ultimately limiting the professional practice of accounting to certified public accountants, after an initial licensing of all persons engaged in public accounting at the time the laws were enacted.

In addition to passing an examination and meeting certain educational requirements, the candidate for a CPA certificate in many states must

---

[6] *The Ontario Securities Act and Regulations—1976* (Toronto: Richard Dee Boo Limited), p. 3.

have from one to five years of public accounting experience. The requirements as to amount of education and public accounting experience differ considerably among the various states. Upon the satisfactory completion of all requirements, a CPA certificate is issued to the candidate by a state or territorial government.

American Institute of Certified Public Accountants

The AICPA is the national organization of certified public accountants engaged in promoting and maintaining high professional standards of practice in the United States. During the 85 years of its existence the Institute has contributed enormously to the evolution of generally accepted accounting principles as well as to development of auditing standards. The many technical divisions and committees of the Institute (such as the Auditing Standards Executive Committee) provide a means of focusing the collective experience and ability of the profession on current problems.

The development of a Code of Professional Ethics and the enforcement of this code represent another achievement of the AICPA. Governmental agencies such as the Securities and Exchange Commission (SEC) and the Internal Revenue Service continually seek the advice and cooperation of the Institute in improving laws and regulations relating to accounting matters.

Since its inception, the AICPA has been concerned with divergences in accounting practice which tend to reduce the comparability of financial statements. A research program designed to cope with controversial accounting issues was launched in 1938 and led to the publication of a series of 51 *Accounting Research Bulletins* and four *Accounting Terminology Bulletins* between 1939 and 1959.

The Accounting Principles Board of the AICPA was formed in 1959 to carry on a new and more ambitious program of research publication. The serially numbered *Opinions* issued by the Accounting Principles Board provide substantial authoritative support in clarifying the phrase "generally accepted accounting principles" used in the audit report. These APB *Opinions* must be followed in the preparation of financial statements, or any departures from these recommended principles must be disclosed in notes attached to the statements or in the report of the independent auditors. The Accounting Principles Board was superseded in 1973 by the Financial Accounting Standards Board, a smaller, full-time, and well-paid group.

Financial Accounting Standards Board

The Financial Accounting Standards Board is an independent private body recognized by the AICPA as the source of authoritative accounting standards for the guidance of AICPA members. The FASB has seven full-time members including representatives from public accounting, industry, government, and the field of accounting education. Aiding in the work of the FASB are an advisory council and a large research staff. Among the principal publications are *Statements on Accounting Standards,* interpretations, and exposure drafts. The use of exposure drafts as a means of securing public reaction to proposed *Statements* enables the FASB to obtain a wide range of comment and criticism before taking an official position on controversial issues. The earlier *Opinions* of the Accounting Principles Board continue in full force except when specifically modified by *FASB Statements.*

The goal of the FASB is to build public confidence in the dependability and comparability of audited financial statements. It is committed to the belief that the establishment of financial accounting standards should be a function of the private sector of the economy rather than the work of a governmental agency. Other basic assumptions are that the FASB must operate independently of the AICPA and other organizations, that it must be responsive to the needs of all sections of the economic community, not merely to professional accountants, and that it should conduct public hearings enabling all interested persons to express themselves on proposed standards. Thus the development and publication of *FASB Statements* stresses a "due process" approach designed to encourage public acceptance of its decisions.

U.S. Securities and Exchange Commission

The SEC is an independent, quasi-judicial agency of the U.S. government. It administers the Securities Act of 1933, the Securities Exchange Act of 1934, and other legislation concerning securities and financial matters. The function of the SEC is to protect the interests of investors and the public by requiring full disclosure of financial information by companies offering securities for public sale. A second objective is to prevent misrepresentation, deceit, or other fraud in the sale of securities. The "disclosure doctrine" of protecting investors was extended by the Securities Exchange Act of 1934 to all securities listed on national stock exchanges. At present all over-the-counter companies with total assets exceeding $1 million and with 500 or more shareholders are subject to the same disclosure requirements previously applicable only to companies listed on major stock exchanges.[7]

The term *registration statement* is an important one in any discussion of the impact of the SEC on accounting practice. To *register* securities means to qualify them for sale to the public by filing with the SEC

---

[7] Certain over-the-counter companies having as few as 300 shareholders may be required to file periodic reports with the SEC subsequent to registering a new securities issue with the Commission under provisions of the Securities Act of 1933.

financial statements and other data in a form acceptable to the Commission. A registration statement varies by type of company but generally calls for (a) description of the business, (b) description of the securities offered and other outstanding securities, (c) information on management, and (d) *audited financial statements,* including a balance sheet and income statements for a three-year period. The legislation creating the SEC made the Commission responsible for determining whether the financial statements presented to it reflect proper application of accounting principles. To aid the Commission in discharging this responsibility, the Securities Acts provided for an examination and report by an *independent* public accountant. Thus, from its beginning, the Securities and Exchange Commission has been a major user of audited financial statements and has exercised great influence upon the development of accounting principles, the strengthening of auditing standards, and especially upon the concept of independence.

If the SEC believes that a given registration statement does not meet its standards of disclosure, it may require amendment of the statement or may issue a stop order preventing sale of the securities. However, the fairness of the pricing of the securities or the prospects for successful operation of the business are not factors bearing on registration—the only standard to be met is that of adequate disclosure. Certain security offerings are presently exempt from the requirements of registration; these include certain offerings not in excess of $500,000, those restricted to residents of a single state, private offerings to a limited number of persons, and government securities. In appraising the impact of the SEC upon the practice of certified public accountants, it should be borne in mind that annual financial statements as well as registration statements must be filed with the Commission by all companies with securities listed on national stock exchanges.

To improve the quality of the financial statements filed with it and the professional standards of the independent accountants who report on these statements, the SEC has adopted a basic accounting regulation known as *Regulation S-X,* entitled *Form and Content of Financial Statements.* The Commission has also published, in *Accounting Series Releases,* its decisions on accounting issues presented in important cases and opinions of the Commission's Chief Accountant on many complex accounting problems. These publications, along with the studies and recommendations of professional accounting societies, have been most influential in the improvement of accounting practices and auditing standards.

The audit report

The principal purpose of most audits is to enable an independent public accountant to form an opinion as to the fairness of the client's financial statements. This opinion is given in the form of a written report, which usually consists of only two short paragraphs. The first, or "scope," paragraph is a concise statement of the scope of the examination; the second paragraph is an equally concise statement of the auditor's opinion based on this examination.

The following auditors' standard report is suggested by the CICA Auditing Standards Committee:

Auditors' Report

To the shareholders of XYZ Limited:

We have examined the balance sheet of XYZ Limited as at December 31, 19— and the statements of income, retained earnings and changes in financial position for the year then ended. Our examination was made in accordance with generally accepted auditing standards, and accordingly included such tests and other procedures as we considered necessary in the circumstances.

In our opinion, these financial statements present fairly the financial position of the company as at December 31, 19— and the results of its operations and the changes in its financial position for the year then ended in accordance with generally accepted accounting principles applied on a basis consistent with that of the preceding year.

Blue, Gray and Company

Blue, Gray and Company
Chartered Accountants

Windsor
February 26, 19—

The auditors' report is addressed to the person or persons who retained the auditors; in the case of corporations, shareholders appoint the auditors. Although the auditors are paid by the client company and address their report to the shareholders, the report is intended for use by shareholders and others such as bankers, investors, and creditors. Unless the auditors are truly independent and free from any restraint or influence by the client, their report would be of little value to these users of the company's financial statements. It is the *independent status* of the auditors which gives value and significance to the auditors' report.

The long-form report

In most audit engagements, the auditors are requested to submit only the standard report previously discussed. In other engagements, however, they will also prepare a long-form report intended for use by management and including discussion of the company's financial position and operating results, analyses and ratios, and comments on various phases of the examination.

Importance of the auditors' report

The writing of the auditors' report is the *final* step in completing an examination. Why, then, should we study the auditors' report at the *beginning* of a course in auditing? The answer is that if we appreciate the significance of the auditors' report, understand why it is prepared and how it is used as a basis for financial decisions, we are then in an excellent position to understand the purpose of the various audit procedures which comprise an examination. Every step in the auditing process is taken to enable the auditors to express an informed opinion on the fairness of the client's financial statements. Later chapters of this book present the auditors' work in verification of cash, inventories, and other financial statement topics. In these chapters students may appropriately ask themselves at each step: How does this verification work relate to the preparation of the auditors' report?

Since the auditors' report is so very briefly and concisely worded, a full understanding of its meaning requires that we consider the significance of each of the phrases included. Phrases such as "generally accepted auditing standards" and "generally accepted accounting principles" mean very different things, and a clear understanding of each is essential to an appreciation of the purpose and nature of auditing. In the following sections of this chapter we shall, therefore, give careful consideration to each of the main ideas in the auditors' standard report.

Auditors' reports and clients' financial statements

In the scope paragraph of the auditors' report, the first sentence reads: "We have examined the balance sheet of XYZ Limited as at December 31, 19— and the statements of income, retained earnings and changes in financial position for the year then ended." To gain a full understanding of this sentence we need to emphasize the following three points:

1.   *The client company is primarily responsible for the financial statements.*

The management of a company has the responsibility of maintaining adequate accounting records and of preparing proper financial statements for the use of shareholders and creditors. These reporting obligations cannot be discharged merely by arranging for an audit by public accountants. However, the retaining of auditors is an important step toward meeting obligations of financial reporting. Even though the financial statements are sometimes constructed and typed in the auditors' office, primary responsibility for the statements remains with management.

The auditors' product is their report. It is a separate document from the client's financial statements, although the two are closely related and often transmitted together to shareholders and creditors.

Once we recognize that the financial statements are the statements of the company and not of the auditors, we realize that the auditors have no right to make changes in the financial statements. What action then should the auditors take if they do not agree with the presentation of a material item in the balance sheet or income statement? Assume, for example, that the allowance for doubtful accounts is not sufficient (in the auditors' opinion) to cover the probable collection losses in the accounts receivable.

The auditors will first discuss the problem with management and point out why they believe the valuation allowance to be inadequate. If management agrees to the desirability of increasing the allowance for doubtful accounts, an adjusting entry will be made for that purpose, and the problem is solved. If management and the audit committee are not convinced by the auditors' arguments and decline to increase the doubtful accounts allowance, the auditors will probably qualify their opinion by stating in the report that the financial statements reflect fairly the company's financial position and operating results, except that the provision for doubtful account losses appears to be insufficient.

Usually such issues are satisfactorily disposed of in discussions between the auditors and the client, and a qualification of the auditors' opinion is avoided. The point to be stressed, however, is that only the management has the power to change the financial statements. The auditors often recommend changes, and generally these changes are agreed to by management. A full consideration of the use of qualifications in the auditors' report is presented in Chapter 20.

2. The auditors' examination and opinion cover not only the balance sheet but also the statements of income, retained earnings, and changes in financial position.

In the early days of public accounting when audit reports were used principally by short-term creditors, the auditors often limited their investigation to the balance sheet, and the examination was referred to as a "balance sheet audit." Many companies considered the income statement confidential and did not release it to outsiders. This situation no longer exists. The measurement of periodic income is perhaps the most important step in the accounting process, and figures for annual earnings are of great interest to investors; consequently, the auditors' examination covers revenue and expense accounts as well as assets and liabilities. The auditors' opinion on the fairness of the net income reported for the period is just as important as their opinion on the fairness of the balance sheet.

Section 5400 of the *CICA Handbook* recommends that the auditors' report "should cover all financial statements required for fair presentation" and indicates that "such statements will normally include the balance sheet and statements of income, retained earnings and changes in financial position." Consequently, the auditors have a responsibility to examine and express an opinion on these statements.

3. The auditors render a report on the financial statements, not on the accounting records.

The auditors investigate every item on the financial statements; this investigation includes reference to the client's accounting records but is not limited to these records. The auditors' examination includes observation of tangible assets, inspection of such documents as purchase orders and contracts, and the gathering of evidence from outsiders (such as banks, customers, and suppliers) as well as analysis of the client's accounting records.

It is true that a principal means of establishing the validity of a balance sheet and income statement is to trace the statement figures to the accounting records and back through the records to original evidence of transactions. However, the auditors' use of the accounting records is merely a part of the examination. It is, therefore, appropriate for the auditors to state in their report that they have made an examination of the *financial statements* rather than to say that they have made an examination of the accounting records.

Auditing standards

The second sentence in the scope paragraph of the auditors' report indicates whether the examination was made in accordance with generally accepted auditing standards and included all auditing procedures which the auditors considered necessary. The sentence reads as follows: "Our examination was made in accordance with generally accepted auditing standards, and accordingly included such tests and other procedures as we considered necessary in the circumstances."

Standards are authoritative rules for measuring the *quality* of performance. The existence of generally accepted auditing standards is evidence that auditors are much concerned with the maintenance of a uniformly high quality of audit work by all independent public accountants. If every public accountant has adequate technical training and performs audits with skill, care, and professional judgment, the prestige of the profession will rise, and the public will attribute more and more significance to the auditor's opinion attached to financial statements.

The CICA Auditing Standards Committee has set forth the following as generally accepted auditing standards:

General standard

> The examination should be performed and the report prepared by a person or persons having adequate technical training and proficiency in auditing, with due care and with an objective state of mind.

Field work standards

(i) The work should be adequately planned and properly executed. If assistants are employed they should be properly supervised.

(ii) There should be an appropriately organized study and evaluation of those internal controls on which the auditor subsequently relies in determining the nature, extent and timing of auditing procedures.

(iii) Sufficient appropriate audit evidence should be obtained, by such means as inspection, observation, enquiry, confirmation, computation and analysis, to afford a reasonable basis to support the content of the report.

Reporting standards

(i) The scope of the auditor's examination should be referred to in the report.

(ii) The report should contain either an expression of opinion on the financial statements or an assertion that an opinion cannot be expressed. In the latter case, the reason therefor should be stated.

(iii) Where an opinion is expressed, it should indicate whether the financial statements present fairly the financial position, results of operations and changes in financial position in accordance with an appropriate disclosed basis of accounting, which except in special circumstances should be generally accepted accounting principles. The report should provide adequate explanation with respect to any reservation contained in such opinion.

(iv) Where an opinion is expressed, the report should also indicate whether the application of the disclosed basis of accounting is consistent with that of the preceding period. Where the basis or its application is not consistent, the report should provide adequate explanation of the nature and effect of the inconsistency.

The above statement of standards is referred to in the audit report as the "generally accepted auditing standards."

Application of auditing standards

In addition to setting forth the generally accepted auditing standards, the Auditing Standards Committee provides explanations of the applicability of the standards and the term "disclosed basis of accounting."

Applicability of the standards

The auditing standards . . . apply to engagements in which the objective is the expression of an opinion on financial statements. The general and field work standards are also applicable to other types of attest engagements.

The general standard . . . is intended to express the spirit of the related rule(s) of professional conduct of each provincial Institute or Order, to which rule(s) the auditor is referred.

Disclosed basis of accounting

Reporting standard (iii) . . . contains a reference to "an appropriate disclosed basis of accounting, which except in special circumstances should be generally accepted accounting principles." [There are] circumstances where the auditor should express his opinion as to the conformity of the financial statements with generally accepted accounting principles. There are [also] special circumstances where a different basis of accounting may be appropriate, for example in financial statements prepared in accordance with regulatory legislation or with contractual requirements such as may be set out in trust indentures or buy/sell agreements.

In special circumstances where a basis of accounting other than generally accepted accounting principles is appropriate, the auditor would express his opinion as to the conformity of the financial statements with such appropriate disclosed basis of accounting. The auditor would express a reservation of opinion on financial statements which did not disclose information appropriate and adequate in the circumstances.

The eight standards set forth by the CICA Auditing Standards Committee also include such intangible and subjective terms of measurement as "adequate planning," "appropriately organized study and evaluation of internal control," "sufficient appropriate audit evidence," and "adequate explanation." To decide under the circumstances of each audit engagement what is adequate, appropriate, and sufficient requires the exercise of professional judgment. Auditing cannot be reduced to rote; the exercise of judgment by the auditor is vital at numerous points in every examination. However, the formulation and publication of carefully worded auditing standards are an immense aid in raising the quality of audit work, even though these standards require professional judgment in their application.

Training and proficiency

How does the independent auditor achieve the "adequate technical training and proficiency in auditing required by the general standard? Both pre-entry education and continuing education are essential. The practising CA must be given on-the-job training during every audit assignment, must participate in formal training programs and professional development courses of the CA firm and the CICA and/or the provincial institutes, and must continually read and study current literature in accounting and related fields. This dedication to continuing education and training is essential to meet the requirements of the first general standards.

An objective state of mind or independence— the most important consideration

An opinion by an independent public accountant as to the fairness of a company's financial statements is of no value unless the accountant is truly objective. Consequently, the general standard states that "the examination should be performed and the report prepared . . . with an objective state of mind." This requirement is perhaps the most essential factor in the existence of a public accounting profession.

If an auditor owned stock in a company which he audited or if he served as a member of the board of directors, he might subconsciously be biased in the performance of auditing duties. The CA should therefore avoid any relationship with a client which would cause an outsider who had knowledge of all the facts to doubt the CA's objective state of mind. It is not enough that the CA be objective; he must conduct himself in such a manner that informed members of the public will have no reason to doubt his objectivity.   perspective

A possible difficulty in the maintenance by the auditor of an attitude of objectivity lies in the fact that he is selected by the shareholders but paid by the management of the company he audits. Moreover, he often serves as a financial adviser and consultant to management. These circumstances naturally create in the auditor a tendency to react sympathetically toward the attitudes and objectives of management and to identify himself with the management group.

The long-run welfare of the public accounting profession—in fact, its very existence and recognition as a profession—is dependent upon the objectivity and integrity of the auditor. If he assumes the role of a partisan spokesman for management, he thereby sacrifices his professional status as an independent public accountant.

Auditing standards contrasted with auditing procedures

Auditing standards must not be confused with auditing procedures. Auditing standards are basic principles governing the nature and extent of the investigation necessary on each examination; auditing procedures, on the other hand, are the detailed acts or steps comprising the auditors' investigation. A familiar example of an audit procedure is the inspection and counting of a client's assets such as cash, marketable securities, and notes receivable.

To illustrate the distinction between auditing standards and procedures, let us consider the auditors' work on inventories. One of the standards of field work stated by the CICA Auditing Standards Committee is the obtaining of "sufficient appropriate audit evidence" to afford a reasonable basis to support the content of the report. As related to inventory, this standard requires evidence as to quantities and prices of merchandise owned by the client. One phase of the standard requires that the auditors satisfy themselves that the inventory is fairly priced. To meet this standard, the auditors might utilize such auditing *procedures* as (a) observe the taking of physical inventory, (b) compare prices applied to the inventory with those prices on purchase invoices, and (c) determine that the carrying value of items in inventory does not exceed current market price. These three investigative steps are auditing procedures.

A decision as to how many purchase invoices should be examined and how extensive the comparison with current market prices should be requires the exercise of judgment by the auditors and invokes an auditing standard—the judging of how much evidence is sufficient under the circumstances. This decision should ideally be the same if made by different auditors facing the same set of circumstances.

No single set of procedures will fit all examinations. In each engagement the nature of the accounting records, the quality of internal control, and other circumstances peculiar to the company will dictate the audit procedures to be used. Auditing standards, however, do not and should not vary from one examination to the next. Standards should be uniform; procedures should vary to fit the circumstances of each engagement.

Audit procedures not determined by the client

The independent status of the auditors is indicated by the fact that the auditors, and not the client, determine the procedures to be employed. The management of a company instructs its employees as to the procedures they are to follow; the management cannot, however, specify the procedures to be followed by the public accounting firm auditing the company. The auditors' report states that the auditors used all procedures which *they* considered necessary in the circumstances. This statement indicates that the audit work was in no way restricted or guided by the client and that the auditors assume full responsibility for the adequacy and scope of their work. The procedures are not listed in the report; the users of audited financial statements must rely upon the professional competence of the auditors for assurance that the procedures selected were appropriate under the circumstances.

The opinion paragraph of the auditors' report

In preceding sections of this chapter, the scope paragraph of the auditors' report has been analyzed, with particular emphasis being placed on the reference to generally accepted auditing standards. Now that we have examined the basis for the auditors' opinion, as set forth in the scope paragraph, we are ready to consider the nature of the opinion itself.

The opinion paragraph consists of only one sentence, which is restated here with certain significant phrases shown in italics:

> *In our opinion,* these financial statements *present fairly* the financial position of XYZ Limited as at December 31, 19— and the results of its operations and the changes in its financial position for the year then ended in accordance with *generally accepted accounting principles* applied on a basis *consistent with that of the preceding year.*

Each of the italicized phrases has a special significance. The first phrase, "in our opinion," makes clear that the auditors are expressing nothing more than an informed opinion; they are not guaranteeing or certifying that the statements are accurate, correct, or true. In an earlier period of public accounting, the wording of the audit report contained the phrase "We certify that . . . ," but this expression was discontinued on the grounds that it was misleading. To "certify" implies a positive assurance of accuracy which an audit simply does not provide.

The auditors cannot guarantee the correctness of the financial statements because the statements themselves are largely matters of opinion rather than of absolute fact. Furthermore, the auditors do not make a complete and detailed examination of all transactions. Their examination is limited to a program of tests which leaves the possibility of some errors going undetected. Because of limitations inherent in the accounting process, and because of practical limitations of time and cost in the making of an audit, the auditors' work culminates in the expression of an opinion and not in the issuance of a guarantee of accuracy. The growth of public accounting and the increased confidence placed in audited statements by all sectors of the economy indicate that the auditors' opinion is usually sufficient assurance that the statements may be relied upon.

In the opinion paragraph of the report, the auditors are really making four assertions about the financial statements: (1) the statements present fairly the financial position and results of economic activity (this is the primary and overriding assertion); (2) the presentation is in conformity with generally accepted accounting principles; (3) generally acceptable accounting principles have been consistently applied; and (4) by implication, disclosure is adequate.

The financial statements "present fairly . . ."

The next phrase of the opinion paragraph which requires special consideration is the expression "present fairly." Since many of the items in financial statements cannot be measured exactly, the auditors cannot say that the statements "present exactly" the financial position or operating results.

The meaning of the words "present fairly" as used in the context of the auditors' report has been much discussed in recent court cases and in auditing literature. This controversy has hinged on the question of whether financial statements which conform to generally accepted accounting principles will *necessarily constitute a fair presentation.* In other words, is the word *fairly* a redundant term in the auditors' report, or does it mean something over and above conforming to generally accepted accounting principles? If the latter view is adopted, what criteria other than conformity with generally accepted accounting principles should be used in judging whether financial statements are fairly presented?

Court cases concerning the fairness of financial statements usually take place several years after the statements have been issued. Events in the intervening years may have weakened the company or caused it to fail. To judge the fairness of financial statements according to whether in retrospect they were a reliable forecast of future earnings represents a contradiction of the traditional concept of the purpose and nature of financial statements.

The CICA Auditing Standards Committee has adopted a position that the auditors' judgment as to "present fairly" can be applied "only within the framework of generally accepted accounting principles."[8] In brief, no better set of specific criteria is available for use in measuring fairness. The exercise of professional judgment by auditors with respect to a decision on the overall fairness of financial statements may include determining whether the accounting principles used have general acceptance; whether the principles selected are appropriate in the circumstances; whether the information in the statements is summarized and classified in a reasonable manner, neither too detailed nor too condensed; and whether the financial statements in an overall sense are informative rather than misleading.

The argument on the meaning of "present fairly" does not appear to have been fully resolved. Future court cases are likely to explore further the quality of fairness in financial statements. In the opinion of the authors, the essence of the Auditing Standards Committee's position is to equate the quality of *presenting fairly* with that of *not being misleading*. Financial statements are not forecasts, but they must not be so presented as to lead users to forecasts or conclusions which a company and its independent auditors know are unsound or unlikely.

Adequate informative disclosure

If financial statements are to *present fairly* the financial position and operating results of a company, there must be adequate disclosure of all essential information. A financial statement may be misleading if it does not give a complete picture. For example, if an extraordinary item arising from an uninsured flood loss of plant and equipment were combined with operating income and not clearly identified, the reader might be misled as to the earning power of the company.

"Adequate informative" disclosure is not "full" disclosure. Premature disclosure of a prospective merger, for example, might injure a company's position. Disclosure of tentative plans for introduction of a new product or discontinuance of an existing line of products might also injure the company by weakening its competitive position. Some very difficult deci-

---

[8] CICA, *CICA Handbook,* p. 5601 (1), sec. 5400.12.

sions become necessary in distinguishing between adequate disclosure and unnecessary harmful publicity.

Materiality

The preceding paragraphs have indicated that disclosure of essential information is necessary if the statements are to *present fairly* the financial position and operating results of a company. In achieving adequate disclosure, however, it is important not to clutter up the statements with unimportant details. Disclosure is needed only for *material* facts. A general definition of the adjective *material* is "of substantial importance, of great consequence, pertinent or essential to, likely to influence." The concept of materiality as used in accounting may be defined as a state of relative importance. Unfortunately, there is no handy rule of thumb to tell us whether a given item is material. Some accountants have tended to dismiss the concept of materiality as meaning nothing more than "if it isn't important, don't bother with it." In actual auditing practice, however, one of the most significant elements of professional judgment is the ability to draw the line between material and immaterial errors or departures from good accounting practice. The auditor who raises objections and creates crises over immaterial items will soon lose the respect of both clients and associates. On the other hand, the auditor who fails to identify and disclose material information may be liable for the losses of those who rely upon audited financial statements. In brief, applying the concept of materiality to corporate financial statements is one of the most complex problems faced by accountants.

An item which is material to one company may not be material to another. For example, the uninsured destruction of $15,000 worth of inventory in a small store would be a relatively important transaction. This $15,000 loss might represent perhaps one fourth of a year's net income and perhaps 10 percent of the total assets of a small store. On the other hand, destruction of inventory costing $15,000 would definitely not be a material item in the financial statements of a giant corporation which has net income and total assets in millions of dollars.

The relative dollar amounts involved are an important consideration in judging materiality, but they are not necessarily the controlling factor. If a corporation sells assets to a member of its top-management group and that individual in turn sells the same assets back to the corporation at a profit, this *related party transaction* warrants disclosure even though the dollar amounts are not large in relation to the financial statements as a whole. Such a transaction suggests the possibility of a conflict of interest and warrants disclosure. Both quantitative and qualitative elements warrant consideration in the determination of materiality.

Perhaps the most useful working rule in applying the test of materiality is to ask: "Is the item of sufficient importance to influence the conclusions which will be reached by users of the financial statements?" This view of materiality has been well expressed in the *CICA Handbook:* "While materiality is a matter of professional judgement in the particular circumstances, . . . , as a general rule, materiality may be judged in relation to the reasonable prospect of its significance in the making of decisions by the readers of the financial statements. If the item might reasonably be expected to affect the decision, it should be deemed to be material."[9]

Similarly, this view of materiality has been expressed by the American Accounting Association in *Accounting and Reporting Standards for Corporate Financial Statements:* "The materiality of an item may depend on its size, its nature, or a combination of both. An item should be regarded as material if there is reason to believe that knowledge of it would influence the decisions of an informed investor."

As a rough rule of thumb, some accountants tend to regard items which are less than 4 or 5 percent of net income as not material. Such an approach is oversimplified in the opinion of the authors. For example, the percentage relationship of an item to total net income or to earnings per share will vary widely when computed for companies which are profitable as compared with companies which are barely breaking even or operating at a loss. For a company which is breaking even, the percentage relationship of an item to net income has no significance; the more important criteria may then become the nature of the item in question, its absolute amount, and its relationship to such factors as total assets, current assets, and shareholders' equity.

Criteria for judging materiality. The CICA study groups and the Financial Accounting Standards Board have carried out lengthy studies seeking to establish criteria for judging materiality which would result in consistent financial reporting. Consideration was given to the feasibility of using quantitative or non-quantitative criteria; criteria for specific items as opposed to an overall criterion; relationship of the item being judged to sales, working capital, and retained earnings; and the effect of the item upon the trend of net income or upon the change in net income from the prior year. Consideration was also given to separate criteria for so-called "sensitive" situations which may receive wide attention in the news media or raise questions as to moral standards. Most of these studies stressed that materiality could not be measured by any single quantitative device.

Trend toward more disclosure. The movement toward more and more disclosure necessarily means shifting more items across the threshold of materiality. Several factors have forced disclosure to become more extensive year after year. Legal actions against companies and their independent auditors have led to more detailed disclosure as a self-protective

---

[9] Ibid., p. 10.

measure. Governmental regulators appear to be disclosure oriented. As a practical matter, disclosure in financial statements may already be so voluminous as to overwhelm and confuse the reader, as evidenced by the many pages of notes typically attached to financial statements. Such proliferation of disclosure indicates the need for a better measurement of what is material.

Current status of the materiality issue. In summary, materiality requires informed judgment based on the particular facts in each set of circumstances. Guidelines, both quantitative and non-quantitative, are needed, at least to identify items clearly not material; but the auditors' judgment cannot be replaced by an arbitrary percentage relationship. Specific rules cannot be formulated which would be valid for determining materiality for all situations. Materiality decisions will probably continue to constitute an area requiring broad experience and informed judgment.

Generally accepted accounting principles

In our study of the main ideas contained in the auditors' report, the next key phrase to be considered is "generally accepted accounting principles." Of all the phrases we have considered, this one is by far the most difficult to define. Yet a clear definition and widespread understanding of "generally accepted accounting principles" are essential to the preparation of financial statements which will permit comparisons between companies.

Comparability in financial statements is not possible unless business enterprise as a whole follows generally accepted accounting principles. The importance of comparability in financial statements can hardly be overemphasized. Financial statements indicate which companies and which industries are employing capital most successfully; and under our free enterprise system, capital flows toward the areas in which earnings are highest. This method of allocating our economic resources works efficiently only if the measurement and reporting of business income are comparable for all sectors of the economy. The public accountant thus serves a vital function in the economy by improving the quality and comparability of financial statements. Further progress in this direction, however, is dependent in large part upon the ability of the accounting profession to reach a clearer, better defined agreement upon the meaning of generally accepted accounting principles.

What are generally accepted accounting principles? No official list exists, but the recommendations of the CICA Accounting Research Committee constitute a major authoritative source. These *CICA Handbook* recommendations are recognized as generally acceptable accounting principles by the Canada Business Corporations Act and the provincial securities commissions.[10] The *CICA Handbook* defines generally accepted accounting principles to include "not only specific rules, practices and procedures relating to particular circumstances but also broad principles and conventions of general application."[11]

Consistency

Another key phrase in the opinion paragraph of the auditors' report is the statement that accounting principles have been applied on a basis *consistent with that of the preceding year.* The privilege of choosing from among a number of alternative accounting methods carries with it an obligation to use the selected methods in a consistent manner. Inventory, for example, may be valued by such diverse methods as Lifo, Fifo, and average cost, even by companies in the same industry. Whichever method is selected by a given company, however, must be followed consistently to obtain comparable statements from year to year. In this regard, the *CICA Handbook* held that in the preparation of financial statements there is a presumption that an accounting principle once adopted should not be changed in accounting for events and transactions of a similar type.

A change in the application of accounting principles may cause a distortion of net income for the period in which the change is made. In consequence, the nature of and justification for a change in accounting principle and its effect on income should be disclosed in the financial statements of the period in which the change is made. The justification for the change should explain clearly why the newly adopted principle is preferable. In this situation the auditors cannot issue the standard report as previously illustrated; they must revise the wording of the opinion paragraph to point out the break in consistency of application of accounting principles. In summary, we may say that the doctrine of consistency does not make a choice of accounting method an irrevocable decision; it does, however, prevent a continual switching from one method to another and also requires disclosure of the effect on net income of any change in method, and the justification for the change.

Other types of auditors' reports

The form of auditors' report discussed in this chapter is called an *unqualified opinion.* Such a report may be regarded as a "clean bill of health" issued by the auditors. An unqualified opinion denotes that the examination was adequate in scope and that the financial statements present fairly the financial position and results of operations in accordance

---

[10] *Canada Business Corporations Act and Regulations,* 2d ed. (Toronto: Richard Dee Boo Limited), reg. 44, p. 189.

[11] CICA, *CICA Handbook,* p. 5601 (1), sec. 5400.11.

with generally accepted accounting principles applied on a basis consistent with that of the preceding year. Under these circumstances the auditors are taking no exceptions and inserting no qualifications in the report. An unqualified opinion is the type of report the client wants and also the type auditors prefer to issue. In some audits, however, the circumstances will not permit the auditors to give their unqualified approval to the financial statements. The other possible alternatives are a *qualified opinion,* an *adverse opinion,* and a *denial of opinion.*

In some audit engagements, the auditors may find that one or more items in the financial statements are not presented in accordance with generally accepted accounting principles. Perhaps the auditors do not regard as reasonable the valuation assigned to certain assets by management. If the auditors cannot persuade the client company to change the unsatisfactory items in the financial statements, they will issue a qualified opinion or an adverse opinion. The choice between these two options depends upon the materiality of the shortcomings in the financial statements. A decision to issue a qualified opinion would indicate that the auditors believed that the deficiencies, although significant, were not so material as to invalidate the financial statements viewed as a whole.

An *adverse opinion* is one which states that the financial statements *are not fairly presented.* In practice an adverse opinion is rare because it would be useless to the client. If the financial statements are so deficient as to warrant rejection by the auditors, this situation will be discussed between the auditors and the client early in the engagement. At this point, the management of the client company probably will agree to make the changes necessary to avoid an adverse opinion.

The auditors will issue a *denial of opinion* if they are unable to determine the overall fairness of the financial statements. This type of result might occur if the audit revealed the system of internal control to be grossly inadequate, or if the auditors for any reason did not perform sufficient work to have a basis for an opinion. Sometimes, the client may restrict the scope of the auditors' work and therefore understands that a denial of opinion will be the only type of audit report possible. However, if the auditors *know* that the financial statements do not constitute a fair presentation, they must not deny an opinion but must issue an adverse opinion. In other words, the fact that the audit was not complete would not justify the auditors in denying an opinion on financial statements which they knew to be misleading.

Extensions of the auditors' attest function

In recent years many suggestions have been made for the extension of the auditors' attest function beyond reporting on annual financial statements. Among the various reports currently issued by auditors are reports on a client's internal control, reports to various regulatory agencies, and letters to the underwriters of an issue of securities and other special reports (discussed in Chapter 20). As a consequence of the growth of multinational corporations, auditors have learned to report on the financial statements of foreign subsidiaries which utilize the accounting principles of the countries in which these companies operate. In addition to this increasing range of reports, however, pressures by government and other sources are mounting for public accounting firms to develop further extensions of the attest function.

Securities analysts are giving increasing attention to companies' financial forecasts and are requesting the auditor to review these "forward-looking" data. A forecast of earnings, or at least a cash budget, may soon be included in a prospectus describing a new issue of securities. The growing interest in the capabilities of a company's managers has generated proposals that the auditor conduct "management audits" and attest to management's performance. Finally, the rising importance of the quarterly earnings reported by publicly owned companies has created pressures for the auditor to attest to the fairness of these reports in addition to the annual financial statements. Both the CICA and the American Institute of Certified Public Accountants have viewed this matter with considerable interest and urgency. The Securities and Exchange Commission, which has significant influence on accounting and auditing matters, has recently urged certified public accountants to review the quarterly statements of their clients before these interim statements are issued to the public and to consult with clients on reporting problems as they arise.

In making decisions on the possible extension of the attest function to these many new proposed areas, we should keep in mind certain basic conditions necessary for successful performance of the attest function. These conditions include objectivity and technical competence of the attestor, the existence of evidential matter and of accepted standards for presentation, adequate disclosure, and a clear indication of the responsibility assumed by the attestor.

A vigorous profession in a rapidly changing society should expect that its role will change to meet changing needs. The public accountant may appropriately ask: "How can I expand or modify my services to make them of greater value to my clients and to the entire community?"

KEY TERMS INTRODUCED OR EMPHASIZED IN CHAPTER 1

Accounting Principles Board (APB)   The unit of the AICPA in the United States which from 1959 to 1973 was authorized to issue authoritative pronouncements to establish a clear meaning for generally accepted accounting principles; superseded in 1973 by the Financial Accounting Standards Board.

Accounting Research Committee (ARC)   The unit of the CICA which was established on June 1, 1973, to issue recommendations with respect to matters of accounting practices. The committee's recommendations are recognized as an authoritative source of generally accepted accounting principles.

adverse opinion   An opinion issued by the auditors that the financial statements which they have examined *do not present fairly* the financial position, results of operation, or changes in financial position in accordance with generally accepted accounting principles.

American Institute of Certified Public Accountants (AICPA)   The national professional organization of CPAs engaged in promoting high professional standards and improving the quality of financial reporting in the United States.

attest function   The primary function of the independent public accountant—to attest to financial statements; that is, to bear witness as to their reliability and fairness—the independent opinion of the public accountant lends credibility to audited financial statements.

audit   An examination or analytical review by independent public accountants of a set of financial statements, and the accounting records and other supporting evidence both within and outside the client's business.

auditing procedures.   Detailed steps comprising an audit; for example, counting cash on hand, confirming accounts receivable, and observing the physical inventory.

Auditing Standards Committee (ASC)   The unit of the CICA which was established on June 1, 1973, to issue recommendations with respect to matters of auditing practices. The committee's recommendations constitute a body of generally accepted auditing standards and the interpretations of such standards.

auditor's report   A very precise document designed to communicate exactly the character and limitations of the responsibility being assumed by the auditor; in standard form, the report consists of a "scope" paragraph and an "opinion" which cover the basic financial statements.

Canada Business Corporations Act   A federal act which governs business corporations (other than bank, insurance, trust, and loan companies) incorporated to carry on business throughout Canada. The purposes of the act are to advance uniformity of business corporation law and to provide a means for an orderly transferal of certain federal companies incorporated under various acts of Parliament to this act.

Canadian Certified General Accountants' Association   A national organization of certified general accountants whose purposes are "to fix standards of skill and competence for its members and thereby promote efficiency in accountants."

Canadian Institute of Chartered Accountants (CICA)   The national organization of chartered accountants engaged in promoting and maintaining high professional standards of practice and providing significant input to the public and private sectors in respect to business practices and government legislation.

Certified General Accountant (CGA)   A member of the Certified General Accountants Association.

Certified Public Accountant (CPA)   A person licensed by the state in the United States to practise public accounting, based on having passed the Uniform

CPA Examination and having met certain education and experience requirements.

Chartered Accountant (CA)   A member of a provincial Institute/Order of Chartered Accountants and the CICA.

CICA Handbook   A publication of the Canadian Institute of Chartered Accountants. It contains background information on the Institute, its charter, by-laws, policy statements, the recommendations of the Accounting Research Committee and of the Auditing Standards Committee, and Accounting/Auditing Guidelines.

consistency   The concept of using the same accounting principles from year to year so that the successive financial statements issued by a business entity will be comparable. Disclosure of the effects of any break in consistency by reason of accounting changes is necessary.

denial of opinion   A form of report in which the auditors state that they do not express an opinion on the financial statements. It should include a separate paragraph stating the auditors' reasons for denying an opinion and also disclosing any reservations they may have concerning the consistent application of generally accepted accounting principles. It should not be used in lieu of an adverse opinion (that is, cases in which the auditors know that material departures from generally accepted accounting principles exist).

disclosure   Making public all material information about financial affairs.

due professional care   One of the key elements of the general standard of the CICA's auditing standards; requires the auditors to exercise due professional care in the performance of their examination and the preparation of their report—a higher level of care than required of the "ordinarily prudent person" under the definition of negligence.

Financial Accounting Standards Board   A seven-member, full-time board with members from public accounting, industry, government, and education, formed in 1973 to formulate financial accounting standards and to improve the quality of financial reporting in the United States.

fraud   Misrepresentation by a person of a material fact, known by that person to be untrue or made with reckless indifference as to whether the fact is true, with intent to deceive and with the result that another party is injured.

generally accepted accounting principles (GAAP)   Concepts, standards, or practices established primarily by the CICA and accepted by the accounting profession as essential to proper financial reporting.

generally accepted auditing standards (GAAS)   A set of eight standards adopted by the CICA and binding on its members—designed to ensure the quality of the auditor's work.

internal control   All the measures used by a business for the purposes of (1) safeguarding its resources from waste, fraud, and inefficiency; (2) promoting accuracy and reliability in accounting and operating data; (3) encouraging compliance with company policy; and (4) judging the efficiency of operations in all divisions of the business.

management fraud   Exists when the client management makes a deliberate effort to present misleading financial statements, supported by falsified accounting records.

material   Being of substantial importance. Significant enough to affect evaluations by users of financial statements. Information which should be disclosed in order that financial statements constitute a fair presentation. Involves both quantitative and qualitative criteria.

non-management fraud   Dishonest actions that occur within a company despite management's efforts to prevent such actions.

objectivity (independence)   A most important auditing standard which prohibits CAs from expressing an opinion on financial statements of an enterprise unless they can maintain an objective state of mind with respect to such enterprise; objectivity is impaired by a material financial interest, service as an officer or trustee, and various other relationships.

Provincial Certified General Accountants Association   A provincial organization of CGAs (in Quebec, the Professional Corporation of Certified General Accountants) incorporated under a provincial act.

Provincial Institute of Chartered Accountants   A provincial organization of CAs (in Quebec, the Order of Chartered Accountants) incorporated under a provincial act and empowered to confer the CA designation on its members.

Provincial Securities Commission   A provincial government unit whose primary objective is to ensure proper protection of the investing public and adequate financial statement disclosure.

public accountant   A person who is licensed by the provincial Public Accountants Acts to engage in the practice of public accountancy, the primary function of which is to attest to the fairness of financial statements.

qualified opinion   The appropriate form of audit report when some factor is sufficiently significant to require mention in the auditors' report but not so material as to necessitate the expression of an adverse opinion or the denial of an opinion. May be viewed as falling into two groups: "except for" and "subject to" opinions. The "except for" clause indicates such limitations as a lack of sufficient evidence, a departure from generally accepted accounting principles, or a change between periods in the application of accounting principles. The "subject to" clause is used when an uncertainty is not subject to reasonable estimation.

Securities and Exchange Commission (SEC)   A government agency in the United States, authorized to review financial statements of companies seeking approval to issue securities for sale to the public.

unqualified opinion   The form of audit report issued when the examination was adequate in scope and the auditors believe that the financial statement present fairly financial position and operating results in accordance with generally accepted accounting principles applied on a basis consistent with that of the preceding year.

GROUP I
REVIEW QUESTIONS

1–1.   The attest function is said to be the principal reason for the existence of a public accounting profession. What is meant by attesting to a client's financial statements, and what two steps are required?

1–2. Identify the two principal qualifications which should be possessed by a person who is to perform the attest function for a company's financial statements.

1–3. Which of the following statements is preferable?
   a. The X Company retains a public accounting firm to conduct an annual audit of its accounting records.
   b. The X Company retains a public accounting firm to conduct an annual audit of its financial statements.
   Give reasons for your answer.

1–4. What actions and objectives distinguish management fraud from non-management fraud?

1–5. In judging the *materiality* of a transaction or an item on a financial statement, are the auditors concerned with anything other than the relative dollar amounts involved? Explain.

1–6. Pike Company has had an annual audit performed by the same firm of public accountants for many years. The financial statements and copies of the audit report are distributed to shareholders each year shortly after completion of the audit. Who is primarily responsible for the fairness of these financial statements? Explain.

1–7. An objective state of mind is a most essential element of an audit by a firm of public accountants. Describe several situations in which the public accounting firm might find it somewhat difficult to maintain this objective point of view.

1–8. Draft the standard form of audit report commonly issued after a satisfactory examination of a client's financial statements.

1–9. Jane Lee, a director of the Ralston Limited suggested that the corporation appoint as controller, John Madison, a chartered accountant on the staff of the auditing firm that had made annual audits of Ralston Limited for many years. Lee expressed the opinion that this move would effect a considerable saving in professional fees as annual audits would no longer be needed. She proposed to give the controller, if appointed, sufficient staff to carry on such continuing investigations of accounting data as appeared necessary. Evaluate this proposal.

1–10. The role of the auditor in the economy has changed over the years in response to changes in our economic and political institutions. Consequently, the nature of an audit today is quite different from that of an audit performed in the year 1900. Classify the following phrases into two groups: (1) phrases more applicable to an audit performed in 1900, and (2) phrases more applicable to an audit performed today.
   a. Complete review of all transactions.
   b. Evaluation of the system of internal control.
   c. Balance sheet audit.
   d. Emphasis upon use of sampling techniques.
   e. Determination of fairness of financial statements.
   f. Audit procedures to prevent or detect fraud on the part of all employees and managers.

  g. Primary emphasis upon verification of balance sheet amounts.
  h. Responsibility of the auditor for the fairness of reported income.
  i. Influence of stock exchanges and the investing public upon use of independent auditors.
  j. Generally accepted auditing standards.
  k. Bankers and short-term creditors as principal users of audit reports.
  l. Certification by the auditor.

1–11. What professional services other than auditing are commonly offered by CAs?

1–12. Under what circumstances may the auditors be unable to issue an unqualified opinion after completing an examination?

1–13. "I have never issued a qualified report," said Accountant X. "Such reports satisfy no one. I find it much simpler to change the financial statements if the client is using unacceptable accounting methods." Criticize this quotation.

1–14. A CA firm does not guarantee the financial soundness of a client when it renders an opinion on financial statements, nor does the CA firm guarantee the absolute accuracy of the statements. Yet the CA firm's opinion is respected and accepted. What is expected of the CA firm in order to merit such confidence? (AICPA, adapted)

1–15. What is the principal use and significance of an audit report to a large corporation with securities listed on a stock exchange? To a small family-owned enterprise?

1–16. State four principal assertions made by the auditors in the opinion paragraph of the standard report.

1–17. Alan Weston, CA, completed an examination of Kirsten Manufacturing Company and issued an unqualified standard audit report. What does this tell us about the extent of the auditing procedures included in the examination?

1–18. Contrast the objectives of auditing in the late 19th century with the objectives of auditing today.

1–19. What were some of the factors that caused auditors to adopt a sampling technique rather than make a complete review of all transactions?

1–20. Describe several business situations which would create a need for a report by an independent public accountant concerning the fairness of a company's financial statements.

1–21. Why should the province license public accountants?

1–22. A student of auditing, when asked to distinguish between auditing standards and auditing procedures, stated that auditing standards relate to the preparation of the audit report whereas auditing procedures are concerned with the examination of the financial statements prior to writing the report. Do you agree? Explain.

1–23. If a CA firm has made a thorough professional examination of a client's financial statements, should it not be able to issue a report dealing with facts rather than the mere expression of an opinion? Explain.

1–24. Why did the auditors of a generation or more ago usually limit their examinations principally to balance sheet accounts?

1–25. The standard audit report usually contains a sentence such as the following: "Our examination was made in accordance with generally accepted auditing standards, and accordingly included such tests and other procedures as we considered necessary in the circumstances."
  a. Distinguish between auditing standards and auditing procedures.
  b. Quote or state in your own words four generally accepted auditing standards. (AICPA, adapted)

1–26. "The auditors' work is essentially complete when they have determined that the dollar amounts in the financial statements are in agreement with the amounts in the client company's ledger accounts." Do you agree with this quotation? Explain.

1–27. Select the best answer for each of the following items:
  1. A qualification as to consistency would ordinarily not be required when the client—
    a. Changed his inventory pricing method from Fifo to Lifo.
    b. Changed his depreciation from straight line to an accelerated basis.
    c. Lowered his pension fund contribution as a result of changes in actuarial assumptions which were based upon experience.
    d. Discontinued the amortization of goodwill.
  2. A client company has changed its accounting practices during the year, materially affecting its financial statements, so as to render them seriously misleading and not in conformity with generally accepted accounting principles. The CA examining these financial statements should—
    a. Render an adverse opinion and give his reasons therefor.
    b. Qualify his opinion with respect to the consistency standard and in a middle paragraph of his report explain the changes and their effects on the net income of the period.
    c. Deny an opinion and give his reasons therefor.
    d. Qualify his opinion with respect to the consistency standard, referring to explanatory footnotes of the financial statements to fulfill disclosure requirements.
  3. A CA may be justified in rendering a qualified opinion except when—
    a. He has omitted a normally required audit procedure such as the confirmation of accounts receivable.
    b. The client's financial statements, in some particular, do not conform to generally accepted accounting principles.
    c. He has not obtained sufficient evidence to form an opinion on the financial statements as a whole.
    d. Generally accepted accounting principles have not been consistently applied compared with the preceding year.
  4. The use of the phrase "subject to" in an auditor's opinion is appropriate when the qualification pertains to—

    a. Non-adherence to generally accepted accounting principles.

    b. Inability to perform an essential audit procedure.

    c. Lack of consistency with the preceding year.

    d. Uncertainty as to the outcome of a material event. (CICA, adapted)

GROUP II
QUESTIONS REQUIRING ANALYSIS

1–28. It is now doubtful if an auditor can defend a challenge to his opinion simply by having adhered to generally accepted auditing standards and by stating that the financial statements have been prepared in accordance with generally accepted accounting principles.

Required:

    Discuss the above statement indicating its implications for the auditing profession. (CICA)

1–29. A newspaper story indicated that Warren Green, president of Meat Products Ltd., was accused of large-scale management fraud in conducting the affairs of the corporation over a period of years. In the court proceedings which followed, Green acknowledged that he possessed considerable wealth, but he was able to prove that he had never stolen even one dollar of the corporation's assets. He presented conclusive evidence that his personal resources had been accumulated through saving a considerable portion of his salary and annual bonus and by successful investment of these savings.

    On the basis of this information, would you conclude that Warren Green is innocent of the charge of management fraud? Explain.

1–30. In a political speech, a candidate for public office stated: "If a large corporation takes any action which violates moral standards, it is the responsibility of that corporation's independent auditors to make full and prompt disclosure of such action." Evaluate this quotation.

1–31. James Chan, while working as a member of the audit staff of Wilkins and Lee, CAs, was assigned to the audit of Bayside Limited. During the next several years, Chan regularly participated in the audit of this client and eventually was placed in charge of the Bayside engagement. During this period he received his CA certificate. Finally, Chan, who had made a very favourable impression upon the officers of Bayside Limited, was offered a position as controller of the company. He accepted the position. Immediately after this appointment, a member of the board of directors introduced a motion for discontinuance of the annual audit on the grounds that the corporation now had the services of Chan on a full-time basis.

    While considering this motion, the board invited Chan to express his views. Put yourself in the role of the new controller and explain fully your views on the proposed discontinuance of the annual audit.

1–32.   Jensen and Landry, CAs, in its first audit of Milltown Limited, found that certain assets of material amount had been valued by the client by use of methods which Jensen and Landry did not approve. Should the auditors change the financial statements to reflect proper valuation of the items in question, or should they qualify the audit report by indicating that generally accepted accounting principles had not been followed in certain respects? Explain.

1–33.   For several years you have made annual audits of Harwell Limited and have issued unqualified audit reports. You have also suggested to management several steps for improving internal control and accounting procedures. One of your recommendations has been for a change in the method of inventory valuation from first-in, first-out to last-in, first-out. Assuming that the change is made, what effect, if any, would this action have upon the audit report at the time of the next annual examination?

1–34.   Assume that you are a partner in a CA firm retained by the Dot Company to perform an examination in accordance with generally accepted auditing standards and are satisfied with the results of your work.

Required:

a.   What effect, if any, would there be on your issuing an audit opinion if the client company had a loan payable to a finance company in which your brother was the principal shareholder? Assume that the loan was material in relation to the other elements in Dot Company's financial statements. Discuss.

b.   Assume that your son, age 16, owns 100 shares of the 50,000 shares of Dot Company's common stock outstanding at the balance sheet date. Would this fact have any effect on your issuance of an opinion as an independent auditor? Discuss. (AICPA, adapted)

1–35.   Assume that you are a senior member of an audit staff and are in charge of the audit of a medium-sized manufacturing company whose unaudited financial statements show total assets, $950,000; shareholders' equity, $400,000; net sales, $2,000,000; and net income, $140,000. One of your less-experienced assistants, John Call, informs you that he has discovered several irregularities while performing the audit tasks assigned to him, but that he is uncertain whether these errors are sufficiently material to warrant any action. The errors noted were as follows:

1.   Petty cash fund of $200 shown by count at the balance sheet date to be $3 short.

2.   An expenditure of $400 for stationery had been charged to the Miscellaneous Office Expense account, although other expenditures of similar nature were charged to Office Supplies Expense, which had a balance of $3,800.

3.   A few entries for amounts less than $100 had been entered directly in general ledger accounts without the use of journal entries.

Do you think that any of these items should be disclosed in the financial statements or in the audit report, or that any other action by you as auditor is called for? Explain fully.

1–36.   Select the best answer for each of the following items and give reasons for your choice.

 a. The concept of materiality will be **least** important to a CA firm in determining the—

  (1) Scope of its audit of specific accounts.

  (2) Specific transactions which should be reviewed.

  (3) Effects of audit exceptions upon its opinion.

  (4) Effects of its direct financial interest in the client company upon its independence.

 b. The general standard of the generally accepted auditing standards includes a requirement that—

  (1) The auditor maintain an objective state of mind.

  (2) The audit be conducted in conformity with generally accepted accounting principles.

  (3) Assistants, if any, be properly supervised.

  (4) There be a proper study and evaluation of internal control.

 c. The general standard of the generally accepted auditing standards is primarily concerned with—

  (1) The personal qualifications of CAs.

  (2) Negotiation with the client about the audit engagement and arrangements for the audit.

  (3) Conformity to generally accepted accounting principles.

  (4) The overall audit program including provision for a review of internal control.

 d. An unqualified standard report by a CA normally does not explicitly state—

  (1) The CA's opinion that the financial statements comply with generally accepted accounting principles.

  (2) That generally accepted auditing standards were followed in the conduct of the audit.

  (3) That the internal control system of the client was found to be satisfactory.

  (4) The subjects of the audit examination. (AICPA, adapted)

GROUP III
PROBLEMS

1–37.   The business activities of Casa Royale Ltd., consist of the administration and maintenance of approximately 400 condominiums and common property owned by individuals in a suburban residential development. Revenue consists of monthly fees collected from each condominium owner, plus some miscellaneous revenue. The principal expenses are property taxes and maintenance of all the buildings, shrubbery, swimming pools, lakes, parking lots, and other facilities. The furniture, fixtures, and equipment owned by the corporation and used to perform its maintenance functions represent about 25 percent of its total assets of $400,000.

 The corporation retained Howard Macklin, CA, to perform an audit of its financial statements for the current year and received from him the following audit report.

Shareholders of Casa Royale Ltd.

I have examined the balance sheet of Casa Royale Ltd. as at December 31, 19— and the statements of income and retained earnings and changes in financial position for the year then ended. My examination was made in accordance with generally accepted auditing standards, and accordingly included such tests and other procedures as I considered necessary in the circumstances.

As further amplified in Note 3 to the financial statements, my engagement did not include an examination of records relating to furniture, fixtures, equipment, or other plant assets indicated on the balance sheet.

In my opinion, except for the effects, if any, on the financial statements that an examination of plant assets might have produced, these financial statements present fairly the financial position of Casa Royale Ltd. as at December 31, 19— and the results of its operations and the changes in its financial position for the year then ended in accordance with generally accepted accounting principles applied on a basis consistent with that of the preceding year.

Howard Macklin, CA

The note to the financial statements referred to in the audit report read as follows "The equipment necessary for administration and maintenance was acquired in various years going back as far as the origin of the corporation ten years ago. Therefore, the records do not lend themselves readily to application of standard auditing procedures and are not included in my engagement of independent auditors. The equipment is being depreciated using the straight-line method over various estimated useful lives."

Required:

a. What type of audit did the CA issue? Was this the appropriate type of report under the circumstances? Explain.
b. What contradiction, if any, exists between the scope paragraph of the audit report and the note to the financial statements? Do you consider the note to be a reasonable statement? Why or why not?
c. Did the omission of the examination of plant assets from the audit engagement have any bearing on the evidence needed by the auditor in order to express an opinion on the income statement? Explain fully.

1–38. Janet Knight, president of Knight Limited, has become convinced that the quality of work being performed in the company's accounting operations has not shown the progress achieved in some other sections of the company. To remedy this situation, Knight decides to retain the services of a firm of chartered accountants. The company has never been audited. On October 1, Knight invites you, as a CA, to conduct an audit covering the current calendar year. The request includes mention of the fact that subsidiary ledgers are not in balance with control accounts, the posting of transactions is approximately two months in arrears, and bank statements have not been reconciled for several months.

Required:

You are to evaluate each of the following courses of action and state which, if any, you would follow. Give reasons for your choice. If none of the suggested courses of action is satisfactory, in your opinion, describe what you consider to be the appropriate action by the auditor. In drafting your answer to this problem, prepare a separate section for each of the six alternative courses of action.

a. Urge the management to take whatever steps are necessary to have the accounting records in balance and all transactions recorded on a current basis before the end of the year, so that the audit work can begin as scheduled and be completed in a reasonable time.

b. Advise the management of the serious deficiencies in operation of the accounting department, and explain that one of the benefits of your audit will be the balancing of subsidiary ledgers with control accounts and the bringing of the posting work up to date.

c. Offer to make an immediate analysis of the condition of the records, and then to undertake the necessary corrective work as a separate engagement, prior to the year-end audit already agreed upon.

d. Offer to make an immediate analysis of the records and a review of accounting personnel with the objective of making recommendations which will aid the client's own staff in getting the records into acceptable condition.

e. Advise the client that no corrective action is feasible until after the year-end audit. Explain that the performance of that audit will provide information on the nature and source of accounting shortcomings which should permit more efficient operation in the future.

f. Advise the client that you cannot accept the engagement, as you would not be able to express an opinion on the financial statements of a business having such poorly kept records.

1–39. Joe Rezzo, a college student majoring in accounting, helped finance his education with a part-time job maintaining all accounting records for a small company, White Company, located near the campus. Upon graduation, Rezzo joined the audit staff of a CA firm. However, he continued to perform all accounting work for White Company during his "leisure time." Three years later Rezzo received his CA certificate and decided to give up his part-time work with White Company. He notified White that he would no longer be available after preparing the year-end financial statements.

On January 7, Rezzo delivered the annual financial statements as his final act for White Company. The owner then made the following request "Joe, I am applying for a substantial bank loan, and the bank loan officer insists upon getting audited financial statements to support my loan application. You are now a CA and you know everything that's happened in this company and everything that's included in these financial statements, and you know they give a fair picture. I would appreciate it if you would write out the standard audit report and attach it to the financial statements. Then I'll be able to get some fast action on my loan application."

Required:

a. Would Rezzo be justified in complying with White's request for an auditor's opinion? Explain.

b. If you think Rezzo should issue the audit report, do you think he should first perform an audit of the company despite his detailed knowledge of the company's affairs? Explain.

c. If White had requested an audit by the CA firm for which Rezzo worked, would it have been reasonable for that firm to accept and assign Rezzo to perform the audit? Explain.

1–40. The following audit report is deficient in a number of respects. You are to criticize the report systematically from beginning to end, considering each sentence in turn. Use a separate paragraph with identifying heading for each point, as for example, Paragraph 1, Sentence 1. You may also wish to make comments on the overall contents of each paragraph and upon any omissions. Give reasons to support your views. After completing this critical review of the report, draft a revised report, on the assumption that your examination was adequate in all respects and disclosed no significant deficiencies.

To Whom It May Concern:

We have examined the accounting records of Garland Limited for the year ended June 30, 19—. We counted the cash and marketable securities, studied the accounting methods in use (which were consistently followed throughout the year), and made tests of the ledger accounts for assets and liabilities. The system of internal control contained no weaknesses.

In our opinion the accompanying balance sheet and income statement present correctly the financial condition of the corporation at June 30, 19—.

The accounting records of Garland Limited are maintained in accordance with accounting principles generally observed throughout the industry. Our examination was made in accordance with generally accepted auditing standards, and we certify the records and financial statements without qualification.

1–41. Bart James, a partner in the CA firm of James and Day, received the following memorandum from John Gray, president of Gray Manufacturing Limited, an audit client of many years.

Dear Bart:

I have a new type of engagement for you. You are familiar with how much time and money we have been spending in installing equipment to eliminate the air and water pollution caused by our manufacturing plant. We have changed our production processes to reduce discharge of gases; we have changed to more expensive fuel sources with less pollution potential; and we have discontinued some products because we couldn't produce them without causing considerable pollution.

I don't think the shareholders and the public are aware of the efforts we have made, and I want to inform them of our accomplishments in avoiding damage to the environment. We will devote a major part of our annual report to this topic, stressing that our company is the leader of the entire industry in combating pollution. To make this publicity more convincing, I would like to retain your firm to study what we have done and to attest as independent accountants that our operations are the best in the industry as far as preventing pollution is concerned.

To justify your statement, you are welcome to investigate every aspect of our operations as fully as you wish. We will pay for your services at your regular audit rates and will publish your "pollution opinion" in our annual report to shareholders immediately following some pictures and discussion of our special equipment and processes for preventing industrial pollution. We may put this section of the annual report in a separate cover and distribute it free to the public. Please let me know at once if this engagement is acceptable to you.

Required:

Put yourself in Bart James's position and write a reply to this client's request. Indicate clearly whether you are willing to accept the engagement and explain your attitude toward this proposed extension of the auditor's attest function.

1–42. After completing the audit field work on September 17, 19—, Dennis Wheeler prepared and delivered the following standard report to the shareholders of Wheat Limited.

To the Shareholders of Wheat Limited:

We have examined the balance sheet and the statement of income and retained earnings of Wheat Limited at July 31, 19—. In accordance with your instructions, a complete audit was conducted.

In many respects, this was an unusual year for Wheat Limited. The weakening of the economy in the early part of the year and the strike of plant employees in the summer led to a decline in sales and net income. After making several tests of sales records, nothing came to our attention that would indicate that sales have not been properly recorded.

In our opinion, with the explanation given above, and with the exception of some minor errors that are considered immaterial, these financial statements present fairly the financial position of Wheat Limited at July 31, 19— and the results of its operations for the year then ended in accordance with the *CICA Handbook* recommendations applied consistently throughout the period.

Toronto   Dennis Wheeler, CA
September 17, 19—

Required:

List and explain deficiencies and omission in the auditor's report. The type of opinion (unqualified, qualified, adverse, or denial) is not the issue and need not be discussed.

Organize your answer by paragraph (scope, explanatory, and opinion) of the auditors' report. (AICPA, adapted)

2

Professional ethics

The need for professional ethics

All recognized professions have developed codes of professional ethics. The fundamental purpose of such codes is to provide members with guidelines for maintaining a professional attitude and conducting themselves in a manner which will enhance the professional stature of their discipline.

To understand the importance of a code of ethics to public accountants and other professionals, one must understand the nature of a "profession" as opposed to other vocations. Unfortunately, there is no universally accepted definition of what constitutes a profession; yet, for generations, certain types of activities have been recognized as professions while others have not. Medicine, law, engineering, architecture, and theology are examples of disciplines long accorded professional status. Public accounting is a relative newcomer to the ranks of the professions, but it has achieved widespread recognition in recent decades.

All of the recognized professions have several common characteristics, and to a great extent it is these characteristics which distinguish the professions from other disciplines. The following characteristics, contained in the "Foreword" of the various provincial institutes' *Rules of Professional Conduct* and the CICA's recommended *Uniform Rules of Professional Conduct,* constitute the criteria which merit chartered accountancy as a profession:

> There is mastery by the practitioners of a particular intellectual skill, acquired by lengthy training and education;

The foundation of the calling rests in public practice—the application of the acquired skill to the affairs of others for a fee;

The calling centres on the provision of personal services rather than entrepreneurial dealing in goods;

There is an outlook, in the practice of the calling, which is essentially objective;

There is acceptance by the practitioners of a responsibility to subordinate personal interests to those of the public good;

There exists a developed and independent society or institute, comprising the members of the calling, which sets and maintains standards of qualification, attests to the competence of the individual pratitioner, and safeguards and develops the skills and standards of the calling;

There is a specialized code of ethical conduct, laid down and enforced by that society or institute, designed principally for the protection of the public;

There is a belief, on the part of those engaged in the calling, in the virtue of interchange of views, and in a duty to contribute to the development of their calling, adding to its knowledge and sharing advances in knowledge and technique with their fellow members.

The most important of these characteristics may be summarized as (a) the responsibility to serve the public, (b) a complex body of knowledge, and (c) the need for public confidence. Let us briefly discuss each.

Responsibility to serve the public.   The public accountant is the representative of the public—creditors, shareholders, consumers, employees, and others—in the financial reporting process. The role of the independent auditor is to assure that financial statements are *fair to all parties* and not biased to benefit one group at the expense of another. This responsibility to serve the public interest must be a basic motivation for the professional. If a public accountant's primary concern were to maximize income, he would presumably work for the benefit of whichever group offered the highest fee.

There is a saying in public accounting that "the public is our only client." This expression is an oversimplification, since the entity being audited pays the auditor's fee and is, in fact, the "client." Yet the saying conveys an ideal which is essential to the long-run professional status of public accounting. Public accountants must maintain a high degree of objectivity from their client (the company) if they are to be of service to the larger community. Objectivity is perhaps the most important concept embodied in public accounting's code of professional ethics.

Complex body of knowledge.   Any practitioner or student of accounting has only to look at the abundance of authoritative pronouncements governing financial reports to realize that accounting is a complex body of knowledge. One reason why such pronouncements continue to proliferate is that accounting must reflect what is taking place in an increasingly complex environment. As the environment changes—such as the trend toward business combinations in the 1960s and the increase in litigation and governmental regulation in the 1970s—accounting principles and auditing practices must adapt. The continual growth in the "common body of knowledge" for practicing accountants has led to serious proposals to establish continuing education requirements for CAs. The need for technical competence and familiarity with current standards of practice is embodied in the code of professional ethics.

Need for public confidence.   A physician, lawyer, chartered accountant, and all other professionals must have the confidence of the public to be successful. To the public accountant, however, public confidence is of special significance. The public accountant's product is *credibiliy;* without public confidence in the attestor, the attest function serves no useful purpose.

Professional ethics in public accounting, as in other professions, has developed gradually and is still in a process of change as the practice of accounting itself changes. Often new concepts are added as a result of unfortunate incidents which reflect unfavourably upon the profession, although not specifically in violation of existing standards.

Professional ethics in public accounting

A principal factor in maintaining high professional standards of practice has been the development of the rules of professional conduct by the provincial institutes and the Canadian Institute of Chartered Accountants. Careless work or lack of integrity on the part of any CA is a reflection upon the entire profession. Consequently, members of the profession have acted in unison through their provincial and national organizations to devise rules of professional conduct. These rules provide practical guidance to the individual member in maintaining a professional attitude. In addition, they give assurance to clients and to the public that the profession intends to maintain high standards and to enforce compliance by individual members.

Evidence that public accounting has achieved the status of a profession is found in the willingness of its members to accept voluntarily standards of conduct more rigorous than those imposed by law. These standards cover the relationships of the CA with clients, fellow practitioners, and the public. To be effective, a body of professional ethics must be attainable and enforceable; it must consist not merely of abstract ideals but of attainable goals and practical working rules which can be enforced.

In the short run the restraints imposed on the individual CA by a body of professional ethics may sometimes appear to constitute a hardship. From a long-run point of view, however, it is clear that the individual practitioner, the profession as a whole, and the public will benefit from the existence of a well-defined body of professional ethics.

The Rules of Professional Conduct

The *Rules of Professional Conduct* of the various provincial institutes and the recommended *Uniform Rules of Professional Conduct* of the CICA consist of four parts.[1] The first part, "Foreword," discusses the distinguishing characteristics of the chartered accountancy profession and the fundamental principles underlying the rules. The second part, "Definitions, Applications, and Interpretations," provides brief clarifications on definitions, applicability of rules, and the importance of the interpretation of the rules by the council of the respective institutes. The third part, "Rules of Conduct," is a group of enforceable ethical standards. The fourth part, "Interpretations," represents the interpretations of the rules issued by the institute council for the guidance of its members and students.

The *Rules of Professional Conduct*, by their very nature, set forth a minimum level of acceptable conduct. Consequently, CAs should strive for conduct beyond that indicated merely by prohibitions. The conduct toward which CAs should strive is embodied in the following fundamental principles underlying the rules:

1. A member or student shall conduct himself at all times in a manner which will maintain the good reputation of the profession and its ability to serve the public interest.
2. A member or student shall perform his professional services with integrity and care and accept an obligation to sustain his professional competence by keeping himself informed of, and complying with, developments in professional standards.
3. A member who is engaged to express an opinion on financial statements shall hold himself free of any influence, interest, or relationship, in respect of his client's affairs, which impairs his professional judgment or objectivity or which, in the view of a reasonable observer, has that effect.
4. A member or student has a duty of confidence in respect of the affairs of any client and shall not disclose, without proper cause, any information obtained in the course of his duties, nor shall he in any way exploit such information to his advantage.
5. The development of a member's practice shall be founded upon a reputation for professional excellence, and the use of methods com-

---

[1] The recommended Uniform Rules of Professional Conduct of the CICA are patterned after the rules of the Ontario Institute and have been adopted by most provincial institutes. It is most likely that all provincial institutes will adopt the Uniform Rules and thus will result in a set of rules uniform throughout Canada. The recommended Uniform Rules have not yet been officially adopted by the CICA even though such an action will be taken in the near future.

monly characterized as self-promotion or solicitation is not in keeping with this principle.

6. A member shall act in relation to any other member with the courtesy and consideration due between professional colleagues and which, in turn, he would wish to be accorded by the other member.

These principles may be summarized as (a) responsibilities to the profession; (b) integrity, due care, and competence; (c) objectivity; and (d) responsibilities to clients and colleagues.

RULES OF CONDUCT

Applicability and enforcement of rules

While most of the *Rules of Professional Conduct* are applicable to those members practicing public accounting, many are also applicable to all members and students. The applicability of the rules is stated in the "Foreword" of the Institute's *Rules of Professional Conduct.*

> A member not engaged in the practice of public accounting must observe these rules except where the wording of any rule makes it clear that it relates specifically to the practice of public accounting or there is a specific exception made in a particular rule.
>
> Where the term "professional services" is used it means, in its application to a member not engaged in the practice of public accounting, those of his activities where the public or his associates are entitled to rely on his membership in the Institute as giving him particular competence.
>
> A member is responsible to the Institute for compliance with these rules by others associated with him in the public practice of the functions covered by the rules, who are either under his supervision or share with him proprietary interest in the practice, and must not permit others to carry out on his behalf acts which, if he carried them out himself, would place him in violation of the rules.
>
> A member who is resident outside Canada is expected to abide by the rules of the organized accounting profession in the jurisdiction in which he resides and to ensure that his actions do not bring disrepute upon the Institute.

Each provincial institute is empowered by its by-laws to enforce compliance with the *Rules of Professional Conduct* by its members. The institute's professional conduct, discipline, and appeal committees are charged with the responsibility of the administration, enforcement, and disciplinary processes. A member or student who is found guilty of violating any provisions of the rules will be reprimanded, suspended, or expelled. A member who is expelled from the institute will lose his or her CA certificate and will not be allowed to engage in the practice of public accounting. Obviously, neither the institute nor its members should take such a penalty lightly, for the damage to the individual's professional reputation can be disastrous.

Interpretations of Rules of Professional Conduct

In order to ensure that the *Rules of Professional Conduct* are properly and clearly understood, interpretations of the rules are issued by the council of the provincial institute. These interpretations provide further information and guidance for members and students and constitute an integral part of the rules. Each member and student should be extremely familiar with such interpretations. Since the interpretations are generally lengthy, they will not be discussed here but are included as an Appendix to this chapter.[2]

Specific rules[3]

The following *Rules of Professional Conduct* are classified into four categories: (*a*) general, (*b*) standards of conduct affecting the public interest, (*c*) relations with fellow members and with non-members engaged in public accounting, and (*d*) organization and conduct of a professional practice.

General

101   Members and students shall comply with the by-laws, rules and regulations and rules of professional conduct of the Institute as they may be from time to time and with any order or resolution of the council or officers of the Institute under the by-laws.

102   Any member or student who has been convicted of any criminal or similar offence may be charged with professional misconduct by the professional conduct committee; in such cases, a certificate of conviction by any competent court shall be sufficient evidence of the conviction and of the commission of the offence.

Standards of conduct affecting the public interest

201   A member or student shall conduct himself at all times in a manner which will maintain the good reputation of the profession and its ability to serve the public interest.

---

[2] Since the interpretations are uniform for most provincial institutes and will likely be uniform for all provincial institutes in the near future, and since the provincial institutes are responsible for the enforcement of the rules, a provincial institute's interpretations appears to be more relevant. The interpretations of the Ontario Institute have been arbitrarily selected for purposes of illustration. Members and students should, of course, refer to their respective institutes' interpretations for guidance.

[3] For the same reasons as stated in footnote 2, the Rules of Professional Conduct of the Ontario Institute are used as illustration. Members and students should, of course, refer to their respective institute's Rule of Professional Conduct for guidance.

202   A member or student shall perform his professional services with integrity and due care.

203   A member shall sustain his professional competence by keeping himself informed of, and complying with, developments in professional standards in all functions in which he practises or is relied upon because of his calling.

204   A member who is engaged to express an opinion on financial statements shall hold himself free of any influence, interest or relationship, in respect of his client's affairs, which impairs his professional judgment or objectivity or which, in the view of a reasonable observer, has that effect.[4]

205   A member or student shall not sign or associate himself with any letter, report, statement, representation or financial statement which he knows, or should know, is false or misleading, whether or not the signing or association is subject to a disclaimer of responsibility.

206.1   In expressing an opinion on financial statements examined by him a member shall not

(1)   fail to reveal any material fact known to him which is not disclosed in the financial statements, the omission of which renders the financial statements misleading, nor

(2)   fail to report any material misstatement known to him to be contained in the financial statements.

.2   A member shall not express an opinion on financial statements examined by him

(1)   if he fails to obtain sufficient information to warrant an expression of opinion, or

(2)   if he has not complied in all material respects with the auditing standards of the profession, or

(3)   if the exceptions or qualifications to the opinion are sufficiently material to nullify the value of such opinion.

.3   Subject to item (3) of Rule 206.2 a member shall not express an opinion on financial statements examined by him which are not prepared in accordance with the accounting standards of the profession unless such opinion is suitably qualified; without limiting the generality of the foregoing, if a member expresses an opinion without qualification or exception that financial statements are presented in accordance with generally accepted accounting principles and if such statements depart in any material respect from the recommendations of the Accounting and Auditing Research Committee of the Canadian Institute of Chartered Accountants or its successor(s) (the Ac-

---

[4] It should be noted that the specific interpretations of objectivity or independence, as used in federal and some provincial business corporations acts, may differ somewhat. Some acts are more restrictive than the council's interpretations. A member should be familiar with the specific act under which his client company is incorporated. To the extent that the act is more restrictive, the auditor should comply with such statutory requirement.

counting Research Committee), such departure must be capable of justification as proper in the particular circumstances.

207 A member shall inform his client of any business connections, any affiliations, and any interests of which the client might reasonably expect to be informed but this does not necessarily include disclosure of professional services he may be rendering or proposing to render to other clients.

208.1 A member or student shall not, in connection with any transaction involving a client, hold, receive, bargain for, become entitled to or acquire any fee, remuneration or benefit without the client's knowledge and consent.

.2 A member or student shall not, in connection with any transaction involving his employer, hold, receive, bargain for, become entitled to or acquire any fee, remuneration or benefit without the employer's knowledge and consent.

209 A member or student shall not take any action, such as acquiring any interest, property or benefit, in connection with which he makes improper use of confidential knowledge of a client's affairs obtained in the course of his duties.

210.1 A member or student shall not disclose or use any confidential information concerning the affairs of any client except when properly acting in the course of his duties or when such information is required to be disclosed by order of lawful authority or by the council, the professional conduct committee, the discipline committee or the appeal committee in the proper exercise of their duties.

.2 A member or student shall not disclose or use any confidential information concerning the affairs of his employer except when properly acting in the course of his duties or when such information is required to be disclosed by order of lawful authority or by the council, the professional conduct committee, the discipline committee or the appeal committee in the proper exercise of their duties.

211 Subject to the provisions of Rule 210, a member shall bring to the attention of the professional conduct committee any apparent breach of these rules or any instance involving or appearing to involve doubt as to the competence, reputation or integrity of a member, student or applicant.

212 A member or student who handles money or other property in trust shall do so in accordance with the terms of the trust and the general law relating to trusts and shall maintain such records as are necessary to account properly for the money or other property; unless otherwise provided for by the terms of the trust, money held in trust shall be kept in a separate trust bank account or accounts.

213 A member or student shall not knowingly lend himself, his name or his services to any unlawful activity.

214 A member shall not respond to any call for tenders for the

provision of professional services in respect of the practice of public accounting.

215   A member engaged in the practice of public accounting shall not offer or agree to render any professional service for a fee contingent on the results of such service, nor shall he represent that he does any service without fee except services of a charitable, benevolent or similar nature.

216   Other than in relation to the sale and purchase of an accounting practice, a member engaged in the practice of public accounting shall not directly or indirectly pay to any person who is not a public accountant a commission or other compensation to obtain a client, nor shall he accept directly or indirectly from any person who is not a public accountant a commission or other compensation for a referral to a client of products or services of others.

217   Except to the extent permitted in any Interpretations adopted and published by the council from time to time interpreting the intent or meaning of this rule, a member engaged in the practice of public accounting shall not advertise.

Relations with fellow members and with non-members engaged in public accounting

301   A member engaged in the practice of public accounting shall not directly or indirectly solicit professional engagements which have been entrusted to another public accountant; without limiting the generality of the foregoing, a member shall not seek to secure such an engagement by representing that he is able to carry out the engagement at a lower fee than that of the other public accountant.

302   A member shall not accept an appointment with respect to any function relating to the practice of public accounting, where he is replacing another public accountant, without first communicating with such public accountant and enquiring whether there are any circumstances he should take into account which might influence his decision whether or not to accept the appointment.

303   A member who accepts any appointment jointly with another public accountant shall accept joint and several responsibility for any portion of the work to be performed by either; no member shall proceed in any matter within the terms of such joint appointment without due notice to the other accountant.

304   A member engaged in the practice of public accounting shall, before commencing any special assignment for a client of another public accountant who is the duly appointed auditor, when not limited or restricted in writing by the terms of his assignment, first notify such accountant of the assignment.

305.1   A member who accepts a special assignment, whether by referral or otherwise, from a client of a public accountant who is continuing in his relationship with that client shall not take any action which would tend to impair the position of the other public accountant in his ongoing work with his client.

.2   A member who receives an engagement for services by referral from another public accountant shall not provide or offer to provide any different services to the referring accountant's client without the consent of the referring accountant; the interest of the client being of overriding concern, the referring accountant shall not unreasonably withhold such consent.

306   A member engaged in the practice of public accounting shall not directly or indirectly offer employment to an employee of another member who is a public accountant without first informing such member. A member engaged in the practice of public accounting may publicly advertise for staff and may negotiate with a respondent to such advertisement or with anyone who on his own initiative applies to the member for employment, providing the member informs the other member of his intention to offer employment to such applicant. [Added in the CICA Uniform Rules]

Organization and conduct of a professional practice

401   A member shall not engage in the practice of public accounting, or in the public practice of any function not inconsistent therewith, under a name or style which is misleading as to the nature of the organization (proprietorship, partnership or, where permitted, corporation) or the nature of the function performed.

402.1   The practice of public accounting shall be carried on under the descriptive style of either "chartered accountant(s)" or "Public accountant(s)"; regardless of the functions actually performed, the use of either or both of these descriptive styles, in offering services to the public, shall be regarded as carrying on the practice of public accounting for the purposes of these rules.

.2   A member engaged in the practice of public accounting who is associated with non-members in such practice shall be responsible to the Institute for any failure of such associates, in respect of such practice, to abide by the rules of professional conduct of the Institute.

403.1   Except to the extent permitted in any Interpretations adopted and published by the council from time to time interpreting the intent or meaning of this rule, a member engaged in the practice of public accounting shall not operate a part-time office.

.2   Each office in Ontario [name of the relevant province] of any member or firm of members engaged in the practice of public accounting shall be under the personal charge and management of a member who is a licensed public accountant and who shall be normally in attendance in such office; no member shall have the personal charge of more than one such office, except as provided in Rule 403.1.

.3 Each office in Ontario [name of the relevant province] of any firm engaged in the practice of public accounting and composed of one or more members sharing proprietary interest with other licensed public accountants who are not members shall practice under the style of "public accountants" and shall be under the personal charge and management of a member or other licensed public accountant who shall be normally in attendance in such office; no member or other licensed public accountant in such firm shall have the personal charge of more than one such office, except as provided in Rule 403.1.

.4 For the purposes of Rules 403.2 and 403.3 and to establish whether or not a person is "normally in attendance," any office which is held out as that of a public practitioner shall be operated on a regular daily full-time basis with a member or other licensed public accountant (as the context requires) personally in charge and normally available there to serve the public.

404 A member shall not hold out or imply that he has an office in any place where he is in fact only represented by another public accountant or a firm of public accountants and, conversely, a member who only represents a public accountant or a firm of public accountants, shall not hold out or imply that he maintains an office for such public accountant or such firm.

405 A member engaged in the practice of public accounting shall not adopt any method of obtaining or attracting clients which tends to bring disrepute on the profession.

406 The practice of public accounting as a sole proprietor or as a firm shall be subject to the following provisions:

(1) A member shall not associate in any way with an individual or a firm carrying on the practice of public accounting under a non-personal title or name.

(2) A member engaged in the practice of public accounting as a sole proprietor shall practice under his own name unless permitted by the council, in special circumstances, to practise under the name of a predecessor sole proprietor or where permitted by council, on a temporary basis, some other predecessor firm name.

(3) Subject to clauses (2) and (4) hereof, firm names shall be restricted to the names of professional colleagues who are, or were previously, partners with the firm, the number of surnames used not to exceed the number of partners currently active with the firm; the addition of "& Co." or appropriate similar wording is allowed only where the number of partners currently active with the

firm exceeds the number of surnames used in the firm name.

(4) Notwithstanding the foregoing clause (3)

(a) firm names need not include the names of all partners,

(b) the council may, in its discretion, in appropriate circumstances, permit the use in a firm name of the names of persons who have practised as public accountants in Canada or any other country.

(c) a firm may continue to use a name which it is permitted to use in Ontario [name of the relevant province] at June 11, 1973 except that, after June 10, 1975,[5] the use or continued use of "& Co." or appropriate similar wording shall be allowed only where the number of partners currently active with the firm exceeds the number of surnames used in the firm name.

(5) A member shall not associate in any way with any firm practising as chartered accountants in Ontario [name of the relevant province] unless:

(a) all partners resident in Ontario [name of the relevant province] are members,

(b) at least one partner is a member, and

(c) all the partners are professional colleagues or professional corporations provided each such corporation is recognized and approved for the practice of public accounting by the provincial institute in the province concerned.[6]

Association with a corporation engaged in the practice of public accounting

407 A member shall not be associated in any way with any corporation engaged in Canada in the practice of public accounting, except to the extent permitted in Rule 409 and in clauses (1), (2) and (3) of this rule:

(1) a member or his firm

(a) may be the auditor(s) of the corporation,

(b) may be the appointed accountant(s) to prepare the financial statements of the corporation,

(c) may give tax advice to the corporation with respect to the financial affairs of the corporation;

(2) a member, other than a practising member, may be associated with a corporation which provides taxation ser-

---

[5] These dates may vary from province to province, for example, the Nova Scotia rules read "at June 21, 1975" and "after June 30, 1977."

[6] The provincial laws of Alberta now permit "professional corporations" for public accountants.

vices involving advice and counselling in an expert capacity provided such services are only a small part of the corporation's activities;

(3)   a member may be associated with a professional corporation engaged in the practice of public accounting in a province other than Ontario if the corporation is recognized and approved for such practice by the provincial institute in the province concerned and the corporation does not engage in the practice of public accounting in Ontario.

408   A member engaged in the practice of public accounting may engage in a business or practice as a department or part of such public accounting practice, in one or more of the following functions, hereinafter sometimes referred to as the related functions:

(1)   management consulting,

(2)   trustee in bankruptcy,

(3)   electronic data processing, and

(4)   such other functions as council may, from time to time, designate,

Subject to the following provisions:

(a)   he may use, in each such business or practice, separate stationery, name plate, professional card, brochure or announcement in which the functions listed as items (1), (2), and (3) herein, shall be designated, "management consultant(s)," "trustee(s) in bankruptcy" and "electronic data processing" respectively; but he shall not use, in any such business or practice, any stationery, name plates, professional card, brochure or announcements of his accounting practice, except to the extent permitted in sub-clause (b) hereof;

(b)   where applicable, the descriptive style "trustee(s) in bankruptcy" may appear together with the descriptive style "chartered accountant(s)" or "public accountant(s)" in stationery, name plates, professional cards, brochures or announcements;

(c)   except as provided in sub-clause (b) hereof, no reference to such functions shall be made in stationery, name plates, professional cards or announcements of his public accounting practice nor shall reference be made to his public accounting practice nor to the other related functions in the stationery, name plates, professional cards or announcements of the business or practice of the related functions;

409.1   A member engaged in the practice of public accounting may carry on a business or practice through an organization separate from such public accounting practice, either as a proprietor, a partner, or as a director, officer or shareholder of a corporation and may associate with non-members for this purpose, in one or more of the following functions, hereinafter sometimes referred to as the related functions:

(1)   management consulting,

(2)   trustee in bankruptcy,

(3)   electronic data processing, and

(4)   such other functions as council may, from time to time, designate,

subject to the following provisions:

(a)   the functions listed as items (1), (2) and (3) herein, shall be designated "management consultant(s)," "trustee(s) in bankruptcy" and "electronic data processing," respectively;

(b)   the business or practice shall not be designated "chartered accountant(s)" or "public accountant(s)";

(c)   subject to the provisions of sub-clauses (d), (e) and (f) hereof, the name of any such business or practice shall not be used until it has first been approved by the council as a name which in its opinion is a personal name distinguishable from the name of any related public accounting practice;

(d)   where there is identity of ownership, the name of any such business or practice may be identical with the name of a related public accounting practice (with the addition of "& Co." or appropriate similar wording permitted where such addition accords with this rule) and such a name may be used without the prior approval of the council;

(e)   where any such business or practice is that of management consulting the name may include the words "management consultant(s)";

(f)   where any such business or practice is that of electronic data processing, the council may approve a name which is non-personal and descriptive of the function performed and which in the opinion of council is not objectionable;

(g)   subject to sub-clause (h) hereof the number of surnames used in the name of any such business or practice shall not exceed the number of partners or shareholders currently active with such business or practice and the addition of "& Co." or appropriate similar wording is allowed only where the number of partners or shareholders currently active with the business or practice exceeds the number of surnames used in such name;

(h)   notwithstanding the foregoing sub-clause (g) any such business or practice may continue to use a name which it was permitted to use in Ontario [name of the relevant province] at June 11, 1973 except that, after June 10,

1975,[7] the use or continued use of "& Co." or appropriate similar wording shall be allowed only where the number of partners or shareholders currently active with such business or practice exceeds the number of surnames used in the name of the business or practice;

(i) where any such business or practice is a corporation there shall be added to its name "Ltd."; "Limited," "Inc." or "Incorporated," "Corp." or "Corporation";

(j) where applicable, the descriptive style "trustee(s) in bankruptcy" may appear together with the descriptive style, "chartered accountant(s)" or "public accountant(s)" in stationery, name plates, professional cards, brochures or announcements;

(k) except as provided in sub-clause (j) hereof, no reference to any such business or practice shall be made in the stationery, name plates, professional cards, or announcements of the public accounting practice nor shall reference be made to the public accounting practice nor to the other related functions in the stationery, name plates, professional cards or announcements of any such business or practice;

(l) except to the extent permitted in sub-clause (j) hereof, a member shall not use, in any such business or practice, any stationery, name plate, professional card, brochure or announcement of his public accounting practice;

(m) except in the case of electronic data processing, beneficial ownership in any such business or practice must be restricted to members and such non-members as are or were actively engaged in the operation of the business or practice; and

(n) for the purpose of this rule the term "identity of ownership" means that the persons who, as proprietors, partners, directors, officers or shareholders, exclusively own and manage any such business or practice are the same persons as exclusively own and manage any related public accounting practice.

.2 Before commencing an assignment in any of the related functions from a client of another public accountant who is the duly appointed auditor, a member engaged in the practice of public accounting who is associated with a firm or corporation carrying on a business or practice in any of the related functions shall first notify, or shall ensure that the associated firm or corporation first notifies, such accountant of the assignment.

.3 A member engaged in the practice of public accounting who

---

[7] These dates may vary from province to province, for example, the Nova Scotia rule reads "at June 21, 1975," and "after June 30, 1977."

is associated with a firm or corporation carrying on a business or practice in one or more of the related functions, either as principal, partner, director, officer or shareholders, shall be responsible to the Institute for any failure of such firm or corporation to abide by the rules of professional conduct of the Institute as if such firm or corporation were a member engaged in the practice of public accounting.

410.1   A member engaged in the public practice of a function not inconsistent with public accounting, and who is not also engaged in the practice of public accounting, may, in carrying on his practice, conduct his affairs (or his firm's or corporation's affairs) free of the constraints imposed upon members engaged in the practice of public accounting by Rules 215, 216, 217, 301, Rules 403 to 406 inclusive and Rules 408, and 409, but not in such a fashion as to tend to bring disrepute on the profession.

.2   A member so engaged shall not refer a client for services to another member or firm engaged in the practice of public accounting for identifiable personal advantage.

Analysis of Rules of Professional Conduct

Many of the rules stated in the *Rules of Professional Conduct* are self-explanatory, but discussion and illustration may be necessary to a full understanding of some of the rules.

Objectivity.[8]   Rule 204 is concerned with the problem of objectivity, which has two distinct aspects. First, public accountants must *in fact* be objective toward any enterprise they audit. Second, the relationships of public accountants with clients must be such that they will *appear* objective to third parties.

Objectivity in fact refers to the public accountant's ability to maintain an unbiased and impartial mental attitude or state of mind in all aspects of his work, regardless of whether or not existing circumstances might have an apparent effect on his objectivity. As such, it is not subject to objective measurement and therefore can be judged only by the public accountant himself.

Objectivity in appearance refers to the public accountant's freedom from conflict of interest which third parties may infer from circumstantial evidence. It is a third party's perception of the public accountant's objectivity based on the facts of a given situation. For example, if a public accountant owns shares in the corporation which he audits, he is most likely perceived by third parties as lacking objectivity. Whether the

---

[8] The term *objectivity* is sometimes referred to as *independence*. The Canada Business Corporations Act and some provincial business corporations acts use the term *independence*.

public accountant can maintain his objective state of mind is beside the question, he *does not appear* to be objective because of his conflict of interest, being a shareholder and the auditor of the same corporation. Since objectivity in fact is subjective and elusive to prove, objectivity in appearance has become more important in judging the public accountant's objectivity. A public accountant who is lacking objectivity in appearance is not qualified to serve as an auditor under the Canada Business Corporations Act.[9] An investor or banker using audited financial statements would prefer that the audit be performed by a public accountant who had no financial or management interest in the company and therefore had no conflict of interest. Moreover, this may also be beneficial to the public accountant. For example, if a public accountant failed to discover a material fraud, the reaction of creditors, investors, and the public would be far more critical if it were discovered that the public accountant was also part owner of the company, even if that ownership interest was quite small. Under these circumstances the publicity which always stems from fraud cases would surely lessen public confidence in the public accounting profession.

Auditing standards and accounting principles.   Rule 206 obligates a CA performing an audit to comply with the CICA Auditing Standards Committee's eight generally accepted auditing standards discussed in Chapter 1. It also requires the CA to recognize the recommendations of the CICA Accounting Research Committee and its predecessor, the Accounting and Auditing Research Committee, as generally accepted accounting principles.

The consequence of this rule is a strengthening of the authority of the CICA and its Accounting Research and Auditing Standards Committees, and a lessening of the opportunity for wide variations in the quality of auditing services or the options available for accounting principles.

Confidential client information.   Rule 210 stresses the confidential nature of information obtained by CAs from their clients. The nature of the public accountants' work makes it necessary for them to have access to their client's most confidential financial affairs. Public accountants may thus gain knowledge of impending business combinations, proposed financing, prospective stock splits or dividend changes, contracts being negotiated, and other confidential information which, if disclosed or otherwise improperly used, could bring the accountants quick monetary profits. Of course, the client would be financially injured, as well as embarrassed, if the CAs were to "leak" such information. Accountants must

---

[9] The *Canada Business Corporations Act and Regulations, 1976,* 3d ed. (Toronto: Richard Dee Boo Limited, 1976), sec. 155, pp. 91–92. This legal requirement only prohibits the auditor from having material interest in the securities of the client corporation. For a comparison with the Rules of Professional Conduct, see Chapter 2, page 68.

not only keep quiet as to their clients' business plans, but they rarely even mention in public the names of their clients. Any loose talk by public accountants concerning the affairs of their clients would immediately brand them as lacking in professional ethics. On the other hand, the confidential relationship between the CA and the client is *never* a justification for the CA to cooperate in any deceitful act. The personal integrity of the CA is essential to the performance of the attest function.

The auditors' reaction to dishonest or illegal acts. Rule 213 requires that a CA "shall not knowingly lend himself, his name or his services to any unlawful activity." It must also be emphasized that unswerving commitment to honourable behaviour is the essence of ethical conduct. If CAs permit doubts to arise about their personal integrity, they have destroyed their usefulness as independent auditors. CAs must always keep this concept of integrity and honourable behaviour in mind when they encounter dishonest, illegal, or possible illegal acts by a client.

Under no circumstances should a CA condone or ignore actions which he *knows* to be dishonest or illegal. This does not mean that the CA should report such acts to governmental authorities; it does mean that he should not permit his firm's name to be associated with financial statements which are misleading, or which conceal morally indefensible actions by a client. If the CA has knowledge of dishonest or clearly illegal actions by a client, he should discuss the situation with the top-management group, including the board of directors, and with the client's and his own firm's legal counsel. The CA should try to persuade the client to disclose all the relevant facts and to take corrective action. Should the client refuse, the CA should withdraw from the engagement. This action on the part of the CA makes clear that he will not be associated in any way with dishonourable or illegal activities. The performance of the attest function by public accountants is a valuable and important service to society if two conditions are met: personal integrity and professional competence on the part of the CA.

The auditors' reaction to "possibly illegal" actions. How should auditors respond when a transaction or conduct appears to be in possible violation of the law? Every large and complex business organization is subject to a maze of laws and regulations at the federal, provincial, and local levels, some of which almost defy understanding. Even a client in the not-for-profit sector of society (such as a university or a hospital) may be unintentionally in violation of some laws. Since some laws are so complex that a court may take years to reach a decision, it is apparent that a CA cannot, during the course of an annual audit, reach definite conclusions about the legality of all actions by a client.

Nevertheless, public accountants may sometimes become aware of transactions which may be illegal. Multinational corporations, for example, may take certain actions which are legal in the country in which the actions occurred but which are illegal in Canada. To what extent should the independent auditor insist on the disclosure in audited financial statements of any such questionable actions by the client? No simple answer exists. An old adage says that "an auditor is neither a reformer nor an informer." Even if the auditor's doubts about the honesty or legality of a client's actions impelled him to sever all relationships with the client, he would ordinarily not be justified in reporting the client's questionable actions to governmental authorities. To do so would be a violation of the confidential relationship of auditor and client. Of course, rare and extraordinary circumstances might outweigh this basic concept of confidentiality. In any event, the auditors should consult with the client's legal counsel and their own firm's counsel regarding possible illegal client acts.

Contingent fees.   Rule 215 prohibits a CA from rendering any professional service on a contingent fee basis. For example, a company in need of an auditor's report to support its application for a bank loan might offer to make the auditor's fee contingent upon approval of the loan by the bank. Such an arrangement would affect the auditor's objectivity, both in fact and in appearance. There would be the potential temptation for the auditor to abandon an objective viewpoint and lend support to the statements prepared by management, and the conflict of interest would probably cause informed third parties to doubt the auditor's objectivity.

Encroachment.   Rules 301 to 306 stipulate that a CA should not encroach upon the practice and other professional activities of another CA or public accountant. The need for such a prohibition is apparent; without it, distrust and hostility would pervade relationships between public accountants.

These rules also contain a safeguard against the undesirable practice known as "shopping for principles." For example, a CA firm which takes a stand against what it considers improper accounting presentation or disclosure by a client might be discharged by the client and replaced by another firm of CAs whose professional judgment sanctions the disputed presentation or disclosure. Such an occurrence obviously would have a detrimental effect upon the relationship between the two CA firms and upon the public accounting profession as a whole. The requirement that a public accountant who is approached by the audit client of another CA must consult with the other accountant before rendering professional services should contribute a great deal toward curbing any "shopping for principles."

Moreover, these rules should also discourage overly aggressive, unprofessional actions by a CA firm in seeking to attract new clients presently served by another CA. An awareness that discussions with a company's present auditors must precede acceptance of a new client will perhaps serve as an additional deterrent to encroachment by one CA firm upon the practice of another.

Furthermore, these rules protect a CA from accepting an appointment before knowing the circumstances under which the previous auditor's services were discontinued, circumstances which might well influence the CA's decision of whether or not to accept the audit engagement.

Advertising, solicitation, and competitive bidding. Rule 217 bans any advertising that is a form of solicitation. Rule 405 prohibits a CA from adopting "any method of obtaining or attracting clients which tends to bring disrepute on the profession." Rule 214 states that a CA "shall not respond to any call for tenders for the provision of professional services in respect of the practice of public accounting."

Accordingly, the use of radio or television advertising, outdoor signs, stationery with heading describing services offered, and similar practices are all unacceptable for a member of the profession. A business executive may appropriately advertise the merits of the products his firm offers for sale, but professional persons cannot appropriately advertise their own intelligence, integrity, and knowledge.

To illustrate the breadth of application of this rule, let us assume that John Wells, CA, appears on television during the income tax season on an educational program discussing some of the problems commonly encountered by taxpayers in the preparation of tax returns. Such appearances are in the public interest and are entirely within the bounds of professional ethics, *provided* Wells does not at any time during the program mention his business address or otherwise intimate that he is available for tax work, and *provided* that he is not introduced by the announcer as available for tax services.

Competitive bidding is considered a form of solicitation, and thus unprofessional and not in the public interest. Obviously, all these rules are intended to protect the public interest, as stated in the "Foreword" of the *Rules of Professional Conduct.*

> . . . strictures against advertising, against publicly claiming special skills above those possessed by colleagues with equal qualifications, and against solicitation for engagements, are readily understood by a member of a profession. He regards these acts, almost instinctively, as the very antithesis of professionalism—a scrambling for clientele inappropriate to an essentially intellectual calling which emphasizes quality of service. So, too, with responding to calls for tenders for engagements.

> . . . It would not be in the public interest, for example, that the selection of a practitioner by a client was a function of the skill of the practitioner's advertising agency and the size of his advertising budget; nor that a practitioner could, publicly, claim for himself professional skills exceeding those of similarly qualified practitioners, in a purely subjective fashion and without let, hindrance or reasonable constraint; nor that quality of service in the important realms of right and property, in which chartered accountants function, should become secondary to price—for example, a

public accounting engagement being tailored to a bid price rather than to the needs of the engagement, as they emerge, in the professional judgment of the chartered accountant; nor that self-promotion replace the building of a reputation for professional competence.

It is not an exaggeration to suggest that the rules concerned are basic to a profession and that their removal would lead, in the long run, to downgrading the quality of service given and to the disintegration of the profession. Since the public interest in the quality of services provided by chartered accountants is assumed in the continuing existence and growth of the profession, that interest would not be served by any act which tended to destroy the profession.

Independence of auditor in the Canada Business Corporations Act

The Canada Business Corporations Act uses the term *independence* rather than *objectivity* to describe the auditor's lack of conflict of interest. Section 155 of the act stipulates that a person must be independent to be qualified as an auditor of a corporation, unless a court exempts such a requirement. Independence is considered "a question of fact," and the following facts constitute non-independence:

a person is deemed not to be independent if he or his business partner
  (i)   is a business partner, a director, an officer or an employee of the corporation, of any of its affiliates, or of any director, officer or employee of any such corporation or its affiliates,
  (ii) beneficially owns or controls, directly or indirectly, a material interest in the securities of the corporation or any of its affiliates, or
  (iii) has been a receiver, receiver-manager, liquidator or trustee in bankruptcy of the corporation or any of its affiliates within two years of his proposed appointment as auditor of the corporation.

The concept of independence (objectivity) required by the act differs from that set forth in the *Rules of Professional Conduct* in three aspects. First, the act defines independence in terms of independence in appearance, while the rules encompass both independence in appearance and in fact. Second, the act allows the auditor to have *immaterial* interest in the client's securities, while the rules do not allow *any* interest in the client's securities. Third, the act disqualifies a person from serving as auditor if he has been a receiver, receiver-manager, liquidator, or trustee in bankruptcy of the corporation or any of its affiliates within the past two years.[10] The Interpretations of the *Rules of Professional Conduct*, however, only deem it inadvisable for a CA to serve as trustee in bankruptcy of a company if he has been the auditor within the past two years. Also, the rules do not preclude a CA who is or has acted as auditor for a

---

[10] Certain provincial corporations act contains the same or similar requirements. For example, see the Ontario Business Corporations Act.

client from accepting an appointment as receiver, receiver-manager, or liquidator of such client. Obviously, the auditor must follow a statutory prohibition in cases where it applies.

The CA as tax adviser—ethical problems

Since the *Rules of Professional Conduct* contain no specific provisions for tax practices, what are the responsibilities of the CA in serving as tax adviser? The CA has a primary responsibility to the client, namely, to see that the client pays the proper amount of tax and no more. The CA may properly resolve questionable issues in favour of the client as long as the solution is within the reasonable interpretation of the tax laws and regulations and the client is appropriately advised of the implications involved; the CA is not obliged to maintain the posture of independence required in audit work. When CAs express an opinion on financial statements, they must be unbiased; however, freedom from bias is not required in serving as a tax adviser. On the other hand, CAs must adhere to the same standards of truth and personal integrity in tax work as in all other professional activities. Any departure from these standards on a tax engagement would surely destroy the reputation of CAs, especially in performing their work as independent auditors.

A second responsibility of CAs on a tax engagement is to ensure that the information contained in the tax returns is not false or misleading, whether or not the returns are signed by CAs. This is required by Rule 205 which states "a member or student shall not sign or associate himself with any letter, report, statement, representation or financial statement which he knows, or should know, is false or misleading, whether or not the signing or association is subject to a disclaimer of responsibility."

To comply with this responsibility, what steps must the CA take? The CA is not required to perform an audit; knowledge of the tax return may be limited to information supplied to him by the taxpayer. However, if this information appears unreasonable or contradictory, the CA is obligated to make sufficient investigation to resolve these issues. Information which appears plausible to a layman might appear unreasonable to a CA, since he is an expert in evaluating financial data. The CA is not obligated to investigate any and all information provided by the taxpayer, but he cannot ignore clues which cast doubt on the accuracy of these data.

Unless CAs approach tax engagements with full recognition of the responsibilities imposed on them by the profession, they may quickly destroy public confidence in the profession. The interests of the taxpayer and of the government are directly opposed, and this conflict of interest requires a most careful delineation of the responsibility of CAs. Because of public confidence in the high professional standards of the CAs and the reputation of the profession for integrity, any financial data to which

CAs lend their names gain in credibility even though no examination is made and no opinion is expressed. This level of public confidence and respect is an invaluable asset of the profession and it deserves to be guarded with the greatest care.

Management advisory services and professional ethics

The rendering of management advisory services has in recent years represented a steadily rising proportion of the work performed by public accounting firms. CAs serve clients as system analysts, data processing advisers, financial consultants, operations researchers, and budgetary experts.

Do the *Rules of Professional Conduct* apply to the field of management advisory services? The answer is "yes." In addition to the rules applicable to all members, there are specific rules relating to CAs engaged in management advisory services, either as part of their public practice or as a separate organization distinct from their public practice. These rules reflect the same high standards as required in the area of public practice. It would be most confusing to the public and damaging to the prestige of a profession if its members were to adopt a double standard of ethics: a set of rules for one segment of practice and a different set for another segment. For example, elaborate newspaper advertising by CAs describing in glowing terms their proficiency as management consultants would surely have considerable impact upon their professional status as auditors. The principal unanswered question in defining management advisory services is whether the range of activities which may reasonably be performed by public accounting firms shall be limited to those relating to accounting and financial matters or shall be unlimited in scope.

Does rendering of management advisory services threaten the auditor's objectivity?

A problem to be considered in rendering management advisory services is the possible threat to the auditors' objectivity when auditing and a variety of consulting services are performed for the same client. Can a public accounting firm which renders extensive management advisory services for a client still maintain the objective status so essential in an audit and in the expression of an opinion on the client's financial statements?

To begin with, it is clear that a CA who becomes in effect a part-time controller for a client and assumes a *decision-making* role in the client's affairs is not in a position to make an independent audit of the financial statements. On the other hand, public accounting firms have long been rendering certain purely *advisory* services to management while continuing to perform audits in an objective manner which serves the public interest. Advisory services can generally be distinguished from management proper; the work of the consultant or adviser consists of such functions as conducting special studies and investigations, making suggestions to management, pointing out the existence of weaknesses, outlining various alternative corrective measures, and making recommendations. The new elements in the problem of maintaining objectivity appear to be the rendering of services relating to general management areas rather than accounting and financial management, and the extent of the services rendered.

If an auditor becomes deeply and continuously involved in rendering a great many management advisory services for a given client, the relationship could conceivably become so significant as to create doubt, at least in appearance, as to the auditor's objectivity in performing periodic audits of the business. At present, the Auditing Standards Committee of the CICA and the *Rules of Professional Conduct* provide no specific guidelines on this issue. It is left to the members of the profession to judge the objectivity issue on an individual case basis.

In the United States, an AICPA Committee on Independence has issued a report advising CPAs to consult with the members of the client's board of directors or audit committee to make certain they concur as to the propriety of the rendering of management advisory services by the company's independent auditors. The report also recommends that CPAs report periodically to the board or audit committee on the nature of all important services being rendered for the client.

Possible modifications of the Rules of Professional Conduct

The ethical standards of the various professions are not static; they are constantly changed in response to the changing needs of the publics which the professions serve. The extension of the federal competition policy to cover the professions under the amended Combines Investigation Act, administered by the Departmeent of Consumer and Corporate Affairs, might result in modifications of the rules of professional conduct of the various professions.[11]

KEY TERMS INTRODUCED OR EMPHASIZED IN CHAPTER 2

appeal committee A committee of the provincial institute that is responsible for confirming, rejecting, or changing the findings and any orders of the discipline committee.

---

[11] The Ontario Law Reform Commission has begun a study of the largest professional groups in Ontario, including the accounting profession. The results of the Commission may have a significant impact on the professions' Rules of Professional Conduct.

council   An elected governing body of the provincial institute whose function is to carry out the objects of the institute.

discipline committee   A committee of the provincial institute that is responsible for administering and enforcing the Rules of Professional Conduct.

interpretations of the Rules of Professional Conduct   Specific guidelines issued by the council of the provincial institute regarding the scope and applications of the Rules of Professional Conduct.

profession   An activity which involves a responsibility to serve the public, which has a complex body of knowledge, and which has a need for public confidence.

professional conduct committee   A committee of the provincial institute that is responsible for initiating disciplinary work on ethical matters and referring them to the discipline committee for appropriate action.

objectivity   One of the most important Rules of Professional Conduct which prohibits CAs from expressing an opinion on financial statements of an enterprise unless they are objective with respect to such enterprise. Objectivity has two aspects—objectivity in fact and in appearance, a biased state of mind impairs objectivity in fact and a conflict of interest impairs objectivity in appearance.

Rules of Professional Conduct   A group of enforceable ethical standards developed for members by the national and provincial institutes of the chartered accountancy profession to enable them to maintain a professional attitude and conduct themselves in a manner which will enhance the professional stature of their discipline.

GROUP I
REVIEW QUESTIONS

2–1.   Select the best answer for each of the following:

   a.   Gray and Moore, CAs, is the firm which audits the financial statements of Mock Company. Mock's board of directors has requested Gray and Moore to perform management advisory services in the area of inventory management, which the board believes to be inefficient. Which of the following services by Gray and Moore could impair the CA firm's audit objectivity?

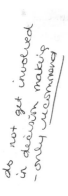

   (1)   Identify the inventory-management problem as caused by the procedures presently operative in the purchasing, receiving, storage, and issuance operations.

   (2)   Study and evaluate the inventory-management problem and suggest several alternative solutions.

   (3)   Develop a time schedule for implementation of the solution adopted by Mock Company's board, to be carried out and supervised by Mock personnel.

   (4)   Supervise the purchasing, receiving, storage, and issuance operations.

   b.   Glen Page, CA, accepted the audit engagement of Todd Company. During the audit, Page became aware of his lack of competence required for the engagement. What should Page do?

    (1)   Deny an opinion.
    (2)   Issue a qualified opinion.
 √ (3)   Suggest that Todd Company engage another CA to perform
          the audit.
    (4)   Rely on the competence of client personnel. (AICPA,
          adapted)

2–2.   Sara Kole, CA, has been requested by the president of Noyes Company,
       a closely held corporation, to co-sign Noyes Company cheques with the
       Noyes treasurer when the president is away on business trips. Would
       Kole violate the Rules of Professional Conduct if she accepted this re-
       quest? Explain.

2–3.   Is it ethical for a CA firm to determine its fee for audit services in con-
       nection with a bond issuance as a percentage of the proceeds of the
       bond issue? Explain.   contingency

2–4.   Lane Rhoads, CA, ran a classified advertisement for staff accountants
       in a local newspaper. Applicants were directed to write to a post office
       box number. James Hope, an employee of Karl Leeds, CA, answered
       the advertisement and was employed by Rhoads. Leeds has accused
       Rhoads of violating the Rules of Professional Conduct. Is Leeds cor-
       rect? Explain.

2–5.   Laura Clark, wife of Jon Clark, CA, is a life insurance agent. May Jon
       Clark refer audit clients needing officer life insurance to Laura Clark, or
       to another life insurance agent who will share a commission with Laura
       Clark? Explain.

2–6.   David Hall, a CA who had reached retirement age, arranged for the
       sale of his practice to another CA. Their agreement called for the trans-
       fer of all working papers and business correspondence to the accountant
       purchasing the practice. Comment on the propriety of this plan.

2–7.   Wallace Company is indebted to John Greer, a CA, for unpaid fees and
       has offered to issue to him unsecured interest-bearing notes. Would the
       CA's acceptance of these notes have any bearing upon his objectivity
       in his relations with Wallace Company? Discuss. (AICPA, adapted)

2–8.   Susan Hines, CA, gave tax advice on a technical question to Hillard
       Company, a client of many years. Subsequently, Hillard Company, with
       the consent of Hines, submitted the same question to Gerard &
       Swank, CAs, who, after consultation with Hines, concurred with her
       advice on the tax question. Afterwards, Gerard & Swank mailed a gen-
       eral client memorandum on income taxes to Hillard Company. Was
       Gerard & Swank's action ethical? Explain.

2–9.   Roy Mason, CA, was favourably impressed with a staff member of an-
       other CA firm whom he met at a cocktail party. He called the staff
       member the next day and invited her out for dinner to discuss the pos-
       sibility of joining Mason's staff. Did Mason's actions constitute a viola-
       tion of the Rules of Professional Conduct? Discuss.

GROUP II
QUESTIONS REQUIRING ANALYSIS

2–10.   Ralph Davis, managing partner of the rapidly growing CA firm of Davis, Ellis, and Foley, desired to obtain new staff assistants from Metropolitan University, which had an excellent undergraduate program in accounting. Accordingly, Davis submitted an advertisement to *The Daily Metro*, the campus newspaper of Metropolitan University. The advertisement stated that a representative of the CA firm of Davis, Ellis, and Foley would be on campus on a specified day to interview students interested in a career in public accounting. Did Davis, Ellis, and Foley, CAs, violate the Rules of Professional Conduct? Explain.

2–11.   Jean Adams, a staff accountant of the CA firm, Rhodes & Co., is participating in the audit of Fashions, Inc., a manufacturer of women's apparel. During a conversation with the vice president of sales, Adams is offered any items of apparel which she might want for her wardrobe, at no cost to her. Should Adams accept the gifts? Explain.

2–12.   A CA is approached by a prospective tax client who promises to pay the CA a fee of "5 percent of whatever amount you save me in taxes." Can the CA accept the tax engagement under this fee arrangement? Explain.

2–13.   *a.*   Since the accounting profession is one of the learned professions, its members are considered as highly competent, disciplined, and responsible professionals. If this is so, why is it still necessary for the profession to establish and enforce the Code of Professional Ethics? Explain fully.

   b.   Rule 214 of the "Rules of Professional Conduct" of the institute states: "A member shall not respond to any call for tenders for the provision of professional services in respect of the practice of public accounting." Briefly discuss the justification for the institute's rule prohibiting its members from bidding for professional services.

   c.   Rule 204 of the "Rules of Professional Conduct" of the institute states: "A member who is engaged to express an opinion on financial statements shall hold himself free of any influence, interest or relationship, in respect of his client's affairs, which impairs his professional judgment or objectivity or which, in the view of a reasonable observer, has that effect." What is the rationale for this rule and how is this rule related to the two important aspects of the auditor's objectivity? Explain briefly.

2–14.   With the approval of its board of directors, Thames Limited made a sizable payment for advertising during the year being audited by Leslie Wade, CA. The corporation deducted the full amount in its federal and provincial income tax returns. The controller, John Warren, acknowledges that this deduction probably will be disallowed because it related to political matters. He has not provided for this disallowance in his income taxes provision and refuses to do so because he fears that this will cause the Department of National Revenue to believe that the deduction is not valid. What is the CA's responsibility in this situation? Explain. (AICPA, adapted)

2–15. Ward Nolan retired from the large CA firm of Oates, Pyle and Company after an association of 20 years. Nolan then accepted directorships with several corporate clients of Oates, Pyle and Company. Nolan has requested permission from the managing partner of Oates, Pyle and Company to maintain a small office in the firm's suite, to receive mail and telephone calls through the firm, and to perform occasional consulting services for the firm on a fee basis. May the managing partner of Oates, Pyle and Company ethically grant Nolan's request? Explain.

2–16. Carl Swift, CA, is an alumnus of Wright College. Wright's alumni magazine publishes a section on recent promotions, and so forth, of alumni. May Swift send a notice to the alumni magazine that he has just opened an office as "an accountant and tax consultant"? Explain.

2–17. The Rules of Professional Conduct prohibit a CA from making a direct or indirect offer of employment to an employee of another CA without first informing the other CA.

Required:

a. What are the justifications for this rule?

b. What action, if any, may the employees of a CA take should they learn that another CA firm has an open position for which they would like to apply? (AICPA, adapted)

2–18. A CA owns a one-tenth interest in an investment club composed of six members. The investment club periodically meets to invest pooled resources in listed securities, or to sell portions of the securities portfolio and invest in other securities. At the current meeting of the investment club, the president, who owns a one-fifth interest, proposes that the club make a substantial investment in shares of common stock of a major corporation which is the audit client of the CA's employer firm. What should the CA do? Explain.

2–19. Mark Riley, CA, was requested by John Gray, president of Gray Industries Ltd., to call at his office to discuss the possibility of having Riley's CA firm perform an annual audit of Gray Industries. During the discussion, Riley made the following statement:

"We will need your permission to contact your former auditors, Green and Handler; we will be able to get a lot of helpful background information from them. Also, by referring to their working papers, we can save a great deal of time in establishing the beginning balances of accounts this year and consequently our audit fee will be much less than if such information had to be developed from the accounting records."

Gray replied as follows: "No, I prefer that you start from scratch and develop on your own all the information you need. I realize this will require more audit time, but we are willing to pay for it. Frankly, I don't feel our former auditors were too competent; that's why we are inviting you to take over our audit work. I prefer that you do not contact the Green and Handler CA firm at all. Just do whatever is necessary to develop your own working papers from our records."

How should Mark Riley, CA, respond to John Gray's statements? Explain fully.

2–20. What effect, if any, does each of the following have upon the auditor's objectivity? Explain.

   a. The auditor's acceptance of a fee from the client.

   b. The client's preparation of working papers for the auditor's files.

   c. The auditor's enquiries of client employees in the course of gathering evidence.

2–21. Auditors must not only appear to be objective but they must also be objective in fact.

Required:

   a. Explain the concept of an "auditor's objectivity" as it applies to third-party reliance upon financial statements.

   b. (1) What determines whether or not an auditor is objective in fact?

       (2) What determines whether or not an auditor appears to be objective?

   c. Explain how an auditor may be objective in fact but not appear to be objective.

   d. Would Joe Marks, CA, be considered objective for an examination of the financial statements of a—

       (1) Church for which he is serving as treasurer without compensation? Explain.

       (2) Women's club for which his wife is serving as treasurer-accountant if he is not to receive a fee for the examination? Explain. (AICPA, adapted)

2–22. Donald Moss, CA, resigned from his position with a national firm of chartered accountants to establish his own practice in the field of management advisory services. Since Moss was well known for his skill and knowledge in the field of electronic data processing, he quickly acquired a considerable number of clients.

   Moss deliberately avoided all auditing work because he felt his specialized abilities could be more profitably utilized in the area of management advisory services. To aid the growth of his practice he arranged with a newspaper to have an advertisement published once a week on the financial page. The advertisement consisted only of Moss's name, business address, and the phrase "Consulting Services in the Field of Data Processing." The advertisement did not identify him as a CA.

   Did Donald Moss violate the Rules of Professional Conduct? Explain fully.

2–23. CA is a member of a committee responsible for reviewing situations which may require disciplinary action against other chartered accountants. The following unrelated situations have come to the committee's attention:

(i)   A chartered accountant was criticized by a court for "not doing enough work to justify expressing an opinion."

(ii)   A chartered accountant placed an advertisement in a magazine which is distributed widely to the retail trade. The advertisement carried the slogan, "Better audit service."

(iii) During the annual meeting of a public company a chartered accountant, who had just been appointed auditor of the company, commented that his predecessor, another chartered accountant, had been an "incompetent auditor."

(iv)   During the trial of a businessman charged with income tax evasion, the businessman testified that his income tax affairs had been arranged entirely according to the advice of his tax advisor, a chartered accountant.

(v)   The report of a Royal Commission enquiry into financial aspects of the food processing industry was recently published. (The chairman of the Commission was a chartered accountant.) Another chartered accountant, well known for his knowledge of the food processing industry, wrote a newspaper article which was severely critical of the Royal Commission's report. The article has since gained national attention, as have the author and the firm of chartered accountants of which he is a partner.

Required:

State the factors that you believe should govern CA's reaction to each of the above five situations. (CICA)

GROUP III
PROBLEMS

2–24. Hillcrest Limited was formed on October 1, Year 5, and its fiscal year will end on September 30, Year 6. You audited the corporation's opening balance sheet and rendered an unqualified opinion on it.

A month after issuing your report you are offered the position of secretary of the company because of the need for a complete set of officers and for convenience in signing various documents.

You will have no financial interest in the company through stock ownership or otherwise, will receive no salary, will not maintain any corporate records, and will not have any influence on Hillcrest's financial matters other than occasional advice on income tax matters and similar advice normally given a client by a CA.

Required:

a. Assume that you accept the offer but plan to resign the position prior to conducting your annual audit with the intention of again assuming the office after rendering an opinion on the statements. Can you render an objective opinion on the financial statements? Discuss.

b. Assume that you accept the offer on a temporary basis until the corporation has gotten under way and can elect a secretary. In any event you would permanently resign the position before conducting your annual audit. Can you render an objective opinion on the financial statements? Discuss. (AICPA, adapted)

2–25. Roland Company, a retail store, has utilized your services as independent auditor for several years. During the current year the company opened a new store; in the course of your annual audit, you verify the cost of the fixtures installed in the new store by examining purchase orders, invoices, and other documents. This review brings to light an understated invoice nearly a year old in which a clerical error by the supplier, Western Showcase, Inc., caused the total of the invoice to read $4,893.62 when it should have been $8,493.62. The invoice was paid immediately upon receipt without any notice of the error, and subsequent statement and correspondence from Western Showcase, Inc., showed that the account with Roland Company had been "paid in full." Assume that the amount in question is material in relation to the financial position of both companies.

Required: ↗ auditor

a. What action should you take in this situation?
b. If the client should decline to take any action in the matter, would you insist that the unpaid amount of $3,600 be included in the liabilities shown on the balance sheet as a condition necessary to your assurance of an unqualified audit report?
c. Assuming that you were later retained to make an audit of Western Showcase, Inc., would you utilize the information gained in your examination of Roland Company to initiate a reopening of the account with that company?

2–26. Bell & Davis, CAs, has been requested by the shareholders of Worthmore, Inc., to audit the company's financial statements for the year ended November 30, Year 5. For each of the following cases, indicate whether Bell & Davis would be objective with respect to Worthmore, Inc., and explain why.
a. Two directors of Worthmore, Inc., became partners in Bell & Davis, CAs, on July 1, Year 5, resigning their directorship on that date.
b. During Year 5, Lee Bell, the former controller of Worthmore, Inc., now a partner of Bell & Davis, was frequently called upon for assistance by Worthmore. He made decisions for Worthmore's management regarding plant and equipment acquisitions and the company's marketing mix. In addition, he conducted a computer feasibility study for Worthmore. (AICPA, adapted)

2–27. An audit client, March Limited, requested that you conduct a feasibility study to advise management of the best way the corporation can utilize electronic data processing equipment and which computer, if any, best meets the corporation's requirements. You are technically competent in this area and accept the engagement. Upon completion of your study the corporation accepts your suggestions and installs the computer and related equipment that you recommended.

Required:

a. Discuss the effect acceptance of this management advisory services engagement would have upon your objectivity in expressing an opinion on the financial statements of March Limited.

b. Instead of accepting the engagement, assume that you recommended Ike Mackey, of the CA firm of Brown and Mackey, who is qualified in management advisory services. Upon completion of the engagement your client requests that Mackey's partner, John Brown, perform services in other areas. Should Brown accept the engagement? Discuss.

c. A local company printing data processing forms customarily offers a commission for recommending it as supplier. The client is aware of the commission offer and suggests that Mackey accept it. Would it be proper for Mackey to accept the commission with the client's approval? Discuss. (AICPA, adapted)

2–28. In each of the following four *unrelated* circumstances, explain what course of action a CA should follow in order to discharge his professional and ethical responsibilities:

(i) CA is employed by a firm of chartered accountants practising in a small town. Early in 1978, he reviews with the principal shareholder, the draft audited 1977 financial statements of G Ltd., a building contractor. CA notes that the company's deteriorating cash position is so serious that he believes that the company is facing bankruptcy.

CA subsequently reviews the draft audited 1977 financial statements of K Ltd., also a client, and notes that the company has a large overdue account receivable from G Ltd., against which no allowance for doubtful accounts has been provided. When CA questions the owner of K Ltd. on the collectibility of the account, CA is convinced that the owner is not aware of the actual financial condition of G Ltd.

√(ii) CA is approached by J, an insurance agent, with the following proposal. When counselling his clients on the purchase of key man life insurance, CA will refer his clients to J. In return J will pay CA 10 percent of his commission on all policies sold through such referrals. In addition, J will undertake to refer to CA certain of his clients who require estate planning services. J points out that he has a similar arrangement with X, another chartered accountant and that, in fairness to all concerned, he will refer to CA only those clients for which CA offers a lower fee than that offered by X.

(iii) CA is in charge of the audit of P Ltd., a public company. CA is asked by an economist, who is doing research for a thesis on the financial operations of firms in the same industry as P Ltd., if CA would contribute any information or views on the financial operations of P Ltd. The economist promises to keep confidential any information received from CA.

√ (iv)   R Ltd. is a small mining company whose principal shareholders are actively promoting the company's shares. CA, the auditor of the company for several years, is in the company's offices conducting his test of transactions before the year-end when he discovers a copy of a set of interim financial statements recently prepared and apparently sent to the company's bank. These were prepared by the company's accounting staff without CA's knowledge. They are clearly marked "unaudited," and CA's name does not appear on them. A quick scrutiny reveals that the statements appear to overstate net income by a material amount. (CICA, adapted)

2–29.   "Professional status as a chartered accountant in Canada carries with it an obligation to maintain a position of independence (objectivity)."

Required:

Outline the rules and guidelines pertaining to the professional standards of independence that apply to the chartered accountant as an auditor. What are the other services a chartered accountant can provide to a client and what are their implications with respect to his independence as an auditor? (CICA, adapted)

APPENDIX

THE INSTITUTE OF CHARTERED ACCOUNTANTS OF ONTARIO

Council Interpretations*
(under powers contained in By-law 3)

INTRODUCTION

Administration of the rules of professional conduct, and their enforcement, is the responsibility of the Professional Conduct Committee. It is one of the prime functions of that committee to give guidance to individual members and students on questions of ethics. When in doubt, therefore, members and students should not hesitate to seek advice from the committee concerning any problem of an ethical nature or concerning the ethical propriety of a proposed course of action in connection with their professional work.

Arising from the committee's experience with ethical problems the council publishes, from time to time, Interpretations on professional conduct matters.

---

* Adopted by the Council June 11, 1973; revisions from time to time are as footnoted.

These Interpretations are made by resolution under the authority of By-law 3 and are issued for the information and guidance of members and students. They should be read in conjunction with the rules of professional conduct, including the Foreword and the Application section.

CI 101—COMPLIANCE WITH BY-LAWS

Employing students

1   By-law 97 provides that the office of a practising member must be approved for the instruction of students before any offer of employment is made to a student. A breach of this by-law is a breach of Rule 101 and, as such, exposes a member to disciplinary action.

CI 102—CRIMINAL OR SIMILAR OFFENSES

Incorporating companies

1   The act of preparing and filing documents of incorporation for Ontario companies by persons other than lawyers has been held to be contrary to the Solicitors Act, in that it is part of the practice of law. A member of the Institute was tried and found guilty under Part XVI of the Criminal Code on a charge that he practised as a solicitor or, for gain or reward, acted as a solicitor, contrary to the Solicitors Act, since he had incorporated a number of companies.

2   Quite apart from the legal position, the relationship existing in this province between the members of the legal profession and members of the Institute is a favourable one, built on the basis of mutual respect for and understanding of each other's fields of endeavour. Members of the Institute should avoid any action which might be interpreted as contrary to the Solicitors Act.

CI 201—GENERAL STANDARDS OF CONDUCT

Public Accountancy Act

1   All members who offer public accounting services in Ontario, whether full or part-time, should be familiar with the provisions of the Public Accountancy Act and must ensure that they obtain a license to practise before offering services to the public; the license must be kept up to date during the time that such services are offered.

Law Society reports

2   Members who are asked to report to the Law Society of Upper Canada concerning lawyers' trust accounts should note that the reports can be signed only by a licensed public accountant.

3   The Law Society report requires the public accountant to certify certain specific items set out in the form of report; a member requiring clarification or guidance concerning these requirements should contact the Law Society.

Employment Agencies Act

4   The Employment Agencies Act, and regulations thereto, requires that those who, for a fee, procure persons for employment or employment for persons must obtain a licence under the legislation to perform the service. A license is required for each office in Ontario undertaking such assignments.

Criticism of a professional colleague or other public accountant

5   During the course of his professional work, a member may on occasion find that he has a responsibility to criticize a professional colleague or other public accountant; such criticism may be direct, or may be implied by material adjustments to a client's accounts considered necessary to correct work performed by the professional colleague or other public accountant. It may be, however, that there are facts or explanations known to the professional colleague or other public accountant concerned which would have a bearing on the matter.

6   A member, unless limited or restricted in writing in special circumstances by the terms of his engagement, shall first submit any proposed criticism to the professional colleague or other public accountant involved so that any eventual criticism takes into account all the available information. This is a step dictated by considerations both of professional courtesy and of simple prudence.

7   When a member does criticize a professional colleague or other public accountant, and due to limitations or restrictions in writing by the terms of his engagement he has not been permitted to submit his criticism to his professional colleague or other public accountant, the member should be on record with the person placing the restriction that such consultation has not taken place.

Refer also to Rule 305.

CI 202—INTEGRITY AND DUE CARE

Documentation

1   Cases may arise from time to time where a member may be asked by a court, or by the professional conduct committee, to substantiate procedures carried out in the course of an assignment. If the member's files do not contain sufficient documentation to confirm the nature and extent of the work done, the member concerned may well have great difficulty in showing that proper procedures were in fact carried out. The importance

of adequate documentation cannot be overemphasized; without it, a member's ability to outline and defend his professional work is seriously impaired.

CI 203—PROFESSIONAL COMPETENCE

Refer to Rule 206 and CI 206, *Professional Standards*

CI 204—OBJECTIVITY

1   Rule 204 requires that a member engaged to express an opinion on financial statements hold himself free of any influence, interest or relationship, in respect of his client's affairs, which impairs his professional judgment or objectivity or which, in the view of a reasonable observer, has that effect.

2   This is one of the principles expressed in the foreword to the rules and the foreword includes some exposition of the reasoning underlying the principle and thus underlying the rule. The "reasonable observer" does not, of course, exist as an individual. The term simply expresses the standard by which impairment, or the possibility of impairment, can be judged. The standard is that of a reasonable man having knowledge of all the facts involved and applying judgment objectively—that is, as an impartial observer.

3   To provide guidance for members, the council issues this Interpretation to set out how, in its opinion, a reasonable observer might be expected to view certain situations.

4*   The council believes that a member would not be complying with Rule 204 if he or his partners in a public accounting practice were engaged to express an opinion on financial statements of a client, and any of the following circumstances were present;

(a) In the case of a corporate client, he or any of his partners or his or their immediate families, directly or indirectly, had any investment in
—shares of the corporation or any associate thereof,
—bonds or debentures of the corporation or any associate thereof (but not such other evidence of indebtedness as annuity contracts, insurance policies or guaranteed investment receipts),
—mortgages of the corporation or any associate thereof, or
—notes or other advances to the corporation or any associate thereof.
(b) Where the client is any other type of organization, he or any of his partners or his or their immediate families, directly or indirectly, had any investment in the organization, or any affiliate thereof, similar to those listed in (a) above.
(c) He or any of his partners was a director, officer or employee of the client organization or of any associates thereof, or a member of his

---

* *Amended, October 26, 1973.*

or their immediate families was a director or officer of the client organization or of any associate thereof.

For purposes of this Interpretation:

(i) The term "immediate family" when used to indicate a relationship with any person means:

—any spouse, son or daughter of that person who has the same home as that person; or

—any other relative of that person or of his spouse who has the same home as that person.

(ii) the term "associate" means in relation to a corporate client:

—any affiliate thereof.

—any "investor" (whether or not it is an affiliate), as that term is defined in subparagraph (b) of paragraph 3050.04 of the Research Recommendations contained in the CICA Handbook, where the investor uses the equity method on the bases recommended in Section 3050 thereof to account for its investment in the corporate client and where the amounts relating to the corporate client reflected in the annual financial statements of the investor constitute more than 5% of total assets or gross revenues of the investor, or

—any "investee" as that term is defined in subparagraph (c) of paragraph 3050.04 and where the corporate client is an investor and uses the equity method in the same circumstances as described in the case of the "investor" referred to above.

(iii) The term "affiliate" has the same meaning as is given to the term "affiliated body corporate" in *The Business Corporations Act* (RSO 1970 c. 53), except that the meaning is extended to include any unincorporated body.

5   Where one or more close relatives of a member, even if not having the same home as the member, hold a material interest in any organization, the member, and his firm, is unlikely to have the appearance of objectivity. The facts in each case determine whether or not there appears to be an acceptable degree of objectivity; the professional conduct committee is willing to give ruling in individual cases.

6*   A member would not be complying with Rule 204 if he or his partners in a public accounting firm were members of a private mutual fund or an investment club which held any investments, set out in 4(a) above, of a client of the member or any of his partners. A member would not be in violation of Rule 204, however, if he or his partners invest in a public mutual fund not audited by the member or his partners, which held investments of a client of the member or his partners, nor would a member be in violation if he held qualifying shares in a social club such as a golf or curling club where the shareholding is a pre-requisite of membership.

7   *Borrowings*—a member would not be considered to violate Rule 204 if he was engaged to report on financial statements of an institution (such

---

* CI 204(6) *as amended June 9, 1975.*

as a chartered bank, trust company, finance or acceptance company) from which he or any of his partners, or his or their immediate families, had borrowed funds in the normal course of business, by way of a loan or mortgage, provided that the amount borrowed bears a reasonable relationship to the borrower's income and his net worth and that the loan is of the sort that would be granted to other customers of the institution in the normal course of events. This assumes, of course, the absence of any specific statutory prohibition on such borrowing by the auditor of the institution, his partners, or his or their immediate families.

8   *Commercial transactions*—similarly, a member would not be considered in breach of Rule 204 if he was engaged to report on the financial statements of a client with whom he or any of his partners, or his or their immediate families, carried out a commercial transaction, provided that the transaction was on the same terms and conditions as are normally allowed to other customers—this would include receiving the client's normal terms for payment of accounts. The member or any of his partners, or his or their immediate families, should not receive any special treatment or preference over and above that granted to other customers.

9**   *Deposits and Shareholdings in Savings and Loan Institutions, Cooperatives, Caisses Populaires and Credit Unions*—a member would not be considered to be in violation of Rule 204 if he was engaged to report on financial statements of a savings and loan institution, cooperative, caisse populaire, a credit union or similar institution in which he or any of his partners, or his or their immediate families, had deposited funds in the normal course of business provided that the amount deposited bears a reasonable relationship both to the borrower's income and net worth and to the total assets of the institution. This assumes, of course, the absence of any specific statutory prohibitions on such deposits by the auditors of the institution, his partners, or his or their immediate families. If such deposits entitle the depositor to vote at the annual or special meetings of the institution, this right to vote should not be exercised. In some cases, it may be necessary for a depositor in such institutions to hold a share in the institution. The holding of such a qualifying share by a member, or any of his partners, or his or their immediate families would not disqualify the member from reporting on financial statements of such institutions, provided that the vote attaching to that share is not exercised at annual or special meetings of the institution.

10   *Non-profit-seeking organizations*—any non-profit-seeking organization which is incorporated under the provisions of Part III of The Ontario Corporations Act (RSO 1970, Ch. 89 as amended) or within Part II of the Canada Corporations Act (RSC 1970 c.C-32) is subject to statutory provisions which preclude a member or his firm serving as auditor if the member or any of his partners is an officer or director of the organization.

** CI 204(9) *new, June 9, 1975, subsequent paragraphs renumbered.*

11   Since April 18, 1973, members have been prohibited from entering into any new arrangements which result in a member serving on the governing body of any non-profit-seeking organization not covered by the above statutory provisions, where he or his firm, or a partner, acts as auditor of the organization. Members serving in such circumstances as at April 18, 1973, are required by April 17, 1976, to complete steps to change the arrangements so as to comply with the prohibition.

12**   *Executor/Trustee/Trusts*—occasions may arise where the acceptance by a member or any of his partners, or his or their immediate families, of a position as executor or trustee, might create a conflict with Rule 204. For example, a member would face a conflict of interest if he or any of his partners or a member of his or their immediate families was

a) the auditor of the related trust or estate; or

b) an executor or trustee of an estate or trust which held a material interest in an organization or in an associate* of an organization of which the member or his firm was the auditor; or

c) a trustee of a profit sharing plan of an audit client or of any associate thereof; or

d) a trustee of a pension plan of an audit client or of any associate thereof; or

e) a trustee of a private charitable foundation which held a material interest in an organization or in an associate of an organization of which the member or his firm was the auditor.

In circumstances of this nature, the member, or his firm, would be expected to resign the position of auditor, if the conflict with the position of executor or trustee could not otherwise be resolved.

13**   The council considers, however, that a member would not be in breach of Rule 204 if a trust, an estate, a custodian or a guardianship, in which he, or any of his partners, or his or their immediate families, has a beneficial interest, held, in market lots, investments similar to those listed in paragraph 4(a) hereof in an audit client or any associate thereof, provided that the member or his partners or his or their immediate families did not have direct or indirect control over the investment policies of the trust, estate, custodianship or guardianship.

The council also considers that a member would not be in breach of Rule 204 only by reason of the fact that he or any of his partners, or his or their immediate families, serves on the governing body of an organization which may hold an interest in an audit client or in any associate of an audit client of the member or his firm, provided that (i) the holding of such interest does not make the organization an "insider" of the audit client or any associate thereof within the terms of the Business Corporations Act of Ontario and (ii) the member serving on the governing body refrains from participating in discussions and decisions relating to investments in the audit client or any associate thereof. Any

---

** *as amended, May 16, 1974.*
* *refer to the meaning of "associate" in paragraph 4(c)(ii).*

member who serves in any such position, where the organization concerned holds a material interest in an audit client or any associate thereof should consider his position carefully; if the circumstances are such that his appearance of objectivity is impaired then the member, or his firm, would be expected to resign the position of auditor if the conflict could not otherwise be resolved.

14   *Retired partners*—a member or his partners would not be considered to violate Rule 204 if they were making payments to a retired partner who holds a direct or indirect financial interest in, or a position or an appointment with, a client provided such payments to the retired partner were determined as of the date of retirement in accordance with the terms of the partnership agreement and are not affected by subsequent events.

15   *Application of Ontario Business Corporations Act*—members are cautioned that the provisions of The Business Corporations Act (Ontario) (Section 170) impose somewhat more restrictive requirements (in respect of audit appointments to corporations covered by the Act) than those set out in this Interpretation. The council has made known to the provincial government its view that the Act requires amendment in this respect, since it is the council's feeling that the section imposes unrealistic and impractical restrictions. The relevant provisions are:

> *"Section 170*
> (1) No person shall be appointed or act as auditor of a corporation who is a director, officer or employee of the corporation or of an affiliate of the corporation or who is a partner, employer or employee of any such director, officer or employee or who is a related person to any director or officer of the corporation or of an affiliate of the corporation. R.S.O. 1960, c.71, s.81(1), amended.
> (2) No person shall be appointed or act as auditor of a corporation if he or any partner or employer of or related person to him beneficially owns, directly or indirectly, any securities of the corporation or of a subsidiary thereof or, if the corporation is a subsidiary, any securities of its holding corporation.
> (3) Subsection 2 does not apply to a person, partner, employer or related person, as the case may be, if the person, partner, employer or related person is not empowered to decide whether securities of the corporation or its holding corporation, as the case may be, are to be beneficially owned, directly or indirectly, by him, or if he is not entitled to vote in respect thereof.
> (4) Where, on the date this section comes into force, an auditor or his partner, employer or related person owns securities as set out in subsection 2, notwithstanding subsection 2, he may for a period of two years from the date this section comes into force continue to act as auditor if he discloses in the report required under subsection 2 of section 171 that he or his partner, employer or related person so owns such securities but, at the expiration of such period, he shall cease to act as auditor unless he or his partner,

employer or related person, as the case may be, has disposed of such securities.

(5) No person shall be appointed a receiver or a receiver and manager or liquidator of any corporation of which he or any partner or employer of or a related person to him is the auditor or has been auditor within the two years preceding his appointment as receiver or receiver and manager or liquidator.

(6) No person who is appointed a trustee of the estate of a corporation under the Bankruptcy Act (Canada) or any partner or employer of or a related person to him shall be appointed or act as auditor of the corporation."

16   *Commissions and Finder's Fee:* From time to time members may be asked by investment dealers, and possibly by insurance brokers, to act as agents or sub-agents for the sale of securities or the placement of insurance. A member in public practice receives fees from his clients for his services which, in some cases, will include advice on the utilization of surplus funds and, often, counseling on insurance coverages. There is bound to be a conflict of interest between this position and that of acting as an agent or sub-agent for the sale of securities or the placement of insurance.* In the opinion of the council, acceptance by a practising member of a commission or other remuneration from third parties for such agency services, would be incompatible with the principle of objectivity which is fundamental to our profession.

17   Instances have also occurred where third parties have offered to pay finder's fees to practising members in connection with arranging a client's mortgage or other financing or in connection with the purchase or sale of a business by a client. A practising member should not accept such a fee without his client's knowledge and consent.

18   In the rare instances where a practising member is able to render independent advice to two or more clients who are parties to the same transaction, the member must inform each of his clients that his services have been retained by other parties to the transaction and that he will derive fees from such parties.

Member acting as trustee under the Bankruptcy Act or as liquidator, receiver or receiver/manager

19   *Trustee under the Bankruptcy Act*—members who hold, or have held, an appointment as auditor, accountant or business adviser may be asked to act as trustee in the bankruptcy of the client or as trustee under a proposal to be made by the client to creditors under the Bankruptcy Act. A potential conflict of interest may exist in such circumstances

---

(* *Note: The Insurance Act prohibits the payment of compensation by an insurer, agent or broker to anyone not licensed as an agent for placing or negotiating insurance. The acceptance of fees or other compensation by a person not licensed under the Act is an offence under the Act, which renders such a person subject to a penalty.*)

because the member, in carrying out his duties, may have acquired confidential information concerning his client's affairs which he would be duty-bound to pass on to the creditors.

20   Notwithstanding that there will likely in fact be no conflict of interest existing in such appointments, council is aware that many creditors facing losses tend to be highly critical of all persons who were in any way connected with the insolvent debtor, including those who have had knowledge of his financial affairs. Where a member acts as trustee under the Bankruptcy Act and he has previously acted for the client in another capacity, doubt may be raised in the business community concerning a "possible conflict of interest," even though the doubt may not be justified by the facts.

21   Council considers that, as a profession, we should avoid not only possible conflicts of interest, but also any position which to a reasonable observer would have the appearance of a conflict of interest. Accordingly, a member or his associate may not be a trustee in bankruptcy or in a proposal, for a client while holding, or within two years of having held, the position of auditor of that client. Furthermore, when a member or his associate has acted for a client in any capacity other than as auditor, he should accept an appointment as trustee only when he can act with objectivity. As a guide, and without attempting to cover all circumstances, it probably would be inadvisable for a member acting as an accountant (say, preparation of unaudited financial statements) or business adviser (say, advice on taxation and other financial matters) to be appointed a trustee under the Bankruptcy Act if he had been advising such client within the preceding two-year period; on the other hand, a member acting as a business adviser (say, consideration of financial reorganization which involved a proposal to creditors under the Bankruptcy Act) may readily be able to act with objectivity as a trustee under a proposal that was related to the reorganization. Before accepting an assignment under the Bankruptcy Act, a member should also be satisfied that his or his associates' relationship with any other clients having an interest in the bankrupt estate is not such as to impair his objectivity.

22   The attention of members is drawn to Section 170(6) of the Business Corporations Act, 1970 (Ontario) which precludes a trustee of the estate of a bankrupt corporation from being auditor of that corporation.

23   *Liquidator*—the council believes that there is no inherent conflict of interest between the positions of auditor, accountant or business adviser, and that of liquidator. A liquidator is appointed to act on behalf of the shareholder or owners in realizing the value of the assets of the company, meeting its debts and distributing any balance to the shareholders. The dictates of normal commercial ethics and law apply and, within these bounds, it is the duty of the liquidator to act in the interest of the shareholders or owners, while seeing that all legal liabilities are settled. A member may, therefore, *in the absence of a statutory prohibition* (see Section 170(5) of The Business Corporations Act, 1970

(Ontario)) act as liquidator for a company of which he or an associate holds or has held the position of auditor, accountant or business adviser, provided that he can act with objectivity.

24   An auditor who accepts an appointment as liquidator would, of course, resign his audit position as otherwise he would be expressing an opinion on the results of the business which he was responsible for liquidating.

25   *Receiver, Receiver/Manager*—the council believes that there is not normally a conflict of interest which would preclude a member or his associate, who is acting or who has acted as auditor, accountant or business adviser for a client, from accepting an appointment as receiver or receiver/manager of such client *in the absence of a statutory prohibition* (see Section 170(5) of The Business Corporations Act, 1970 (Ontario)), provided that he can act with objectivity. In fact, the member's specialized knowledge of the client's affairs may well make him the logical appointee.

26* If a member is asked to act as a receiver or receiver/manager by the shareholders or owners and he is not prevented by statute, or by some other conflicting circumstances, he may accept the appointment. A member who proposes to accept such an appointment where it is being made by parties other than the shareholders or owners of the client, or former client, must observe the following requirements:
a) The offer of appointment must not be accepted without first having secured the consent of the client or former client. Where a corporation is involved, if it is impracticable to seek the consent of the shareholders, the consent of a responsible officer of the corporation must first be secured. It must be made clear, in seeking such consent, that the terms of the appointment may require the member to place his responsibility to the shareholders and/or management second to those attached to the new appointment, and that he may have to disclose information which he may have obtained as auditor, accountant or business adviser and which may conceivably affect the position of the shareholders and/or management.
b) The discussion should be followed up immediately by a letter to the client or former client reiterating the member's position.
c) The member must make it known to those who are appointing him that he has complied with the above requirements, so that his position is clear to all concerned. A copy of the letter to the client or former client, in which the member's position is set out, should be filed with those persons who are making the appointment.

27   An auditor who accepts an appointment as receiver or receiver/manager would, of course, resign his audit position as otherwise he would be expressing an opinion on the results of the business which he was responsible for operating. In any event, a member shall not accept any appointment unless he can act with objectivity.

---

* CI 204(26) *amended, June 9, 1975.*

28   *General*

Frequently, secured creditors require assistance in disposing of assets which have been seized as security for a debt owing. A member should be guided by the foregoing provisions of this Interpretation before accepting an appointment to act as agent for a secured creditor in administration or disposing of such assets.

29   References to "members" in this Interpretation are to be read as applying equally to firms and as applying also as between partners in the same or associated firms. References to trustee in bankruptcy, liquidator, receiver or receiver/manager would apply equally to companies incorporated to perform these functions.

CI 205—FALSE OR MISLEADING STATEMENTS

Application to members not in public practice

A member who is employed other than in public practice is subject to Rule 205 just as is the member in public practice. It is recognized that under exceptional circumstances, this may place such a member in a difficult position *vis-a-vis* the organization with which he is employed; however, a member fails in his professional duty if he allows himself to be associated with financial statements or other documents which he knows, or should know, are false or misleading.

CI 206—PROFESSIONAL STANDARDS

Auditing standards

1   Rule 206.2 of the Rules of Professional Conduct states, *inter alia*, that no member shall express opinion on financial statements examined by him if he fails to obtain sufficient information to warrant an expression of opinion.

2   The council is of the opinion that it would be useful to members to have before them a statement of certain generally accepted auditing standards which are in addition to those dealt with in the *CICA Handbook*. Auditing standards relate to the quality of work to be performed and the suitability of the resulting audit report to the objectives of an audit. These are pre-eminently matters of judgment.

3   The council considers that the following auditing standards are generally accepted; some of these, while implied in the *CICA Handbook*, may not be specifically set out therein. [This is no longer the case, see Section 5100 of the *CICA Handbook*]:

a) The examination of the records and underlying data is to be performed by a person or persons having adequate technical training and proficiency in auditing, with due care and with an objective state of mind.

b) The work is to be adequately planned and properly executed. If assistants are employed, they are to be adequately supervised.

c) There is to be an organized study and evaluation of internal control as a basis for any reliance thereon in determining the extent of test audit procedures.

d) Sufficient appropriate evidential matter is to be obtained through inspection, observation, enquiry, and confirmation to afford a reasonable basis for expressing an opinion on the financial statements.

Accounting standards

4   Rule 206.3: this rule, subject to item (3) of rule 206.2, requires that a member shall not express an opinion on financial statements examined by him which are not prepared in accordance with the accounting standards of the profession unless such opinion is suitably qualified. The rule further provides that, without limiting the generality of the foregoing, if a member expresses an opinion without qualification or exception that financial statements are presented in accordance with generally accepted accounting principles and if such statements depart in any material respect from the recommendations of the Accounting and Auditing Research Committee of the Canadian Institute of Chartered Accountants or its successor(s) (herein collectively referred to as the Research Committee), such departure must be capable of justification as proper in the particular circumstances.

5   As the term "accounting *standards* of the profession" and reference to the recommendations of the Research Committee are appearing in the rules of professional conduct for the first time, council issues this Interpretation to provide guidance for members. While the term "accounting *principles*" is widely used and is embodied in statute law, it does present difficulties. Sometimes it is held to refer only to broad general principles, while at other times its meaning has been extended to cover practices *as well* as principles.

6   Where the term "accounting *standards* of the profession" is used in the rule it expresses this wider meaning, i.e., that body of principles *and practices* which have been generally adopted by the profession and which are applied in the preparation of financial statements, taken together with the requirements of any governing act, such as The Business Corporations Act and The Securities Act (subject to the comment in 7(d) below).

7*   The accounting standards of the profession include the following:

a) accounting practices recommended by the Research Committee;

b) accounting practices that differ from those recommended by the Research Committee, provided that there is substantial authoritative support for alternative treatment and the departure from the Research Committee's recommendations is disclosed;

c) accounting practices not specifically dealt with by the Research

---

* CI 206(7) *as amended, June 9, 1975.*

Committee but which are generally accepted for ordinary industrial and commercial enterprises, e.g., accrual accounting; and

d) requirements of any governing act or regulation, providing however, in the rare event that there is a conflict between the other accounting standards of the profession and a specific statutory or regulatory requirement the member, subject to the comment in 8 (below), is not relieved of the responsibility of making appropriate qualification in his report.

8   It should be noted that in connection with 7(d) (above) the recommendations of the Research Committee to-date do not cover the whole spectrum of financial reporting. The Preface to the committee's Research Recommendations (dated December 1971) states:

> "Recommendations are intended to apply to all types of profit oriented enterprises, unless a particular recommendation makes a specific exemption or extension. However, pending further study, the recommendations do not necessarily apply to the special problems of banks and insurance companies. No recommendation is intended to override the requirements of a governing statute."

The form and content of financial reports of banks and insurance companies are controlled, or heavily influenced, by statute or by governmental regulation. While the Research Committee is silent as to accounting methods appropriate to the circumstances of such financial institutions some accounting practices are prescribed or permitted for them by law or regulation which are different from those that would be considered normal for ordinary commercial and industrial enterprises. In these circumstances it is considered appropriate for an auditor to omit a reference to generally accepted accounting principles in his report and not to qualify his report.

9   The latter part of rule 206.3, while not ruling out circumstances in which financial reporting may depart from the recommendations of the Research Committee, places the burden of justification upon the member if he issues an unqualified report in such circumstances.

10   Apart from general requirements of rule 206.3, members should keep in mind policy statement No. 27, effective December 18, 1972, of the Securities Administrators in Canada which reads as follows:

> "Where the term 'generally accepted accounting principles' is used, either in Securities Legislation, Regulations, and Companies Legislation and Regulations, the Securities Administrators will regard pronouncements by the Accounting and Auditing Research Committee of the Canadian Institute of Chartered Accountants to the extent set out in the research recommendations in the 'CICA Handbook' as 'generally accepted accounting principles'."

Council understands that in the implementation of this policy, the Securities Administrators have adopted the standards referred to in paragraph 7 above.

*   *   *   *   *

Refer also to Rule 202 and CI 202, *Documentation.*

CI 207—INFORMING CLIENT OF BUSINESS CONNECTIONS

Refer to Rule 204 and CI 204, paragraphs 16–18, *Commissions and Finders Fees.*

CI 208—FEE FOR TRANSACTION INVOLVING CLIENT

Refer to Rule 204 and CI 204, paragraphs 16–18, *Commissions and Finders Fees.*

CI 209—IMPROPER USE OF CONFIDENTIAL KNOWLEDGE OF CLIENTS' AFFAIRS

Refer to Rule 204 and CI 204, paragraphs 16–18, *Commissions and Finders Fees.*

CI 210—CONFIDENTIALITY

Legal privilege

1   Members and students should be aware of a judgment of the Supreme Court of Ontario (Cronkwright v Cronkwright (1970) 3 O.R. 784). Mr. Justice Wright, in the course of the action, recognized a duty on professional persons or other persons in a position of confidence and testifying at a trial to ask the court for a ruling before divulging information obtained by them in their confidential capacity.

2   While His Lordship qualified his comments as being "my personal opinion" and while that opinion was not essential to his decision on the point in issue and is therefore not binding on other courts, a member or student testifying at a trial could quite properly point to this opinion in requesting a ruling of this kind. Indeed, as His Lordship stated, he has "a duty" to do so.

Information about client's affairs

3   Members and students who may be asked by a banker, or other third party, to pass on information concerning a client's affairs should clearly understand that the information requested must not be divulged without the client's consent. The third party's request for information, or for authority to make such an approach direct, should be made to the client.

CI 214—TENDERS FOR PROFESSIONAL APPOINTMENTS

Refer to Rule 301 and CI 301, *Professional Appointments.*

CI 217—PUBLICITY AND ADVERTISING

General policy

1   Council is of the opinion that it is in the interest of all members of the Institute that individual members receive publicity, identifying them as members of the Institute, in areas which reflect their competence and knowledge, in matters which are within the scope of activities of all members of the Institute, and in matters of civic or public interest. At the same time council wishes to ensure that such publicity will contribute to public respect for the profession and thus to the professional standing of all the members. It is also important to ensure as far as possible that no member or group of members obtains an unfair advantage over other members.

2   As guidance to members engaged in the practice of public accounting, council sets out below its views on desirable conduct in a number of different areas. Except in those cases specifically noted, all the views expressed in this Interpretation apply to firms or companies engaged in the practice of functions related to public accounting if such firms or companies are associated with members engaged in the practice of public accounting.

Stationery

3   The stationery of a member or firm of members engaged in the practice of public accounting may contain no more than:

a) the name of the member or firm including, in appropriate circumstances, a statement that the member or firm are successors to a named predecessor practising member or firm;
b) the business, telegraph and telephone address or addresses;
c) the home telephone number of the practising member or partners of the firm;
d) the occupation of chartered accountant or public accountant, and/or in appropriate circumstances other designations as permitted by the rules of conduct or approved by council;
e) the names of the partners in the firm together with such academic degrees, titles, military rank, decorations, etc., which such persons may be entitled to use, including the initials C.M.C. or F.M.C. (denoting membership in The Institute of Management Consultants of Ontario) and initials denoting membership in such other organizations as, in the opinion of council, have developed meaningful standards and whose objectives do not conflict with the aims of the Institute;
f) the names of other members employed by the practising member or firm provided they are licensed to practise as public accountants, are clearly separated from the names of partners and designated by an appropriate descriptive term such as "manager(s)", "supervisor(s)", or "other chartered accountant(s)";

g) where an office is in the charge of a member who is not a partner, the manager's name may be listed provided he is so designated;

h) reference to other cities in which the firm has offices;

i) reference to other firms which act as representatives of the member or firm giving the names and the business, telegraph and telephone addresses of such other firms.

4*   The stationery of a member or firm, engaged in the practice of public accounting, and of separate organizations which engage solely in the practice of functions related to public accounting, should be in professional good taste. The use of crests and photographs is not permitted. A separate organization which engages solely in the practice of functions related to public accounting may refer on its stationery to membership in The Canadian Association of Management Consultants.

5**   Members who hold dual designations, one of which is unrelated to public accounting or the related functions (such as "chartered accountant" and "barrister & solicitor"), should not use them together on the same stationery.

6*   The stationery of a practising member or firm should not be used for a mailing to the public soliciting support for a charity or other cause, although it may be used to solicit such support from other practising members. This does not prevent the use of the office address (without the name of the practising member or firm) as a mailing address for replies to such mailings to the public.

Name plates

7   Name plates making known the location of the office of a member or firm engaged in the practice of public accounting may show the name of the member or firm, the occupation chartered accountant or public accountant and/or in appropriate circumstances other designations as permitted by the rules of conduct or approved by council and, in the case of a firm, the names of the partners. Such name plates should be restricted in size, should not be designed to advertise the business of the member or firm, and should be in keeping with professional standards.

Professional cards and announcements

8   Members or firms engaged in the practice of public accounting may place their professional card in any publication which is open to all members and in which such placement does not, in the opinion of council, tend to lower public respect for the profession.

9   As in the case of stationery, professional cards of members or firms engaged in the practice of public accounting may contain no more than:

---

* as amended, May 16, 1974 and further amended, October 1977.
** as amended, October 1977.

a) the name of the member or firm including, in appropriate circumstances, a statement that the member or firm are successors to a named predecessor practising member or firm;

b) the business, telegraph and telephone address or addresses;

c) the home telephone number of the practising member or partners of the firm;

d) the occupation of chartered accountant or public accountant and/or in appropriate circumstances other designations as permitted by the rules of conduct or approved by council;

e) the names of the partners in the firm together with such academic degrees, titles, military rank, decorations, etc., which such persons may be entitled to use, including the initials C.M.C. or F.M.C. (denoting membership in The Institute of Management Consultants of Ontario) and initials denoting membership in such other organizations as, in the opinion of council, have developed meaningful standards and whose objectives do not conflict with the aims of the Institute;

f) the names of other members employed by the practising member or firm provided they are licensed to practise as public accountants, are clearly separated from the names of partners and designated by an appropriate descriptive term such as "manager(s)", "supervisor(s)", or "other chartered accountant(s)";

g) where an office is in the charge of a member who is not a partner, the manager's name may be listed provided he is so designated;

h) reference to other cities in which the firm has offices;

i) reference to other firms which act as representatives of the member or firm giving the names and the business, telegraph and telephone addresses of such other firms.

10   In addition, in such a card, members may include an announcement of a change of address, the opening of a new office, the admission of a new partner or partners, a change in firm name, or the appointment to a position (e.g. manager or resident manager) of a member who is not a partner, provided such member is appropriately designated and is licensed as a public accountant.

11*   Separate organizations which engage solely in the practice of functions related to public accounting, even though associated with a member or firm engaged in the practice of public accounting, may make reference in their professional cards to membership in the Canadian Association of Management Consultants.

12   A professional card containing the information set out above may be circulated by mail to clients and to close associates.

13   To provide for a uniform practice in connection with professional cards and announcements, council has established as a general guideline that cards published in newspapers should be kept to a maximum size of two newspaper columns wide by three inches deep. Similarly, as a general guideline, cards sent through the mail should be of no larger

---

* as amended, May 16, 1974.

proportions than 5½″ x 4½″. Cards appearing in other publications should have the same relative size and not be out of proportion to other similar cards appearing in the publication.

14   The above restrictions on the contents of printed professional cards and announcements are not intended to apply to announcements which members may wish to make by way of letters addressed to individual clients.

15   A firm of public accountants, or its associates, will sometimes join a consortium, usually inter-disciplinary, which is formed to provide a unique or highly specialized service. A firm of public accountants, or its associates, is permitted to have its name associated with an announcement concerning the formation of such a consortium, but subsequent disclosure of the name of the firm of public accountants, or its associates, should be avoided. A subsequent change in the membership of the consortium is not sufficient cause to place an announcement which would again publicize the participation of the firm of public accountants or its associates, since it would be sufficient to note that a specific firm (which may be a firm of public accountants or its associate) has been added to the consortium. If the consortium wishes to announce the expansion or contraction of the sphere of operations in any specific area, the publication of the name of the firm of public accountants, or the name of its associates, should also be avoided.

16   It is not intended that members use the medium of such consortiums for publicity when offering services that a reasonable observer would assume any competent firm of public accountants or its associates would be able to offer.

Business or calling cards

17   Members engaged in the practice of public accounting may have business cards printed for their own use. Such cards may show the member's name, his designation (C.A. or F.C.A.) together with such academic degrees, titles, military rank, decorations, etc., which he may be entitled to use, including the initials C.M.C. or F.M.C. (denoting membership in The Institute of Management Consultants of Ontario) and initials denoting membership in such other organizations as, in the opinion of council, have developed meaningful standards and whose objectives do not conflict with the aims of the Institute. Business and home addresses and telephone numbers may also be shown. In the event the designation C.A. or F.C.A. is not used, the occupation, chartered accountant or public accountant, could be used. The name of the firm of which the member is a partner or employee may also be shown with the occupation chartered accountant or public accountant, and the address and telephone number. Photographs are not permitted.

Telephone directories

18   Members engaged in the practice of public accounting should comply with the Public Accountants Council's Rule (m), as follows:

> *A licensee may permit to be inserted, under the heading "Account-ants-Public" or a similar heading in the advertising section (yellow pages) of a telephone directory, only a listing of his name, firm name, profession, address and telephone number all without any border or means of emphasis. Bold-faced type may be used only in the alphabetical listing (white pages).*

(Yellow pages)
Example:
John Doe, *Chartered Accountant,* 1 Young Street 111-0000
Doe & Co., *Chartered Accountants,* 5 Old Road 220-0000

19   Members should review their directory listing to avoid the following common faults:

a) Sole practitioners must not use the plural form "chartered account-ants";

b) Practising members are not permitted to list under yellow page headings such as "tax consultants", "business consultants" or "indus-trial consultants".

Listings under "Trustees in Bankruptcy", "Management Consultants" and "Data Processing Services" are permitted, where applicable.

Cooperative advertising

20   This form of advertising arises when a group of business men join together to express greeting to a mutual customer on the occasion of some special observance. These advertisements also take the form of a "salute" to some charitable, religious, educational or artistic organiza-tion.

21   Council is of the opinion that participation in cooperative advertising is not professional, and such participation by a member or firm engaged in the practice of public accounting is considered objectionable.

Advertising for staff

22   Members engaged in the practice of public accounting are likely to ad-vertise for staff under three sets of circumstances:

a) advertising for accounting or audit staff where the main market is other public accounting firms;

b) advertising for other staff who are probably not on the staff of other public accounting firms;

c) advertising for executives or other staff on behalf of clients.

23   Council believes that these three sets of circumstances require different treatment by members engaged in the practice of public accounting and considers the approach outlined below should be followed.

24*   When advertising for accounting or audit staff, where the main market is other public accounting firms, members should avoid extravagant, self-laudatory terminology and references to salary or remuneration offered, either by quoting a figure or by any general allusions. A general statement to the effect that the salary is negotiable or dependent on qualifications and experience is permitted; members should avoid any terms which could give the impression that they are prepared to pay premium salaries to attract staff. The advertisement should give the facts of the opening. The member should bear in mind that similar opportunities for experience are probably available with other members and it is unlikely that there is anything unique about the position advertised except that it is open. When advertising for new students, members should adhere to the rules set out for other audit staff and should not imply that the opportunity offered is any greater than is available with other public accounting firms.

25   In advertising for other staff such as non-C.A. specialist staff for a management consulting division of a firm, or clerical or stenographic staff, a member is directing his advertisement to potential employees who are being sought by both members and non-members. Members must be permitted to be competitive in such advertising and references to salary are not objectionable. Members, however, must avoid using language that can be construed as an advertisement for the firm rather than an attempt to locate suitable personnel. A factual statement of the position to be filled is permitted but extravagant language is undesirable.

26   When advertising for executives or other staff for clients the views of the client will have to be considered. A member, of course, should not be prepared to be associated with a client who wishes to advertise a position in an unrealistic or false manner. A reference to remuneration will usually be required. If clients authorize the use of the radio or television media there is no objection to this. The major concern of council, in this area, is that the member avoid using his executive placement advertisements as a method of advertising his own firm.

27   Under each of the three circumstances the name of the member or firm should appear only once in the text of the advertisement, at the foot, giving the address to which inquiries should be directed. It is recognized that in radio and television advertising more than one reference to the name may be necessary but, in any form of advertising, the name of the member or firm should not be given undue prominence. Members are aware of the medium in which they are advertising and the prominence given to the names of other advertisers in that medium. The general position of members should be that their name should never be given more prominence than that generally given to other similar organizations

---

* *as amended, May 16, 1974.*

in that medium. Preferably we will provide leadership in giving less prominence to the advertiser's name.

28   In all cases it is desirable to obtain a proof or script of the advertisement in the form in which it will be used in order to ensure that the member's instructions have been followed.

29   Advertisements for staff, placed outside Canada, should conform with rules of the accounting profession in the country where the advertisement is placed.

Publication of articles

30   Members may submit articles for publication to any newspaper or magazine in which publication of an article by a member would not reflect unfavourably on the profession. Members engaged in the practice of public accounting, when submitting articles, should avoid references in the text of such articles to their particular practices and should avoid giving the impression that there is anything unique to them or their firm in the work being described. Most articles can be written to reflect favourably on the work of the profession as a whole rather than on an individual or a firm.

31   A member engaged in the practice of public accounting, when submitting an article, may permit his name, designation (C.A. or F.C.A.) and firm name to be published, as the author. He should not permit his address to be published but reference to the city in which his practice is carried on is not objectionable. Suggestions as to photographs and biographies are referred to below.

32   It is not considered proper for a member engaged in the practice of public accounting to submit one article for publication in, say, all newspapers in the province. An article should be written for a particular publication or a limited number of appropriate publications, but syndication of articles is permitted and the reporting of all or part of an article through the facilities of news services or otherwise is not considered objectionable.

33   Members should accept an obligation to avoid publication of statements which are derogatory of the profession or of other members of the Institute. This does not mean that members should not express their views on matters where there may be differences of opinion—such as developing accounting principles, Institute policies or the views of Institute committees. If a member writes an article which disagrees with an official position taken by the Institute, however, he should, as a matter of courtesy, forward a copy of such article to the Secretary prior to publication so that council will be informed of the subject of disagreement.

34   It is undesirable for a member engaged in the practice of public accounting, having had an article accepted and printed, to circulate it to non-clients. There is no objection to circulating reproductions of the article to existing clients, close associates and, on request, to non-clients.

Speeches

35   Speeches made by members are subject to the same general rules as those set out above for articles. In particular, except when speaking to C.A. groups (e.g. at Institute conferences), members engaged in the practice of public accounting, in making speeches, should avoid references to their own practices or to the unique nature of work performed in such practices. Every effort should be made to reflect favourably on the profession as a whole rather than on an individual or firm.

36   Speeches, after delivery, may be submitted to appropriate newspapers or magazines for publication. Wholesale distribution to a large number of publications, however, should be avoided. When a speech is published, a member engaged in the practice of public accounting may permit the use of his name, designation and firm name but not his address, except reference to the city in which his practice is carried on.

37   Reproductions of speeches may be circulated by members engaged in the practice of public accounting only to existing clients, close associates and, on request, to non-clients.

38   If a member plans a speech which disagrees with an official position of the Institute, he should, as a matter of courtesy, forward a copy of such speech to the Secretary before the speech is made.

Comments to the press

39   Members from time to time will receive calls from members of the press asking their comments on some current matter. Members engaged in the practice of public accounting are permitted to express their opinions and to allow their names, their firm names and their professional qualifications to be used by the press. Members should take great care in replying to such inquiries to ensure that they have sufficient knowledge in the area to express a considered opinion. They should also be very careful to consider whether the opinion they express could be based on information which they have obtained as a result of a confidential relationship with their clients.

40   Council considers it important that members of the profession should be recognized by the public as knowledgeable people who have views that are of value in areas within our collective or particular knowledge. Members should be prepared to put these views forward and be identified with them. It is the responsibility of each member, however, to use his own good judgment to ensure that he is acting within both the letter and spirit of the rules.

Radio and television appearances

41   From time to time members will be requested to appear on radio and television programmes. The general guidelines set out above for the

publication of articles and comments to the press should be followed. A member engaged in the practice of public accounting, in being introduced, may permit his name, the name of his firm, and his professional qualifications to be mentioned. Thereafter he should attempt to focus attention on his professional identification. Members should avoid giving any impression of soliciting business during such an appearance.

Use of photographs and biographies

42   There are various occasions when it is appropriate for a member engaged in the practice of public accounting to give permission, when requested, for the publication of his photograph and/or a biography in newpapers or magazines. These occasions are as follows:

a) in conjunction with the publication of an article written by the member;
b) in conjunction with a speech given or to be given by a member, or when a member is a participant in a public discussion as a member of a panel;
c) when a member is appointed to an office or position of national or local importance, or is awarded a distinction;
d) in conjunction with the seeking by the member of election to public office;
e) upon the establishment of a new practice or firm;
f) upon the admission of a new partner or partners to an existing firm;
g) upon the merger of existing firms;
h) upon graduation as a chartered accountant, or upon a student being awarded an Institute or a district C.A. association prize.

43   On such occasions, it is the responsibility of the member to ensure that the biographical material published is factual, and that commentary in narrative form relating to his particular accomplishments is restrained and in good taste.

44   Paid advertisements concerning members engaged in the practice of public accounting, or their students, and including photographs and/or biographies are considered appropriate in respect of items c, d, e, f, g and h above. An advertisement in this respect should appear only once in any particular paper or magazine, and only in media cirrculating in the area in which the practice is carried on. Such advertisements may include the following information:

a) the name of the person;
b) the names of the partners in the firm together with such academic degrees, titles, military rank, decorations, etc., which such persons may be entitled to use, including the initials C.M.C. or F.M.C. (denoting membership in The Institute of Management Consultants of Ontario) and initials denoting membership in such other organizations as, in the opinion of council, have developed meaningful standards and whose objectives do not conflict with the aims of the Institute;
c) the name (but not address) of his firm;

d) the name of the town in which his office is situated;

e) reasonable biographical material of a factual nature, i.e. place of birth, education and positions held. Comments, in narrative form, related to particular accomplishments of the individual should be avoided.

f) facts as to the position to be occupied or the award or distinction obtained.

45   In the case of announcements of graduation, or the award of an Institute prize, the following additional information would be appropriate:

g) the examination passed, with details of any prize;

h) names of parents;

i) school and local background;

j) name of employer (member or firm).

46   When a member engaged in the practice of public accounting *arranges* for the publication of a photograph or biographical comment, it should not be wider than one newspaper column for each photograph. However, when a member *consents* to such publication, it should not be of greater size or prominence than that generally allotted in similar circumstances by the publishing media concerned.

Certificates used by clients in advertising

47   Members engaged in the practice of public accounting may sometimes be asked by a client to report on the accuracy of figures to be used in advertising by the client. In such a case, there is no objection to the use of the complete statement which has been reported on and the complete report of the member. Anything less than the full statement and report is not acceptable. The difficulty in controlling the use of such a report is recognized, but it is the responsibility of the member to ensure that his report and the related statement are quoted in their entirety.

Recruitment brochures

48   Members or firms engaged in the practice of public accounting may circulate, or cause to be circulated, a brochure designed to attract students. In preparing such brochures, members should be guided by the following criteria as to form and content:

a) the brochure must be in good taste and show professional restraint;

b) contents must be factual;

c) pictures of members or students may be included;

*d)   without restricting the generality of the foregoing:

　　(i)   the amounts of salaries usually paid must not be included, although it is permissible to cover the firm's policy with respect to salary reviews and fringe benefits;

　　(ii)   the names of the firm's clients may not be included;

---

* *as amended, October 1977.*

(iii) testimonials from clients or others may not be included;

(iv) a recruitment brochure may include reference to non-audit services in which a student may be engaged during part of his training, or to related departments or firms of management consultants in which he might be employed at the completion of his training.

49   Approval of recruiting brochures by council is not required, but members who so wish may submit their brochures for review by the Institute to ensure that the established criteria have been met.

50   The following rules apply with respect to distribution of recruitment brochures:

a) brochures contemplated under this Interpretation may be used only for recruitment purposes;

b) brochures may be given only to individuals who have expressed an interest in employment with the member firm concerned by attending an interview, writing or asking for information or otherwise;

c) members and firms are permitted, however, to place a supply of brochures with the placement office of any educational institution where they propose to recruit, so that the placement service can make the brochures available to students on the same basis as those of industrial companies.

51   For the purpose of this Interpretation, the term "recruitment brochure" includes any literature designed for the recruitment of students, whether a booklet, a form letter or similar material.

52   Members or firms engaged in the practice of public accounting may insert an advertisement in any publication, circulation of which is primarily directed to students who are attending degree-granting institutions, provided that such advertisements follow the criteria, as to form and content, set out for recruitment brochures, with the exception that pictures of members or students may *not* be included.

53   Members engaged in the practice of public accounting who serve as part-time lecturers at universities or other educational institutions should exercise care so as not to take unfair advantage of their teaching positions for the purpose of recruiting students for or otherwise promoting the interests of their own firms.

Distribution of tax circulars, newsletters and firm literature on special subjects

54   Members engaged in the practice of public accounting may circulate to their clients and close associates tax circulars, newsletters and firm literature on special subjects. Members will also, on occasion, receive requests from non-clients for copies of material circulated to their clients. These requests may be complied with.

55°   Members may not permit further distribution of such material by clients, associations or others, except for distribution by either the CICA or a provincial Institute. If a client or other party (except for

---

° *as amended, October 1977.*

CICA or a provincial Institute) requests material for further circulation it can only be provided on the terms that it be circulated with no identification of the related member or firm.

56   Circulars should not be used as a method of general advertising and it is not permissible to distribute them except under the circumstances noted above.

Brochures describing related functions

57°   Separate organizations which engage solely in the "related functions" referred to in Rules 408 and 409, and divisions of public accounting firms which are so engaged, may use brochures to describe, in a factual way, the services offered. Approval by council of such brochures is not required but members may, if they wish, submit them for review by the Institute. The distribution of such brochures is to be governed by the provisions of paragraphs 54–56 of this Interpretation.

Use of public relations counsel/recruitment agencies

58°   The employment of a public relations officer, or the engagement of a public relations consultant or executive/employee recruitment agency by a member or firm engaged in the practice of public accounting is not of itself objectionable. Members who follow such a course, however, are responsible for ensuring that no activity of the public relations officer, consultant or recruitment agency, in respect of the firm, contravenes the rules of professional conduct and related Interpretations. Accordingly, while there are matters in which the use of skilled assistance in these areas can be advantageous, members should recognize that there is also an inherent danger of contravention of the rules and Interpretations and that close control must be exercised to avoid breaches. Public relations or recruitment advertising copy should be closely scrutinized by the members or firms engaging the services of such organizations to ensure that it contains nothing which might be considered objectionable.

Refer also to Rule 214, Rule 301 and CI 301, paragraphs 1–12, *Professional Appointments*.

CI 301—PROFESSIONAL APPOINTMENTS

1   A number of the rules of conduct relate to the responsibilities of a member in undertaking or withdrawing from a professional appointment. These rules are based on a number of fundamental assumptions:
    —the client's interests must always be placed ahead of the personal interests of the member;

° CI 217(57), (58) *as amended, June 9, 1975.*

—the client is, and must be, free to have his work performed by the practitioner of his choice;

—the fee for professional services cannot be measured until full information is available about the assignment;

—professional courtesy should be maintained between members in complying with a client's wishes.

The purpose of this Interpretation is to outline the course of conduct which should be followed in different situations.

Selection of professional advisers

2   A client in selecting professional advisers is entitled to information which will help him in making his selection. In addition, members have a responsibility to ensure that a transfer of professional work is carried out in an orderly fashion in the best interests of the client.

3   When approached by a prospective client about the assumption of work, it is proper for a member to meet with him to discuss his problems. There are, however, inquiries which must be made at the beginning of the discussion:

    —does the prospective client already engage the services of another public accountant?

    —if so, has he decided to dispense with the services of the present accountant?

    —has the prospective client notified the present accountant (incumbent) of this intention?

4   These inquiries are a matter of professional courtesy and are intended to ensure that the member is fully aware of the relationship existing between the prospective client and any incumbent accountant; having made them, a member is entitled to discuss, with the potential client, his work and its scope.

5   The potential client will wish to discuss with the member the services that he is in a position to offer and to obtain some indication of the cost of such services. There is no objection to the member supplying such information. In doing so, however, there are certain things that must be borne in mind.

6   A member must avoid giving any indication that he has exclusive knowledge or abilities which are not available from other members of the profession. The member is, however, entitled to give factual information as to his organization and as to the skills available within his organization.

7   Normally, professional fees are based on the time required to perform the services undertaken. There is no objection to a member stating what his per diem rates are, based on his standard rates for all clients. A member discussing a new assignment is not in a position to quote a fee or fee range, however, until he has been assured that the client has decided to dispense with the services of the incumbent accountant and

has had an opportunity to become fully familiar with the problems which he may encounter in carrying out the assignment, since otherwise he will not know how many days will be required to carry out his professional responsibilities. This is one reason why the rules of conduct provide that a member shall not seek to secure an engagement by representing that he can perform professional services for a lower fee than another public accountant and why responding to calls for tenders is prohibited.

8   A member should not reach any firm understanding with a client who already has a professional adviser until he has communicated with the incumbent accountant as required by Rule 302.

Changes in professional appointments

9*   Many members in practice are unclear on the purpose of the rule relating to changes in professional appointments (Rule 302), their impression being that on receipt of a communication from a proposed successor they may object to him assuming the appointment and thus prevent the change. There is no such intention; the purpose of the rule is as follows:

a) It protects a potential successor from accepting an appointment before he has knowledge of the circumstances under which the previous accountant's services were discontinued. Knowledge of these circumstances might well influence him against accepting the engagement which is offered.

b) If two separate practitioners are dealing with the same client, one as incumbent and one as successor, they should only do so in complete cooperation. There should be no period when one believes he is the incumbent whereas the other has been appointed. They must both be aware of the proposed change before the successor accountant accepts the appointment.

In all circumstances relating to changes in professional appointments (Rule 302) the recommended procedure outlined in paragraph 10 —below—should be followed.

10*   The recommended procedure is that when a member has been asked by a prospective client to accept a professional appointment he should advise the client that the retiring accountant should first be notified of the proposed change by the client. The successor should then inquire of the incumbent whether there are any circumstances he should take into account which might influence his decision whether or not to accept the appointment. The incoming accountant should not take up any work on the account until he has communicated with the retiring accountant, except that in the client's interest, acceptance of the offered appointment should not be unduly delayed through the failure of the retiring accountant to reply, if every reasonable effort has been made

---

Amended, October 26, 1973.

to communicate with him. As a matter of professional courtesy the retiring accountant should respond promptly to a communication of this nature. If there are no circumstances that the successor should be made aware of, a simple response to this effect is all that is necessary. If, on the other hand, the retiring accountant is aware of circumstances that the potential successor should take into account which might influence his decision whether or not to accept the appointment, he will need to consider first the question of confidentiality. If it appears that the circumstances cannot be disclosed because of confidentiality, the response to the potential successor should state that there are, in the opinion of the retiring accountant, circumstances which should be taken into account, but that they cannot be disclosed without the consent of the client.[1] Although the circumstances which the retiring accountant has in mind may be matters of public record, the retiring accountant must still consider whether confidentiality precludes him from disclosing the exact circumstances to his successor. Where confidentiality is in doubt, legal advice should be sought.

11[°]   The successor should also enquire of the predecessor whether there is any ongoing business of which he should be aware, in order to ensure that the client's interests are protected. On the part of the predecessor, there must be readiness to co-operate with the successor, recognizing that the client's interests are paramount. Generally, a member should be prepared to transfer promptly to the client or, on the client's instructions, to the newly-appointed accountants all books and documents belonging to the client which are in his possession, whether or not the terminal billing has been paid.

12   A member should also be prepared to supply reasonable information to his successor about the work being assumed. Where the time and trouble involved in giving information to the new accountant is not significant it should be regarded, in normal circumstances, as best professional practice to make no charge for this work.

Resignation of auditors

13   On occasion, the question arises of the duty of a chartered accountant appointed to act as an auditor at the annual general meeting of an Ontario or Canadian company, who is asked by the directors to resign before reporting.

14   In the Canada Corporations Act and the Ontario Business Corporations Act the statutory provisions with regard to auditors form a very important part of the legislation. The whole background of companies' legis-

---

[1] Section 161(7) of the Canada Business Corporations Act requires the successor auditor to obtain a written statement of the circumstances and the reasons why, in the predecessor auditor's opinion, that he is to be replaced. For a more detailed discussion, see Chapter 3.

[°] *Amended, October 26, 1973 and further amended June 9, 1975.*

lation makes it clear that the auditor fulfills an essential statutory and independent function and assumes statutory duties when he accepts his appointment. It is the council's view that, as a general rule, the proper course for an appointed auditor to follow is the completion of his statutory duties: having been appointed by the shareholders he should report, as required in the legislation. He should lay down his duties only when a successor has been properly elected, after he has been relieved or disqualified.

15   This being the proper course, the question remains whether there are exceptions when a duly authorized auditor may resign at the request of a board of directors without fulfilling his statutory duties. The answer depends on the circumstances. Certainly, the auditor of a company should not lightly resign under such circumstances, and should not resign at all, before reporting to the shareholders, if he has any reason to believe that his resignation is required by reason of any sharp practice, impropriety or concealment which it is his duty to report upon.

16   However, exceptional circumstances may exist in a particular case which would justify an auditor in acceding to a request for his resignation; one example would be where he has reason to believe that if a special meeting of the shareholders was called to relieve him of his appointment the necessary percentage of shareholders specified in the governing statute would require his resignation—in such a case it may not be necessary for the auditor to insist on a special meeting being called.

17   In summary, the auditor of a company is appointed to represent the shareholders and has a duty to them, he should never lightly resign his appointment before reporting and should not resign at all before reporting if he has reason to suspect that his resignation is required by reason of any sharp practice, impropriety or concealment, which it is his duty to report upon. Subject to that general statement, however, there may be exceptional circumstances in a particular case which would justify his resignation and this will be a matter of individual judgment in each case.

Non-member public accountants

18   It is emphasized that the approaches outlined in this Interpretation are to be followed, where applicable, not only in dealing with fellow members and professional colleagues but in dealing with licensed public accountants generally.

❖   ❖   ❖   ❖   ❖

Refer also to Rule 214 and Rule 302.

CI 302—COMMUNICATION WITH INCUMBENT PUBLIC ACCOUNTANT

Refer to Rule 214, Rule 301 and CI 301, paragraphs 1–12, *Professional Appointments*.

CI 305—ASSIGNMENTS FOR CLIENTS OF ANOTHER PUBLIC ACCOUNTANT

Refer also to Rule 201 and CI 201, paragraphs 5–7, *Criticism of a Professional Colleague or other Public Accountant.*

CI 401—MISLEADING NAMES

Refer also to Rule 406, *Practice of Public Accounting.*

CI 403*—PART-TIME AND "CONVENIENCE" OFFICES

1   Rule 403 clearly contemplates that where an office is held out to the public as offering public accounting services, the office is to be in the personal charge and management of a qualified professional (member or other licensee as the rule may require) normally in attendance to serve the public. Reinforcing this is the provision that no member or other licensee shall have the personal charge of more than one office.

2   The whole purpose of these provisions is to ensure to the public that its public accounting needs will be met in each instance by properly qualified professional personnel. It is in the light of this ethical requirement that the Council issues this interpretation laying down guidelines for the operation of part-time offices and "convenience" offices.
The essence of the differences between a part-time and a convenience office is that of holding out to the public. If there is holding out to the public about the existence of an office, then the guidelines governing holding out, contained here, have to be met. If there is no holding out, the office classifies as a private office of convenience.

3   *Part-time office:* a part-time office is defined as being an office which is held out to the public as that of a public accountant, but where the member (or licensee) having personal charge and management is not normally in attendance to serve the public throughout the business hours of the community in which the office is located. The following guidelines apply:

(a) a part-time office is to be under the personal charge and management of a member who is a licensed public accountant (or in the case of a Rule 403.3 firm, a non-member licensed public accountant) and who shall be present in the community during the published office hours of the part-time office;

(b) except with the specific approval of Council in special cases (see paragraph 4 below), a part-time office shall not be open to the public, nor staffed, other than during such published office hours;

(c) the office shall not be operated without the prior approval of the Council. Once such approval has been received the public can be advised of the existence of the office only in the following ways

(i) by the display of a suitable card on the door of the office or

---

* CI 403 *as amended, October 1977.*

on the directory board of the building in which the office is located,

(ii) by insertion of a professional card—specifying the hours/days of attendance by the practitioner—in publications whose distribution is restricted to the immediate area in which the office is located, the cards otherwise to conform to the general provisions of CI 217 (paras 8–14),

(iii) by a listing in the telephone directory white pages, and, if desired,

(iv) by a listing in the telephone directory yellow pages, restricted to the immediate area in which the office is located, specifying the hours/days of attendance by the practitioner;

(d) no other public references to a part-time office shall be made in letterheads, other professional cards, or other published material.

4   *Special cases:* the above guidelines provided that a part-time office shall not be open to the public, nor staffed, other than during the published office hours. There are, however, communities in the province, usually in the north, where there is a need for a public accounting office to be open to the public throughout the normal business hours of the community but where the full-time attendance of a member (or licensee as the case may be) is not justified economically. Members or firms wishing to operate an office on the basis of it being open full-time but with the practitioner present in the community only on a part-time basis may request special consideration. The service arrangements proposed should be outlined for Council so that, if it is in the public interest to do so, Council may grant appropriate remission from the normal requirements.

5   *Private office of convenience:* the distinguishing feature of a private office of convenience, as opposed to a part-time office, is that its existence is not held out to the public. Such an office is not, therefore, to be advertised publicly (in newspapers and telephone directory yellow pages, for example) or listed on letterhead or professional cards. There is one exception to this—that a member who is practising public accounting on a less than full-time basis is not precluded from having letterhead and financial statement paper for such practice; typically this member is retired, semi-retired or is engaged, regularly, in an occupation other than public accounting. The name of the practice is not, in any event, to appear on the exterior of the building in which the convenience office is located, on exterior doors or windows, for example. To enable existing clients to locate the office, a listing in the telephone directory white pages is permissible, and the name may appear on the building directory board, as well as on the interior door leading directly into the office.

CI 405—OBTAINING OR ATTRACTING CLIENTS

Organizations offering tax services

1   Any arrangement made by practising members with an organization offering tax services to the public, which results in a franchise or referral

scheme whereby that organization benefits from supplying clients to a practitioner, would be objectionable as a form of indirect solicitation.

       *   *   *   *   *

Refer also to: Rule 217 and CI 217, *Publicity and Advertising*, and Rule 301.

CI 406—PARTNERSHIPS

Refer to Rule 401 and CI 401, *Misleading Names*.

CI 407*—ASSOCIATION WITH A CORPORATION ENGAGED IN THE PRACTICE OF PUBLIC ACCOUNTING

In Rule 407, the term "corporation engaged in Canada in the practice of public accounting" does not include a corporation primarily engaged in the publishing business which publishes information on the subject of auditing, accounting or taxation.

---

* CI 407—*new, October 1977.*

3

Auditors' legal responsibility and liability

Legal responsibility and liability

Public accountants must comply with certain statutory and contractual requirements. These requirements delineate their legal responsibility. Of course, they should also observe the rules of professional conduct and generally accepted auditing standards discussed in the previous chapters. Those who fail to fulfill their professional and legal responsibility satisfactorily may be faced with legal action. Thus, public accountants must be keenly aware of their legal responsibility and liability.

Legal responsibility

The auditors' legal responsibility can be statutory, contractual, or both. Statutory responsibility is based on the mandatory audit requirement in the federal or provincial business corporations act. Contractual responsibility derives from an agreement mutually decided upon by the auditor and his client. Both may also agree to certain functions in addition to the statutory requirements; in such a case, the auditor will be responsible to the client for both the statutory and the additional contractual requirements.

A business corporation may be incorporated under the federal or provincial business corporations act. Certain types of corporations such as banking, insurance, trust, and loan are incorporated under special acts. The auditors must be familiar with the specific act applicable to each of their clients. The discussion of the auditors' responsibility in the following sections of this chapter is related to the Canada Business Corporations Act because it governs some of the largest corporations and is one of the most recently revised corporation acts in Canada. It is also similar to some provincial acts, such as the Ontario Business Corporations Act.

Mandatory audit requirement

Sections 154, 156, and 157 of the federal Business Corporations Act require a corporation that is or has offered its securities to the public, or with gross revenues exceeding $10 million, or with assets exceeding $5 million to appoint an auditor by an ordinary resolution of its shareholders at the first annual shareholders meeting. Section 157 does specify that the shareholders of a corporation by unanimous consent may choose not to appoint an auditor. The auditor's qualifications are stipulated in Section 155, which was briefly discussed in Chapter 2.

The details of these four sections are as follows:

154. (1) Copies to Director—A corporation
(a) any of the securities of which are or were a part of a distribution to the public, remain outstanding and are held by more than one person, or
(b) the gross revenues of which, as shown in the most recent financial statements referred to in section 149, exceed ten million dollars or the assets of which as shown in those financial statements exceed five million dollars.

shall, not less than twenty-one days before each annual meeting of shareholders or forthwith after the signing of a resolution under paragraph 136 (1) (b) in lieu of the annual meeting, and in any event not later than fifteen months after that last date when the last preceding anual meeting should have been held or a resolution in lieu of the meeting should have been signed, send a copy of the documents referred to in section 149 to the Director.

(2) Affiliates.—For the purposes of paragraph (1) (b), the gross revenues and assets of the corporation include the gross revenues and assets of its affiliates.

(3) Exemption.—A corporation may apply to the Director for an order exempting the corporation from the application of subsection (2) in such circumstances as may be prescribed.

(4) Further disclosure.—If a corporation referred to in subsection (1)
(a) sends to its shareholders, or
(b) is required to file with or send to a public authority or a recognized stock exchange

interim financial statements or related documents, the corporation shall forthwith send copies thereof to the Director.

(5) Subsidiary corporation exemption.—A subsidiary corporation is not required to comply with this section if

(a)   the financial statements of its holding corporation are in consolidated or combined form and include the accounts of the subsidiary; and

(b)   the consolidated or combined financial statements of the holding corporation are included in the documents sent to the Director by the holding corporation in compliance with this section.

(6)   Offence.—A corporation that fails to comply with this section is guilty of an offence and liable on summary conviction to a fine not exceeding five thousand dollars.

155.   (1)   Qualification of auditor.—Subject to subsection (5), a person is disqualified from being an auditor of a corporation if he is not independent of the corporation, any of its affiliates, or the directors or officers of any such corporation or its affiliates.

(2)   Independence.—For the purposes of this section,

(a)   independence is a question of fact; and

(b)   a person is deemed not to be independent if he or his business partner

(i)   is a business partner, a director, an officer or an employee of the corporation, of any of its affiliates, or of any director, officer or employee of any such corporation or its affiliates,

(ii)   beneficially owns or controls, directly or indirectly, a material interest in the securities of the corporation or any of its affiliates, or

(iii) has been a receiver, receiver-manager, liquidator or trustee in a bankruptcy of the corporation or any of its affiliates within two years of his proposed appointment as auditor of the corporation.

(3)   Duty to resign.—An auditor who becomes disqualified under this section shall, subject to subsection (5), resign forthwith after becoming aware of his disqualification.

(4)   Disqualification order.—An interested person may apply to a court for an order declaring an auditor to be disqualified under this section and the office of auditor to be vacant.

(5)   Exemption order.—An interested person may apply to a court for an order exempting an auditor from disqualification under this section and the court may, if it is satisfied that an exemption would not unfairly prejudice the shareholders, make an exemption order on such terms as it thinks fit, which order may have retrospective effect.

156.   (1)   Appointment of auditor.—Subject to section 157, shareholders of a corporation shall by ordinary resolution, at the first meeting of shareholders and at each succeeding annual meeting, appoint an auditor to hold office until the close of the next annual meeting.

(2)   Eligibility.—An auditor appointed under section 99 is eligible for appointment under subsection (1).

(3)   Incumbent auditor.—Notwithstanding subsection (1), if an auditor is not appointed at a meeting of shareholders, the incumbent auditor continues in office until his successor is appointed.

(4)   Remuneration.—The remuneration of an auditor may be fixed by ordinary resolution of the shareholders or, if not so fixed, may be fixed by the directors.

157.   (1)   Dispensing with auditor.—The shareholders of a corporation that is not required to comply with section 154, may resolve not to appoint an auditor.

(2)   Limitation.—A resolution under subsection (1) is valid only until the next succeeding annual meeting of shareholders.

(3)   Unanimous consent.—A resolution under subsection (1) is not valid unless it is consented to by all the shareholders, including shareholders not otherwise entitled to vote.

Auditors' statutory rights and responsibilities

Sections 162, 163, 164, and 166 of the federal Business Corporations Act delineate the auditors' rights and responsibilities. The specifics of these sections are:

162.   (1)   Right to attend meeting.—The auditor of a corporation is entitled to receive notice of every meeting of shareholders and, at the expense of the corporation, to attend and be heard thereat on matters relating to his duties as auditor.

(2)   Duty to attend.—If a director or shareholder of a corporation, whether or not the shareholder is entitled to vote at the meeting, gives written notice, not less than ten days before a meeting of shareholders, to the auditor or a former auditor of the corporation, the auditor or former auditor shall attend the meeting at the expense of the corporation and answer questions relating to his duties as auditor.

(3)   Notice to corporation.—A director or shareholder who sends a notice referred to in subsection (2) shall send concurrently a copy of the notice to the corporation.

(4)   Offence.—An auditor or former auditor of a corporation who fails without reasonable cause to comply with subsection (2) is guilty of an offence and liable on summary conviction to a fine not exceeding five thousand dollars or to imprisonment for a term not exceeding six months or to both.

(5)   Statement of auditor.—An auditor who

(a)   resigns,

(b)   receives a notice or otherwise learns of a meeting of shareholders called for the purpose of removing him from office,

(c)   receives a notice or otherwise learns of a meeting of directors or shareholders at which another person is to be appointed to fill the office of auditor, whether because of the resignation or removal of the incumbent auditor or because his term of office has expired or is about to expire, or

(d)   receives a notice or otherwise learns of a meeting of shareholders at which a resolution referred to in section 157 is to be proposed,

is entitled to submit to the corporation a written statement giving the reasons for his resignation or the reason why he opposes any proposed action or resolution.

(6) Circulating statement.—The corporation shall forthwith send a copy of the statement referred to in subsection (5) to every shareholder entitled to receive notice of any meeting referred to in subsection (1) and to the Director unless the statement is included in or attached to a management proxy circular required by section 144.

(7) Replacing auditor.—No person shall accept appointment or consent to be appointed auditor of a corporation if he is replacing an auditor who has resigned, been removed or whose term of office has expired or is about to expire until he has requested and received from that auditor a written statement of the circumstances and the reasons why, in that auditor's opinion, he is to be replaced.

(8) Exception.—Notwithstanding subsection (7), a person otherwise qualified may accept appointment or consent to be appointed as auditor of a corporation if, within fifteen days after making the request referred to in that subsection, he does not receive a reply.

(9) Effect of non-compliance.—Unless subsection (8) applies, an appointment as auditor of a corporation of a person who has not complied with subsection (7) is void.

163. (1) Examination.—An auditor of a corporation shall make the examination that is in his opinion necessary to enable him to report in the prescribed manner on the financial statements required by this Act to be placed before the shareholders, except such financial statements or part thereof that relate to the period referred to in subparagraph 149(1)(a)(ii).

(2) Reliance on other auditor.—Notwithstanding section 164,

(a)   an auditor of a holding corporation may reasonably rely upon the report of the auditor of a body corporate that is a subsidiary of the holding corporation if the fact of his reliance is disclosed in his report as auditor of the holding corporation; and

(b)   an auditor of a corporation may reasonably rely upon the report of the auditor of a body corporate that is not a subsidiary of that corporation but is, as prescribed, effectively controlled by the corporation, if the fact of his reliance is disclosed in his report as auditor of the corporation.

(3) Reasonableness.—For the purpose of subsection (2), reasonableness is a question of fact.

(4) Application.—Subsection (2) applies whether or not the financial statements of the holding corporation reported upon by the auditor are in consolidated form.

164. (1) Right to information.—Upon the demand of an auditor of a corporation, the present or former directors, officers, employees or agents of the corporation shall furnish such

(a)   information and explanations, and

(b)   access to records, documents, books, accounts and vouchers of the corporation or any of its subsidiaries

as are, in the opinion of the auditor, necessary to enable him to make the examination and report required under section 163 and that the directors, officers, employees or agents are reasonably able to furnish.

(2) Idem.—Upon the demand of an auditor of a corporation, the directors of the corporation shall obtain from and furnish to the auditor such information and explanations from the present or former directors, officers, employees or agents of any subsidiary of the corporation as are, in the opinion of the auditor, necessary to enable him to make the examination and report required under section 163 and that the directors, officers, employees or agents are reasonably able to furnish.

166. Qualified privilege (defamation).—Any oral or written statement or report made under this Act by the auditor or former auditor of a corporation has qualified privilege.

The main thrust of these sections is to strengthen the auditor's position, which in turn would enhance the reliability and credibility of audited financial statements, for the protection of shareholders and other investors.

Two items in Section 162 deserve special attention: first, the auditor's right and duty to attend the shareholders meetings; and, second, the right and duties of the predecessor and successor auditors in the change of appointment. The first item is significant because it provides a formal and direct channel of communication between the auditor and shareholders whereby the auditor has the opportunity to explain and respond to matters concerning his duties. This would contribute to the effective and efficient functioning of the auditor. The second item is significant because it provides the auditor who resigns or is being asked to resign with an opportunity to explain his position. Also, the successor auditor is required to request and to receive a written statement from the predecessor auditor concerning the circumstances and reasons for his resignation or removal. This would probably serve as a deterrent for unreasonable dismissal of the auditor. The auditor's position would be further strengthened if the Business Corporations Act had compelled the predecessor auditor to respond to the successor auditor's request. The act permits the auditor to accept the appointment if he does not receive a response from the predecessor auditor after 15 days. The act, however, goes beyond the rules of professional conduct by requiring the auditor to disclose the *circumstances and reasons* for his replacement rather than to state whether there are circumstances for the successor auditor to consider before he accepts the engagement. To the extent that this legal requirement overrides the auditor's right to maintain professional confidentiality, he may decline to respond. However, if the predecessor auditor does respond, he should seek legal advice on the matter.

The provisions in Section 163 concerning the auditor's examination and right to rely on other auditors warrant further elaboration. First, the auditor is responsible for an examination of the client's financial statement. He is, of course, also responsible for his opinion on such statements based on his examination. The reporting standards and contents of these financial statements are governed by the following regulations of the Business Corporations Act.

General

44.   The financial statements referred to in section 149 of the Act and the auditor's report referred to in section 163 of the Act shall, except as otherwise provided by this Part, be prepared in accordance with the recommendations of the Canadian Institute of Chartered Accountants set out in the C.I.C.A. Handbook.   *GAAP*

Interpretation

45.   For the purposes of paragraph 163 (2) (b) of the Act, a body corporate is "effectively controlled" by a corporation when the corporation accounts for its investment in the body corporate on an equity basis.

Contents of Financial Statements

46.   (1)   The financial statements referred to in section 149 of the Act shall include at least

(a)   a balance sheet;
(b)   a statement of retained earnings;
(c)   an income statement; and
(d)   a statement of changes in financial position.

(2)   Financial statements need not be designated by the names set out in paragraphs (1) (a) to (d).

Reporting Classes of Business

47.   (1)   In this section "corporation" means a corporation that carries on a diversified as distinct from an integrated business and that sends its financial statements to the Director pursuant to subsection 154 (1) of the Act.

(2)   The financial statements of a corporation shall disclose separately or in a schedule thereto a summary of financial information for each class of business the revenue from which is 10 per cent or more of the corporation's total revenues for the period.

(3)   The financial statements or schedule referred to in subsection (2) shall contain a note stating that the directors of the corporation have determined its classes of business at a meeting of directors and have recorded them in the minutes of the meeting.

(4)   Subject to subsection (5), the classes of business referred to in subsection (2) shall be designated in accordance with the Statistics Canada Standard Industrial Classification Code.

(5)   Where the directors of the corporation do not adopt the Statistics Canada Standard Industrial Classification Code to identify the corporation's classes of business, the financial statements or note thereto shall contain a description of the basis used to determine the corporation's classes of business.

Regulations 48, 49, and 50 prescribe certain circumstances under which a corporation may be exempted from public disclosure of its financial statements.

It is important to stress that the Business Corporations Act requires financial statements to be prepared in accordance with the recommendations set out in the *CICA Handbook*. This statutory sanction of the recommendations of the accounting profession strengthens the authority of the CICA and its Accounting Research Committee, and, at the same time, it places an added heavy responsibility on the accounting profession to provide sound accounting and reporting standards.

Second, the auditor of a holding corporation may reasonably rely upon the auditor's report of a subsidiary or effectively controlled corporation if the fact of such reliance is disclosed in the auditor's report of the holding corporation. Reasonableness is defined by the Business Corporations Act as "a question of fact." To establish such reasonableness, the auditor of the holding corporation should make "a professional judgment as to the competence of his professional colleague, and it is for him to decide how he will satisfy himself on the matter."[1] But how does the auditor decide on the matter? Section 5530 of the *CICA Handbook* provides the following guidelines where there is no agency relationship between the auditor of the holding corporation and the subsidiary auditor:

> The steps taken by the parent company auditors to entitle them to rely on the work and opinion of the subsidiary company auditors should normally include:
>
> (a)   assurance that the subsidiary company auditors are independent practising public accountants, licensed where required or otherwise appropriately qualified;
>
> (b)   direct communication with the subsidiary company auditors to ensure that they are aware:
>
>   (i)   that the audited financial statements of the subsidiary are to be included in the consolidated financial statements, and that their work and opinion will be relied on by the parent company auditors for the purpose of forming an opinion on the consolidated financial statements;
>
>   (ii)   of the financial reporting requirements relevant to the consolidated financial statements;
>
> (c)   consideration of the content of the report of the subsidiary company auditors as supporting the credibility of the related financial statements;
>
> (d)   enquiry into the extent to which accounting policies reflected in the financial statements of the subsidiary company differ from those of the parent company or from those followed in the preceding year.

---

[1] Robert W. V. Dickerson et al., *Proposals for a New Business Corporations Law for Canada* (Ottawa: Queen's Printer, 1971), I, p. 111.

In addition, the parent company auditors may consider it necessary to enquire into the scope of the examination conducted by the subsidiary company auditors.

The enquiries referred to above may be made by any methods reasonable in the circumstances, such as personal consultation, correspondence or review of working papers. In determining the extent of their enquiries, the auditors of the parent company will have regard to the materiality of the accounts of the subsidiary company and any other significant circumstances in each individual case.

Section 164 grants the auditor the right to demand the information he needs to perform his duties. He is allowed to have access to records, documents, books, accounts, and vouchers of the corporation or any of its subsidiaries, and to obtain information and explanations from the *present* or *former* directors, officers, employees, or agents of the corporation. The necessity of this right is obvious, without it the scope of the audit may be limited or restricted by the corporation.

Section 166 gives the auditor a "qualified privilege" for any oral or written statement or report made under the Business Corporations Act. This protects the auditor from legal action against him for slander or libel, provided that his statement or report is made in good faith and without malice. Thus, it encourages the auditor to make full and frank statements on matters related to his examination and opinion on the financial statements. Since the auditor is probably entitled to such a "qualified privilege" under common law, this provision is to ensure that he is aware of the common law position.[2]

Subsequent discovery of errors in financial statements

Section 165 contains two important provisions: first, the right and responsibilities of the auditor and directors of a corporation for subsequent discovery of errors in published financial statements; and, second, the audit committee. The first item is discussed below and the second in the next section.

The details of the first provision are:

165. (6) Notice of errors.—A director or an officer of a corporation shall forthwith notify the audit committee and the auditor of any error or mis-statement of which he becomes aware in a financial statement that the auditor or a former auditor has reported upon.

(7) Error in financial statements.—If the auditor or former auditor of a corporation is notified or becomes aware of an error or mis-statement in a financial statement upon which he has reported, and if in his opinion the error or mis-statement is material, he shall inform each director accordingly.

---

[2] Ibid., p. 112.

(8) Duty of directors.—When upon subsection (7) the auditor or former auditor informs the directors of an error or misstatement in a financial statement, the directors shall

(a) prepare and issue revised financial statements; or

(b) otherwise inform the shareholders and, if the corporation is one that is required to comply with section 154, it shall inform the Director of the error or mis-statement in the same manner as it informs the shareholders.

(9) Offence.—Every director or officer of a corporation who knowingly fails to comply with subsection (6) or (8) is guilty of an offence and liable on summary conviction to a fine not exceeding five thousand dollars or to imprisonment for a term not exceeding six months or to both.

This provision imposes upon the auditor, director, and officer of a corporation a duty to take the necessary action to inform the shareholders and probably other users of the errors they discover in published financial statements of the corporation. This is essential to ensure the reliability and credibility of financial statements.

Audit committee[3]

Section 165 requires a corporation that is or has offered its securities to the public to have an audit committee. The specific provisions are:

165. (1) Audit committee.—Subject to subsection (2), a corporation described in subsection 97 (2) [requiring a corporation offering its securities to the public to have no fewer than three directors] shall, and any other corporation may, have an audit committee composed of not less than three directors of the corporation, a majority of whom are not officers or employees of the corporation or any of its affiliates.

(2) Exemption.—A corporation may apply to the Director for an order authorizing the corporation to dispense with an audit committee, and the Director may, if he is satisfied that the shareholders will not be prejudiced by such an order, permit the corporation to dispense with an audit committee on such reasonable conditions as he thinks fit.

(3) Duty of committee.—An audit committee shall review the financial statements of the corporation before such financial statements are approved under section 152 [approval by one or more directors].

(4) Auditor's attendance.—The auditor of a corporation is entitled to receive notice of every meeting of the audit committee and, at the expense of the corporation, to attend and be heard thereat; and, if so re-

---

3 For a more detailed and in-depth discussion on audit committees, see R. K. Mautz and F. L. Newmann, *Corporate Audit Committees* (Urbana: Bureau of Economics and Business Research, University of Illinois, 1970); Wai P. Lam, "Corporate Audit Committees in Ontario, Canada: An Empirical Study" (Ph. D. diss., Michigan State University, 1974); Wai P. Lam, "The Development and Significance of Corporate Audit Committees," *CA Magazine* (April 1975); and Wai P. Lam and Alvin A. Arens, "Audit Committees in Practice: A Survey," *CA Magazine* (October 1975).

quested by a member of the audit committee, shall attend every meeting of the committee held during the term of office of the auditor.

(5) Calling meeting.—The auditor of a corporation or a member of the audit committee may call a meeting of the committee.

The most salient rationale for establishing an audit committee is the need to assure the independence or objectivity of the external auditor. This need arises because the close relationship between the auditor and management frequently poses a threat to the auditor's independence. The audit committee, composed chiefly or entirely of nonofficer directors, provides a degree of objectivity and a direct channel of communication between the auditor and directors, and thus will help to minimize or avert this threat to the auditor's independence.[4]

In practice, the objectives and functions of an audit committee usually are broader than those set forth or implied in the statutory requirements. The most important objectives are:

1. To relieve the board of directors, as a whole, of details regarding the review of the results of the independent audit.
2. To perform as an independent review function of the corporation's operations and its annual financial statements before their submission to the board of directors for approval.
3. To relieve the board of directors, as a whole, of details regarding the review of the annual financial statements.
4. To give attention to the internal control functions of the corporation.
5. To give additional attention to the audit function performed by the independent auditors.
6. To provide non-officer directors with direct and more personal contact with the independent auditors.

Although the functions of an audit committee may vary from corporation to corporation, the most important functions should include:

1. Review with the independent auditors, on completion of the audit, their experience, any restrictions on their work, cooperation received, their findings, and their recommendations.
2. Review with the independent auditors their evaluation of the corporation's internal control systems.
3. Review the corporate annual financial statements before their submission to the board of directors for approval.
4. Review the scope of internal audit procedures with the chief internal auditor.

---

[4] Ontario, Legislative Assembly, *1967 Interim Report of the Select Committee on Company Law* (Toronto, 1967), pp. 91–92. Also see, Ontario, *Report of the Royal Commission—Atlantic Acceptance Corporation Limited* (Toronto, 1967), iv, p. 1512, which noted that with an audit committee the auditor would have been more independent of management and "it was probable that the story of Atlantic Acceptance would have been different."

5. Discuss with the independent auditors, before the audit, its scope, purpose, and the procedures to be included.
6. Review interim financial reports to shareholders before these reports are approved by the board of directors.

Since the creation of an audit committee introduces a new organizational unit within the corporate structure, it gives rise to a new set of relationships among the auditor, directors, and management. An audit committee, in performing a variety of its functions, should take extreme care not to encroach upon management's operating duties. Any unnecessary and unwarranted encroachment would eventually undermine the effective functioning of the committee.

Audit committees usually are small, three members being most common. This perhaps reflects the thinking that a small committee would make in-depth discussions on important matters more effective and efficient. The committee generally meets at least once or twice a year, usually with the auditor in attendance. These meetings are devoted to the discussion of the functions cited earlier.

In general, audit committees are considered useful for most corporations, including not-for-profit organizations, and are effective in fulfilling their objectives and functions. They represent a positive force in assuring the auditor's independence from management and enhance the reliability and credibility of corporate financial statements. They can also contribute other benefits, such as resolving major disagreements between auditors and management and providing added protection for the directors of the corporation, especially for non-officer directors.

In addition to the federal Business Corporations Act, the Ontario and British Columbia acts also contain an audit committee provision. It appears that the audit committee will probably be a common practice in the near future, both in Canada and the United States.[5]

Other statutory requirements relevant to the auditor

The relevance and importance of the following sections of the federal Business Corporations Act should be self-evident.

> 20. (1) Corporate records.—A corporation shall prepare and maintain, at its registered office or at any other place in Canada designated by the directors, records containing
>
> (a) the articles and the by-laws, and all amendments thereto, and a copy of any unanimous shareholder agreement;
> (b) minutes of meetings and resolutions of shareholders;
> (c) copies of all notices required by section 101 or 108; and

---

[5] While audit committees are mostly voluntary in the United States, the New York Stock Exchange recently adopted a policy requiring its listed domestic companies to have an audit committee. This policy will be effective June 30, 1978.

(d)   a securities register complying with section 46.

(2)   Directors records.—In addition to the records described in subsection (1), a corporation shall prepare and maintain adequate accounting records and records containing minutes of meetings and resolutions of the directors and any committee thereof.

(4)   Place of directors records.—The records described in subsection (2) shall be kept at the registered office of the corporation or at such other place as the directors think fit and shall at all reasonable times be open to inspection by the directors.

(5)   Records in Canada.—Where accounting records of a corporation are kept at a place outside Canada, there shall be kept at the registered office or other office in Canada accounting records adequate to enable the directors to ascertain the financial position of the corporation with reasonable accuracy on a quarterly basis.

(6)   Offence.—A corporation that, without reasonable cause, fails to comply with this section is guilty of an offence and liable on summary conviction to a fine not exceeding five thousand dollars.

22.   (1)   Form of records.—All registers and other records required by this Act to be prepared and maintained may be in a bound or loose-leaf form or in a photographic film form, or may be entered or recorded by any system of mechanical or electronic data processing or any other information storage device that is capable of reproducing any required information in intelligible written form within a reasonable time.

(2)   Precautions.—A corporation and its agents shall take reasonable precautions to

(a)   prevent loss or destruction of,

(b)   prevent falsification of entries in, and

(c)   facilitate detection and correction of inaccuracies in the records and registers required by this Act to be prepared and maintained.

(3)   Offence.—A person who contravenes this section is guilty of an offence and liable on summary conviction to a fine not exceeding five thousand dollars or to imprisonment for a term not exceeding six months or to both.

23.   Corporate seal.—An instrument or agreement executed on behalf of a corporation by a director, an officer or an agent of the corporation is not invalid merely because a corporate seal is not affixed thereto.

117.   (1)   Duty of care of directors and officers.—Every director and officer of a corporation in exercising his powers and discharging his duties shall

(a)   act honestly and in good faith with a view to the best interests of the corporation; and

(b)   exercise the care, diligence and skill that a reasonably prudent person would exercise in comparable circumstances.

(2)   Duty to comply.—Every director and officer of a corporation shall comply with this Act, the regulations, articles, by-laws and any unanimous shareholder agreement.

(3)   No exculpation.—No provision in a contract, the articles, the

by-laws or a resolution relieves a director or officer from the duty to act in accordance with this Act or the regulations or relieves him from liability for a breach thereof.

149.   (1)   Annual financial statements.—Subject to section 150, the directors of a corporation shall place before the shareholders at every annual meeting

(a)   comparative financial statements as prescribed relating separately to

    (i)   the period that began on the date the corporation came into existence and ended not more than six months before the annual meeting or, if the corporation has completed a financial year, the period that began immediately after the end of the last completed financial year and ended not more than six months before the annual meeting, and

    (ii)   the immediately preceding financial year;

(b)   the report of the auditor, if any; and

(c)   any further information respecting the financial position of the corporation and the results of its operations required by the articles, the by-laws or any unanimous shareholder agreement.

(2)   Exception.—Notwithstanding paragraph (1)(a), the financial statements referred to in sub-paragraph (1)(a)(ii) may be omitted if the reason for the omission is set out in the financial statements, or in a note thereto, to be placed before the shareholders at an annual meeting.

150.   Exemption.—A corporation may apply to the Director for an order authorizing the corporation to omit from its financial statements any item prescribed, or to dispense with the publication of any particular financial statement prescribed, and the Director may if he reasonably believes that disclosure of the information therein contained would be detrimental to the corporation, permit such omission on such reasonable conditions as he thinks fit.

151.   (1)   Consolidated statements.—A holding corporation may prepare the financial statements referred to in section 149 in consolidated or combined form as prescribed, and in any case the corporation shall keep at its registered office copies of the financial statements of each subsidiary body corporate.

(2)   Examination.—Shareholders of a corporation and their agents and legal representatives may upon request therefor examine the statements referred to in subsection (1) during the usual business hours of the corporation, and may make extracts therefrom, free of charge.

(3)   Barring examination.—A corporation may, within fifteen days of a request to examine under subsection (2), apply to a court for an order barring the right of any person to so examine, and the court may, if it is satisfied that such examination would be detrimental to the corporation or a subsidiary body corporate, bar such right and make any further order it thinks fit.

(4)   Notice to Director.—A corporation shall give the Director and the person asking to examine under subsection (2) notice of an applica-

tion under subsection (3), and the Director and such person may appear and be heard in person or by counsel.

152. (1) Approval of financial statements.—The directors of a corporation shall approve the financial statements referred to in section 149 and the approval shall be evidenced by the signature of one or more directors.

(2) Condition precedent.—A corporation shall not issue, publish or circulate copies of the financial statements referred to in section 149 unless the financial statements are

(a)   approved and signed in accordance with subsection (1); and

(b)   accompanied by the report of the auditor of the corporation, if any.

158. (1) Ceasing to hold office.—An auditor of a corporation ceases to hold office when

(a)   he dies or resigns; or

(b)   he is removed pursuant to section 159.

(2) Effective date of resignation.—A resignation of an auditor becomes effective at the time a written resignation is sent to the corporation, or at the time specified in the resignation, whichever is later.

159. (1) Removal of auditor.—The shareholders of a corporation may by ordinary resolution at a special meeting remove from office the auditor other than an auditor appointed by a court under section 161.

(2) Vacancy.—A vacancy created by the removal of an auditor may be filled at the meeting at which the auditor is removed or, if not so filled, may be filled under section 160.

160. (1) Filling vacancy.—Subject to subsection (3), the directors shall forthwith fill a vacancy in the office of auditor.

(2) Calling meeting.—If there is not a quorum of directors, the directors then in office shall, within twenty-one days after a vacancy in the office of auditor occurs, call a special meeting of shareholders to fill the vacancy and, if they fail to call a meeting or if there are no directors, the meeting may be called by any shareholder.

(3) Shareholders filling vacancy.—The articles of a corporation may provide that a vacancy in the office of auditor shall only be filled by vote of the shareholders.

(4) Unexpired term.—An auditor appointed to fill a vacancy holds office for the unexpired term of his predecessor.

161. (1) Court appointed auditor.—If a corporation does not have an auditor, the court may, upon the application of a shareholder or the Director, appoint and fix the remuneration of an auditor who holds office until an auditor is appointed by the shareholders.

(2) Exception.—Subsection (1) does not apply if the shareholders have resolved under section 157 not to appoint an auditor.

Auditors' contractual responsibilities

Auditors' contractual responsibilities stem from three different types of engagements, statutory, statutory with additional agreements, and non-statutory. For the first type, the statutory responsibilities are the auditors' contractual responsibilities. The second type of engagement requires the auditor to be responsible for both the statutory requirements and other additional functions agreed upon by the auditors and their clients. The terms of the third engagement depend completely on the auditors and their clients. The terms of the contract, once agreed upon by auditors and clients, are binding on both parties. In all engagements the auditors should make certain that the parties to the contract understand clearly and precisely what the terms are. To avoid misunderstanding, the contract, usually in the form of an engagement letter, should be in writing and should be confirmed by the client. In the case of repeat engagements, the auditors should confirm in writing the terms of the contract with their clients every year to ensure that any changes in the contract are not overlooked.

Legal liability

We live in an "age of litigation." Persons having real or fancied grievances against business and professional persons are likely to take their grievances to court. Consumer advocate groups, environmentalists, and other aggressive organizations often request courts to assess damages against professionals and business executives for alleged wrongs to society.

The rapid growth of the public accounting profession during the past several years has been accompanied by a sharp increase in the number of court cases involving independent public accountants. These court cases have included criminal charges as well as lawsuits involving civil matters. A man or woman entering the public accounting profession today should be aware of the legal liability inherent in the practice of public accounting. The following sections will describe briefly some aspects of common law having a bearing on the work of the CA, and some related court cases in Canada, the United Kingdom, and the United States. It should be emphasized, however, that the court cases discussed in this chapter are isolated occurrences; the tens of thousands of satisfactory audits performed each year by public accountants do not result in court cases or newspaper headlines.

By way of comparison, let us assume that one million commercial air line flights are safely completed during a year, but that two crashes occur. It would seem unreasonable to assert on the basis of these assumed facts that commercial aviation is unsafe and should be prohibited by law. On the other hand, there is every reason to investigate every detail relating to the two crashes with the goal of improving the safety record of commercial aviation.

Definition of terms

Discussion of auditors' liability is best prefaced by a definition of some of the common terms of business law. Among these are the following:

Breach of contract is a failure of one or both parties to a contract to perform in accordance with the contract's provision. A CA firm might be sued for breach of contract, for example, if the firm failed to deliver its audit report to the client by the date specified in the *engagement letter* representing the contractual arrangement between the CA firm and the client.

Fraud is defined as misrepresentation by a person of a material fact, known by that person to be untrue or made with reckless indifference as to whether the fact is true, with the intention of deceiving the other party and with the result that the other party is injured. Rule 205 of the *Rules of Professional Conduct* (discussed in Chapter 2) states that a CA shall not knowingly misrepresent facts. A CA found to have violated this provision might be sued for fraud by the client or another injured party. Charges of fraud might also be made against a CA who violates Rule 206.

Constructive fraud differs from fraud as defined above in that constructive fraud does not involve a misrepresentation of fact *with intent to deceive.* Instead, a person who violates a legal duty or contractual obligation which requires the exercise of exceptional good faith might be accused of constructive fraud because of the very lack of good faith. A CA firm which failed to comply with generally accepted auditing standards during an audit engagement might be charged with constructive fraud.

An *independent contractor* is a party to a contract who performs contractual obligations essentially without control or supervision by the other contracting party. The generally accepted auditing standard dealing with objectivity makes it essential that a CA firm's role in the examination of a client's financial statements be that of an independent contractor rather than an employee, despite the firm's receipt of a fee from the client.

Negligence is violation of a legal duty to exercise a degree of care which an ordinarily prudent person would exercise under similar circumstances, with resultant damages to another party. The two subdivisions of negligence are *ordinary negligence,* defined as lack of reasonable care; and *gross negligence,* which is lack of even *slight* care, indicative of reckless disregard for fact. A public accounting firm which failed to gather sufficient appropriate evidence to support the figure for cash in the client's balance sheet might be accused of *ordinary negligence* by an injured party if all other phases of the audit conformed to generally accepted auditing standards. In contrast, if the public accounting firm failed substantially to comply with generally accepted auditing standards, it might be charged with *gross negligence* by an aggrieved party. Gross negligence by auditors may constitute constructive fraud.

Proximate cause exists when damage to another is directly attributable to a wrongdoer's act.

Contributory negligence is negligence on the part of a party damaged by another party's negligence. For example, a public accounting firm charged by a client with *ordinary negligence* for failure to discover a cash shortage during the course of the audit might countercharge the client with *contributory negligence* for failing to establish an adequate system of internal control for cash.

Privity is the relationship between parties to a contract. A public accounting firm is in privity with the client which it is serving, as well as with any *third-party beneficiary,* such as a creditor bank, named in the engagement letter representing the contract between the public accounting firm and its client.

A *third-party* beneficiary is a person—not the promisor or promisee—who is named in a contract or intended by the contracting parties to have definite rights and benefits under the contract. For example, if Warren & Co., CAs, is engaged to examine the financial statements of Arthur Company and to send a copy of its audit report to Third National Bank, the bank is a third-party beneficiary under the contract between Warren & Co. and Arthur Company.

Auditors' liability to clients and to third-party beneficiaries

We have pointed out that public accounting firms are independent contractors in their performance of audit engagements. In undertaking the customary audit engagement—the examination of and the expression of an opinion on the client's financial statements—auditors are responsible for carrying out their assignment in accordance with generally accepted auditing standards, and for complying with the Rules of Professional Conduct. Under common law, if the auditors do not comply with their obligations to the client and there is consequent harm to the client, the latter may sue the auditors for breach of contract, or for torts such as fraud or negligence. An injured client need only prove that the auditors were guilty of *ordinary negligence* in order to collect damages under the common law.

A recent Canadian case, *Toromont Industrial Holding Ltd.,* involved the liability of auditors to a client because of ordinary negligence. The parties were a CA firm and its client, *Cimco Ltd.,* which was controlled by Toromont. The action against the CA firm for negligence was brought by Toromont on behalf of Cimco. The High Court of Justice of Ontario ruled in June 1975 that the CA firm was negligent and was in breach of its duty to its client, with a resulting damage of $7,967. The counterclaim by the CA firm for audit fees of $4,750 was disallowed in view of the admitted negligence of the defendant.

A similar case in the United States is the *Westec* case. Westec Corporation was a rapidly growing, diversified company, and the market price of its stock increased from $2 per share to more than $67 per share over a two-year span. The stock's market price thereafter began to decline, and trading in the stock was suspended when an order for approximately 160,000 shares purchased by or on behalf of Westec's president was not paid for.

Westec Corporation subsequently entered into corporate reorganization under Chapter 10 of the Bankruptcy Act. On behalf of Westec and its shareholders, the bankruptcy trustee sued the CPA firm which had audited the financial statements of Westec during its "high-flying" period. The trustee charged the CPA firm with negligence in conducting the audits and with consequently failing to discover significant related party transactions, fictitious sales of assets, and improper application of the pooling-of-interests accounting method for business combinations completed by Westec. The CPA firm subsequently settled the trustee's suit by a payment of $1,875,000 to compensate for damages to Westec and its shareholders and by withdrawing a claim for fees and interest totaling approximately $133,000.

Not all damages paid by public accounting firms for negligence to their clients result from lawsuits. Litigation is extremely costly in demands upon the time of public accountants involved as well as expenditures for legal fees. Therefore, some public accounting firms have made payments to aggrieved clients voluntarily, before the client initiated a suit.

Liability to third-party beneficiaries. Since a third-party beneficiary is *in privity* with the public accounting firm and the client being audited, the third-party beneficiary has the same rights as the client under common law. Thus, an aggrieved third-party beneficiary, such as a creditor bank, need only prove that the auditors were guilty of *ordinary negligence* in order to recover damages from the public accounting firm.

Auditors' liability to other third parties

The liability of public accounting firms to third parties not in privity has developed under the common law. The responsibility of auditors to third parties who may rely upon the audit report has evolved through several significant court cases. These cases involve the auditors' liability to third parties for negligence, gross negligence, and fraud. Since court decisions in the United Kingdom and the United States are cited in Canadian court decisions (for example, the decision of the Supreme Court of Canada in *Haig v. Bamford et al.* in 1976), it is important to discuss cases in those two countries as well as Canada. The principal aspects of the following cases, arranged in chronological order, are discussed.

In *Ultramares* v. *Touche & Co.*, 255 N.Y. 170 (1931), in the United States, the defendant CPAs issued what was in essence an unqualified opinion on the balance sheet of a company engaged in the importation and sale of rubber. On the strength of the CPAs' opinion, the plaintiff, a factor, made a number of loans to the company. Shortly thereafter, the company was declared bankrupt.

The factor originally sued the CPAs for negligence; later, during trial, fraud was added to the complaint. The court found that the CPAs were **grossly negligent** in not discovering obvious material overstatements of sales and receivables, among other audit shortcomings; and that consequently the factor, although not a third-party beneficiary in the case, could recover its losses from the auditors. As a result of the landmark *Ultramares* case, the defence of privity is invalid in the event of gross negligence.

However, the court also held that the auditors could not be liable for negligence to the plaintiff, a third party identifiable only in a general way.

> If liability for negligence exists, a thoughtless slip or blunder, the failure to detect a theft or forgery beneath the cover of deceptive entries, may expose accountants to a liability in an indeterminate amount for an indeterminate time to an indeterminate class.

In *Hedley Byrne & Co. Ltd.* v. *Heller & Partners Ltd.* (1963) 2 all ER 575, in the United Kingdom, Hedley Byrne & Co. Ltd., a third-party advertising agency, sued Heller & Partners Ltd., a banking company, for negligence. The plaintiff suffered a loss resulting from relying on the defendant's favourable references on a client company which subsequently went into liquidation. The plaintiff's action failed because the defendant had expressly disclaimed any responsibility for his references. The observations of the court on the broader issue of negligence to third parties are especially significant to auditors. The court stated that anyone making negligent statements in a business or professional capacity would be liable to third parties that were known or should have been known to him.

> . . . if in a sphere in which a person is so placed that others could reasonably rely upon his judgment or his skill or upon his ability to make careful inquiry, a person takes it upon himself to give information or advice to, or allows his information or advice to be passed on to, another person, who, as he knows or should know, will place reliance upon it, then a duty of care will arise.

Hence, the defence of privity of contract may be invalid if the auditors know or should know that certain third parties will be relying on their report. To prove whether the auditors know or should know the third parties, a principle called the **Hedley Byrne** principle of foreseeability or special relationship is used. Its influence on Canadian court decisions is evident in two cases discussed later.

In another case in the United States, *Rusch Factors, Inc.* v. *Levin,* 284 F. Supp. 85 (1968), the court held that an accountant should be liable in negligence for careless financial misrepresentations relied upon by actually foreseen and limited classes of persons. It also declared that an accountant who **commits fraud** in issuing a report is **liable to all third parties** he could *foresee* being injured, despite his lack of knowledge of actual third parties who might rely upon his report.

In *Haig* v. *Bamford et al.* (1972) 6 W.W.R. 557 in Canada, the Saskatchewan court found the accountants liable to a third party for negligence. The third party, Haig, relied on the accountants' audit report and invested $20,075 in an apparently profitable company which in fact was losing money. The profit figure was distorted by an erroneous treatment of a customer's advances as sales. The accountants submitted the auditors' report on the financial statements without performing an audit, the performance of which would have discovered the error. After the error was revealed and when the company was in financial trouble, Haig invested another $2,500 in an attempt to save the company. The attempt proved futile, and the company ceased operation shortly thereafter.

The court found the accountants negligent and, in applying the **Hedley Byrne** principle of foreseeability, held the accountants liable to Haig, for both the original investment ($20,075) and the additional investment ($2,500), because they knew or ought to have known that a third party would be relying on the financial statements.

> On the facts I hold that the defendants knew or ought to have known that [the auditors' report] would be used by a potential investor. Although Haig was not in the picture when the defendants were preparing [the report], he must be included in the category of persons who could be foreseen by the defendants as relying on [the report] in a matter affecting their economic interests. The defendants therefore had a duty to Haig. The negligence which I have found was a breach of that duty, and it follows therefore that the defendants are liable.

The successful appeal of the accountants in the Saskatchewan Court of Appeal was reversed by the Supreme Court of Canada in 1976. In reinstating the trial judge's decision that the defendants were negligent and therefore liable, the Supreme Court stated:

> The outcome of this appeal rests, it would seem, on whether, to create a duty of care, it is sufficient that the accountants knew that the information was intended to be disseminated among a specific group or class, . . . or whether the accountants also needed to be apprised of the plaintiff's identity.

> The increasing growth and changing role of corporations in modern society has been attended by a new perception of the social role of the profession of accounting. . . . The complexities of modern industry combined with . . . the separation of ownership from management . . .

have led to marked changes in the role and responsibilities of the accountant, and in the reliance which the public must place upon his work. The
financial statements of the corporations upon which he reports can affect
the economic interests of the general public as well as of shareholders and
potential shareholders.

With the added prestige and value of his services has come, as the leaders
of the profession have recognized, a concomitant and commensurately
increased responsibility to the public. It seems unrealistic to be oblivious
to these developments. It does not necessarily follow that the doors must
be thrown open and recovery permitted whenever someone's economic
interest suffers as the result of a negligent act on the part of an accountant . . . it appears that several possible tests could be applied to involve
a duty of care on the part of accountants vis-a-vis third parties (i) foreseeability of the use of the financial statements and the auditor's report
thereon by the plaintiff and reliance thereon; (ii) actual knowledge of
the limited class that will use and rely on the statement; (iii) actual
knowledge of the specific plaintiff who will use and rely on the statement.

The choice in the present case, it seems to me, is between test (ii) and
test (iii), actual knowledge of the limited class or actual knowledge of the
specific plaintiff. I have concluded on the authorities that test (iii) is too
narrow and that test (ii), actual knowledge of the limited class, is the
proper test to apply in this case.

In the present case the accountants knew that the financial statements
were being prepared for the very purpose of influencing . . . a limited
number of potential investors. The names of the potential investors were
not material to the accountants. What was important was the nature of
the transaction or transactions for which the statements were intended, for
that is what delineated the limits of potential liability.

The court then allowed Haig to recover the $20,075 but not the additional
investment of $2,500 because he was then fully aware of the true state of
affairs of the company.

In another Canadian case, *Toromont Industrial Holdings Ltd. et al.* v.
Thorne, Gunn, Helliwell & Christenson (1975) 3-10 OR, the plaintiff, a
third party, sued the auditors for about $1.6 million in damages for the
auditors' negligence. The High Court of Justice of Ontario held that the
auditors were not liable for the damages, but this was only because the
plaintiff failed to prove any loss flowing from the auditors' negligence.

In order for there to be liability for negligent misrepresentation, there must
be first a duty of care; second, a negligent misrepresentation; third, reliance on the misrepresentation by the plaintiff; and fourth, loss resulting
from that reliance. Since Hedley Byrne & Co. Ltd. v. Heller & Partners
Ltd. . . . , liability for negligent misrepresentation can arise whenever
there is a special relationship exisiting between the parties which casts a
duty on the one making the statement to exercise reasonable care. The
defendant through one of its partners was aware that the plaintiff was

relying on the financial statements in connection with the purchase of the shares, and this knowledge was enough to create a special relationship imposing a duty of care on the defendant.

The court also found that the audited financial statements did reflect the true financial position of the company at the time, but the auditors' report was false because "no adequate audit had in fact been completed for the year in question," and "the defendant being too prone to accept the advice of the management of [the company] in conducting their audit."

The plaintiff appealed the decision, but the Ontario Court of Appeal upheld the ruling of the High Court of Justice.

From the analysis of the above cases it appears that, under common law, bankers and other creditors or investors who utilize financial statements covered by an audit report can recover damages from the auditors if it can be shown that the auditors were guilty of *fraud* or *gross negligence* in the performance of their professional duties. Fraud is obviously present if the auditors surrender their objectivity and cooperate with the client to give outsiders a false impression of the financial position or operating results of the business. Gross negligence exists if the auditors have not conducted an examination of any real substance and consequently have no real basis for an opinion. To express an opinion in their role of independent experts when in fact they have no basis for an opinion is considered gross negligence and provides a basis for legal action by injured third parties.

Moreover, the auditors can also be held liable for negligence to a limited class of third parties if the auditors have actual knowledge of such third parties or if there exists a special relationship between the auditors and the third parties.

The burden of proof.   Legal actions under common law require the plaintiffs to bear most of the burden of affirmative proof. Thus, the plaintiffs must prove that they sustained losses, that they relied upon audited financial statements which were misleading, that this reliance was the proximate cause of their losses, and that the auditors were negligent. The auditors named as defendants in a common law action are in the position of having to refute the charges brought by the plaintiffs.

Auditors' responsibility for the detection of fraud

Any discussion of the legal liability of auditors would be incomplete without the inclusion of auditors' obligations to discover fraud. As pointed out in Chapter 1, the typical audits performed prior to this century by public accountants were primarily concerned with the discovery of management and non-management fraud. In later years, however, the public accounting profession has directed its auditing emphasis to the determination of the fairness of the client's financial statements.

In recognition of this change in audit emphasis, the *CICA Handbook* states:

> *The prevention and detection of errors and irregularities is a management responsibility.* . . .
>
> In conducting an audit, the auditor recognizes that the financial statements may be mis-stated as a result of errors or irregularities. Accordingly, in obtaining sufficient appropriate audit evidence to afford a reasonable basis to support the content of his report, *the auditor seeks reasonable assurance, through the application of procedures which comply with generally accepted auditing standards, that errors or irregularities which may be material to the financial statements have not occurred,* or that if they have occurred, they are either corrected or properly accounted for in the financial statements. *The auditor has no separate or additional responsibility to detect fraud or other irregularities.* . . . Some irregularities, because of their nature or the manner in which they are concealed, may not be detected by audit procedures which comply with generally accepted auditing standards.
>
> If the auditor does not discover a particular error or irregularity—even where the error or irregularity is material—that fact does not necessarily indicate that he has failed to adhere to generally accepted auditing standards. Rather, the question of adherence to generally accepted auditing standards would be determined by the adequacy of the procedures undertaken in the circumstances and the suitability of the auditors' report.[6]

Similarly, *Statement on Auditing Standards No. 1* of the AICPA stresses that—

> . . . *the ordinary examination directed to the expression of an opinion on financial statements is not primarily or specifically designed, and cannot be relied upon, to disclose defalcations and other similar irregularities, although their discovery may result.* . . .
>
> The responsibility of the independent auditor for failure to detect fraud . . . *arises only when such failure clearly results from failure to comply with generally accepted auditing standards.*
>
> . . . if his examination was made with due professional skill and care in accordance with generally accepted auditing standards, he has fulfilled all obligations implicit in his undertaking.[7]

A recent AICPA statement, "The Independent Auditor's Responsibility for Detection of Errors or Irregularities," reiterates the above position and adds the following:

> . . . under generally accepted auditing standards the independent auditor has the responsibility, within the inherent limitations of the auditing

---

[6] CICA, *CICA Handbook* (Toronto), sec. 5215.07–.09. (Emphasis supplied.)

[7] AICPA, "Codification of Auditing Standards and Procedures," *Statement on Auditing Standards No. 1* (New York, 1973), pp. 2–4. (Emphasis supplied.)

process . . . , to plan his examination . . . to search for errors or irregularities that would have a material effect on the financial statements, and to exercise due skill and care in the conduct of his examination.[8]

The statement recommends that the auditor should extend the scope of his examination and inform the board of directors or the audit committee if he believes material irregularities may exist and senior management may be involved. Furthermore, it illustrates three types of circumstances that may suggest the possibility of errors or irregularities.

1.   (a)   discrepancies within the accounting records such as a difference between a control account and its supporting subsidiary records;
      (b)   differences disclosed by confirmations;
      (c)   significantly fewer responses to confirmation requests than expected;
      (d)   transactions not supported by proper documentation;
      (e)   transactions not recorded in accordance with management's general or specific authorization; and
      (f)   the completion of unusual transaction at or near year end.
2.   (a)   (a company) is in an industy that is experiencing a large number of business failures; or that lacks sufficient working capital or credit to continue operations.
3.   (a)   the company does not correct material weaknesses in internal accounting control that are practicable to correct;
      (b)   key financial positions, such as controller, have a high turnover rate; or
      (c)   the accounting and financial functions appear to be understaffed resulting in constant crisis conditions and related loss of controls.[9]

If the auditor encounters one or more of the above circumstances in an audit, he should seek reasonable assurance that material errors or irregularities do not in fact exist.

However, the auditors' failure to detect errors or irregularities does not necessarily constitute proof of negligence. Auditors do not guarantee the accuracy of financial statements; they merely express an opinion as to the fairness of the statements. Furthermore, auditors do not make a complete and detailed examination of all records and all transactions. To do so would entail an almost prohibitive cost, which would certainly not be warranted under ordinary business conditions. The auditors' examination is based upon a study and evaluation of the client's system of internal control; the extent and nature of specific auditing procedures will be determined in accordance with the strengths and weaknesses found in

---

[8] AICPA, "The Independent Auditor's Responsibility for the Detection of Errors or Irregularities," *Statement on Auditing Standards No. 16* (New York, 1976), p. 2.

[9] Ibid., pp. 4–6.

the controls. If the scope and direction of the audit procedures have been well chosen, the conclusions of the auditors should generally be sound. However, there can never be any absolute assurance that fraud did not exist among the transactions not included in the auditors' tests. There is also the possibility that fraudulent documents have been so skillfully forged or other irregularities so expertly concealed that the application of generally accepted auditing techniques would not reveal the fraud.

When the auditors' examination has been made in accordance with generally accepted auditing standards, they are not liable for failure to detect the existence of fraud. Throughout the course of the examination auditors must exercise their professional judgment as to the procedures to be employed and the extent of the tests to be made. Because so many difficult, technical decisions must be made by auditors, it is inevitable that some errors in judgment will occur. If auditors act in good faith and employ the same care and degree of skill commonly followed within the public accounting profession, an error in judgment is not regarded as negligence.

This view of the limits or boundaries of the auditors' responsibility for detection of fraud is widely held within the public accounting profession. However, some court decisions in the United States have rejected the view that compliance with generally accepted auditing standards is a complete defense for the auditor when audited financial statements are proved to be misleading. Such decisions, however, would appear incompatible with a viable public accounting profession.

In summary, a client can ordinarily recover losses arising as a result of the auditors' failure to disclose localized fraud only if it can be shown that they were guilty of negligence. Nevertheless, every competent auditor is continuously alert to detect any evidence of possible existence of fraud. If the auditors do discover evidence of possible material fraud, they should discuss their findings with the client's board of directors or the audit committee of the board to determine whether client personnel or the auditors should pursue the matter. Under no circumstances should auditors abandon their customary examination to carry out a fraud investigation without obtaining the client's permission to do so.

The Equity Funding Corporation of America fraud in the United States. The AICPA's posture on auditors' responsibility for discovery of fraud was challenged by many critics in the United States as a result of the celebrated Equity Funding Corporation of America fraud. Nineteen persons—principally employees of Equity Funding—pleaded guilty to criminal fraud associated with Equity Funding's published financial statements covering a period of several years. Three accountants who were tried and found guilty of comparable criminal charges appealed their convictions. These accountants were members of the CPA firm retained to audit Equity Funding's financial statements.

Because of the furor caused by the Equity Funding case, the AICPA appointed a five-member Special Committee on Equity Funding to consider whether the fraud suggested a need for changes in generally accepted auditing standards or in the auditing procedures by which auditing standards are implemented. The Committee also sought to determine any need for a change in the scope, or a clarification, of auditors' responsibilities for the detection of fraud.

In the *Report of the Special Committee on Equity Funding,* the Committee concluded that, with few exceptions, generally accepted auditing standards are adequate and no changes are required in procedures commonly used by auditors. The exceptions dealt with confirmation of an insurance company's insurance in force, and with the audit of related party transactions. The Committee further concluded that *customary auditing procedures properly applied* would have provided reasonable assurance of detection of fraud at Equity Funding.

The Committee reached the following conclusions with respect to auditors' responsibilities for the detection of fraud:

> In sum, the committee reaffirms the soundness of the accounting profession's understanding with respect to the role of audits in the detection of fraud. A change in this basic understanding to make the auditor's opinion into more of a guarantee of the absence of fraud would represent a major change in the conception and performance of audits and would vastly increase their expense—yet still not furnish a complete guarantee. To ask that a professional opinion be made into an absolute assurance would, moreover, be to seek a degree of certainty which is seldom to be found in any other area of commercial life—or, for that matter, in any area of our lives, private or public. However, even though such absolute assurance is not feasible, the application of generally accepted auditing standards will often result in the discovery of material frauds. Audits also can be expected to deter fraud which might otherwise occur.[10]

Accountants' liability for unaudited financial statements

To this point, we have discussed the liability of public accounting firms which serve their clients as *external auditors.* Many small public accounting firms do little or no auditing; instead, a major part of their practice is the preparation of *unaudited financial statements* for their clients. In this capacity the public accounting firms serve their clients as *accountants* rather than as *external auditors.*

In providing these accounting services, it is essential for the public accounting firms and their clients to have a clear understanding as to the nature, extent, and limitation of such an engagement. The terms mutually

---

[10] AICPA, *Report of the Special Committee on Equity Funding* (New York, 1975), pp. 39–40.

agreed upon by the two parties should be in writing to avoid future misunderstanding. Otherwise, the consequences could be enormously expensive, as evidenced by the *1136 Tenants' Corporation* v. *Rothenberg* case in the United States.

In this common law case, an incorporated apartment cooperative, which was owned by its shareholder-tenants and managed by a separate realty agent, orally retained a CPA firm for a period of 17 months to perform services leading to the preparation of financial statements for the cooperative, and also including letters containing tax information to the shareholders. The CPA firm's fee was to be only $600 per year.

The CPA firm submitted financial statements of the corporation for one full year and the first six months of the following year. The financial statements bore the notation "subject to comments in letter of transmittal." The referenced letter of transmittal read in part:

> Pursuant to our engagement, we have reviewed and summarized the statements of your managing agent and other data submitted to us by . . . (the agent), pertaining to 1136 Tenants' Corporation. . . .
>
> The following statements were prepared from the books and records of the Corporation. No independent verifications were undertaken thereon. . . .

The client corporation later sued the CPA firm for damages totaling $174,000 for the CPA's alleged failure to discover defalcations of the corporation's funds committed by the managing agent. The client contended that the CPAs had been retained to render all necessary accounting and *auditing* services for it. The CPAs maintained they had been engaged to do "write-up work" only, although a working paper they had prepared supporting accrued expenses payable in the balance sheet included an entry for "audit expense."

The New York state trial court ruled in favour of the plaintiff client, as did the Appellate Court of New York. The latter found that the CPAs' working papers indicated that the CPAs had examined the client's bank statements, invoices and bills, and had made notations in their working papers concerning "missing invoices." The New York Court of Appeals (the state's highest court) affirmed the decision.

There are many lessons for public accounting firms in the *1136 Tenants' Corporation* case. First, public accountants who prepare unaudited financial statements should adhere closely to the Rules of Professional Conduct. Rule 205 states that a CA shall not sign or associate himself with statements which he knows, or should know, are false or misleading.

Second, engagement letters are as essential for accounting services as they are for independent audits. Oral arrangements for accounting services are of scant assistance when there is a dispute as to the nature of the services to be rendered by the public accounting firm to the client.

Third, a public accountant engaged to perform *accounting* services that include unaudited financial statements should be alert for, and follow up on, unusual items like "missing invoices." As professional persons, public accountants are bound to exercise due professional care, even though their engagements do not encompass independent audits of the client's financial statements.

Fourth, public accountants should *clearly* and *concisely* disclaim an opinion on unaudited financial statements, using wherever possible standardized language set forth in the *CICA Handbook*, Section 8100. In addition, each page of the financial statements and footnotes should be marked "unaudited."

Subsequent to the courts' decision in the 1136 Tenants' Corporation case, the AICPA published the Guide for Engagements of CPAs to Prepare Unaudited Financial Statements. The Guide discusses the nature of unaudited financial statements, engagement letters, professional care, and types of disclaimers of opinion for unaudited financial statements. Unaudited statements and the *CICA Handbook*, Section 8100, are considered further in Chapter 20.

Auditors' liability under the securities acts of the United States

Legal actions against auditors which are brought under the United States' securities acts tend to shift much of the burden of proof to the auditors. The plaintiffs must prove only that they sustained losses and that the financial statements were misleading. The auditors must then bear the burden of proof to show that they were not negligent or that the misleading financial statements were not the proximate cause of the plaintiffs' losses. For these and other reasons, it is important in considering specific cases involving auditors' liability to third parties in the United States to determine whether the legal action is being brought under the statutes administered by the Securities Exchange Commission (SEC).

Auditors' liability under the U.S. securities acts. The Securities Act of 1933 and the Securities Exchange Act of 1934 place heavy responsibility on independent public accountants who prepare or examine any part of a registration statement or periodic report required under the acts. The inclusion of an untrue statement of material fact, or failure to state a material fact when such omission makes the statement misleading, opens the door to legal action against the public accountants by any person acquiring the security.

Securities Act of 1933. The Securities Act of 1933 states that accountants who express an opinion in a *registration statement* concerning a proposed offering of corporate securities may be liable to third parties for their losses if the statements are later shown to include untrue statements of material fact or to omit material facts necessary to prevent the statements from being misleading. The wording of Section 11(a) of the act on this point is as follows:

> In case any part of the registration statement, when such part became effective, contained an untrue statement of a material fact or omitted to state a material fact required to be stated therein or necessary to make the statements therein not misleading, any person acquiring such security (unless it is proved that at the time of such acquisition he knew of such untruth or omission) may . . . sue. . . .

The third parties who have sustained losses may sue for recovery from the accountants and *need not prove that they relied upon the statements or that the accountants were negligent.* The burden of proof is placed upon the accountants to show that their audit work was adequate to support their opinion (the "due diligence" defence) or that the losses of third parties were not the result of errors or omissions in the statements.

The effect of the Securities Act of 1933 is therefore to give third parties who purchase securities in reliance upon registration statements the same rights against auditors as are possessed by the client under common law. In audits for registration statements, the auditors are liable not only for fraud and gross negligence but also for losses to third parties resulting from ordinary negligence. This legislation inaugurated a new era in the professional responsibilities of independent public accountants.

A significant case involving auditors' liability under the Securities Act of 1933 was the *BarChris* case. *Escott* v. *BarChris Construction Corporation,* 283 F. Supp. 643 (1968), was an action under Section 11 of the Securities Act of 1933 undertaken by purchasers of BarChris's registered debentures against the directors, underwriters, and independent auditors of BarChris. Subsequent to issuance of the debentures, BarChris, a builder of bowling alleys, became bankrupt. The plaintiffs claimed that the registration statement for the debentures contained material false statements and material omissions; the defendants all countered with "due diligence" defenses. The court found that the registration statement was false and misleading, and that, with a few exceptions, none of the defendants had established their due diligence defenses. The court also found that the CPA firm had failed to comply with generally accepted auditing standards. The court was especially critical of the CPA firm's conduct of the S-1 review, so-called because it is a special investigation carried out by a CPA firm some time after completion of the audit but just prior to the effective date of the "S-1," or similar registration statement filed with the SEC. In an S-1 review, the CPAs look for any evidence that events since their audit have made the registration statement misleading as filed. The court cited the CPA firm's excessive reliance on questioning of client management during the S-1 review, with no follow-up by the firm of the management's answers.

Subsequent to the decision of the court in *BarChris*, the AICPA's Auditing Standards Executive Committee issued a statement entitled "Subsequent Events," now a section of *SAS No. 1*. This statement, which clarified the auditing procedures required in an "S-1 review," is discussed in Chapter 7.

Securities Exchange Act of 1934. In addition to the registration statements required in connection with new issues of securities, companies which are listed on the stock exchanges and certain companies whose stock is traded over the counter *must file audited financial statements each year* with the SEC, in accordance with provisions of the Securities Exchange Act of 1934. Section 18(a) of that act provides the following liability for misleading statements:

> Any person who shall make or cause to be made any statement in any application, report, or document filed pursuant to this . . . (Act) or any rule of regulation thereunder . . . , which statement was at the time and in the light of the circumstances under which it was made false or misleading with respect to any material fact, shall be liable to any person (not knowing that such statement was false or misleading) who, in reliance upon such statement, shall have purchased or sold a security at a price which was affected by such statement, for damages caused by such reliance, unless the person sued shall prove that he acted in good faith and had no knowledge that such statement was false or misleading.

In addition, Rule 10b-5, promulgated by the SEC under the 1934 act, reads as follows:

> It shall be unlawful for any person, directly or indirectly, . . .
> (1)   to employ any device, scheme, or artifice to defraud,
> (2)   to make any untrue statement of a material fact or to omit to state a material fact necessary in order to make the statements made . . . not misleading, or
> (3)   to engage in any act, practice, or course of business which operates or would operate as a fraud or deceit upon any person, in connection with the purchase or sale of any security.

Most lawsuits against certified public accountants have been filed under Section 18(a) and Rule 10b-5 of the Securities Exchange Act of 1934. The wording of this act implies that the act was written to create liability for fraudulent misrepresentations. In some court decisions, however, the act has been interpreted more broadly and auditors have been held liable for losses proximately caused by their negligence even though fraudulent intent was not established. The recent Hochfelder decision (discussed below) should lead to more uniform interpretations of the criteria for liability under the 1934 act.

The Hochfelder case and its impact on accountants' liability. The expansion of auditors' liability to third parties may have been slowed by the decision of the U.S. Supreme Court in *Ernst* v. *Hochfelder* (44 LW 4451

[1976]). This decision was in a suit instituted against a national public accounting firm which for 21 years had audited the financial statements of First Securities Company of Chicago, a small brokerage firm. The president of First Securities, who was also its majority shareholder, committed suicide, leaving a note stating that the firm was insolvent and disclosing a fraud which he had perpetrated upon several investors. The president had persuaded the investors to mail him their personal cheques, the funds from which he was to invest in "escrow accounts" yielding high returns to the investors. There was no such "escrow accounts" in the accounting records of First Securities Company; instead, the president converted the investors' cheques to his own use immediately upon receipt.

The investors filed suit under SEC Rule 10b-5 (and the related Securities Exchange Act of 1934 Section 10[b]) against the CPA firm, charging it with negligence and thus with responsibility for the investors' losses in the fraud. During the court hearings, the plaintiffs acknowledged that they had not relied upon the audited financial statements of First Securities Company or upon the auditors' reports; further, they did not accuse the CPA firm of fraud or intentional misconduct. The basis for the plaintiffs' charge of negligence was that the CPA firm failed during its audits to discover a weakness in First Securities Company's internal control that enabled the president of First Securities to carry on the fraud. The internal control weakness was manifested in the president's rule that *only he* could open mail addressed to him at First Securities, or addressed to First Securities to his attention.

The U.S. district court which heard the case dismissed it, holding that there was no issue of material fact as to whether the CPA firm had conducted its audits of First Securities in accordance with generally accepted auditing standards. The U.S. Court of Appeals, in reversing the district court's dismissal of the case, stated that the CPA firm was liable for damages for aiding and abetting the First Securities president's fraud, because the CPA firm had breached its duty of enquiry and disclosure regarding the First Securities internal control weakness.

The U.S. Supreme Court reversed the court of appeals, deciding that an action for damages under Section 10(b) of the 1934 act and the related SEC Rule 10b-5 was not warranted in the absence of *intent* to deceive, manipulate, or defraud on the CPA firm's part. In the Court's opinion, Mr. Justice Powell wrote:

> The words "manipulative or deceptive" used in conjunction with "device or contrivance" strongly suggest that (Section) 10(b) was intended to proscribe knowing or intentional misconduct.
>
>   ❖   ❖   ❖   ❖   ❖
>
> When a statute speaks so specifically in terms of manipulation and deception, and of implementing devices and contrivances—the commonly under-

stood terminology of intentional wrongdoing—and when its history reflects no expansive intent, we are quite unwilling to extend the scope of the statute to negligent conduct.

Many accountants believe that the *Hochfelder* case, despite its narrow application to a CPA firm's responsibility for discovering a weakness in internal control, should help limit auditors' responsibility to third parties who are not third party beneficiaries, and restrain the SEC's efforts to widen that responsibility. In *Hochfelder,* the Supreme Court rejected the SEC's *amicus curiae* brief supporting the plaintiffs, pointing to the Commission's acknowledgement that the CPA firm was unaware of the existence of the plaintiffs, and thus could not foresee that its audit reports could influence the plaintiffs' investments—as indeed they did not.

Auditors' criminal liability under the U.S. securities acts.   Both the Securities Act of 1933 and the Securities Exchange Act of 1933 include provisions for criminal charges against persons violating provisions of the act. These provisions are found in Section 17(a) of the Securities Act of 1933 and Section 32(a) of the Securities Exchange Act of 1934.

The *Continental Vending Machine Corporation* civil case was accompanied by a celebrated criminal case involving three members of the CPA firm which audited Continental's financial statements. A jury found the three CPAs guilty of criminal fraud in issuing an unqualified opinion on the financial statements of Continental. The verdict of guilt was affirmed by a U.S. court of appeals, and the U.S. Supreme Court refused to review the case. The three CPAs were later pardoned by the president of the United States. The president of Continental, who had originally been indicted with the three CPAs and who pleaded guilty, received a six-month jail sentence.

The principal facts of the *Continental Vending* case (*United States* v. *Simon,* 425 F. 2d 796 [1969]) are as follows. The U.S. government's case of fraud against the three CPAs hinged upon a footnote to Continental's audited financial statements which read:

> The amount receivable from Valley Commercial Corp. (an affiliated company of which . . . (Continental's president) is an officer, director, and stockholder) bears interest at 12 percent a year. Such amount, less the balance of the notes payable to that company, is secured by the assignment to the Company of Valley's equity in certain marketable securities. As of . . . (the date of the auditors' report) . . . the amount of such equity at current market quotations exceeded the net amount receivable.

The U.S. government charged the CPAs should have insisted that the note be worded as follows:

> The amount receivable from Valley Commercial Corp. (an affiliated company of which . . . (Continental's president is an officer, director,

and stockholder), which bears interest at 12 percent a year, was uncollectible at . . . (the balance sheet date), since Valley had loaned approximately the same amount to . . . (Continental's president) who was unable to pay. Since that date . . . (Continental's president) and others have pledged as security for the repayment of his obligation to Valley and its obligation to Continental (now $3,900,000, against which Continental's liability to Valley cannot be offset) securities which as of . . . (the date of the auditors' report) . . ., had a market value of $2,978,000. Approximately 80 percent of such securities are stock and convertible debentures of the Company.

The receivable from Valley amounted to $3.5 million, of which more than $2.1 million was included in current assets (totaling $20.1 million), with the $1.4 million balance in other assets. The amount payable to Valley was slightly more than $1 million, of which about one half was included in total current liabilities of $19 million and the remainder in long-term debt.

The CPA firm had been auditors for Continental for several years. The court found that the CPAs had been concerned with the amounts receivable from and payable to Valley for at least five years, especially as they involved loans to Continental's president; yet the CPAs had continued to issue opinions on Continental's financial statements despite the continued growth of the receivable from Valley. The court also found that the CPAs were not furnished audited financial statements for Valley, in spite of their repeated requests, and that the CPAs had never themselves been auditors for Valley. In response to the defendant CPAs' claims that they had no motive for the alleged fraud, the U.S. government demonstrated to the appellate court's satisfaction that the CPAs were motivated to preserve their firm's reputation and to conceal the alleged derelictions of their predecessors and themselves in preceding years.

The *Continental Vending* case has significant implications for the public accounting profession. Not only is civil liability an ever-present hazard for public accountants but criminal charges may also be involved.

The SEC's regulation of accountants.   The SEC has issued rules for the appearance and practice of CPAs, attorneys, and others before the Commission under the statutes which it administers. Rule of Practice 2(e), giving the SEC the power of suspension and disbarment, has the following wording:

> The Commission may deny, temporarily or permanently, the privilege of appearing or practicing before it in any way to any person who is found by the Commission . . . (1) not to possess the requisite qualifications to represent others, or (2) to be lacking in character or integrity or to have engaged in unethical or improper professional conduct.

On several occasions the Commission has taken punitive action against public accounting firms when it has found the audit work deficient with regard to financial statements filed with the Commission. These actions against public accounting firms usually arise when a listed corporation encounters financial difficulties and it later appears that misleading financial statements had served to conceal for a time the losses being incurred by the company. In recent years the SEC has taken action against CPA firms by use of the consent decrees in which the CPAs have agreed to certain penalties or restrictions. For example, a CPA firm may agree under pressure from the SEC not to accept new clients during a specified period and to permit a review of its practice.

The public accountants' posture in the "age of litigation"

It is apparent that lawsuits will continue to plague the public accounting profession, as they have the legal and medical professions. The question thus is: What should be the public accountants' reaction to this "age of litigation"?

In the opinion of the authors, positive actions helpful to public accountants in withstanding threats of possible lawsuits include the following:

1. Greater emphasis upon compliance with the public accounting profession's generally accepted auditing standards and rules of professional conduct. Close analysis of the court cases and other actions described in this chapter discloses numerous instances in which the auditors appear not to have complied fully with one or more auditing standards and rules of professional conduct.

2. Emphasis on professionalism rather than growth. Some public accounting firms may have emphasized growth of their practices more than high quality of their work. Very rapid growth may bring excessive overtime work by overextended staff members and responsibilities too heavy for insufficiently "seasoned" accountants.

3. Thorough investigation of prospective clients. As indicated in preceding sections of this chapter, many court cases involving public accountants have been accompanied by criminal charges against top management of the public accountants' clients. Public accountants should use great care in screening prospective clients to avoid the risks involved in professional relationships with the criminally inclined.

4. Use of engagement letters for all professional services. Controversies over what services are to be rendered by a public accountant can be minimized by a clearly written contract describing the agreed-upon services and pointing out that the ordinary audit is not designed to uncover fraud. Engagement letters are discussed in Chapter 4.

5. Exercising extreme care in audits of clients in financial difficulties. Creditors and shareholders of companies which are insolvent or in bankruptcy are likely to seek scapegoats to blame for their losses. As the court

cases described in this chapter demonstrate, litigation involving public accountants tends to centre around auditing of clients which later become bankrupt.

6. Use of engagement letters for non-audit services, stating explicitly the nature, extent, and limitations of the engagement. This is important in order to avoid misunderstanding. Of course, the public accountant should exercise due professional skill and care in his work and avoid associating himself with misleading statements.

7. Maintenance of adequate liability insurance coverage. Although liability insurance coverage should not be considered a substitute for the public accountant's compliance with the six preceding recommendations, public accountants must protect themselves against possible financial losses from lawsuits. Adequate liability insurance is essential.

8. More extensive use of "peer reviews." Since public accounting firms are not required to be audited, they might voluntarily engage other public accounting firms to review their quality controls and other aspects of their professional practice. The interchange of professional skills among public accountants is a policy worthy of encouragement.

KEY TERMS INTRODUCED OR EMPHASIZED IN CHAPTER 3

audit committee   A committee of the board of directors, composed of not less than three directors, of whom a majority are not officers or employees of the corporation or any of its affiliates, that is responsible for reviewing the audited financial statements and other audit related matters.

common law   Uncodified principles of law developed through court decisions.

constructive fraud   Violation of a legal duty or a contractual obligation which requires the exercise of exceptional good faith.

due diligence defence   A CPA firm's contention that its audit work was adequate to support its opinion on financial statements included in a registration statement filed with the SEC under the Securities Act of 1933.

fraud   Misrepresentation by a person of a material fact, known by that person to be untrue or made with reckless indifference as to whether the fact is true, with the intent to deceive and with the result that another party is injured.

gross negligence   Lack of even slight care. (A term more relevant in the United States, where it may be used as grounds for an action against an accountant by a person other than his client.)

management fraud   When management of the client company makes a deliberate effort to present misleading financial statements, supported by falsified accounting records.

negligence   Violation of a legal duty to exercise a degree of care which an ordinarily prudent person would exercise under similar circumstances, with resultant damages to another party.

non-management fraud   Dishonest actions that occur within a company despite management's efforts to prevent such actions.

peer review   Review of a public accounting firm's or practitioner's public accounting practice—especially quality control—by another public accounting firm or practitioner.

related party transaction   A transaction in which one party has the ability to influence significantly the management or operating policies of the other party, to the extent that one of the transacting parties might be prevented from pursuing fully its own separate interests.

third-party beneficiary   A person—not the promisor or promisee—who is named in a contract (or known to the contracting parties) with the intention that he should have definite rights and benefits under the contract.

GROUP I
REVIEW QUESTIONS

3–1.   Why does the Canada Business Corporations Act provide an audit requirement for corporations offering securities to the public?

3–2.   Describe fully the auditor's statutory rights and responsibilities.

3–3.   Briefly describe the statutory rights and duties of the predecessor and successor auditors in the change of appointment. Are they the same as those set forth in the Interpretations of the *Rules of Professional Conduct?*

3–4.   What are the statutory rights and responsibilities of the auditor, director, or officer of a corporation regarding subsequent discovery of errors in the published financial statements?

3–5.   What is the significance of the statutory sanction of the *CICA Handbook* recommendations.

3–6.   With respect to the audit committee, discuss:
   a.   Its composition.
   b.   The rationale for its establishment.
   c.   Its purposes and functions.
   d.   The rights and duties of the auditor.

3–7.   Watts and Williams, CAs, audited the balance sheet of Sampson Skins, Inc., a closely held corporation that imports and deals in fine furs. Upon completion of the examination the auditors supplied Sampson Skins with 20 copies of the audited balance sheet. The firm knew that Sampson Skins wanted that number of copies of the auditors' report to furnish to banks and other potential lenders.

   The balance sheet in question was in error by approximately $800,-000. Instead of having shareholders' equity of $600,000, the corporation was insolvent. The management of Sampson Skins had "doctored" the accounting records to avoid bankruptcy. The assets had been overstated by $500,000 of fictitious and non-existing accounts receivable and $300,000 of non-existing skins listed as inventory when in fact there were only empty boxes. The audit failed to detect these fraudulent entries. Martinson, a factor, relying on the audited balance sheet, loaned Sampson Skins $200,000. He seeks to recover his loss from Watts and Williams.

Required:

State whether each of the following statements is true or false under common law, and explain why.

a. If Martinson alleges and proves ordinary negligence on the part of Watts and Williams, he would be able to recover his loss.

b. If Martinson alleges and proves constructive fraud or gross negligence on the part of Watts and Williams, he would be able to recover his loss.

c. Martinson is not in privity of contract with Watts and Williams.

d. Unless gross negligence or actual fraud on the part of Watts and Williams could be shown, Martinson could not recover.

e. Martinson is a third-party beneficiary of the contract Watts and Williams made with Sampson Skins. (AICPA, adapted)

3–8. Dandy Container Corporation located in the United States engaged the accounting firm of Adams and Adams, CPAs, to examine financial statements to be used in connection with a public offering of securities. The audit was completed, and an unqualified opinion was expressed on the financial statements which were submitted to the Securities and Exchange Commission along with the registration statement. Two hundred thousand shares of Dandy Container common stock were offered to the public at $11 a share. Eight months later the stock fell to $2 a share when it was disclosed that several large loans to two "paper" corporations owned by one of the directors were worthless. The loans were secured by the stock of the borrowing corporations which was owned by the director. These facts were not disclosed in the financial statements. The director involved and the two corporations are insolvent.

Required:

State whether each of the following statements is true or false, and explain why.

a. The Securities Act of 1933 applies to the above-described public offering of securities in interstate commerce.

b. The accounting firm has potential liability to any person who acquired the stock in reliance upon the registration statement.

c. An insider who had knowledge of all the facts regarding the loans to the two "paper" corporations could nevertheless recover from the accounting firm.

d. An investor who bought shares in Dandy Container would make a prima facie case if he alleges that the failure to explain the nature of the loans in question constituted a false statement or misleading omission in the financial statements.

e. The accountants could avoid liability if they could show they were neither negligent nor fraudulent.

f. The accountants could avoid or reduce the damages asserted against them if they could establish that the drop in the stock's market price was due in whole or in part to other causes.

g. It would appear that the accountants were negligent in respect to handling of the secured loans in question—if they discovered the facts regarding the loans to the "paper" corporations and failed to require adequate disclosure in the financial statements.

h. The Securities and Exchange Commission would defend any action brought against the accountants in that the SEC examined and approved the registration statement. (AICPA, adapted)

3–9. Compare auditors' common law liability to client and third-party beneficiaries with their common law liability to other third parties.

3–10. Should auditors who are engaged in the examination of a client's financial statements thoroughly investigate suspected material non-management fraud? Explain.

3–11. Is privity a valid defense against third-party charges of negligence against an auditor? Explain.

3–12. How does the SEC regulate CPAs who appear and practice before the Commission?

3–13. What is the impact of the *1136 Tenants' Corporation* v. *Rothenberg* case on CPAs engaged to prepare audited financial statements?

GROUP II
QUESTIONS REQUIRING ANALYSIS

3–14. "As increasing numbers of lawsuits against auditors are demonstrating, the public accountant incurs very real risks as auditor of a corporation. In his own interest, he should be more aware of the factors that must be considered in any attempt to measure the risk of an audit engagement."

Required:

What factors affect the risk of a specific audit engagement? Explain each briefly. (CICA)

3–15. A CA firm's accounting services to a client sometimes involve the preparation of unaudited financial statements. Discuss the need for an engagement letter for unaudited financial statements preparation. (AICPA, adapted)

3–16. The partnership, Watkins, Miller, & Fogg, CAs, was engaged for the first time to examine the financial statements of Flinco Ltd. Flinco is the largest manufacturing concern in the locale. It is engaged in a multi-province business and its stock is traded on the over-the-counter market. The CA firm has enjoyed considerable stature in the business community but has traditionally served small to medium-sized businesses. The firm has never audited a publicly held corporation before.

Required:

State the general guidelines which a CA firm may look to in assessing its legal liability when assuming the responsibility for a publicly held client. (AICPA, adapted)

3–17.   Wanda Young, doing business as Wanda Young Fashions, engaged the
        CA partnership of Small & Brown to examine her financial statements.
        During the examination, Small & Brown discovered certain irregularities
        which would have indicated to a reasonably prudent accountant that
        James Smith, the chief accountant, might be engaged in a fraud. More
        specifically, it appeared to Small & Brown that serious defalcations were
        taking place. However, Small & Brown, not having been engaged to
        discover defalcations, submitted an unqualified opinion in its report and
        did not mention the potential defalcation problem.

Required:

        What are the legal implications of the above facts as they relate to
        the relationship between Small & Brown and Wanda Young? Explain.
        (AICPA, adapted)

3–18.   Donald Sharpe recently joined the CA firm of Spark, Watts, and Wil-
        cox. He quickly established a reputation for thoroughness and a stead-
        fast dedication to following prescribed auditing procedures to the letter.
        On his third audit for the firm, involving a partnership client, Sharpe
        examined the underlying documentation of 200 disbursements as a com-
        pliance test of purchasing, receiving, vouchers payable, and cash dis-
        bursement procedures. In the process he found 12 disbursements for the
        purchase of materials with no receiving reports in the documentation.
        He noted the exceptions in his working papers and called them to the
        attention of the in-charge accountant. Relying on prior experience with
        the client, the in-charge accountant disregarded Sharpe's comments, and
        nothing further was done about the exceptions.
             Subsequently, it was learned that one of the client's purchasing agents
        and a member of its accounting department were engaged in a fraudu-
        lent scheme whereby they diverted the receipt of materials to a public
        warehouse while sending the invoices to the client. When the client dis-
        covered the fraud, the conspirators had obtained approximately $700,-
        000, of which $500,000 was gained after the completion of the audit.

Required:

        Discuss the legal implications for and liabilities of Spark, Watts, and
        Wilcox as a result of the above facts. (AICPA, adapted)

3–19.   The partnership of Porter, Potts, & Farr, CAs, was engaged by Revolu-
        tionary Products, Inc., to examine its financial statements for the year
        ended June 30, 1978. The engagement letter said nothing about the
        CA firm's responsibility for defalcations. Porter, Potts, & Farr performed
        its examination in a careful and competent manner, following generally
        accepted auditing standards and using appropriate auditing procedures
        and tests under the circumstances.
             Subsequently, it was discovered that the client's chief accountant
        was engaged in major defalcations. However, only an audit specifically

designed to discover possible defalcations would have revealed the fraud. Revolutionary Products asserts that Porter, Potts, & Farr is liable for the defalcations.

Required:

Is Porter, Potts, & Farr liable? Explain. (AICPA, adapted)

3-20. Barton and Company. CAs, has been engaged to examine the financial statement of Mirror Manufacturing Corporation Ltd. for the year ended September 30, 1978. During that year, Mirror needed additional cash to continue its operations. To raise the cash, it sold its common stock investment in a subsidiary. The buyers insisted upon having the proceeds placed in escrow because of the existence of a major loss contingency involving additional income taxes assessed to the subsidiary by the Department of National Revenue for Taxation. William Carter, president of Mirror, explained this to Carl Barton, the partner in charge of the Mirror audit. Carter indicated that he wished to show the proceeds from the sale of the subsidiary as an unrestricted current account receivable. He stated that in his opinion the claim of the Department of National Revenue against the subsidiary was groundless, and that he needed an "uncluttered" balance sheet and a "clean" auditor's opinion to obtain additional working capital through loans. Barton acquiesced in this request. The Department's claim proved to be valid, and pursuant to the agreement with the buyers the purchase price of the subsidiary was reduced by $450,000. This coupled with other adverse developments caused Mirror to become insolvent. Barton and Company is being sued by several of Mirror's creditors who loaned money in reliance upon the audited financial statements.

Required:

What is the liability, if any, of Barton and Company to the creditors of Mirror Manufacturing? Explain. (AICPA, adapted)

3-21. In conducting the examination of the financial statements of Farber Corporation for the year ended September 30, 1978, Anne Harper, CA, discovered that George Nance, the president who was also one of the principal shareholders, had borrowed substantial amounts of money from the corporation. Nance indicated that he owned 51 percent of the corporation, that the money would be promptly repaid, and that the financial statements were being prepared for internal use only, and would not be distributed to the other six shareholders. He requested that these loans not be accounted for separately in the financial statements but be included in the other current accounts receivable. Harper acquiesced in this request. Nance was correct as to his stock ownership and the fact that the financial statements were for internal use only. However, he subsequently became insolvent and was unable to repay the loans.

Required:

What is Harper's liability? Explain. (AICPA, adapted)

3–22. The CA firm of Bigelow, Barton, and Brown was expanding very rapidly. Consequently it hired several staff assistants, including James Small. Subsequently, the partners of the firm became dissatisfied with Small's production and warned him that they would be forced to discharge him unless his output increased significantly.

At that time Small was engaged in audits of several clients. He decided that to avoid being fired, he would reduce or omit entirely some of the required auditing procedures listed in audit programs prepared by the partners. One of the CA firm's clients, Newell Corporation Ltd. was in serious financial difficulty and had adjusted several of its accounts being examined by Small to appear financially sound. Small prepared fictitious working papers in his home at night to support purported completion of auditing procedures assigned to him, although he in fact did not examine the Newell adjusting entries. The CA firm rendered an unqualified opinion on Newell's financial statements, which were grossly misstated. Several creditors subsequently extended large sums of money to Newell Corporation Ltd. relying upon the audited financial statements.

Required:

Would the CA firm be liable to the creditors who extended the money in reliance on the erroneous financial statements if Newell Corporation Ltd. should fail to pay the creditors? Explain. (AICPA, adapted)

3–23. In connection with current problems relating to external accounting statements it has been stated that:

. . . the bulk of the problems can be traced to a single crucial flaw in the basic structure (of the financial disclosure process): despite the fact that external accounting statements are meant to report on managerial operation of owner resources, it is management that controls the content of these reports.

The obvious question is: 'What about the shareholders' auditor in this situation?' My hypothesis is that the auditor is just not sufficiently independent to overcome the power position of management.

Required:

Analyze and comment on the relative positions of, and the causes of the potential conflict between, management and the shareholders' auditor. (CICA)

3–24. It is now doubtful if an auditor can defend a challenge to his opinion simply by having adhered to generally accepted auditing standards and by stating that the financial statements have been prepared in accordance with generally accepted accounting principles.

Required:

Discuss the above statement indicating its implications for the auditing profession (CICA)

GROUP III
PROBLEMS

3–25.   Risk Capital Limited was considering the purchase of a substantial amount of the treasury stock held by Sunshine Corporation Ltd., a closely held corporation. Initial discussions with the Sunshine Corporation Ltd. began late in 1978.

Wilson and Wyatt, CAs, Sunshine's public accountants, regularly prepared quarterly and annual unaudited financial statements. The most recently prepared unaudited financial statements were for the fiscal year ended September 30, 1978.

On November 15, 1978, after protracted negotiations, Risk Capital agreed to purchase 100,000 shares of no-par treasury stock of Sunshine at $12.50 per share. However, Risk Capital insisted upon audited statements for the calendar year 1978. The contract specifically provided: "Risk Capital shall have the right to rescind the purchase of said stock if the audited financial statements of Sunshine for calendar year 1978 show a material adverse change in the financial position of the Corporation."

At the request of Sunshine, Wilson and Wyatt audited the company's financial statements for the year ended December 31, 1978. The December 31, 1978, audited financial statements furnished to Sunshine by Wilson and Wyatt showed no material adverse change from the September 30, 1978, unaudited statements. Risk Capital relied upon the audited statements and purchased the treasury stock of Sunshine. It was subsequently discovered that as of the balance sheet date, the audited statements contained several misstatements and that in fact there had been a material adverse change in the financial position of the corporation. Sunshine has become insolvent, and Risk Capital will lose virtually its entire investment.

Risk Capital seeks recovery against Wilson and Wyatt.

Required:

a.   Discuss each of the theories of liability that Risk Capital will probably assert as its basis for recovery.

b.   Assuming that only ordinary negligence by Wilson and Wyatt is proven, will Risk Capital prevail? State "yes" or "no" and explain. (AICPA, adapted)

3–26.   Dale Williams, CA, was engaged by Jackson Financial Development Company to audit the financial statements of Apex Construction Company, a small closely held corporation. Williams was told when he was engaged that Jackson Financial needed reliable financial statements which would be used to determine whether or not to purchase a substantial amount of Apex Construction's convertible debentures at the price asked by the estate of one of Apex's former directors.

Williams performed his examination in a negligent manner. As a result of his negligence he failed to discover substantial defalcations by Carl Brown, the Apex controller. Jackson Financial purchased the debentures but would not have if the defalcations had been discovered. After discovery of the fraud Jackson Financial promptly sold them for the highest price offered in the market at a $70,000 loss.

Required:

a. What liability does Williams have to Jackson Financial? Explain.
b. If Apex Construction also sues Williams for negligence, what are the probable legal defenses which Williams's attorney would raise? Explain.
c. Will the negligence of a CA as described above prevent him from recovering on a liability insurance policy covering the practice of his profession? Explain. (AICPA)

3–27. Charles Worthington, the founding and senior partner of a successful and respected CA firm, was a highly competent practitioner who always emphasized high professional standards. One of the policies of the firm was that all reports by members or staff be submitted to Worthington for review.

Recently, Arthur Craft, a junior partner in the firm, received a phone call from Herbert Flack, a close personal friend. Flack informed Craft that he, his family, and some friends were planning to create a corporation to engage in various land development ventures; that various members of the family are presently in a partnership (Flack Ventures) which holds some land and other assets; and that the partnership would contribute all of its assets to the new corporation and the corporation would assume the liabilities of the partnership.

Flack asked Craft to prepare a balance sheet of the partnership that he could show to members of his family, who were in the partnership, and to friends, to determine whether they might have an interest in joining in the formation and financing of the new corporation. Flack said he had the partnership general ledger in front of him and proceeded to read to Craft the names of the accounts and their balances at the end of the latest month. Craft took the notes he made during the telephone conversation with Flack, classified and organized the data into a conventional balance sheet, and had his secretary type the balance sheet and an accompanying letter on firm stationery. He did not consult Worthington on this matter or submit his work to him for review.

The transmittal letter stated "We have reviewed the books and records of Flack Ventures, a partnership, and have prepared the attached balance sheet at March 31, 1978. We did not perform an examination in conformity with generally accepted auditing standards, and therefore do not express an opinion on the accompanying balance sheet." The balance sheet was prominently marked "unaudited." Craft signed the letter and instructed his secretary to send it to Flack.

Required:

What legal problems are suggested by these facts? Explain. (AICPA, adapted)

3–28. Chriswell Corporation Ltd. decided to raise additional long-term capital by issuing $3,000,000 of 8 percent subordinated debentures to the public. May, Clark & Company, CAs, the company's auditors, were engaged to examine the June 30, 1978, financial statements which were included in the registration statement for the debentures.

May, Clark & Company completed its examination and submitted an unqualified auditors' report dated July 15, 1978. The registration statement was filed and became effective on September 1, 1978. Two weeks prior to the effective date, one of the partners of May, Clark & Company called on Chriswell Corporation Ltd. and had lunch with the financial vice president and the controller. He questioned both officials on the company's operations since June 30 and enquired whether there had been any material changes in the company's financial position since that date. Both officers assured him that everything had proceeded normally and that the financial position of the company had not changed materially.

Unfortunately, the officers' representation was not true. On July 30, a substantial debtor of the company failed to pay the $400,000 due on its account receivable and indicated to Chriswell that it would probably be forced into bankruptcy. This receivable was shown as a collateralized loan on the June 30 financial statements. It was collateralized by stock at the debtor corporation which had a value in excess of the loan at the time the financial statements were prepared but was virtually worthless at the effective date of the registration statement. This $400,-000 account receivable was material to the financial position of Chriswell Corporation Ltd. and the market price of the subordinated debentures decreased by nearly 50 percent after the foregoing facts were disclosed.

The debenture holders of Chriswell are seeking recovery of their loss against all parties connected with the debenture registration.

Required:

Is May, Clark & Company liable to the Chriswell debenture holders under the U.S. securities acts? Explain. (AICPA, adapted)

3–29. Meglow Corporation Ltd., a closely held manufacturer of dresses and blouses, sought a loan from Busch Factors. Busch had previously extended $25,000 credit to Meglow but refused to lend any additional money without obtaining copies of Meglow's audited financial statements.

Meglow contacted the CA firm of Winslow & Watkins to perform the audit. In arranging for the examination, Meglow clearly indicated that its purpose was to satisfy Busch Factors as to the corporation's sound financial condition and to obtain an additional loan of $50,000. Winslow & Watkins accepted the engagement, performed the examination in a negligent manner, and rendered an unqualified opinion. If an adequate examination had been performed, the financial statements would have been found to be misleading.

Meglow submitted the audited financial statements to Busch Factors and obtained an additional loan of $35,000. Busch refused to lend more than that amount. After several other factors also refused, Meglow finally was able to persuade Maxwell Department Stores, one of its customers, to lend the additional $15,000. Maxwell relied upon the financial statements examined by Winslow & Watkins.

Meglow is now in bankruptcy, and Busch seeks to collect from Winslow & Watkins the $60,000 it loaned Meglow. Maxwell seeks to recover from Winslow & Watkins the $15,000 it loaned Meglow.

Required:

a.   Will Busch recover? Explain.

b.   Will Maxwell recover? Explain. (AICPA, adapted)

3–30. Cragsmore & Company, a medium-sized partnership of CAs, was engaged by Marlowe Manufacturing, Inc., to examine its financial statements for the year ended December 31, 1978.

Prior to preparing the audit report William Cragsmore, a partner, and Joan Willmore, a staff senior, reviewed the disclosures necessary in the notes to the financial statements. One note involved the terms, costs, and obligations of a lease between Marlowe and Acme Leasing Company.

Willmore suggested that the note disclose the following: "The Acme Leasing Company is owned by persons who have a 35 percent interest in the capital stock and who are officers of Marlowe Manufacturing, Inc."

On Cragsmore's recommendation, this was revised by substituting "minority shareholders" for "persons who have a 35 percent interest in the capital stock and who are officers."

The audit report and financial statements were forwarded to Marlowe Manufacturing for review. The officer-shareholders of Marlowe who also owned Acme Leasing objected to the revised wording and insisted that the note be changed to describe the relationship between Acme and Marlowe as merely one of affiliation. Cragsmore acceded to this request.

The audit report was issued on this basis with an unqualified opinion. But the working papers included the drafts that showed the changes in the wording of the note.

Subsequent to delivery of the audit report, Marlowe suffered a substantial uninsured fire loss and was forced into bankruptcy. The failure of Marlowe to carry any fire insurance coverage was not noted in the financial statements.

Required:

What legal problems for Cragsmore & Company are suggested by these facts? Discuss. (AICPA, adapted)

3–31.   Ralph Jones, CA, was engaged by Dee Company to examine and report on its financial statements which were required by the National Bank to accompany Dee's application for a $50,000 loan. Jones was informed that the primary purpose of the financial statements was to obtain the bank loan. National Bank previously had loaned Dee Company $100,-000 for five years at 6 percent with the typical call provisions requiring immediate repayment upon default or for failing to maintain certain current ratio tests. This loan was still unpaid when Jones was engaged.

Jones discovered that Dee's accounting records were seriously deficient. He informed Dee's president of the deficiencies and that he would have to deny an opinion on any financial statements which might be prepared from the records. The president then prevailed upon Jones to assist the company accountant to "get the books in shape and, if possible, to prepare unaudited financial statements for internal use only."

With the assistance of Dee's accountant, Jones was able to prepare a set of unaudited statements. During this time Jones learned that a physical inventory count had not been taken, and that the inventory per the accounting records was an estimate made by management. This disclosure was not made in the financial statements. The inventory reported in the balance sheet was material in relation to the financial statements taken as a whole.

Jones had the statements typed on his stationery without marking each statement "unaudited—for internal use only." He delivered a copy of the statements to each member of the board of directors (all were members of management) accompanied by his report as follows:

> The accompanying balance sheet of Dee Company, as of (date), and the related statements of income, retained earnings and changes in financial position for the year then ended were not audited by me and are restricted to internal use only and accordingly I express no opinion on them.

Dee's president removed Jones's report and used the financial statements to obtain the additional loan from National Bank. Jones had no knowledge of these acts.

It was subsequently learned that Dee's inventory in the accounting records was significantly overstated. Dee became insolvent and suit was brought against Jones by National.

Required:

Discuss the possibilities including countering arguments of Jones being liable to National. (AICPA, adapted)

3–32.   The limitations on professional responsibilities of CAs when they are associated with unaudited financial statements are often misunderstood. These misunderstandings can be reduced substantially if CAs carefully follow professional pronouncements in the course of their work and take other appropriate measures.

Required:

The following list describes seven situations CAs may encounter in their association with and preparation of unaudited financial statements. Briefly discuss the extent of the CAs' responsibilities and, if appropriate, the actions to be taken to minimize misunderstandings. Identify your answers to correspond with the letters in the following list.

a. A CA was engaged by telephone to perform accounting work including the preparation of financial statements. His client believes that the CA has been engaged to audit the financial statements and examine the records accordingly.

b. A group of business executives who own a farm managed by an independent agent engage a CA to prepare quarterly unaudited financial statements for them. The CA prepares the financial statements from information given to her by the independent agent. Subsequently, the business executives find the statements were inaccurate because their independent agent was embezzling funds. The executives refuse to pay the CA's fee and blame her for allowing the situation to go undetected, contending that she should not have relied on representations from the independent agent.

c. In comparing the trial balance with the general ledger a CA finds an account labeled "Audit Fees" in which the client has accumulated the CA's quarterly billings for accounting services including the preparation of quarterly unaudited financial statements.

d. Unaudited financial statements were accompanied by the following letter of transmittal from a CA:

"We are enclosing your company's balance sheet as of June 30, 1978, and the related statements of income, retained earnings, and changes in financial position for the six months then ended which we have reviewed."

e. To determine appropriate account classification, a CA reviewed a number of the client's invoices. He noted in his working papers that some invoices were missing but did nothing further because he felt they did not affect the unaudited financial statements he was preparing. When the client subsequently discovered that invoices were missing he contended that the CA should not have ignored the missing invoices when preparing the financial statements and had a responsibility to at least inform him that they were missing.

f. A CA has prepared a draft of unaudited financial statements from the client's records. While reviewing this draft with her client, the CA learns that the land and building were recorded at appraisal value.

g. A CA is engaged to review without audit the financial statements prepared by the client's controller. During this review, the CA learns of several items which by generally accepted accounting principles would require adjustment of the statements and footnote disclosure. The controller agrees to make the recommended adjustments to the statements but says that he is not going to add the footnotes because the statements are unaudited. (AICPA, adapted)

3–33. In a preliminary discussion, prior to beginning your audit of Mark Company, the chairman of the board of directors audit committee states that he would like to ascertain whether any key employees have interests which conflict with their duties at Mark Company. He asks that during your regular audit you be watchful for signs of these conditions and report them to him.

Required:

Briefly discuss your professional position in this matter. Include the following aspects in your discussion:

a. The responsibility of the CA for the discovery of conflicts of interest. Give reasons for your position.

b. The advisability of requesting that the client furnish you with a letter of representations which contains a statement that no conflict of interests is known to exist among the company's officers and employees. What action, if any, would you take if the client refused to provide the letter? How would his refusal affect your opinion?

c. At the same time that you are conducting the audit of Mark Company you are also conducting the audit of Timzin Company, a supplier of Mark Company. During your audit of Timzin Company you determine that an employee of Mark Company is receiving kick backs.

(1) Discuss your responsibility, if any, to reveal this practice to the audit committee of Mark Company.

(2) Discuss your professional relationships with Timzin Company after discovering the kick backs. (AICPA, adapted)

4

The public accounting profession
and planning the audit:
An overview

The public accounting profession

The public accounting profession encompasses all those who are licensed or entitled to be licensed to practice public accounting. Since all provinces automatically grant chartered accountants the privilege of practising public accounting, most public accountants are chartered accountants. Accordingly, the chartered accountancy profession is used in this chapter to demonstrate the public accounting profession and the public accounting firm.

In the past, two or more chartered accountants wishing to carry on a joint practice would organize a partnership because the rules of professional conduct of the provincial institutes and provincial laws prohibited public accounting practice by corporations. This prohibition was founded on the premise that CAs using the traditional corporate form of organization might avoid personal responsibility for their professional acts by "hiding behind the corporate veil." A further objection to public accounting corporations was that a controlling interest might be acquired by someone other than a CA—someone whose objective might be the earning of maximum profits without regard for professional ethics or auditing standards.

The opposition to incorporation of public accountants' practices has changed in recent years. The province of Alberta now sanctions *professional corporations* for public accountants and other professionals such as lawyers, medical doctors, and dentists. The Alberta legislation requires that shareholders and directors of a professional corporation must be members of the profession who are licensed to practice and that the shareholders have no limited liability. The officers of a professional corporation, however, do not have to be members of the profession. Because of the Alberta legislation and the fact that certain other provinces are contemplating similar laws, the rules of professional conduct of the provincial institutes have been or will be changed to permit their members to associate with professional corporations. While a professional corporation may provide certain benefits for public accountants, the main benefit of the Alberta legislation appears to be the minimization of income taxes.

It should be emphasized that a *professional corporation* differs from a *traditional corporation* in a number of respects. Usually, all shareholders, directors, and officers of a professional corporation must be licensed practitioners of the profession. Shares of a professional corporation can only be transferred to licensed practitioners or to the corporation itself. Professional corporations must also maintain adequate insurance for potential claims of negligence, and shareholders have no limited liability.

In the United States, a number of states have recognized the professional corporation as a permissible form of organization for a public accounting firm. In recognition of this trend in state laws, the AICPA *Code of Professional Ethics* has been amended to make the professional corporation form of organization available to AICPA members. However, a public accounting firm may not organize as a professional corporation unless all states in which the firm will practice permit this form of organization. The large national public accounting firms therefore will remain as partnerships for the foreseeable future. Many local CPA firms, on the other hand, are organized as professional corporations.

While the professional corporation concept is gaining acceptance in both Canada and the United States, it is still more common for public accounting firms to remain sole proprietorships or partnerships.

Organization of the public accounting firm

Human resources—the competence, judgment, and integrity of personnel—represent the greatest asset of any public accounting firm. The professional staff of a typical public accounting firm includes partners, managers or supervisors, senior accountants, and staff assistants. Since all *partners* in a public accounting firm must be CAs, some firms have created the position of *principal* for top-ranking individuals in the area of management advisory services or personnel who do not hold CA certificates. The position of principal is roughly equivalent to that of partner in responsibilities and compensation. In addition to these various levels of professional accounting personnel, the firm will also necessarily employ typists, computer operators, receptionists, and other general office employees.

The profession of public accounting embraces a variety of accounting-related services, including auditing, tax work, and management advisory services. Since auditing requires a larger staff, many small public accounting firms specialize in tax work and management advisory services. Larger public accounting firms are often departmentalized into separate auditing, tax, and management advisory services sections, with perhaps a "small business" department integrating all three types of services for smaller clients. Large firms may also have a separate professional development department to keep all members of the firm abreast of current developments within the profession.

Responsibilities of the partner.   A partner maintains contacts with clients. These contacts include the arrangement of the objectives, scope, and timing of examinations; consultations with clients over important issues; and the review and signing of audit reports. Recruitment of new staff members, professional development programs, establishment of the quality control policies of the firm, and general supervision of staff members are other responsibilities of the partner.

Specialization by each partner in a different area of the firm's practice is often advantageous. One partner, for example, may become expert in tax matters and head the firm's tax department; another may specialize in bankruptcy; and a third may devote full time to design and installation of the data processing systems.

The partnership level in a public accounting firm is comparable to that of top management in an industrial organization. Executives at this level are concerned with the long-run well-being of the organization and of the community it serves. They should and do contribute important amounts of time to civic, professional, and educational activities in the community. Participation in the provincial institute of chartered accountants and in the CICA is, of course, a requisite if the partners are to do their share in building the profession. Contribution of their specialized skills and professional judgment to leadership of civic organizations is equally necessary in developing the economic and social environment in which business and professional accomplishment is possible.

A secondary aspect of partners' active participation in professional institutes and in various business and civic organizations is the prestige and recognition which may come to their firms. The development of new business is an important responsibility of CA firm partners. Since professional firms do not advertise for clients, the obtaining of new business may hinge to an important extent upon a wide acquaintance by partners in the business community. However, the obtaining of new business is not the motivating factor in the partners' participation in civic affairs. By the time they have reached the partnership level, they have usually acquired an appreciation of the ideals and basic values of a profession which enables them to contribute their services to the community without thought of direct personal gain. Partners who lend their professional talents to expanding and enriching college and university accounting courses, for example, may contribute greatly to the quality of accounting education; the possibility that their contribution may attract promising graduates to their firm is a secondary consideration, not the motivating reason for their assistance to educational institutions.

Responsibilities of the manager or supervisor. In large public accounting firms, managers or supervisors perform many of the duties which would be discharged by partners in smaller firms. The manager is often responsible for general supervision of two or more concurrent audit engagements. This supervisory work includes the review of audit reports and working papers and the making of arrangements with the client for settlement of various accounting problems which may arise during the course of the engagement. The manager is responsible for determining the audit procedures applicable to specific audits and for maintaining uniform standards of field work. Familiarity with tax laws and with business legislation, as well as a broad and current knowledge of accounting theory and practice, are essential qualifications for a successful manager. Like the partner, the audit manager may specialize in specific industries or other areas of the firm's practice. Often the manager has the administrative duties of compiling and collecting the firm's billings to clients. In addition to the other duties mentioned, the manager may also assume responsibility for a program of staff training. In large CA firms some managers may be assigned on a full-time basis to the function of professional development.

Responsibilities of the senior auditor. The senior auditor is an individual competent to assume full responsibility for the planning and conducting of an audit and the writing of the audit report, subject to review and approval by the manager or partner. This requires that the senior delegate audit operations to assistants based upon an appraisal of the ability and capacity of each assistant to perform particular phases of the work. A well-qualified university graduate with extensive formal education in accounting may progress from the position of a beginning assistant to that of a senior auditor within two or three years, or even less time.

One of the major responsibilities of the senior is on-the-job staff training. When assigning work to staff assistants, the senior should make clear the end objectives of the particular audit operation. Constructive criticism of the work of assistants and judicious rotation of their duties in a manner that will provide diversified experience are important elements of the senior's work.

The review of working papers as rapidly as they are completed is another duty of the senior in charge of an audit. This enables the senior to control the progress of the work and to ascertain that each phase of the engagement is adequately covered. At the conclusion of the field work, the senior will make a final review, tracing all items from individual working papers to grouping sheets, and from the grouping sheets to the financial statements.

The senior will also maintain a continuous record of the hours devoted by all members of the staff to the various phases of the examination. In addition to maintaining uniform professional standards of field work, the senior is responsible for preventing the accumulation of excessive staff-hours on inconsequential matters and for completing the entire engagement within budgeted time, if possible.

Responsibilities of the staff assistant.   The first position of a university graduate entering the public accounting profession is that of a staff assistant (student-in-accounts). Staff assistants usually encounter a variety of assignments which fully utilize their capacity for analysis and growth. Of course some routine work must be done in every audit engagement, but those graduates with thorough training in accounting need have no fear of being assigned for long to extensive routine procedures when they enter the field of public accounting. Most firms are anxious to assign more and more responsibility to younger staff members as rapidly as they are able to assume it. The demand for accounting services is so far beyond the available supply of competent individuals that every incentive exists for rapid development of promising assistants.

Staff and pool systems.   Generally, a public accounting firm adopts either a staff or a pool system. In a staff system, professional personnel (managers or supervisors, senior auditors, and staff assistants) are organized into specific *staff groups,* each of which is assigned the responsibility for a group of clients and reports to a partner or partners. The pool system, on the other hand, treats the entire professional staff as a large group, and the personnel required for each engagement are drawn from the entire pool. Both systems have strengths and weaknesses. Regardless of which system is used, it is important that all professional personnel be provided with significantly broad training and experience to assure their professional development.

The larger public accounting firms maintain well-organized training programs designed to integrate new staff members into the organization with maximum efficiency. One of the most attractive features of the public accounting profession is the richness and variety of experience acquired even by the beginning staff member. Because of the high quality of the experience gained by chartered accountants as they move from one audit engagement to another, many business concerns select individuals from the public accounting field to fill such executive positions as controller or treasurer.

The tax department

Most large public accounting firms maintain separate tax departments, staffed by accountants who are experts in all aspects of income tax laws and regulations. Partners, managers, and seniors of the tax department review or prepare income tax returns for corporations, individuals, partnerships, estates, and trusts as well as gift tax and inheritance tax returns. In addition, they assist clients in tax planning and consult with members of the audit department as to tax problems encountered during audits. Tax work, though not as significant as auditing in the production of fees for most firms, represents an increasingly important source of revenue in public accounting.

The audit staff also must have a working familiarity with taxes. Many audit engagements include the preparation of the client's tax return. Even if a tax return is not prepared, the auditors must satisfy themselves as to the fairness of the client's tax expense and tax liability. Taxes play such an important role in financial reporting that an extensive knowledge of income taxes can be very useful to an auditor.

Management advisory services

Traditionally the services rendered by chartered accountants have centred about auditing and income tax work. Although these activities could reasonably be described as services to business management, the term *management advisory services* has acquired a specific meaning. Management advisory services describes advisory (consulting) services rendered by a CA to improve a client's use of its capabilities and resources to achieve the objectives of the organization.

When firms of chartered accountants in the course of performing annual audits have discovered unsatisfactory situations in a client's business, it has been natural for them to offer suggestions for corrective action. Often the client has requested the accounting firm to undertake as a special assignment an extensive study of the problem and to plan in detail the new procedures, policies, and organization required for a solution. In this evolutionary manner many public accounting firms found themselves gradually becoming involved in management consulting work. At first their engagements were mostly in the fields of accounting, finance, and office operations. Typical problems were the development of cost accounting systems, budgetary controls, improved general accounting procedures, and streamlined office operations. The prevalence in many companies of cumbersome, obsolete procedures, duplication of record keeping, and lack of information on product costs made consulting work a fertile field for public accounting firms. The chartered accountants' intimate knowledge of how things were done in the best-managed companies in the industry, plus their familiarity with a client's records and personnel, enabled them to devise highly effective recommendations for improved accounting methods and more efficient office operation.

After thus having extended their services from auditing and tax work to areas of systems design, costs, budgets, procedures, and office operations, public accounting firms found their field of work continuing to broaden. Up to this point the services being rendered were clearly related to accounting processes; these services could be rendered efficiently by persons with extensive experience in public accounting. Let us assume, however, that a CA firm made an analytical study for a manufacturing client of the cost of certain products; assume further that the product cost information indicated that factory production costs were excessive in comparison with the costs of other firms in the industry or in relation to selling prices in a competive market. Further progress in this situation called for study of factory production processes and physical facilities by industrial engineers. The public accounting firm then faced the alternatives of (a) employing as staff members industrial engineers who could handle the plant production aspects of consulting work, or (b) limiting the range of their management advisory services. Those firms which decided to take the step of employing industrial engineers soon faced the need of expanding further by adding experts in other technical areas.

Most of the national public accounting firms have now established separate management advisory services (MAS) divisions or organizations. Such a division or organization may have a hundred or more full-time staff members, including cost accountants, industrial engineers, computer specialists, electronic engineers, mathematicians, statisticians, psychologists, market analysts, and numerous other specialists.

Management advisory services by small public accounting firms

The small public accounting firm has both an opportunity and a responsibility to render management advisory services to its clients. These clients are for the most part small business concerns—too small to maintain a variety of specialists as full-time employees. Such clients should be able to call on their public accountants not only for auditing and tax services but also for expert assistance on all problems relating to accounting, finance, statistics, office methods and equipment, and electronic data processing. In some cases, counselling on general management problems may appropriately be added to the list.

Some small public accounting firms have been rendering such services to their clients for many years and have developed outstanding ability as management counsellors. As the field of management advisory services gains greater recognition, the principal difficulty confronting small accounting firms is how to deal with problems requiring specialized skills quite apart from accounting.

Obviously the small public accounting firm cannot offer as broad a range of consulting services as a firm with a large management advisory services division including scores of specialists. When the rendering of management advisory services brings accountants into contact with problems having engineering aspects, or requiring other skills not possessed by the CA firm, they can suggest to clients the desirability of calling in other professional consultants. Perhaps, in time, standard practices for referral to other public accounting firms for specialized services may develop along the lines followed by the medical profession. At present most small public accounting firms are reluctant to make referrals to national firms for fear that the client may decide to utilize the larger firm for all its needs. In a few instances, however, accountants have referred their clients to other accounting firms for specialized services, and the arrangement has worked out well. Many leaders of the profession believe that the practice of referrals will eventually become much more common.

The chartered accountant serving a clientele of small businesses may appropriately consider the following questions: "Are tax services, accounting services, systems work, and auditing the most important and valuable services which I can perform for my clients? Am I competent, or can I become competent, to aid clients in the solution of a wide range of management problems for which independent outside counsel is desirable?" Management is spending more each year for consulting services; if CA firms do not expand the area of services they now render, other consultants, perhaps less qualified, will surely move to meet this rising demand. Problems in general management and in production, industrial engineering, and marketing all demand skills other than accounting, yet they often require a thorough accounting knowledge of the client's operations. No independent consultant other than the chartered accountant has this accounting background.

Professional development within the CA firm

A major problem in public accounting is keeping abreast of current developments within the profession. New business practices, the shift to computer-based information systems, new pronouncements by the Auditing Standards Committee, the Accounting Research Committee, and changes in the tax laws are only a few of the factors which require members of the profession to continually update their technical knowledge. To assist in this updating process, most large public accounting firms maintain a separate professional development section.

Professional development sections offer a wide range of seminars and educational programs to personnel of the firm. The curriculum of each program is especially designed to suit the needs and responsibilities of participants. Partners, for example, may attend programs focusing on the firm's policies on audit quality control or means of minimizing exposure to lawsuits; on the other hand, programs designed for staff assistants may cover audit procedures or use of the firm's computer facilities.

The professional development section may also have a research staff which studies emerging issues in the profession. This staff assists in developing the "firm's position" on complex accounting issues arising in clients' financial statements or CICA Exposure Drafts and Discussion Memoranda. Often, a "position paper" conveying the firm's viewpoint is prepared by the research staff and sent to the research staff of the CICA. Thus, the professional development section may take an active hand in shaping current developments in the profession as well as in updating and informing personnel of the firm.

Continuing education—the CA's response to change

The need for CAs to expand their knowledge and improve their skills continues throughout their professional careers. In recognition of this need, all provincial institutes encourage their members to take appropriate professional development courses. Professional development sections of CA firms, the CICA, various provincial institutes of chartered accountants, and many universities provide numerous programs which meet the continuing education needs. Home study materials providing continuing education needs are also available through the CICA.

Seasonal fluctuations in public accounting work

One of the traditional disadvantages of the public accounting profession has been the concentration of work during the "busy season" from December through March, followed by a period of slack demand during the summer months. This seasonal trend was caused by the fact that most companies kept their records on a calendar-year basis and desired auditing services immediately after the December 31 closing of the accounts. Another important factor has been the spring deadline for filing of federal income tax returns. A generation ago it was customary, because of the seasonal concentration of work, for many audit firms to increase their staffs in December and to reduce them again a few months later. Such seasonal fluctuation in employment undoubtedly deterred many qualified persons from entering the field of public accounting.

In recent years the seasonal pattern of employment in public accounting has largely disappeared. A number of factors have contributed toward a more stable working force and more uniform distribution of work throughout the year. These factors include (a) the decision of many business concerns to adopt a fiscal year ending at a date of seasonal inactivity rather than a calendar year, and (b) recognition by the public accounting profession that much of the audit work traditionally performed after the annual closing of the accounts could just as effectively be performed on an interim basis throughout the year. Coupled with these changes has been a growing awareness of the need for personnel policies which tend to minimize overtime work and to provide stability of employment. Public accounting firms now offer the same stability of employment found in other professions.

The CA as an expert witness

As business affairs have grown more complex, the number of court cases involving accounting issues has increased greatly. The testimony of accountants and other experts is needed in order that the judge or jury gain the necessary understanding of the pertinent facts. *Expert witnesses* are persons who have special knowledge, experience, or training in a given field or profession. They are able to analyze and evaluate matters within a specialized body of knowledge, on which the judge or jury lacking such specialized experience could not readily form an opinion.

The role of the expert witness is sharply different from that of other witnesses. Lay witnesses are permitted to testify only as to facts they have seen or heard; they must usually leave the drawing of opinions or conclusions to the judge or jury. In some situations the lay witness may include an opinion in testimony if that opinion is based on facts the witness personally has seen or heard. The expert witnesses, on the other hand, may draw opinions based on the testimony of others and upon information acquired from others before or during the trial. For the expert's opinion to carry weight, the information on which it is based must, of course, come from a reliable source.

Courtroom tactics

The CA will achieve maximum effectiveness as an expert witness by responding to all questions from counsel on both sides clearly and in an impartial, courteous manner. An expert witness should speak slowly enough that the court reporter can record all statements, and should bear in mind that expert opinions will be of little value unless they are expressed in language which the judge or jury can understand.

A preliminary step when the CA takes the witness stand is usually a series of questions designed to establish professional qualifications and competence. Education, experience, publications, and professional affiliations are factors in qualifying a person as an expert. Special knowledge of the field or industry involved in the case is particularly helpful.

As a result of pretrial conferences with the attorney, the CA will be aware of most of the questions to be answered during direct examination. In cross-examination by the opposing counsel, however, a great variety of questions may arise. The objective of the attorney conducting the cross-examination is to destroy the significance of the opinion expressed by the expert witness. This situation requires that the CA consider each question carefully and answer it in a professional and deliberate manner. If the CA does not know the answer to a given question, it is usually best to say so. Thorough preparation and intimate knowledge of the issues are the best means by which the expert witness can uphold a position under rigorous cross-examination.

Types of cases in which the CA may testify

The CA is retained as an expert witness by one of the parties to the litigation in the belief that the CAs testimony will strengthen his case. Among the types of cases in which a CA may appropriately serve as an expert witness are the following: (*a*) income tax cases, including both criminal fraud cases and civil tax cases; (*b*) partnership dissolutions; (*c*) interpretations of contracts involving valuation of assets, bonuses, or determination of net income; (*d*) suits by minority shareholders who believe corporate officers and directors have been deficient in handling corporate affairs; (*e*) rates and earnings of public utilities; and (*f*) other cases involving complex accounting measurements.

Obtaining clients

Members of a profession—whether it be law, architecture, medicine, public accounting, or any similar field—do not advertise their services. New business is obtained through personal recommendations by present clients, bankers, attorneys, and insurance agents and adjusters, and by other business and professional people whose work brings them into contact with persons needing accounting services.

To a young accountant trying to establish a new practice, the bans against advertising and solicitation of clients may seem at first glance to be barriers imposed by established public accountants to protect themselves from new competition. However, if advertising were permissible for professional accountants, the larger, well-established firms would be able to outdo the new practitioner. Most members of the professions have traditionally believed advertising to be incompatible with the dignity and prestige of a professional practice. Nearly everyone prefers to engage an attorney, physician, or accountant who has been recommended by friends rather than to trust professional persons who speak to the public in glowing terms of their own accomplishments.

But how does the young accountant attract clients and establish a practice? One answer is to buy an existing practice, or to enter partnership with an established, older practitioner who is contemplating retirement and wants to effect a gradual transition of work to a younger man or woman. Another possibility is that the previous CA firm employer of the young accountant may "cede" some of its smaller clients to the former employee to help in getting the new practice established. Clients may also be obtained through a circle of friends and acquaintances. Participation in community activities, clubs, and organizations is an acceptable and proven method for the young professional person to obtain recognition. Speaking engagements before local groups is another useful step in becoming known to business executives.

By far the most effective way of gaining new clients is the enthusiastic recommendation of a present client. It is not unusual for satisfied clients to go out of their way to recommend an independent accountant to business associates, with the result of generating new business in a short time. Consequently, the competent accountant, once having established a nucleus of satisfied clients, often finds the new practice snowballing suddenly into a demand for services that is difficult to meet.

Relationships with clients

The wide-ranging scope of public accountants' activities today demands that CAs be interested in and well informed about economic trends, political developments, sports events, and the many other topics that play a significant part in business and social contacts. Although an in-depth knowledge of accounting is a most important qualification of the CA, an ability to meet people easily and gain their confidence and goodwill may be no less important in achieving success in the profession of public accounting. The ability to work effectively with clients will be enhanced by a sincere interest in their problems and by a relaxed and cordial manner.

The question of the auditors' objectivity or independence inevitably arises in considering the advisability of social activities with clients. The partner in today's public accounting firm may play golf with the executives of client companies and other business associates. These relationships actually may make it easier to resolve differences of opinions which arise during the audit, if the client has learned to know and respect the CA partner. This mutual understanding need not prevent the CA from standing firm on matters of accounting principle. This is perhaps the "moment of truth" for the practitioners of a profession.

However, the CA must always remember that the concept of objectivity embodies an *appearance* of objectivity. This appearance of objectivity may be impaired if an auditor becomes excessively involved in social activities with clients. For example, if a CA frequently attends lavish parties held by a client, or dates an officer or employee of a client corporation, the question might be raised as to whether the CA will appear objective to outsiders. This dilemma is but one illustration of the continual need for judgment and perspective on the part of an auditor.

PLANNING THE AUDIT

Background information on clients

The recent wave of litigation involving auditors has placed a new emphasis on the need for CAs to investigate prospective audit clients before undertaking the engagement. The CAs should investigate the history of the prospective client, including such matters as product lines, credit rating, working capital position, and the identities and reputations of major shareholders, directors, officers, and legal counsel. Many CAs choose to avoid engagements which entail a relatively high risk of overstated operating results or management fraud; others may accept such engagements, recognizing the need to expand audit procedures to compensate for the unusual level of risk.

It is always important for the auditors to discover why a new client wants an audit and what specific results the client hopes to attain. Audit procedures are not the same for all types of engagements; the audit work to be done will depend to a considerable extent upon any special objectives, such as (a) statutory audits, (b) sale of the business, or (c) change in a partnership agreement. In some cases, the auditors may find that the client company is in need of services quite different from those it had in mind in engaging the independent auditors.

Numerous sources of information on prospective clients are available to auditors. Trade publications and government agency and CICA publications are useful in obtaining orientation in the client's industry. Previous audit reports, annual reports to shareholders, securities commission filings, and prior years' tax returns are excellent sources of financial background information. Informal discussions between the auditor-in-charge and key officers of the prospective client can provide information about the history, size, operations, accounting records, and internal controls of the enterprise.

Communication with predecessor auditors. An excellent source of information about a prospective client which previously has been audited is the predecessor auditors. The successor auditors' examination may be greatly facilitated by consulting with the predecessor auditors and reviewing the predecessors' working papers. Communication with predecessor auditors can provide the successor CAs with background information about the client, details about the client's system of internal control, and evidence as to the account balances at the beginning of the year under audit.

On occasion, a client may seek to change auditors because of disagreements with the predecessor auditors over accounting principles or audit procedures. For this reason, the rules of professional conduct and business corporations acts require the successor auditors to make certain enquiries of the predecessor auditors *before accepting the engagement.* These enquiries should include questions regarding disagreements with management over accounting principles, the integrity of management and other matters which will assist the successor auditors in deciding whether to accept the engagement.[1] In the United States, SEC regulations require companies subject to its jurisdiction to report changes in independent auditors, and the reasons therefor, to the Commission.

Auditors are ethically prohibited from disclosing confidential information obtained in the course of an audit without the consent of the client. The successor auditors should therefore obtain the prospective client's consent before making enquiries of the predecessor auditors. In addition, they should ask the client to authorize the predecessor auditors to respond fully.

If a prospective client is reluctant to authorize communications with the predecessor auditors, the successor CAs should consider the implications in deciding whether to accept the engagement.

Tour of plant and offices.   Another useful preliminary step for the auditors is to arrange an inspection tour of the plant and offices of a prospective client. This tour will give the auditors some understanding of the plant layout, manufacturing process, principal products, and physical safeguards surrounding inventories. During the tour, the auditors should be alert for signs of potential problems. Rust on equipment may indicate that plant assets have been idle; excessive dust on raw materials or finished goods may indicate a problem of obsolescence. A knowledge of the physical facilities will assist the auditors in planning how many audit staff members will be needed to participate in observing the physical inventory.

The tour affords the auditors an opportunity to observe first-hand what types of internal documentation are used to record such activity as receiving raw materials, transferring materials into production, and shipping finished goods to customers. This documentation is essential to the auditors' study and evaluation of internal control.

In going through the offices the auditors will learn the location of various accounting records. The auditors can ascertain how much subdivision of duties is practical within the client organization by observing the number of office employees. In addition, the tour will afford an opportunity to meet the key personnel whose names appear on the organization chart. The auditors will record the background information about the client in a *permanent file* available for reference in future engagements.

---

[1] Some guidance regarding a first audit engagement is contained in *The First Audit Engagement,* an audit technique study published by the CICA in 1975.

Preliminary arrangements with clients

The auditors' approach to an engagement is not that of detectives looking for evidence of fraud; instead, the approach is the positive, constructive one of gathering evidence to prove the fairness and validity of the client's financial statements.

A conference with the client prior to beginning the engagement is a useful step in avoiding misunderstandings. The conference should include discussion of the nature, purpose, and scope of the audit and any matters which conceivably could produce friction. Since the fee is usually in the mind of both client and auditors, it should be frankly discussed, but without creating the impression that the auditors' chief interest is in the earning of a fee.

As a basis for a worth-while conference prior to the engagement, the auditors may make a preliminary survey of the client's accounting records and monthly statements to help determine the client's needs and the existence of any special problems. The cost of the survey is usually not large; this cost is usually included in the total fee for the audit.

A clear understanding between the client and the auditors concerning the scope of the examination and the condition of the accounting records at the starting date is an essential step in planning an audit. Otherwise, the auditors may arrive to begin an examination only to find that transactions for the period to be examined have not yet been fully recorded. It is not the auditors' job to draft routine adjusting entries or to balance the subsidiary ledgers with the control accounts. By doing this type of work for an audit client, the auditors would be acting as accountants for the client.

A new client should be informed as to the extent of investigation of the beginning balances of such accounts as plant and equipment and inventories. To determine the propriety of depreciation expense for the current year and the proper balances in plant and equipment accounts at the balance sheet date, the auditors must investigate the validity of the property accounts at the beginning of the current period. If the auditors are unable to obtain satisfactory evidence as to the balance of *beginning inventory*, it maybe necessary to deny an opinion on the income statement in the first audit of a new client.

In some cases, satisfactory audits of the business in preceding years by other reputable auditing firms may enable the auditors to accept the opening balances of the current year with a minimum of verification work; in other cases, in which no satisfactory recent audit has been made, an extensive analysis of transactions of prior years will be necessary to establish account balances as of the beginning of the current year. In these latter situations the client should be made to understand that the scope and cost of the initial audit may exceed that of repeat engagements, which will not require analysis of past years' transactions.

Fees. When a business engages the services of independent public accountants, it will usually ask for an estimate of the cost of the audit. In supplying this estimate after being engaged, the accountants will give first consideration to the time probably required for the audit. Staff time is the basic unit of measurement for audit fees. Each public accounting firm develops a per hour or per diem fee schedule for each category of audit staff, based on direct salaries and such related costs as payroll taxes and insurance. The "direct" rate is then increased for allocated overhead costs and a profit element.

In addition to basic per diem or per hour fees, clients are charged for direct costs incurred by the public accounting firm for staff travel, report processing, and other "out-of-pocket" expenditures.

Estimating a fee for an audit thus usually involves the application of the CA firm's daily or hourly rates to the estimated time required. Since the exact number of days cannot be determined in advance, the auditors may merely give a rough estimate of the fee. Or they may multiply the rates by the estimated time, add an amount for unforeseen problems, and quote a range or bracket of amounts within which the total fee will fall. Once the auditors have given an estimate of the fee to a client, they naturally feel some compulsion to keep the charges within this limit.

Per diem rates for audit work vary considerably in different sections of the country, and even within a given community, in accordance with the reputation and experience of the accounting firm. Of course, the salaries paid to audit staff members are much less than the rates at which audit time is billed to clients. In many firms salaries represent about 40 percent of billing rates; the remainder is required to cover the cost of "non-billable" time when auditors are not assigned, overhead expenses of the office, and a profit to the partners.

Use of the client's staff. Another issue to be discussed in the preliminary conference is what the client's staff can do to prepare for the audit. As previously mentioned, the client's staff should have the accounting records up to date when the auditors arrive. In addition, many audit working papers can be prepared for the auditors by the client's staff, thus reducing the cost of the audit and freeing the auditors from routine work. The auditors may set up the columnar headings for such working papers and give instructions to the client's staff as to the information to be gathered. These working papers should bear the label **Prepared by Client** or **P.B.C.**, and also the initials of the auditor who verifies the work performed by the client's staff. Working papers prepared by the client should never be accepted at face value; such papers must be reviewed and tested by the auditors in order that the CA firm maintain its objective status.

Among the tasks which may be assigned to the client's employees are the preparation of a trial balance of the general ledger, preparation of an aged trial balance of accounts receivable, analyses of accounts receivable written off, lists of property additions and retirements during the year, and analyses of various revenue and expense accounts. Many of these working papers may be in the form of computer print-outs.

Engagement letters

These preliminary understandings with the client should be recorded in an *engagement letter* by the auditors, making clear the nature of the engagement, any limitations on the scope of the audit, work to be performed by the client's staff, and the basis for computing the auditors' fee. Since this letter specifies the terms of the audit engagement, it is essential for both statutory and non-statutory audits. Theoretically, the letter should be accepted by the shareholders of the company as the auditors are appointed by them. As a practical matter, however, it is usually accepted by either the chairman of the board of directors, the chief executive officer, or the audit committee on behalf of the shareholders. Since the format and content of an engagement letter vary considerably in practice, the letter for a statutory audit presented in Figure 4–1 is adapted from the suggested wordings of the special committee of the *Ontario Institute*. A similar letter may also be used for a non-statutory audit.

The use of engagement letters is not limited to audit engagements; documentation of the mutual understanding between the CAs and the client is desirable before rendering any type of professional service. The importance of such a letter can be seen from the following case.

> In the 1136 Tenants' *Corporation* v. *Rothenberg* case in the United states, an incorporated apartment cooperative sued its CPAs for failing to detect embezzlement losses caused by a managing agent. The CPAs maintained they had been engaged only to do "write-up" work and not to perform any audit procedures. The court found that the CPAs had not made it sufficiently clear to the client that the engagement did not include audit procedures and held the CPAs liable for damages totaling $174,000. (The CPAs' fee for the engagement had been only $600.) Had the CPAs clearly set forth the scope of the engagement in an engagement letter, the case might never have been brought to court.

Audit plans

The first standard of field work states:

> The work should be **adequately planned** and **properly executed.** If assistants are employed they should be **properly supervised.** (Emphasis added.)

FIGURE 4–1
Engagement letter for a statutory audit

December 1, 1979

Mr. J. B. Barker, President (or the Secretary, chairman of the audit committee)
Barker Tool Ltd.
Anycity, Ontario
Canada

Dear Mr. Barker:

As a result of our conversation on November 1, 1979, we are summarizing our understanding of the terms of our engagement as auditors of the Company for the financial year ending December 31, 1980.

Our statutory function as auditors of your company is to report to the shareholders whether the annual financial statements present fairly the financial position, results of operations, and changes in financial position. To meet this obligation and in accordance with generally accepted auditing standards in Canada, our audit will include an examination of the accounting system, internal controls and such tests and other procedures as we considered necessary in the circumstances. Our assessment of the reliability of the accounting system and internal controls will affect the nature, extent, and timing of our audit work.

Because the audit examination will be planned and conducted primarily to enable us to express a professional opinion on the annual financial statements, it will not be designed to identify and cannot necessarily be expected to disclose defalcations and other irregularities. Of course, the discovery of irregularities may still result from our examination and should any significant ones be encountered, they will be reported to you.

In properly organized accounting systems, reliance is placed principally upon the maintenance of an adequate degree of internal control to prevent or detect errors and irregularities. If we believe that it is desirable and practicable to make important improvements in the system of internal control, or if material errors or irregularities are encountered by us during our audit, we shall bring these to your attention.

The foregoing comments deal only with our statutory obligation as your company's auditors. We are always prepared to broaden our procedures if feasible, at your request.

Yours truly,

Charles Adams

Charles Adams
Adams, Barnes & Co.,
Chartered Accountants

We agree with your understanding of the terms of your engagement as auditor of the company as set out in this letter.

Barker Tool Ltd.

J. B. Barker

December 16, 1979   J. B. Barker, President

Source: Adapted from the report of the Special Committee on Professional Incorporation and Professional Liability of the Ontario Institute of Chartered Accountants, 1972.

To conduct an audit in compliance with this standard, the auditor-in-charge must develop a "plan of action" to organize, coordinate, and schedule the activities of the audit staff and must ensure that the activities are properly performed. This advance planning is usually accomplished through the preparation of audit plans, audit programs, and time budgets.

An audit plan is an overview of the engagement. Although audit plans differ in form and content among public accounting firms, a "typical" plan includes details on the following:

1. Description of the client company—its structure, business, and organization.
2. Objectives of the audit (e.g., statutory audit, special-purpose audit).
3. Nature and extent of other services, such as preparation of tax returns, to be performed for the client.
4. Timing and scheduling of the audit work, including determining which procedures may be performed before the balance sheet date, what must be done on or after the balance sheet date, and setting dates for such critical procedures as cash counts, accounts receivable confirmations, and inventory observation.
5. Work to be done by the client's staff.
6. Staffing requirements during the engagement.
7. Target dates for completing major segments of the engagement, such as the study and evaluation of internal control, tax returns, the audit report, and filings with the appropriate government agencies.
8. Any special problems to be resolved in the course of the engagement.

The audit plan is normally drafted prior to starting work at the client's offices. However, the plan may be modified throughout the engagement as special problems are encountered and as the auditors' study and evaluation of internal control lead to identification of areas requiring more or less audit work.

Audit programs

An audit program is a detailed outline of the auditing work to be performed, specifying the procedures to be followed in verification of each item in the financial statements and giving the estimated time required. As each step in the audit program is completed, the date, the auditor's initials, and the actual time consumed may be entered opposite the item. An audit program thus serves as a useful tool both in scheduling and in controlling audit work. It indicates the number of persons required and the relative proportions of senior and staff assistant hours needed, and it enables supervisors to keep currently informed on the progress being made.

The inclusion of detailed audit instructions in the program gives assurance that essential steps in verification will not be overlooked. These written instructions enable inexperienced auditors to work effectively with less personal supervision than would otherwise be required, and they thus permit seniors and managers to concentrate upon those features of the examination which demand a high degree of analytical ability and the discriminating exercise of professional judgment.

Audit programs are considerably more detailed than audit plans. The audit plan outlines the objectives of the engagement, while the audit program lists the specific procedures which must be performed to accomplish these objectives.

Illustrative audit program. A typical example of the detailed audit procedures set forth in an audit program is the following partial list of procedures for the audit of investments in marketable securities:

X COMPANY
Partial Audit Program—Securities
December 31, 19—

Working paper reference	*Date and initials*		*Time*	
			Estimated	*Actual*
		1. Inspection of securities:		
		a. Obtain or prepare list of securities owned as of balance sheet date.		
		b. Compare list of securities with corresponding ledger account.		
		c. Inspect securities on hand at or near date of balance sheet and compare with list of securities at balance sheet date. Reconcile securities to date of balance sheet and vouch transactions for intervening period. Maintain control of securities during this period.		
		d. Compare serial numbers of securities inspected with serial numbers listed for these securities in prior year's audit.		

Tailor-made audit programs. Since the conditions and problems encountered differ with every audit engagement, it is necessary for the auditor-in-charge of each examination to determine what procedures are appropriate under the circumstances. At the beginning of an engagement, only a tentative audit program can be prepared. The auditor should expect this "first draft" of the program to be modified during the audit as strengths and weaknesses in the client's system of internal control and other special considerations are encountered.

Weak internal control, as manifested by poor accounting records, incompetent personnel, or lack of internal auditing, necessitates much more extensive auditing than would be necessary for a well-staffed concern with strong internal controls, good accounting records, and an effective internal auditing department. Internal control is sometimes adequate for certain operations of the company but weak or absent in other areas. The amount of testing by the auditors should be increased in areas of operations for which internal controls are deficient and may properly be minimized in areas subject to strong internal controls. The great variation in quality of internal controls encountered, coupled with the variety of accounting methods and special problems peculiar to individual business concerns, requires that the audit program be modified as the auditors learn more about the circumstances of the individual audit engagement.

The value of the audit program as a means of giving coherence, order, and logical sequence to the investigation is beyond dispute. The audit program must not, however, be considered a substitute for an alert, resourceful attitude on the part of the audit staff. They should be encouraged to explore fully any unusual transactions or questionable practices which come to their attention from any source and cautioned not to restrict themselves to the investigative routines set forth in a prearranged audit program. As the examination progresses, the desirability of making certain modifications in the work contemplated by the audit program will usually become apparent. The selection of audit procedures appropriate to the circumstances requires professional judgment based on extensive auditing experience.

Time budgets for audit engagements

Public accounting firms usually charge clients on a time basis, and detailed time records must therefore be maintained on every audit engagement. A time budget for an audit is constructed by estimating the time required for each step in the audit program for each of the various grades of auditors and totaling these estimated amounts. Time budgets serve other functions in addition to providing a basis for estimating fees. The time budget is an important tool of the audit senior—it is used to measure the efficiency of staff assistants and to determine at each stage of the engagement whether the work is progressing at a satisfactory rate.

There is always pressure to complete an audit within the estimated time. The staff assistant who takes more than the normal time for a task is not likely to be popular with supervisors or to win rapid advancement. Ability to do satisfactory work when given abundant time is not a sufficient qualification, *for time is never abundant in public accounting.*

The development of time budgets is facilitated in repeat engagements by reference to the preceding year's detailed time records. Sometimes time budgets prove quite unattainable because the client's records are not in satisfactory condition, or because of other special circumstances which arise. Even when time estimates are exceeded, there can be no compromise with qualitative standards in the performance of the field work. The CA firm's professional reputation and its legal liability to clients and third parties do not permit any short-cutting or omission of audit procedures to meet a predetermined time estimate.

The audit trail

In developing audit procedures, the auditors are assisted by the organized manner in which accounting systems record, classify, and summarize data. The flow of accounting data begins with the recording of thousands of individual transactions on documents such as invoices and cheques. The information recorded on these original documents is summarized in journals; and at the end of each month, the totals of the journals are computed and posted to ledger accounts. At the end of the year the balances in the ledger accounts are arranged in the form of a balance sheet and income statement.

In thinking of the accounting records as a whole, we may say that a continuous trail of evidence exists—a trail of evidence which links the thousands of individual transactions comprising a year's business activity with the summary figures in the financial statements. In a manual accounting system, this *audit trail* consists of source documents, journal entries, and ledger entries. An audit trail also exists within a computer-based accounting system, although it may have a substantially different form; this will be discussed in Chapter 6.

Just as a hiker may walk in either direction along a mountain path, an auditor may follow the audit trail in either of two directions. For example, the auditor may follow specific transactions from their origin forward to their inclusion in the financial statement summary figures. This approach provides the auditor with assurance that the transactions have been properly interpreted and processed.

On the other hand, the auditors may follow the stream of evidence back to its sources. This type of verification consists of tracing the various items in the statements (such as cash, receivables, sales, and expenses) back to the ledger accounts, and from the ledgers back through the journals to original documents evidencing transactions. This process of working backward from the statement figures to the detailed evidence of individual transactions is the exact opposite of the accounting process. Working backward along the audit trail provides assurance that financial statement figures are based upon actual transactions.

Although the technique of working along the audit trail is a useful one, bear in mind that the auditors must acquire other types of evidence obtained from sources other than the client's accounting records.

The audit process

Although specific audit procedures vary from one engagement to the next, the fundamental steps underlying the audit process are essentially the same in almost every engagement. These fundamental steps are:

1. Review and prepare a written description of the client's system of internal control.
2. Test the operation of the system of internal control for compliance with the written description.
3. Evaluate the effectiveness of the system of internal control.
4. Prepare a report to management containing recommendations for improving the system of internal control.
5. Complete the audit: conduct tests to substantiate specific account balances and perform other auditing procedures.
6. Issue the audit report.

The sequence of these steps provides a logical framework for the audit process. However, the auditors need not complete each of these tasks before moving on to the next; several steps of the process may be undertaken concurrently. Of course the audit report cannot be issued until all other audit work is complete.

1. Review internal control.

The nature and extent of the audit work to be performed on a particular engagement depend largely upon the effectiveness of the client's system of internal control in preventing material errors in the financial statements. Before auditors can evaluate the effectiveness of the system, they need a knowledge and understanding of how it works: what procedures are performed and who performs them, what controls are in effect, how various types of transactions are processed and recorded, and what accounting records and supporting documentation exist. Thus, a review of the client's system of internal control is a logical first step in every audit engagement.

Sources of information about the client's system include interviews with client personnel, audit working papers from prior years' engagements, plant tours, and the client's procedures manuals. In gathering information about a system, it is often useful to study the sequence of procedures used in processing major categories of transactions. A manufacturing business, for example, typically has four major categories of transactions; (a) *sales transactions,* involving sales, accounts receivable, and cash receipts; (b) *purchase transactions,* involving various assets and expenses, accounts payable, and cash disbursements; (c) *production transactions,* involving production costs, inventories, and the cost of goods sold; and (d) *payroll transactions,* involving labour costs, payroll tax liabilities, and cash disbursements.

To illustrate one of these transaction groups, let us consider sales transactions. The procedures used in processing sales transactions might include receiving a customer's purchase order, credit approval, shipment of merchandise, preparation of sales invoices, recording the sale, recording the account receivable, billing, and handling and recording the cash received from the customer.

A working knowledge of the client's system of internal control is needed throughout the audit; consequently the auditors should prepare a working paper fully describing their understanding of the system. Frequent reference to this working paper will be made to aid in designing audit procedures, ascertaining where documents are filed, familiarizing new audit staff with the system, and as a refresher in beginning next year's engagement.

The description of the system of internal control is usually prepared in the form of a written narrative, flowcharts, or a questionnaire; all of these working papers are discussed in Chapter 5.

2. Test the system.

The auditors' written description of the system of internal control is prepared, in large part, from information obtained from the client's procedures manuals and from interviews with client personnel. In reality, however, a system may operate quite differently from what is described in manuals and interviews. When interviewed, client personnel may pay "lip service" to the procedures manuals by describing how the system *should* function rather than how it really *does* function. The auditors must therefore test the system to ascertain that accounting control procedures are actually being applied as indicated in manuals and interviews.

Compliance tests.   The auditors' tests of the client's system of internal control are termed *tests of compliance* because they test the system's compliance with the written description contained in the auditors' working papers. If the auditors find that the system functions differently from the working paper description, they will amend the working papers to describe the actual system.

Compliance tests are of two types: transactions tests and functional tests. *Transactions tests* are designed to determine the "flow" of data through the client's system, that is, the nature and sequence of procedures used in processing the major categories of transactions. To perform a transactions test of the sale of merchandise on credit, for example, an auditor might begin by selecting a sample of sales orders and following the related transactions through the client's sequence of procedures. The auditor would determine whether such procedures as credit approval, preparation of shipping documents, shipment of merchandise, preparation of sales invoices, recording the account receivable, and recording the receipt of cash from the customer were performed by appropriate client personnel and in the sequence indicated in the audit working papers. Notice that a transactions test follows *specific transactions* along the audit trail from *beginning to end;* the purpose of the test is to identify the procedures being performed and the persons performing them.

The second type of compliance tests is the functional test. *Functional tests* provide the auditor with reasonable assurance that specific control procedures have been performed *consistently and effectively* throughout the period under audit. For example, an auditor may wish to obtain assurance that sales invoices were prepared for all shipments of merchandise during the year. An appropriate test might consist of selecting a sample of shipping documents prepared at various times throughout the year and inspecting the related sales invoices. In conducting functional tests, the auditors focus their attention upon the effectiveness with which a single procedure has been performed, rather than upon the entire sequence of procedures performed in processing a transaction.

The second standard of field work states:

> There should be an **appropriately organized study and evaluation** of those internal controls on which the auditor subsequently relies in determining the nature, extent and timing of audit procedures. (Emphasis added.)

The first two steps of the audit process complete the auditors' "study" of internal control by providing them with an understanding of the system and with reasonable assurance that the procedures are in use and operating effectively. The next logical step in the audit process is for the auditors to evaluate the system of internal control.

3. Evaluate the system.

Auditors evaluate the system of internal control in order to determine the *nature, extent,* and *timing* of the audit procedures necessary to complete the audit. A major objective of internal control is to produce accurate and reliable accounting data. Thus, auditors should make an intensive investigation in areas for which internal control is weak; however, they are justified in performing less extensive auditing work in areas for which internal controls are strong. This process of deciding upon the matters to be emphasized during the audit, based upon the evaluation of internal control, means that the auditors will modify their audit program by expanding audit procedures in some areas and reducing them in others.

Not all weaknesses in internal control require action by the auditors. Some weaknesses would cost more to correct than the benefit which could be derived from the improvement. For example, poor internal control over a small petty cash fund is not likely to have a material impact upon the fairness of the financial statements. On the other hand, if one employee is responsible for initiating cash disbursements and also for signing cheques, this combination of duties might result in material errors in the financial statements and substantial defalcations. In each instance, the auditors must exercise professional judgment in determining whether to modify the nature, timing, and extent of their audit procedures and whether to make recommendations to the client for improving the system of internal control.

4. Report to management.

When serious deficiencies in internal control are discovered, the auditors should issue a recommendation letter to the client containing suggestions for overcoming the weaknesses. This *internal control letter* (sometimes called management letter) not only provides the client with valuable suggestions for improving internal control but also serves to minimize the liability of the auditors in the event that a major defalcation or other serious loss is later discovered. The internal control letter should be issued as soon as possible after the auditors complete the evaluation of internal control. If the evaluation of internal control is completed prior to the balance sheet date, the auditors' recommendations may be implemented quickly enough to contribute to the reliability of the financial statements for the year under audit.

5. Complete the audit.

Some procedures for verifying account balances may be performed early in the audit. However, only after completing the study and evaluation of internal control are the auditors in a position to determine fully the nature, timing, and extent of the procedures necessary to substantiate account balances.

Tests designed to substantiate the fairness of a specific financial statement item are termed *substantive tests.* Examples of substantive tests include confirmation of accounts receivable, observation of the taking of physical inventory, and determination of an appropriate *cutoff* of transactions to be included in the year under audit. A significant distinction may be made between substantive tests and tests of compliance. Substantive tests are designed to *detect* errors in the financial statements; compliance tests are a step in evaluating how effectively the system of internal control has operated to *prevent* errors from occurring. In addition to conducting substantive tests, the auditors will perform other audit procedures in completing the audit, as, for example, investigating related party transactions which may warrant special disclosure.

6. Issue the report.

The date upon which the last audit procedures are completed is termed the *last day of field work.* Although the audit report is dated as of the last day of field work, it is not actually issued on that date. Since the audit report represents an acceptance of considerable responsibility by the CA firm, a partner must first review the working papers from the engagement to ascertain that a thorough examination has been completed. If the auditors are to issue anything other than an unqualified opinion of standard form, considerable care must go into the precise wording of the audit report. Consequently, the audit report is usually issued a week or more after the last day of field work.

Timing of audit work

The value of audited financial statements is enhanced if the statements are available on a timely basis after the year-end. To facilitate an early release of the audit report, auditors normally begin the audit well before the balance sheet date. The period before the balance sheet date is termed the *interim period.* Audit work which can be performed during the interim period includes the study and evaluation of internal control, issuance of the internal control or management letter, and some of the substantive testing. Other substantive tests, such as confirmation of year-end bank balances, establishing a proper cutoff of transactions to be included in the year, and searching for unrecorded liabilities must necessarily be performed on or after the balance sheet date.

Performing audit work during the interim period has numerous advantages in addition to facilitating the timely release of the audited financial statements. The independent auditors may be able to evaluate internal control more effectively by observing and testing the system at various times throughout the year. Also, they will be on hand to advise the client whether complex transactions, such as business combinations, are being recorded in conformity with generally accepted accounting principles. Another advantage is that interim auditing creates a more uniform workload for CA firms. With a large client, the auditors may have office space within the client's buildings and carry on auditing procedures throughout the entire year.

Auditing terminology

The terms used to describe the various phases of audit work need to be precisely defined in order that audit programs, other working papers, and reports may be clearly understood. The following terms are among those most commonly employed; others will be defined as they are introduced in later chapters.

Analyze—the process of identifying and classifying for further study all the debit and credit entries contained in a ledger account. Accounts are analyzed in order to ascertain the nature of all the transactions which give rise to the balance. An account such as Miscellaneous Expense, for example, requires analysis before any real understanding of its contents is possible.

Compare—the process of observing the similarity or variations of particular items in financial statements from one period to the next. If the comparison of a given type of revenue or expense for two successive years shows substantial change, further investigation to ascertain the cause of the change is necessary. The term "compare" may also be used by the auditor to mean ascertaining the agreement or lack of agreement between a journal entry and the corresponding entry in a ledger account, or between such related documents as a purchase order and an invoice.

Confirm—the process of proving the authenticity and accuracy of an account balance or entry by direct written communication with the debtor, creditor, or other party to the transaction. Obtaining proof from a source outside the client's records is thus a basic element of confirmation. It is standard practice to confirm bank balances by direct correspondence with the bank, and to confirm accounts receivable by direct correspondence with customers. The letters or forms sent to outsiders for this purpose are called *confirmation requests.*

Examine—to review critically or to investigate. An "examination of the financial statements" has the same meaning as an "audit of the financial statements."

Extend—to compute by multiplication. To "extend" the client's physical inventory listing is to multiply the quantity in units by the cost per unit. The resultant product is the "extension."

Footing (or down-footing)—the process of proving the totals of vertical columns of figures; *cross-footing* means the proving of totals of figures appearing in horizontal rows. By footing and cross-footing schedules and records the auditor derives positive assurance of their arithmetical accuracy.

Inspect—a careful reading or point-by-point review of a document or record. Other terms frequently used by the auditor to convey the same or a similar meaning are "scrutinize" and "examine."

Reconcile—to establish agreement between two sets of independently maintained but related records. Thus, the ledger account for Cash in Bank is reconciled with the bank statement, and the home office record of shipments to a branch office is reconciled with the record of receipts maintained by the branch.

Test—to select and examine a representative sample from a population of similar items. If the sample is properly chosen, the results of this limited test should reveal the same characteristics as would be disclosed by an examination of the entire lot of items.

Trace—the process of following a transaction from one accounting record to another. The purchase of machinery, for example, might be verified by tracing the transaction from the voucher register to the cheque register.

Verify—to prove the validity and accuracy of records or to establish the existence and ownership of assets. Verification of plant and equipment, for example, might include analysis of ledger accounts, proof of footings, tracing of postings from journals, examination of documents authorizing acquisitions and retirements, and physical observation of the assets.

Voucher—a term used to describe any document supporting a transaction. Examples are petty cash receipts, receiving memoranda, and paid cheques.

Vouching—establishing the accuracy and authenticity of entries in ledger accounts or other records by examining such supporting evidence of the transactions as invoices, paid cheques, and other original papers.

KEY TERMS INTRODUCED OR EMPHASIZED IN CHAPTER 4

(Note: The preceding section of this chapter contains definitions of specific audit terminology which are not repeated in this glossary.)

audit plan   A broad overview of an audit engagement prepared in the planning stages of the engagement. Audit plans usually include such matters as the objectives of the engagement, nature of the work to be done, a time schedule for major audit work and completion of the engagement, and staffing requirements.

audit program   A detailed listing and explanation of the specific audit procedures to be performed in the course of an audit engagement. Audit programs provide a basis for assigning and scheduling audit work and for determining what work remains to be done. Audit programs are specially tailored to each engagement.

audit trail   A "trail" of evidence linking individual transactions to the summary totals in the financial statements. In a manual accounting system, this trail consists of source documents, journal entries, and ledger entries.

compliance tests   Audit procedures designed to provide reasonable assurance that prescribed control procedures within the client's system are (1) in use and (2) operating as planned.

engagement letter   A formal letter sent by the auditors to the client at the beginning of an engagement summarizing the nature of the engagement, any limitations on the scope of audit work, work to be done by the client's staff, and the basis for the audit fee. The purpose of engagement letters is to avoid misunderstandings, and they are essential on non-audit engagements as well as audits.

interim period   The period under audit prior to the balance sheet date. Many audit procedures can be performed during the interim period to facilitate early issuance of the audit report.

internal control letter   A report to management containing the auditors' recommendations for correcting any deficiencies disclosed by the auditors' study and evaluation of internal control. In addition to providing management with useful information, an internal control letter may also help limit the auditors' liability in the event a control weakness subsequently results in a loss sustained by the client.

last day of field work   The last day on which auditing procedures are performed. This is also the date used in the audit report.

management advisory services **(MAS)**   A department within many CA firms which offers a wide range of consulting services to clients. In addition to accountants, the staff of a management advisory department often includes industrial engineers, statisticians, market analysts, and numerous other specialists.

predecessor auditors   The CA firm which formerly served as auditor but has resigned from the engagement or has been notified that its services have been terminated.

pool system   A system adopted within a public accounting firm which regards the firm's entire professional staff as one large group from which the required personnel for each audit engagement is drawn.

professional corporation   A form of organization for professional practices which is now permitted. Professional corporations enable practitioners to obtain the tax benefits of incorporation. All shareholders and directors of a professional corporation must be licensed practitioners of the profession, and the corporation must carry adequate amounts of professional liability insurance.

staff system   A system adopted within a public accounting firm which organizes the firm's entire professional staff into specific groups; each group is responsible for a number of clients and reports to a partner or partners.

substantive tests   Tests of account balances and transactions designed to detect any material errors in the financial statements. The nature, timing, and extent of substantive testing is determined by the auditors' study and evaluation of the client's system of internal control.

successor auditor   An auditor who has accepted an engagement or who has been invited to make a proposal for an engagement to replace the CA firm which formerly served as auditors.

time budget   An estimate of the time required to perform each step in the audit program.

GROUP I
REVIEW QUESTIONS

4–1. How does a professional corporation differ from the traditional corporation?

4–2. Describe the various levels or grades of accounting personnel in a large public accounting firm.

4–3. Distinguish between the responsibilities of a senior auditor and a staff assistant.

4–4. List three of the more important responsibilities of a partner in a public accounting firm.

4–5. What are "management advisory services"?

4–6. Describe the activities of a professional development department in a large public accounting firm.

4–7. In recent years the work of public accounting firms has tended to be spread more uniformly over the year rather than being heavily concentrated in a few months. What are the principal reasons for this change?

4–8. List four types of court cases in which the CA may serve as an expert witness.

4–9. What information should a CA firm seek in its investigation of a prospective client?

4–10. What topics should be discussed in a preliminary meeting with a prospective audit client?

4–11. Are auditors justified in relying upon the accuracy of working papers prepared for them by employees of the client?

4–12. State the purpose and nature of an engagement letter.

4–13. Define and differentiate between an *audit plan* and an *audit program.*

4–14. Should a separate audit program be prepared for each audit engagement, or can a standard program be used for most engagements?

4–15. "An audit program is desirable when new staff members are assigned to an engagement, but an experienced auditor should be able to conduct an examination without reference to an audit program." Do you agree? Discuss.

4–16. Suggest some factors which might cause an audit engagement to exceed the original time estimate. Would the extra time be charged to the client?

4–17. The following statements illustrate incorrect use of auditing terms. You are to substitute the proper terms for the italicized words.
  a. We *checked* the cash on hand.
  b. We *analyzed* the bank statement with the ledger balance for Cash in Bank.
  c. We *confirmed* the ledger account for Miscellaneous Expense by classifying and reviewing the various kinds of debit and credit entries in the account.
  d. We *vouched* the accounts receivable by direct written communication with customers.
  e. We *reconciled* the minutes of directors' meetings for the entire period under audit.

GROUP II
QUESTIONS REQUIRING ANALYSIS

4–18. In a discussion between Peters and Ferrel, two auditing students, Peters made the following statement:
  "A CA is a professional person who is providing an independent expert opinion on the fairness of financial statements. To maintain an attitude of mental independence and objectivity in all phases of his audit work, it is advisable that he not fraternize with client personnel. He should be courteous but reserved and dignified at all times. If he indulges in social contacts with clients outside of business hours, this will make it more difficult for him to be firm and objective if he finds evidence of fraud or of unsound accounting practices."
  Ferrel replied as follows:

"You are 50 years behind the times, Peters. An auditor and a client are both human beings. The auditor needs the cooperation of the client to do a good job; he's much more likely to get cooperation if he's relaxed and friendly rather than being cold and impersonal. Having a few beers or going to a football game with a client won't keep the CA from being independent. It will make the working relationship a lot more comfortable, and will probably cause the client to recommend the CA to other business people who need auditing services. In other words, the approach you're recommending should be called 'How to Avoid Friends and Alienate Clients.' I will admit, though, that with so many women entering public accounting and other women holding executive positions in business, a few complications may arise when auditor-client relations get pretty relaxed."

Evaluate the opposing views expressed by Peters and Ferrel.

4–19. Should a CA accept a request to serve as an expert witness for the plaintiff in a case involving another CA as defendant? Explain.

4–20. Arthur Samuels, CA, agreed to perform an audit of a new client engaged in the manufacture of power tools. After some preliminary discussion of the purposes of the audit and the basis for determination of the audit fee, Samuels asked to be taken on a comprehensive guided tour of the client's plant facilities. Explain specific ways that the knowledge gained by Samuels during the plant tour may help in planning and conducting the audit.

4–21. How can a CA make use of the preceding year's audit working papers in a recurring examination? (AICPA, adapted)

4–22. The audit plan, the audit program, and the time budget are three important working papers prepared early in an audit. What functions do these working papers serve in the auditor's compliance with generally accepted auditing standards? Discuss.

4–23. Henry Bailey, CA, is planning the audit of The Neighbourhood Store, a local grocery co-operative. Because The Neighbourhood Store is a small business operated entirely by part-time volunteer personnel, internal controls are weak. Bailey has decided that he will not be able to rely on internal control to restrict audit procedures in any area. Under these circumstances, may Bailey omit study and evaluation of the system of internal control in this engagement?

4–24. Ann Knox, president of Knox Ltd., is a close friend of a client of yours. In response to a strong recommendation of your audit work by her friend, Ann Knox has retained you to make an audit of Knox Ltd.'s financial statements. Although you have had extensive auditing experience, you have not previously audited a company in the same line of business as Knox Ltd.

Ann Knox informs you that she would like to have an estimate of the cost of the audit. List all the steps you would take in order to have an adequate basis for providing an estimate of the audit fee for the Knox Ltd. engagement. (AICPA, adapted)

4–25.   Select the best answer for each of the following. Explain the reasons for your selection.

  a.   One step in the audit process involves preparing a written description of the client's system of internal control. The next step should be:

  (1)   Determine the extent of audit work necessary to complete the audit.

  (2)   Gather enough evidence to determine if the system of internal control is functioning as described.

  (3)   Write a letter to management describing the weaknesses in the system of internal control.

  (4)   Form a final judgment on the effectiveness of internal control.

  b.   Which of the following portions of an audit may *not* be completed prior to the balance sheet date?

  (1)   Compliance testing.

  (2)   Issuance of a management or internal control letter.

  (3)   Substantive testing.

  (4)   Evaluation of the system of internal control.

  c.   A CA firm conducting its first examination of TDX, Inc., is considering the propriety of reducing its work by consulting with the predecessor auditor and reviewing the predecessor's working papers. This procedure is:

  (1)   Acceptable, providing the client consents.

  (2)   Unacceptable because of the confidential nature of the predecessor auditor's working papers.

  (3)   An acceptable substitute for the new auditors conducting a study and evaluation of internal control.

  (4)   Unacceptable because the CA firm should bring an independent viewpoint to a new engagement. (AICPA, adapted)

GROUP III
PROBLEMS

4–26.   The president of R Ltd. has just telephoned CA to ask if CA would "do an audit of the company." The president explained that R Ltd. had applied for a substantial bank loan and had been informed that the bank would require audited financial statements of the company. CA's name had been selected by the president from a list of local CA firms supplied by the bank.

  The president indicated that the company had never had an audit and that he was not sure what the audit would involve and what benefits would result from it. He asked CA to come to the company's offices to discuss the terms and arrangements for the engagement with him and other officers of the company.

  Required:

  a.   CA intends to explain carefully to the officers of R Ltd. the extent and limits of the responsibilities he would assume if he accepted the audit engagement. What points would he make?

b. What other matters would CA want to discuss at the meeting? (CICA)

4–27. CA was recently appointed auditor of W Ltd., a public company. He had been approached by the audit committee of the board of directors and had communicated with the company's previous auditor before indicating that he would be prepared to accept the appointment. He attended the shareholders' meeting at which he was appointed but has not yet visited the company's offices.

Required:

List the matters that CA should attend to between the time of his appointment and the commencement of his detailed audit work in order to plan an effective audit of W Ltd. (CICA)

4–28. You are invited by John Bray, the president of Cheviot Ltd., to discuss with him the possibility of your conducting an audit of the company. The corporation is a small, closely held manufacturing organization which appears to be expanding. No previous audit has been made by independent public accountants. Your discussions with Bray include a review of the recent monthly financial statements, inspection of the accounting records, and review of policies with the chief accountant. You also are taken on a guided tour of the plant by the president. He then makes the following statement:

"Before making definite arrangements for an audit, I would like to know about how long it will take and about how much it will cost. I want quality work and expect to pay a fair price, but since this is our first experience with independent auditors, I would like a full explanation as to how the cost of the audit is determined. Will you please send me a memorandum covering these points?"

Write the memorandum requested by John Bray.

4–29. McKay Company found its sales rising rapidly after the opening of a large military installation in its territory. To finance the increase in accounts receivable and the larger inventory required by the increased volume of sales, the company decided for the first time in its history to seek a bank loan. The president of the local bank informed McKay Company that an audit by a CA would be a necessary prerequisite to approval of the loan application. Jill McKay, sole proprietor of the business, engaged the newly formed CA firm of Marshall and Wills to conduct the audit and provide the report requested by the bank. McKay Company had not previously been audited.

From the beginning of the audit engagement, nothing seemed to go well. Robert Corning, the staff accountant sent out by Marshall and Wills to begin the work, found that the accounting records were not up to date and not in balance. He worked for a week assisting the McKay Company accountant to get the accounting records in shape. The problem was not reported to the partners until the following week because Marshall was out of town and Wills was suddenly taken ill. In the meantime, the McKay accountant complained to Jill McKay that the auditor was impeding his work.

After the audit work was well under way during the second week, → no compliance
McKay refused to permit the auditor to confirm accounts receivable,
which were the largest current asset. She also stated that the pressure of
current business prevented interrupting operations for the taking of a
physical inventory. Corning protested that confirmation of accounts receivable and observation of a physical inventory were mandatory auditing procedures, but Jill McKay rejected this protest.

Upon his return to town Marshall was informed of the difficulties and
went immediately to McKay's office. He explained to McKay that the
omission of work on receivables and inventories would force the auditors to deny an opinion on the financial statements taken as a whole.
McKay became quite angry; she asserted that she could borrow the
money she needed from her mother-in-law and thereby eliminate any
need for bankers or auditors in her business. McKay ordered Marshall
and Corning off the premises and asserted that she would pay them
nothing. Marshall replied that he had the McKay Company general
ledger and other accounting records in his own office, and that he would
not return them until he received payment in full for all time expended,
at the firm's regular per diem rates for Corning plus a charge for his
own time.

Evaluate the actions taken by Marshall and Wills in this case and
advise on the action to be taken at this point.

4–30. Valley Finance Company opened four personal loan offices in neighbouring cities on January 2. Small cash loans are made to borrowers who
repay the principal with interest in monthly installments over a period
not exceeding two years. Ralph Norris, president of the company, uses
one of the offices as a central office and visits the other offices periodically for supervision and internal auditing purposes.

Required:

Assume that you agreed to examine Valley Finance Company's financial statements for the year ended December 31. No scope limitations
were imposed.

a. How would you determine the scope necessary to complete your
examination satisfactorily? Discuss.

b. Would you be responsible for the discovery of fraud in this examination? Discuss. (AICPA, adapted)

4–31. Fredrika Taubitz, an experienced CA, was asked by the federal government to serve as an expert witness in a case aimed at assessing additional income tax upon the PBM Corporation Ltd.

Taubitz had written several articles on inventory pricing. The publication of these articles in professional journals had been influential in
causing the government to request her services in this case. Also considered important was the fact that Taubitz's prior experience had included several years as a member of the accounting faculty in a large
university. Since Taubitz had never served as an expert witness, she
had some doubts as to whether she should accept the engagement.

However, she decided to meet with the attorneys for the government and discuss the issues.

The conference indicated that the PBM Corporation Ltd., a manufacturer of machinery and electronic equipment, had valued its inventories of work in process and finished goods on the basis of "prime costs" only. These "prime costs" included only raw materials and direct labour. All overhead had been deducted from revenue as incurred. The government's view was that this treatment violated generally accepted accounting principles and caused an undervaluation of inventories and an understatement of net income. The point was stressed that Taubitz was not being asked to interpret tax laws but to express an expert opinion on generally accepted accounting principles with reference to inventory pricing. After some discussion, Taubitz agreed to serve as an expert witness at the per diem rate she normally charged for consulting services. This rate was also applicable to time spent in preparing for her court appearance.

Prior to her appearance on the witness stand, Taubitz spent most of a day in court while the taxpayer presented arguments supporting his position. Another CA known to Taubitz testified that he had designed PBM Corporation Ltd.'s accounting system and that the omission of overhead from inventories was justified because of rapid change in product design, which made obsolescence of inventories a continuing problem. A well-known bank official also appeared as a defense witness. He testified that the bank made large loans to PBM Corporation Ltd. and regarded its financial statements as of excellent quality. He particularly approved the valuation of inventories at "prime cost" only and stated he would prefer to see all the bank's customers follow this practice.

When Taubitz was called to the witness stand, her qualifications as an expert were established without difficulty. In the direct examination which followed, she was asked her opinion on a hypothetical question concerning the exclusion of factory overhead as part of inventory cost. Taubitz replied that the exclusion of all overhead from inventory cost was not an acceptable accounting method. She stressed the point that the determination of net income required the matching of costs and revenue, and that the cost of producing a manufactured article necessarily included a share of overhead as well as material and direct labour cost.

During cross-examination, the attorney for the defendant asked Taubitz the following questions:

a. Have you discussed the issues in this case with anyone prior to your appearance in court?

b. Does accounting literature recognize the existence of a variety of methods for computing inventory costs?

c. In a business in which product obsolescence is a major threat, would you favour the valuation of inventories in a manner that would lead to a maximum or minimum valuation?

d. Do you think a banker who daily makes loans on the basis of financial statements presented in support of loan applications is well qualified to recognize good methods of financial reporting?

e. If the production of a factory or a section thereof is shut down for a period of several months, would you include the continuing overhead expense as a part of inventory costs?

Required:

Draft the answers you think Taubitz should give to each of the five questions. Give full explanations of the reasons underlying your answer. In choosing your language bear in mind that the judge is not a professional accountant. Try to answer the questions in a manner that will not destroy or weaken the value of the testimony previously given by Taubitz.

5

Internal control

Our consideration of internal control has three major objectives: first, to explain the meaning and significance of internal control; second, to outline the steps required to create and maintain strong internal control; and third, to show how auditors go about their study and evaluation of internal control. No attempt is made in this chapter to present in detail the internal control procedures applicable to particular kinds of assets or to particular phases of operations, such as purchases or sales. Detailed information along these lines will be found in succeeding chapters as each phase of the auditors' examination is presented.

The meaning of internal control

Many people interpret the term *internal control* to mean the steps taken by a business to prevent employee fraud. Actually, such measures are rather a small part of internal control. The *CICA Handbook* defines internal control as follows:

> Internal control comprises the plan of organization and all the coordinate systems established by the management of an enterprise to assist in achieving management's objective of ensuring, as far as practical, the orderly and efficient conduct of its business, including the safeguarding of assets, the reliability of accounting records and the timely preparation of reliable financial information.[1]

Thus, the basic purpose of internal control is to *promote the efficient operation of an organization.* More specifically, internal control is designed to (1) safeguard assets from waste, fraud, and inefficient use; (2)

---

[1] CICA, *CICA Handbook* (Toronto), p. 5303.

promote accuracy and reliability in the accounting records and timely preparation of reliable financial information; (3) encourage and measure compliance with company policies; and (4) evaluate the efficiency of operations. In short, internal control consists of all measures taken to provide management with assurance that everything is functioning as it should.

Internal control extends beyond the accounting and financial functions; its scope is company-wide and touches all activities of the organization. It includes the methods by which top management delegates authority and assigns responsibility for such functions as selling, purchasing, accounting, and production. Internal control also includes the program for preparing, verifying, and distributing to various levels of supervision those current reports and analyses which enable executives to maintain control over the variety of activities and functions which constitute a large corporate enterprise. The use of budgetary techniques, production standards, inspection laboratories, time and motion studies, and employee training programs involve engineers and many other technicians far removed from accounting and financial activities; yet all of these devices are part of the mechanism now conceived of as a system of internal control.

This broad, sweeping concept of internal control is most significant when viewed against the backdrop of a large nation-wide industrial organization, for internal control has developed into a technique of vital importance in enabling management of large complex enterprises to function efficiently. Since internal control has attained greatest significance in large-scale business organizations, the greater part of the discussion in this chapter is presented in terms of the large corporation. A separate section is presented at the end of the chapter, however, dealing with the problem of achieving internal control in a small business.

Internal accounting controls versus internal administrative controls and business policies

Auditors are primarily interested in internal controls of an accounting nature—those controls which bear directly upon the dependability of the accounting records and the financial statements. For example, preparation of monthly bank reconciliations by an employee not authorized to issue cheques or handle cash is an *internal accounting control* which increases the probability that cash transactions are presented fairly in the accounting records and financial statements.

Some internal controls have no bearing on the financial statements and consequently are not of direct interest to the independent public accountant. Controls of this category are often referred to as *internal administrative controls.* Management is interested in maintaining strong internal control over factory operations and sales activities as well as over accounting and financial functions. Accordingly, management will establish administrative controls to provide operational efficiency and adherence to prescribed policies in all departments of the organization.

An example of an internal control device of an administrative nature is a written directive to the personnel department of a company establishing specific guidelines as to race and ethnic background to be observed in the selection of new employees. Important though such a control device may be to the successful operation of the company, it is not directly related to the dependability of the financial statements.

In *Statement on Auditing Standards No. 1,* the AICPA provided the following definitions to assist in the distinction between accounting and administrative internal control:

> *Administrative control* includes, but is not limited to, the plan of organization and the procedures and records that are concerned with the decision processes leading to management's authorization of transactions. Such authorization is a management function directly associated with the responsibility for achieving the objectives of the organization and is the starting point for establishing accounting control of transactions.
>
> *Accounting control* comprises the plan of organization and the procedures and records that are concerned with the safeguarding of assets and the reliability of financial records and consequently are designed to provide reasonable assurance that:
>
> a.   Transactions are executed in accordance with management's general or specific authorization.
>
> b.   Transactions are recorded as necessary (1) to permit preparation of financial statements in conformity with generally accepted accounting principles or any other criteria applicable to such statements and (2) to maintain accountability for assets.
>
> c.   Access to assets is permitted only in accordance with management's authorization.
>
> d.   The recorded accountability for assets is compared with the existing assets at reasonable intervals and appropriate action is taken with respect to any differences.

Both administrative and accounting controls are derived from **business policies** established by management; they are the means by which business policies are satisfactorily accomplished. Thus, auditors should be aware of these policies and review them in terms of their impact on internal controls. The review of internal controls of a purely administrative nature does not ordinarily fall within the responsibility of the independent auditors, whose objective is to express an opinion on the fairness of financial statements. However, the auditors' study and evaluation of internal control will always include review and testing of major accounting controls.

Public accounting firms often perform management advisory services for their clients in addition to making audits. In rendering management advisory services, public accountants will frequently evaluate internal administrative controls and suggest modifications therein; such work, however, is not necessary to the expression of an opinion as to the fairness of financial statements. The internal auditing staff in most large corporations *does* review internal administrative controls as well as those in the accounting areas. Internal auditing will be considered in another section of this chapter.

The need and objectives for internal control

The long-run trend for corporations to evolve into organizations of gigantic size and scope, including a great variety of specialized technical operations and numbering employees in tens of thousands, has made it impossible for corporate executives to exercise personal, first-hand supervision of operations. No longer able to rely upon personal observation as a means of appraising operating results and financial position, the corporate executive has, of necessity, come to depend upon a stream of accounting and statistical reports. These reports summarize current happenings and conditions throughout the enterprise; the units of measurement employed are not only dollars but also labour-hours, material weights, customer calls, employee terminations, and a host of other denominators.

The information carried by this stream of reports enables management to control and direct the enterprise. It keeps management informed as to whether company policy is being carried out, whether governmental regulations are being observed, and whether the financial position is sound, operations profitable, and interdepartmental relations harmonious.

Business decisions of almost every kind are based at least in part on accounting data. These decisions range from such minor matters as authorizing overtime work or purchasing office supplies to such major issues as a shift from one product to another or making a choice between leasing or buying a new plant. Internal control provides reasonable assurance to management of the dependability of the accounting data used in making these decisions.

Decisions made by management become company policy. To be effective, this policy must be communicated throughout the company and consistently followed. Internal control aids in securing compliance with company policy. Management also has a direct responsibility of maintaining accounting records and producing financial statements which are adequate and reliable. Internal control provides reasonable assurance that this responsibility is being met.

Thus, management's objectives for internal control are to (1) obtain a reasonable assurance that managerial policies are effectively and efficiently complied with, and (2) ensure that the business is conducted in an orderly and efficient manner. To accomplish these objectives management needs an adequate and reliable system of internal control, for which management bears the primary and sole responsibility.

To the external auditors, internal control is of equal importance. The quality of the internal controls in force, more than any other factor, determines the pattern of their examination. Therefore, both external auditors and management need a system of internal control to perform their respective functions. However, the auditors' objective for internal control is not the same as management's. The external auditors' objective in their study and evaluation of the system of internal control is to determine the nature, extent, and timing of the audit work necessary to permit them to express an opinion as to the fairness of the financial statements.[2]

MEANS OF ACHIEVING INTERNAL ACCOUNTING CONTROL

Systems of internal control vary significantly from one organization to the next. The specific control features in any system depend upon such factors as size, organizational structure, nature of operations, and objectives of the organization for which the system was designed. Yet, certain factors are essential to satisfactory internal control in almost any large-scale organization. These factors include a logical plan of organization, a well-designed accounting structure, an internal audit function, and the quality and training of personnel.[3]

Plan of organization

An *organization plan* refers to the division of authority, responsibilities, and duties among members of an organization. A well-designed organization plan should provide assurance that transactions are executed in conformity with company policies, enhance the efficiency of operations, safeguard assets, and promote the reliability of accounting data. These objectives may be achieved in large part through adequate separation of responsibilities for (1) initiation or approval of transactions, (2) custody of assets, and (3) record keeping.

Internal control over transactions. A fundamental concept of accounting control is that *no one person or department should handle all aspects of a transaction from beginning to end.* If management is to direct the

---

[2] For a more detailed discussion on management's and auditors' objectives for internal control, see sec. 5205.01–.12 and sec. 5210.01–.11 of the *CICA Handbook.*

[3] These factors encompass the seven basic components of internal control systems discussed in the *CICA Handbook,* sec. 5205.13–26. They are (1) plan of organization, (2) recording of transactions, (3) personnel, (4) authorizations, (5) limitation of access to assets, (6) comparison of accounting records with assets, and (7) management supervision.

activities of a business according to plan, every transaction should involve four steps; it should be *authorized, approved, executed,* and *recorded.* Accounting control will be enhanced if each of these steps is performed by relatively independent employees or departments. No single department will then be in a position to complete a transaction which has not been reviewed, approved, and recorded by other departments.

A credit sales transaction may be used to illustrate an appropriate division of responsibilities. Top management of a company may authorize the sale of merchandise at specified credit terms to customers who meet certain criteria. Orders from customers are received in the sales department and sent to the credit department for approval. The credit department reviews the transaction to ascertain that the extension of credit and terms of sale are in compliance with company policies. Once the sale is approved, the shipping department executes the transaction by obtaining the merchandise from the inventory stores department and shipping it to the customer. The accounting department uses copies of the documentation created by the sales, credit, and shipping departments as a basis for recording the transaction and billing the customer.

When responsibilities for authorizing, approving, executing, and recording transactions are separated in this manner, no one department can initiate and complete an unauthorized transaction. The possibility of unrecorded transactions is greatly reduced because of the documentation which must be prepared as information concerning the transaction moves from one department to another. (Sequential numbering of this documentation will assist the accounting department in determining that all transactions have been accounted for.) Also, division of responsibilities permits specialization of labour, which should contribute to the overall efficiency of operations.

Accountability for assets. A traditional step in achieving internal accounting control is separation of the accounting function from custody of related assets. When the accounting and custodial departments are relatively independent, the work of each department serves to verify the accuracy of the work of the other. Periodic comparisons should be made of accounting records and the physical assets on hand. Investigation as to the cause of any discrepancies will uncover weaknesses either in procedures for safeguarding assets or in maintaining the related accounting records. If the accounting records were not independent of the custodial department, the records could be manipulated to conceal waste, loss, or theft of the related assets.

ILLUSTRATIVE CASE. A manufacturer of golf clubs operated a large storeroom containing thousands of sets of golf clubs ready for shipment. Detailed perpetual inventory records were maintained by the employees in charge of the storeroom. A shortage of several sets of clubs developed as a result of theft by another employee who had acquired an unauthorized key to the storeroom. The employee responsible for the storeroom discovered the discrepancy between the clubs in stock and the quantities of clubs as shown by the records. Fearing criticism of his record keeping, he changed the inventory records to agree with the quantities on hand. The thefts continued, and large losses were sustained before the shortages were discovered. If the inventory records had been maintained by someone not responsible for physical custody of the merchandise, there would have been no incentive or opportunity to conceal a shortage by falsifying the records. The internal control principle involved is a simple one; separate the function of record keeping from that of custody of assets, and have periodic verification of assets by an employee not connected with record keeping or asset custody.

Figure 5–1 illustrates the use of an independently maintained record to establish accountability for assets. It is not essential that all three parties in the diagram (**A, B,** and **C**) be employees of the company; one or more may be an outside party or a mechanical device. For example, if **A** is a bank with custody of cash on deposit, **B** would be the company employees maintaining records of cash receipts and disbursements, and **C** might be a computer program which performs periodic bank reconciliations. Or, if **A** is a salesclerk with custody of cash receipts from sales, **B** could be a cash register with a locked-in tape, and **C** could be the central cashier. Regardless of the nature of the parties involved, the principle remains the same: accounting records should be maintained independently of custody of the related assets and periodically should be compared to asset quantities on hand.

Efficiency of operations. An effective organization plan should enhance the efficiency of operations as well as contribute to internal accounting control. When two or more departments participate in every transaction, the work of one department is reviewed by another. Also, each

FIGURE 5–1
Establishing accountability for assets

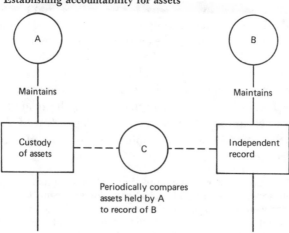

department has an incentive to demand efficient performance from the others.

A typical purchase transaction illustrates how good organizational structure enhances both internal control and the efficiency of operations. If the purchasing department fails to place a purchase order promptly upon receipt of a purchase requisition from the material stores department, the latter department may find itself without materials required by production departments. The material stores department, therefore, has an incentive to follow up purchase requisitions and to demand prompt action by the purchasing agent. If the purchasing department ordered an excessive or insufficient quantity, the responsibility for the error will be pinned down by reference to the purchase requisition, the purchase order, and the receiving report, each of which is prepared by an independent department.

Errors made by the receiving department in counting goods received will normally be brought to light by the accounting department when it compares the receiving report with the vendor's invoice and the purchase order. If defective materials are accepted by the receiving department, responsibility will be placed on the negligent department by personnel of the storekeeping or production departments, which must utilize the materials in question.

On the other hand, if the various functional activities are not segregated by independent departments and all aspects of a purchase transaction are handled by employees reporting to the purchasing agent, then top management has no convenient means of informing itself about the efficiency of the purchasing activities. Duplication of orders, delays in shipment, acceptance of defective goods, and secret rebates (kick backs) to buyers could all be covered up. The possibilities of fraud would be greatly increased if a single department head were given the authority to place an order, receive the goods, approve the invoice for payment, and record the transaction. When these functions are assigned to independent departments, fraud becomes difficult, if not impossible, without the collusion of large numbers of key personnel.

Organizational independence of departments.   Internal control is achieved largely through the organizational independence of accounting, operating, and custodial departments. This degree of independence is usually obtained by having designated department heads who are evaluated on the basis of the performance of their respective departments. The top executives of the major departments should be of equal rank and should report directly to the president or to an executive vice president. The partial organization chart in Figure 5–2 illustrates such an arrangement. If, for example, the controller were a line subordinate to the vice president of production, the organizational independence of the accounting department would be greatly impaired.

FIGURE 5–2
Partial organization chart

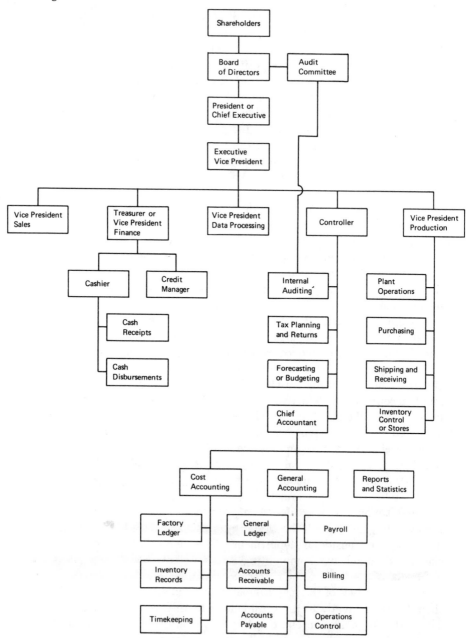

ILLUSTRATIVE CASE. During an examination of the Foster Company, the auditors' study of organizational lines of authority and their use of an internal control questionnaire disclosed that the receiving department personnel were under the direction of the purchasing agent. Accounts payable department employees had also been instructed to accept informal memoranda from the purchasing agent as evidence of receipt of merchandise and propriety of invoices.

Because of this deficiency in internal control, the auditors made a very thorough examination of purchase invoices and came across a number of large December invoices from one supplier bearing the notation: "Subject to adjustment at time of delivery of merchandise." Investigation of these transactions disclosed that the merchandise had not yet been delivered, but the invoices had been paid. The purchasing agent explained that he had requested the advance billing in an effort to reduce taxable income for the year under audit, during which profits had been higher than usual. Further investigation revealed that the purchasing agent held a substantial personal interest in the supplier making the advance billings, and that his actions had not been authorized by the management of the client company.

Responsibilities of finance and accounting departments. Finance and accounting are the two departments most directly involved in the financial affairs of a business enterprise. The division of responsibilities between these departments illustrates the separation of the accounting function from operations and also from the custody of assets. Under the direction of the *treasurer,* the finance department is responsible for financial operations and custody of liquid assets. Activities of this department include planning future cash requirements, establishing customer credit policies, and arranging to meet the short- and long-term financing needs of the business. In addition, the finance department has custody of bank accounts and other liquid assets, invests idle cash, handles cash receipts, and makes cash disbursements. In short, it is the finance department which *conducts* financial activities.

The accounting department, under the authority of the *controller,* is responsible for all accounting functions and the design and implementation of internal control. With respect to financial activity, the accounting department *records* financial transactions but does not handle financial assets. Accounting records establish *accountability* over assets, as well as provide the information necessary for financial reports, tax returns, and daily operating decisions. With respect to internal control, the accounting department maintains the independent records with which quantities of assets and operating results are compared. Often, this reconciliation function is performed by the operations control group or some other subdepartment within accounting.

Many of the subdepartments often found within accounting are illustrated in Figure 5–2. It is important for many of these subdepartments to be relatively independent of one another. For example, if the operations control group reconciles assets on hand to the accounting records, it is essential that the operations control personnel not maintain those records. Therefore, each subdepartment shown in the organization chart usually has its own employees and supervisor.

The accounting structure

To achieve internal control through separation of duties, the accounting system must be able to measure the performance and efficiency of the individual organizational units. An accounting system with this capability should include:

1. Adequate internal documentation to focus responsibility.
2. A chart of accounts classified in accordance with the responsibilities of individual supervisors and key employees.
3. A manual of accounting policies and procedures, and flowcharts depicting the established methods of processing transactions.
4. A financial forecast consisting of a detailed forecast of operations with provision for prompt reporting and analysis of variations between actual performance and budgetary standards.
5. A manufacturing cost accounting system, if appropriate to the industry.

Adequate documentation.   A system of well-designed forms and documents is necessary to create a record of the activities of all departments. For example, how is the accounting department notified when a credit sale takes place? Usually notification is through a sales ticket prepared by the salesclerk when the sale occurs. Without such documentation, there would be virtually no record or control over the activities of the operating departments. Internally created documents are also used to create accountability for assets transferred from one department to another. Copies of these documents provide a "trail" of evidence that focuses responsibility for any shortages which may develop as the assets move from department to department.

The reliability of internally created documents is increased if two parties with opposing interests participate in preparation of the document. For example, when the stores department releases materials to production, a *production order* is initialed by employees of each department. The stores department has an incentive to ascertain that quantities shown on the production order are not *understated;* otherwise, the stores department will be held responsible for goods no longer on hand. The production department, on the other hand, has an incentive to see that materials charged to its operations are not *overstated.*

Serial numbering of documents.   An internal control device of wide applicability is the use of serial numbers on documents. Serial numbers provide control over the number of documents issued. Cheques, tickets, sales invoices, purchase orders, share certificates, and many other business papers can be controlled in this manner. For some documents, such as cheques, it may be desirable to account for every number of the series by a monthly or weekly inspection of the documents issued. For other situations, as in the case of serially numbered admission tickets, control may be achieved by noting the last serial number issued each day, and thereby computing the total value of tickets issued during the day. Adequate safekeeping and numerical control should be maintained at all times for unissued prenumbered documents.

Chart of accounts.   A chart of accounts is a classified listing of all accounts to be used, accompanied by a detailed description of the purpose and content of each. Some companies use both a chart of accounts and a text of accounts, the former being limited to a classification of ledger accounts and the latter consisting of explanatory material describing the transactions properly to be charged and credited to each account.

How many accounts are needed? The number will depend upon the extent to which a company uses the accounts as a means of holding individuals responsible for custody of assets, for earning revenue, and for incurring expenses. In too many cases the classification of accounts is looked upon as a mere listing of the items to be separately enumerated in the financial statements. A better approach is to view the chart of accounts as an internal control device consisting of separate accounts for recording the responsibilities of individual supervisors and employees.

For example, a petty cash fund should be in the custody of a single employee; a separate account for such a fund is required if the accounts are to measure individual responsibility. The principle of relating accounts and personal responsibility is by no means limited to the custody of assets; it is equally applicable to revenue and expense control. For every manager charged with obtaining revenue or incurring expense, separate revenue and expense accounts should be established to permit a clear measurement of the manager's performance. Just as machine operators may be held responsible for units of output, so should the department managers be held to account for the performance of the function entrusted to them.

Use of a chart of accounts which classifies operating results by responsible decision makers is often termed *responsibility accounting.* A prerequisite to responsibility accounting is adequate internal documentation to focus responsibility for operating results. Responsibility accounting is hindered by any vagueness or inconsistency in the plan of organization and lines of responsibility. It is commonly found that for a given type of expense, such as repair, several individuals have authority to make commitments; hence no one individual can be held responsible for excessive expenditures in this direction. Careful analysis of the chart of accounts and application of the test of clear segregation of individual responsibilities will often indicate a need of revision in lines of organizational responsibility. Even under the best of organization plans, certain expenses probably will not be clearly assignable to a single responsible individual. Obsolescence of plant and equipment, cost of performing work under product guarantees, and expenses associated with strikes or other industrial disputes are examples of such expenses. These expenses often result from policy decisions rather than from departmental operations and therefore should be segregated and clearly labeled.

Although classification of accounts along lines of individual responsibility is an essential step in achieving control of costs, it does not serve the purpose of providing management with cost figures for individual products. The techniques of cost accounting must be utilized for a reclassification, or distribution, of costs from the primary classification to a product basis.

Manual of accounting policies and procedures. Every business organization, large or small, has a body of established methods of initiating, recording, and summarizing transactions. These procedures should be stated in writing, and in the form of flowcharts in a loose-leaf manual, and they should be revised as the pattern of operating routines changes. If accounting procedures are clearly stated in writing, the policies set by management can be enforced efficiently and consistently. Uniform handling of like transactions is essential to the production of reliable accounting records and reports, and uniformity in the handling of transactions is possible only when definite patterns for processing routine transactions are made known to all employees.

Financial forecasts. A financial forecast for an enterprise is an estimate of the most probable financial position, results of operations, and changes in financial position for one or more future periods.[4] It establishes definite goals and thus provides management with a yardstick for evaluating actual performance. Forecasting is often associated with standard cost systems because both involve the setting of predetermined standards and the continuing analysis of variations between these standards and actual operating figures. Although most concerns which employ standard costs also have well-developed financial and operating forecasts, the use of forecasts is by no means limited to businesses which utilize standard costs. On the contrary, nearly all concerns make use of forecasts to some extent.

The simplest and most common application of forecasting is the cash forecast, in which the treasurer estimates, for perhaps a year in advance, the flow of cash receipts and disbursements classified by source of receipt and object of disbursement. The principal aim of the cash forecast is to ensure that sufficient funds are available at all times to meet maturing liabilities. In addition, the scheduling of anticipated receipts from all sources makes fraud involving the withholding of receipts more susceptible of detection. Similarly, the detailed planning of cash disbursements discourages the potential embezzler from any attempt to falsify the records of cash disbursements.

---

[4] AICPA, *Guidelines for Systems for the Preparation of Financial Forecasts* (New York, 1975), p. 3.

A more comprehensive forecasting program would include:

1. A sales forecast, consisting of estimated sales by product and territory, based on analysis of past sales performance, current trends of prices and business volume, and appraisal of new products, territories, and distribution methods.
2. A production forecast, specifying the quantities necessary to meet the sales forecast, and detailing the quantity and cost of material, labour, and manufacturing overhead for given levels of output.
3. A distribution cost forecast, consisting of estimates of costs of selling, advertising, delivery, credit and collection, and other expenses appropriate to the estimated sales volume, classified by product or territory, and as variable, semivariable, and fixed.
4. A plant and equipment forecast, consisting of estimates of amounts required for the acquisition of new equipment and the maintenance of presently owned equipment.
5. A cash forecast, including an estimate of cash receipts and disbursements, short-term investments, and borrowing and repayments.
6. An estimated income statement, balance sheet, and statement of changes in financial position for the period encompassed by the forecast.

The completed forecast is summarized by preparing estimated financial statements for the coming year, supported by detailed analyses for segments of the business such as territories, divisions, or branches. During the year, monthly income statements should be prepared comparing actual operating results with forecast figures. These statements should be accompanied by explanations of all significant variations between forecast and actual results, with a definite fixing of responsibility for such variances.

In brief, a forecast is a control device, involving the establishment of definite standards of performance throughout the business. Failure to attain these standards is promptly called to the attention of appropriate levels of management through variance reports.

Internal control through accounting techniques is most fully attained when a comprehensive forecasting program is combined with a classification of accounts that provides a separate account to record the commitments made by each individual responsible for initiating transactions.

Cost accounting system. Cost accounting systems have at least two separate basic objectives:

1. To provide information for management decision making, planning, and control over operations.
2. To develop historical data for determination of the inventory and cost of goods sold figures used in the balance sheet and income statement.

The information function of cost accounting provides reports to top management which will facilitate decisions on pricing of products, plant expansion, wage rates, and related issues. Reporting by the cost accountant also embraces reports to factory management on the details of operating performance, which should enable product supervisors to spot waste and inefficiency in the operations they direct. Cost data are most valuable for factory executives when the data are classified by operation, stressing individual responsibilities. For the use of sales executives and general management, reclassification of costs to a product basis is necessary.

Much remains to be accomplished in the establishment of cost standards for selling and administrative expenses. Progress toward more effective control in these areas appears to lie in the extension of budgetary techniques, the development of more effective denominators for measuring output, and a sharper distinction between fixed and variable items of expense.

Internal auditing—its relationship to internal control

Another basic component of strong internal control is an internal auditing staff. The job of internal auditors is to investigate and appraise the system of internal control and the efficiency with which the various units of the organization are carrying out their assigned functions. In a small concern, the owner or manager can give personal attention to each phase of operations and thus become aware of any failure to protect assets or any wastefulness in operating routines. In a large corporation, however, top management usually creates a large number of departments, divisions, or other organizational units, and assigns a manager to each unit. The managers of each unit are guided by policies established by top management, but they enjoy a considerable amount of freedom within the limits of these policy directives. This decentralization of authority to a great number of organizational units sets the stage for the internal auditors. It is their function to visit and appraise the problems and performance of every department in the company. As representatives of top management, the internal auditors are interested in determining whether each branch or department has a clear understanding of its assignment, whether it is adequately staffed, maintains good records, protects cash and inventories and other assets properly, cooperates harmoniously with other departments, and in general carries out effectively the function provided for in the overall plan and organization of the business.

Internal auditors are *not* responsible for performing routine control procedures, such as reconciling bank statements, balancing subsidiary ledgers, or verifying the mathematical accuracy of invoices. These functions are usually performed by a separate unit within the accounting department, such as the operations control group shown in Figure 5–2.

Internal auditors provide a higher level of internal control; they design and carry out audit procedures which test the efficiency of virtually all aspects of company operations.

Internal auditors contrasted with independent auditors. The independent auditors' objective is the expression of an opinion on the client's financial statements; the internal auditors' objective is not to verify financial statements but to aid management in achieving the most efficient administration of the business. To this end, they appraise the effectiveness of internal controls in various departments, branches, or other organizational units of the company. Internal auditors' work is not limited to accounting controls; they also monitor administrative controls and business policies.

The similarities between independent audits and internal auditing pertain to mechanics and techniques, not to objectives and end results. Both internal auditors and independent auditors examine accounting records and procedures and prepare working papers, but the reasons motivating the two lines of work and the end results obtained are entirely different.

For example, in the examination of accounts receivable, independent auditors are concerned primarily with establishing that the receivables fairly reflect the amount likely to be collected. Internal auditors are concerned with studying the system of billing to see whether it provides for accumulation of all the information necessary and ensures that all the company's customers are properly billed for goods or services delivered. They are interested in seeing that the credit system is operated so that charges in excess of credit limits are not permitted, and in the collection system to see that working capital invested in receivables is realized in cash as quickly as possible. They are also interested in the effect of credit policies—do the credit policies provide adequate safeguards without being too restrictive?

In companies which stress growth through acquisitions and mergers, the internal auditors may perform investigations of companies being considered for acquisition. In such an assignment, the role of the internal auditors is similar to that of an independent auditor. The investigation consists of gathering evidence to substantiate or disprove the other company's representations as to the collectibility of receivables, valuation of inventories, loss contingencies, volume of sales, trend of earnings, and related data in the financial statements.

Internal audit reports. The first draft of the internal auditors' report should be discussed in detail with the managers and key employees of the unit being investigated prior to issuance of the report. This review provides departmental personnel with an opportunity to draw attention to any points they consider to be inaccurate, and to suggest any additional matters which deserve to be considered. The quality of the report may thus be improved and better relations maintained between internal auditors and other company personnel. The internal audit report thus serves as a vehicle by which supervisors may secure the attention of top management to problems that have long been troubling them. When department heads are aware that they will be informed of the contents of the internal auditors' report before it is released, and will have an opportunity to present their views, they are sure to act in a more cooperative manner throughout the internal auditors' investigation of their departments.

The final version of the internal auditors' report will be transmitted to the member of top management in direct charge of the internal auditing function, and probably to the audit committee of the board of directors as well. After submitting the report, the internal auditors may later make another visit to the department investigated to determine the nature and extent of corrective actions taken in response to recommendations contained in the report.

Independence of internal auditors.   Since internal auditors are employees of the company they serve, they obviously cannot achieve the external auditors' independence in fact and in appearance. However, if internal auditors report directly to the audit committee of the board of directors, to the president, or other senior officer, they may achieve a greater degree of freedom, independence, and objectivity than if they report to an official of lesser rank in the organization.

Limitations of internal control

Internal control can do much to protect against fraud and assure the reliability of accounting data. Still, it is important to recognize the existence of inherent limitations in any system of internal control. Errors may be made in the performance of control procedures as a result of carelessness, misunderstanding of instructions, or other human factors. As dramatically illustrated in the Equity Funding management fraud, top management may circumvent internal control. Also, those control procedures which depend upon separation of duties may be circumvented by collusion among employees. Moreover, most controls tend to be directed at regularly recurring types of transactions. Besides, the efficiency of controls may vary with volume of transactions or changes of staff.

The extent of the internal controls adopted by a business is limited by cost considerations; to maintain a system of internal control so perfect as to make any fraud "impossible" would usually cost more than was warranted by the threat of loss from fraud. Particularly in a small business, it is often impracticable to separate completely the custody of assets from the function of record keeping. When a business has only a few employees, the opportunities for subdivision of duties are obviously somewhat limited. Despite these limitations, however, many actual defalcations could have been prevented or disclosed at an early stage if even the most simple and inexpensive of internal control practices had been followed.

Fidelity bonds

Strong internal control is not a guarantee against losses from dishonest employees. Neither is it possible to prevent fraud by emphasizing the selection of trustworthy employees. It is often the most trusted employees who engineer the biggest embezzlements. The fact that they are so highly trusted explains why they have access to cash, securities, and company records and are in a position which makes embezzlement possible.

Fidelity bonds are a form of insurance in which a bonding company agrees to reimburse an employer, within limits, for losses attributable to theft or embezzlement by bonded employees. Most employers require employees handling cash or other negotiable assets to be bonded. Individual fidelity bonds may be obtained by concerns with only a few employees; larger concerns may prefer to obtain a blanket fidelity bond covering many employees. Before issuing fidelity bonds, underwriters investigate thoroughly the past records of the employees to be bonded. This service offers added protection by preventing the employment of persons with dubious records in positions of trust. Bonding companies are much more likely to prosecute fraud cases vigorously than are employers; general awareness of this fact is another deterrent against dishonesty on the part of bonded employees.

Fidelity bonds are neither part of the system of internal control nor a substitute for internal control. If internal control is weak, losses may accumulate undiscovered until they exceed the fidelity coverage. Theft or defalcation must be discovered and the loss proved before recovery can be obtained from a bonding company. Moreover, inadequate internal control often causes other losses, as when management places reliance on inaccurate and misleading accounting data. In connection with their evaluation of internal control, auditors should give consideration to the fidelity bonds in force and may appropriately call the client's attention to any apparent inadequacies in fidelity insurance coverage.

To protect a business adequately from losses through embezzlement requires three things: (1) a strong system of internal control, (2) regular audits by independent public accountants, and (3) fidelity bonds protecting the company up to an agreed amount against loss from employee dishonesty.

THE AUDITORS' REVIEW OF INTERNAL CONTROL

The generally accepted auditing standards set forth by the CICA were presented in Chapter 1. The second standard of field work reads as follows:

There should be an appropriately organized study and evaluation of those internal controls on which the auditor subsequently relies in determining the nature, extent and timing of auditing procedures.

In formulating this standard, the CA recognized that it is not possible for auditors to verify all, or even a major portion, of the great number of transactions comprising a year's operations in a large enterprise. In order that auditors make the most effective and searching investigation possible within reasonable time limits, they must determine whether the internal control in force is such as to ensure the integrity of the financial statements. The decisions based on an analysis of internal control will govern the extent of substantive testing and will designate those areas which require most intensive examination.

Reliance by the auditors upon internal control

In expressing an opinion as to the fairness of financial statements, auditors rely upon (1) the effectiveness of internal control in preventing material errors in the accounting process, and (2) substantive tests to verify the amounts in the financial statements. In cases where internal accounting controls are strong, the auditors need rely less upon substantive testing. Conversely, where internal controls are weak, the auditors must place greater reliance upon their substantive tests. Thus, the auditors' study and evaluation of internal control is a major factor in determining the *nature, extent, and timing of the substantive testing* necessary to verify the financial statement items.

Since an adequate system of internal control is a major factor in the audit conducted by independent public accountants, the question arises as to what action they should take when internal control is found to be seriously deficient. Can the auditors complete a satisfactory audit and properly express an opinion on the fairness of financial statements of a company which has little or no internal control over its transactions? Although in theory the auditors might compensate for the lack of internal control by making a detailed verification of all entries in the accounts and of all transactions, this approach would generally be beyond the realm of practicability unless the business were quite small. In a large business the existence of adequate internal control over at least a considerable portion of the company's activities seems to be a prerequisite if the auditors are to establish that the company's financial statements reflect fairly its financial position and operating results.

Scope of the auditors' investigation of internal control

The auditors' investigation of internal control consists of two phases—the *study* and the *evaluation.* The study phase encompasses the first two steps of the audit process, as discussed in Chapter 4. First, the auditors review the client's internal control and prepare a description of the system in their working papers. Next, they conduct tests of compliance to determine how effectively the system is functioning. The critical evaluation of the weaknesses and strengths of internal control comprises the third step in the audit process. As part of their evaluation, the auditors expand their audit program to compensate for deficiencies in internal control. In areas where internal control is very strong, the auditors will limit their substantive testing to the minimum necessary under the circumstances.

Review and description of internal control

How do auditors obtain the information about a client's system of internal control that enables them to describe this system in their working papers? One approach is to review the audit working papers from examinations made in prior years. When auditors are involved in repeat engagements, they will of course utilize all information about the client obtained in previous engagements. Their investigation will then stress the areas shown as having questionable controls in prior years. It is imperative, however, that auditors recognize that the pattern of operations is an ever-changing one, that internal controls which were adequate last year may now be obsolete, and that the established use of a given control procedure is no assurance that it is currently being applied in an effective and intelligent manner.

Auditors may ascertain the duties and responsibilities of client employees from organization charts, job descriptions, and interviews with client personnel. A review of the client's chart and text of accounts may provide information about employees' responsibilities as well as about accounting policies and procedures. Most clients have procedures manuals and flowcharts describing the approved practices to be followed in all phases of operations. Other excellent sources of information are the reports, working papers, and audit programs of the client's internal auditing staff. As the independent auditors obtain a working knowledge of the system of internal control, this information is recorded in the form of an internal control questionnaire, a written narrative, or flowcharts.

Internal control questionnaire. The traditional method of describing a system of internal control is the filling in of a standardized internal control questionnaire. Many public accounting firms have developed their own questionnaires for this purpose. These usually consist of several separate sections devoted to such topics as petty cash, cash receipts, cash disbursements, notes receivable, and so on. The questionnaire may thus conveniently be divided, completed in sections by different audit staff members, and later reassembled for review by the auditor in charge. Space is usually provided for explanatory comments for those questions which cannot be answered adequately without discussion.

Most internal control questionnaires are so designed that a "no" answer to a question indicates a weakness in internal control. In addition, questionnaires usually provide for distinction between major and minor control weaknesses, indication of the sources of information used in answering questions, and explanatory comments regarding control deficiencies. An internal control questionnaire relating to cash receipts is illustrated on page 224.

Written narrative of internal control.   An internal control questionnaire is intended as a means for the auditors to study a system of internal control. If completion of the questionnaire is regarded as an end in itself, there may be a tendency for the auditors to fill in the "yes" and "no" answers in a mechanical manner, without any real understanding or study of the problem. For this reason, some public accounting firms prefer to use written narratives or flowcharts in lieu of questionnaires.

Written narratives usually follow the flow of each major category of transaction, identifying the employees performing various tasks, documents prepared, records maintained, and the division of duties. After preparing this written description of control procedures, the auditors usually summarize each major section of the internal control system as "strong," "adequate," or "weak." A weak system of internal control usually exists when there is insufficient subdivision of duties—as, for example, when one employee functions as both cashier and accountant.

Flowcharts of internal control.   Many CA firms now consider *systems flowcharts* to be more effective than questionnaires or narrative descriptions in developing an understanding of a client's data processing system and the related internal controls. A systems flowchart is a diagram—a symbolic representation of a system or a series of procedures with each procedure shown in sequence. To the experienced reader, a flowchart conveys a clear image of the system, showing the nature and sequence of procedures, division of responsibilities, sources and distribution of documents, and types and location of accounting records and files. The standard symbols used in systems flowcharting are illustrated in Figure 5-3.

Separate systems flowcharts are usually prepared for each major category of transaction. For example, auditors might prepare separate flowcharts to describe a client's internal control over cash receipts, cash disbursements, credit sales, purchases, production, and payroll. Each flowchart is subdivided into vertical columns representing the various departments (or employees) involved in the transaction. Departmental responsibility for procedures, documents, and records is shown by locating the related flowcharting symbol beneath the appropriate departmental heading. Flowcharts usually begin in the upper left-hand corner; directional "flowlines" then indicate the sequence of activity. The normal flow of activity is from top to bottom and from left to right. These basic concepts of systems flowcharting are illustrated in Figure 5-6, on page 225.

We have previously indicated that questionnaires, narrative descrip-

FIGURE 5–3
Standard systems flowcharting symbols adopted by the American National
Standards Institute, Inc. (These symbols are identical or similar to those used
in the CICA literature.)

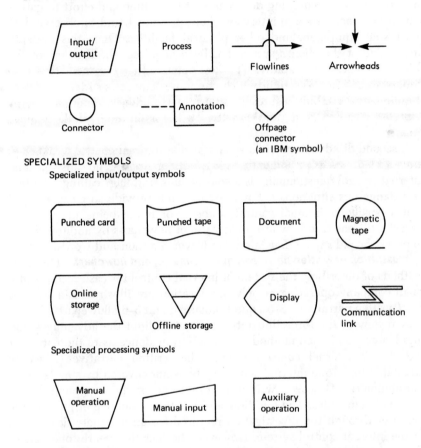

tions, and flowcharts are the three most common approaches to gaining an
understanding of a system of internal control and describing that system
in the auditors' working papers. What are the advantages and disadvantages of flowcharts in comparison to the two older techniques? The
special advantage of a flowchart is that it provides a clearer, more specific
portrayal of the client's system. There is less opportunity for misunderstanding, "blank spots," or ambiguous statements when one uses lines and
symbols rather than words to describe an internal control system. Furthermore, in each successive annual audit, the updating of a flowchart is a
simple process requiring only that the auditor add or change a few lines
and symbols.

A possible disadvantage of flowcharts as compared to the alternative techniques is that they may require more time and skill to prepare. However, any extra time required may be well spent, because the time-consuming aspects of flowcharting lie in the necessity for acquiring a first-hand knowledge of the client's organizational structure, processing procedures, and accounting documents. It takes time and effort to gather samples of documents, to interview client personnel, and to observe data processing equipment and other physical facilities. Once this in-depth knowledge of the client's system has been acquired, the drawing of the flowcharts goes very rapidly. The key point is that the more thorough understanding of the system which one must acquire in order to portray it in lines and symbols ensures a better understanding of internal control, a better audit program, and a better basis for an audit of the highest quality.

A second disadvantage of flowcharts is that internal control weaknesses are not identified as prominently as in questionnaires. A "no" answer in an internal control questionnaire is a conspicuous "red flag" calling attention to a dangerous situation. A flowchart may not provide so clear a signal that a particular internal control is absent or is not being properly enforced. Still, the trend toward greater use of flowcharts by auditors seems to prove the old saying that "a picture is worth a thousand words."

Illustration of written narrative, questionnaire, and flowchart. The three methods of describing the system of internal control for cash receipts of a small company operating at only one location are illustrated in Figures 5–4 (written narrative), 5–5 (questionnaire), and 5–6 (flowchart).

A review of the three illustrations brings to light the advantages and disadvantages of each method for gathering evidence as to the nature of the client's internal control system. The written narrative is readily adaptable to unique internal control systems not covered by standardized questionnaires. However, written narratives generally are practical only for small companies. The questionnaire has the advantage of guiding the preparer through the investigation required for an adequate description of the internal control system. However, the fact that nearly one half of the questions are not applicable to a client as small as the illustrated Bennington Co., Inc. implies a major weakness of the questionnaire—its inflexibility. The flowchart, like the written narrative, can be readily tailored to a specific client system; but more expertise is required to prepare a flowchart than to write a narrative or to complete a questionnaire.

Compliance tests of internal control

Auditors must continually bear in mind that the procedures described in accounting manuals or other management directives may not be in actual use. In some instances, client personnel may pay lip service to

FIGURE 5–4

Bennington Co., Inc.
Cash Receipts Procedures
December 31, 1979

All cash receipts are received by mail in the form of cheques. Lorraine Martin, cashier, picks up the mail every morning at the post office and delivers it unopened to Helen Ellis, the head bookkeeper.

Ellis opens and distributes the mail. Customers' cheques are given to Martin who records the remittances in the cash receipts journal, prepares duplicate deposit slips, and mails the day's receipts intact to National Bank. The bank returns the validated duplicate deposit slips by mail and Ellis files them in chronological order. Ellis posts the accounts receivable subsidiary ledger from the cash receipts journal on a daily basis.

Any customers' cheques charged back by the bank are given by Ellis to the manager, William Dale, who follows up and redeposits the cheques. Ellis also forwards monthly bank statements unopened to Dale. Dale reconciles the monthly bank statement, compares the dates and amounts of deposits to the entries in the cash receipts journal, and reviews the propriety of sales discounts recorded in the cash receipts journal.

Martin, Ellis, and Dale are all bonded.

Conclusion:
Internal control over cash receipts is weak; there is no separation of cash handling and record keeping functions.

V. M. H.
June 6, 79

certain prescribed controls but ignore them in the daily routine of operations. Whenever possible, the auditors' study of internal control should be based on evidence other than statements by supervisors or employees. For this reason, auditors conduct compliance tests to determine whether the internal controls described in their working papers are actually in use and functioning effectively.

ILLUSTRATIVE CASE. In their first examination of a radio and television manufacturing company, the auditors were informed by the controller that credit memoranda for merchandise returned by dealers were issued only after the returned merchandise had been inspected by receiving department personnel and an executive in the sales department had approved in writing the issuance of the credit.

FIGURE 5-5

INTERNAL CONTROL QUESTIONNAIRE
CASH RECEIPTS

Client _Bennington Co., Inc._   Audit Date _December 31, 1979_

Names and Positions of Client Personnel Interviewed:
Lorraine Martin - Cashier; Helen Ellis - head bookkeeper; Wm. Dale - Manager

QUESTION	NOT APPL.	YES	NO	WEAKNESS MAJOR	WEAKNESS MINOR	REMARKS
1. Are all persons receiving or disbursing cash bonded?		✓				
2. Is all incoming mail opened by a responsible employee who does not have access to accounting records and is not connected with the cashier's office?			✓	✓		H. Ellis is head bookkeeper
3. Does the employee assigned to the opening of incoming mail prepare a list of all cheques and money received?			✓		✓	See mitigating control in #13
4. a) Is a copy of the listing of mail receipts forwarded to the accounts receivable department for comparison with the credits to customers' accounts?	✓					
b) Is a copy of this list turned over to an employee other than the cashier for comparison with the cash receipts book?	✓					
5. Are receipts from cash sales and other over-the-counter collections recorded by sales registers, cash registers, and serially numbered receipts?	✓					
6. Are the daily totals of cash registers or other mechanical devices verified by an employee not having access to cash?	✓					
7. Are physical facilities and mechanical equipment for receiving and recording cash adequate and conducive to good control?		✓				
8. Is revenue from investments, rent, concessions, and similar sources scheduled in advance so that nonreceipt on due date would be promptly investigated?	✓					
9. Do procedures for sale of scrap materials provide for direct reporting to accounting department concurrently with transfer of receipts to cashier?	✓					
10. Are securities and other negotiable assets in the custody of someone other than the cashier?	✓					
11. Are collections by branch offices deposited daily in a bank account subject to withdrawal only by home-office executives?	✓					
12. Are each day's receipts deposited intact and without delay by an employee other than the accounts receivable bookkeeper?		✓				
13. Are duplicate deposit tickets signed by the bank teller and compared with the cash receipts record and mailroom list of receipts by an employee other than the cashier or accounts receivable bookkeeper?		✓				W. Dale Manager
14. Are the duplicate deposit tickets properly filed and available for inspection by auditors?		✓				Chronological sequence
15. Are N.S.F. cheques or other items returned by the bank delivered directly to an employee other than the cashier and promptly investigated?		✓				W. Dale Manager
16. Is the physical arrangement of offices and accounting records designed to prevent employees who handle cash from having access to accounting records?			✓		✓	Small Company doesn't permit this.

Prepared By _V. M. Harris_   Date _June 6, 79_   Manager Review _____ Date_____

Senior Review _____ Date_____   Partner Review _____ Date_____

The auditors wished to verify that this control procedure was being followed in practice. They therefore obtained a number of credit memoranda from the files. Several of these documents lacked any approval signature. Comparison of the dates on the credit memoranda with the dates on related receiving reports for the returned goods showed that the credits had been issued in some cases several weeks prior to the return of the goods, and that in other cases, merchandise for

FIGURE 5–6

BENNINGTON CO., INC.
CASH RECEIPTS SYSTEMS FLOWCHART
DECEMBER 31, 1979

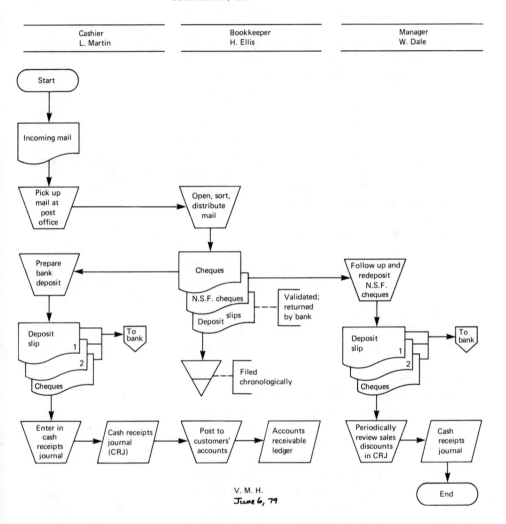

| Cashier
L. Martin | Bookkeeper
H. Ellis | Manager
W. Dale |

V. M. H.
June 6, 79

which credit had been granted had never been returned to the company. Discussions with various employees who prepared credit memoranda indicated disagreement as to the authorized procedures.

The basic purpose of compliance testing is to provide the auditors with assurance that accounting control procedures are (1) in use and (2) operating as planned. Such tests are necessary if the auditors are to rely upon the client's system of internal control to determine the nature, extent, and timing of the audit work necessary to substantiate the financial statement items. As discussed in Chapter 4, compliance tests may be subdivided into the categories of transactions tests and functional tests. Transactions tests provide assurance that the sequence of procedures actually performed within the client's system corresponds to that described in the auditors' working papers. Functional tests, on the other hand, are designed to determine how effectively the major accounting controls have been functioning throughout the period under audit.

Transactions tests are performed for each major category of transaction occurring within the client's system. In a transactions test, the auditors trace specific transactions through the records from the point of initiation to that of completion. The tracing of a sales transaction, for example, might begin with a sales order and be concluded by tracing the customer's remittance to a bank deposit. Or, the auditors might verify the processing of a sales transaction by examining the customer's remittance, then tracing back through the system to the originating sales order. A single credit sales transaction affects sales revenue, accounts receivable, and cash. For clearness of presentation in an auditing textbook, it seems preferable to describe in a single section all verification procedures pertaining to a specific balance sheet item, such as cash or accounts receivable; but the student of auditing should realize that all aspects of specific transactions must be tested in conjunction with the study of internal control.

Functional tests focus upon specific control procedures rather than complete transactions. For example, the auditors may wish to test the effectiveness of the client's billing procedures. This test might consist of tracing records of shipments made at various times throughout the year to the related sales invoices. Errors in quantities or prices shown in the invoices would indicate weaknesses in the billing procedures. The results of this test provide the auditors with a basis for determining whether the client's system may be relied upon with respect to the billing of customers. If the system appears weak, the auditors will expand their audit procedures in the area of accounts receivable and sales.

Omission of compliance tests in weak systems.   In some engagements, auditors may find that (*a*) internal controls in some areas are so weak that they provide no basis for reliance, or (*b*) compliance tests would require more effort than any reduction in substantive testing which might result from reliance upon internal control. When internal control will not be relied upon, there is no purpose in conducting tests of compliance. For this reason, auditors perform a *preliminary* evaluation of internal control after reviewing the system and describing it in their working papers. If this preliminary evaluation indicates that it will not be feasible to rely upon internal control in certain portions of the system, the auditors may omit compliance tests in those areas and concentrate upon substantiating the financial statement items. In areas where compliance tests are omitted, however, the auditors may place *no reliance* upon internal control in determining the nature, extent, and timing of the procedures necessary to complete the audit.

In the audit of a small business, it may be possible to do sufficient substantive testing to express an opinion on the financial statements while placing little or no reliance upon internal control. In the audit of a large business, however, the auditors would normally deny an opinion if they were not able to place a reasonable degree of reliance upon the system of internal control.

Evaluation of internal control

After the auditors have carried out their study of internal control (review and compliance testing), they must evaluate the system to determine the extent to which they may rely upon internal control. Based upon this evaluation, modifications are made in the audit program; audit procedures are expanded in areas of weak internal control and limited in areas of unusually strong controls. Only after an evaluation of internal control are the auditors in a position to draft a complete audit program which is suitably tailored to the engagement.

The study of internal control will have identified the areas of strength and weakness in the system. Significant weaknesses, as well as features of unusual strength, are summarized on a working paper which provides space for developing additional substantive tests to be performed in areas of weak controls and setting limitations on audit procedures in areas of strong controls. This working paper also contains a summary of recommendations to the client for strengthening weak points in the system. A working paper used to summarize the auditors' evaluation of internal control is illustrated in Figure 5–7. Notice that the extensions and limitations of audit procedures are described in detail to facilitate drafting a final version of the audit program.

Reliance on the work of internal auditors. Many of the audit procedures performed by internal auditors are similar in nature to those employed by independent auditors. This raises the question of whether the independent auditors may rely on the work already performed by the internal auditors. The CICA has addressed this issue in the internal control section of the *Handbook*.

The position taken in the *Handbook* is that the work of internal auditors cannot be substituted for the work of independent auditors. However, the independent auditors should consider the existence and quality of an internal audit function in their evaluation of the client's system of internal control. Through its contribution to internal control, the work of the internal auditors may affect the nature, extent, and timing of the audit

FIGURE 5-7

a. Manufacturing Company
Evaluation of Internal Control
December 31, 1979

Weakness in Internal Control

1. There is no established procedure for investigating and following up debit balances in accounts payable.

2. The accounts receivable book-keeper prepares and issues all credit memoranda for sales returns and allowances.

Weakness Strength in Internal Control

1. The depository bank reconciles all of the client's bank accounts on the bank's data processing equipment.

Extension of Auditing Procedures

1.
   a. Obtain or prepare a listing of accounts payable debit balances at December 31, 1979.
   b. Mail confirmation requests to vendors having debit balances.
   c. Review credit standing of vendors having debit balances.
   d. Discuss with purchasing agent the prospects of additional purchases from debit balance vendors.
   e. Consider the need for an allowance for uncollectible debit balances.

2.
   a. Inspect copies of all credit memos issued during the period.
   b. Review with sales manager and controller all credit memoranda issued during the period.
   c. Confirm accounts of all customers to whom credit memoranda were issued during the period.

Limitation of Auditing Procedures

1. Perform no independent bank reconciliation at December 31, 1979. Obtain and review the bank's reconciliations.

Recommendation to Client

1. The accounts payable departments should furnish a list of vendors with debit balances to the purchasing agent and the credit manager monthly. These individuals should follow-up for procurement possibilities or collection of the debit balance.

2. The sales department should initiate all credit memoranda. Credit memos in excess of a stated minimum should be reviewed by the controller before being posted to the accounts receivable subsidiary ledger.

procedures performed by the independent auditors. In assessing the contribution of the internal audit function to internal control, the independent auditors should consider the competence and objectivity of the internal audit staff and evaluate its work.

On a test basis, the independent auditors should examine the work of the internal audit staff, considering such factors as the scope and quality of its audit procedures, the extent of the documentation in its working papers, and the appropriateness of its conclusions. In addition, the independent auditors should test specific transactions and compare their results with those obtained by the internal auditors. Upon completion of this investigation, the independent auditors have a sound basis for determining the extent to which they may limit their audit procedures in reliance upon the internal auditors' contribution to internal control.

To reduce the time and cost of an audit, the internal auditors may provide direct assistance to the CAs in preparing working papers and performing certain audit procedures. The CAs, however, should supervise and test any audit work done for them by the internal auditors. Also, the judgments regarding matters to be investigated, the effectiveness of internal control, and the fairness of the financial statements must be those of the independent auditors.

Preparation of an "internal control letter"

Deficiencies in internal control brought to light by the auditors' study and evaluation of the system should be communicated to the client along with the auditors' recommendations for corrective action. Discussions with management are the most effective way for auditors to communicate their findings to the client and explore possible courses of action. The content of these discussions is formally summarized and conveyed in writing to the client in a report called an *internal control letter.* Although internal control letters are not required by generally accepted auditing standards, it is in the best interests of both the client and the auditors to have written documentation of their discussions. This report serves as a reference document for management, and may also serve to minimize the auditors' liability in the event that a major defalcation or other loss stemming from a weakness in internal control is later discovered.

Internal control letters are usually addressed to the chief executive officer or the audit committee of the board of directors. Many auditing firms place great emphasis upon providing clients with a thorough and well-planned internal control letter. These firms recognize that such a report can be a valuable and constructive contribution to the efficiency of the client's operations. The quality of the auditors' recommendations reflects their professional expertise and creative ability and the thoroughness of their investigation. No specific format exists for the preparation of internal control letters, since they are a communication sent only to the client. Reports on internal control which are prepared for distribution to third parties are distinct from internal control letters and are discussed in Chapter 20.

The internal control letter is usually prepared at the conclusion of the auditors' evaluation of internal control. It is desirable to submit this report well in advance of the balance sheet date. The amount of substantive testing necessary to complete the audit may be reduced if management is able to implement significant improvements in internal control prior to year-end.

Electronic data processing—effect upon internal control

The generally accepted auditing standard which requires a study and evaluation of internal control applies to the audit of all companies, regardless of whether the record keeping is performed by an electronic computer or by manual methods.

In manual accounting systems, an important element of internal control consists of the division of duties among several persons in such a manner that the work of one employee verifies that of another, and no one person handles a transaction in its entirety. When an electronic data processing system is installed, the work formerly done by numerous employees will be done by the machines. The employees operating the electronic machines do not have custody of assets nor do they initiate transactions; their function is solely to process the data furnished by other departments.

Adequate internal control in this situation requires assurance that the employees operating the data processing machines do their work accurately and honestly. This assurance may be provided by creating a separate control group, whose function it is to verify the accuracy of the work of the data processing center. The separate control group may carry out its verification function by maintaining memorandum records to accumulate key totals for comparison with totals produced by the machines.

For example, if payrolls are handled by the data processing centre, the control group might compute independently such key figures as the total number of employees in selected departments and the total dollar amount of deductions authorized by these employees. These figures could be accumulated on adding machines for comparison with corresponding totals produced by the data processing centre. If the volume of transactions is so great as to render the maintenance of such memorandum records burdensome, another approach is for the control group to make its tests by using the computer, at appropriate intervals, to process its own memorandum records. Internal control would not permit the control group to turn this task over to the employees of the data processing centre, since the whole point is to prove the accuracy of the work of employees regularly operating the machines.

Traditionally, accountants have felt that every accounting system, whether manual, mechanical, or electronic, should provide a trail of audit evidence. With the advent of more sophisticated electronic equipment, some relaxation of this view has taken place. This matter, together with the entire field of electronic data processing, is considered further in Chapter 6.

Internal control in the small company

The preceding discussion of the system of internal control and its evaluation by the independent auditors has been presented in terms of large corporations. In the large concern, excellent internal control may be achieved by extensive subdivision of duties, so that no one person handles a transaction completely from beginning to end. In the very small concern, however, with only one or two office employees, there is little or no opportunity for division of duties and responsibilities. Consequently, internal control tends to be weak, if not completely absent, unless the owner-manager recognizes the importance of internal control and participates in key activities.

Because of the absence of adequate internal control in small concerns, the independent auditors must make a much more detailed examination of accounts, journal entries, and supporting documents than is required in larger organizations. Although it is well to recognize that internal control can never be adequate in a small business, this limitation is no justification for ignoring those forms of control which are available. There is seldom any excuse for failure to deposit cash receipts intact daily, but it is not uncommon to find this basic rule violated in small concerns. The violation is often defended on the grounds that internal control is not possible, anyway, so that cash receipts may as well be used for disbursements when convenient. The use of cheques and invoices not controlled by serial numbers and the purchase of merchandise or materials without the issuance of formal purchase orders are other examples of negligence in operations sometimes encountered in small companies. Auditors can make a valuable contribution to small client companies by encouraging the installation of such control procedures as are practicable in the circumstances. The following specific practices are almost always capable of use in even the smallest business:

1. Record all cash receipts immediately.
   a. For over-the-counter collections, use cash registers easily visible to customers. Record register readings daily.
   b. Prepare a list of all mail remittances immediately upon opening of the mail and retain this list for subsequent comparison with bank deposit tickets and entries in the cash receipts journal.
2. Deposit all cash receipts intact daily.

3. Make all payments by serially numbered cheques, with the exception of small disbursements from petty cash.
4. Use an imprest petty cash fund entrusted to a single custodian for all payments other than by cheque.
5. Reconcile bank accounts monthly and retain copies of the reconciliations in the files.
6. Use serially numbered sales invoices, purchase orders, and receiving reports.
7. Issue cheques to vendors only in payment of approved invoices which have been matched with purchase orders and receiving reports.
8. Balance subsidiary ledgers with control accounts at regular intervals; prepare and mail customers' statements monthly.
9. Prepare comparative financial statements monthly in sufficient detail to disclose significant variations in any category of revenue or expense.
10. Account for numerical sequence of all pre-numbered documents such as purchase orders, receiving reports, sales invoices, and cheques.
11. Retain a CA firm for an annual audit.

Conscientious enforcement of the practices listed above will significantly reduce the opportunity for substantial errors or major fraud to go undetected. If the size of the business permits a segregation of the duties of cash handling and record keeping, a fair degree of control can be achieved. If it is necessary that one employee serve as both accounting clerk and cashier, then active participation by the owner in certain key functions is necessary to guard against the concealment of fraud or errors. In a few minutes each day the owner, even though not trained in accounting, can create a significant amount of internal control by personally (*a*) reading daily cash register totals, (*b*) reconciling the bank account monthly, (*c*) signing all cheques and cancelling the supporting documents, (*d*) approving all general journal entries, and (*e*) critically reviewing comparative monthly statements of revenue and expense.

KEY TERMS INTRODUCED OR EMPHASIZED IN CHAPTER 5

accounting controls   Internal controls of a nature which can directly affect the reliability of the accounting records and financial statements.

administrative controls   Internal controls of a nature having no direct bearing upon the reliability of accounting data.

compliance tests   Audit procedures designed to provide reasonable assurance that significant accounting controls within a client's system are (1) in use and (2) operating as planned.

fidelity bonds   A form of insurance in which a bonding company agrees to re-

imburse an employer for losses attributable to theft or embezzlement by
bonded employees.

financial forecast   An estimate of financial position, results of operations, and
changes in financial position for one or more future periods.

internal auditors   Corporation employees who design and execute audit programs to test the efficiency of all aspects of internal control. The primary
objective of internal auditors is to evaluate and improve the efficiency of
the various operating units of an organization, rather than to express an
opinion as to the fairness of financial statements.

internal control questionnaire   One of several alternative methods of describing
a system of internal control in audit working papers. Questionnaires are
usually designed so that "no" answers prominently identify weaknesses in
internal control.

organization plan   The division of authority, responsibility, and duties among
members of an organization.

responsibility accounting   An accounting system which separately accumulates
the operating results attributable to specific decision makers. Separate accounts for the assets, revenue, and expenses under the control of specific
decision makers and adequate internal documentation to focus responsibility are the basic elements of a responsibility accounting system.

systems flowcharts   A symbolic representation of a system or series of procedures with each procedure shown in sequence. Systems flowcharts are the
most widely used method of describing a system of internal control in audit
working papers.

written narrative of internal control   A written summary of a system of internal
control for inclusion in audit working papers. Written narratives are more
flexible than questionnaires but are practical only for describing relatively
small, simple systems.

GROUP I
REVIEW QUESTIONS

5–1.   What is the basic purpose of a system of internal control? What measures comprise the system?

5–2.   What is meant by internal accounting controls as contrasted with internal administrative controls? Give examples of each, and explain which
category is of more importance to the auditor.

5–3.   Identify the basic features of a strong system of internal control.

5–4.   How does separation of the record-keeping function from custody of assets contribute to internal control?

5–5.   The owner of a medium-sized corporation asks you to state two or three
principles to be followed in dividing responsibilities among employees
in a manner that will produce strong internal control.

5–6.   One basic concept of internal control is that no one employee should
handle all aspects of a transaction. Assuming that a general category of
transactions has been authorized by top management, how many employees (or departments) should participate in each transaction, as a

minimum, to achieve strong internal accounting control? Explain in general terms the function of each of these employees.

5–7. Explain the term "responsibility accounting." Why is this concept an important factor in achieving internal control?

5–8. Compare the objectives of the internal auditor with those of the independent auditor.

5–9. "The principal distinction between independent audits and internal audits is that the latter activity is carried on by an organization's own employees rather than by independent auditors." Criticize this statement.

5–10. What reliance, if any, may independent auditors place upon the work of a client's internal audit staff?

5–11. What is the purpose of the study and evaluation of internal control required by generally accepted auditing standards?

5–12. A prospective client informs you that all officers and employees of the company are bonded, and he requests that under these circumstances you forego an evaluation of internal control in order to reduce the cost of an audit. Construct a logical reply to this request.

5–13. Suggest a number of sources from which auditors might obtain the information needed to prepare a description of internal control in the audit working papers.

5–14. Tests of compliance may be subdivided into transactions tests and functional tests. Distinguish between these two categories.

5–15. Under what circumstances might auditors elect to forego tests of compliance for certain portions of a client's system of internal control?

5–16. After completing the study of internal control, how do auditors evaluate the system?

5–17. What is an "internal control letter"? At what stage of the audit should it be prepared?

5–18. During your first examination of a manufacturing company with approximately 100 production employees, you find that all aspects of factory payroll are handled by one employee and that none of the usual internal controls over payroll is observed. What action would you take?

5–19. In view of the reliance which the auditor places upon the system of internal control, how do you account for the fact that the standard audit report makes no reference to internal control in describing the scope of the examination?

5–20. Name the three factors you consider of greatest importance in protecting a business against losses through embezzlement.

GROUP II
QUESTIONS REQUIRING ANALYSIS

5–21. The audit process was described in Chapter 4 as a series of basic steps. Explain the relationship of each step of the audit process to the auditors' study and evaluation of internal control. For example—(1) **Review the** *system and prepare a description in the audit working papers* is the first step in the audit process and is the first part of the "study" phase of the auditors' investigation of internal control.

5-22. Adherence to generally accepted auditing standards requires, among other things, a proper study and evaluation of the existing internal control. The most common approaches to reviewing the system of internal control include the use of a questionnaire, preparation of a written narrative, preparation of a flowchart, and combinations of these methods.

Required:

a. What is the CAs' objective in conducting a study and evaluation of internal control during an audit?
b. Discuss the advantages to CAs of reviewing internal control by using
   (1) An internal control questionnaire.
   (2) A written narrative.
   (3) A flowchart.
c. If they are satisfied after completing their description of internal control that no material weaknesses exist in the system, is it necessary for the CAs to conduct tests of compliance? Explain. (AICPA, adapted)

5-23. The process of gathering evidential matter to support an opinion on a client's financial statements involves several types of testing procedures. In the course of the examination, auditors perform detailed tests of samples of transactions from large-volume populations. Auditors may also audit various types of transactions by tracing a few transactions of each type through all stages of the accounting system.

Required:

What are the audit objectives associated with—

a. A sample of transactions from a large-volume population?
b. Tracing a few transactions of each type through all stages of the accounting system? (AICPA, adapted)

5-24. At the Main Street Theatre the cashier, located in a box office at the entrance, receives cash from customers and operates a machine which ejects serially numbered tickets. To gain admission to the theatre a customer hands the ticket to a doorman stationed some 50 feet from the box office at the entrance to the theatre lobby. The doorman tears the ticket in half, opens the door for the customer, and returns the stub to him. The other half of the ticket is dropped by the doorman into a locked box.

Required:

a. What internal controls are present in this phase of handling cash receipts?
b. What steps should be taken regularly by the manager or other supervisor to give maximum effectiveness to these controls?

    c. Assume that the cashier and the doorman decided to collaborate in an effort to abstract cash receipts. What action might they take?

    d. Continuing the assumption made in (*c*) of collusion between the cashier and the doorman, what features of the control procedures would be likely to disclose the embezzlement?

5–25. During your first examination of a medium-sized manufacturing company, the owner explains that in order to establish clear-cut lines of responsibility for various aspects of the business, he has made one employee responsible for the purchasing, receiving, and storing of merchandise. A second employee has full responsibility for maintenance of accounts receivable records and collections from customers. A third employee is responsible for personnel records, timekeeping, preparation of payrolls, and distribution of payroll cheques. The client asks your opinion concerning this plan of organization. Explain fully the reasons supporting your opinion.

5–26. Internal auditing is a staff function found in virtually every large corporation. The internal audit function is also performed in many smaller companies as a part-time activity of individuals who may or may not be called internal auditors. The differences between the audits by independent auditors and the work of internal auditors are more basic than is generally recognized.

Required:

    a. Briefly discuss the auditing work performed by the independent public accountant and the internal auditor with regard to—
    (1) Auditing objectives.
    (2) General nature of auditing work.

    b. In conducting their audit, the independent auditors must evaluate the work of the internal auditors. Discuss briefly the reason for this evaluation.

    c. List the auditing procedures used by independent auditors in evaluating the work of the internal auditors. (AICPA, adapted)

5–27. The Carleton Company did not utilize the services of independent public accountants during the first several years of its existence. In the current year, at the suggestion of its banker, the company decided to retain McTavish and Company, a CA firm, to conduct an audit of its financial statements in order to qualify for a larger bank loan. The auditors found the system of internal control to be "extremely weak or non-existent." Under these circumstances what kind of audit report, if any, could McTavish and Company issue? Explain fully.

5–28. The Auditing Standards Committee of the CICA has stated that an ordinary examination directed to the expression of an opinion on financial statements is not designed to disclose fraud, although discovery of defalcations or other fraud may sometimes result. How can this concept of an audit be reconciled with the standard practice which requires CAs to expand the scope of their audit work when they find weaknesses in internal control?

5–29.   *a.*   A newspaper article about embezzlement contained this comment, "Both the management of a company and the chartered accountant (as the shareholders' auditor) have certain responsibilities with respect to the prevention of defalcations by employees."
     What is the extent of the responsibilities of each?

     b.   What general measures should be taken by management in attempting to prevent defalcations by employees? (CICA)

5–30.   CA is employed by M & Co., chartered accountants, and has been put in charge of the audit of a new client, The Family Clothing Store Ltd.

     The Family Clothing Store Ltd. is owned by three men, Messrs. X, Y, and Z. Only one of the owners, Mr. X, is active in the business—the other two live and work in another city. Mr. X operated the business as a proprietorship until a few years ago, when he incorporated it and obtained additional capital for store improvements by selling to each of Y and Z 24 percent of his equity. In addition to Mr. X, the store employs three salesclerks and Miss R, the cashier-bookkeeper. Miss R has worked for Mr. X for many years.

     CA and the partner responsible for The Family Clothing Store Ltd. examination have agreed that one of the first things CA should do when he starts work on the examination is evaluate the internal control.

Required:

     a.   Why would CA bother to evaluate the internal control of this small company?

     b.   What particular features of internal control would CA enquire into in the circumstances described above? Do not give detailed procedures. (CICA)

GROUP III
PROBLEMS

5–31.   A description of some of the operating procedures of Old World Manufacturing Company, is given in succeeding paragraphs. For each of the activities described, you are to point out (*a*) the deficiencies, if any, in internal control, including an explanation of the errors or manipulations which might occur; and (*b*) recommendations for changes in procedures which would correct the existing weakness.

     1.   When materials are ordered, a duplicate of the purchase order is sent to the receiving department. When the materials are received, the receiving clerk records the receipt on the copy of the order, which is then sent to the accounting department to support the entry to Accounts Payable and to Purchases. The materials are then taken to the inventory storeroom, where the quantity is entered on bin records.

     2.   Time reports of employees are sent to a data processing department which prepares punched cards for use in the preparation of payrolls, payroll cheques, and labour cost distribution records. The payroll cheques are compared with the payrolls and signed by the

treasurer of the company, who returns them to the supervisor of the data processing department for distribution to employees.

3. A sales branch of the company has an office force consisting of John Lane, the manager, and two assistants. The branch has a local bank account in which it deposits cash receipts. Cheques drawn on this account require the manager's signature or the signature of the treasurer of the company. Bank statements and paid cheques are returned by the bank to the manager, who retains them in his files after making the reconciliation. Reports of disbursements are prepared by the manager and submitted to the home office on scheduled dates. (AICPA, adapted)

5–32. Island Trading Company, a client of your CA firm, has requested your advice on the following problem: It has three clerical employees who must perform the following functions:

1. Maintain general ledger.
2. Maintain accounts payable ledger.
3. Maintain accounts receivable ledger.
4. Maintain cash disbursements journal and prepare cheques for signature.
5. Issue credit memos on sales returns and allowances.
6. Reconcile the bank account.
7. Handle and deposit cash receipts.

Required:

Assuming that there is no problem as to the ability of any of the employees, the company requests your advice on assigning the above functions to the three employees in such a manner as to achieve the highest degree of internal control. It may be assumed that these employees will perform no other accounting function than the ones listed, and that any accounting functions not listed will be performed by persons other than these three employees.

a. List four possible unsatisfactory combinations of the above-listed functions.
b. State how you would recommend distributing the above functions among the three employees. Assume that, with the exception of the nominal jobs of the bank reconciliation and the issuance of credits on returns and allowances, all functions require an equal amount of time (AICPA, adapted)

5–33. Prospect Corporation Inc., your new audit client, processes its sales and cash receipts in the following manner:

A. **Sales.** Salesclerks prepare sales invoices in triplicate. The original and second copy are presented to the cashier, the third copy is retained by the salesclerk in the sales book. When the sale is for cash, the customer pays the salesclerk, who presents the money to the cashier with the invoice copies.

A credit sale is approved by the cashier from an approved credit list. After receiving the cash or approving the invoice, the cashier validates the original copy of the sales invoice and gives it to the customer. At the end of each day the cashier recaps the sales and cash received, files the recap by date, and forwards the cash and the second copy of all sales invoices to the accounts receivable clerk.

The accounts receivable clerk balances the cash received with cash sales invoices and prepares a daily sales summary. Cash sales are posted by the accounts receivable clerk to the cash receipts journal, and the daily sales summary is filed by date. Cash from cash sales is included in the daily bank deposit (preparation of bank deposit is described with cash receipts in the following section). The accounts receivable clerk posts credit sales invoices to the accounts receivable ledger, and then sends all invoices to the inventory control clerk in the sales department.

The inventory clerk posts to the inventory control cards and files the sales invoices numerically.

B. **Cash receipts.**   The mail is opened each morning by a mail clerk in the sales department. The mail clerk prepares a remittance advice (showing customer and amount paid) for each cheque and forwards the cheques and remittance advices to the sales department supervisor. The supervisor reviews the remittance advices and forwards the cheques and advices to the accounting department supervisor.

The accounting department supervisor, who also functions as credit manager in approving new credit and all credit limits, reviews all cheques for payments on past-due accounts and then gives the cheques and remittance advices to the accounts receivable clerk, who arranges the advices in alphabetical order. The remittance advices are posted directly to the accounts receivable ledger cards. The cheques are endorsed by stamp and totaled. The total is posted to the cash receipts journal. The remittance advices are filed chronologically.

After receiving the cash from the previous day's cash sales from the cashier, the accounts receivable clerk prepares the daily deposit slip in triplicate. The original and second copy of the deposit slip accompany the bank deposit and the third copy is filed by date. The bank deposit is sent directly to National Bank.

Required:

a.   Prepare a systems flowchart of internal control over sales transactions as described in part A above.

b.   Prepare a systems flowchart of internal control over cash receipts as described in part B above.

5–34.   "In general, the literature dealing with auditing uses as its tacit frame of reference the examination of statements of large-scale enterprises. The implication usually made is that audits of small companies are similar in nature to those of large companies; such differences as exist are held to be not differences of kind but only of size. These prevailing views are not correct."

Required:

Discuss the important ways in which "audits of small companies" differ from "audits of large companies" and the particular problems usually associated with the small ones. (CICA)

5–35.　In early September the Vista Corporation Ltd. retained you to make an examination of its financial statements for the current year ending December 31. Your appointment occurred shortly after the death of the CA who had audited the company in prior years. Assume that you have completed your examination during the following February and have prepared a draft of your audit report containing an unqualified opinion on the financial statements. Your report, as required by your engagement letter, was addressed to the shareholders. You also have drafted a letter describing weaknesses in the system of internal control observed during your examination and setting forth your recommendations for the correction of these weaknesses.

During your review of the drafts of these reports with Jon Hall, president of Vista Corporation Ltd., he expressed his satisfaction with the unqualified report on the financial statements but indicated that the letter on internal control was unnecessary. The president stated that he was aware of the weaknesses in internal control and that he would personally take steps to remedy them. Finally, the president instructed you not to render the internal control letter. He explained that he felt the board of directors should deal with major policy decisions and not be burdened with day-to-day management problems.

Required:

a.　Enumerate at least five separate factors which should be considered before reaching a decision whether to render the internal control letter.

b.　In the event that you decide to render the internal control letter to Vista Corporation Ltd., would you render it to the board of directors or to the president? Explain fully. (AICPA, adapted)

5–36.　Jewellery Ltd. sells and services expensive jewelry and watches. The company employs four jewelers, eight salesclerks, a manager, and a bookkeeper. The salesclerks serve all customers, but the jewelers often assist them in answering queries and providing repair estimates.

Required:

Outline a system to account for service revenue and provide adequate internal control over customers' jewelry and watches received for service. (CICA)

5–37.　You have been asked by the board of trustees of a local church to review its accounting procedures. As a part of this review you have prepared the following comments relating to the collections made at weekly services and record keeping for members' pledges and contributions:

1.　The church's board of trustees has delegated responsibility for financial management and internal audit of the financial records to the finance committee. This group prepares the annual forecast and approves major disbursements but is not involved in collections or record keeping. No internal or independent audit has been considered necessary in recent years because the same trusted employee has kept church records and served as financial secretary for 15 years.

2. The collection at the weekly service is taken by a team of ushers. The head usher counts the collection in the church office following each service. He then places the collection and a notation of the amount counted in the church safe. Next morning the financial secretary opens the safe and recounts the collection. He withholds about $100 to meet cash expenditures during the coming week and deposits the remainder of the collection intact. In order to facilitate the deposit, members who contribute by cheque are asked to draw their cheques to "Cash."

3. At their request a few members are furnished prenumbered predated envelopes in which to insert their weekly contributions. The head usher removes the cash from the envelopes to be counted with the loose cash included in the collection and discards the envelopes. No record is maintained of issuance or return of the envelopes, and the envelope system is not encouraged.

4. Each member is asked to prepare a contribution pledge card annually. The pledge is regarded as a moral commitment by the member to contribute a stated weekly amount. Based upon the amounts shown on the pledge cards, the financial secretary furnishes a letter to requesting members to support the tax deductibility of their contributions.

Required:

Describe the weaknesses and recommended improvements in procedures for—

a. Collections made at weekly services.
b. Record keeping for members' pledges and contributions.

Organize your answer sheets as follows:

Weakness	Recommended improvement

(AICPA)

5–38.   After completing the interim examination of the accounts of B Ltd., CA
sent an internal control letter to the controller, commenting on several
matters which he felt required improvement.

The controller discussed the comments with his staff, then sent a
reply rejecting all of CA's suggested improvements.

Excerpts from CA's letters are marked (L) below; excerpts from the
controller's reply are marked (R).

1. *Petty cash*
    (L)   The positions of petty cash custodian and cashier should be
          filled by different people. At present, the cashier controls the
          $500 petty cash fund—this situation results in weak internal
          control because of the possibility of cash being temporarily
          transferred between petty cash and cash receipts.
    (R)   A $500 fund is too small to warrant segregation of the duties.
          If the cashier, for example, were involved in a lapping
          operation of the cash receipts, and was using the petty cash
          fund to cover the shortage, $500 would not go very far. Simi-
          larly, if part of the $500 were borrowed by the cashier, the
          amount would not be significant. The cashier is covered by
          our blanket bond.

2. *Bank reconciliation*
    (L)   The bank reconciliation should be prepared by an employee
          who takes no part in the regular cash receipts or disburse-
          ments functions. The reconciliation is now prepared by the
          bookkeeper, who also prepares the cheques and is a singing
          officer.
    (R)   We do not wish to segregate the duties with respect to the
          bank reconciliation and cash disbursements because the pay-
          roll cheques are included with the returned cheques. The
          confidential nature of the payroll amounts must be pre-
          served.

3. *Purchase orders*
    (L)   A purchase order when accepted by the supplier is a binding
          agreement to purchase the merchandise or services ordered,
          and should therefore include unit prices. Approximately 75
          percent of the purchase orders presently issued do not show
          unit prices.
    (R)   As we deal with a limited number of suppliers and as all of
          their prices are published in catalogues (to which the ac-
          counts payable department checks invoice prices), entering
          the unit price on the purchase order is an unnecessary cleri-
          cal step.

4. *Cancellation of documents*
    (L)   Suppliers' invoices and supporting documents should be can-
          celled by, or under the direct supervision of, a second cheque-
          signing officer. At present, vouchers are not cancelled; this

could lead to a fraudulent or accidental duplicate payment of an invoice.

(R) Our cash disbursement policy is that all invoices be paid within 15 days of receipt. The chance of a duplicate payment is minimal because a signing officer would notice an old invoice at the time the cheque was signed. The clerical effort to cancel the vouchers is therefore not warranted.

5. *Sales invoices*

(L) Sales invoices should be prenumbered by the printer. Without the control provided by prenumbering, the company has no assurance that employees are not suppressing invoices and misappropriating sales proceeds.

(R) We discontinued prenumbering sales invoices because we found that the time spent controlling them was quite significant. Sales invoices in our organization can originate in a number of places; accordingly, the clerk charged with the responsibility of accounting for the numbers had a very difficult time with the many numerical sequences. This problem was further aggravated when we switched to the present prebilling system. The invoices are prepared before the merchandise is shipped, so the shipping department sometimes will hold an invoice for a considerable period of time awaiting receipt of the items from production or from an outside supplier.

6. *Vouchers payable*

(L) The trial balance of vouchers payable should be reconciled monthly with the general ledger control account, by someone other than the accounts payable clerk. At the time of my examination there was a substantial difference between the accounts payable detail listing prepared by the accounts payable clerk and the control account in the general ledger.

(R) We have a new clerk in the accounts payable department; unfortunately your examination was conducted after she had been in the position for only two weeks. Our usual practice is to have the accounts payable clerk prepare a listing of unpaid vouchers at the month-end and pass this listing to the general ledger control account. At the time of your examination the listing had been returned to the clerk as a large number of errors had become apparent—she was instructed to locate the errors in her listing as a training exercise.

Required:

For each of the six matters above, suggest what CA's position should be in his reply to the controller, supporting the position you suggest by listing factors CA would consider in drafting his reply. (CICA, adapted)

6

The audit of electronic
data processing systems

The rapid growth of electronic data processing (EDP) for business use
is having a greater impact upon public accounting than perhaps any other
event in the history of this profession. Although the computer has created
some challenging problems for professional accountants, it has also
broadened their horizons and expanded the range and value of the
services they offer. The computer is more than a tool for performing
routine accounting tasks with unprecedented speed and accuracy. It
makes possible the development of information which could not have
been gathered in the past because of time and cost limitations. When a
client maintains accounting records with a complex and sophisticated
EDP system, auditors may find it helpful, and even necessary, to utilize
the computer in performing many auditing procedures.

This chapter will call attention to some of the most significant ways in
which auditing work is being affected by EDP, but cannot impart extensive knowledge of technical computer skills. Independent auditors will
find additional familiarity with the computer, including technical skills
such as programming, to be of ever-increasing value in the accounting
profession.

Nature of an electronic data processing system

Before considering the impact of electronic data processing systems on
the work of the independent public accountant, some understanding of
the nature of a computer and its capabilities is needed. A business EDP

system usually consists of a digital computer and peripheral equipment known as *hardware;* and equally essential *software,* consisting of various programs and routines for operating a computer.

Hardware.   The principal hardware component of a digital computer is the *central processing unit* (CPU). The CPU consists of a *control unit,* which processes a program of instructions for manipulating data; a *storage unit,* consisting of many tiny magnetic rings or cores, for storing the program of instructions and the data to be manipulated; and an *arithmetic unit* capable of addition, subtraction, multiplication, division, and comparison of data at speeds measured in *microseconds or nanoseconds.*

Peripheral to the central processing unit are devices for recording input and devices for auxiliary storage, output, and communications. Peripheral devices in direct communication with the CPU are said to be *online,* in contrast to *offline* equipment not in direct communication with the CPU.

A first step in the functioning of an electronic data processing system is to convert the data to machine-sensible form. This is the role of recording and input devices, such as card punches and readers, paper tape punches and readers, magnetic tape encoders, magnetic ink character readers, and optical scanners. Each of these devices either records data in some medium for later "reading into" the storage unit or communicates data direct to the CPU.

Auxiliary storage devices are utilized to augment the capacity of the storage unit of the CPU. Examples of auxiliary storage devices are magnetic tape, magnetic drums, and magnetic disk packs. Magnetic drums and disk packs have the advantage of *random access,* while data on magnetic tapes must be stored sequentially.

Computers use special codes called *machine language* to represent data being stored or processed within the computer. The purpose of a machine language is to permit all data to be expressed by combinations of only two symbols. Digital computer circuitry has two states in that any given circuit may be "on" or "off." By using an internal code capable of representing with two symbols any kind of data, the computer makes an "on" circuit represent one symbol and an "off" circuit represent the other. All data may then be expressed internally by the computer by a combination of "on" and "off" circuits. An example of a machine language is the *binary* number system.

Machines must also be used to translate the output of the computer back to a recognizable code or language. Output equipment includes card punches, printers, cathode ray tubes, and console display panels.

Software.   Most important of the software components is the *program* —a series of instructions written in a language comprehensible to the computer. These instructions order the computer to process data. Early-day programs were labouriously written in machine language, but today, programming languages such as COBOL (common business-oriented language) are much like English. Programming in COBOL and other *source languages* is made possible by another element of software called the *compiler,* which is a computer program utilized in translating a *source-language program* into machine language. The machine-language version of a program is called an *object program.*

Another important software component is the prewritten utility program for recurring tasks of data processing, such as sorting, sequencing, or merging data, language processing, and other routines closely related to the functioning of the computer. These prewritten utility programs are available from the computer manufacturer and do not generally pose any problem to the auditors because they are not likely to be the source of errors in computer output. Furthermore, they are technically so complex as to make examination by the auditors impracticable in most cases.

In concluding this brief discussion of the nature of an EDP system, two points deserve emphasis. First, computer *hardware* is extremely reliable, but this machine precision does not assure that the computer output will be reliable. Second, auditors have the same responsibility in auditing an EDP system as a manual system—which is to satisfy themselves that the financial statements produced reflect the interpretation and processing of transactions in conformity with generally accepted accounting principles. GAAP

Internal control in the electronic data processing system

The discussion of internal control in Chapter 5 stressed the need for a proper division of duties among employees operating a manual or punched card accounting system. In such a system no one employee has the complete responsibility for a transaction, and the work of one person is verified by the work of another handling other aspects of the same transaction. This division of duties gives assurance of accuracy in records and reports, and protects the company against loss from fraud or carelessness.

When a company converts to an EDP system, however, the work formerly divided among many people is performed by the computer. Consolidation of activities and integration of functions are to be expected, since the computer can conveniently handle many related aspects of a transaction. For example, when payroll is handled by a computer, it is possible to carry out a variety of related tasks with only a single use of the master records. These tasks could include the maintenance of personnel files with information on seniority, rate of pay, insurance, and the like; a portion of the timekeeping function; distribution of labour costs; and preparation of payroll cheques and payroll records.

Despite the integration of several functions in an EDP system, the importance of internal control is not in the least diminished. The essential factors described in Chapter 5 for satisfactory internal control in a large-scale organization are still relevant. Separation of duties and clearly defined responsibilities are still key ingredients despite the change in departmental boundaries, as will be explained in later sections of this chapter. These traditional control concepts are augmented, however, by controls written into the computer program and controls built into the computer hardware.

In recognition of the effect of EDP upon traditional control concepts, the CICA has issued two research studies: *Computer Control Guidelines* and *Computer Audit Guidelines.* The first study was designed to assist external auditors and others in evaluating the controls in EDP systems. It classified EDP controls into (1) preinstallation, (2) organizational, (3) development, (4) operations, (5) processing, (6) documentation, and (7) outside data centre. The second study is closely related to the first and was designed to provide guidance to auditors in their audit of EDP systems.

Similarly, the AICPA issued SAS No. 3, "The Effects of EDP on the Auditor's Study and Evaluation of Internal Control." SAS No. 3 classifies accounting controls in an EDP system into the categories of **general controls** and **application controls.** General controls relate to all EDP applications and include such considerations as (a) the organization of the EDP department; (b) procedures for documenting, testing, and approving the original system and any subsequent changes; (c) controls built into the hardware (equipment controls); and (d) security for files and equipment. Application controls, on the other hand, relate to specific accounting tasks performed by EDP, such as the preparation of payrolls. Controls of this nature include measures designed to assure the reliability of input, controls over processing, and controls over output.

Organizational controls in an electronic data processing system

Because of the ability of the computer to process data efficiently, there is a tendency to combine many data processing functions in an EDP department. In a manual or mechanical system, certain combinations of functions are considered incompatible from a standpoint of achieving strong internal control. For example, the function of recording cash disbursements is incompatible with the responsibility for reconciling bank statements. Since one of these procedures serves as a check upon the other, assigning both functions to one employee would enable the employee to conceal his own errors. A properly programmed computer, however, has no tendency or motivation to canceal its errors. Therefore, what appears to be an "incompatible" combination of functions may be combined in an EDP department without weakening internal control.

When "incompatible" functions are combined in the EDP department, compensating controls are necessary to prevent improper human intervention with computer processing. A person with the opportunity to make unauthorized changes in computer programs or data files is in a position to exploit the concentration of data processing functions in the EDP department. For example, a computer program used to process accounts payable may be designed to approve a vendor's invoice for payment only when that invoice is supported by a purchase order and receiving report. An employee able to make unauthorized changes in that program could cause unsubstantiated payments to be made to specific vendors.

EDP programs and data files cannot be changed without the use of EDP equipment. With EDP equipment, however, they can be changed without leaving any visible evidence of the alteration. Thus, the organization plan of an EDP department should prevent EDP personnel from having unauthorized access to EDP equipment, programs, or data files. This is accomplished by providing definite lines of authority and responsibility, segregation of functions, and clear definition of duties for each employee in the department. The organizational structure of a well-staffed EDP department, as illustrated in Figure 6–1, should include the following separation of responsibilities:

Data processing manager.   A manager should be appointed to supervise the operation of the data processing department. This data processing manager may report to the controller, or perhaps to a vice president of data processing or information systems. It is desirable for the data processing department to have a substantial degree of autonomy from major user departments. When EDP is a section within the accounting department, the controller should not have direct contact with computer operations.

Systems analysis.   Systems analysts are responsible for designing the EDP system. After considering the objectives of the business and its data processing needs, they determine the goals of the system and the means of achieving these goals. Utilizing system flowcharts and detail instructions, they outline the data processing system.

FIGURE 6–1
Organization of EDP department

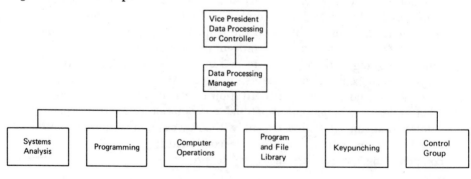

Programming. Guided by the specifications provided by the systems analysts, the programmers design program flowcharts for computer programs required by the system. They then code the required programs in computer language, generally making use of specialized programming languages, such as COBOL, and software elements, such as assemblers, compilers, and utility programs. They test the programs with *test decks* composed of genuine or dummy records and transactions, and perform the necessary debugging. Finally, the programmers prepare necessary documentation, such as the computer operator instructions.

Computer operations. The computer operators manipulate the computer in accordance with the instructions developed by the programmers. On occasion the computer operators may have to intervene through the computer console during a run in order to correct an indicated error. All operator entries into the computer should be made through a console typewriter so that printed copies of the entries are available. The separation of computer operations from programming is an important one from the standpoint of achieving internal control. An employee performing both functions would have an opportunity to make unauthorized changes in computer programs.

Program and file library. The purpose of the file library is to protect computer programs, master files, transaction (detail) tapes, and other records from loss, damage, and unauthorized use or alteration. To assure adequate control, the librarian maintains a formal "check-out" system for making records available to authorized users.

Keypunching. Keypunch operators transcribe data from source documents to punched cards which are read into the computer by an input device. Keypunching is primarily associated with *batch processing* systems, in which a group (batch) of source documents is processed at one time. In an *online, real-time system,* data may be entered directly into the computer by user departments through remote *terminals* without being transcribed into punched cards. Even in the most sophisticated systems, however, many applications are handled by batch processing.

Control group. The control group of a data processing department reviews and tests all input procedures, monitors computer processing, handles the reprocessing of errors detected by the computer, and reviews and distributes all computer output. This group also reviews the console log of operator interventions with computer processing and the library log of program usage.

Besides segregation of functions, the data processing organization plan should provide for rotation of programmer assignments, rotation of operator assignments, mandatory vacations, and adequate fidelity bonds for employees. At least two of the qualified data processing personnel should be present whenever the computer facility is in use. Careful screening procedures in the hiring of EDP personnel are also an important factor in achieving strong internal control.

Organizational controls and computer-centred fraud

The history of computer-centred fraud shows that the persons responsible for frauds typically set up the system and "run the whole show" as programmer and operator.

ILLUSTRATIVE CASE. A programmer for a large bank wrote a program for identifying and listing all overdrawn accounts. Later, as operator of the bank's computer, he was able to insert a "patch" in the program to cause the computer to ignore overdrafts in his own account. The programmer-operator was then able to overdraw his bank account at will, without the overdraft coming to management's attention. The fraud was not discovered until the computer broke down and the listing of overdrawn accounts had to be prepared manually.

The number of personnel and the organizational structure will, of course, determine the extent to which segregation of duties is possible. As a minimum, the function of programming should be separated from the functions controlling input to the computer programs, and the function of the computer operator should be segregated from functions requiring detailed knowledge or custody of the computer programs. If one person is permitted to perform duties in several of these functions, internal control is weakened, and the opportunity exists for fraudulent data to be inserted in the system.

Access to assets by EDP personnel. Whenever the responsibilities for record keeping and custody of the related assets are combined, the opportunities for an employee to conceal the abstraction of assets are increased. Since EDP is basically a record-keeping function, it is highly desirable to limit the access of EDP personnel to company assets. However, EDP personnel have direct access to cash if EDP activity includes the preparation of signed cheques. EDP personnel may also have indirect access to assets if, for example, EDP is used to generate shipping orders authorizing the release of inventory.

The combination of record keeping with access to assets seriously weakens internal control unless adequate *compensating controls* are present. One type of compensating control is the use of predetermined *batch totals,* such as document counts and totals of significant data fields, prepared in departments independent of EDP. For example, if EDP performs the function of printing cheques, another department should be responsible for authorizing the preparation of the cheques. The authorizing department should maintain a record of the total number and dollar amount of cheques authorized. These independently prepared batch totals should then be compared with the computer output before the cheques are released.

It is difficult for compensating controls to eliminate entirely the risk which results from EDP personnel having access to company assets. Auditors should therefore realize that the risk of computer-centred fraud is greatest in those areas in which EDP personnel have access to assets.

Management fraud. Organizational controls are reasonably effective in preventing an individual employee from perpetrating a fraud, but they do not prevent fraud involving collusion. If key employees or company officers conspire in an effort to commit fraud, internal controls which rely upon separation of duties can be rendered inoperative.

ILLUSTRATIVE CASE. The U.S. firm Equity Funding Corporation of America went into bankruptcy after it was discovered that the company's financial statements had been grossly and fraudulently misleading for a period of years. A life insurance subsidiary of the company had been manufacturing bogus insurance policies for fictitious persons and then selling these policies to other insurance companies. When the fraud was discovered, Equity Funding's balance sheet included over $120 million in fictitious assets, far exceeding the $75 million net income reported over the 13-year life of the company.

Perhaps the most startling revelation of the Equity Funding scandal was that numerous officers and employees of the company had worked together for years to perpetrate and conceal the fraud. The fictitious transactions had been carefully integrated into the company's computer-based accounting system. A wide variety of fraudulent supporting documents had been prepared for the sole purpose of deceiving auditors and governmental regulatory agencies. Upon disclosure of the activities, several members of top management were convicted of criminal charges.

The Equity Funding scandal is often described as a computer-based fraud. It was not because of the use of computers, however, that the company was able to deceive auditors and governmental investigators. Rather, the fraudulent activities were successfully concealed for a number of years because of the unprecedented willingness of a large number of company officers and employees to participate in the scheme. Collusion of the magnitude existing at Equity Funding would render any system of internal control ineffective.

Documentation

Internal control in an EDP department requires not only subdivision of duties but also the maintenance of adequate documentation describing the system and procedures used in all data processing tasks. Although several *runs* through the computer may be necessary to perform all of the elements of a specific data processing task, the run is usually the basic unit of computer documentation. Documentation of each computer run is included in a *run manual.*

A run manual is prepared by either the systems analyst or the programmer and contains a complete description of the program used for the run. As a minimum, run documentation should include:

1. A statement of the problems to be solved by elements of the system.
2. System flowcharts showing sources and nature of input, operations, and output.
3. A list and explanation of processing controls associated with the run.
4. Record layouts showing the placement of data on punched cards, magnetic tape, and print-outs.
5. Program flowcharts showing the major steps and logic of each computer program.
6. Program listings showing the detailed assembler and compiler print-outs.
7. Program approval and change sheets showing proper authorization for all initial programs and subsequent changes.
8. Operator instructions for processing the programs.
9. Test decks utilized in testing and debugging programs.

Complete run manuals may be utilized by systems analysts and programmers for making authorized changes in programs. Computer operators, on the other hand, should have access only to the instructions for processing the programs. If operators have access to the complete run manual, the opportunities for an operator to change or patch a program are increased.

Documentation is helpful to the auditors in reviewing the controls over program changes, evaluating controls written into programs, and determining the program logic. The auditors must also refer to format and layout information in the documentation in order to prepare test decks or special audit programs for testing the client's processing programs and computerized files. In other words, the auditors' study of internal control and their planning of an audit program to test the client's system require them to utilize the client's documentation.

Equipment controls

Modern electronic data processing equipment is highly accurate and reliable. Most errors in computer output result from erroneous input or an error in the program. Auditors, however, should be familiar with the equipment controls within a given system in order to appraise the reliability of the hardware, either for evaluating output or for searching for probable causes of erroneous output. Equipment controls are built into the computer by the computer manufacturer. Among the more common equipment or hardware controls are the following:

1. *Read after write.* The computer reads back the data after they have been recorded in storage and verifies their accuracy.
2. *Dual read or read after punch.* Data on magnetic tape or punched cards are read twice during the input phase, and the two readings are compared.

3. *Parity check.* Data are processed by the computer in arrays of *bits* (binary digits of "1" or "0"). In addition to bits necessary to represent the numeric or alphabetic character, a *parity* bit is added when necessary to make the sum of all the "1" bits always odd or even, depending upon the make of the computer. As data are transferred at rapid speeds between computer components, the parity check is applied by the computer to assure that bits are not lost during the transfer process.

4. *Echo check.* The echo check involves transmitting data received by an output device back to the source unit for comparison with the original data.

5. *Reverse multiplication.* In reverse multiplication, the roles of the original multiplicand and multiplier are reversed and the resultant product is compared to the original product.

A program of preventive maintenance is essential to assure the proper functioning of the equipment controls.

Security for files and equipment

All magnetic tape and punched card files should be properly identified by external labels and machine-readable internal *header* labels. The librarian should maintain a log recording all files checked out and returned to the library, and the signature of the authorized person responsible for the file during the check-out period.

Generally, three "generations" of master files should be retained to enable reproduction of files lost or destroyed. Under this *grandfather-father-son* principle of file retention, the current updated master file is the *son;* the master file utilized in the updating run which produced the son is the *father;* and the previous father is the *grandfather.* Records of transactions for the current period and for the prior period also should be retained to facilitate updating the older master files in the event that the current master file is accidentally destroyed. The three generations should be stored in separate sections of the library, or in separate locations, to minimize the risk of losing all three generations at once.

When programs are stored in online storage devices, users should be required to enter a secret password in order to gain access to the programs. The computer should maintain a log of all program usage, and should produce a warning if repeated attempts are made to gain access to programs by the use of incorrect passwords.

Safeguards are also necessary to protect the equipment against sabotage, fire, and water damage. The best way to prevent deliberate damage is to limit access to the facility to authorized personnel. Outsiders should be kept away from the facility, and EDP personnel should be carefully screened prior to employment. Management should always be alert to the possibility of damage by a disgruntled employee. Frequently, the location of the computer facility is kept relatively secret. The facility should have no windows and few doors; entrances should be controlled by guards or badge-activated locks. In addition, the computer room should be fire-resistant, air-conditioned, and above possible flood levels.

Controls over input

Input controls are designed to provide assurance that data received for processing represent properly authorized transactions and are accurate and complete when read into the computer. Control over input begins with proper authorization for initiation of the transactions to be processed. EDP is primarily a record-keeping department and therefore should not be authorized to initiate transactions. When transaction data are originally recorded on "hard-copy" source documents, such as sales orders, authorization may be indicated by the appropriate person initialing the document. In online systems, transaction data may be entered directly into the computer from remote terminal devices located in the departments initiating the transactions. In these cases, access to the terminals must be limited to those persons authorized to initiate transactions. This may be accomplished by assigning to authorized terminal users an identification number which must be read into the terminal before the computer will accept the input data.

In most systems, transaction documents are collected into batches for processing in sequence as one lot. Input controls are necessary in batch processing to determine that no data are lost or added to the batch. The sequence of serial numbers of source documents comprising each batch should be accounted for. In addition, such batch totals as item counts and totals for significant data fields should be developed for each batch; these totals may be verified during each stage of the processing of the batch.

Provision should be made for verifying the accuracy of the conversion of source documents to machine-readable media. For keypunch operations, a verifier punch should test the accuracy of the mechanical key strokes, or, as an alternative, the punched cards may be interpreted and visually compared to the source documents. A *self-checking number* may also be utilized to promote the reliability of identification and account numbers included in the input data.

Control over processing

Processing controls are designed to assure the reliability and accuracy of data processing. A major method of achieving control over processing is the use of *program controls,* which are written into the computer programs. Common program controls include:

1. *Item (or record) count.* A count of number of items or transactions to be processed in a given batch.
2. *Control total.* The predetermined total of one field of information for all items in a batch. An example would be total sales for a batch of sales orders. This control protects against missing amounts, duplication, and transposition errors in input or processing.
3. *Hash total.* A total of one field of information for all items in a batch, used in much the same manner as a control total. The difference between a hash total and a control total is that a hash total has no intrinsic meaning. An example of a hash total would be the sum of the employee numbers in a payroll application.
4. *Validity (code validity) test.* A comparison of employee, vendor, and other codes against a master file for authenticity.
5. *Limit test.* A test of the reasonableness of a field of data, given a predetermined upper and/or lower limit.
6. *Character mode.* A test to verify that all characters within a field are alphabetic, numeric, or alphanumeric, as required.
7. *Self-checking number.* A number containing redundant information, such as the sum of digits in another number, permitting a check for accuracy after the number has been transmitted from one device to another.
8. *File labels.* Labels used to ensure that the proper transaction file or master file is being used on a specific run. A *header label* is a machine-readable message at the beginning of a tape file, identifying the file and its release date. A *trailer label* is the last record in a file and contains such control devices as an item count and/or control totals.

In cases of exceptions or errors disclosed by program controls, the computer processing will halt, or the errors will be printed out. Error print-outs should be transmitted directly to the control group for follow-up. The control group's responsibility includes ascertaining that corrections of errors are properly entered into the appropriate batches, and that duplicate corrections are avoided.

The control group also monitors the operator's activities. A log maintained by the operator should be available to the control group. The log records the description of each run, the elapsed time for the run, operator console interventions, machine halts, master files utilized, and so on.

Controls over output

Output controls are designed to assure the reliability of computer output and to determine that output is distributed only to authorized personnel. Departments external to EDP can appraise the reliability of output by maintaining independent control totals of input and by reviewing the output returned by the data processing department. The EDP control group should have the responsibility for distributing the computer output to the appropriate recipients, and for following up on exceptions and errors reported by the recipients.

Internal auditing and EDP

An internal audit function should exist separate and distinct from the work of the control group in the data processing department. The control group is primarily concerned with day-to-day maintenance of the internal accounting controls for data processing, whereas the internal auditors are interested in evaluating the overall efficiency of data processing operations and the related internal controls.

The internal auditors should participate in the design of the data processing system to ensure that the system provides a proper *audit trail* and includes adequate internal controls. Once the system becomes operative, internal auditors review all aspects of the system on a test basis to determine that prescribed internal controls are operating as planned. Among other things, the internal auditors will test to determine that no changes are made in the system without proper authorization, programming personnel are functionally separate from computer operating personnel, adequate documentation is maintained, input controls are functioning effectively, and the control group is performing its assigned functions.

Integrated test facility. One method used by internal auditors to test and monitor accounting controls in EDP applications is an *integrated test facility*. An integrated test facility is a subsystem of dummy records and files built into the regular data processing system. These dummy files permit test data to be processed simultaneously with regular (live) input without adversely affecting the live data files or output. The test data, which include all conceivable types of transactions and exceptions, affect only the dummy files and dummy output. For this reason, an integrated test facility is often termed the "mini-company approach" to testing the system. Integrated test facilities may be used in either online, real-time, or batch processing systems.

The internal auditing staff monitors the processing of test data, studying the effects upon the dummy files, error reports and other output produced, and the follow-up of exceptions by the control group. An integrated test facility for payroll applications, for example, could be set up by including a fictitious department and records for fictitious employees in the payroll master file. Input data for the dummy department would be included with input data from actual departments. Internal auditors would monitor all output relating to the dummy department, including payroll records, error reports, and payroll cheques. (In this situation, strict control would be necessary to prevent misuse of the dummy payroll cheques.)

One problem with integrated test facilities is the risk that someone may manipulate the real data files by transferring data to or from the dummy files. Controls should exist to prevent unauthorized access to the dummy files, and the internal auditors should monitor all activity in these files.

Impact of EDP on the audit trail

In a manual or mechanical data processing system, an audit trail of hard copy documentation links individual transactions with the summary figures in the financial statements. Computers, on the other hand, are able to create, update, and erase data in computer-based records without any visible evidence of a change being made. During the early development of EDP systems, this capability led to some concern among accountants that electronic data processing would obscure or even eliminate the audit trail. While it is technologically possible to design an EDP system which would leave no audit trail, such a system would be neither practical nor desirable. Valid business reasons exist for the inclusion of a hard copy audit trail in even the most sophisticated EDP systems.

An adequate audit trail is necessary to enable management to direct and control the operations of the business, to permit file reconstruction in the event of processing errors or computer failure, and to accommodate the needs of independent auditors and governmental agencies.

Thus, fears that EDP would obscure the audit trail have not materialized. During the design of an EDP system, management will normally consult with both its internal auditors and independent auditors to assure that an adequate audit trail is built into the system. In an EDP system, of course, the audit trail may consist of computer print-outs and data stored on punched cards and magnetic tapes, rather than the more traditional handwritten source documents, journals, and ledgers.

Implications of online, real-time systems

An online, real-time system is one in which users have direct (online) access to the computer, and the recording of transactions causes instantaneous updating of all relevant files. An example of an online, real-time (OLRT) system is frequently encountered in savings and loan associations. These systems allow a teller at any branch to update a customer's account immediately by recording deposits or withdrawals on a computer terminal.

When an OLRT system is in use, input need not be entered to the computer in batch runs. Elimination of the batch concept poses several problems for auditors. For example, original source documents may not be available to support input to the computer, and batch controls, such as control totals and item counts, may not be applicable. Also, the overall amount of hard copy included in the audit trail may be substantially reduced.

For the purpose of providing an audit trail in an OLRT system, account balances should be printed out periodically. In addition, daily print-outs should be prepared listing the transactions entered through each terminal. If specified terminals are used for certain types of transactions, the transaction records will be grouped by type of transaction. Print-outs of account balances and transactions should be stored in a separate location from the computer files so they can be used for file reconstruction if necessary.

In an OLRT system there is a greater degree of reliance upon the computer for internal control. Input and output errors are detected primarily through program controls. Control must be exercised to prevent manipulation of the system as a whole, since the amount of hard copy and the possibilities for output verification are substantially reduced. Security should be provided at each terminal to assure that transactions are initiated only by authorized personnel. A validity check of an identification number should be made before a terminal user can gain access to files. Passwords should be required to gain access to specific programs and files, and a self-checking digit should be used with account numbers to prevent input into the wrong accounts. Terminals should be operative only during regular processing hours.

A log of all input should be maintained at each input terminal. These logs should be reconciled with the daily record of transactions maintained and printed out by the computer.

A special problem in an OLRT system is the need to provide for continuing operations in the event of computer failure. Mechanical equipment should be kept available, whenever feasible, to permit the continuance of operations during computer "down time." For processing which can be handled only by computer, arrangements should be made for another computer facility to provide back-up computer services on short notice.

The auditors' study and evaluation of internal control in an EDP system

Whether financial statements are produced by a manual, mechanical, or electronic data processing system, the auditors must conduct a proper study and evaluation of internal control. This investigation provides the auditors with a basis for assessing the extent to which the client's internal controls may be relied upon in determining the nature, timing, and extent of work necessary to complete the audit. In addition, their evaluation of internal control serves as the basis for the auditors' recommendations to the client for improving the system.

Regardless of the type of data processing system used by the client, the auditors' study and evaluation of internal control involves three distinct steps. The auditors must (1) review internal control and prepare a description of the system in their working papers, (2) conduct tests of compliance to determine that accounting controls are functioning as prescribed, and (3) evaluate the system to determine the extent to which internal controls may be relied upon.

Review of internal control

Auditors acquire an understanding of an EDP system by making enquiries, observing operations, inspecting records and documents, studying flowcharts, and reviewing run manuals. This understanding is then documented in the audit working papers by the use of their systems flowcharts or a specially designed internal control questionnaire.

Systems flowcharts. As explained in Chapter 5, systems flowcharts are the most commonly used technique for describing a system of internal control in audit working papers. An advantage of flowcharting, with respect to EDP systems, is that the EDP department should have systems flowcharts available for all computer applications as part of the standard documentation.

An illustration of a system flowchart for sales, accounts receivable, and cash receipts appears in Figure 6–2. The following description of the illustrated procedures and processing steps should be helpful in studying the illustrated flowchart.

1. Orders are received from sales representatives, and sales invoices are mechanically produced by a posting machine. A punched paper tape is a by-product of the writing of the sales invoice. Two copies of the invoice are mailed to the customer, one copy is sent to the shipping department, and one copy is filed offline. The punched paper tape of sales invoice transactions is converted to magnetic tape. The items on the magnetic tape are then sorted into the proper sequence on another magnetic tape.

2. Individual cash remittance advices from customers are received from the mail room and verified against a batch total, which is also received from the mail room. These remittances are keypunched on cards, and the cards are verified. The deck of punched cards is then converted to magnetic tape. The items on the magnetic tape are in turn sorted into proper sequence on another magnetic tape.

3. The accounts receivable master file is updated by processing both the sales transactions tape and the cash receipts transactions tape. A by-product of the updating of the accounts receivable master file is an *error report* for the run and a print-out (on an online typewriter) of any job messages.

FIGURE 6–2
System flowchart

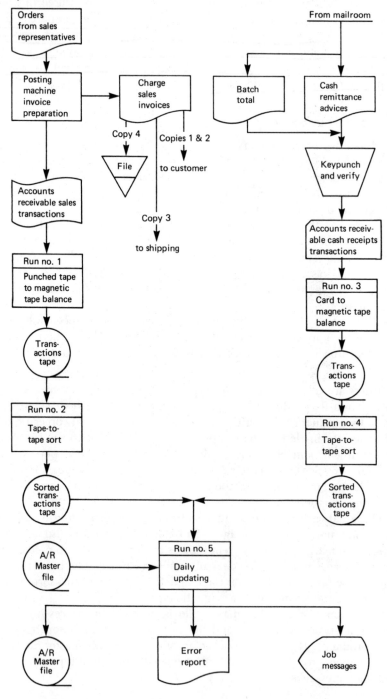

The client's documentation of EDP activities usually includes *program flowcharts* as well as systems flowcharts. Program flowcharts illustrate the detailed logic of specific computer programs. Auditors capable of interpreting program flowcharts may evaluate the program controls contained in specific computer applications and draw inferences regarding the computer output. Many computers will accept software routines which generate computer-made flowcharts of the programs in use. Auditors may use such routines to ensure that the program flowcharts contained in the documentation actually describe the programs in use. A shortcoming of this method is that even trained auditors may overlook a major deficiency within a program unless they know in advance what type of problem they should be looking for.

Internal control questionnaires for EDP systems.   The use of internal control questionnaires was discussed in Chapter 5. In the audit of EDP systems, questionnaires are best suited for a study of organizational controls and controls over input and output. The questionnaire approach is not well suited to studying the effectiveness of program controls because neither the auditor nor the respondent is usually aware of situations in which program controls are inadequate. A portion of the EDP control questionnaire used by one national CA firm is illustrated in Figure 6–3.

Preliminary evaluation of internal control.   After completing their initial review of the system, the auditors are in a position to make a preliminary appraisal of the reliability of the client's accounting controls. If it appears that accounting controls may be sufficiently strong to provide a basis for reliance, the auditors must conduct tests of compliance before making their final evaluation of internal control. On the other hand, it may appear that accounting controls in some areas will not prove sufficiently reliable to justify the audit effort of compliance testing. In the interest of efficiency, the auditors may elect to place no reliance upon those accounting controls and omit the related compliance testing procedures.

Tests of compliance

Regardless of the nature of the client's data processing system, auditors must conduct tests of compliance if they are to place any reliance upon the client's internal controls. The purpose of these tests is to provide reasonable assurance that the internal controls described in the audit working papers are actually in use and operating as planned. The nature of the data processing system may, however, affect the specific procedures employed by the auditors in their compliance testing. In this regard, the CICA's *Computer Audit Guidelines* research study should provide useful guidance to auditors in developing appropriate tests of compliance.

Auditors usually test general controls by observing the performance of duties by client personnel; reviewing authorizations, documentation,

FIGURE 6-3
Internal control questionnaire for EDP systems—input controls

B. Input controls	*Yes*	*No*	*n.a.*

B. Input controls

1. Are source documents submitted for processing date-stamped or otherwise cancelled by EDP to prevent duplicate processing (such as keypunching the same document twice)?

   If so, describe policy below.

         ____   ____   ____

2. Are control techniques that eliminate all or a part of the input preparation function (such as preprinted or prepunched data cards) used in the preparation of source information by originating department(s)?

   If so, describe below.

         ____   ____   ____

3. Does the originating department prepare a transmittal document that includes the batch number, date, control totals of important fields, transaction counts, and so on?

   Describe the batching and transmittal procedures.

         ____   ____   ____

4. Are source documents reviewed for proper authorization and preparation prior to their conversion to machine-readable form?

   If so, describe procedures.

         ____   ____   ____

5. Are input control totals checked after processing by someone independent of the EDP function?

   By whom? _____

   Describe the procedure.

         ____   ____   ____

FIGURE 6–3 (*continued*)   *Yes*   *No*   *n.a.*

6. Are transactions representing error resolutions and correcting entries that are resubmitted into the EDP system processed through all of the same checking and edit routines as the original transactions?   ____ ____ ____

7. Are error correction procedures adequate to insure that errors are ultimately corrected or resolved?   ____ ____ ____

8. Do the company records provide the means to adequately:
   a. Trace any transaction forward to a final total?   ____ ____ ____
   b. Trace any transaction back to the original source document or input?   ____ ____ ____
   c. Trace any final total back to the component transactions?   ____ ____ ____

9. When ledgers (general or subsidiary) are maintained on computer media, do the systems of processing provide:
   a. A historical record of activity in the accounts?   ____ ____ ____
   b. A periodic trial balance of the accounts?   ____ ____ ____

10. Are original source documents retained for an adequate period of time in a manner that allows identification with related output records?

11. Describe the edit tests performed on the input data (e.g. codes, characters, fields, transactions, sequence, limit checks, etc.) to verify completeness, accuracy, and reasonableness of input data.

12. If an edit test causes the rejection of data, what media is utilized to notify the user?

Source: Reprinted with special permission of Laventhol & Horwath.

and approvals of programs and program changes; inspecting the equipment in use; and observing the security measures in force. The nature of general controls is such that their presence usually must be observed rather than determined by the examination of accounting data.

Procedures used to test applications controls vary significantly from one system or application to another. In a batch system, for example, input controls may be tested by accounting for the serial sequence of source documents in selected batches, verifying the computation of batch control totals, and comparing control totals to computer output. In an online, real-time system, on the other hand, batch data are not available, and the auditors must design entirely different compliance tests.

In testing processing controls, the auditors examine error reports printed by the computer, review the procedures performed by the EDP control group, and review the working papers of any testing done by the client's internal auditors. In addition, they must test the effectiveness of significant accounting controls written into the computer programs. Methods commonly used in compliance testing program controls include auditing "around the computer" and the use of test decks, controlled programs, and generalized audit software packages.

Auditing "around the computer." One approach to testing processing controls in an EDP system is for the auditors to process input data manually on a test basis. The auditors' results are then compared to those obtained by the client's EDP department and any discrepancies are investigated. This technique is termed auditing "around the computer" because the auditors by-pass the computer rather than utilize it in conducting their tests. As auditors have acquired greater expertise in auditing computer-based systems, testing procedures which make use of the computer (auditing *through the computer*) have tended to replace this older audit technique. However, auditing around the computer still can be very effective with respect to computer activities which involve a risk of improper manipulation by EDP personnel.

Test decks. In the audit of a manual accounting system, the auditors trace sample transactions through the records from their inception to their final disposition. In the audit of an EDP system, a comparable approach is the use of a *test deck*. The test decks developed by the client's programmers may be utilized by the independent auditors once they have satisfied themselves by study of flowcharts and print-outs that the tests are valid. Less desirably in terms of audit effort, the auditors may develop their own test decks.

Test decks should include all conceivable types of exceptions and errors in a process. Among these would be missing transactions, erroneous transactions, illogical transactions, out-of-balance batches, and out-of-sequence records. The auditors will carefully appraise the program controls and control group functions with respect to the test deck errors and exceptions. Dummy transactions and records used in test decks can be specially coded to avoid contamination of the client's genuine records and files.

Controlled programs. As an alternative or supplement to the test deck approach, the auditors may monitor the processing of current data by a duplicate program which has been under their control. They then compare the output to that developed by the client's copy of the program. They may also request the reprocessing of historical data with their controlled program for comparison with the original output. Reprocessing historical data may alert the auditors to undocumented changes in the client's programs.

Controlled programs are advantageous because the auditor may test the client's program with both genuine (live) and test data. A problem arises in testing historical data, however, since the client may not retain tape files beyond three generations.

Through controlled programs, auditors may test program controls without risk of contaminating the client's files. Also, the testing may be conducted at an independent computer facility without utilizing the client's computer or data processing personnel.

Generalized audit software. Many large public accounting firms have developed *generalized audit software* (computer programs) which may be used to test the reliability of the client's programs as well as to perform many specific auditing functions.

One application of computer audit software is to verify the reliability of the client's programs through a process termed *parallel simulation.* The generalized audit software includes programs that can perform processing functions essentially equivalent to those of the client's programs. The generalized audit programs use the same files (transaction files and master files) as do the client's programs, and should ideally produce the same results as were produced by the client. Thus, the generalized audit programs "simulate" the client's processing of live data.

Although the generalized audit programs are likely to be less efficient than the client's programs, the output should be comparable in all material respects. The generalized audit software compares the simulated output to the client's records and prepares a listing of discrepancies. These discrepancies, of course, should be followed up and reconciled by the auditors. A flowchart of the parallel simulation process is illustrated in Figure 6–4.

The value of generalized audit software lies in the fact that the auditors are able to conduct independent processing of live data. Often, the verification of the client's output would be too large a task to be undertaken manually but can be done efficiently through a parallel computer program. Even when manual verification would be possible, the use of a parallel program allows the auditors to expand greatly the size of the

FIGURE 6–4
Flowchart of parallel simulation process

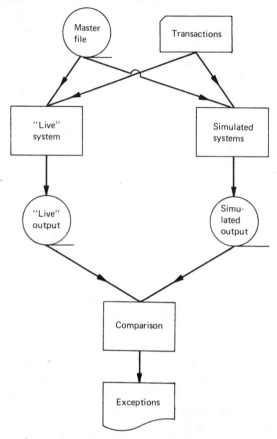

Source: Reprinted with special permission from *Tempo,*
a quarterly journal published by Touche Ross & Co.

sample of transactions to be tested. An extensive examination of the client's files may become a feasible and economic undertaking. It is not necessary, however, to duplicate all of the client's data processing. Testing should be performed only to the extent necessary to determine the reliability of the client's financial reporting systems.

Generalized audit software and substantive testing. Audit software is available for a wide variety of audit applications. It is most widely used for retrieving data from the client's system for use by the auditors in substantiating account balances. In performing retrieval functions, the audit software *interfaces* with the client's master files and locates specific data requested by the auditors. Applications of this nature include:

1. Stratification of populations for sampling.
2. Selection of random samples of transactions for testing.
3. Selection of accounts receivable for confirmation.
4. Identification of slow-moving inventory.
5. Identification of past-due receivables.
6. Comparison of budgeted and actual data.
7. Comparison of inventory test counts and perpetual inventory records.
8. Comparison of sales prices in master files to sales prices on invoices.
9. Verification of inventory extensions and footings.

Auditors do not need extensive technical EDP knowledge in order to make use of generalized computer audit programs. They will find it necessary to perform only a modest amount of programming. In fact, many public accounting firms have found that they can train audit staff members to code specification sheets and operate a generalized audit program within a time span of a week or two. Because of the simplified procedures which have been developed, auditors can, after limited training, program and operate the generalized audit software independently—that is, without assistance from the client's EDP personnel. On occasion, prepackaged software may not be available for a specific audit application. Most large public accounting firms, however, have technical support groups which can design software routines to meet the specifications of the audit staff.

As previously mentioned, a number of the larger public accounting firms have developed their own generalized audit software. In the United States similar programs are available to other members of the profession through the AICPA.

Evaluation of internal control

Auditors evaluate internal control to determine the extent to which it may be relied upon to produce reliable accounting data. The extent of this reliance, in turn, determines the nature, timing, and extent of the substantive testing necessary for the auditors to express an opinion as to the fairness of the financial statements.

Conceptually, evaluating internal accounting controls over EDP activities is no different from evaluating other aspects of the system. Substantive testing procedures must be expanded in those areas where internal accounting controls are weak and may be restricted in areas where control is unusually strong. In evaluating accounting control over EDP activity, the auditors should consider the controls applied by user departments and internal auditing, as well as controls applied within the EDP department.

Computer service centres

Computer service centres provide data processing services to customers who do not do enough data processing to justify having their own computers. The customer delivers the input to the computer service centre, and the service centre processes the data and returns the output to the customer.

Computer service centres actually strengthen internal control because of increased subdivision of duties. Deliberate manipulation of a company's records is less likely because the persons doing the data processing do not have access to the company's assets. Also, since the service centre processes input in small batches and provides hard-copy output to the customer, the independent auditors usually will have an adequate audit trail for evaluation of the processing conducted by the computer service centre. Control totals, hash totals, and item counts may also be used effectively to ensure the reliability of the batch processing.

When their client uses a service centre for data processing, the auditors ordinarily are able to evaluate internal control by auditing "around" the service centre's computer, and possibly by using test decks. On occasion, the data processed by the service centre may be material to the client's operations and the client's controls over the data may not be adequate. In such situations, the auditors should consider visiting the service centre to review, test, and evaluate the accounting controls in effect. To assist the auditors of clients using computer service centres, the AICPA in the United States has issued an audit guide entitled *Audit of Service-Center-Produced Records.*

Third-party reviews of service centres. Some service centres perform similar processing services for numerous clients. If the auditors of each client (termed "user auditors") were to visit the service centre for the purpose of reviewing accounting controls, they would probably all ask similar questions. To avoid such repetition, it may be advantageous for the service centre to engage its own auditors to review and test the system of internal control at the service centre, and issue a report describing the system and their findings. The user auditors may then elect to rely upon this ***third-party review*** as an alternative to visiting the service centre themselves. The cost of the third-party review may be borne by the service centre, customers of the service centre, or the user auditors.

Before relying upon a third-party review, the user auditors should take steps to satisfy themselves as to the independence and professional reputation of the third-party auditors. In addition, they should enquire of the service centre management and the third-party auditors as to whether any significant changes have been made in accounting control at the service centre subsequent to the third-party review.

Time-sharing systems

A time-sharing system consists of a large, fast, central computer which may be used simultaneously by a number of independent users at remote locations. Communication devices related to the computer permit translation of computer input into codes which are transmitted over telephone lines. Each user (subscriber) has online access to the central computer through a remote terminal. To use this terminal, either to enter input or receive output, the subscriber merely dials a telephone number and is automatically connected to the computer. The subscriber's files are maintained at the central computer facility. To prevent access to these files or other use of the computer by an unauthorized person, each subscriber is required to type an identification code into the terminal.

The subscribers to a commercial time-sharing system can, through their terminals, run programs, store these programs in the computer for subsequent use, use the programs developed by the time-sharing company, and store files of data in the computer for subsequent use. In brief, the user of a time-sharing system has available most of the services which would be available through ownership of a computer.

The central computer centre should maintain controls to prevent unauthorized use of each customer's proprietary programs, loss or destruction of customers' data files, and alteration of customers' programs. Provision should also be made for file reconstruction. The internal controls most important to the auditors of a company having a time-sharing terminal are the client's control over input data and the program controls, such as item counts and control totals. Substantial hard-copy output is usually generated at the subscriber's access terminal; thus an adequate audit trail usually exists for verifying the reliability of data processing.

In most cases it is not feasible or necessary for the auditors to test or evaluate the internal control for the central computer; however, they may test the client's proprietary programs. Care must be taken so that test data do not permanently contaminate the client's files.

Some large public accounting firms have terminals in their offices across the country, all linked to national time-sharing networks. These terminals are used for such projects as forecasting financial statements with numerous input variables, preparation of tax returns, selection of random samples for testing, staff training in computer skills, and also for administrative processes within the firm.

Auditing EDP systems—a look to the future

The computer was once viewed by some as a potential menace to auditors—a black box which threatened to make their task impossible by eliminating the audit trail. However, the public accounting profession has responded impressively to the challenges posed by the computer. Auditors have modified their procedures to fit electronic data processing systems and have harnessed the power of the computer to assist in the performance of many audit functions. Generalized computer audit programs have been developed which not only test the client's files and programs but also perform simulations, capital budgeting applications, and other functions useful to both auditors and client. No longer are auditors dependent upon programmers in communicating with the computer. They have acquired the independent capacity to utilize the computer in achieving their goals.

As the routine clerical aspects of auditing are increasingly being delegated to the computer, auditors are able to broaden the scope of their activities and to emphasize the testing of management plans and policies. The use of computerized audit techniques may pave the way to the audit of quarterly financial statements as well as annual statements. Since interim financial statements are used as a basis for investment decisions, adding to their credibility through extension of the auditors' role is a logical consideration. (The auditors' responsibilities with respect to interim financial statements are discussed in Chapter 20.)

The challenges of EDP are continuing to grow, and auditors will have to become increasingly familiar with EDP systems if they are to meet these challenges. While staff auditors must have a good working knowledge of computer-based systems, they need not be computer specialists. In the audit of clients using sophisticated EDP systems, specialists in electronic data processing and specialists in statistical sampling may work with the audit team. The staff auditors, however, should have sufficient familiarity with EDP to design appropriate audit procedures for computer-based systems.

Computer audit programs for use with an online, real-time system may eventually be designed as part of the client's EDP system. These programs and related special-purpose hardware might select random samples of the data processed for subsequent review by the auditors. Other audit functions made part of the system might be to ensure that all transactions processed meet stipulated criteria.

The painstaking work of developing input for a computer by use of punched cards or tape may be solved by improvements in optical scanning devices. A typewriter may be a sufficient input device if optical scanners capable of reading ordinary printed or typed material are available. In fact, auditors may type the evidence they gather on working papers which will be read by optical scanners, automatically recorded on magnetic tape, and made available for processing by the computer.

KEY TERMS INTRODUCED OR EMPHASIZED IN CHAPTER 6

application controls   Internal controls relating to a specific accounting task, such as preparation of a payroll.

batch   A group of transactions processed in sequence as one lot.

boundary protection   Protection against unauthorized entry (read or write) to a tape, disk, or other storage device.

control total   A total of one information field for all the records of a batch, such as the total sales dollars for a batch of sales invoices.

disk   A random access storage device consisting of a circular metal plate with magnetic material on both sides.

file   An organized collection of related records, such as a customer file, which is usually arranged in sequence according to a key contained in each record.

file integrity   The accuracy and reliability of data in a file.

general controls   Internal accounting controls which relate to all EDP applications. The category includes organizational controls, documentation, equipment controls, and security controls.

hard copy   Computer output in printed form, such as printed listings, reports, and summaries.

hash total   A meaningless control total, such as the total of all invoice numbers in a batch of sales invoices, utilized to determine whether data are lost between operations.

header label   A machine-readable record at the beginning of a file which identifies the file.

integrated test facility   A set of dummy records and files included in an EDP system enabling test data to be processed simultaneously with live input.

interface   To run two or more files or programs simultaneously in a manner permitting data to be transferred from one to another.

master file   A file of relatively permanent data or information which is generally updated periodically.

offline   Pertaining to peripheral devices or equipment which are not in direct communication with the central processing unit of the computer.

online   Pertaining to peripheral devices or equipment which are in direct communication with the central processing unit of the computer.

patch   A new section of coding added in a rough or expedient way to modify a program.

program flowchart   A graphic representation of the major steps and logic of a computer program.

random access   Pertaining to a storage technique in which the time required to gain access to data is not significantly affected by the location of the data in storage. A disk is a random access device.

record   A group of related items or fields of data handled as a unit.

record layout   A diagram showing all the fields of data in a record and their arrangement in the record.

self-checking number   A number which contains a redundant suffixed digit (check digit) permitting the number to be verified for accuracy after it has been transferred from one device or medium to another.

sequential access   Pertaining to a storage technique in which the time required to gain access to data is related to the location of the data in storage. Magnetic tape is a sequential storage device.

terminal   An online input device. Many terminals are portable and may be connected to the computer through ordinary telephone lines. The method of entering data is usually a typewriter keyboard or an optical scanner.

test deck   A set of dummy records and transactions developed to test the adequacy of a computer program or system.

third-party review (of a computer service centre)   An evaluation and report by an independent auditor on the internal accounting controls at a computer service centre. Other auditors make use of this report in evaluating the internal control over data processing performed for their clients by the service centre.

GROUP I
REVIEW QUESTIONS

6–1.   Distinguish general controls from application controls, and give examples of the types of controls included in each of these broad categories.

6–2.   Auxiliary storage devices used to augment the capacity of the storage unit of a computer include which of the following: (*a*) cathode ray tubes, (*b*) magnetic drums, (*c*) card punches, (*d*) magnetic tape, (*e*) magnetic disk packs, (*f*) console display panels, (*g*) compilers, and (*h*) magnetic tape encoders?

6–3.   An EDP department usually performs numerous data processing functions which would be separated in a manual system. Does this imply that separation of duties is not a practical means of achieving internal control in a computerized system? Explain.

6–4.   What are the principal responsibilities of the "control group" in an electronic data processing department?

6–5.   Explain briefly the term "online, real-time system."

6–6.   Explain brieflly the meaning of the terms "documentation" and "run manual" as used in an EDP department. How might a client's "documentation" be used by the auditors?

6–7.   The number of personnel in an EDP department may limit the extent to which subdivision of duties is feasible. What is the minimum amount of segregation of duties that will permit satisfactory internal control?

6–8.   Compare the responsibilities and objectives of the EDP control group to those of the internal auditors with respect to EDP activities.

6–9.   What is an "integrated test facility?" How is it used?

6–10.   Define and give the purpose of each of the following program or equipment controls:

    a.   Record counts.

    b.   Limit test.

    c.   Reverse multiplication.

    d.   Hash totals. (AICPA, adapted)

6–11.   Most electronic data processing equipment manufacturers have built-in controls to ensure that information is correctly read, processed, transferred within the system, and recorded. One of these built-in controls is the parity bit.

    a.   What is the parity bit?

    b.   When would the parity bit control be used? (AICPA)

6–12.   Distinguish equipment controls from program controls, and give examples of each.

6–13.   Differentiate between a systems flowchart and a program flowchart.

6–14.   Auditors should be familiar with the terminology employed in electronic data processing. The following statements contain some of the terminology so employed. Indicate whether each statement is true or false.

    a.   A recent improvement in computer hardware is the ability to automatically produce error listings. Previously, this was possible only when provisions for such a report were included in the program.

    b.   The control of input and output to and from the EDP department should be performed by an independent control group.

    c.   An internal-audit computer program which continuously monitors computer processing is a feasible approach for improving internal control in OLRT systems.

    d.   An internal label is one of the controls built into the hardware by the manufacturer of a magnetic tape system.

    e.   A limit test in a computer program is comparable to a decision that an individual makes in a manual system to judge a transaction's reasonableness.

    f.   A principal advantage of using magnetic tape files is that data need not be recorded sequentially.

    g.   A major advantage of disk files is the ability to gain random access to data on the disk.

    h.   The term "grandfather-father-son" refers to a method of computer record security rather than to generations in the evolution of computer hardware.

    i.   A control total is an example of a self-checking number within a batch control.

    j.   When they are not in use, tapes, disks, and card files should be stored apart from the computer room under the control of a librarian.

6–15.   Explain the fundamental differences between the use of a test deck and the use of generalized audit software.

6–16.   Is it probable that the use of EDP will eventually eliminate the audit trail, making it impossible to trace individual transactions from their origin to the summary totals in the financial statements. Explain the reasons for your answer.

6–17.   Is the term "parallel simulation" associated with auditing "around the computer" or "through the computer"?

6–18.   What is a "computer service centre"? Does the use of a computer service centre tend to strengthen or weaken a client's internal control? Explain.

6–19.   Does a time-sharing system require the subscriber to deliver batches of data to a centre for processing?

GROUP II
QUESTIONS REQUIRING ANALYSIS

6–20. Distinguish between batch processing and online, real-time (OLRT) processing. In which of these systems is strong internal accounting control over input most easily attained? Explain.

6–21. The first requirement of an effective system of internal control is a satisfactory plan of organization. Explain the characteristics of a satisfactory plan of organization for an EDP department, including the relationship between the department and the rest of the organization.

6–22. An effective system of internal control requires a sound system of records control, of operations and transactions (source data and their flow), and of classification of data within the accounts. For an EDP system, these controls include input controls, processing controls, and output controls. List the characteristics of a satisfactory system of input controls. (Confine your comments to a batch-controlled system employing punched cards and to the steps that occur prior to the processing of the input cards in the computer.) (AICPA, adapted)

6–23. The use of test decks is one method of performing compliance tests of processing controls in an EDP system. Identify and discuss several other methods by which auditors may test internal processing controls over EDP activity.

6–24. The Central Valley Utility District is installing an electronic data processing system. The CA who conducts the annual examination of the utility district's financial statements has been asked to recommend controls for the new system.

Required:

Discuss recommended controls over:

    a. Program documentation.
    b. EDP hardware.
    c. Tape files and programs. (AICPA, adapted)

6–25. Many companies have part or all of their data processing done by computer service centres.

    a. What controls should the company maintain to assure the accuracy of processing done by a service centre?
    b. How do auditors test and evaluate internal control over applications processed for an audit client by a service centre?
    c. What is a "third-party review" of a computer service centre? Explain the rationale behind third-party reviews and the procedures which user auditors must employ before relying upon such reviews.

6–26. Select the best answer for each of the following questions. Explain the reasons for your selection.

    a. A customer inadvertently ordered part number 12368 rather than part number 12638. In processing this order, the error would be

detected by the vendor with which of the following four controls?
  (1)   Batch total.
  (2)   Key punch verifying.
  (3)   Self-checking digit.
  (4)   Limit test.
b.   When auditing a computerized system, auditors may use the "in-
      tegrated test facility" technique, sometimes referred to as the mini-
      company approach, as an audit tool. This technique—
  (1)   Is more applicable to independent audits than internal audits.
  (2)   Involves using test decks of punched cards.
  (3)   Is the most commonly used audit tool for "auditing through
        the computer."
  √ (4)   Involves introducing simulated transactions into the system
        simultaneously with actual transactions.
c.   If a trailer label is used on a magnetic tape file, it is the last record
      and summarizes the file. Which of the following information is not
      typically found on a trailer label?
  (1)   Record (item) count.
  (2)   Identification number.
  (3)   Control totals for one or more fields.
  (4)   End-of-file or end-of-reel code.
d.   Data Corporation Ltd. has just completely computerized its billing
      and accounts receivable record keeping. You want to make maxi-
      mum use of the new computer in your audit of Data Corporation
      Ltd. Which of the following audit procedures could not be per-
      formed through a computer program?
  (1)   Tracing audited cash receipts to accounts receivable credits.
  (2)   Selecting on a random number basis accounts to be con-
        firmed.
  (3)   Examining sales invoices for completeness, consistency be-
        tween different items, and reasonableness of amounts.
  (4)   Resolving differences reported by customers on confirmation
        requests.

6–27. During a meeting of his firm's Auditing Committee, CA and his partners
      have been discussing methods of auditing those of the firm's clients
      having computer installations. The main topic of discussion was whether
      to use a client's computer to test the records produced by the com-
      puter system.
          At the end of the meeting, the partners decided to investigate the
      subject further, each partner agreeing to look into different parts of the
      subject before the next meeting. CA agreed to prepare:

  (*i*)   A list of the auditing tasks that computer programs could perform
        for the firm; and
  (*ii*) A list describing the practical problems involved in the use of
        test decks.

Required:

Compose the two lists. (CICA)

6–28. Select the best answer for each of the following questions.

    a. A fundamental programming technique which allows computers to be utilized effectively in solving repetitive problems is—
      (1) Dynamic reallocation.
      (2) Indexed sequential access.
      (3) Blocking.
      (4) Looping.
      (5) None of the above.

    b. In connection with his examination of financial statements, a CA may use duplicate programs which he controls to process a client's current data. This procedure may be an acceptable alternative to—
      (1) Examining a sample of source documents.
      (2) Reviewing controls over data processing.
      (3) Reviewing data processing flowcharts.
      (4) Using a test data deck with client programs.
      (5) None of the above.

    c. On magnetic disks more than one file may be stored on a single physical file while in multiprogramming computer operations, several programs may be in core storage at one time. In both cases, it is important to prevent the intermixing or overlapping of data. This is accomplished by a technique known as—
      (1) Boundary protection.
      (2) File integrity.
      (3) Paging.
      (4) Interleaving.
      (5) None of the above.

    d. A technique for controlling identification numbers (part number, man number, etc.) is—
      (1) Self-checking digits.
      (2) Echo checks.
      (3) Parity control.
      (4) File protection.
      (5) None of the above.

    e. In a batch processing system, control over the punching into cards of hours worked could be most efficiently established by use of—
      (1) Dual punching.
      (2) Batch verification.
      (3) Hash totals.
      (4) Sight checking.
      (5) None of the above.

    f. The basic form of back-up used in magnetic tape operations is called—
      (1) Odd parity check.
      (2) Dual-head processing.
      (3) File protection rings.

(4)   The son-father-grandfather concept.

(5)   None of the above.

g.   Maintenance of proper internal control within an electronic data processing system requires physical controls and separation of duties similar to those required in a manual system. However, proper internal control will still exist in an EDP system if—

(1)   The programmer also acts as the operator during production runs.

(2)   The programmer is responsible for security over the operating programs.

(3)   The operator has the authority to amend input data.

(4)   The operator also acts as input/output control clerk.

(5)   None of the above. (CICA, adapted)

GROUP III
PROBLEMS

6-29.   A CA's client, The Outsider, Inc., is a medium-sized manufacturer of products for the leisure time activities market (camping equipment, scuba gear, bows and arrows, and so on). During the past year, a computer system was installed, and inventory records of finished goods and parts were converted to computer processing. The inventory master file is maintained on a disk. Each record of the file contains the following information:

> Item or part number.
> Description.
> Size.
> Unit of measure code.
> Quantity on hand.
> Cost per unit.
> Total value of inventory on hand at cost.
> Date of last sale or usage.
> Quantity sold or used this year.
> Economic order quantity.
> Code number of major vendor.
> Code number of secondary vendor.

In preparation for year-end inventory, the client has two identical sets of preprinted inventory count cards. One set is for the client's inventory counts, and the other is for the CA's use to make audit test counts. The following information has been keypunched into the cards and interpreted on their face:

> Item or part number.
> Description.
> Size.
> Unit of measure code.

In taking the year-end inventory, the client's personnel will write the actual counted quantity on the face of each card. When all counts are complete, the counted quantity will be keypunched into the cards. The cards will be processed against the disk file, and quantity-on-hand figures will be adjusted to reflect the actual count. A computer listing will be prepared to show any missing inventory count cards and all quantity adjustments of more than $100 in value. These items will be investigated by client personnel, and all required adjustments will be made. When adjustments have been completed, the final year-end balances will be computed and posted to the general ledger.

The CA has available generalized audit software which can process both cards and disk files.

Required:

a. In general and without regard to the facts above, discuss the nature of generalized audit software and list the various types of uses of such software.

→ b. List and describe at least five ways general-purpose audit software can be used to assist in the audit of inventory of The Outsider, Inc. (For example, the software can be used to read the disk inventory master file and list items of high unit cost or total value. Such items can be included in the CA's test counts to increase the dollar coverage of the audit verification.)

6–30. M Corporation Ltd. has been following a policy of increasingly computerizing its financial and management information records. Recently, the controller of M Corporation Ltd. approached CA, the company's auditor, with a problem he had encountered that, he felt, jeopardized the success of this policy. He confided to CA that the systems and data processing department personnel were becoming flippant and arrogant —that they appeared to view their department as separate from the rest of the company and beyond reproach. He felt that this situation pointed to a need for greater control over compliance with management policy, and better safeguards against possible destruction of data as well as an overall review of the computerization policy.

The controller therefore asked CA the following questions:

(i) What methods should be used for continuous monitoring of the operations of a systems and data processing department to ensure compliance with management's policies and objectives?

(ii) What steps could be taken to ensure that only authorized use is made of the computer?

(iii) What steps could be taken to guard against loss from destruction of magnetic records by malicious acts?

(iv) What steps could be taken to ensure the adequacy of security and protection over confidential data, such as executive payrolls, customer lists, and so forth?

(v) What procedures could be used to ensure that development efforts are made only for the most worth-while systems?

Required:

CA's answers to the controller's five questions. (CICA.)

6-31. CAs may audit "around" or "through" computers in the examination of the financial statements of clients who utilize computers to process accounting data.

Required:

a. Describe the auditing approach referred to as auditing "around" the computer.

b. Under what conditions do CAs decide to audit "through" the computer instead of "around" the computer?

c. In auditing "through" the computer, CAs may use test decks.
  (1) What is a "test deck"?
  (2) Why do CAs use test decks?

d. How can the CAs be satisfied that the computer programs presented to them for testing are actually those used by the client for processing accounting data? (AICPA, adapted)

6-32. Lee Wong, CA, is examining the financial statements of the Alexandria Corporation, which recently installed an offline electronic computer. The following comments have been extracted from Wong's notes on computer operations and the processing and control of shipping notices and customer invoices:

To minimize inconvenience Alexandria converted without change its existing data processing system, which utilized tabulating equipment. The computer company supervised the conversion and has provided training to all computer department employees (except keypunch operators) in systems design, operations, and programming.

Each computer run is assigned to a specific employee, who is responsible for making program changes, running the program, and answering questions. This procedure has the advantage of eliminating the need for records of computer operations because each employee is responsible for his own computer runs.

At least one computer department employee remains in the computer room during office hours, and only computer department employees have keys to the computer room.

System documentation consists of those materials furnished by the computer company—a set of record formats and program listings. These and the tape library are kept in a corner of the computer department.

The corporation considered the desirability of program controls, but decided to retain the manual controls from its existing system.

Company products are shipped directly from public warehouses which forward shipping notices to general accounting. There a billing clerk enters the price of the item and accounts for the numerical sequence of shipping notices from each warehouse. The billing clerk also prepares daily adding machine tapes ("control tapes") of the units shipped and the unit prices.

Shipping notices and control tapes are forwarded to the computer department for keypunching and processing. Extensions are made on the computer. Output consists of invoices (in six copies) and a daily sales register. The daily sales register shows the aggregate totals of units shipped and unit prices which the computer operator compares to the control tapes.

All copies of the invoice are returned to the billing clerk. The clerk mails three copies to the customer, forwards one copy to the warehouse, maintains one copy in a numerical file, and retains one copy in an open invoice file that serves as a detailed accounts receivable record.

Required:

Describe weaknesses in internal control over information and data flows and the procedures for processing, shipping notices and customer invoices, and recommend improvements in these controls and processing procedures. Organize your answer sheet as follows:

Weakness	Recommended improvement

(AICPA, adapted)

6–33.   You will be examining for the first time the financial statements of Central Savings and Loan Association for the year ending December 31. The CA firm which examined the association's financial statements for the prior year issued an unqualified audit report.

At the beginning of the current year, the association installed an online, real-time computer system. Each teller in the association's main office and seven branch offices has an online, input-output terminal. Customers' mortgage payments and savings account deposits and withdrawals are recorded in the accounts by the computer from data input by the teller at the time of the transaction. The teller keys the proper account by account number and enters the information in the terminal keyboard to record the transaction. The accounting department at the main office has both punched card and typewriter input-output devices. The computer is housed at the main office.

Required:

You would expect the association to have certain internal controls in effect because an online, real-time computer system is employed. List the internal controls which should be in effect solely because this system is employed, classifying them as:

a.   Those controls pertaining to input of information.

b.   All other types of computer controls. (AICPA, adapted)

6–34.   Porter & Klein Ltd., a drug manufacturer, has the following system for billing and recording accounts receivable:

1.   An incoming customer's purchase order is received in the order department by a clerk who prepares a prenumbered company sales order form in which is inserted the pertinent information, such as the customer's name and address, customer's account number, quantity, and items ordered. After the sales order has been prepared, the customer's purchase order is stapled to it.

2.   The sales order form is then passed to the credit department for credit approval. Rough approximations of the billing values of the orders are made in the credit department for those accounts on which credit limitations are imposed. After investigation, approval of credit is noted on the form.

3.   Next, the sales order form is passed to the billing department, where a clerk types the customer's invoice on a billing machine that cross-multiplies the number of items and the unit price, then adds the automatically extended amounts for the total amount of the invoice. The billing clerk determines the unit prices for the items from a list of billing prices.

   The billing machine has registers that automatically accumulate daily totals of customer account numbers and invoice amounts to provide "hash" totals and control amounts. These totals, which are inserted in a daily record book, serve as predetermined batch totals for verification of computer inputs.

   The billing is done on prenumbered, continuous, carbon-interleaved forms having the following designations:

   a.   "Customer's copy."
   b.   "Sales department copy," for information purposes.
   c.   "File copy."
   d.   "Shipping department copy," which serves as a shipping order. Bills of lading are also prepared as carbon copy byproducts of the invoicing procedure.

4.   The shipping department copy of the invoice and the bills of lading are then sent to the shipping department. After the order has been shipped, copies of the bill of lading are returned to the billing department. The shipping department copy of the invoice is filed in the shipping department.

5.   In the billing department, one copy of the bill of lading is attached to the customer's copy of the invoice and both are mailed to the customer. The other copy of the bill of lading, together with the sales order form, is then stapled to the invoice file copy and filed in invoice numerical order.

6.   A keypunch machine is connected to the billing machine so that punched cards are created during the preparation of the invoices. The punched cards then become the means by which the sales data are transmitted to a computer.

   The punched cards are fed to the computer in batches. One

day's accumulation of cards comprises a batch. After the punched cards have been processed by the computer, they are placed in files and held for about two years.

Required:

List the procedures that the CAs would employ in their examination of selected audit samples of the company's:

a. Typed invoices, including the source documents.
b. Punched cards.

(The listed procedures should be limited to the verification of the sales data being fed into the computer. Do not carry the procedures beyond the point at which the cards are ready to be fed to the computer.) (AICPA, adapted)

6–35. L Limited is a dry goods chain selling mainly staples: practical clothing for the family, work clothes, shoes, notions, piece goods, and a relatively small amount of housewares. Its 170 stores are distributed across the country. Ten years ago, the president authorized the introduction of a credit card system, and within 2½ years the company had issued 300,000 credit cards. In 1976, some 450,000 credit cards were in circulation of which some 430,000 showed monthly activity. Seventy percent of the company's sales are made on credit, with some 75 percent of the credit sales made to company credit card holders, the other credit sales being made to holders of other credit cards.

The credit card system is one of several computerized systems processed on the company's computer.

Relevant procedures for the computerized credit card system are as follows:

There are 140 stores located in areas other than the head office. All credit card purchase, credit, adjustment and payment documents are batched daily by each store, and record counts represent the input control. The batches are delivered each evening to a local data centre for keypunching. After verification and check to the record count, the data are transmitted via teleprocessing on the following day to L Limited's computer.

For the 30 stores in the head office area, the system works similarly except that the batches are delivered directly to head office.

Cyclical billing is done at the head office. Credit card holders have been divided into groups, the size of the group having been determined by dividing the number of customers (credit cards) by the number of working days in the month. Each group is billed once a month.

Remittances received by mail or in person at the head office, write-offs, and other adjustments including service charges on overdue accounts are processed at the head office.

The credit department at the head office is responsible for the issuance of credit cards and for a weekly advice to all stores of cards which have been inactive for 90 days and of delinquent credit cards. Credit cards are delinquent as soon as:

(i)   The customer exceeds his credit limit;

(ii)   The customer has made no payments for 60 days since the last billing;

(iii) The credit card is reported stolen;

(iv)   The customer has given notice of cancellation.

In addition to the above information, the auditor finds the following in the accounts:

Accounts receivable—credit cards .... $8,218,374 debit
Allowance for doubtful accounts (manually controlled) ...   1,221,000 credit

During the discussion of the computerized system, the data processing manager indicated that he would be pleased to have one of his programmers write a program to extract information from the credit card master file according to the auditor's specification.

Required:

a. As auditor, assuming you accept the data processing manager's offer, describe with reasons the information you would hope to obtain through the program prepared by the client.

b. How would you control that no account in the credit card master file would be excluded from the program prepared by the client? (CICA)

6–36. A Company Limited, a food wholesaler, has combined the purchasing, accounts payable, and inventory systems into one integrated computerized system.

The file updating process automatically generates reorder messages in a punched card format.

These punched cards are repeatedly processed in the system in order to:

(i)   Generate the printed purchase orders;

(ii)   Update the inventory file to reflect the new orders;

(iii) Serve as the receiving report in the receiving department; and

(iv)   Update the inventory file to record the receipts.

The inventory master file contains fields for the following information for each item:

Inventory code number
Item name
Quantity on hand
Open purchase order—quantity on order
                   —date of order
                   —purchase order number
Minimum quantity (reorder point)
Reorder quantity
Reorder code (automatic or discretionary)
Vendor number
Date and purchase order number of most recent shipment received

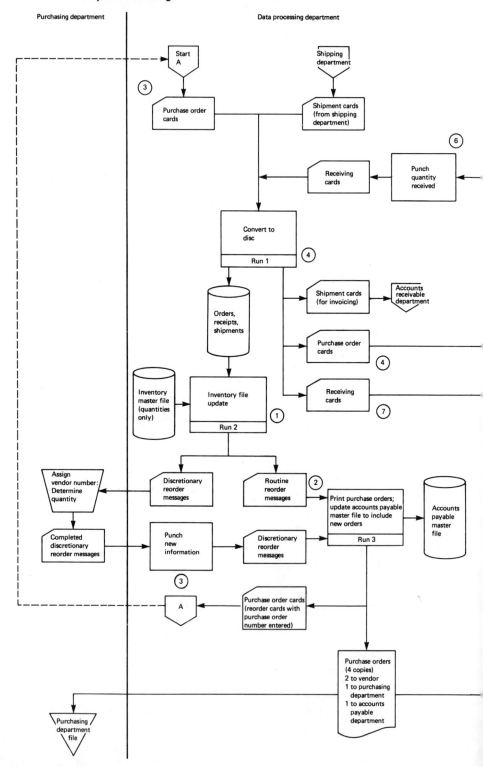

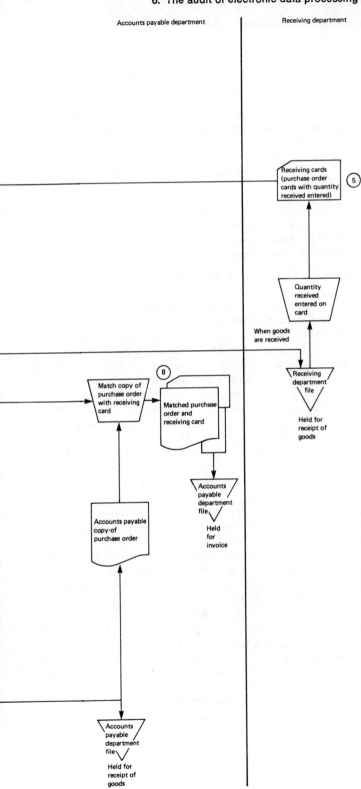

Accounts payable department

Receiving department

Receiving cards
(purchase order
cards with quantity
received entered)
⑤

Quantity
received
entered on
card

When goods
are received

Match copy of
purchase order
with receiving
card
⑧
Matched purchase
order and
receiving card

Receiving
department
file

Held for
receipt of
goods

Accounts
payable
department
file

Held
for
invoice

Accounts payable
copy·of
purchase order

Accounts
payable
department
file

Held for
receipt of
goods

Number of reorders year-to-date
Total issues year-to-date
Total issues last year.

System description (keyed to numbered points on flowchart on pages 284 and 285):

① When the quantity on hand plus the quantity on order for an inventory item falls below the reorder point, a reorder message is punched by the computer into a card. If the master file contains an *automatic reorder* code for the item, a routine reorder message is punched which contains the following information, both printed and punched:

Date
Inventory code number
Vendor number
Standard order quantity.

In addition, a brief name or description of the item is printed on the card.

If the master file contains a *discretionary reorder* code, or if there is no vendor number in the inventory master file, a discretionary reorder message is produced which contains the date and inventory code number punched and printed, and the item name and standard order quantity printed only. These discretionary message cards are then sent to the purchasing department.

The purchasing department decides whether or not to order, enters the quantity and vendor number on the card, and returns the card to the data processing department, where the additional information is punched into the card.

② The routine reorder message cards and the returned discretionary message cards are used as the input to a computer program which prints four copies of the purchase orders and which updates the accounts payable master file (on disc) to include the items ordered in the vendor file as "ordered, not received." The vendor name and address are obtained from the accounts payable master file. The copies of the purchase order are distributed as shown on the flowchart. The purchase orders are automatically numbered and dated by the computer, and the purchase order number is punched into the reorder message card, thereby changing it to a purchase order card. No check is made of the numerical sequence of complete or incomplete purchase orders, and no attempt is made to identify missing purchase order numbers or open orders outstanding for a long period of time.

③ The purchase order cards are re-entered into the system in the next day's processing in order to update the inventory master file to show the quantity on order. In addition, shipment cards generated by the shipping department update the inventory file to reduce the quantity on hand and to update the total issues field.

Purchase order cards and receiving cards (described below) are processed before shipment cards.

④ After conversion to disc for the updating, the purchase order cards are sent to the receiving department where they are filed for use as receiving reports.

⑤ When goods are received, the receiving clerk pulls the card for that order, enters the quantity received (if different from the quantity ordered) and sends the card back to the data processing department where the quantity received is punched into the card (when necessary) and the card re-enters the inventory up-

⑥ dating cycle to move the quantity received from the "on order" to the "on hand" field in the master file.

⑦ The receiving cards then are sent to the accounts payable department where they are matched with the accounts payable copy of

⑧ the purchase order and held for receipt of the invoice from the vendor. The receipt and payment of the invoice, and the updating of the accounts payable master file to delete the open purchase order, to enter the invoice, and to record the eventual payment, are all later steps in the processing and are not included in this part of the system description or flowchart.

The auditor has at his disposal a general-purpose audit program (GPAP), which can directly access any of the machine-readable files and perform a variety of standard audit procedures.

Required:

a. Describe the weak control points in this system. For each weakness identified, show what improvement you would recommend.

b. For each weakness identified in part (*a*), list what compensating audit procedures you would use in performing an audit of the purchasing—accounts payable—inventory area. (Remember that you have a GPAP—general-purpose audit program—at your disposal.) (CICA)

7

Evidence — what kind and how much?

The financial statements of a business constitute representations by management as to the financial position, operating results, and changes in financial position of the business. An audit report, on the other hand, is an expression of opinion by an independent expert on the fairness of the client's financial statements. Although in some engagements the auditors may participate in the preparation of the financial statements, the completed statements are nonetheless the statements of the client. The role of the auditors is that of independent professional critics who investigate, analyze, and evaluate the information underlying the financial statements as a means of reaching a conclusion as to their fairness.

Auditors' opinion based on evidence

Before expressing an opinion on financial statements, the independent auditors must have evidence that—

1. The items in the financial statements are supported by the balances in the ledger accounts.
2. The balances in the ledger accounts summarize correctly the numerous debit and credit entries.
3. These debit and credit entries in the accounts represent proper accounting interpretation of all the transactions entered into by the business.

Although the accounting records provide much of the evidence needed to support the expression of an opinion by the auditors, these records are not the only source of evidence. The auditors also gather evidence through first-hand observation of assets, by interviews with numerous client personnel, and from a variety of sources outside the client company.

In a company using a manual accounting system, the chain of audit evidence extends from documents describing individual transactions through the journals to ledger accounts, and from ledger accounts to financial statements. For a company using electronic data processing, the form of the records will differ, but the chain of evidence linking business transactions to financial statements is still essential to permit verification by the auditors. An audit may be thought of as the process of gathering and evaluating sufficient evidence to provide an adequate basis for expression of an opinion on financial statements.

Auditing procedures—a means of gathering evidence

The scope paragraph of the audit report tells in very concise language what the auditors have done to develop a basis for their opinion:

> Our examination was made in accordance with generally accepted auditing standards, and accordingly included such tests and other procedures as we considered necessary in the circumstances.

Why do the auditors make "tests"? The purpose is to gather evidence. They need evidence that transactions have been properly analyzed and recorded, evidence of arithmetical accuracy in the records, and evidence that the work of summarizing the accounts and preparing the statements has been performed accurately in accordance with generally accepted accounting principles.

Why do the auditors carry out "other procedures"? Again, the purpose is to gather evidence. They need evidence by physical observation that the assets listed on the balance sheet actually exist and are owned by the client, evidence that all liabilities owed by the client are included in the financial statements, and evidence from banks, customers, and other sources outside the business that will tend to substantiate the evidence gathered from the accounting records.

Evidence needed for material items

The purpose of an audit is to enable the auditors to express an opinion on the financial statements *as a whole.* It follows that the auditors should gather evidence on the material items in the statements—those items of sufficient size and importance to have a significant bearing on the statements viewed as a whole. The more material an item, the greater the need for evidence of its validity. The concept of materiality was defined in Chapter 1 as a state of relative importance, and the point made that an asset of $15,000 might be a material item in a small company but quite immaterial on the statements of a large corporation. We also stressed that materiality cannot be judged solely in quantitative terms. For example, transactions between related parties, and transactions which suggest fraud or violation of the law, may be considered to be material even though the dollar amounts are not large.

If an item is definitely not material, the auditors may be quite undisturbed over the fact that its treatment in the accounts violates generally accepted accounting principles. As a somewhat extreme example, consider the audit of a motion picture theatre: the inventory of popcorn on hand would probably not be of material amount, and the auditors would not care whether this inventory was listed as an asset or charged directly to expense when purchased. Experienced auditors are always careful to avoid making an issue of an inconsequential matter.

Sufficient appropriate audit evidence

The third standard of field work states:

> Sufficient appropriate audit evidence should be obtained, by such means as inspection, observation, enquiry, confirmation, computation and analysis, to afford a reasonable basis to support the content of the report.

What constitutes "sufficient appropriate audit evidence"? *Audit evidence* is any information which corroborates or refutes a premise. The auditors' premise is that the financial statements present fairly the client's financial position and operating results. Section 5300.13 of the CICA *Handbook on Audit Evidence* recommends that the auditors' judgment as to what is sufficient appropriate audit evidence is influenced by the following factors:

1. the adequacy of internal control;
2. materiality;
3. the degree of risk of mis-statement through errors or irregularities. This risk may be affected by (a) the nature of the item, (b) the nature of the business carried on by the enterprise, (c) situations which may exert an unusual influence on management, and (d) the financial strength or weakness of the client;
4. the experience gained during previous audit examinations as to the reliability of the client's records and representations;
5. the persuasiveness of the evidence and;
6. errors or irregularities found while performing the audit procedure.

In addition to the above general factors, however, we ought to look into what is specifically meant by "appropriate" and "sufficient."

Appropriateness of audit evidence relates to its *quality*. Several factors contribute to the quality of audit evidence. When the auditors are able to obtain audit evidence from independent sources outside of the client enterprise, the reliability of the evidence is increased. Strong internal accounting controls contribute substantially to the quality of accounting records and other evidence created within the client organization. The quality of evidence is also increased when the auditors obtain the information *directly*—that is, by first-hand examination, observation, and computation, rather than by obtaining the information "second-hand." In addition, the appropriateness of audit evidence is enhanced when the auditors are able to obtain additional related information which supports the original evidence. Thus, the quality of evidence is related to its relevance and reliability.

The term *sufficient* relates to the *quantity* of evidence obtained by the auditors. The amount of audit evidence which is considered sufficient to support the independent auditors' opinion on the clients' financial statements is a matter of judgment. However, the amount of audit evidence which is sufficient in a specific audit engagement varies inversely with the appropriateness of the evidence available. In every audit, CAs take a *calculated risk* as to the propriety of their opinion on the client's financial statements; they are never *certain.* The *sufficient* evidence required for the auditors' professional opinion—to justify the conclusions presented in the audit report—falls short of "proof beyond a reasonable doubt," the standard of sufficient evidence used in criminal law.

Types of audit evidence

A fuller understanding of the appropriateness of audit evidence may be gained by a brief consideration of the more important types of evidence gathered by the independent auditors as a basis for their opinion. The types of evidence to be discussed are as follows:

1. Internal control.
2. Physical evidence.
3. Documentary evidence.
   a. Documentary evidence created outside the client organization and transmitted directly to the auditors.
   b. Documentary evidence created outside the client organization and held by the client.
   c. Documentary evidence created and held within the client organization.
4. Accounting records.
5. Computations.
6. Oral evidence.
7. Comparisons and ratios.
8. Evidence provided by specialists.

1. Internal control as evidence.

An adequate system of internal control promotes accuracy and reliability in accounting data. Errors are quickly and automatically brought to light by the built-in proofs and cross-checks inherent in the system.

Consequently, if the auditors find that the client company has a carefully devised system of internal control and that practices prescribed by management are being consistently followed in day-to-day operations, they will regard the existence of this system of internal control as strong evidence of the validity of the amounts in the financial statements.

In verifying the financial statements by working back through the accounting records, it is not practicable for the auditors to examine every invoice, cheque, or other piece of documentary evidence. The solution lies in a study of the methods and procedures by which the company carries on its accounting processes. If these procedures are well designed and consistently followed, the end results in the form of financial statements will be valid. The auditors' approach is, therefore, to study and evaluate the system of internal control, including in this study a series of compliance tests to determine that the company's accounting procedures are actually working as intended. Much of the auditors' professional skill lies in their ability first to evaluate the effectiveness of various control devices and then to select the appropriate substantive tests to prove the agreement of the financial statements with the underlying transactions data.

The adequacy of the system of internal control is a major factor in determining how much evidence the auditors will need to gather from documents, records, enquiries, and other sources. The stronger the internal control, the less evidence of other nature that will be required as a basis for the auditors' opinion. When internal control is weak, the auditors must gather a correspondingly greater amount of evidence of other kinds.

2. Physical evidence.

Actual observation or count of certain types of assets is the best evidence of their physical existence. The amount of cash on hand is verified by counting; inventories are also observed and counted. The existence of property and equipment such as automobiles, buildings, office equipment, and factory machinery may also be established by physical observation.

At first thought, it might seem that physical observation of an asset would be conclusive verification, but this is often not true. For example, if the cash on hand to be counted by the auditors includes cheques received from customers, the making of a count provides no assurance that all of the cheques will prove to be collectible when deposited. There is also the possibility that one or more worthless cheques may have been created deliberately by a dishonest employee as a means of concealing from the auditors the existence of a cash shortage.

The physical observation of inventory may also leave some important questions unanswered. The quality and condition of merchandise or of goods in process are vital in determining salability. If the goods counted by the auditors contain hidden defects or are obsolete, a mere counting of units does not substantiate the dollar value shown on the balance sheet.

ILLUSTRATIVE CASE.   During the observation of the physical inventory of a company manufacturing costly aircraft instruments, an auditor counted more than a hundred instruments of a given type, each of which had cost several hundred dollars to manufacture. After the inventory taking had been completed, the auditor was informed by the client that these instruments were defective and could not be sold. The defective instruments were identical in appearance with other satisfactory instruments.

There are many similar situations in which a physical observation and count by the auditors serve to verify the quantity but not the quality of an asset. The auditors do not claim to be expert in judging the quality of materials. Their responsibility for the detection of shortcomings in quality of goods is much less than their responsibility for accuracy in quantities. Since auditors examine such widely differing businesses as breweries, mines, and jewelry stores, it is not possible for them to become expert in appraising the products of all their clients. However, CAs should be alert to any clues which raise a doubt as to the quality or condition of inventories. CAs often request clients to hire independent specialists to provide the auditors with information on quality or condition of inventories. Evidence provided by specialists is discussed in a subsequent section of this chapter.

In the case of plant and equipment, the auditors' physical observation verifies the existence of the asset but gives no proof of ownership. A fleet of automobiles used by salesmen and company executives, for example, might be leased rather than owned—or if owned might be subject to a mortgage.

In summary, the physical observation of an asset implies identification of the thing being examined, determination of quantity, and at least an effort to determine the quality or genuineness of the article. It does not establish ownership. Physical evidence is available only for the asset elements in the financial statements. Although physical evidence is important in the verification of a number of assets, it generally must be supplemented by other types of evidence. For some types of assets such as accounts receivable or intangible assets, there may be no opportunity to gather physical evidence

3. Documentary evidence.

The most important type of evidence relied upon by auditors consists of documents. The worth of a document as evidence depends in part upon whether it was created within the company (for example, a sales invoice) or came from outside the company (as in the case of a vendor's invoice). Some documents created within the company (cheques, for example) are sent outside the organization for endorsement and processing; because of this critical review by outsiders these documents are regarded as very reliable evidence.

In appraising the reliability of documentary evidence, the auditors should consider whether the document is of a type which could easily be forged or created in its entirety by a dishonest employee. A share certificate evidencing an investment in marketable securities is usually elaborately engraved and would be most difficult to falsify. On the other hand, a note receivable may be created by anyone in a moment merely by filling in the blank spaces in one of the standard note forms available at any bank.

Documentary evidence created outside the client organization and transmitted directly to the auditors. The best quality of documentary evidence consists of documents created by independent agencies outside the client's organization and transmitted directly to the auditors without passing through the client's hands. For example, in the verification of accounts receivable, the customer is requested by the client to write directly to the auditors to confirm the amount owed to the auditors' client. To assure that the customer's reply comes directly to the auditors and not to the client, the auditors will enclose with the confirmation request a return envelope addressed to the auditors' office. If the replies were addressed to the auditors at the client's place of business, an opportunity would exist for someone in the client's organization to intercept the customer's letter and alter the amount of indebtedness reported, or even destroy the letter.

Similar precautions are taken in the verification of cash in bank. The client will request the bank to advise the auditors directly in writing of the amount the client has on deposit.

Other types of documents created outside the client's organization and transmitted directly to the auditors include letters from the client's attorneys describing any pending litigation and listings of insurance in force provided by the client's insurance broker. In each case, the client requests the outsider to furnish the information directly to the auditors in an envelope addressed to the auditors' office; and the auditors mail the request.

Documentary evidence created outside the client organization and held by the client. Many of the externally created documents referred to by the auditors will, however, be in the client's possession. Examples include bank statements, vendors' invoices and statements, property tax bills, notes receivable, contracts, customers' purchase orders, and share and bond certificates. In deciding how much reliance to place upon this type of evidence, the auditors should consider whether the document is of a type that could be easily created or altered by someone in the client's employ. The auditors should be particularly cautious in accepting as evidence any documents which have been altered in any way. Of course, an alteration may have been made by the company originating the document to correct an accidental error. In general, however, business concerns do not send out documents marred by errors and corrections. The auditors cannot afford to overlook the possibility that an alteration on a document may have been made deliberately to misstate the facts and to mislead auditors or others who relied upon the document.

In pointing out the possibility that externally created documents in the client's possession *might* have been forged or altered, it is not intended to discredit this type of evidence. Externally created documents in the possession of the client are used extensively by auditors and are considered, in general, as a stronger type of evidence than documents created by the client.

Documentary evidence created and held within the client organization. No doubt the most dependable single piece of documentary evidence created within the client's organization is a paid cheque. The cheque bears the endorsement of the payee and a perforation or stamp indicating payment by the bank. Because of this review and processing of a cheque by outsiders, the auditors will usually look upon a paid cheque as a strong type of evidence. The paid cheque may be viewed as evidence that an asset was acquired at a given cost, or as a proof that a liability was paid, or an expense incurred. Of course the amount of the cheque might have been raised by an alteration subsequent to its payment, but protection against this possibility is afforded through the preparation of bank reconciliations, and also through comparison of paid cheques with the entries on the bank statement and in the cash payment records.

Most companies place great emphasis on proper internal control of cash disbursements by such devices as the use of serial numbers on cheques, signature (or two signatures) by responsible officials, and separation of the cheque-signing function from the accounting function. This emphasis on internal control over cash payments lends additional assurance that a paid cheque is a valid document.

Most documents created within the client organization represent a lower quality of evidence than a paid cheque because they circulate within the company only and do not receive critical review by an outsider. Examples of internally created documents which do not leave the client's possession are sales invoices, shipping notices, purchase orders, receiving reports, credit memoranda, and a variety of other business papers. Of course, the original copy of a sales invoice or purchase order is sent to the customer or supplier, but the carbon copy available for the auditors' inspection has not left the client's possession.

The degree of reliance to be placed on documents created and used only within the organization depends on the adequacy of the system of internal control. If the accounting procedures are so designed that a document prepared by one person must be critically reviewed by another, and if all documents are serially numbered and all numbers in the series accounted for, these documents may represent reasonably good evidence. Adequate internal control will also provide for extensive subdivision of duties so that no one employee handles a transaction from beginning to end. An employee who maintains records or creates documents, such as credit memoranda, should not have access to cash. Under these conditions there is no incentive for an employee to falsify a document since the employee creating documents does not have custody of assets.

On the other hand, if internal control is weak, the auditors cannot place much reliance on documentary evidence created within the organization and not reviewed by outsiders. There is the danger not only of fictitious documents created to cover theft by an employee but also the possibility, however remote, that management is purposely presenting misleading financial statements and has prepared false supporting documents for the purpose of deceiving the auditors.

One important type of internally created document is the letter of representations prepared by officers of the client company at the auditors' request setting forth certain facts about the company's financial position or operations. For example, the controller of a client company may be asked to write a letter stating that to the best of his knowledge all liabilities of the company are reflected in the financial statements. The auditors' purpose in requesting such a formal written statement is to bring to light any unrecorded liabilities, and also to impress upon the officers of a client *their primary and personal responsibility for the financial statements.* A document of this nature may serve a useful function, but it does not relieve the auditors of their duty to verify management's representations. The financial statements themselves constitute a representation by management; a letter signed by management as to the inclusiveness of the liability figure shown in the balance sheet is merely a further representation. Consequently, a letter of representations by management, although important, does not rank very high in our scale for evaluation of various types of evidence.

ILLUSTRATIVE CASE. The income statement of National Student Marketing Corporation (NSMC), a company in the United States, included total gains of $370,-000 from the sale of two subsidiary companies to employees of the subsidiaries. Consideration for the sales was notes receivable collateralized by 7,700 shares of NSMC shares. Because both subsidiaries had been operating at substantial losses, NSMC's independent auditors obtained written representations from three officers of NSMC that there were no indemnification or repurchase commitments given to the purchasers.

In *Accounting Series Release No. 173,* the SEC criticized the auditors for too great reliance on management representations regarding the sales. The SEC considered the "sales" to be sham transactions which would have been brought to light had the auditors sufficiently extended their auditing procedures. NSMC had executed various side agreements to assume all risks of ownership after the "sale" of one subsidiary, and had agreed to make cash contributions and guarantee a bank line of credit after "sale" of the other subsidiary. Further, the NSMC shares collateralizing the notes receivable had been given to the subsidiaries' "purchasers" by officers of NSMC.

Many CA firms obtain a single letter of representations from client management covering numerous aspects of the financial position and operations of the client. Other auditors obtain separate representations for individual items. Subsequent chapters illustrate the latter type of letters of representations from clients.

4. Accounting records as evidence.

When auditors attempt to verify an amount in the financial statements by tracing it back through the accounting records, they will ordinarily carry this tracing process through the ledgers to the journals and on back to such basic documentary evidence as a paid cheque, invoice, or other original papers. To some extent, however, the ledger accounts and the journals constitute worth-while evidence in themselves.

The dependability of ledgers and journals as evidence is indicated by the extent of internal control covering their preparation. Whenever possible, subsidiary ledgers for receivables, payables, and plant equipment should be maintained by persons not responsible for the general ledger. All general journal entries should be approved in writing by the controller or other official. If ledgers and journals are produced by an electronic data processing system, the safeguards described in Chapter 6 should be in effect. When controls of this type exist and the records appear to be well maintained, the auditors may regard the ledgers and journals as affording considerable support for the financial statements.

As a specific example, assume that the auditors wish to determine that the sale of certain old factory machinery during the year under audit was properly recorded. By reference to the subsidiary ledger for plant and equipment, they might ascertain that the depreciation accumulated during the years the machine was owned agreed with the amount cleared out of the Accumulated Depreciation account at the time of sale. They might also note that the original cost of the machine as shown in the plant ledger agreed with the credit to the Plant and Equipment control account when the machine was sold, and that the proceeds from sale were entered in the cash receipts journal. Assuming that the plant ledger, general ledger, and the cash receipts journal are independently maintained by three different employees, or are produced by an electronic data processing department with effective internal control, the agreement of these records offers considerable evidence that the sale of the machine was a legitimate transaction and properly recorded. Whether the auditors should go beyond this evidence and examine original documents, such as the bill of sale or a work order authorizing the sale, would depend upon the relative importance of the amount involved and upon other circumstances of the audit.

In addition to journals and ledgers, other accounting records providing evidential matter for independent auditors include sales summaries, trial balances, interim financial statements, and operating and financial reports prepared for management.

5. Computations as evidence.

A form of quantitative audit evidence consists of calculations made independently by the auditors to prove the arithmetical accuracy of the client's records. In its simplest form, this evidence might consist of footing a column of figures in a sales journal or in a ledger account to prove the accuracy of the column total.

Computations also provide evidence when the auditors test the depreciation expense for the year, using rates adopted by the client, and thus prove the arithmetical accuracy of the depreciation expense entered in the accounting records. If the client determines uncollectible accounts expense as a percentage of sales, or takes up income on long-term contracts on the basis of percentage of completion, the results obtained by the client should be verified by means of independent calculations by the auditors. Other familiar examples in which the auditors' computations provide important evidence are bonus plans and profit-sharing agreements with executives, earnings-per-share data, and provisions for federal, provincial, and foreign income taxes.

6. Oral evidence.

Throughout their examination the auditors will ask a great many questions of the officers and employees of the client's organization. Novice auditors are sometimes afraid to ask questions for fear of seeming to be uninformed and inexperienced. Such an attitude is quite illogical; even the most experienced and competent auditors will ask a great many questions. These questions cover an endless range of topics—the location of records and documents, the reasons underlying an unusual accounting procedure, the probabilities of collecting a long past-due account receivable.

The answers which auditors receive to these questions constitute another type of evidence. Generally, oral evidence is not sufficient in itself, but it may be useful in disclosing situations that require investigation or in corroborating other forms of evidence. For example, an auditor after making a careful analysis of all past-due accounts receivable will normally sit down with the credit manager and get that official's views on the prospects for collection of accounts considered doubtful. If the opinions of the credit manager are in accordance with the estimates of uncollectible accounts losses that have been made independently by the auditor, this oral evidence will constitute significant support of the conclusions reached. In repeat examinations of a business, the auditor will be in a better position to evaluate the opinions of the credit manager based on how well the manager's estimates in prior years have worked out.

In asking questions the auditors should be neither apologetic nor authoritarian. They are conducting the audit at the request of the client; consequently, it is in the client's own interest that all employees cooperate in providing any information they have which is needed by the auditors.

On the other hand, the auditors should avoid a "police" attitude; they do not cross-examine employees or demand information. A deficiency in tact and courtesy will spell failure in public accounting work even faster than a deficiency in technical skill.

7. Comparisons and ratios as evidence.

Comparison of the amount of each asset, liability, revenue, and expense with the corresponding balance for the preceding period is a simple means of spotting any significant changes. Any unusual changes from year to year should be explored until the auditors are satisfied that a valid reason exists for the variation in amount.

Besides comparing dollar amounts from year to year, the auditors also will study the percentage relationships of various items on the financial statements. For example, the auditors noticed that the uncollectible accounts expense, which had been running about 1 percent of net sales for several years, had increased in the current year to 8 percent of net sales. This significant variation caused the auditors to make a very careful investigation of all accounts written off during the year and those presently past due. Most of the "uncollectible" accounts examined were found to be fictitious, and the cashier-bookkeeper then admitted that he had created these accounts to cover up his abstraction of cash receipts.

Comparison of the gross profit on sales percentages from year to year affords a means of verifying the overall reasonableness of the cost of goods sold and of the ending inventory. The relative proportions of the various types of inventory (raw materials, goods in process, and finished goods) should also be related to the rate of production and the trend of sales. Other useful comparisons are the relationship of accounts receivable changes to sales trends, actual revenue and expenses versus budgeted amounts, and the comparison of accounts payable changes to trends for cost of goods sold. These overall substantive tests supplement the detailed verification of individual accounts and provide assurance that the auditors will not "fail to see the forest for the trees."

8. Evidence provided by specialists.

We have pointed out in a previous section of this chapter that CAs are not experts in judging the quality of materials in a client's inventories. Other phases of an audit in which CAs lack the special qualifications necessary to determine the fairness of the client's representations include actuarial computations supporting pension liabilities and estimated productive contents of a natural resource used in depletion computations.

In SAS No. 11, "Using the Work of a Specialist," the AICPA recognized the necessity for CPAs to consult with experts, when appropriate, as a means of gathering competent audit evidence.[1] SAS No. 11 defined a

---

[1] The Canadian Institute of Chartered Accountants has not issued recommendations in this area.

specialist as a person or firm possessing special skill or knowledge in a field other than accounting or auditing, giving as examples actuaries, appraisers, attorneys, engineers, and geologists. Desirably, a specialist consulted by CAs should be unrelated to the client; in any event, the CAs are responsible for ascertaining the professional qualifications and reputation of the specialist consulted. The auditors should prepare an engagement letter to identify the services to be performed by the specialist. The CAs cannot accept the specialist's findings blindly; they must obtain an understanding of the methods or assumptions used by the specialist and test accounting data furnished to the specialist by the client. The CAs may accept the specialist's findings as competent audit evidence unless their tests cause them to believe the findings are unreasonable. If the auditors accept the specialist's findings as competent audit evidence, the specialist should not be mentioned in an unqualified audit report. If the auditors are not satisfied with the findings of the specialist, and issue a qualified or adverse opinion, or a denial of opinion, they may refer to and identify the specialist in support for the modification of the audit report.

The cost of obtaining evidence

CAs can no more disregard the cost of alternative auditing procedures than a store manager can disregard a difference in the costs of competing brands of merchandise. Cost is not the primary factor influencing the auditors in deciding what evidence should be obtained, but cost is always an important consideration.

The cost factor may preclude the gathering of the "ideal" form of evidence and necessitate the substitution of other forms of evidence which are of lesser quality yet still satisfactory. For example, assume that the auditors find that the client has a large note receivable from a customer. What evidence should the auditors obtain to be satisfied that the note is authentic and will be paid at maturity? One alternative is for the auditors to correspond directly with the customer and obtain written confirmation of the amount, maturity date, and other terms of the note. This confirmation is evidence that the customer issued the note and regards it as a valid obligation. Second, the auditors might test the collectibility of the note by obtaining a credit report on the customer from Dun & Bradstreet or from a local credit association. They might also obtain copies of the customer's most recent financial statements accompanied, if possible, by the opinion of an independent CA. To carry our illustration to an extreme, the auditors might obtain permission to make an audit of the financial statements of the customer. The cost of conducting this separate audit could conceivably amount to more than the note receivable which the auditors wished to verify.

The point of this illustration is that auditors do not always insist upon obtaining the strongest possible evidence. They do insist upon obtaining evidence which is adequate under the circumstances. The more material the item to be verified, the stronger the evidence required by the auditors, and the greater the cost they may be willing to incur in obtaining it.

Relative risk

Is the risk of misstatement, or of fraud, or of violation of accounting principles about the same in all audits? Certainly not. In certain situations, which the auditors must learn to recognize, the risk of substantial error and misstatement in the accounts and in the financial statements is far greater than in other audits. When relative risk is above normal, the auditors should demand more and better evidence than they would normally require as a basis for their opinion. The following examples illustrate some relatively high-risk auditing situations:

1. *Weak internal control.* The system of internal control is itself one of the more important types of evidence utilized by the auditors. Internal control may be weak or absent in certain areas of the client's affairs or throughout the business. In this situation the auditors are on notice to exercise added caution and to gather other forms of detailed evidence to compensate for the weakness in internal control. This topic has already received attention in the chapter devoted to internal control.

2. *Unsound financial condition.* A company operating at a loss or hard pressed to pay its creditors is more likely to postpone writing off worthless receivables or obsolete inventories of merchandise, or perhaps to "forget" to record a liability, than is a strong, well-financed, profitable company.

3. *Revision of income tax rates or regulations.* When income tax rates are suddenly raised significantly, the reaction of some clients may be to look harder than ever for ways to minimize taxable income. The pressure of a heavy tax burden sometimes leads to the twisting of accounting principles and to interpretations of business transactions in a manner inconsistent with that of prior years. When any sharp change in tax rates or regulations is anticipated for the following year, an incentive exists for the client to shift income from one period to another.

4. *Unreliable management.* Despite careful investigation of the backgrounds of directors and management of a prospective client a CA firm may nevertheless be involved with clients having unscrupulous executives. Auditors should be wary of managers whose oral representations are found to be wholly or partially untrue.

5. *Complex business transactions.* Clients whose operations involve extremely complicated transactions represent a far greater risk to

auditors than do clients with conventional operations. There is ever-present danger that the auditors, despite all of their evidence-gathering efforts, will not comprehend the *substance* of the complex activity.

6. *Clients which change auditors without clear justification.* A satisfactory client-auditor relationship should be a continuous one. When a company changes its independent CA firm, the change may have resulted from dissatisfaction with the predecessor firm's services. All too often, however, companies change auditors because of disputes over financial statement presentation and disclosure. The new client who has changed auditors thus represents a high-risk situation for the successor auditors. (We have already pointed out in Chapter 2 the obligation of successor auditors to consult with the predecessor auditors to ascertain, among other matters, the predecessors' understanding of the reason for the client's change of auditors.)

7. *"High-flyer" speculative ventures.* The history of business is replete with examples of the rise and fall of companies which attempted to capitalize on fads, innovations, and other speculative ventures. Auditors of such operations are subject to far greater risk than are the auditors of long-time, successful, and more conventional companies.

The concept of relative risk may also be applied to the gathering of evidence on particular items in the financial statements. The very nature of some assets makes the risk of misstatement greater than for others. Assume that in a given business the asset of cash amounts to only half as much as the Buildings account. Does this relationship indicate that the auditors should spend only half as much time in the verification of cash as in the verification of the buildings? Cash is much more susceptible to error or theft than are plant and equipment, and the great number of cash transactions affords an opportunity for errors to be well hidden. The amount of audit time devoted to the verification of cash balances and of cash transactions during the year will generally be much greater in proportion to the dollar amounts involved than will be necessary for such assets as plant and equipment.

In some special audit engagements the auditors are aware in advance that fraud is suspected and that the accounting records may include fictitious or altered entries. Perhaps the auditors have been engaged because of a dispute between partners, or because of dissatisfaction on the part of shareholders with the existing management. The risks involved in such engagements will cause the auditors to assign different weights to various types of evidence than they otherwise would.

ILLUSTRATIVE CASE. Bruce Henry, a resident of Toronto, owned a 90 percent share interest in a Halifax automobile agency. The other 10 percent of the share was owned by James Barr, who also had a contract to act as general manager of the business. As compensation for his managerial services, Barr received a percentage of net income rather than a fixed salary. The reported net income in recent years had been large and increasing each year, with correspondingly larger payments to Barr as manager. However, during this period of reported rising income, the cash position of the business as shown by the balance sheet had been deteriorating rapidly. Working capital had been adequate when Barr took over as manager but was now critically low.

Henry, the majority shareholder in Toronto, was quite concerned over these trends. He was further disturbed by reports that Barr was making frequent trips to Bermuda, and that he had placed several relatives on the payroll of the automobile agency. Henry decided to engage a CA firm to make an audit of the business. He explained fully to the CAs his doubts as to the fairness of the reported net income and his misgivings as to Barr's personal integrity. Henry added that he wished to buy Barr's shareholdings but first needed some basis for valuing the shares.

An audit initiated under these circumstances obviously called for a greater amount of evidence and a greater degree of caution by the auditors than would normally be required. Oral evidence from Barr could not be given much weight. Documents created within the business might very possibly have been falsified. In brief, the degree of risk was great, and the auditors' approach was modified to fit the circumstances. More evidence and more conclusive evidence was called for than in a more routine audit of an automobile agency.

The outcome of the audit in question was a disclosure of a gross overstatement of inventories and the reporting of numerous fictitious sales. Commission payments were also found to have been made to persons not participating in the business.

Evidence provided by subsequent events

The CA firm's opinion about items in the financial statements may be considerably changed by subsequent events—those events occurring after the date of the balance sheet but prior to completion of the audit and issuance of the report. Evidence not available at the close of the period under audit often becomes available before the auditors finish their field work and write the audit report.

As an example, let us assume that a client's accounts receivable at December 31 included one large account and numerous small ones. The large amount due from the major customer was regarded as good and collectible at the year-end, but during the course of the audit engagement the customer entered bankruptcy. As a result of this information, the auditors might have found it necessary to insist on an increase in the December 31 allowance for uncollectible accounts. The bankruptcy of the customer shortly after the balance sheet date indicates that the financial strength of the customer had probably deteriorated before December 31, and the client was simply in error in believing the receivable to be good and collectible at that date. Evidence becoming available after the balance sheet date should be used in making judgments about the valuation of receivables on the balance sheet date.

Other examples of evidence coming into existence subsequent to the period under audit include the following:

1. Customers' cheques included in the cash receipts of the last day of the year prove to be uncollectible and are charged back to the client's account by the bank. If the cheques were material in amount, an adjustment of the December 31 cash balance may be necessary to exclude the cheques now known to be uncollectible.
2. Rejection by inspectors of manufactured units. If inspectors reject an unusually large number of completed units leaving the client's assembly line in January, this situation indicates that a considerable part of the goods in process inventory at December 31 consisted of defective units. Reduction of the year-end figure for goods in process may be necessary.
3. A six-month note receivable held by the client which matured two weeks after the balance sheet date was dishonoured by the maker. This evidence may justify a reduction in the carrying value of notes receivable as of the balance sheet date.
4. Settlement of a pending lawsuit during the course of the audit caused a large and unexpected cash payment by the client to become necessary. The settlement of the lawsuit constitutes evidence that a *real,* rather than a *contingent,* liability may have existed as of December 31, although there had been no admission of the obligation by the client nor any entry in the accounting records to reflect such a liability.

The first three of the preceding examples may be regarded as falling into one specific class: events directly affecting amounts shown in the balance sheet. If the amounts involved in this category of subsequent events are material, the client should include them in the year-end financial statements.

The fourth example, that of a pending lawsuit settled after the balance sheet date by a ruling against the client, is essentially of the same category. The existence of a loss contingency in the form of a pending lawsuit was known at the balance sheet date; if the outcome of the suit becomes known during the course of the audit, disclosure is called for, and probably the most useful method of disclosure is to insert the liability in the balance sheet.

In summary, the first class of subsequent events includes those which *provide additional evidence with respect to conditions that existed at the balance sheet date* and affect the estimates inherent in the process of preparing financial statements. The effects of these subsequent events should be reflected in the financial statements for the period under audit.

Footnote disclosure of subsequent events

Having considered examples of subsequent events which the client should include in the financial statements by revising dollar amounts, let us turn next to a second class of subsequent events which do not alter the financial position of the company as of the balance sheet date, but may be significant in any appraisal of future prospects. In considering the following examples, assume that the event occurred after the balance sheet date but prior to completion of the audit field work and issuance of the report.

1. Plant and equipment seriously damaged by flood or earthquake.
2. Business combination with competing company.
3. Material loss on receivables resulting from a customer's major casualty.
4. Death of company treasurer in airplane crash.
5. Introduction of a new line of products.
6. Plant closed by a strike.
7. New labour contract.
8. Newspaper story that a large shareholder may launch a proxy fight to secure control of company.

Although these events may be significant in the future operations of the company, and of interest to many who read the audited financial statements, none of these occurrences has any bearing on the results of the year under audit, and their bearing on future results is not easily determinable. Prophecies as to the effect of specific events on future operations may be inappropriate. The question facing the independent auditors is: Which, if any, of these events should be reflected in footnotes to the financial statements in order to achieve adequate informative disclosure?

It is generally agreed that subsequent events involving business combinations, substantial casualty losses, and other significant changes in a company's financial position or financial structure should be disclosed in footnotes. Otherwise the financial statements might be misleading rather than informative. Consequently, the first three of the preceding examples (major property loss, combination with a competing company, and significant loss on receivables resulting from customer's casualty) should be disclosed in notes to the financial statements.

ILLUSTRATIVE CASE. Joe Morgan, CA, in his year-end examination of Wilson Company found that all accounts receivable from customers were current, that credit losses in prior years had been nominal, and that all customers had good credit ratings. A few days after the end of the year, Wilson Company's largest customer sustained a major flood loss which destroyed virtually all its plant and inventories. As a result of this disaster, collection by Wilson Company of its largest account receivable became very doubtful.

The probable loss on this account receivable should be recognized in the accounting period in which the disaster occurred. Since the customer was in good financial condition at the end of the year under audit, there is no reason why the auditor's client, Wilson Company, should treat the receivable as uncollectible before the date of the customer's casualty loss.

Subsequent events and pro forma financial statements. In a few rare cases, subsequent events may be so material that supplementary pro forma financial statements should be provided giving effect to the events as though they had occurred as of the balance sheet date. The use of pro forma supplementary data does not affect the application of generally accepted accounting principles to the basic financial statements.

Subsequent events not requiring footnote disclosure. The last five types of subsequent events mentioned on page 305 (personnel changes, product line changes, strikes, new labour contracts, and rumors of an impending proxy fight) are *non-accounting matters* and are *not disclosed in footnotes* unless particular circumstances make such information essential to the proper interpretation of the financial statements.

Footnotes are an integral part of the financial statements, and are used for many purposes other than disclosure of subsequent events. The published financial statements of virtually every listed corporation include a long list of footnotes, perhaps too long to be read and understood by most users of the statements. Pressure by government agencies and the courts for more disclosure has caused disclosure by footnotes to reach somewhat extreme lengths. Disclosure in a footnote of any events not essential to proper interpretation of the financial statements raises questions as to the reason for disclosure and creates a possibility that misleading inferences may be drawn. Some subsequent events may be regarded as "favourable" and others as "unfavourable," but not all readers of the statements will agree as to these qualities. Conceivably, the financial statements might be made misleading, rather than more informative, if disclosure were made of "favourable" events but not of other "unfavourable" events, or vice versa. Primary responsibility for disclosure of significant subsequent events rests with management, just as primary responsibility for the financial statements rests with management. Management has other means of disclosure apart from the financial statements, such as the president's letter to shareholders which usually appears in the annual report, or in unaudited quarterly financial statements and news releases.

The auditors' responsibility for subsequent events

Section 1500.14 of the *CICA Handbook* recommends that "any event or transaction between the date of the balance sheet and the date of the auditors' report thereon, which may have a material effect on the financial position or net income of the business, should be disclosed." Thus the auditors must ensure that these subsequent events are properly disclosed or change their unqualified opinion accordingly.

In *SAS No. 1*, the AICPA also outlined the auditors' responsibility for subsequent events. During the period subsequent to the balance sheet date, the auditors should always determine that proper "cutoffs" of cash receipts and disbursements and sales and purchases have been made, and should examine data to aid in the evaluation of assets and liabilities as of the balance sheet date. In addition, the auditors should—

1. Review the latest available interim financial statements, and minutes of directors', shareholders', and appropriate committees' meetings.
2. Enquire about matters dealt with at meetings for which minutes are not available.
3. Enquire of appropriate client officials as to loss contingencies, changes in capital stock, debt or working capital, changes in the current status of items estimated in the financial statements under audit, or any unusual adjustments made subsequent to the balance sheet date.
4. Obtain a letter from the client's attorney describing pending litigation, other loss contingencies, and unasserted claims.
5. Obtain a letter of representations from the client.

Throughout the course of their field work, the auditors should maintain an alert attitude as to the impact of current happenings on the financial position of the client at the balance sheet date.

Generally, the independent auditors' responsibility for evidence as to subsequent events extends only to the date they complete the audit field work. However, even after completing normal audit procedures, the auditors have the responsibility to evaluate subsequent events *which come to their attention.* Suppose, for example, that the auditors completed their field work for a July 31 audit on September 3, and thereafter began writing their report. On September 12, before completing their report, the auditors were informed by the client that a lawsuit which had been footnoted as a loss contingency in the July 31 financial statements had been settled on September 11 by a substantial payment by the client. The auditors would have to insist that the loss contingency be changed to a real liability in the July 31 balance sheet, and that the footnote be revised to show the settlement of the lawsuit subsequent to the balance sheet date. If the client agrees, the auditors would *dual-date* their report "September 3, except for Note ___, as to which the date is September 12." Alternatively, the auditors might decide to return to the client's facilities for further review of subsequent events through September 12; in this case, the audit report would bear that date only.

Dual-dating extends the auditors' liability for disclosure through the later date *only with respect to the specified item.* Using the later date for the date of the report will extend the auditors' liability with respect to all areas of the financial statements.

The auditors' "S–1 review" in an SEC registration in the United States. The Securities Act of 1933 (Section 11[a]) extends the auditors' liability in connection with the registration of new securities with the SEC to the *effective date* of the registration statement—the date on which the securities may be sold to the public. In many cases, the effective date of the registration statement may be several days or even weeks later than the date the auditors completed their field work. Accordingly, on or as close as practicable to the effective date, the auditors return to the client's facilities to conduct an "S–1 review," so-called because of the "Form S–1" title of the traditional SEC registration statement for new securities issues. In addition to completing the subsequent events review described in the preceding section, the auditors should read the entire prospectus and other pertinent portions of the registration statement. In addition, they should enquire of officers and other key executives of the client whether any events not reported in the registration statement have occurred which require amendment of the registration statement to prevent the audited financial statements therein from being misleading.

The auditors' subsequent discovery of facts existing at the date of their report

In some unfortunate cases, CA firms have learned subsequent to the issuance of their reports on audited financial statements that there were material misstatements in the financial statements or footnotes. Section 165 of the Canada Business Corporations Act requires a director or an officer of a company who is aware of any error or misstatement in the published financial statements to inform the auditor accordingly. The auditor then is responsible for ensuring that each director of the company is likewise informed if the error or misstatement is material. The directors are responsible to either issue revised financial statements or inform the shareholders by other appropriate means. A failure by the auditor to take prompt and appropriate action in this area can bring serious consequences. The following case in the United States amply demonstrates this point.

Early in 1964 a national CPA firm issued an unqualified opinion on the December 31, 1963, financial statements of Yale Express System, Inc., a trucking and freight forwarding concern. Three months later, the CPAs' opinion was included in the 1963 annual report filed with the SEC. The 1963 audited income statement of Yale showed net income of $1.1 million on gross revenue of $65.9 million.

Sometime in 1964 (the CPA firm claimed *after* the 1963 audit report was issued), Yale retained the CPAs to perform a management advisory services engagement—a "special study" of Yale's past and current revenue and expenses. During the course of the special study, Yale issued unaudited quarterly earnings reports required by the New York Stock Exchange; for the nine months ended September 30, 1964, Yale reported net income of $904,000. However, in March 1965 Yale announced that its interim reported profits for 1964 were in error and that it estimated a net loss of $3.3 million for all of 1964. Then, in May 1965, Yale's CPAs reported a revised 1963 net loss for Yale of $1.3 million (later increased to $1.9 million) and a 1964 net loss of $2.9 million. The CPAs stated the previously reported audited 1963 net income of $1.1 million was in error because of omission of liabilities and overstatement of receivables.

Subsequently, Yale went into bankruptcy and a number of shareholders and creditors filed suit against the CPA firm, charging the firm with deceit (deception). The basis of the plaintiffs' deception claim was that the CPAs knew before the end of 1964 that the 1963 audited financial statements as well as the unaudited 1964 quarterly earnings reports were false and misleading, but they had not disclosed this knowledge until mid-1965. The court (*Fischer* v. *Kletz*, 266 F. Supp. 180 [1967]), denied the CPAs' motion for dismissal and held that there were no reasons for barring the action of deceit against the CPAs. The court also found that there were no reasons why a duty to disclose such knowledge is not imposed upon a CPA, despite the lack of privity of those interested in Yale's financial statements.

Subsequent to the case described above, the AICPA provided guidelines in *SAS No. 1* for CPAs who become aware, subsequent to the issuance of their report on audited financial statements, of facts existing at the date of their report which might have affected their report had they then been aware of those facts. The auditors must investigate immediately such subsequently discovered facts. If the auditors ascertain that the facts are significant and existed at the date of the audit report, they should advise the client to make appropriate disclosure of the facts to anyone actually or likely to be relying upon the audit report and the related financial statements. If the client refuses to make appropriate disclosure, the CPAs should inform each member of the client's board of directors of such refusal and then should notify regulatory agencies having jurisdiction over the client, and, if practicable, each person known to be relying upon the audited financial statements, that the CPAs' report can no longer be relied upon.

Evidence for related party transactions

Thus far, we have discussed sufficient appropriate audit evidence for client transactions with *outside interests,* such as unrelated customers and vendors. The auditors must give special attention to accumulating evidence supporting *related party transactions*—client transactions not at arm's length with parties having interests adverse to those of the client. Many cases of management fraud coming to light in recent years have involved fraudulent related party transactions.

In *Statement on Auditing Standards No. 6,* the AICPA discussed related party transactions as follows:

Examples of related party transactions include transactions between a parent company and its subsidiaries, transactions between or among subsidiaries of a common parent, and transactions in which the reporting entity participates with other affiliated businesses, with management or with principal stockholders (or other ownership interests). Transactions between or among the foregoing parties are considered to be related party transactions even though they may not be given accounting recognition. For example, an entity may provide services to a related party without charge.[2]

The primary concern of the auditors is that related party transactions are adequately disclosed in the client's financial statements or footnotes. Disclosure of related party transactions should include: the nature of the relationship; a description of the transactions, including dollar amounts; and amounts due to and from related parties, together with terms and manner of settlement.

Enquiry of management is not a reliable procedure to obtain audit evidence to support related party transactions. The audit procedures for related party transactions must concentrate on obtaining confirmations and other evidence from the related parties and from intermediaries such as banks, agents, and attorneys. It is essential that the auditors learn the *substance* of related party transactions, which often differs from the *form* of the transactions.

KEY TERMS INTRODUCED OR EMPHASIZED IN CHAPTER 7

appropriateness   The appropriateness of audit evidence relates to its quality.

audit evidence   Any information which corroborates or refutes the auditors' premise that the financial statements present fairly the client's financial position and operating results.

confirmation   A type of documentary evidence which is created outside the client organization and transmitted directly to the auditors.

inspection   The auditors' evidence-gathering technique which provides documentary evidence.

letter of representations   A single letter or separate letters prepared by officers of the client company at the auditors' request setting forth certain facts about the company's financial position or operations.

material   Of substantial importance. Significant enough to affect evaluations or decisions by users of financial satements. Information which should be disclosed in order that financial statements constitute a fair presentation. Involves both qualitative and quantitative considerations.

observation   The auditors' evidence-gathering technique which provides physical evidence.

pro forma financial statements   Financial statements which give effect to subsequent events as though they had occurred as of the balance sheet date.

---

[2] AICPA, "Related Party Transactions," *Statement on Auditing Standards No. 6* (New York, 1975), p. 2.

related party transaction   A transaction in which one party has the ability to influence significantly the management or operating policies of the other party, to the extent that one of the transacting parties might be prevented from pursuing fully its own separate interests.

relative risk   The danger in a specific audit engagement of substantial error and misstatement in the accounts and the financial statements.

S-1 review   Procedures carried out by auditors at the client company's facilities on or as close as practicable to the effective date of a registration statement filed under the U.S. Securities Act of 1933.

specialist   A person or firm possessing special skill or knowledge in a field other than accounting or auditing, such as an actuary.

subsequent event   An event occurring after the date of the balance sheet but prior to completion of the audit and issuance of the audit report.

substantive test   A test designed to substantiate the fairness of a specific financial statement item, such as accounts receivable.

sufficient   Sufficient audit evidence is a measure of the quantity of the evidence.

GROUP I
REVIEW QUESTIONS

7-1.   Give at least four examples of *specialists* whose findings might provide appropriate evidence for the independent auditors.

7-2.   What are *related party transactions?*

7-3.   In a conversation with you, Mark Rogers, CA, claims that both the *sufficiency* and the *appropriateness* of audit evidence are a matter of judgment in every audit. Do you agree? Explain.

7-4.   "The best means of verification of cash, inventory, office equipment, and nearly all other assets is a physical count of the units; only a physical count gives the auditors complete assurance as to the accuracy of the amounts listed on the balance sheet." Evaluate this statement.

7-5.   What are "subsequent events?"

7-6.   Give three examples of subsequent events which might influence the auditors' opinion as to one or more items on the balance sheet.

7-7.   In verifying the asset accounts Notes Receivable and Marketable Securities, the auditors examined all notes receivable and all share certificates. Which of these documents represents the stronger type of evidence? Why?

7-8.   As part of the verification of accounts receivable as of the balance sheet date, the auditors might inspect copies of sales invoices. Similarly, as part of the verification of accounts payable, the auditors might inspect purchase invoices. Which of these two types of invoices do you think represents the stronger type of evidence? Why?

7-9.   Explain how comparisons and ratios may be used by the auditors as evidence to support their opinion on the fairness of the financial statements.

7-10.   *a.*   What is a letter of representations?
      b.   What information should a letter of representations contain?

    c. What effect does a letter of representations have on the auditors' examination of a client's financial statements? (AICPA, adapted)

7–11. "In deciding upon the type of evidence to be gathered in support of a given item on the financial statements, the auditors should not be influenced by the differences in cost of obtaining alternative forms of evidence." Do you agree? Explain.

7–12. Identify and explain the considerations that guide the auditors in deciding how much evidence they must examine as a basis for expressing an opinion on a client's financial statements.

7–13. What are the factors that may influence the auditors' judgment on the sufficiency and appropriateness of audit evidence?

GROUP II
QUESTIONS REQUIRING ANALYSIS

7–14. The following statement is representative of attitudes and opinions sometimes encountered by CAs in their professional practices: "Today's audits consist of compliance tests and substantive tests. This is dangerous because testing depends upon the auditors' judgment, which may be defective. An audit can be relied upon only if every transaction is verified."

Required:

    Evaluate the above statement and indicate:

    a. Areas of agreement with the statement, if any.

    b. Areas of misconception, incompleteness, or fallacious reasoning including in the statement, if any. (AICPA, adapted)

7–15. On July 27, 1979, Arthur Ward, CA, issued an unqualified audit report on the financial statements of Dexter Ltd. for the year ended June 30, 1979. Two weeks later, Dexter Ltd. mailed annual reports including the June 30, 1979, financial statements and Ward's audit report to 150 shareholders and to several creditors of Dexter Ltd. Dexter Ltd's. shares are not actively traded on stock exchanges or over the counter.

    On September 5, 1979, the controller of Dexter Ltd. informed Ward that an account payable for consulting services in the amount of $90,000 had inadvertently been omitted from Dexter's June 30, 1979, balance sheet. As a consequence, net income for the year ended June 30, 1979, was overstated $40,500, net of applicable federal and provincial income taxes. Both Ward and Dexter's controller agreed that the misstatements were material to Dexter's financial position at June 30, 1979, and operating results for the year then ended.

Required:

    What should Arthur Ward's course of action be in this matter? Discuss.

7–16. *a.* What are the objectives of the client's representations letters?

    b. Who should prepare and sign the client's representations letters?

    c. When should the client's representations letters be obtained?

    d. Why should the client's representations letters be obtained for each examination? (AICPA, adapted)

7–17. Rank each of the following examples of audit evidence in their order of *appropriateness*. Arrange your answer in the form of a separate paragraph for each item. Explain fully the reasoning employed in judging the appropriateness of each item.

    a. Copies of client's sales invoices.

    b. Auditors' independent computation of earnings per share.

    c. Paid cheques returned with bank statement.

    d. Response from customer of client addressed to auditors' office confirming amount owed to client at balance sheet date.

    e. Letter of representations by controller of client company stating that all liabilities of which he has knowledge are reflected in the company's accounts.

7–18. The financial statements of Yale Company show sales of $10 million for the year. What evidence might the auditors utilize in verifying this amount?

7–19. Marshall Land Company owns substantial amounts of farm and timber lands, and consequently property taxes represent one of the more important types of expense. What specific documents or other evidence should the auditors examine in verifying the Property Taxes Expense account?

7–20. Coldstream Corporation Ltd. has large investments in marketable securities. What documentary evidence should the auditors examine in verifying (*a*) the Marketable Securities account and (*b*) interest and dividends revenue?

7–21. In auditing the financial statements of a manufacturing company that were prepared from data processed by electronic data processing equipment, CAs have found that the traditional "audit trail" has been obscured. As a result CAs may place increased emphasis upon overall tests of the data under audit. These overall tests, which are also applied in auditing manual accounting systems, include the computation of ratios, which are compared to prior year ratios or to industry-wide norms. Examples of such overall ratios are the computation of the rate of inventory turnover and computation of the number of day's sales in receivables.

Required:

    a. Discuss the advantages to the auditors of the use of ratios as overall tests in an audit.

    b. In addition to the computations given above, list the ratios that the auditors may compute during an audit as overall tests on balance sheet accounts and related income statement accounts. For each ratio listed name the two (or more) accounts used in its computation.

    c. When the auditors discover that there has been a significant change in a ratio when compared to the prior year's ratio, they consider the possible reasons for the change. Give the possible reasons for the following significant changes in ratios:

(1)   The rate of the inventory turnover (ratio of cost of goods sold and average inventory) has decreased from the prior year's rate.

(2)   The number of day's sales in receivables (ratio of average daily accounts receivable and sales) has increased over the prior year. (AICPA, adapted)

GROUP III
PROBLEMS

7–22.   In the examination of financial statements, auditors must judge the validity of the audit evidence they obtain.

Required:

Assume that the auditors have evaluated internal control and found it satisfactory.

a.   In the course of examination, the auditors ask many questions of client officers and employees.

(1)   Describe the factors that the auditors should consider in evaluating oral evidence provided by client officers and employees.

(2)   Discuss the validity and limitations of oral evidence.

b.   The auditors' examination may include computation of various balance sheet and operating ratios for comparison to prior years and industry averages. Discuss the validity and limitations of ratio analysis.

c.   In connection with an examination of the financial statements of a manufacturing company, the auditors are observing the physical inventory of finished goods, which consists of expensive, highly complex electronic equipment.

Discuss the validity and limitations of the audit evidence provided by this procedure. (AICPA, adapted)

7–23.   In connection with his examination of the financial statements of Flowmeter, Inc., for the year ended December 31, 1978, John Hirsch, CA, is aware that certain events and transactions that took place after December 31, 1978, but before he issues his report dated February 28, 1979, may affect the company's financial statements.

The following material events or transactions have come to his attention:

a.   On January 3, 1979, Flowmeter, Inc., received a shipment of raw materials. The materials had been ordered in October 1978 and shipped f.o.b. shipping point in November 1978.

b.   On January 15, 1979, the company settled and paid a personal injury claim of a former employee as the result of an accident which occurred in March 1978. The company had not previously recorded a liability for the claim.

c.   On January 25, 1979, the company agreed to purchase for cash

the outstanding shares of Porter Electrical Company. The business combination is likely to double the sales volume of Flowmeter, Inc.
d. On February 1, 1979, a plant owned by Flowmeter, Inc., was damaged by a flood, resulting in an uninsured loss of inventory.
e. On February 5, 1979, Flowmeter, Inc., issued to an underwriting syndicate $2,000,000 in convertible bonds.

Required:

For each of the above events or transactions, indicate the audit procedures that should have brought the item to the attention of the auditor, and the form of disclosure in the financial statements including the reasons for such disclosures. Arrange your answer in the format shown below.

Item letter	Audit procedures	Required disclosure and reasons

(AICPA, adapted)

7–24. The financial statements of Wayne Ltd. indicate that large amounts of notes payable to banks were retired during the period under audit. Evaluate the reliability of each of the following types of evidence supporting these transactions:
a. Debit entries in the Notes Payable account.
b. Entries in the cheque register.
c. Paid cheques.
d. Notes payable bearing bank perforation stamp "PAID" and the date of payment.
e. Statement by client's treasurer that notes had been paid at maturity.
f. Letter received by auditors directly from bank stating that no indebtedness on part of client existed as of the balance sheet date.

7–25. During your examination of the accounts receivable of a new client, you notice that one account is much larger than the rest, and you therefore decide to examine the evidence supporting this customer's account. Comment on the relative reliability and adequacy of the following types of evidence:
a. Computer print-out from accounts receivable subsidiary ledger.
b. Copies of sales invoices in amount of the receivable.
c. Purchase order received from customer.

    d. Shipping document describing the articles sold.

    e. Letter received by client from customer acknowledging the correctness of the receivable in the amount shown on client's accounting records.

    f. Letter received by auditors directly from customer acknowledging the correctness of the amount shown as receivable on client's accounting records.

7–26. In an examination of financial statements CAs are concerned with the accumulation of audit evidence.

Required:

    a. What is the objective of the CAs' accumulation of audit evidence during the course of their examination?

    b. The source of documentary evidence is of primary importance in the CAs' evaluation of its quality. Documentary evidence may be classified according to source. For example, one class originates within the client's organization, passes through the hands of third parties, and returns to the client, where it may be examined by the auditors. List the classification of documentary evidence according to source, briefly discussing the effect of the source on the reliability of the evidence. (AICPA, adapted)

7–27. What would you accept as satisfactory documentary evidence in support of entries in the following:

    a. Sales register.

    b. Sales returns register.

    c. Voucher or invoice register.

    d. Payroll register.

    e. Cheque register. (AICPA, adapted)

7–28. One of the field work standards requires the auditor to obtain sufficient appropriate audit evidence to afford a reasonable basis to support the content of his report.

Required:

    a. Identify the general sources of audit evidence available to the auditor.

    b. Comment on the degree of reliance the auditor may place upon evidence originating from each source.

    c. Give an example of the type of evidence that would originate from each source.

    Arrange your answer in the following format.

a. *General source*	b. *Degree of reliance*	c. *Example*

(CICA, adapted)

7–29.   Robertson Ltd. had accounts receivable of $100,000 at December 31, 1978, and had provided an allowance for uncollectible accounts of $3,000. After performing all normal auditing procedures relating to the receivables and to the valuation allowance, the independent auditors were satisfied that this asset was fairly stated and that the allowance for uncollectible accounts was adequate. Just before completion of the audit field work late in February, however, the auditors learned that the entire plant of Thompson Limited, a major customer, had been destroyed by a flood early in February, and that as a result Thompson Limited was hopelessly insolvent.

The account receivable from Thompson Limited in the amount of $22,000 originated on December 28; terms of payment were "net 60 days." The receivable had been regarded as entirely collectible at December 31, and the auditors had so considered it in reaching their conclusion as to the adequacy of the allowance for uncollectible accounts. In discussing the news concerning the flood, the controller of Robertson Ltd. emphasized to the auditors that the probable loss of $22,000 should be regarded as a loss of the year 1979 and not of 1978, the year under audit.

What action, if any, should the auditors recommend with respect to the receivable from Thompson Limited?

7–30.   In connection with your examination of the financial statements of Hollis Manufacturing Corporation Ltd. for the year ended December 31, 1978, your review of subsequent events disclosed the following items:

1.   January 7, 1979: The mineral content of a shipment of ore en route to Hollis Manufacturing Corporation Ltd. on December 31, 1978, was determined to be 72 percent. The shipment was recorded at year-end at an estimated content of 50 percent by a debit to Raw Materials Inventory and a credit to Accounts Payable in the amount of $20,600. The final liability to the vendor is based on the actual mineral content of the shipment.

2.   January 15, 1979: Culminating a series of personal disagreements between Ray Hollis, the president, and his brother-in-law, the treasurer, the latter resigned, effective immediately, under an agreement whereby the corporation would purchase his 10 percent share ownership at book value as of December 31, 1978. Payment is to be made in two equal amounts in cash on April 1 and October 1, 1979. In December the treasurer had obtained a divorce from his wife, who is Ray Hollis's sister.

3.   January 31, 1979: As a result of reduced sales, production was curtailed in mid-January and some workers were laid off. On February 5, 1979, all the remaining workers went on strike. To date the strike is unsettled.

Required:

Assume that the above items came to your attention prior to completion of your audit field work on February 15, 1979. For each of the above items, discuss the disclosure that you would recommend for the item, listing all details that you would suggest should be disclosed. Indicate those items or details, if any, that should not be disclosed. Give your reasons for recommending or not recommending disclosure of the items or details. (AICPA, adapted)

7–31. CA is the auditor of F Ltd., which has a December 31 year-end. On January 31, CA's staff completed the field work for the year 1978. On February 15, CA is in the process of finalizing his auditor's report dated January 31, 1979, when he becomes aware of a material subsequent event which occurred on February 10. Management prefers not to disclose the subsequent event.

Required:

What factors should CA take into account before signing his report? (CICA)

8

Statistical sampling

The preceding chapter discussed the need for sufficient, appropriate audit evidence as the basis for the auditors' report. Since the evolution of large business entities, auditors increasingly have had to rely upon sampling procedures as the only practical means of obtaining this evidence. This reliance upon sampling procedures is one of the basic reasons why the auditors' report is regarded as an expression of opinion rather than absolute certification of the fairness of financial statements.

Sampling, whether statistical or judgmental, is the process of selecting a sample from a larger group of items (called the *population, field,* or *universe*) and using the characteristics of the sample to draw inferences about the characteristics of the entire field of items. The underlying assumption is that the sample is *representative* of the population, meaning that the sample will possess essentially the same characteristics as the population. Inherent in the techniques of sampling is the risk of *sampling error*—the possibility of selecting a sample which, purely by chance, *is not* representative of the population. Due to the ever-present risk of sampling error, there is always some degree of risk that sampling will lead to incorrect conclusions concerning the population.

Comparison of statistical with judgmental sampling

Some degree of sampling error is likely to be present in any sample.

Thus, sampling results are always an *estimate* rather than an exact determination of the true population characteristics. As a general rule, the risk of material sampling error is reduced by increasing the sample size. When sample size is 100 percent of the population, the sample is by definition perfectly representative of the population and the risk of sampling error is eliminated. Larger samples, however, are more costly and time-consuming. A key element in utilizing sampling effectively is to balance the risk of material sampling error against the cost of increasing the sample size.

Judgmental sampling. Sampling can be either "judgmental" or "statistical," and one or both techniques may be used by the auditors in their audit. In *judgmental sampling,* the determination of sample size or composition of the sample is based on the auditors' professional judgment rather than on a combination of professional judgment and the laws of probability. When sample size or composition is determined solely by the auditors' professional judgment, the sample results are not subject to statistical interpretation. Thus, judgmental sampling provides the auditors with no objective or statistical means of measuring the risk of material sampling error. The auditors must use their professional experience and judgment to evaluate the risk of material sampling error and to interpret the sample results. Consequently, the auditors may find themselves either taking larger and more costly samples than are justified "just to be on the safe side," or unknowingly running an unacceptably high risk that their conclusions regarding the population are materially in error. Despite these shortcomings, judgmental sampling is still used in practice.

Statistical sampling. In *statistical sampling,* the determination of sample size and composition of the sample are based on both the auditors' professional judgment and the laws of probability. Thus, the auditors may specify in advance the reliability which they require in their sample results, and then compute a sample size which affords that degree of reliability. Since statistical sampling techniques are based upon the laws of probability, the auditors are able to control the extent of their risk in relying upon sample results. Consequently, an advantage of statistical sampling over judgmental sampling is that the *risk of material sampling error may be measured and controlled.*

Sampling plans. Auditors may use sampling procedures to estimate many different characteristics of populations, but basically every estimate is either of a numerical quantity or of a rate of occurrence. The sampling terms corresponding to "numerical quantities" and "occurrence rates" are, respectively, *variables* and *attributes.*

The statistical sampling procedures used to accomplish a specific audit objective are termed a *sampling plan.* Sampling plans most frequently used by auditors include *estimation sampling for attributes, discovery sampling, estimation sampling for variables,* and *ratio and difference estimation.* The application of any of these sampling plans involves five distinct steps in which the auditors must—

1. Define the objectives and nature of the test.
2. Determine the method of sampling to be used.
3. Calculate the appropriate sample size.
4. Select the sample.
5. Interpret the sample results.

The specific procedures used in completing these five steps vary somewhat from one sampling plan to another. Also, these five steps can be used in judgmental sampling as well as statistical sampling.

In order for auditors to measure or control the risk of sampling error, they must calculate the appropriate sample size by statistical methods and select the items for inclusion in the sample on a *random* basis. If either of these steps is performed on a judgmental (nonstatistical) basis, the sample results must be interpreted judgmentally.

Random selection

A common misinterpretation of statistical sampling is to equate this process with *random sampling.* Random sampling relates only to one step in a statistical sampling plan; it is the method of selecting the items for inclusion in the sample. Random sampling, therefore, is only a part of the statistical sampling procedure and not the entire process. If auditors are to control the risk of sampling error, random sampling procedures must be used in conjunction with statistical procedures for determining sample size and interpreting sample results. To emphasize this distinction, this text will use the term *random selection* rather than random "sampling" to refer to the procedure of selecting the items for inclusion in a sample.

The principle involved in unrestricted random selection is that every item in the population has an equal chance of being selected for inclusion in the sample. Since the items comprising a random sample are selected purely by chance, the person selecting the sample will not influence or bias the selection process. Although random selection results in an *unbiased sample,* that sample is not necessarily representative. The risk still exists that purely by chance a sample will be selected which does not possess essentially the same characteristics as the population. However, since the risk of a non-representative random sample stems from the laws of probability, this risk may be measured by statistical formulas.

The concept of a random sample requires that the person selecting the sample will not influence or bias the selection either consciously or unconsciously. Thus, some type of impartial selection process is necessary to obtain a truly random sample. Techniques often used for selecting random samples include *random number tables, random number generators, systematic selection,* and *cluster selection.*

Random number tables

Perhaps the easiest method of selecting items at random is the use of a random number table. A portion of a random number table is illustrated in Figure 8-1.

The random numbers appearing in Figure 8-1 are arranged into columns of five digits. Except that the columnar arrangement permits the reader of the table to select numbers easily, the columns are purely arbitrary and otherwise meaningless. Each digit on the table is a random digit; the table does *not* represent a listing of random five-digit numbers. The columnar arrangement is for convenience only.

In using a random number table, the first step is to establish correspondence between the digits in the table and the items in the population. This is most easily done when the items in the population are consecutively numbered. On occasion, however, auditors may find it necessary to renumber the population to obtain correspondence. For example, if transactions are numbered A-001, B-001, and so on, the auditors may assign numbers to replace the alphabetic characters. Next, the auditors must select a starting point and a systematic route to be used in reading the random number table. Any route is permissible, as long as it is followed consistently.

To illustrate the use of a random number table, assume that a client's accounts receivable are numbered from 0001 to 5,000, and that the auditors want to select a random sample of 300 accounts for confirmation. Using the table in Figure 8-1, the auditors decide to start at the top of column 2 and to proceed from top to bottom. Reading only the first four digits of the numbers in column 2, the auditors would select 3942, 1968, and 4837 as three of the account numbers to be included in their sample. The next number, 8692, would be ignored since there is no account with

FIGURE 8-1
Table of random numbers

	Columns				
Row	(1)	(2)	(3)	(4)	(5)
1	04734	39426	91035	54839	76873
2	10417	19688	83404	42038	48226
3	07514	48374	35658	38971	53779
4	52305	86925	16223	25946	90222
5	96357	11486	30102	82679	57983
6	92870	05921	65698	27993	86406
7	00500	75924	38803	05386	10072
8	34862	93784	52709	15370	96727
9	25809	21860	36790	76883	20435
10	77487	38419	20631	48694	12638

that number. The next numbers to be included in the sample would be 1148, 592, 2186, and so on.

Duplicate numbers. In using a random number table, it is possible that the auditors will draw the same number more than once. If the auditors ignore a number that is drawn a second time and go on to the next number, they are *sampling without replacement.* This term means that an item once selected is not "replaced" into the population of eligible items, and consequently it cannot be drawn for inclusion in the sample a second time.

The alternative to sampling without replacement is *sampling with replacement.* This method requires that if a particular number is drawn two or more times, the number must be included two or more times in the sample. Sampling with replacement means that once an item has been selected, it is immediately "replaced" into the population of eligible items and may be selected a second time.

Statistical measurement formulas assume sampling with replacement. As a practical matter, however, samples are often selected without replacement. Sampling without replacement is more conservative, since samples are likely to include more items. For example, assume that we select a sample of 100 items sampling without replacement. When we finish selecting the sample we will have exactly 100 different items. If we sampled with replacement, however, we could end up with less than 100 different items, since the same item could be counted two or more times in our sample.

Random number generators

Even when items are assigned consecutive numbers, the selection of a large sample from a random number table may be a very time-consuming process. Computer programs called *random number generators* may be used to provide any length list of random numbers applicable to a given population. Random number generators may be programmed to select random numbers with specific characteristics, so that the list of random numbers provided to the auditors includes only numbers present in the population. A random number generator is a standard program in all generalized audit software packages.

Systematic selection

An approach which is less time consuming than selecting a random number for each item to be included in the sample is *systematic selection.* This technique involves selecting every *n*th item in the population following a *random starting point.*

To illustrate systematic selection, assume that auditors wish to examine 200 paid cheques from a population of 10,000 cheques. If only one random starting point is used, the auditors would select every 50th cheque (10,000 ÷ 200) in the population. In order that 200 items be selected, the auditors must move upward and downward from their random starting point. If a random starting point of Cheque No. 137 were selected, Cheque Nos. 87 (137 − 50) and 37 (137 − 100) would be included in the sample, as well as every 50th cheque number after 137 (Nos. 187, 237, and so on). If the auditors had elected to use five random starting points, 40 cheques (200 ÷ 5) would have to be selected from each random start. Thus, the auditors would select every 250th cheque number (10,000 ÷ 40) before and after each of the random starting points.

Selecting every nth item in the population results in a random sample only when identification numbers were assigned to population items in random order. For example, if expensive inventory parts are always assigned an identification number ending in 9, systematic selection could result in a highly biased sample which included only expensive items or only inexpensive items.

To prevent drawing a non-random or biased sample when systematic selection is used, the auditors should first determine that the population is arranged in random order. If the population is not in random order, each item to be included in the sample should be selected independently. Alternatively, the auditors might *stratify* the population (as explained on page 345) into segments, each of which is arranged in random order, and apply systematic selection within each segment. Another method by which the auditors may guard against a non-random sample is to increase the number of random starting points used in conjunction with systematic selection.

The systematic selection technique has the advantage of enabling the auditors to obtain a sample from a population of unnumbered documents or transactions. If the documents to be examined are unnumbered, there is no necessity under this method to number them either physically or mentally; as required under the random number table selection technique. Rather, the auditors merely count off the sampling interval to select the documents or use a ruler to measure the interval. Generalized audit software packages include routines for systematic selection of audit samples from computer-based files.

Cluster selection

A fourth method of selecting a random sample is the *cluster selection* technique. Frequently, the auditors will encounter a group of items to be examined which may conveniently be broken down into subgroups. Each of these subgroups may be described as a *cluster.* For example, the accounts receivable of a department store may be contained in a number of trays. If there were 10,000 accounts receivable cards in 50 trays, each tray of cards may be considered as a cluster. Under this method, the auditors may select on a random basis (perhaps by using a random number table) a few trays of cards to be examined.

This method of sampling would appear at first glance to be simple, compared with either the random number table or systematic selection methods. However, in cluster sampling, the auditors must evaluate each cluster as if it were a single observation. If this cluster consists of 500 cards, the evaluation becomes a formidable task. Because of these statistical requirements, the auditors will normally find that the apparent saving in time proves to be an illusion because of the need for a larger sample size to achieve the desired results. Cluster selection requires the assistance of a specialist in statistical sampling.

Judgment block samples

Block sampling is a selection technique widely used by auditors in conjunction with *judgmental* sampling plans. A *block sample* usually includes all items in a selected time period, numerical sequence, or alphabetical sequence. For example, in verifying cash disbursements, the auditors might decide to examine all cheques issued for the months of April and December, or all cheques numbered 3,581 through 3,880. In the audit of accounts receivable, all accounts with customers in the alphabetical section from L to N might be examined.

The same months or alphabetical sections should not be chosen for sampling in successive audits, and the auditors should be careful not to indicate in advance the blocks to be sampled. On the other hand, many auditors feel that the last month of the audit period requires testing to a greater extent than other months because of the likelihood of irregularities being introduced just prior to the end of the fiscal year.

A weakness of the block sample is that it ignores changes in the client's accounting personnel during the period under audit. An accounting clerk or cashier who worked for three or four months during the year may have made numerous errors which will not be disclosed if the block sample happens to be taken from other months. However, block samples are especially effective in detecting lapping activities (fraud involving delay in entering cash receipts) by persons handling cash and cash records.

Block sampling is *not* a random selection technique. From a statistical sampling viewpoint, block sampling is deficient in that all items in the population do not stand an equal chance of being included in the sample. The technique is appropriate, however, in a wide variety of auditing situations involving the used of judgmental sampling.

Statistical measurement

Random selection techniques are limited to helping the auditors select items to be sampled; if auditors are to control the risk of sampling error, they must take a further step and use *statistical measurement* methods to determine sample size and interpret sample results. If auditors plan to use statistical measurement techniques, they must employ random selection in drawing the sample.

Statistical measurement techniques may be applied to a wide variety of audit situations. In recognition of the audit uses of statistical sampling, the AICPA has prepared an individual study program entitled *An Auditor's Approach to Statistical Sampling.*[1] This six-volume series provides detailed instructions and case study illustrations of the statistical sampling plans considered most useful to auditors. These are:

1. Estimation sampling for attributes. This sampling plan permits auditors to determine the rate of occurrence of certain characteristics (for example, exceptions) in a population within prescribed ranges of precision and levels of confidence.

2. Discovery sampling. This form of attribute sampling is designed to locate at least one exception item, providing that the exception occurs within the population with at least a specified occurrence rate. Discovery sampling is used to search for *critical* errors, for which the existence of even a very low occurrence rate could have great significance.

3. Estimation sampling for variables. This plan enables auditors to estimate numerical quantities, such as the dollar value of a population, with prescribed precision and reliability.

4. Ratio and difference estimation. Although closely related, ratio estimation and difference estimation are two separate sampling plans. Both are alternatives to estimation sampling for variables as a technique for estimating the dollar value of a population.

In order to understand any of these statistical sampling plans, the auditors must first be familiar with the meanings and interrelationships among certain statistical concepts, such as *occurrence rate, precision, confidence level* (or *reliability*), and *sample size.*

Occurrence rate

Occurrence rate is the frequency with which a given characteristic occurs in the population being studied. Since the characteristic the auditors are interested in is frequently some type of error, an occurrence rate is

---

[1] The CICA published in 1972 a study entitled *Statistical Sampling in an Audit Context* to promote "a broad understanding of the basic concepts of statistical sampling." However, it is not as comprehensive as the AICPA study program.

often referred to as an *error rate*. Since the true occurrence rate of the population is not known, an expected or estimated occurrence rate, either based on past audit experiences or a pilot sample, must be used as one of the factors to determine the sample size.

Precision

Whether the auditors' objective is estimating attributes or variables, the sample results may not be *exactly* representative of the population. Some degree of sampling error is usually present. In utilizing statistical sampling techniques, auditors are able to measure and control the risk of material sampling error by calculating precision and confidence level.

Precision is the range, set by + and − limits from the sample results, within which the true value of the population characteristic being measured is likely to lie. For example, assume a sample is taken to determine the occurrence rate of a certain type of error in the preparation of invoices. The sample indicates an error rate of 2.1 percent. We have little assurance that the error rate in the population is exactly 2.1 percent, but we know that the sample result probably approximates the population error rate. Therefore, we may set an *interval* around the sample result within which we expect the population error rate to be. A precision interval of ±1 percent would indicate that we expect the true population error rate to lie between 1.1 and 3.1 percent. The figures designating the upper and lower boundaries of the precision interval are the *precision limits.*

The less precision we require (meaning the wider the interval we allow), the more confident we may be that the true population characteristic lies within the precision interval. In the preceding example, a precision of ±2 percent would mean that we assume the population error rate to be between 0.1 percent and 4.1 percent. Obviously, it is more probable that the true population error rate will lie within this wider precision interval than within the narrower interval of ±1 percent. Remember, *less precision means a wider interval* and *more precision means a narrower interval* because the true population characteristics is assumed to be closer to the sample results.

Precision may also be stated as a dollar value interval. For example, we may attempt to establish the total dollar value of receivables with a precision of ±$10,000. Precision may be viewed as the allowable margin of sampling error. The precision required by auditors usually is determined in light of the materiality of this allowable margin of error.

Confidence level (reliability)

The true population characteristic may not always lie within our specified range of precision. Our confidence level is the *percentage of the time* we can expect the sample results to represent the true population characteristic within the specified range of precision. Confidence level measures the reliability of the sample, and the risk that the true population characteristic value lies outside the precision interval of the sample. The terms *confidence level* and *reliability* are used interchangeably.

Reliability of 95 percent means we can expect 95 percent of the time the same results will represent the true population characteristic value. Conversely, there is a 5 percent risk that the true population characteristic value is not within the precision interval of our sample result. This represents the risk that the amount of sampling error exceeds that allowed for by the precision interval.

Given a specific sample, the less precision we require the greater our level of confidence that the true population value lies within the precision interval. The greater the required precision, the lower will be our confidence level that the sample represents the population within the desired precision interval.

Sample size

The size of our sample has a direct effect upon both precision and reliability. With a very small sample, we cannot have high reliability unless we allow a very great range of precision. On the other hand, a sample of 100 percent of the population allows us 100 percent reliability with maximum precision (± 0 percent).

In general, both confidence level and the degree of precision can be increased by increasing sample size. In other words, the greater the precision and/or confidence level desired by the auditors, the larger the sample that will be required.

Sample size is also affected by certain characteristics of the population being tested. As the population increases in size, the sample size necessary to represent the population with specified precision and reliability will increase, but not in proportion to the increase in population size. In estimation sampling for attributes, sample size also increases as the expected occurrence rate becomes larger. Finally, in sampling to estimate variables, greater variability among the item values in the population increases the required sample size. These relationships are summarized in Figure 8–2.

Estimation sampling for attributes

Estimation sampling for attributes enables auditors to determine, within prescribed limits of precision and confidence, the frequency of occurrence of specified characteristics in a population. This technique is widely used in compliance testing when auditors want to estimate the frequency of exceptions (errors) in the operation of specific internal accounting control procedures.

FIGURE 8–2
Factors affecting sample size

Factor	Change in factor°	Effect upon required sample size
Auditors' requirements:		
Precision	Increase (tighter)	Increase
Reliability	Increase	Increase
Population characteristics:		
Size	Increase	Small increase
Expected occurrence rate ⎫		
or ⎬	Increase	Increase
Variability of item values ⎭		

° As one factor changes, other factors are assumed to remain constant.

Estimated exception rates are stated in percentages. If a sample indicates an exception rate of 3 percent with a precision interval of ±1 percent, the auditors could infer that between 2 and 4 percent of the items in the population contain the designated exception. Sampling for attributes does not provide dollar value information—that is, the sample results do not indicate the dollar magnitude of the exceptions or their effect upon the fairness of the financial statements.[2] The sample results do provide the auditors with useful *qualitative* information as to whether the client's internal control procedures are operating effectively or in a haphazard manner. Comparison of current exception rates with those of prior years may also give the auditors an indication of whether internal accounting control is improving or deteriorating.

Defining an "exception." When attribute sampling is used for compliance tests, the population usually consists of all transactions subject to a specific control procedure during the period under audit. Exceptions are defined as those control failures which the auditors consider relevant to their evaluation of the effectiveness of the control procedure. The auditors' interpretation of the estimated exception rate will depend largely on how they have defined "exceptions." If exceptions are defined to include all errors, no matter how trivial, a population could contain a relatively high error rate without lessening the reliability of the financial statements. On the other hand, if exceptions are defined only as fictitious transactions recorded in the accounting records, even a very low occurrence rate has serious implications.

If several types of errors are combined in the auditors' definition of exceptions, it is important that these errors are of similar audit significance.

---

[2] Ratio and difference estimation plans may be used to convert the results of attribute sampling into dollar measurements.

If serious and minor types of errors are combined in the definition, the significance of the occurrence rate is obscured.

Determining precision and reliability. How do auditors determine the appropriate precision interval and reliability for their estimations of occurrence rates? The answer depends upon many factors, including the purpose of the test, anticipated occurrence rate, nature of the characteristic being measured, type of transactions involved, and the existence or lack of compensating controls.

Compliance tests usually are designed to provide the auditors with assurance that error rates do not exceed acceptable levels. The *upper precision limit* is therefore of greater importance than the lower limit. Assume, for example, that auditors anticipate an error rate of 5 percent and stipulate a precision of ±3 percent. The relevant question is whether the auditors can accept an error rate ranging up to 8 percent, not whether they can accept an error rate of less than 2 percent. The lower precision limit is not pertinent to the objective of the test. For this reason, auditors generally use *one-sided precision* in estimation sampling for attributes—that is, they state precision only in terms of an upper precision limit. In stipulating an upper precision limit, the auditors must consider both the anticipated occurrence rate and an allowable margin of sampling error.

The upper precision limit may also have some effect on the auditors' determination of confidence level or risk. Should the occurrence rate be uncomfortably high, they may wish to take less risk of being wrong and stipulate a higher confidence level. The converse may also be true.

The nature of the exception and the type of transactions being examined also have a bearing on the determination of precision and confidence level. In estimation sampling for attributes, the auditors may separate the types of exceptions they are testing into two major categories: (1) exceptions of a procedural nature that have no direct effect on the financial statements and (2) exceptions which may directly affect account balances and, therefore, the financial statements. If the exceptions of a procedural nature (such as the failure to obtain two signatures on cheques) are compensated for by other internal controls, the auditors should be able to stipulate a fairly wide range of precision coupled with a relatively high degree of risk. On the other hand, if the exception is of the type which may directly affect the financial statements (such as the incorrect pricing of inventory items), the auditors must generally stipulate a narrow range of precision and a low risk.

Although precision and confidence level are not independent of one another, the auditors may view precision as the allowable margin of error, and the confidence level as establishing the risk of being wrong. Precision, then, should be determined by the potential effect of the exceptions on the financial statements. Confidence levels should be determined in light of the amount of supporting evidence the auditors require for rendering an opinion. Since the results of compliance tests are a factor in determining the nature, timing, and extent of other audit procedures, auditors usually desire a high level of confidence in these results.

Tables for use in estimating error rates. To enable auditors to use estimation sampling for attributes without resorting to complex mathematical formulas, tables such as the one in Figure 8–3 have been developed. This illustration is one page of a set of tables in the AICPA's *An Auditor's Approach to Statistical Sampling, Volume 6.* The horizontal axis of the table is the anticipated occurrence rate in the population, and the vertical axis is the required sample size. The numbers in the body of the table are the upper precision limits (stated in percentages) which result from various sample sizes and occurrence rates.

To use this set of tables, the auditors must stipulate a desired reliability level, an anticipated occurrence rate, and a desired upper precision limit.[3] Sample size then may be determined by selecting the column designated by the anticipated occurrence rate, moving down the column to an acceptable upper precision limit, and reading the corresponding sample size from the extreme left column.

Figure 8–3 also may be used in the evaluation of sample results. When the table is used for this purpose, the horizontal axis is the occurrence rate actually observed in the sample. The intersection of the observed occurrence rate column with the row designating sample size indicates the upper precision limit of the sample results.

Illustration of estimation sampling for attributes

The following procedures for applying estimation sampling for attributes is predicated upon the use of the table in Figure 8–3; however, only slight modifications are necessary if other tables are used.

Determine the nature and objective of the tests to be made. Assume that the auditors wish to test the effectiveness of the client's internal control procedure of matching receiving reports with purchase invoices as a step in authorizing payment for purchases of materials. They are, therefore, interested in the clerical accuracy of the matching process and in determining whether the control procedure which requires the matching of purchase invoices and receiving reports is working. The auditors define an exception as any one or more of the following with respect to each invoice and the related receiver:

1. Any invoice not supported by a receiving document.
2. Any invoice supported by a receiving document which is applicable to another invoice.

---

[3] Some tables require the auditors to specify population size. Figure 8–3 assumes an infinite population. The effect on sample size when populations are finite but of significant size is not material.

FIGURE 8–3
Table for use in estimation sampling for attributes: Determination of sample size, one-sided upper precision limits (reliability level—95 percent)

Sample size	Occurrence rate 0.0	0.5	1.0	2.0	3.0	4.0	5.0	6.0	7.0	8.0	9.0	10.0	12.0	14.0	16.0	18.0	20.0	25.0	30.0	40.0	50.0
50	5.8			9.1		12.1		14.8		17.4		19.9	22.3	25.1	27.0	29.6	31.6		42.4	52.6	62.4
100	3.0		4.7	6.2	7.6	8.9	10.2	11.5	13.0	14.0	15.4	16.4	18.7	21.2	23.3	25.6	27.7	33.1	38.4	48.7	56.6
150	2.0			5.1		7.7		10.2		12.6		15.0	17.3	19.6	21.7	24.0	26.1		36.7	47.0	56.8
200	1.5	2.4	3.1	4.5	5.8	7.1	8.3	9.5	10.8	11.9	13.1	14.2	16.4	18.7	20.9	23.1	25.2	30.5	35.7	45.7	55.6
250	1.2			4.2		6.7		9.1		11.4		13.7	15.9	18.1	20.3	22.4	24.6		34.8	44.8	54.7
300	1.0		2.6	3.9	5.2	6.4	7.6	8.8	10.0	11.1	12.2	13.3	15.5	17.7	19.8	22.0	24.1	29.1	34.1	44.1	54.1
350	0.9			3.7		6.2		8.5		10.8		13.0	15.2	17.4	19.5	21.7	23.6		33.6	43.6	53.6
400	0.7	1.6	2.3	3.6	4.8	6.0	7.2	8.3	9.5	10.6	11.7	12.8	15.0	17.2	19.2	21.2	23.2	28.2	33.2	43.2	53.2
450	0.7			3.5		5.9		8.2		10.4		12.6	14.8	16.8	18.9	20.9	22.9		32.9	42.9	52.9
500	0.6		2.1	3.4	4.6	5.8	6.9	8.0	9.2	10.3	11.4	12.5	14.6	16.7	18.6	20.7	22.6	27.6	32.6	42.6	52.6
550	0.5			3.3		5.7		7.9		10.1		12.3	14.4	16.4	18.4	20.4	22.4		32.4	42.4	52.4
600	0.5	1.3	2.0	3.2	4.4	5.6	6.7	7.8	9.0	10.0	11.2	12.2	14.2	16.2	18.2	20.2	22.2	27.2	32.2	42.2	52.2
650	0.5			3.2		5.5		7.7		10.0		12.1	14.1	16.1	18.1	20.1	22.1		32.1	42.1	52.1
700	0.4		1.9	3.1	4.3	5.4	6.6	7.7	8.8	9.9	10.8	11.9	13.9	15.9	17.9	19.9	21.9	26.9	31.9	41.9	51.9
750	0.4			3.1		5.4		7.6		9.8		11.8	13.8	15.8	17.8	19.8	21.8		31.8	41.8	51.8
800	0.4	1.1	1.8	3.0	4.2	5.3	6.4	7.5	8.7	9.7	10.7	11.7	13.7	15.7	17.7	19.7	21.7	26.7	31.7	41.7	51.7
850	0.4			3.0		5.3		7.5		9.6		11.6	13.6	15.6	17.6	19.6	21.6		31.6	41.6	51.6
900	0.3		1.7	3.0	4.1	5.2	6.3	7.5	8.5	9.5	10.5	11.5	13.5	15.5	17.5	19.5	21.5	26.5	31.5	41.5	51.5
950	0.3			2.9		5.2		7.4		9.4		11.4	13.4	15.5	17.4	19.5	21.4		31.5	41.5	51.5
1,000	0.3	1.0	1.7	2.9	4.0	5.2	6.3	7.4	8.4	9.4	10.4	11.4	13.4	15.4	17.4	19.4	21.4	26.4	31.4	41.4	51.4
1,500	0.2		1.5	2.7	3.8	4.9	5.9	6.9	7.9	8.9	9.9	10.9	12.9	14.9	16.9	18.9	20.9	25.9	30.9	40.9	50.9
2,000	0.1	0.8	1.4	2.6	3.7	4.7	5.7	6.7	7.7	8.7	9.7	10.7	12.7	14.7	16.7	18.7	20.7	25.7	30.7	40.7	50.7
2,500	0.1		1.4	2.6	3.6	4.6	5.6	6.6	7.6	8.6	9.6	10.6	12.6	14.6	16.6	18.6	20.6	25.6	30.6	40.6	50.6
3,000	0.1	0.8	1.4	2.5	3.5	4.5	5.5	6.5	7.5	8.5	9.5	10.5	12.5	14.5	16.5	18.5	20.5	25.5	30.5	40.5	50.5
4,000	0.1	0.7	1.3	2.4	3.4	4.4	5.4	6.4	7.4	8.4	9.4	10.4	12.4	14.4	16.4	18.4	20.4	25.4	30.4	40.4	50.4
5,000	0.1	0.7	1.3	2.3	3.3	4.3	5.3	6.3	7.3	8.3	9.3	10.3	12.3	14.3	16.3	18.3	20.3	25.3	30.3	40.3	50.3

Source: AICPA, *An Auditor's Approach to Statistical Sampling, Volume 6* (New York, 1974).

3. Any differences between the invoice and the receiving document as to quantities shipped.
4. Any irregularities in the documents which were not subsequently corrected.
5. Any evidence of deliberate manipulation or circumvention of the internal control system.

For this type of test, the only testing procedure needed is inspection of the documents and matching of receivers with invoices.

Determine the field to be sampled. The client prepares a serially numbered voucher for every purchase of materials. The receiving report and purchase invoice are attached to each voucher. Since this compliance test is being performed during the interim period, the population to be tested consists of 7,600 vouchers for purchases of material during the first ten months of the year under audit.

Determine the expected occurrence rate. In the audits of the previous three years, the auditors observed that exceptions of the type described above produced occurrence rates of 0.5 percent, 0.9 percent, and 0.7 percent in the respective years. No positive trend can be discerned from the figures for these three years; the auditors, therefore, select an expected occurrence rate of 1 percent, knowing that this rate is higher than any prior observed rates and that they can defend it on the basis of conservatism and reasonableness. The rate, however, is not so high as to result in an unreasonably large sample size. *[handwritten: predet-ermined rate]*

Stipulate precision and confidence level. From their prior experience and their review of the client's internal controls, the auditors conclude that the system of control over the matching of receiving documents with purchase orders, although not weak, is susceptible to improvement. They also realize that mistakes in matching receiving documents with purchase orders can affect the financial statements through overpayment of vendors and overstatement of inventories. On the other hand, they know that certain recommendations they made during the prior audit for improvement of the internal control system in this area have been adopted. Based upon these considerations, the auditors decide upon an acceptable upper precision limit of 2.6 percent with 95 percent reliability.

Determine the required sample size from the table. Since the stipulated confidence level is 95 percent, the table in Figure 8–3 is applicable. Under the column for a 1 percent occurrence rate, the auditors find the stipulated upper precision limit of 2.6 percent; the corresponding sample size is 300 items.

Draw and inspect the sample. The auditors proceed to select 300 vouchers using an appropriate random selection technique. They then examine the vouchers and supporting documents for each of the types of exceptions previously defined.

Interpret the results of the examination. In interpreting the sample results, the auditors must consider not only the actual percentage of exceptions observed but also the nature of the exceptions. There are three possibilities to be considered: (1) the actual occurrence rate is equal to, or less than, the expected rate; (2) the actual occurrence rate is more than the expected rate; and (3) one or more of the exceptions observed contain evidence of a deliberate manipulation or circumvention of the internal control system.

If the actual occurrence rate observed in the sample items examined is equal to or less than 1 percent, and there is no evidence of a deliberate manipulation or circumvention of the internal control system, the auditors have completed their compliance test of this control procedure. They have their desired assurance that the error rate in the population does not exceed 2.6 percent.

Assume, however, that the error rate observed in the sample is 2 percent and none of the observed exceptions indicate deliberate manipulation or circumvention of internal control. Do the auditors still have 95 percent confidence that the population error rate does not exceed 2.6 percent? Referring to Figure 8–3, the auditors will find that a sample of 300 items with a 2 percent error rate provides 95 percent confidence only that the error rate does not exceed 3.9 percent. Thus, the sample results do not provide the auditors with assurance that the error rate does not exceed their stipulated upper precision limit.

In light of these results, the auditors should reduce their reliance upon the client's internal control in this area and increase their reliance upon their own substantive testing procedures. This weakness in internal control may affect the auditors' substantive tests of inventories, accounts payable, and cash disbursements. As a preliminary step to any modification of their audit program, the auditors should investigate the cause of the unexpectedly high error rate. In addition, they may wish to expand their sample of vouchers to provide a more precise estimate of the population error rate.

There is no requirement that the auditors must continue to use statistical sampling techniques after their preliminary sample has indicated that the characteristics of the population do not meet their expectations. If the indicated error rate in the matching of purchase invoices with receivers is too high, the auditors may request that a thorough examination be performed in this area by the client's employees under the auditors' supervision. Or, the auditors may be able to isolate the exceptions noted to a particular time period. Most of the exceptions may have been caused, for instance, by a replacement employee when a regular employee was on sick leave. If that is the case, the auditors may apply appropriate audit procedures to determine the dollar effect of errors occurring during that time period. The auditors should apply whatever audit procedures are appropriate to ensure that the excessive error rate had not led to material error in the financial statements.

Regardless of the occurrence rate observed, if one or more of the exceptions discovered by the auditors indicates fraud or circumvention of the internal control system, other auditing procedures become necessary. The auditors must evaluate the effect of the exception on the financial statements and adopt auditing procedures which are specifically designed to protect against the type of exception observed. The nature of the exception may be more important than its rate of occurrence.

Discovery sampling

Discovery sampling is actually a modified case of attribute sampling. The purpose of a discovery sample is to detect at least *one exception*, with a predetermined level of confidence, providing the exception exists with a specified occurrence rate in the population. One important use of discovery sampling is to locate examples of a suspected fraud.

Although discovery sampling is designed to locate relatively rare items, it cannot locate "a needle in a haystack." If an exception exists within a population but has an insignificant occurrence rate (0.5 percent or less), no sampling plan can provide adequate assurance that an example of the exception will be encountered. Still, discovery sampling can (with a very high degree of confidence) ensure detection of exceptions occurring at a rate as low as 0.5 to 1 percent.

Discovery sampling is used primarily to search for *critical errors.* When an exception is critical, such as evidence of fraud, any occurrence rate may be intolerable. Consequently, if such an exception is discovered, the auditors may abandon their sampling procedures and undertake a thorough examination of the population. If no exceptions are found in discovery sampling, the auditors may conclude (with the specified reliability) that the critical error does not occur to the extent of the stipulated occurrence rate.

To use discovery sampling, the auditors must specify their desired level of confidence and stiplate the occurrence rate for the test. The required sample size then is computed as follows:

$$\text{Sample size} = \frac{\text{Reliability factor}}{\text{Stipulated occurrence rate}}$$

The *reliability factor* is *not* the same thing as the confidence or reliability level. For a given confidence level, the reliability factor for use in this formula is found from a table such as the one in Figure 8–4. The stipulated occurrence rate is stated as a decimal in the above formula—that is, a rate of 3 percent would be entered as 0.03.

To illustrate discovery sampling, assume that auditors have reason to

FIGURE 8–4
Reliability factors for use in discovery
sampling

Confidence level	Reliability factor
90%	2.3
95	3.0
96	3.2
97	3.4
98	3.7
99	4.3
99+	5.4

Source: AICPA, *An Auditor's Approach to
Statistical Sampling, Volume 6* (New York, 1974).

suspect that someone has been preparing fraudulent purchase orders, receiving reports, and purchase invoices in order to generate cash disbursements for fictitious purchase transactions. In order to determine whether
this has occurred, it is necessary to locate only one set of the fraudulent
documents in the client's file of paid vouchers.

Assume the auditors wish to be 95 percent certain that their sample
will bring to light a fraudulent voucher if the population contains 1 percent or more fraudulent items. Figure 8–4 indicates that the reliability
factor corresponding to 95 percent confidence is 3.0. Dividing this reliability factor by the stipulated occurrence rate (0.01) indicates that the
auditors must examine a sample of 300 vouchers. If no fraudulent vouchers are found in this sample, the auditors will have 95 percent confidence
that fraudulent vouchers are not present in the population to the extent of
1 percent. They have not, however, ruled out the possibility that one or
more vouchers are fraudulent.

Discovery sampling and estimation sampling for attributes may be
applied to the same sample. Auditors might examine a sample of vouchers
once, simultaneously using discovery sampling to search for critical errors
and estimation sampling to estimate the occurrence rates of various non-
critical errors.

Sampling for variables

Although estimation sampling for attributes and discovery sampling are
useful for testing internal control, these sampling plans do not provide
results stated in dollars. Techniques which enable auditors to estimate
dollar amounts are termed *sampling for variables.* These techniques are
very useful in such audit applications as estimating the dollar value of a
client's inventories or accounts receivable, or the aggregate dollar value

of each age classification in an aging schedule of accounts receivable. Sampling for variables is used primarily in the auditors' substantive tests of account balances, whereas sampling for attributes is most widely used in compliance tests of internal accounting control procedures.

Auditors may use sampling for variables either when a book value for a population is unavailable or when the book value in the client's accounting records cannot be relied upon. Sampling plans for variables include *estimation sampling for variables* and *ratio and difference estimation.*

Estimation sampling for variables

Estimation sampling for variables, or *mean-per-unit estimation,* enables auditors to estimate the *average* dollar value of items in a population, with specified precision and reliability, by determining the *average* dollar value of items in a sample. If an estimate of the total dollar value of the population is desired, the estimated average value (the *sample mean*) may be multiplied by the number of items in the population.

Precision, in estimation sampling for variables, is the maximum allowable difference between the auditors' estimate and the true population value. Since this sampling technique deals with averages, precision may be stated either with respect to the total population value or with respect to the average value per item. For example, assume that we wish to estimate the total value of a population containing 1,000 items with precision of ±$500. Assume also that the population has a total value of $18,000 and, therefore, a *true mean* of $18. If we select a sample with a mean of $17, we have missed estimating the true mean by only $1. However, our estimate of the total population value is $17,000 ($17 × 1,000 items), which is not within our stipulated precision of ±$500.

If our estimate of the total population is to be within ±$500, our estimate of the average item value must be within ±50 cents. This figure, ±50 cents, is our *sample precision.* Sample precision may be viewed as the required *precision per item;* it is found by dividing the stipulated precision for our estimate of the total population value by the number of items in the population.

Theory of estimation sampling for variables

The assumption underlying estimation sampling for variables is that the mean of a sample will, within a certain precision and confidence level, represent the true mean of the population. Sampling for variables is a more sophisticated statistical process than attribute or discovery sampling. Even if tables are used to determine the required sample size, the auditor needs some familiarity with statistical theory and terminology. Of particular importance are the concepts of *normal distribution, standard devi-*

FIGURE 8–5
Normal distribution

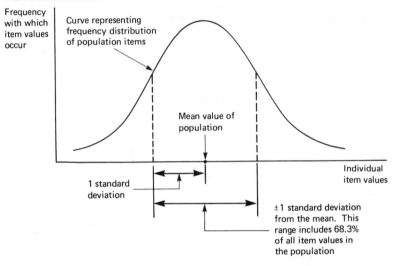

ation, **standard error of the sample means,** and **standard normal deviate.**

Normal distribution. Many populations, such as the heights of all men, may be described as normal distributions. A normal distribution is illustrated by the familiar bell-shaped curve, illustrated in Figure 8–5, in which the values of the individual items tend to congregate around the population **mean.** Notice that the distribution of individual item values is symmetrical on both sides of the mean. There is no tendency for deviations to be to one side rather than the other. Although not all populations are normally distributed, it is often useful to assume normality. In cases where the normal distribution assumption is clearly inappropriate, the auditors should enlist the services of an expert statistician.

Standard deviation. The standard deviation of a population is a measure of the **variability** or **dispersion** of individual item values about the population mean.[4] The less variation among item values, the smaller the standard deviation; the greater the variation among item values, the larger the standard deviation. It is inherent in the definitions of normal distribution and standard deviation that 68.3 percent of the item values in a normal distribution fall within ±1 standard deviation of the popula-

---

[4] The standard deviation is the square root of the following quotient: the sum of the squares of the deviation of each item value from the population mean, divided by the number of items in the population. Symbolically, the formula for calculating the standard deviation is:

$$\sqrt{\frac{\Sigma (x - \overline{X})^2}{N}}$$

tion mean, that 95.4 percent fall within ±2 standard deviations, and that 99.7 percent fall within ±3 standard deviations. These percentage relationships hold true by definition; however, the dollar amount of the standard deviation will vary from one population to another.

Auditors may obtain a reliable estimate of the dollar amount of the standard deviation by taking a *pilot sample.* The procedures for making this estimate are as follows:

1. Select a random sample of 49 items.
2. Group the selected items into seven groups of seven items each, based upon the order in which the items were selected.
3. Find the range (difference) between the highest and lowest item in each group.
4. Compute the average of the seven ranges.
5. Divide this average range by 2.704 to obtain an estimate of the standard deviation of the population.

Generalized audit software packages also include routines designed to estimate the standard deviation of a population either from a sample or from the population itself.[5]

Standard error of the sample means. If a series of samples of a given size are taken from a normal population, the means of these samples should vary from the population (true) mean because of sampling error. The sample means should, however, be normally distributed about the true mean. The standard deviation of this normal distribution of sample means is called the *standard error of the sample means.* The words *standard error* are used in place of *standard deviation* to stress that deviation of sample means from the true mean is caused by *sampling error.*

The number of standard errors in the auditors' desired precision interval *determines the reliability of the sample results.* Since the standard error is the standard deviation of a distribution of all possible sample means, we know the percentage of sample means which will fall within a given number of standard errors of the true mean. For example, we know that 68.3 percent of all sample means fall within ±1 standard error

---

[5] An estimate of the standard deviation may be made from a sample by taking the square root of the following quotient: the sum of the squares of the deviation of each sample item value from the sample mean, divided by one less than the number of items in the sample. Symbolically, the formula for estimating the standard deviation is:

$$\sqrt{\frac{\Sigma (x - \bar{x})^2}{n - 1}}$$ or, restated in a form to facilitate computation:

$$\sqrt{\frac{\sum_{j=l}^{j=n} (x_j)^2 - n\bar{x}^2}{n - 1}}$$

of the true mean, that 95.4 percent fall within ±2 standard errors, and that 99.7 percent fall within ±3 standard errors. The numbers of standard errors in the precision intervals necessary to yield other levels of confidence may be determined from a table of standard normal deviates.

The larger the sample size, the more closely the sample means should represent the population mean. Thus, the standard error of a distribution of sample means may be reduced by increasing the sample size. The fact that a known percentage of sample means falls within a specified number of standard errors of the true mean enables auditors to control the reliability of their sample results. Selecting a sample size that limits the standard error to the desired amount enables them to control the precision of their estimate.

Standard normal deviate. In estimation sampling for variables, reliability expresses the percentage of the time that the sample mean may be expected to fall within a specified interval of the population mean. The **standard normal deviate** is the **number of standard errors in this interval.** For example, we know by definition that 95.4 percent of all possible sample means fall within ±2 standard errors of the true mean. Thus, the reliability level of 95.4 percent has a standard normal deviate of 2, meaning that the sample mean may differ from the true mean by as much as two standard errors. The standard normal deviates corresponding to other levels of confidence are shown in Figure 8–6 below.

FIGURE 8–6
Table of standard normal deviates

Reliability*	Standard normal deviate (U)
68.3	±1.00
70	±1.04
75	±1.15
80	±1.28
85	±1.44
90	±1.64
95	±1.96
95.4	±2.00
99	±2.58
99.7	±3.00

* Percentage of the time that $\bar{x} - \bar{X}$ will be no more than U standard errors.

Determination of sample size

The factors affecting sample size in estimation sampling for variables are (1) desired precision, (2) desired sample reliability, (3) variability among item values in the population, and (4) population size. The relationship of these factors to the required sample size is expressed by the following formula:[6]

$$\text{Sample size} = \left(\frac{\text{Standard normal deviate} \times \text{Estimated standard deviation}}{\text{Sample precision}} \right)^2$$

The procedures for estimation sampling for variables now may be summarized as follows:

1. **Define the objectives of the test.** Estimation sampling for variables is generally used for substantive tests in which the auditors seek to gather evidence to support the value shown in the financial statements for a particular population.

2. **Stipulate the desired precision and reliability.** Since this sampling plan deals with dollar values, the materiality of the tolerable margin of error should be the criterion used to determine precision. The reliability specified by the auditors will depend upon the amount of audit evidence they require to support their opinion, taking into consideration their reliance upon the client's system of internal control. This topic is discussed in more detail later in this chapter.

3. **Estimate the standard deviation of the population.** An estimate of the standard deviation may be made from a pilot sample, following the procedures listed on page 339, or by using an appropriate computer program.

4. **Determine the required sample precision.** The precision with which the sample mean must approximate the true mean is determined by dividing the precision desired for the estimate of the population total by the number of items in the population.

5. **Determine the standard normal deviate corresponding to the desired reliability.** The standard normal deviate is determined from tables such as the one in Figure 8–6.

6. **Solve the formula for the required sample size.**

7. **Draw the sample and compute the sample mean.**

8. **Interpret the sample results.** The sample mean provides the auditors with an estimate of the true population mean, within prescribed precision and reliability. If this estimate does not support the representations made in the client's financial statements, the auditors should investigate further to determine the cause and scope of the discrep-

---

[6] This formula is based upon an infinite population. The effect on sample size when the population is finite but of significant size is not material. Symbolically, this formula may be stated:

$$n = \left(\frac{U\, S_{xj}}{p} \right)^2$$

where n = sample size, U = standard normal deviate, S_{xj} = estimated standard deviation, and p = precision stated in terms of the estimate of the mean value.

ancies. This may involve additional sampling to determine the true value of the population with greater precision and reliability. Ultimately, the auditors must require the client to correct any material misstatement of the population value if they are to render an unqualified report on the financial statements.

Illustration of estimation sampling for variables

Assume that an audit client has an inventory of 10,000 head of beef cattle (steers) located in feedlots. The steers were purchased on various dates and at various prices. The client's records show a value for the inventory equal to the purchase cost of the cattle plus the cumulative costs of feeding these cattle. The current price quotation for beef cattle of this grade is 40 cents per pound. As auditors, we wish to estimate the market value of the inventory to determine that the carrying value of the cattle in the accounting records does not exceed current market value.

In view of the dollar amounts involved, we stipulate a precision of ±$50,000 for our estimate of the market value of the cattle. The client has no internal control procedure that would have caused a market value lower than cost to have been reflected in the accounting records. For this reason, we decide to require 95.4 percent reliability in our substantive test results.

We estimate the standard deviation of the population of cattle values by selecting a random sample of 49 steers, weighing each one to determine its market value, and following the procedures described on page 339. Let us assume that this process results in an estimated standard deviation of $30.

Since estimation sampling for variables deals with average amounts, we must actually estimate the average market value per steer and multiply this estimate by the number of cattle in the inventory. If the estimate of total market value is to have a precision of ±$50,000 at the 95.4 percent confidence level, the estimate of average market value per steer must have a precision of ±$5 ($50,000 ÷ 10,000 steers). Referring to the table in Figure 8–6, we find the standard normal deviate corresponding to 95.4 percent reliability is ±2.00.

Using the sample size formula, we may now compute our required sample size:

$$\text{Sample size:} = \left(\frac{\text{Standard normal deviate} \times \text{Estimated standard deviation}}{\text{Sample precision}} \right)^2$$

$$= \left(\frac{2.00 \times \$30}{\pm \$5} \right)^2 = \frac{3,600}{25} = 144 \text{ steers}$$

Since we have already sampled 49 steers, we need only select on a random basis another 95 to complete our required sample of 144. Assuming our sample mean indicated an average market value of $280 per steer, we could get 95.4 percent confident that the current market value of the inventory is $2,800,000 ± $50,000. If our client's value for the cattle does not exceed our upper precision limit of $2,850,000, we would accept the client's figure as not being materially in excess of market value. If the client's book value exceeds $2,850,000 we would propose an adjusting entry to write down the carrying value of the cattle to market value.

Ratio and difference estimation

Estimation sampling for variables estimates the average item value as the basis for estimating the total value of the population. Two alternatives to this approach are ratio and difference estimation. Although closely related, ratio estimation and difference estimation are two distinct sampling plans; each is appropriate under slightly different circumstances.

In ratio estimation, the auditors use a sample to estimate the *ratio* of the audited (correct) value of a population to its book value. This ratio is estimated by dividing the total audited value of a sample by the total book value of the sample items.[7] An estimate of the correct population value is obtained by multiplying this estimated ratio by the total book value of the population.

In applying difference estimation, the auditors use a sample to estimate the *average difference* between the audited value and book value of items in a population. The average difference is estimated by dividing the net difference between the audited value and book value of a sample by the number of items in the sample.[8] The total difference between the book value of the population and its estimated correct value is determined by multiplying the estimated average difference by the number of items in the population.

---

[7] Symbolically, this process is expressed:

$$\hat{R} = \frac{\Sigma a_j}{\Sigma b_j}$$

where $\hat{R}$ (pronounced R caret) represents the estimated ratio of audited value to book value, a_j represents the audited value of each sample item, and b_j represents the book value of each sample item.

[8] Symbolically, the estimated difference is computed:

$$\hat{d} = \frac{1}{n} \sum_{j=1}^{n} (a_j - b_j)$$

where d represents the estimated average difference between audited value and book value; n represents the number of items in the sample; and a_j and b_j represent the audited and book values, respectively.

Use of ratio and difference estimation.   The use of ratio or difference estimation techniques requires that (1) each population item has a book value, (2) the population book value corresponds to the sum of the item book values, (3) an audited value may be ascertained for each sample item, and (4) differences between audited and book values are relatively frequent. If the occurrence rate of differences is very low, a prohibitively large sample is required to disclose a representative number of errors.

Ratio estimation is most appropriate when the size of errors is nearly proportional to the book values of the items. In many cases, the size of transactions affecting an account may be nearly proportional to the account balance. Thus, mistakes in processing transactions affecting large accounts generally are larger than those affecting small accounts. When the size of errors is not nearly proportional to book value, difference estimation is the more appropriate technique.

Ratio or difference estimation frequently is more effective than estimation sampling for variables. The ratios or the differences in audited and book values of population items form a ratio or difference population. A ratio or difference population generally has a smaller standard deviation than does the population of item dollar values. Consequently, a smaller sample size may be required to estimate the ratio or difference than to estimate the average dollar value.

Illustration of ratio and difference estimation

To illustrate the use of ratio and difference estimation techniques, assume that auditors wish to estimate the total value of a client's accounts payable. The population consists of 4,000 accounts with an aggregate book value of $5,000,000. The auditors calculate the required sample size, randomly select the accounts to be sampled, and apply auditing procedures to establish the correct account balances. Assume that this sample consists of 200 accounts with a book value of $250,000, and that the audited value is determined to be $257,500.

Using ratio estimation, the auditors would estimate the ratio of audited value to book value to be 1.03 (computed $257,500 ÷ $250,000). Their estimate of the total population value, therefore, would be $5,150,000 (computed $5,000,000 × 1.03). If difference estimation is used, the auditors would estimate the average difference per item to be a $37.50 understatement ($7,500 net difference divided by 200 items). Multiplying $37.50 by the 4,000 accounts in the population indicates that the client's book value for accounts payable is understated by $150,000.

Each of these estimates would have a precision interval and reliability related to the auditors' sample size. The procedures for determining the required sample size in these sampling plans are more complex than in estimation sampling for variables. To provide auditors with assistance in this area, the AICPA has issued *An Auditor's Approach to Statistical Sampling, Volume 5,* entitled "Ratio and Difference Estimation."

Stratification

Stratification is the technique of dividing a population into relatively homogeneous subgroups called *strata.* These strata then may be sampled separately; the sample results may be evaluated separately, or combined, to provide an estimate of the characteristics of the total population. Whenever items of extremely high or low values, or other unusual characteristics, are segregated into separate populations, each population becomes more homogeneous. It is easier to draw a representative sample from a relatively homogeneous population. Thus, it is frequently true that a smaller number of items must be examined to evaluate several strata separately than to evaluate the total population.

Besides increasing the efficiency of sampling procedures, stratification enables auditors to relate sample selection to the materiality, turnover, or other characteristics of items, and to apply different audit procedures to each stratum. Frequently, auditors examine 100 percent of the stratum containing the most material items. For example, in selecting accounts receivable for confirmation, auditors might stratify and test the population as follows:

Stratum	Composition of stratum	Method of selection used	Type of confirmation request*
1	All accounts of $10,000 and over	100% confirmation	Positive
2	Wholesale accounts receivable (under $10,000), all numbered with numbers ending in zero.	Random number table selection	Positive
3	All other accounts (under $10,000) in random order	Systematic selection	Negative

* A positive confirmation request asks the respondent to reply, indicating the amount owed; a negative request asks for a response only if the respondent does not agree with the amount indicated on the request. Confirmation of accounts receivable is discussed in more detail in Chapter 13.

In this illustration, the population is stratified not only by dollar amount but also by type of transaction. In addition to stratification on these bases, auditors may also stratify by transaction frequency. For instance, in estimating the error rate in an accounting control procedure, the auditors might stratify the population into high- and low-volume transactions if they believe controls are more likely to be violated during the processing of low-volume transactions. Stratification is appropriate whenever the characteristic being tested by the auditors varies significantly within different portions of the population. This technique almost always is used in sampling for variables, and is frequently used in sampling for attributes.

Measurement of the auditors' risk

The auditors' opinion that financial statements are free from material error is a result of their reliance upon (1) the client's system of internal control to prevent the occurrence of such error, and (2) the substantive tests to disclose any material error that may have occurred. Since the auditors have two bases for reliance, their overall confidence in their audit report is termed *combined reliability.* Although combined reliability may be quite high, every audit engagement involves some degree of risk that the financial statements are materially in error. This *ultimate risk* is the possibility that internal control has failed to prevent the error *and* that the auditors' substantive tests have failed to disclose the existence of the error. Unless auditors were able to perform 100 percent examination, this risk cannot be entirely eliminated.

The ultimate risk of error may be quantified by multiplying (1) the risk of internal control failing to prevent the error by (2) the risk of substantive tests failing to disclose the error. This relationship is expressed by the following formula:

$$1 - R = (1 - C) \times (1 - S)$$

where R represents combined reliability, C represents the auditors' reliance upon internal control to prevent material error, and S represents the reliability of substantive tests to disclose material error if it exists. Risk is the complement of reliability; therefore, if R represents combined reliability, $1 - R$ represents ultimate risk. The terms $1 - C$ and $1 - S$ represent the risk in reliance upon internal control and the risk in reliance upon substantive testing, respectively.

To illustrate the measurement of ultimate audit risk, assume that auditors have 40 percent confidence in the client's system of internal control and 90 percent confidence in the results of their substantive tests. The risk of material error still existing in the financial statements may be computed as follows:

$$1 - R = (1 - 0.4) \times (1 - 0.9)$$
$$1 - R = 0.6 \times 0.1 = 0.06$$

Thus, the auditors still face a 6 percent ultimate risk that material error has evaded both the system of internal control and their substantive tests. Conversely, they have 94 percent combined confidence that the financial statements are free from material error.

Reliability levels in substantive tests. In audit practice, auditors stipulate in advance the ultimate risk that they are willing to accept, rather than compute this statistic at the conclusion of the engagement. Their reliance upon internal control is governed by the quality of the client's system. Thus, the only determinant of ultimate risk which is under the auditors' direct control is the reliability of the substantive tests. To determine the appropriate reliability of substantive tests in a particular audit area, the risk formula may be restated:

$$S = 1 - \frac{1 - R}{1 - C}$$

interrelationship between overall confidence, control, & how it relates to substantive testing

The formula is now arranged to solve for S, the required reliability level for the auditors' substantive tests.

To illustrate, assume that auditors require 95 percent combined reliability on a particular engagement. After studying and evaluating internal control, they subjectively decide to place 70 percent reliance on the system of internal control to have prevented material error. Entering these reliability levels into the formula:

$$S = 1 - \frac{1 - 0.95}{1 - 0.7}$$

$$S = 1 - \frac{0.05}{0.3} = 1 - 0.17 = 0.83$$

combined reliability = overall confidence in their audit report (free from material error)

Thus, the auditors must stipulate a confidence level of at least 83 percent in their substantive tests if they are to achieve 95 percent combined reliability in this area of the financial statements.

KEY TERMS INTRODUCED OR EMPHASIZED IN CHAPTER 8

block sample   A sample including all items in a selected time period, numerical sequence, or alphabetical sequence. Block sampling is used in conjunction with judgmental sampling and is *not* a random selection technique.

combined reliability   The auditors' overall confidence that audited financial statements do not contain material errors. The complement of combined reliability is *ultimate risk.*

confidence level   See *Reliability.*

difference estimation   A sampling plan for estimating the average difference between the audited (correct) values of items in a population and their book values. Difference estimation is used in lieu of ratio estimation when the differences are not nearly proportional to book values.

discovery sampling   A sampling plan for locating at least one exception, providing that the exception occurs in the population with a specified frequency. Discovery sampling is used to search for *critical errors,* such as evidence of fraud.

estimation sampling for attributes   A sampling plan enabling the auditors to estimate the occurrence rate of a specified characteristic in a population, with stipulated precision and reliability.

estimation sampling for variables A sampling plan enabling the auditors to estimate the average dollar value (or other variable) of items in a population by determining the average value of items in a sample. This plan also is called *mean-per-unit estimation.*

exception An item containing the designated error in an attribute sampling plan.

expected occurrence rate An advance estimate of an occurrence rate. This estimate is necessary for determining the required sample size in an attribute sampling plan.

judgmental sampling A sampling plan in which the determination of sample size or composition of the sample is based on the auditor's professional judgment only; thus, the sample results are not subject to statistical interpretation.

mean Average item value, computed by dividing total value by the number of items comprising total value.

mean-per-unit estimation See *Estimation sampling for variables.*

normal distribution A frequency distribution in which item values tend to congregate around the mean with no tendency for deviation toward one side rather than the other. A normal distribution is represented graphically by a bell-shaped curve.

one-sided precision A precision interval defined by only one precision limit. One-sided precision frequently is used in estimation sampling for attributes because auditors are interested only in whether an error rate exceeds some upper limit, and not whether it might be less than some lower limit.

pilot sample A preliminary sample taken for the purpose of estimating the standard deviation of a population or the expected occurrence rate.

population The entire field of items from which a sample might be drawn.

precision An interval around the sample results in which the true population characteristic is expected to lie. Precision may be considered the allowable margin of sampling error.

precision limits The points designating the upper and lower boundaries of the precision interval.

random number generator A computer program which produces a list of random numbers applicable to the numbering scheme of a specific population.

random selection Selecting items from a population in a manner in which every item has an equal chance of being included in the sample.

random starting point A randomly selected point from which to begin the systematic selection of every nth item in the population.

ratio estimation A sampling plan for estimating the ratio of the audited (correct) values of items to their book values. Extending the book value of the population by this ratio provides an estimate of audited total population value. Ratio estimation is a highly efficient technique when errors are nearly proportional to item book values.

reliability (confidence level) The percentage of the time that the true population characteristic lies within the stated precision of the sample results.

representative sample A sample possessing essentially the same characteristics as the population from which it was drawn.

sample   A group of items selected from a larger population for the purpose of estimating the characteristics of the population.

sample precision   Precision stated with respect to an estimate of the average (rather than total) value of a population. Sample precision may be viewed as *precision per item;* it is found by dividing the stipulated precision for the estimate of total value by the number of items in the population.

sampling error   The difference between the characteristics of a sample and the characteristics of the population. Some sampling error is likely to exist in any sample. Auditors are able to control the risk of material sampling error through stipulating precision and reliability.

sampling for attributes   Sampling plans designed to estimate the frequency of occurrence of a specified population characteristic.

sampling for variables   Sampling plans designed to estimate a numerical measurement of a population, such as dollar value.

standard deviation   A measure of the variability or dispersion of item values within a population. In a normal distribution, 68.3 percent of all item values fall within ± 1 standard deviation of the mean, 95.4 percent fall within ± 2 standard deviations, and 99.7 percent fall within ± 3 standard deviations.

standard error of the sample means   The standard deviation of a distribution of sample means. Since known percentages of all sample means fall within a given number of standard errors of the true mean, the number of standard errors in the auditors' precision interval determines the reliability of the sample results.

standard normal deviate   The number of standard errors in the stipulated precision interval. A table of standard normal deviates shows the standard normal deviates corresponding to stipulated confidence levels; this factor is then used in the computation of required sample size.

statistical sampling   A sampling plan in which the determination of sample size and composition of the sample are based on the auditor's professional judgment and the law of probability such that the sample results are subject to statistical interpretation.

stratification   Dividing a population into two or more relatively homogeneous subgroups (strata). Stratification increases the efficiency of most sampling plans by reducing the variability of items in each stratum. The sample size necessary to evaluate the strata separately is often smaller than would be needed to evaluate the total population.

systematic selection   The technique of selecting a sample by drawing every *n*th item in the population, following a random starting point.

ultimate risk   The risk that audited financial statements contain material error. Ultimate risk is the complement of *combined reliability.*

GROUP I
REVIEW QUESTIONS

8–1.   Do statistical sampling techniques preclude the need for auditors to exercise judgment in evaluating a client's accounting records? Explain.

8–2. Explain why a random stratified sample is superior to a judgment sample. (AICPA)

8–3. Distinguish between sampling for attributes and sampling for variables.

8–4. Explain the meaning of *sampling without replacement* and *sampling with replacement.* Which method of sampling is assumed in most statistical formulas? What is the effect upon sample results if the other method is used?

8–5. In selecting items for examination an auditor considered four alternatives (a) random number table selection, (b) systematic selection, (c) random number generator selection, and (d) cluster selection. Which, if any, of the four methods would lead to a random sample if properly applied?

8–6. Explain briefly the term *systematic selection* as used in auditing, and indicate the precautions to be taken if a random sample is to be obtained. Is systematic selection applicable to unnumbered documents? Explain.

8–7. Explain briefly how the auditors using statistical sampling techniques may measure the possibility that the sample drawn has characteristics not representative of the population.

8–8. What relationships exist between confidence level, precision, and sample size? (AICPA)

8–9. Assume population item values are randomly distributed between $0 and $10,000. Do these item values form a normal distribution?

8–10. Define, and differentiate between, judgment sampling and statistical sampling.

8–11. Why is discovery sampling well suited to the detection of fraud?

8–12. What would be the difference in an estimation sampling for attributes plan and an estimation sampling for variables plan in a test of inventory extensions?

8–13. What is meant by the term *standard error of the sample means?* Why is this measurement of significance to the auditor?

8–14. What is meant by the term *one-sided precision?* Explain why this approach frequently is used in estimating error rates.

8–15. If a sample of 100 items indicates an error rate of 3 percent, should the auditors conclude that the entire population also has approximately a 3 percent error rate?

8–16. What relationship exists between the expected occurrence rate and sample size?

8–17. Explain what is meant by a precision of ± 1 percent with reliability of 90 percent. (AICPA, adapted)

8–18. The 12 following statements apply to unrestricted random sampling with replacement. Indicate whether each statement is true or false.

  a. The auditors' prior knowledge of the materiality of the items to be tested may negate the need for random selection.

b. A rigid definition of the population of accounts receivable must specify that only active accounts with balances be included.

c. If a population consists mostly of accounts with large balances, it is acceptable to exclude accounts with small balances from the population to be sampled because the error in a small balance could not be material.

d. Excluding extremely large items from the definition of the population, and evaluating them separately so that they have no chance of being included in the sample, would violate the definition of unrestricted random sampling.

e. To be random a sample must be completely unbiased and its selection governed completely by chance.

f. The precision of an estimate of a population mean from a sample mean increases as the degree of confidence in the estimate increases.

g. It is likely that five different random samples from the same population would produce five different estimates of the true population mean.

h. A 100 percent sample would have to be taken to attain a precision range of ± $0 with 100 percent reliability.

i. The effect of the inclusion by chance of a very large or very small item in a random sample can be lessened by increasing the size of the sample.

j. The standard deviation is a measure of the variability of items in a population.

k. The larger the standard deviation of a population, the smaller the required sample size.

l. The standard error of the sample means will usually be less than the estimated standard deviation computed from a sample estimate. (AICPA, adapted)

8–19. Under what conditions are ratio or difference estimation appropriate methods of estimating the total dollar value of a population? What relationship determines which of these two sampling plans will be most efficient?

GROUP II
QUESTIONS REQUIRING ANALYSIS

8–20. Explain the meaning of the formula $1 - R = (1 - C) \times (1 - S)$ as it relates to the ultimate risk of material error in audited financial statements. (R represents combined reliability, C represents the auditors' reliance upon internal control, and S represents the reliability of the auditors' substantive tests.)

8–21. The professional development department of a large CA firm has prepared the following illustration to familiarize the audit staff with the relationships of sample size to population size and variability and the auditors' specifications as to precision and reliability.

	Characteristics of population 1 relative to population 2		Audit specifications as to a sample from population 1 relative to a sample from population 2	
	Size	Variability	Specified precision	Specified confidence level
Case 1.....	Equal	Equal	Equal	Higher
Case 2.....	Equal	Larger	Wider	Equal
Case 3.....	Larger	Equal	Tighter	Lower
Case 4.....	Smaller	Smaller	Equal	Lower
Case 5.....	Larger	Equal	Equal	Higher

Required:

For each of the five cases in the above illustration, indicate the relationship of the sample size to be selected from population 1 relative to the sample from population 2. Select your answer from the following numbered responses and state the reasoning behind your choice. The required sample size from population 1 is:

1. Larger than the required sample size from population 2.
2. Equal to the required sample size from population 2.
3. Smaller than the required sample size from population 2.
4. Indeterminate relative to the required sample size from population 2. (AICPA, adapted)

8–22. Increasing attention is being given by CAs to the application of statistical techniques to audit testing.

Required:

a. List and explain the advantages of applying statistical sampling techniques to audit testing.
b. List and discuss the decisions involving professional judgment that must be made by the CAs in applying statistical sampling techniques to audit testing.
c. You have applied estimation sampling for attributes techniques to the client's pricing of the inventory and discovered from your sampling that the occurrence rate exceeds your stipulated upper precision limit. Discuss the courses of action you can take. (AICPA, adapted)

8–23. In performing a compliance test of sales order approvals, the CAs stipulate an upper precision limit of 4.5 percent with desired reliability of 95 percent. They anticipate an error rate of 2 percent.

Required:

a. What type of sampling plan should the auditors use for this test?
b. Using the appropriate table or formula from this chapter, compute the required sample size for the test.
c. Assume that the sample indicates an occurrence rate of 3 percent.

May the CAs conclude with 95 percent confidence that the population error rate does not exceed their upper precision limit of 4.5 percent?

8–24. An auditor has reason to suspect that fraud has occurred through forgery of the treasurer's signature on company cheques. The population under consideration consists of 3,000 cheques.

Required:

a. Can discovery sampling rule out the possibility that any forged signatures exist among the 3,000 cheques? Explain.

b. If the population includes 15 forged signatures, how many cheques would the auditor have to examine to have 90 percent confidence of encountering at least one forgery?

8–25. During an audit of Potter Company, an auditor needs to estimate the total value of the 5,000 invoices processed during June. The auditor estimates the standard deviation of the population to be $15. Determine the size sample the auditor should select to achieve a precision of ± $10,000 with 95.4 percent reliability. (AICPA, adapted)

8–26. Bock Company had two billing clerks during the year. Clerk A worked nine months, and Clerk B worked three months. Assume the quantity of invoices per month is constant. If the same maximum tolerable occurrence rate and confidence level are specified for each population, should the ratio of the size of the sample drawn from Clerk A's invoices to the size of the sample drawn from Clerk B's invoices be 3:1? Discuss. (AICPA, adapted)

8–27. During the audit of Dunbar Electronics, the auditors decide that they may place 80 percent reliance upon the client's system of internal control to have prevented any material error in the valuation of accounts receivable. The auditors require combined reliability of 95 percent as a basis for rendering an opinion on financial statements. What is the minimum reliability they must achieve in their substantive tests to verify the valuation of accounts receivable?

8–28. Select the best answer for each of the following questions. Explain the reasons for your selection.

a. What is the primary purpose of using stratification as a sampling method in auditing?

(1) To increase the confidence level at which a decision will be reached from the results of the sample.

(2) To determine the occurrence rate of a given characteristic in the population being studied.

(3) To decrease the effect of variance in the total population.

(4) To determine the precision range of the sample selected.

b. In estimating the total value of supplies on repair trucks, Baker Company draws random samples from two equal-sized strata of trucks. The mean value of the inventory stored on the larger trucks (stratum 1) was computed at $1,500, with a standard deviation of $250. On the smaller trucks (stratum 2), the mean value of inventory was computed as $500, with a standard deviation of $45. If Baker had drawn an unrestricted sample from the entire population of trucks, the expected mean value of inventory per truck would be $1,000, and the expected standard deviation would be:

(1) Exactly $147.50.
(2) Greater than $250.
(3) Less than $45.
(4) Between $45 and $250, but not $147.50.

c. A CA's test of the accuracy of inventory counts involves two storehouses. Storehouse A contains 10,000 inventory items, and Storehouse B contains 5,000 items. The CA plans to use sampling without replacement to test for an estimated 5 percent error rate. If the CA's sampling plan calls for reliability of 95 percent and an upper precision limit of 7.5 percent for both storehouses, the ratio of the size of the CA's sample from Storehouse A to the size of the sample from Storehouse B should be:

(1) More than 1:1 but less than 2:1.
(2) 2:1.
(3) 1:1.
(4) More than 0.5:1 but less than 1:1.

d. Approximately 4 percent of the homogeneous items included in Barletta's finished goods inventory are believed to be defective. The CAs examining Barletta's financial statements decide to test this estimated 4 percent defective rate. They learn that a sample of 284 items from the inventory will permit specified reliability of 95 percent and specified precision of ±2.5 percent. If specified precision is changed to ±5 percent, and specified reliability remains 95 percent, the required sample size becomes—

(1) 72.   (3) 436.
(2) 335.   (4) 1,543.   (AICPA, adapted)

8–29. a. Describe the limitations of statistical sampling as a technique for use by the auditor.

b. In discussing the use of statistical sampling in auditing, reference is often made to two kinds of statistical sampling: estimation sampling and discovery sampling. What is the purpose of each of the two kinds, as used in an auditing situation? Use examples to clarify your answer if you wish.

c. What factors involving the auditor's judgment determine the size of a statistical sample? Explain each factor briefly.

d. In a specific audit application of statistical sampling, what should the auditor consider in establishing values for the factors referred to c above? (CICA, adapted)

GROUP III
PROBLEMS

8–30. The use of statistical sampling techniques in an examination of financial statements does not eliminate judgmental decisions.

Required:

a. Identify and explain four areas where judgment may be exercised by CAs in planning a statistical test.

b. Assume that the auditors' sample shows an unacceptable error rate. Discuss the various actions that they may take based upon this finding.

c. A non-stratified sample of 80 accounts payable vouchers is to be selected from a population of 3,200. The vouchers are numbered consecutively from 1 to 3,200 and are listed, 40 to a page, in the voucher register. Describe four different techniques for selecting a random sample of vouchers for review. (AICPA, adapted)

8–31. To test the pricing and mathematical accuracy of sales invoices, the auditors selected a sample of 500 sales invoices from a total of 100,000 invoices that were issued during the years under examination. The 500 invoices represented total recorded sales of $22,500. Total sales for the year amounted to $5,000,000. The examination disclosed that of the 500 invoices audited, 15 were not properly priced or contained errors in extension and footings. The 15 incorrect invoices represented $720 of the total recorded sales, and the errors found resulted in a net understatement of these invoices by $300.

Required:

Explain what conclusions the auditors may draw from the above information, assuming the sample was selected.

a. On a judgment basis.

b. As part of an estimation sampling for attributes plan using an expected occurrence rate of 3 percent, a stipulated upper precision limit of 5 percent, and reliability of 95 percent.

c. As part of a difference estimation for estimating the total population value with precision of ±$50,000 and 80 percent reliability.

8–32. During your examination of the financial statements of Southwest Oil Company for the year ended June 30, you confirm accounts receivable from credit card customers. For purposes of the confirmation process, an "error" is defined as a misstatement of the June 30 balance of the accounts receivable control account and/or an individual customer's account balance, for other than "in-transit" items. As of June 30, there are approximately 30,000 accounts with balances ranging from $5 to $200 and averaging about $40. You select a sample of 500 accounts on a random basis; and after all accounts have been confirmed or otherwise examined through alternative procedures, your assistant shows you a working paper containing the following description of items considered by the assistant to be exceptions:

Number of sample item drawn	Nature of exception
002	Customer claims that payment was made on June 29. Our investigation discloses that the cheque was received from the customer on June 30,

but it was not processed because of the large volume of cash receipts on that date. However, the cheque was deposited and recorded as a receipt on July 1.

086   The customer had purchased a set of tires which were found to be defective and returned them to one of the company's service stations in June. The service station issued a credit memo on July 2 which was received and recorded by the accounting office the following day.

121   The customer paid one of the company's branches for the entire account balance on July 1. Investigation discloses that the branch held its cash journal open to pick up all July 1 cash receipts as June 30 business.

157   Confirmation was returned by the customer's trustee in bankruptcy. The trustee states that the customer will be unable to pay; however, the credit manager feels that in the long run a partial collection is possible.

212   Customer claims that the account was paid in full before the middle of June. Investigation discloses that all open charges to this customer's account should have been charged to another account. There was a transposition in customer account numbers. Account 99026 was charged instead of Account 99062.

294   Customer claimed payment was mailed on June 29. Investigation shows that the payment was received and recorded on July 2.

302   Customer refuses to pay for delinquent charges on an installment plan purchase of automobile tires. For policy reasons, the client will not press for collection and the amount will be charged off in July.

336   Customer claims that the account balance was paid on June 25. Investigation discloses that the payment was received on June 29 but was not accompanied by the payment slip. The company was unable to identify the payment and credited it to a suspense account pending identification.

426   Customer reported that the account balance should be $129.62 instead of $119.62 as shown by the statement. Investigation disclosed that the detail credit card slips were improperly footed.

487   Customer claims a bulk purchase container was returned for credit several months previously. Investigation discloses that a credit memo for the container inadvertently was not issued.

Required:

Prepare an analysis of each of the items listed in your assistant's working paper explaining whether or not the item should be considered an "error" for the purposes of your test. What error rate (in number or misstated customers' accounts) has your sample disclosed?

8–33.   In the audit of Potomac Mills, the auditors wish to test the costs assigned to manufactured goods. During the year, the company has produced 2,000 production lots with a total recorded cost of $5,900,000. The auditors select a sample of 200 production lots with an aggregate book value of $600,000 and vouch the assigned costs to the supporting documentation. Their examination discloses errors in the cost of 52 of the 200 production lots; after adjustment for these errors, the audited value of the sample is $582,000.

Required:

a.   Show how the auditors would compute an estimate of the total cost of production lots manufactured during the year using each of the following sampling plans. (Do not compute the precision or reliability of these estimates.)

    (1)   Estimation sampling for variables.

    (2)   Ratio estimation.

    (3)   Difference estimation.

b.   Explain why estimation sampling for variables results in a higher estimate of the population value than does ratio estimation in this particular instance.

8–34.   You desire to evaluate the reasonableness of the book value of the inventory of your client, Draper, Inc. You satisfied yourself earlier as to inventory quantities. During the examination of the pricing and extension of the inventory, the following data were gathered using appropriate unrestricted random sampling with replacement:

1.   Total items in the inventory (N) 12,700

2.   Total items in the sample (n) 400

3.   Total audited values of items in the sample $38,400

4.   Formula for estimated population standard deviation ....

$$S_{x_j} = \sqrt{\frac{\sum_{j=1}^{j=n}(x_j - \bar{x})^2}{n-1}}$$

5. $\sum_{j=1}^{400}(x_j - \bar{x})^2$ 312,816

6.   Formula for estimated standard error of the sample means ... $SE = \dfrac{S_{x_j}}{\sqrt{n}}$

7.   Standard normal deviate coefficient corresponding to 95 percent reliability .... ±1.96

Required:

a.   Based on the sample results, use estimation sampling for variables to estimate the total value of inventory. Show computations in good form where appropriate.

b.   With what precision may the estimated population value in (a), above, represent the true population value at the 95 percent reliability level? (Hint: At the 95 percent reliability level, the precision interval is equivalent to a known number of standard errors of the mean.)

c.   Independent of your answers to (a) and (b), assume that the book value of Draper's inventory is $1,700,000, and based on the sample results the estimated total value of the inventory is $1,690,000. The auditors desire a confidence (reliability) level of 95 percent. Discuss the audit and statistical considerations the auditors must evaluate before deciding whether the sampling results support acceptance of the book value as a fair presentation of Draper's inventory. (AICPA, adapted)

9

Audit working papers:
Quality control for audits

Working papers are vitally important instruments of the auditing profession. The need for the auditors to acquire skill and judgment in the design and use of these basic tools is scarcely less than the need for a surgeon to master the use of operating instruments. Working papers are the connecting link between the client's records and the auditors' report. In fact, the work of an audit centres around the systematic preparation of a series of working papers in such form, and with such content, that the auditors may prepare therefrom a report on the financial position and operations of the client. During the course of their verification of the financial statements, the auditors analyze ledger accounts, gather supplementary information to support the accounting records, and draft adjusting entries to correct for errors in amount and errors in accounting principles. It is this analyzing, compiling of audit evidence, and preparation of adjusting entries that necessitate the use of extensive working papers.

AUDIT WORKING PAPERS

Definition of working papers

The CICA's Auditing Standards Committee, in discussing standards of field work, has pointed out that "sufficient appropriate audit evidence should be obtained, by such means as inspection, observation, enquiries, confirmations, computation and analysis, to afford a reasonable basis to support the content of the report." In building up this evidence the auditors prepare working papers. Some of these may take the form of bank reconciliations or analyses of ledger accounts; others may consist of copies of correspondence, copies of minutes of directors' and shareholders' meetings, and lists of shareholders; still others might be organization charts or graphical presentations of plant layout. Working trial balances, audit programs, internal control questionnaires, a letter of representations obtained from the client, returned confirmation forms—all these various schedules, analyses, lists, notes, and documents form parts of the auditors' working papers.

The term "working papers" is thus a comprehensive one; it includes *all the evidence gathered by the auditors* to show the work they have done, the methods and procedures they have followed, and the conclusions they have developed. In their working papers the auditors have the basis for their report to the client, evidence of the extent of their examination, and proof of the professional care exercised in their investigation.

Confidential nature of working papers

To conduct a satisfactory audit the auditors must be given unrestricted access to all information about the client's business. Much of this information is confidential, such as the profit margins on individual products, tentative plans for business combinations with other companies, and the salaries of officers and key employees. Officers of the client company would not be willing to make available to the auditors information which is carefully guarded from competitors and employees unless they could rely on the auditors maintaining a professional silence on these matters.

Much of the information gained in confidence by the auditors is recorded in their working papers; consequently, the working papers are confidential in nature. The *Rules of Professional Conduct* prohibit a CA from disclosing any confidential information obtained in the course of a professional engagement except with the consent of the client, or when he is required to do so by order of lawful authority or by the institute's council or its appropriate committees.

Although the auditor is as careful as a lawyer or physician to hold in confidence all information concerning a client, the communication between a client and a CA is not privileged under the common law. Thus, a CA firm may legally be required to produce its working papers in a court case and to disclose information regarding a client.

Since audit working papers are highly confidential, they must be safeguarded at all times. Safeguarding working papers usually means keeping them locked in a brief case during luncheon and after working hours. If the client company wishes to keep some of its employees uninformed on executive salaries, business combinations, or other aspects of the business, the auditors obviously should not defeat this policy by exposing their working papers to unauthorized employees of the client. The policy of close control of audit working papers is also necessary because if employees were seeking to conceal fraud or to mislead the auditors for any reason, they might make alterations in the papers. The working papers may identify particular accounts, branches, or time periods to be tested; to permit the client's employees to learn of these in advance would weaken the significance of the tests.

Audit working papers are prepared on the client's premises, from the client's records, and at the client's expense, yet these papers are the exclusive property of the auditors. This ownership of working papers follows logically from the contractual relationship between the auditors and the client and has been supported in the courts.

Purposes of audit working papers

Audit working papers include all evidence gathered by the auditors and serve several major purposes:[1] (1) to organize and coordinate all phases of the audit engagement; (2) to aid partners, managers, and senior accountants in reviewing the work performed by audit staff members; (3) to facilitate preparation of the audit report; and (4) to substantiate and explain in detail the opinions and findings summarized in the report.

In addition, working papers provide information for preparation of income tax returns and for registration documents with the securities commissions and other governmental agencies, and also serve as a useful guide in subsequent engagements. Although clients may sometimes find it helpful to request information from the auditors' working papers of prior years, these working papers should not be regarded as a substitute for the client's own accounting records.[2]

Working papers and auditing standards

The four major purposes listed in the preceding section are applicable to the working papers prepared for recurring annual audits, and apply to most non-recurring special investigations as well. Each of these major purposes of audit working papers will now be considered individually and related to the generally accepted standards of field work.

---

[1] The purposes suggested by the CICA study group are (1) support the auditors' report, (2) improve the quality of the examination, (3) provide a source of information, (4) facilitate third-party review, and (5) aid professional development. CICA, *Good Audit Working Papers* (Toronto: The Canadian Institute of Chartered Accountants, 1970), pp. 2–4.

[2] AICPA, "Codification of Auditing Standards and Procedures," *Statement on Auditing Standards No. 1* (New York, 1973), p. 70.

To organize and coordinate audit work. Coordination of all phases of the audit work is achieved through the working papers. As each step of verification and analysis is performed, significant facts and relationships come to the attention of the auditors. Unless these matters are set down in writing when discovered, they are likely to be forgotten before they can be properly appraised in the light of information disclosed by other phases of the audit. By carefully planning the assignment of assistants to work on different papers, a senior auditor may efficiently coordinate and organize many phases of the examination work at one time. Thus the working papers show that the first standard of field work (adequate planning and proper execution of the work and proper supervision of assistants) has been met.

The senior auditor may instruct each assistant to prepare a separate working paper on different items under examination, and then proceed from one assistant to another, supervising the work done. Frequently the senior may prepare working paper headings and enter a few sample transactions, requesting assistants to complete the papers; in this manner, the auditor-in-charge initiates the examination of several items simultaneously and follows each project to completion. It is often not feasible for the auditor to carry out all verification work on a particular account at one time. For example, cash on hand may be counted on the first day of the investigation, but confirmation of bank balances not completed until several days later. As each phase is completed, the working papers are filed, to be expanded and added to as additional information is obtained. Thus the audit file on a given account may be begun early in the engagement but may not be completed until after other phases of the audit have been fully carried out.

To aid supervisors in reviewing the work of audit staff members. When an audit covers several scattered branches of a company, working papers are of great assistance in organizing and coordinating the work. The records of each branch or subsidiary may be examined by different staff members, perhaps by individuals from different offices of the auditing firm. Working papers will then be prepared at each place of examination and sent to a central location, where they can be assembled and reviewed prior to the writing of the report. Working papers of uniformly high quality are obviously of basic importance in audits of this type.

An audit does not end when the accountants leave the client's office. The report must be completed, or in some cases written in its entirety, tax returns prepared, and the entire engagement reviewed by a manager or partner. These last stages of the audit are made possible by the working papers. The managers or partners, with the working papers before them, have a view of the entire audit as an organized and coordinated whole; only then can they judge whether the audit meets professional auditing standards.

To facilitate preparation of the report.   Working papers facilitate the preparation of the auditors' report to the client because they are the source from which the report writers draw material. This report may assume a variety of forms, depending upon the purpose and scope of the engagement. A summary of the principal findings and recommendations constitutes the most essential part of the report for most special investigations and for most long-form reports used for credit purposes. The scope of the work performed and other general background information may accompany the findings and recommendations. For nearly all types of audit situations, the end product of the auditors' work is a report; this report and any related financial statements or schedules will be drawn from the audit working papers.

To substantiate the report.   Since audit reports are prepared from the working papers, it follows that audit working papers substantiate and explain the conclusions reached in the report. The auditors may on occasion be called upon to testify in court concerning the financial affairs of a client, or they may be required to defend in court the accuracy and reasonableness of their report. In all such cases, working papers are the principal means of substantiating the audit report. After completion of the study and evaluation of internal control, the auditors may draft an internal control letter to the client. In identifying existing weaknesses in internal control, and in developing recommendations to correct these weaknesses, the auditors will use the working papers as a principal source of information.

To clearly substantiate the auditors' report, audit working papers must provide evidence of the auditors' compliance with generally accepted auditing standards. The working papers should especially demonstrate adequate planning and proper execution of the audit and proper supervision of all staff members; a comprehensive study and evaluation of the client's system of internal control and the relation of the internal control evaluation to the audit program; and the accumulation of sufficient appropriate evidence to support the auditors' opinion on the client's financial statements. Other essential contents of working papers in order to substantiate the report include the actions taken to resolve exceptions or other unusual matters discovered during the audit, and the auditors' conclusion on specific aspects of the engagement.

Working papers and accountants' liability

The auditors' working papers are the only evidence which documents the extent of the procedures applied and evidence gathered during the audit. If the auditors, after completing an engagement, are charged with negligence, their audit working papers will be a major factor in refuting or substantiating the charge. Working papers, if not properly prepared, are as likely to injure the auditors as to protect them. *To look over a set of working papers for supporting information is one thing; to look over these same papers for details which may be used to attack the auditors' conclusions is quite another.* This latter possibility suggests the need for public accounting firms to make a critical review of working papers at the end of each engagement, and to give thought to the possibility that any contradictory statements, or evidence inconsistent with the conclusions finally reached, may be used to support charges of negligence at a later date.

Part of the difficulty in avoiding inconsistent and conflicting evidence in working papers is that the papers are prepared in large part by less experienced staff members. When the papers are reviewed by a supervisor or partner, the reviewer will give careful consideration to any questionable points. In studying these points the supervisors often give consideration to many other aspects of the audit, and of the client's records with which they are familiar; these other factors may lead the reviewer to the conclusion that an issue raised in the working papers does not warrant any corrective action. In some instances the reviewer may conclude that the assistant who prepared the paper has misinterpreted the situation. Years later, if a dispute arises and the working papers are being subjected to critical study by attorneys representing an "injured" client or third party, these questionable points in the papers may appear in a different light. The supervisor who cleared the issue based on personal knowledge of the client's business may not be available to explain the reasoning involved or the other special considerations present at the time of the audit. This long-range responsibility suggests that the supervisor should, at the time of deciding upon disposition of a troublesome point, insert an adequate explanation of the action in the working papers.

From time to time a public accounting firm should make a critical evaluation of its policies for preparation, review, and preservation of working papers. Recent experience in cases involving legal liability may lead some firms to considerable modification in the traditional handling of working papers.

Essentials of good working papers

The mark of experienced auditors is their ability to produce papers which contain all essential information but do not include any superfluous material. Audit tests usually involve the examination of numerous documents. Nonetheless, in many instances the only appropriate entry in the working papers is a notation by the auditors indicating that certain supporting documents have been inspected. This notation may consist merely of the responsible auditor's initials and the date placed in the audit program to indicate that a specific procedure has been completed.

An audit report may properly include both facts and opinions but should not confuse or intermingle the two. Consequently, the working papers must also clearly identify factual statements and matters of judgment. Every factual statement and every figure in the report should be supported and explained in the working papers. As the examination progresses, the auditors should anticipate the problems of report writing and include in the working papers comments and explanations which will later become part of the report. There should be no hesitancy in adding full explanatory remarks to any schedule or analysis prepared during any part of the audit. Working papers are not limited to quantitative data; they should include notes and explanations which record fully what was done by the auditors, their reasons for following certain audit procedures and omitting others, and their reactions and opinions concerning the quality of the data examined, the adequacy of the internal controls in force, and the competence of the persons responsible for the operations or records under review.

It is inevitable that errors of judgment will be made in the design and preparation of working papers. Occasionally, inexperienced auditors will become absorbed in a line of investigation altogether irrelevant to the objectives of the audit. They may create extensive working papers before the misdirection of their energies is detected. If these working papers have no bearing on the audit, they should not be preserved. There is a very natural reluctance to destroy papers which embody many hours of labour, but to retain such superfluous papers does not serve to regain the time wasted. On the contrary, inclusion of unnecessary working papers in the file detracts from the quality of the papers as a whole and may lead to further wasted effort during subsequent reviews of the work performed. In all cases the ultimate purpose of the papers should be considered the guiding criterion as to what material is included and what is omitted as unnecessary.

Types of working papers

Since audit working papers include all information gathered by the auditors, there are innumerable varieties and types of papers. However, there are certain general categories into which most of these may be grouped; these are (1) audit plans, audit programs, questionnaires, flowcharts and agenda sheets; (2) working trial balance or grouping sheets; (3) adjusting journal entries and reclassification entries; (4) supporting schedules, analyses, and computational working papers; (5) copies of minutes and other records or documents; and (6) clients' letters of representations and lawyers' letters. The original draft of the auditors' report, including the audited financial statements, is also considered part of the audit working papers.

Audit plans, audit programs, questionnaires, flowcharts, and agenda sheets. Audit plans and audit programs were discussed in Chapter 4; questionnaires and flowcharts in Chapter 5. Closely allied to the audit program is the agenda sheet. This is little more than a note sheet upon which questionable points, comments on unfinished items, and matters to be discussed with the client are recorded for "clearing." The agenda sheet will contain not only these comments and notes but also the initials of the persons who investigated them and full explanations as to their disposition or adequate cross references to other working papers showing their final treatment.

Working trial balance. The working trial balance is a schedule listing the balances of all the accounts in the general ledger for the current and previous year, and also providing columns for the auditors' adjustments and reclassifications and for the final amounts which will appear in the financial statements. A working trial balance is the "backbone" of the entire set of audit working papers; it is the key schedule which controls and summarizes all supporting papers.

Each page of a working trial balance will usually include headings similar to the following:

Working paper reference	Account title	Final balance Dec. 31, 19– (last year)	Balance per ledger Dec. 31, 19– (this year)	Adjustments and reclassifications Dr.	Cr.	Final balance Dec. 31, 19– (this year)

Although most of these column headings are self-explanatory, a brief discussion of the third and fourth columns is appropriate. In the third column, the final adjusted balances from the previous year's audit are listed. Inclusion of the previous year's figures facilitates comparison with the corresponding amounts for the current year and focuses attention upon any unusual changes. Inclusion of the final figures from the prior year's audit also gives assurance that the correct starting figure is used if the auditors verify the year's transactions in a balance sheet account in order to determine the validity of the ending balance.

The fourth column provides for the account balances at the close of the year under audit; these balances usually are taken directly from the general ledger. The balances of the revenue and expense accounts should be included even though these accounts have been closed into the Retained Earnings account prior to the auditors' arrival. Since the auditors ordinarily express an opinion on the income statement as well as the balance sheet, it is imperative that the audit working papers include full information on the revenue and expense accounts. The amount to be listed for the Retained Earnings account is the balance at the beginning of the year under audit. Dividends declared during the year are listed as a separate item, as is the computed net income for the year.

In many audits, the client furnishes the auditors with a working trial balance after all normal end-of-period journal entries have been posted. Before accepting the trial balance for their working papers, the auditors should trace the amounts to the general ledger for evidence that all ledger accounts have been included in the client-prepared trial balance.

If the auditors find that the ledger is out of balance, they should ordinarily request that the client's staff locate the error or errors and correct the accounts. If the client prefers that the auditors do the routine work to put the ledger in balance, there should be an understanding that such work is outside the scope of an audit and must be charged for as an additional service. It is generally uneconomical for the auditors' time to be devoted to detailed record keeping which could be performed by the client's employees.

Grouping sheets. A working trial balance is appropriate for the audit of a small client having relatively few general ledger accounts. For larger clients with numerous ledger accounts, the working trial balance method is unwieldy. Many general ledger accounts must be combined into a single figure in the audited balance sheet and income statement.

The grouping sheet technique was designed to overcome this disadvantage of the working trial balance. *Grouping sheets* are working papers with columnar headings similar to those for the working trial balance. Separate grouping sheets (also called *lead schedules* or *summary schedules*) are set up to combine similar general ledger accounts, the total of which appears in the client's balance sheet or income statement as a single amount. For example, a Cash grouping sheet might combine the following hypothetical general ledger accounts: Petty Cash, $500; General Bank Account, $348,216; Office Payroll Bank Account, $1,500; Factory Payroll Bank Account, $2,000; and Dividends Bank Account, $500. Similar grouping sheets would be set up for Accounts Receivable, Inventories, Shareholders' Equity, Net Sales, and for any other balance sheet or income statement caption.

Adjusting journal entries and reclassification entries accepted by the client are posted to the appropriate grouping sheets. All columns of the grouping sheets are totaled; then the columnar totals are recapitulated in a *working balance sheet* or *working income statement*, as appropriate. These two working statements also have columnar headings identical to those for the working trial balance. The working balance sheet, which summarizes all grouping sheets for assets, liabilities, and owners' equity, and the working income statement, which summarizes all grouping sheets for revenue and expenses, thus constitute the basic working papers supporting the balance sheet and income statement appearing in the audit report.

A working balance sheet is illustrated in Figure 9–1; Figure 9–2 illustrates a working income statement. Note particularly the following features of these illustrations:

1. Account numbers are included for individual general ledger accounts presented as separate financial statement captions (Notes Payable, for example, is Account 201).
2. All captions are cross referenced to supporting grouping sheets, schedules, or analyses.

FIGURE 9–1

Process Company Ltd.
Working Balance Sheet   C-1
December 31, 1978

Working Paper Reference	Account No.	Caption	Final Dec. 31, 77	Balance per Ledger Dec. 31, 78	Adjustments Dr. (Cr.)	Adjusted Dec. 31, 78	Reclassifications Dr. (Cr.)	Final Balance Dec. 31, 78
		Assets						
		Current Assets:						
E		Cash	481 413	742 186		742 186		742 186
F-1	111	Short-Term Investments		149 413		149 413		149 413
G		Accounts Receivable—Net	2 298 722	2 053 918	(91 096)	1 962 822		1 962 822
H		Inventories	2 701 814	2 942 117	(129 799)	2 812 318		2 812 318
J-2		Prepaid Expenses	118 322	125 829		125 829		125 829
		Total	5 600 271	6 013 463		5 792 568		5 792 568
K		Property & Equipment—Net	2 982 431	2 997 433	32 766	3 030 199		3 030 199
			8 582 702	9 010 896	(188 129)	8 822 767		8 822 767
		Liabilities & Equity						
		Current Liabilities:						
M-4	201	Notes Payable	500 000	450 000		450 000		450 000
M-1		Accounts Payable	1 651 126	1 585 839	(76 585)	1 662 424		1 662 424
M-2	221	Income Taxes Payable	127 000	323 000	⑧ 132 000	191 000		191 000
M-3		Other Accrued Liabilities	321 418	385 014		385 014		385 014
		Total	2 599 544	2 743 853		2 688 438		2 688 438
N		Long-Term Liabilities	2 000 000	1 960 000		1 960 000		1 960 000
P		Shareholders' Equity	3 983 158	4 307 043	132 714	4 174 329		4 174 329
			8 582 702	9 010 896	188 129	8 822 767		8 822 767

UM It
Feb 24, 79

FIGURE 9–2

Process Company Ltd.
Working Income Statement   C-2
Year Ended December 31, 1978

Working Paper Reference	Account No.	Caption	Final Dec. 31, 77	Balance per Ledger Dec. 31, 78	Adjustments Dr. (Cr.)	Adjusted Dec. 31, 78	Reclassifi- cations Dr. (Cr.)	Final Balance Dec. 31, 78
Q		Net Sales	21 422 719	23 814 882		23 814 882		23 814 882
		Costs and Expenses:						
R-1		Cost of Goods Sold	19 344 723	20 941 887	232 296	21 174 183		21 174 183
R-2		Selling, General, and Administrative Expense	1 713 878	2 124 810	32 418	2 157 228		2 157 228
R-4	582	Interest	110 200	101 300		101 300		101 300
M-2	601	Income Taxes	127 000	323 000	⑧(132 000)	191 000		191 000
			21 295 801	23 490 997	132 714	23 623 711		23 623 711
P		Net Income	126 918	323 885	132 714	191 171		191 171
								U.M.H. Feb 24, 79

3. The only individual adjusting journal entry posted to the working statements is number 8, which affects individual accounts listed in the working statements. Totals of all other adjustments are carried forward from the applicable grouping sheets.

The use of grouping sheets facilitates the review of working papers by supervisors. Minor details are eliminated from the working balance sheet and the working income statement, and the major issues stand forth more clearly. Thus the partner or other reviewer finds that the top pages in the working papers file present an overall view of the audited financial statements. Any critical problems can be quickly recognized, and more detailed information can be readily located in supporting pages.

Adjusting journal entries and reclassification entries

During the course of an audit engagement, the auditors may discover various types of errors in the client's financial statements and accounting records. These errors may be large or small in amount, they may arise from the omission of transactions or from the use of incorrect amounts, or they may result from improper classification or cutoff, or from mis-interpretation of transactions. Generally, these errors are accidental; however, the auditors may discover fraud in *intentional* errors in the financial statements or accounting records.

To correct *material* errors discovered in the financial statements and accounting records, the auditors draft *adjusting journal entries* (AJEs), which they recommend for entry in the client's accounting records. In addition, the auditors develop *reclassification entries* for items which, although not incorrectly recorded in the accounting records, must be reclassified for fair presentation in the client's financial statements.

Proposed adjusting entries are typically identified by numbers, and reclassification entries are assigned letters. The critical component of each type of entry is the *explanation;* without a complete, lucid explanation, an adjusting or reclassification entry is nearly worthless.

To develop adjusting journal entries, the auditors compare the client's erroneous accounting entry for a transaction with the entry which should have been made. To illustrate, assume that The Berkeley Corporation Ltd. on June 30, 1978, erroneously charged to the Repairs and Maintenance Expense account an invoice of $84,000 for construction of a new shipping room for its building. As of June 30, 1978, the building had an estimated remaining service life of 20 years, with no estimated residual value. The auditors would make the following analysis of the client's erroneous entry for the December 31, 1978, audit:

	Entry per Client	Entry Should Be	Adjustment
	Dr. (Cr.)	Dr. (Cr.)	Dr. (Cr.)
Repairs and Maintenance Expense	84 000 –		(84 000 –)
Buildings		84 000 –	84 000 –
Cash	(84 000 –)	(84 000 –)	
Depreciation Expense: Buildings		2 100 –	2 100 –
Accumulated Depreciation: Buildings		(2 100 –)	(2 100 –)

The information in the "Adjustment" column above provides the data for the auditors' formal proposed adjusting journal entry, which is illustrated as entry number 1 in Figure 9–3, together with another illustrative adjusting journal entry.

Note that the client's entry to the Cash account in the preceding illustration was correct. Inexperienced accountants sometimes draft adjusting entries affecting cash when none is required.

Distinction between adjusting entries and reclassification entries

A distinction must be made between reclassification entries used solely in the auditors' working papers for the purpose of obtaining proper

FIGURE 9–3

The Berkeley Corporation Ltd.

Proposed Adjusting Journal Entries   D-1

December 31, 1978

Working Paper Reference	Account No.	Account Title and Explanation	Dr.	Cr.
		①		
K-1-1	151	Buildings	84 000 —	
R-1-1	509	Depreciation Expense-Buildings	2 100 —	
R-1-3	531	Repairs and Maintenance Expense		84 000 —
K-2-1	155	Accumulated Depreciation-Bldg.		2 100 —
		To correct distribution of Lehnberg Co. invoice dated June 30, 78 for construction of new shipping room. Depreciation based on remaining 20-year life of building.		
		②		
K-1-3	153	Office Equipment	1 760 —	
K-2-6	522	Sales Supplies		1 760 —
		To correct distribution of Reese Office Supplies invoice dated Dec. 26, 78. for a calculator.		
				V.M.H. Jan. 19, 79

presentation in the financial statements and adjusting entries intended for recording in the client's accounts. A reclassification entry serves to transfer or reclassify an amount on the auditors' working papers; *it is not turned over to the client for entry in the accounting records.* Typical of the reclassification entries is the one made to reclassify customers' accounts with credit balances so that they will appear on the balance sheet as liabilities, rather than being offset against accounts receivable with debit balances. Such an account will ordinarily regain its normal debit balance within a short time and should therefore be continued in the client's records as part of accounts receivable. A similar reclassification entry is made for debit balances in accounts payable, as shown in Figure 9–4.

The working paper formats for adjusting and reclassification entries are similar, with columns provided for working paper references and account numbers, as well as for account titles and dollar amounts.

Adjusting entries for material items only

A legend has long persisted in business folklore and popular fiction that auditors are persons busily engaged in making minute adjustments to correct accounting records to a state of precise accuracy. This misconception has perhaps been bolstered by textbook illustrations which, as a matter of convenience, have used very small dollar amounts to illustrate the principle of the adjusting entry.

In the examination of some small companies which lack competent accounting personnel, the auditors may in fact assume the burden of making routine end-of-period adjusting entries for depreciation, expired insurance, and accrued expenses, as well as entries to correct numerous errors. In such situations, however, the auditors' role is really a combination of auditor and part-time accountant. In the examination of larger concerns with well-qualified accounting personnel, the auditors will find that all normal year-end adjustments for depreciation, prepay-

FIGURE 9–4

The Berkeley Corporation Ltd.
Proposed Reclassification Entry   D-2
December 31, 1978

Working Paper Reference	Account No.	Account Title and Explanation	Dr.	Cr.
		(A)		
G-1	121	Accounts Receivable	12 000 00	
M-1	200	Accounts Payable		12 000 00
		To transfer debit balance in Accounts Payable to asset classification. (Advance to McZudy Company in connection with purchase order no. 12-73.)		
				U. M. H. Jan. 19, 79

ments, accruals, and similar items have been completed; the accounts may have been closed and transactions recorded for the subsequent period before much of the audit work is performed. Adjusting entries by the auditors will then be few in number and limited to matters which have an important bearing on the financial statements. In other words, the auditors' purpose in proposing an adjusting entry is not to secure greater accuracy of details in the accounting records but to modify financial statements so that they will "present fairly" the financial position and operating results of the company. The adjustments, however, must be entered in the accounting records by client personnel so that the accounts will agree with the financial statements.

No precise rule can be employed to indicate whether a proposed adjustment is sufficiently material to warrant its being made. In reaching a decision the auditors may consider whether the adjustment is of a type that would cause a change in the net income for the year, and the amount of the change expressed as a percentage of net sales and net income. If the proposed adjustment affects balance sheet accounts only, the significance of the amount may be appraised by expressing it as a percentage of total assets, of current assets, or of shareholders' equity. However, as discussed under the heading of *Materiality* in Chapter 1, the qualitative aspects of the adjustment must be considered along with its quantitative importance.

In making decisions as to whether an adjustment should be made or "passed," there is no satisfactory substitute for the judgment of the partners or managers supervising the examination, since they are in a position to consider all the special circumstances of the engagement. In all cases, they will consider the *cumulative* materiality of "passed" adjustments which appear to be immaterial when considered individually. A "Summary of Unadjusted Discrepancies" working paper is a convenient tool for the review of the cumulative effect of "passed" adjustments. This working paper also demonstrates the auditors' awareness of the immaterial discrepancies.

In summary, for the audit of a client with good internal accounting controls and a competent staff, adjusting entries proposed by the auditors probably will not be numerous. If the auditors presented numerous adjustments of minor importance, the client might believe that the audit fee was being inflated by unnecessarily detailed work.

Auditors' adjusting entries recorded by client

Prior to the conclusion of the audit the proposed adjusting journal entries drafted by the auditors will be discussed with the client's controller or chief accountant. In most cases the controller will approve the entries and authorize their recording in the company's accounting records.

The auditors record the approved entries on their working trial balance or grouping sheets and extend the adjusted balances to the "Final" column.

The auditors do not personally make entries in the client's accounts; to do so would be to abandon at least temporarily their role of independent auditors. Some of the adjusting journal entries worked out by the auditors may relate to transactions already recorded by the client in the following period. In such cases the auditors should provide the client with a list of the reversing entries which should be made to offset the adjusting journal entries. The auditors must always verify that the adjusting and reversing entries are recorded in the accounts; otherwise, the financial statements appearing in the audit report will not agree with the client's accounting records.

ILLUSTRATIVE CASE. An auditor found that an unrecorded liability in the amount of $80,000 existed at the balance sheet date for repair to buildings completed during December of the year under audit. The client had recorded the liability as though it were a January transaction of the following year. Since the amount was quite material for this company, the auditor insisted that the repair expense should be reflected in the year in which the work was done and the liability incurred. The auditor therefore drafted an adjusting entry and a reversing entry, both to be recorded by the client in the accounts.

Another practical difficulty sometimes encountered when the auditors do not begin their examination until some time after the end of the period to be audited is that the client company may have closed its books and begun entering revenue and expense items in the accounts for the succeeding year. The only alternative open to the auditors in this situation is to make adjustments affecting revenue or expense directly to the Retained Earnings account. Of course, the prior closing of the accounts affects *only* the entries to be entered in the accounting records—and not the entries on the working papers leading to the statement amounts.

Supporting schedules

Although all types of working papers may loosely be called "schedules," auditors prefer to use this term to describe a listing of the elements or details comprising the balance in an asset or liability account at a specific date. No historical review is involved—simply a listing. Thus, a list of amounts owed to vendors making up the balance of the Trade Accounts Payable account, as illustrated in Figure 9–5, is properly described as a *schedule*.

Analysis of a ledger account

An analysis of a ledger account is another common type of audit working paper. The purpose of an analysis is to show on one paper *all changes*

FIGURE 9–5

Maini Company Limited
Acct. No. 203   Accounts Payable – Trade   M-2
                                 March 31, 1979

Invoice Date	Invoice No.	Vendor				Amount	
		Vouchered invoices:					
	Various	Ace Industries, Inc.				14 418 19	4 X
	Various	Carlsbad Steel Supply				22 819 50	4 r X
	Various	Douglas Mfg. Co. Ltd.				39 416 20	4 X
	Various	Graham Company Ltd.				16 944 89	4 r X
	Various	Jenkins, Inc.				35 193 44	4 r X
Mar. 18, 78	—	Mitchell Supply Co. Ltd.		①		(1 863 50)	
	Various	Parks Fabricators Ltd.				16 419 20	4 r X
		Unmatched invoices (goods not received):					
Mar. 28, 79	614 J	Graham Company Ltd.				4 163 88	4 r
Mar. 26, 79	215 J	Jenkins, Inc.				3 016 40	4 r
		Unbilled receivers:					
Mar. 28, 79	572	Carlsbad Steel Supply				5 216 53	4
Mar. 31, 79	575	Ace Industries, Inc.				2 839 26	4
		Balance per ledger,	Mar. 31, 79			158 583 99	4 ∧
		A.J.E. 17 – Inv. 69 L X of Carlsbad Steel Supply dated Mar. 16, 79,					
		received Mar. 31, 79, per receiver no. 576 4-4-3				4 188 70	
		Adjusted balance,	Mar. 31, 79			162 772 69	∧
		R.J.E. A – Reclassify dr. balance of Mitchell Supply Co. Ltd.		G-4		1 863 50	
						164 636 19	
						C-1	

① Per L. R. Harris, Controller – debit balance is uncollectible.
    〈It arose from Maini's rejection of materials after
       Mitchell had been paid.〉
4 – Footed.
∧ – Traced to general ledger.
4 – Examined supporting documents as applicable.
r – Reconciled to statement received directly from
       vendor 〈remaining vendors do not prepare
       statements〉.
X – Examined April 1979 cheque copy in payment.

Prepared by:
Ellen Miles
〈client's head bookkeeper – V.M.H.〉

                                                               V. M. H.
                                                               May 17, 79

in an asset, liability, equity, revenue, or expense account during the period covered by the audit. If a number of the changes are individually immaterial, they may be recorded as a single item in the analysis working paper.

To analyze a ledger account, the auditors first list the beginning balance and indicate the nature of the items comprising this balance. Next, the auditors list and investigate the nature of all debits and credits to the account during the period. These entries when combined with the beginning balance produce a figure representing the balance in the account as of the audit date. If any errors or omissions of importance are detected during this analysis of the account, the necessary adjusting journal entry approved by the client is entered on the working paper to produce the adjusted balance required for the financial statements. Figure 9–6 illustrates an analysis of the Allowance for Uncollectible Accounts ledger account.

In preparing analyses, it usually is desirable for the auditors to arrive at a figure equal to the general ledger account balance before they make any adjustments to correct such balance. In this manner they account for the balance of the ledger account as it stands; at the same time, by analyzing the account, the auditors disclose any items improperly included therein. In other words, the auditors first record in their working paper all of the current year's entries in the account, even though some of these entries are improper. Then, after having accounted for the balance of the account, and having analyzed the activity therein, they proceed to make any necessary adjusting journal entries to arrive at an adjusted balance. Among the various errors which the analysis of a large account might disclose are errors in addition of items, the entering of debits as credits and vice versa, posting of erroneous amounts, misclassification of entries, and omission of entries. The omission of entries belonging in the account is less easily detected, although comparison of the account with a corresponding analysis for the prior year may sometimes suggest the omission of items.

Computational working papers

Another type of supporting working paper is the computational working paper. The auditors' approach to verifying certain types of accounts and other figures is to make an independent computation and compare their results with the amounts shown by the client's records. Examples of amounts which might be verified by computation are the bonuses paid to executives, pension accruals, royalty expense, interest on notes, and accrued taxes. Bonuses, pensions, and royalties are ordinarily specified in contracts; by making computations based on the terms of the contracts, the auditors determine whether these items are stated in accordance with

FIGURE 9–6

Maini Company Limited

Acct. No. 126   Allowance for Uncollectible Accounts   G-4

March 31, 1979

Balance per ledger, Mar. 31, 78				22 881 75
Deduct: Write-offs during fiscal 1979:				
June 18, 78 Morgan Desk Co. Ltd.	6 581 44 ᵐᶜ			
Feb. 12, 79 Baker Cabinet Co. Ltd.	8 041 60 ᵐᶜ		14 623 04	
				8 258 71
Add: Provision for year ended Mar. 31, 79, based upon aged trial balance of trade accounts receivable at Mar. 31, 79				6 589 81
Balance per ledger, Mar. 31, 79		G-1		14 848 52
A.J.E. 7 - to increase allowance for following doubtful accounts:				
Gibson Furniture Co. Ltd. - see comments regarding this customer at working paper G-3; also see working paper E-2 for Gibson N.S.F. cheque.				3 169 44
Mitchell Supply Co. Ltd. - uncollectible debit balance of vendor - see working paper M-2.				1 863 50 c
Rounding of estimate				118 54
Total provision added per A.J.E. 7				5 151 48
Adjusted balance, Mar. 31, 79				20 000 —
				Ⓖ

ᵐ – Examined Controller L. R. Harris's authorization for
write-off. Board of directors ratified write-off –
see minutes at V-7-79.

c – Confirmation request mailed Mar. 31, 79; returned
by Post Office stamped "Moved - no forwarding
address".

D. M. H.
May 14, 79

contractual requirements. Canada Pension Plan contributions are based on the amount of wages and salaries paid; the auditors' verification in this case consists of applying the tax rates to the contributory wages and salaries for the period.

Copies of minutes and other records or documents

Auditing is not limited to the examination of financial records, and working papers are not confined to schedules and analyses. During the course of an audit the auditors may gather much purely expository material to substantiate their report. One common example is copies of minutes of directors' and shareholders' meetings. Other examples include copies of articles of incorporation and by-laws; copies of important contracts, bond indentures, and mortgages; and memoranda pertaining to examination of records, confirmations of accounts receivable, and bank deposits.

Letters of representations provided by clients

It is customary for the auditors to obtain letters of representations from clients regarding receivables, inventories, liabilities, and other matters. These generally take the form of letters addressed to the auditing firm, signed by officials of the client company, and containing statements as to the correctness and authenticity of inventory quantities and prices; the completeness and correctness of liabilities recorded in the balance sheet; and any other matter concerning which the auditors may see fit to obtain such representation. Although representations by the client officials do not excuse the auditors from any necessary auditing procedures, they do have the effect of reminding the client officials that they are primarily responsible for the correctness of the accounts and the financial statements. Illustrations of client letters of representations are included in subsequent chapters.

Lawyers' letters

Letters from the client company's legal counsel to the auditors are an increasingly important type of working paper. Client officials should request the company's attorneys to furnish the auditors with a description and evaluation of pending or threatened litigation involving the company, and of unasserted claims and assessments against the company which the client officials consider to be probable of assertion and reasonably possible of having an unfavorable outcome to the company. The use of lawyers' letters by the auditors is discussed in greater detail in Chapter 17.

The permanent file

The auditors usually maintain two files of working papers for each client: (1) annual audit files for every completed examination, and (2) a permanent file of relatively unchanging data. The annual file (as for the 1978 audit) pertains solely to that year's examination; the permanent file contains such things as copies of the articles of incorporation which need not be duplicated in subsequent examinations. The permanent file serves three purposes: (1) to refresh the auditors' memory on items applicable over a period of many years; (2) to provide for new staff members a quick summary of the policies and organization of the client; and (3) to preserve working papers on items which show relatively few or no changes, thus eliminating the necessity for their preparation year after year.

Much of the information contained in the permanent file is gathered during the course of the first audit of a client's records. A considerable portion of the time spent on a first audit is devoted to gathering and appraising background information, such as the following:

1. Copies of articles of incorporation and by-laws.
2. Organization charts and scope of authority and responsibility of officers.
3. Charts of accounts, procedure manuals, accounting manuals, and other data concerning internal control.
4. Terms of share issues and bond indentures.
5. Copies of leases, patent agreements, pension plans, labour contracts, profit-sharing and bonus plans, long-term construction contracts, and guarantee agreements.
6. Plant layout, manufacturing processes, and principal products.
7. Copies of minutes of directors', shareholders', and committees' meetings.
8. Analyses of such "permanent" accounts as land, buildings, share capital, long-term debt, retained earnings, and premium on share issues.
9. Copies of income tax returns for prior years (if not maintained in a separate tax file).
10. Summary of accounting principles employed by client.
11. Articles in newspapers or periodicals which deal with the client company.

This information should be carefully preserved by the auditors in a permanent file so that they may avoid any unnecessary repetition of work during subsequent examinations. Most business executives are quite willing to spend considerable time with representatives of an auditing firm during the first audit in order to make them conversant with the history, policies, and key personnel of the business. They do not, however, expect to repeat this indoctrination process in full each year. To fulfill its function, the permanent file must be brought up to date during each examination. Copies of new minutes, recent contracts and agreements, any changes in by-laws, and similar developments should be added each year to the file. In each repeat engagement the system of internal control should be reexamined and any changes or improvements recorded. The permanent file should be properly indexed to provide ready reference and be adequately bound so that it may be carried to each engagement.

Analyses of accounts which show few or no changes over a period of years are also included in the permanent file. These accounts may include land, buildings, accumulated depreciation, long-term investments, long-term liabilities, share capital, and other owners' equity accounts. The initial investigation of these accounts must often include the transactions of many years. But once these historical analyses have been brought up to date, the work required in subsequent examinations will be limited to a review of the current year's transactions in these accounts. In this respect, the permanent file is a timesaving device because current changes in such accounts need only be added to the permanent papers without reappearing in the current working papers. Adequate cross-indexing in the working papers, of course, should be provided to show where in the permanent file such information is to be found.

Arrangement of working papers in the annual file

The working papers which comprise the annual file should be indexed and cross referenced during the course of the audit or upon its completion. There are many alternative methods of arranging and indexing working papers in the annual file; the following tabulation illustrates one such method:

A. Draft of audit report and financial statements.
   A-1. Audit report.
   A-2. Balance sheet.
   A-3. Statements of income and retained earnings.
   A-4. Statement of changes in financial position.
   A-5. Notes to financial statements.
B. Planning working papers.
   B-1. Engagement letter
   B-2. Audit plan.
   B-3. Study and evaluation of internal control.
      B-3-1. Questionnaires, written descriptions, flowcharts.
      B-3-2. Preliminary evaluation of internal control.

            B–3–3. Compliance tests of internal control.

            B–3–4. Final evaluation of internal control.

   B–4. Audit program.

   B–5. Time budget.

   B–6. Agenda sheets.

C. Working balance sheet and working income statement.

D. Adjusting journal entries and reclassification entries.

E. Cash grouping sheet.

   E–1. Petty cash.

   E–2. Bank reconciliations.

            E–2.1. Bank confirmations.

F. Short-term investments.

G. Receivables grouping sheet.

   G–1. Trial balance of trade accounts receivable.

            G–1–1. Accounts receivable confirmations.

   G–2. Notes receivable analysis.

            G–2–2. Notes receivable confirmations.

   G–3. Analysis of allowance for uncollectible accounts and notes.

H. Inventories grouping sheet.

   H–1. Raw materials physical inventory.

   H–2. Goods in process physical inventory.

   H–3. Finished goods physical inventory.

   H–4. Observation of physical inventory.

   H–5. Tests of inventory pricing.

J. Prepaid expenses grouping sheet.

K. Property, plant, and equipment grouping sheet.

   K–1. Summary analysis of plant and equipment.

   K–2. Tests of depreciation.

L. Other assets.

M. Current liabilities grouping sheet.

   M–1. Trade accounts payable trial balance.

   M–2. Analyses of federal and provincial income taxes payable.

   M–3. Accrued liabilities.

N. Long-term liabilities.

P. Shareholders' equity grouping sheet.

Q. Revenue grouping sheet.

   Q–1. Analysis of sales.

   Q–2. Analysis of other revenue.

R. Costs and expenses grouping sheet.

   R–1. Analysis of cost of goods sold.

   R–2. Analysis of selling expenses.

   R–3. Analysis of administrative expenses.

   R–4. Analysis of other expenses.

S. Extraordinary and non-operating gains and losses and prior-period adjustments.
T. Consolidating working papers.

Index references should be marked in coloured pencil on the upper or lower right-hand corner of each working paper, where they will be most conspicuous. Whenever reference is made in one working paper to another, there should be adequate cross-indexing. The index itself should be filed with the working papers, and the index symbols marked alongside the captions in the working trial balance or grouping sheets. Supporting schedules and analyses should always be referenced in some way to the working trial balance.

Storage and retention of working papers

After being arranged and indexed, the working papers are ready for storage. A satisfactory storage procedure is one that gives protection against such hazards as fire and theft and ensures that the working papers may be readily found and referred to when needed. Working papers that are inaccessible are obviously of little use. Public accountants may keep current working papers in their offices for three to five years and place the older papers in public storage. Permanent files, of course, are all kept on hand. It is sometimes advantageous to develop separate working paper files for tax returns and reports to governmental agencies.

The question of how long working papers should be retained is a controversial one. The statute of limitations restricting the time within which legal action may be brought varies by province and by the type of action, but does not often extend beyond six years.[3] The occasions are few and far between, however, when an auditor can say with assurance that certain working papers have no possible future value.

Indefinite retention of working papers creates a serious storage problem; many CA firms microfilm working papers for economy of storage.

Guidelines for preparation of working papers

Auditors are often judged by their working papers. When working papers are prepared in good form with proper attention to layout, design, and legibility, with complete headings, explanations of sources, and verification work performed, they create in supervisors and partners a feeling of confidence in the auditors on the job. Working papers should convey an impression of system and order and of conscientious attention

---

[3] The CICA study group noted that in the province of Quebec the period may be up to 30 years. CICA, *Good Audit Working Paper* (Toronto, 1970), p. 18.

to detail, coupled with a clear distinction between the important and the trivial.

We can now summarize in a few short paragraphs our basic guidelines for preparing working papers that will meet current professional standards.

A separate, properly identified working paper should be prepared for each topic. Only one side of a sheet is used, to prevent the overlooking of material recorded on the back of a paper. Proper identification of a working paper is accomplished by a heading which includes the name of the client company, a clear description of the information presented, and the applicable date or the period covered. Rubber stamps may be used to insert client names and relevant dates on entire sets of working papers.

Complete and specific identification of documents examined, employees interviewed, and sites visited is essential for good working paper practice. The preparer of a working paper should date and sign or initial the working paper; the signatures or initials of the senior, manager, or partner who reviewed the working paper should also appear on the paper.

All working papers should be indexed and should be cross-indexed to the working trial balance or relevant grouping sheet. Where reference is necessary between working papers, there must be adequate cross-indexing.

The nature of verification work performed by the auditors should be indicated on each working paper. A review of paid purchase invoices, for example, might be supplemented by inspection of the related purchase orders and receiving documents to substantiate the authenticity of the invoices examined; a description of this verification procedure should be included on the working paper. As audit working papers are prepared, the auditors will use several different symbols to identify specific steps in the work performed. These symbols, or *tick marks,* provide a very concise means of indicating the auditing procedures applied to particular amounts. Whenever tick marks are employed, they must be accompanied by a legend explaining their significance.

The extent and scope of compliance testing and substantive testing should be clearly stated in the working papers for every phase of the audit. In the examination of the Repairs and Maintenance Expense account, for example, the auditors might, by inspecting 10 percent of all invoices, account for 90 percent of the total charges involved.

A separate agenda sheet listing points to be investigated should be developed as the audit proceeds. In the course of the investigation, many questions will arise which cannot be answered or settled immediately. By listing these points on a working paper designed for that purpose, the auditors can avoid interrupting the work at hand but make sure that the question will not be forgotten. Before the audit is finished, the agenda sheet must be reviewed and each question satisfactorily settled.

The working papers should include comments by the auditors indicating their conclusions on each aspect of the work. In other words, the auditors should take a stand on all findings. For example, after carrying out the audit program for cash, an auditor may write the following conclusion in the working papers:

> As a result of carrying out the auditing procedures for cash set forth in the audit program at B–4–2, I conclude that, after the effects of AJEs 3 and 4, Cash is fairly presented in the current asset section of Maini Company Limited's balance sheet in the rounded amount of $70,874.

The rewriting of working papers should be considered evidence of inefficiency and inadequate planning. There is little or no justification for the practice of recording audit data on a type of paper or in a manner which will necessitate rewriting. The old maxim of "write it once and write it right" is just as applicable to the production of audit working papers as it is to the recording phases of accounting.

Working papers should be placed in the completed file as rapidly as they are finished. As each schedule, analysis, or memorandum is completed, it should be brought together with other completed papers in a file, binder, or folder.

The review of working papers

Working papers are reviewed at every supervisory level of a CA firm. Senior auditors in charge of an engagement review the working papers of staff assistants, managers and supervisors scrutinize all working papers prepared by senior auditors and staff assistants, and partners make a final review of the entire set of working papers before signing the CA firm's name to the audit report.

What do working paper reviewers look for? First, they seek indications that the audit was performed in accordance with generally accepted auditing standards—especially the standards of field work. Next, the reviewers judge whether the evidence accumulated during the audit supported the CA firm's opinion on the client's financial statements.

Review for compliance with standards of field work

In reviewing working papers, managers and partners look for evidence of: (1) proper planning and execution of the audit and supervision of audit staff members, (2) an appropriate study and evaluation of the client's existing internal control, and (3) the gathering of sufficient appropriate audit evidence.

Proper planning is substantiated in the working papers by a copy of the engagement letter, a formalized audit plan, detailed audit programs for specific sections of the audit, and a time budget showing adequate explanations for material differences between actual and budgeted hours for each phase of the audit. Reviewers are especially concerned that the audit plan and audit programs are consistent with the evaluation of internal control.

Supervision of audit staff members and proper execution of the audit are demonstrated by agenda sheets containing reviewers' queries and follow-up comments by audit staff members, and by signatures or initials of reviewers on the various working papers.

The quality of the study and evaluation of internal control is demonstrated in the flowcharts, questionnaires, or written descriptions of internal control; in the preliminary evaluation; in the audit programs for compliance tests, and related working papers describing sampling procedures and conclusions; in the formal working paper for the evaluation of internal control; and in a copy of the internal control letter to the client describing recommendations for improvements in internal control.

Every audit working paper should demonstrate to the reviewer that sufficient appropriate audit evidence was gathered by the audit staff. The "signed-off" audit program is the principal working paper demonstrating the quantity and quality of evidence accumulated during the audit. The working paper reviewer wants to know how exceptions and unusual matters were resolved, as evidenced by written comments in the working papers, and whether the staff auditors' conclusions regarding various sections of the audit were warranted by information presented in the working papers.

Throughout their scrutiny of the working papers, reviewers are alert for any indication that the general standard (proficiency, objectivity, due care) was not complied with.

Review for support of CA firm's opinion

If the reviewing manager and partner are satisfied that the audit working papers demonstrate compliance with generally accepted auditing standards, they next consider whether the draft of the audit report is substantiated by the working papers. In addition to verifying the accuracy of amounts, dates, names, and other key data in the audited financial statements and in the draft report, the reviewers will consider whether the working papers contain answers to the following questions:

Did the client company use generally accepted accounting principles in the preparation of its financial statements (including footnotes)?

Were the accounting principles used in the current period's financial statements consistent with those used in the preceding year's financial statements?

Are disclosures in the financial statements (including footnotes) adequate and informative?

Is the type of opinion (unqualified, qualified, adverse, or denial) in the draft audit report warranted?

QUALITY CONTROL FOR AUDITS

In recent years, the work of independent auditors has come under increasing criticism from the courts, the government, consumer activists, academicians, and CAs themselves. Many critics have charged that the public accounting profession has done little to police its own ranks. The dismal performance of some CA firms, brought to light in court cases, supports these criticisms.

While the CICA has not issued pronouncements in this area, the AICPA has taken steps to counteract the criticism described above. In *SAS No. 4,* "Quality Control Considerations for a Firm of Independent Auditors," the Institute set forth matters to be considered by CPA firms in establishing quality controls over their work. In addition, the AICPA adopted a *voluntary* quality control review program for CPA firms.

Quality control standards

In *SAS No. 4,* the AICPA suggested quality control guidelines in the following areas: independence, assigning personnel to engagements, consultation, supervision, hiring, professional development, advancement, acceptance and continuation of clients, and inspection. Most of the AICPA's quality control guidelines are obvious to professional CPAs; some guideline topics have been considered at length in preceding pages of this textbook. Only the guidelines for *consultation* and *inspection* will be discussed at this point.

Consultation. The AICPA recommended the establishment of policies and procedures to assure that independent auditors will consult with knowledgeable persons on critical questions in accounting and auditing. In large CPA firms, such consultation might be with partners or managers having expertise in specialized industries or SEC practice, or with the firm's technical research staff. Smaller CPA firms may refer questions to an appropriate group in the AICPA or in a state society of CPAs.[4] The point to be stressed is that independent auditors should not attempt to solve complex accounting and auditing questions without the counsel of another expert.

Inspection. The inspection guideline in *SAS No. 4* deals with an internal audit type function. Most large CPA firms have established programs in which "review teams" of partners and managers from various

---

[4] In Canada the practice adviser of the provincial institutes may be consulted, especially by small CA firms, on difficult technical matters.

offices of the firm appraise the quality controls of other offices of the firm.[5] Many smaller CPA firms have participated in a voluntary quality control review program administered by the AICPA. In this voluntary program, quality controls of a local CPA firm are reviewed by practicing CPAs from other CPA firms.

Recent innovations in the inspection area have been one national CPA firm's "peer review" of another national CPA firm, at the latter's request; the appointment of a "public review board" of non-CPAs by a national CPA firm; and independent audits of a major CPA firm's financial statements by another CPA firm.

Review of CPA firms

The review program adopted by the AICPA makes participation voluntary. The quality controls of participating firms are reviewed at least once every three years by another CPA firm or by teams composed of partners and managers from other CPA firms. An AICPA-appointed quality control review committee administers the program. Standards for the reviews are established by the AICPA's Auditing Standards Executive Committee. Reports on quality control reviews are submitted to the reviewed firms, which at their option can provide copies of the reports to the AICPA.

The AICPA's quality control review program appears to be a good one. CPA firms participating in the plan clearly demonstrate their concern about the quality controls for their public accounting practices.

KEY TERMS INTRODUCED OR EMPHASIZED IN CHAPTER 9

adjusting journal entry   A journal entry drafted by the auditors to correct a material error discovered in the financial statements and accounting records.

agenda sheet   A working paper containing questionable points, comments on unfinished items, or matters to be discussed with the client. All items listed on agenda sheets must be cleared before the audit is completed.

analysis   A working paper showing all changes in an asset, liability, equity, revenue, or expense account during the period covered by the audit.

grouping sheet   A working paper with columnar headings similar to those in a working trial balance, set up to combine similar ledger accounts, the total of which appears in the client's balance sheet or income statement as a single amount.

lawyer's letters   Letters from the client company's legal counsel to the auditors, describing and evaluating pending or threatened litigation involving the company. Lawyers' letters also describe unasserted claims and assessments

---

[5] Such a practice is also common for large CA firms in Canada.

against the company which the client officials consider to be probable of assertion and reasonably possible of having an unfavourable outcome to the company.

letter of representations   A single letter or separate letters prepared by officers of the client company at the auditors' request setting forth certain facts about the company's financial position or operations.

permanent file   A file of working papers containing relatively unchanging data, such as copies of articles of incorporation and by-laws, copies of minutes of directors', shareholders' and committees' meetings, and analyses of such ledger accounts as land and retained earnings.

reclassification entry   A working paper entry drafted by the auditors to assure fair presentation in the client's financial statements, such as an entry to transfer accounts receivable credit balances to the current liabilities section of the client's balance sheet. Since reclassification entries do not correct errors in the client company's financial statements or accounting records, they are not posted to the client's ledger accounts.

tick mark   A symbol used in working papers by the auditor to indicate a specific step in the work performed. Whenever tick marks are used, they must be accompanied by a legend explaining their significance.

working balance sheet   A working paper which recapitulates the columnar totals for all grouping sheets for assets, liabilities, and owners' equity. A working balance sheet has columnar headings similar to the headings of grouping sheets or a working trial balance.

working income statement   A working paper which recapitulates the columnar totals for all grouping sheets for revenue and expenses. A working income statement has columnar headings similar to the headings of grouping sheets or a working trial balance.

working papers   Papers including all the evidence gathered by auditors to show the work they have done, the methods and procedures they have followed, and the conclusions they have developed in an examination of financial statements or another type of engagement.

working trial balance   A working paper which lists the balances of all the accounts in the general ledger for the current and the previous year, and which also provides columns for the auditor's adjustments and reclassifications and for the final amounts which will appear in the financial statements.

GROUP I
REVIEW QUESTIONS

9–1.   What has the AICPA done to help assure quality control by CPA firms?

9–2.   Should the auditors prepare adjusting journal entries to correct all errors which they discover in the accounting records for the year under audit? Explain.

9–3.   What are the purposes of audit working papers?

9–4.   Why are the final figures from the prior year's audit included in a working trial balance or grouping sheets? Explain.

9–5.   Should the working trial balance or grouping sheets prepared by the auditors include revenue and expense accounts if the balances of these accounts for the audit year have been closed into retained earnings prior to the auditors' arrival? Explain.

9–6.   Under what circumstances should an adjusting journal entry proposed by the auditors include a debit or credit to a Cash account? Explain.

9–7.   In their review of audit working papers, what do managers and partners look for?

9–8.   "Audit working papers are the property of the auditors, who may destroy the papers, sell them, or give them away." Criticize this quotation.

9–9.   Describe a situation in which a set of audit working papers might be used by third parties to support a charge of gross negligence against the auditors.

9–10. "I have finished my testing of footings of the cash journals," said the assistant auditor to the senior auditor. "Shall I state in the working papers the period for which I verified footings, or should I just list the totals of the receipts and disbursements I have proved to be correct?" Prepare an answer to the assistant's question, stressing the reasoning involved.

9–11. Do generally accepted auditing standards permit the auditors to utilize the services of the client's employees in the preparation of audit working papers? Explain.

9–12. Explain the meaning of the term "permanent file" as used in connection with audit working papers. What kinds of information are usually included in the permanent file?

9–13. To what extent, if at all, should the auditors rely upon statements or explanations by employees of the client in the preparation of the audit working papers? Explain.

9–14. Thomas Walsh, CA, found that his office was becoming crowded with files of audit working papers from completed audit engagements and considered the possibility of throwing away some of the papers. What uses to be made of audit working papers after the audit engagement has been completed should be considered by Walsh in reaching a decision on his problem?

9–15. List several rules to be observed in the preparation of working papers which will reflect current professional practice.

9–16. What advantages do grouping sheets offer in contrast to the working trial balance?

9–17. List the major types of audit working papers and give a brief explanation of each. For example, one type of audit working paper is an account analysis. This working paper shows the changes which occurred in a given account during the period under audit. By analyzing an account the auditors determine its nature and content.

GROUP II
QUESTIONS REQUIRING ANALYSIS

9–18. The partnership of Smith, Frank & Clark, a CA firm, has been the auditor of Greenleaf, Inc., for many years. During the annual examination of the financial statements for the year ended December 31, 1978, a dispute developed over whether certain disclosures should be made in the financial statements. The dispute resulted in Smith, Frank & Clark's being dismissed and Greenleaf's engaging another CA firm. Greenleaf demanded that Smith, Frank & Clark turn over all working papers applicable to the Greenleaf audits to it or face a lawsuit. Smith, Frank & Clark refused. Greenleaf has instituted a suit against Smith, Frank & Clark to obtain the working papers.

Required:

a. Will Greenleaf succeed in its suit? Explain.

b. Discuss the rationale underlying the rule of law applicable to the ownership of audit working papers. (AICPA, adapted)

9–19. "Working papers should contain facts and nothing but facts," said student A. "Not at all," replied student B. "The audit working papers may also include expressions of opinion. Facts are not always available to settle all issues." "In my opinion," said student C, "a mixture of facts and opinions in the audit working papers would be most confusing if the papers were produced as a means of supporting the auditors' position when their report has been challenged." Evaluate the issues underlying these arguments.

9–20. At twelve o'clock when the plant whistle sounded, George Green, an assistant auditor, had his desk completely covered with various types of working papers. Green stopped work immediately, but not wanting to leave the desk with such a disorderly appearance he took a few minutes to sort the papers into proper order, place them in a neat pile, and weight them down with a heavy ash tray. He then departed for lunch. The auditor-in-charge, who had been observing what was going on, was critical of the assistant's actions. What do you think was the basis for criticism by the auditor-in-charge?

9–21. An important part of every examination of financial statements is the preparation of audit working papers.

Required:

a. Discuss the relationship of audit working papers to each of the standards of field work.

b. You are instructing an inexperienced staff assistant on her first auditing assignment. She is to examine an account. An analysis of the account has been prepared by the client for inclusion in the audit working papers. Prepare a list of the comments, commentaries, and notations that the staff assistant should make or have made on the account analysis to provide an adequate working paper as evidence of her examination. (Do not include a description of auditing procedures applicable to the account.) (AICPA, adapted)

9–22. The preparation of working papers is an integral part of the auditors' examination of financial statements. On a recurring engagement the auditors review the working papers from their prior examination while planning the current examination to determine the papers' usefulness for the current engagement.

Required:

a. (1)   What are the purposes or functions of audit working papers?
   (2)   What records of the auditors may be included in audit working papers?
b.   What factors affect the auditors' judgment of the type and content of the working papers for a particular engagement?
c.   To comply with generally accepted auditing standards, the auditors include certain evidence in their working papers, for example, "evidence that the engagement was adequately planned and properly executed and work of assistants was properly supervised and reviewed." What other evidence should the auditors include in audit working papers to comply with generally accepted auditing standards? (AICPA, adapted)

9–23. You have been assigned by your CA firm to complete the examination of the 1978 financial statements of Hamilton Manufacturing Corporation Ltd. because the senior accountant and his inexperienced assistant, who began the engagement, were hospitalized as the result of an accident. The engagement is about one-half completed. Your audit report must be delivered in three weeks, as agreed when your firm accepted the engagement. You estimate that by utilizing the client's staff to the greatest possible extent consonant with independence you can complete the engagement in five weeks. Your firm cannot assign an assistant to you.

The working papers show the status of work on the examination as follows:

1.   *Completed*—Cash, property and equipment, depreciation, mortgage note payable, and shareholders' equity.
2.   *Completed except as noted later*—Inventories, accounts payable, compliance tests of purchase transactions and payrolls.
3.   *Nothing done*—Trade accounts receivable, inventory price testing, accrued expenses payable, unrecorded liability test, compliance tests of sales transactions, payroll deductions compliance tests and observation of payroll cheque distribution, analysis of other expenses, ratio and comparison analysis, vouching of December purchase transactions, audit report, internal control evaluation, internal control report, minutes, preparation of tax returns, subsequent events, and supervision and review.

Your review discloses that the assistant's working papers are incomplete and were not reviewed by the senior accountant. For example, the inventory working papers present incomplete notations, incomplete explanations, and no cross referencing.

Required:

a. What field work standards have been violated by the senior accountant who preceded you on this assignment? Explain why you feel the standards you list have been violated.

b. In planning your work to complete this engagement you should scan working papers and schedule certain work as soon as possible, and also identify work which may be postponed until after the audit report is rendered to the client.

    (1)   List the areas on which you should plan to work first, say in your first week of work, and for each item explain why it deserves early attention.

    (2)   State which work you believe could be postponed until after the audit report is rendered to the client, and give reasons why the work may be postponed. (AICPA, adapted)

9–24.   CA has been the auditor of N Ltd., a medium-sized manufacturing company, for just over two years. After CA billed the company for the first year audit, Mr. H, the president, called CA to his office to discuss the audit fee, expressing surprise and concern as to its size. CA pointed out that an audit fee for a first time audit is always higher than normal, and gave Mr. H several examples of the work he had to do that would not be required in subsequent years. CA reminded Mr. H that they had previously discussed this point in broad terms, and Mr. H accepted the explanation. CA suggested that the audit fee for subsequent years could be reduced if the staff of N Ltd. were to prepare some of the schedules for CA's working papers. Mr. H agreed with this suggestion. For the second year audit, N Ltd.'s staff prepared several of the schedules and CA was able to reduce his fee. However, Mr. H, on receiving the billing for the second year's audit fee, was still concerned as to its size. When discussing the results of the audit with CA, Mr. H expressed surprise as to the quantity of schedules that had to be prepared by his staff particularly considering the fact that CA and his staff prepared additional working papers themselves. He asked CA what were the purposes of audit working papers. Mr. H also expressed concern about all the information in the working papers on his company being in CA's files and asked who owned the working papers.

Required:

In point form explain:

a. The purposes of audit working papers (including the benefits to the client and the auditor).

b. The ownership of audit working papers. (CICA)

GROUP III
PROBLEMS

9–25.   Criticize the following working paper which you are reviewing as senior in charge of the November 30, 1978, audit of Pratt Company Limited.

Pratt Company Limited

Cash   E-2

Per bank		44,874.50 ✓
Deposit in transit		837.50 ✓
Bank charges		2.80
		45,714.80
Outstanding cheques:		
	46.40	
	10.00	
	30.00	
	1,013.60 ✓	
	1,200.00 ✓	
	10.00	
	25.00 ✓	
	15.00 ✓	
	50.00 ✓	
	1,002.00 ✓	3,402.00
Per ledger		42,312.80 ✓

✓ – Verified

R. G. H.
Dec. 2, 78

9–26.   One of the practical problems confronting the auditors is that of determining whether adjusting journal entries or other corrective actions are warranted by errors, omissions, and inconsistencies. The following items were noted by the auditors during their year-end examination of a small manufacturing partnership having net sales of approximately $1,600,-000; net income of approximately $20,000; total assets of nearly $2,000,-000; and total partners' capital of $300,000.

1. Proceeds of $250 from the sale of fully depreciated office equipment were credited to Miscellaneous Revenue rather than to Gain and Loss on Sale of Equipment, a ledger account which had not been used for several years.

2. The Trade Accounts Receivable control account showed a balance of $79,600. The individual accounts comprising this balance included three with credit balances of $320, $19, and $250, respectively.

3. Several debits and credits to general ledger accounts had been made directly without use of journal entries. The amounts involved did not exceed $500.

4. Credit memoranda were not serially numbered or signed, but a file of duplicates was maintained.

5. General journal entries did not include explanations for any but unusual transactions.

6. Posting references were occasionally omitted from entries in general ledger accounts.

7. An expenditure of $200 for automobile repairs was recorded as a December expense, although shown by the invoice to be a November charge.

8. The auditors' count of petty cash disclosed a shortage of $20.

9. Expenditures for advertising amounting to $8,000 were charged to the Advertising Expense account; other advertising expenses amounting to $3,000 had been charged to Miscellaneous Expense.

10. On a bank loan of $300,000, negotiated September 5, for a period of four months at an annual interest rate of 6 percent, the entire amount of interest had been deducted in advance. The client's accountant had charged the full amount of interest to expense. He stated that he did not consider an entry to defer a part of the expense to the following year to be warranted by the amount involved.

Required:

You are to state clearly the position which the auditors should take with respect to each of the above items during the course of an annual audit. If adjusting journal entries are necessary, include them in your solution.

9-27. The following audit working papers from an audit still in process are listed in alphabetical order. You are to rearrange them in logical order and assign an index reference to each.

1. Accounts Receivable Grouping Sheet.
2. Allowance for Uncollectible Accounts.
3. Analysis of Accumulated Depreciation.

4. Analysis of Share Capital.
5. Analysis of Cost of Goods Sold.
6. Analysis of Miscellaneous Expense.
7. Analysis of Repairs and Maintenance Expense.
8. Audit Plan.
9. Audit Program.
10. Automobiles.
11. Buildings.
12. Confirmation from National Bank.
13. Confirmations of Trade Accounts Receivable.
14. Copies of Minutes.
15. Count of Petty Cash.
16. Draft of Audit Report.
17. Federal Income Tax Payable.
18. Financial Statements Prepared by Client.
19. Internal Control Evaluation.
20. Internal Control Questionnaire.
21. Inventories Grouping Sheet.
22. Inventories—Tests of Pricing.
23. Land.
24. Letter of Representations from Client.
25. List of Shareholders.
26. Mortgage Note Payable.
27. Notes on Observation of Physical Inventory.
28. Notes Payable.
29. Prepaid Insurance.
30. Property Tax Expense.
31. Proposed Adjusting Journal Entries.
32. Reconciliation of Bank Account.
33. Reserve for Loss Contingencies.
34. Retained Earnings Analysis.
35. Summary of Administrative and General Expenses.
36. Summary of Property and Equipment.
37. Summary of Sales.
38. Summary of Selling Expenses.
39. Working Trial Balance.

GROUP IV
CASE STUDIES IN AUDITING

9–28.   BRYAN INSTRUMENT MANUFACTURING CO. LTD.
           Audit Working Papers and Legal Liability of Auditors
     During the examination of Bryan Instrument Manufacturing Co. Ltd.,
Dwight Bond, an assistant auditor, was assigned by the auditor-in-
charge to the verification of the trade accounts receivable. The receivables totaled more than $2 million, and included accounts with govern-
mental agencies, national mail-order houses, manufacturers, wholesalers,

and retailers. Bond had recently read a study of credit losses in this industry covering the past ten years; and as a preliminary step, he computed an allowance for uncollectible accounts by applying to the total accounts receivable a percentage mentioned in the ten-year study as the average rate of uncollectible account losses for the sales of the entire industry. Application of this percentage to the Bryan's receivables indicated an uncollectible account loss of $90,000; the allowance provided by the company's management was $25,000. The working paper showing the computation of the $90,000 estimate of uncollectible account losses was placed in the file of working papers by Bond.

After making this preliminary calculation, Bond undertook a careful study of the receivables; as a first step he obtained from the client a classification of the accounts by type of customer and by age. He made a careful analysis of individual accounts which appeared in any way doubtful, discussed all past-due accounts with the credit manager, and reviewed the company's prior history of uncollectible account losses. He then reviewed his findings with the auditor-in-charge who, after further investigation and discussion with the client management, took the position that the allowance for uncollectible accounts must be increased from $25,000 to $40,000 or an unqualified opinion could not be given. The client management was not convinced of the need for the increase but finally agreed to make the change.

While Bond was working on the accounts receivable, another staff assistant, Carla Roberts, was engaged in verification of inventory. Roberts overheard a stock clerk remark that the finished goods inventory was full of obsolete products that could never be sold. As a result of this chance remark, Roberts made tests of a number of items in the inventory, comparing the quantities on hand with the amount of recent sales. These tests indicated the quantities in inventory were reasonable and that the items were moving out to customers. Because of the technical nature of the instruments manufactured by the company. Roberts was not able to determine by observation whether the articles in stock were obsolete or unsalable for any other reason. She made a point of questioning officials of the company on the possibility of obsolescence in the inventory and was assured that no serious problem of obsolescence existed.

In preparing the working papers covering her investigation, Roberts included a separate memorandum quoting the remark she had overheard concerning the obsolescence of the inventory, and added a suggestion of her own that this question of obsolescence be given special attention in succeeding examinations. She prepared a detailed description of certain portions of the inventory and suggested that in the succeeding examination the auditors determine whether these specific units were still on hand. During the review of the working papers, the auditor-in-charge questioned Roberts at length about the tests for obsolescence. He interviewed the employee who had made the remark about the impossibility of disposing of the finished goods inventory; the employee denied having made any such statement. The auditor-in-charge then discussed the issue with client officials and came to the conclusion that the inventory was properly valued and readily salable. In completing his review of the working papers, the auditor-in-charge added the following comment to the memorandum prepared by Roberts: "Question of obsolescence investigated and passed, but we should give consideration to this issue in succeeding examinations."

After all adjustments recommended by the auditors had been made, the financial statements of the company indicated a considerably weaker financial position than in prior years. The president complained that the adjustments insisted on by the auditors made the company's position look so bad that it would be difficult to obtain private long-term financing for which he had been negotiating. An unqualified audit report was issued.

Two months later, Bryan Instrument Manufacturing Co. Ltd. became insolvent. Principal causes of the failure, according to the president, were unexpectedly large credit losses and inability to dispose of inventories which had become obsolete because of newly designed products being offered by competitors in recent years. The president acknowledged that the company had made sales to customers of questionable credit standing because of the need for disposing of inventories threatened by obsolescence. Creditors of the company attempted to recover their losses from the auditors, charging the CA firm with gross negligence and lack of independence in reviewing the valuation of the accounts receivable and inventory. Attention was directed to the working papers prepared by Bond and Roberts; it was charged that these papers showed the auditors had knowledge of the overvaluation of receivables and inventory but under pressure from the client had failed to disclose the facts.

Required:

a. Should the working paper showing the percentage calculation of a $90,000 allowance for uncollectible accounts have been prepared and retained? Explain. Comment on the industry rate of loss.

b. Should the working paper quoting the stock clerk's remark about obsolescence have been prepared and retained? Explain.

c. Did the auditor in charge handle his duties satisfactorily?

d. Do you think the working papers tended to support or injure the auditors' defense against the charges of the creditors? Explain.

e. Do you consider the creditors' charges to be well founded? Give reasons for your answer.

10

Examination of the general records; audit program design

In the early stages of an audit, the independent auditors must become familiar with many aspects of the client's business. For example, the auditors must become informed on the client's organization, financial structure, physical facilities, products, accounting policies, and control procedures. However, information about the internal activities of the client is not in itself sufficient. If this information is to be interpreted and evaluated in a proper perspective, the auditors must also understand the business environment in which the client operates. Provincial and federal laws and regulations, pending or threatened litigation, affiliations with other companies, and contracts with suppliers and customers are only a few of the factors in the business environment which may affect the client's internal activities. The auditors can gain considerable information about both the client's business environment and internal operations by examining the client's general records. The term *general records* is used to include the following categories:

1. Non-financial records.
   a. Articles of incorporation, certificate of incorporation, and by-laws.
   b. Partnership contract.
   c. Minutes of directors' and shareholders' meetings.
   d. Contracts with customers and suppliers.
   e. Contracts with officers and employees, including union agreements, stock option, profit-sharing, bonus, and pension plans.
   f. Governmental regulations directly affecting the enterprise.
   g. Correspondence files.

2. Financial records.
   a. Income tax returns of prior years.
   b. Financial statements and annual reports of prior years.
   c. Registration statements and periodic reports filed with the securities commission and other government agencies.
3. Accounting records.
   a. General ledger.
   b. General journal.

Examining these records should provide the auditors with a concise picture of the client's policies and plans. As the engagement progresses, this understanding will enable the auditors to determine whether the transactions reflected in the accounts were properly authorized and executed in accordance with the directives of management. If audit staff members are thoroughly familiar with the history and problems of the business, the duties and responsibilities of key officials, and the nature and quality of the accounting records and procedures, then they are prepared to carry out each phase of the audit with confidence and understanding. If they do not acquire this background information before beginning the work of analyzing transactions and substantiating account balances, they are almost certain to proceed in a mechanical and routine manner, unaware of the real significance of much of the evidence examined.

Articles of incorporation, certificate of incorporation, and by-laws

In the first audit of a client's financial statements, a senior auditor will obtain copies of the articles of incorporation (or letters patent, or memorandum of association), certificate of incorporation, and by-laws, reviewing them for such information as the exact name of the corporation, the date and place of incorporation, the authorized capital structure, and the number of directors authorized.

The articles of incorporation and the certificate of incorporation are the basic documents evidencing the existence of a corporate entity and are, therefore, the most appropriate source of information for the above-listed items. Accuracy is of paramount importance in compiling this information—even for the most minute points. The name of the corporation will appear prominently in the heading of the auditors' formal report, and there is no excuse for error in its statement. For example, "The Blank Manufacturing Company, Inc." must not be called "Blank Manufacturing Corporation" or "The Blank Manufacturing Company, Incorporated." In reorganizations the corporate name is sometimes changed in only the slightest degree, and care is required to avoid confusing the new corporate entity with its predecessor. Apart from any practical consequences, independent auditors, by virtue of their traditional reputation for accuracy and precision, cannot afford to allow minor irregularities as to names and dates to creep into their reports because such slips are sure to lessen the confidence and respect of clients. The articles of incorporation contain information on the corporate structure, powers, and restrictions conferred upon the company by the federal or provincial business corporation act. The by-laws, on the other hand, indicate the administrative organization, rules, and procedures adopted by the corporate shareholders. For example, the by-laws may stipulate the frequency of shareholders' meetings, the date and method for election of directors and selection of officers, and the powers and duties of directors and officers.

Copies of the corporate charter, the certificate of incorporation, and the by-laws will, as previously mentioned, be obtained during the first audit engagement with a client and will be preserved in the auditors' permanent file for convenient reference during repeat engagements. Although repetition of this original investigative work is to be avoided in subsequent audits, the auditors must be alert to recognize and review any amendments or additions to these documents. Copies of such revisions should be entered in the permanent file so that the usefulness of that record may be maintained.

Partnership contract

In the audit of a business organized as a partnership, the partnership contract should be examined in much the same manner as the articles and certificate of incorporation and by-laws of corporate clients. The partnership contract represents an agreement among partners on the rules to be followed in the operation of the enterprise. The information available in a copy of the partnership contract usually includes:

1. The name and address of the firm.
2. The names and addresses of the individual partners.
3. The amount, date, and nature of the investment made by each partner.
4. The profit-sharing ratio, partners' salaries, interest on partners' capital, and restrictions on withdrawals.
5. The duties, responsibilities, and authority of each partner.
6. The provision for insurance on lives of partners.
7. The provisions concerning liquidation of the firm and distribution of assets.

In repeat examinations the auditors must ascertain whether any modification of the partnership contract has been made and obtain copies of the modifications for the permanent file. If no change has occurred since the preceding audit, a notation to that effect should be made.

Corporate minutes book

The corporate minutes book is an official record of the actions taken at meetings of directors and shareholders. Typical of the actions taken at meetings of shareholders is the appointment of auditors, the extension of authority to management to issue or to reacquire securities, to acquire or dispose of subsidiaries or other important properties, and to adopt or modify pension or profit-sharing plans for officers and employees. Also, the shareholders may request the auditors to attend the shareholders meeting for the purpose of answering any questions that may arise concerning the operations or financial position of the business.

Minutes of the directors' meetings usually contain a record of authorizations for important transactions and contractual arrangements, such as the establishment of bank accounts, setting of officers' salaries, declaration of dividends, and formation of long-term agreements with vendors, customers, and lessors. In large corporations the board of directors often finds it necessary to work through committees appointed to deal with special phases of operations and bearing descriptive titles such as "Executive Committee" or "Investment Committee." Minutes of the meetings of such committees are, of course, just as essential to the auditors' investigation as are the minutes covering meetings of the entire board.

Procedure for review of minutes.   In the first audit of a client, it may be necessary to review minutes recorded in prior years. Copies of these minutes will be preserved in the permanent file; as succeeding annual audits are made, the file will be appropriately expanded.

The auditor-in-charge will obtain from the secretary or other corporate officer copies of all minutes, including those of board committees, directors, and shareholders, for both regular and special meetings. These copies should be certified by a corporate officer and should be compared with the official minutes book to an extent sufficient to establish their completeness and authenticity. The recent trend toward spreading audit work uniformly over the year is reflected in the practice of some public accounting firms which request their audit clients to forward copies of the minutes immediately after each meeting. Verification of these copies at year-end is an essential part of such practices.

In reviewing the minutes, the auditors will (1) note the date of the meeting and whether a quorum was present, and (2) underscore or otherwise highlight in the permanent file copies of the minutes such actions and decisions as, in their judgment, have a significant effect on the company's financial position or operations or should influence the conduct of the audit. Non-essential material can be scanned rapidly, and highlighting can be limited to issues which warrant investigation during the course of the audit. For this phase of the audit work, there is no substitute for breadth of experience and maturity of judgment; these factors make possible a sharp distinction between matters of real import to the audit and those which may safely be passed by.

Major decisions in the minutes, such as declaration of dividends or authorization for borrowing, usually result in actions which need to be recorded in the accounting records. As the audit progresses, the auditors should trace authorized events from the minutes into the accounting records and cross reference their copies of the minutes to the underlying account analyses. Similarly, events recorded in the accounting records which normally require authorization by directors should be traced and cross referenced to the auditors' copies of the minutes.

Relationship of corporate minutes to substantiation procedures.   The nature of the information to be highlighted in the minutes copies and the uses to be made of this information as the audit progresses can be made clear by a few examples. The following list shows several audit procedures and indicates for each such phase of the audit certain transactions which require authorization by the board of directors.

1. Substantiation of cash in bank.
    a. The opening and closing of corporate bank accounts are acts requiring authorization by the board of directors.
    b. The authority to sign cheques is delegated to specific officers by the board.
    c. The obtaining of loans from banks requires approval in advance by directors.
2. Substantiation of investments.
    a. Purchases, sales, and exchanges of securities should be authorized in advance by the board of directors or a committee thereof.
    b. Designation of two officers to have dual custody of securities is customarily made by the board.
    c. The location of securities, whether in the company's own safe, a bank safe-deposit box, or elsewhere, should conform to instructions by the board.
    d. Pledging of securities as a basis for obtaining credit or guaranteeing performance of a contract requires board approval.
3. Proof of liabilities.
    a. Authority for declaration of dividends rests exclusively with the board of directors.
    b. Liabilities for pending lawsuits, income tax disputes, accommodation endorsements, guarantees, and other loss contingencies should receive approval of directors when recorded in the accounting records.
    c. The assumption of long-term debt by issuance of bonds or mortgage notes should be supported by the approval of shareholders and should also be covered in the minutes of directors' meetings.

    d. Unusual purchase commitments and contracts for extensive future deliveries of raw materials are often referred to the board for approval.

This list does not purport to show all the various areas of an audit in which reference to authorizations by the board would be appropriate. On the contrary, it is safe to say that in virtually every area of an audit, the auditors may need to refer to actions by the board of directors.

The review of the minutes, including those for directors' and shareholders' meetings taking place subsequent to the balance sheet date but prior to completion of the audit field work, is a mandatory step. Corporate management generally is aware of the significance of this record in the auditors' investigation. In rare instances, however, the auditors may encounter reluctance on the part of management to make the minutes available for their review, or they may find that the minutes book has not been properly maintained. In these cases the auditors must make it clear that if they are to express an unqualified opinion concerning the financial statements, they must have unlimited access to all documents and records having any bearing on the integrity of the financial statements. Any other position taken by the auditors would be in violation of generally accepted auditing standards. If the minutes book has not been kept up to date, the auditors should explain to the client the importance of this record and urge that the missing data be promptly recorded. Lack of complete minutes warrants comment in the auditors' report to the client on internal control.

Contracts held or issued by client

Early in the audit engagement the auditors should obtain copies of the major contracts to which the client is a party. Information obtained from an analysis of contracts may be helpful in interpreting such accounts as Advances from Suppliers, Progress Payments under Government Contracts, and Stock Options. In addition to production contracts with governmental agencies and other companies, the auditors may review contracts with suppliers for future delivery of materials, royalty agreements for use of patents, union labour contracts, leases, pension plans, stock options, and bonus contracts with officers.

The terms of existing contracts are often material factors in the measurement of debt-paying ability and in the estimating of futures earnings. When examinations are being made in behalf of prospective investors, creditors, or purchases of a business, the nature of contracts with customers may outweigh all other considerations in determining a market value for the business.

The procedure for examination of contracts will depend upon the length and nature of the contract in question. A contract from the federal government to an aircraft manufacturer may be a sizable volume with hundreds of pages of exhibits and specifications. Such contracts are generally accompanied by large numbers of change orders issued at frequent intervals throughout the life of the contract. When contracts are extremely long and technical, the auditors may find it necessary to rely upon summaries prepared by the client's staff or legal counsel. Data obtained in this manner should, of course, be verified by comparison with the basic contract to an extent considered reasonable in the circumstances.

The auditors may at times require the assistance of engineers, attorneys, and other specialists in the interpretation of important contracts. Most contracts include such accounting concepts as net income or working capital, but unfortunately those who draft the contracts may not in all cases understand the true meaning of the accounting terminology they employ. Skill in analyzing and interpreting the financial aspects of contracts appears to be a qualification of increasing importance to independent auditors.

Among the items auditors should usually note in reviewing contracts are the names and addresses of parties, effective date and duration of the contract, schedule for performance, provisions for price redetermination (such as cost-of-living adjustments), settlement of disputes, cancellation clauses, and provisions requiring audit of records to determine amounts owed.

Government regulations

Although independent auditors are not licensed to give legal advice or to interpret federal or provincial laws, they must be familiar with laws and regulations that affect the client's financial statements. Auditors should consult with the client's legal counsel—and their own attorneys if necessary—when they believe a legal problem affects performance of the audit or requires disclosure in the financial statements.

Among the laws and regulations with which the auditors should be familiar are the following:

Federal and provincial business corporations acts. Laws governing the formation and operation of corporations vary between the federal and provincial acts, and also among the provincial acts. The auditor should obtain a copy of the act of each client's place of incorporation and become familiar with provisions of the act which affect such matters as legal or stated capital, par or no-par-value shares, dividend declarations, and treasury shares.

Provincial partnership acts. These acts govern the operations of partnerships in areas not covered by the partnership contract.

Provincial securities laws. Since securities legislation is substantially within provincial jurisdiction, the auditors should be familiar with the securities laws governing the issue and trading of their clients' securities as well as the disclosure requirements for their clients' financial statements.

Combines Investigation Act. This act is designed to promote competition and prescribes penalties for certain unfair business and trading practices such as price fixing, predatory pricing, discriminatory allowance, and misleading advertising about price.

Labour laws. The federal and provincial labour codes govern collective bargaining and other labour matters.

Unemployment Insurance, Canada Pension and Workmen's Compensation laws. These laws are relevant to auditors because they affect payroll deductions and contributions.

Special acts for specific industries. Clients in industries such as insurance, banking, air lines, railroads, public utilities, and broadcasting are governed by special acts of both the federal and provincial governments. Auditors with clients in these industries will need to be familiar with the special laws and regulations that directly affect operation of these companies.

"Temporary" controls. In addition to the seemingly permanent statutes listed above, various "temporary" regulations are occasionally imposed by government which affect the transactions subject to review by the auditors. Examples include controls over wages, prices, profits, and dividends. If violations are apparent, the auditors should inform both management and legal counsel of the client company and consider the possible existence of unrecorded liabilities in the form of fines or penalties.

Correspondence files

The general correspondence files of the client may contain much information of importance to the independent auditors, but it would be quite out of the question for them to plow through the great mass of general correspondence on file in search of pertinent letters. When the reading of corporate minutes, contract files, or other data indicates the existence of significant correspondence on matters of concern to the auditors they should request the client to provide them with copies of such letters. In addition, the audit staff will usually review the client's correspondence with banks and other lending institutions, attorneys, and governmental agencies. Correspondence may generally be accepted as authentic; but if reason for doubt exists, the auditors may wish to confirm the contents of letters directly with the responsible persons.

Income tax returns of prior years

A review of federal, provincial, and foreign income tax returns of prior years will aid the auditors in planning any tax services required by the terms of the engagement. The possibility of assessment of additional income taxes exists with respect to the returns of recent years not yet cleared by tax authorities. By reviewing tax returns and assessment notices, the auditors may become aware of any matters which pose a threat of additional assessments; they may also find a basis for filing a claim for a tax refund.

Other information which the auditors can obtain from reviewing the prior-year tax returns of a new client includes the accounting principles used by the client for uncollectible accounts, inventory valuation, and depreciation, as well as the compensation and share ownership of officers and the existence of affiliated organizations.

Financial statements and annual reports of prior years

Study of the financial statements and annual reports of prior years and of any available monthly or quarterly statements for the current year is a convenient way for the auditors to gain a general background knowledge of the financial history and problems of the business. If independent auditors have submitted audit reports in prior years, these documents may also be useful in drawing attention to matters requiring special consideration.

Reports to securities commissions and other government agencies

Registration statements and periodic reports filed by the client with the securities commissions and other government agencies contain valuable information for the auditors—especially in a first audit. Included in this information will be the client's capital structure, a summary of earnings for the past five years, identity of affiliated companies, descriptions of the business and property of the client, pending legal proceedings, names of directors and executive officers of the client and their remuneration, stock option plans, and principal shareholders of the client.

Review and testing of the accounting records

Soon after beginning the examination, the auditors should review and test the journals and general ledger as part of the study of the client's internal control. A review of these records will inform the auditors as to the client's accounting procedures, the accounting records in use, and the control procedures in effect. The compliance testing verifies the mechanical accuracy of the records and provides assurance that the journals and ledger are actually achieving their respective purposes of recording and classifying transaction data.

The quality of accounting records may vary widely from one engagement to the next. Many clients maintain records that are carefully designed, well maintained, and easy to comprehend. The journals and ledgers of such clients are generally up to date, in balance, and virtually free from mechanical error. When the auditors ascertain that a client's accounting records are highly reliable, the audit work necessary to substantiate account balances may justifiably be minimized. At the other extreme, the accounting records of some clients may be typified by unrecorded transactions, unsupported entries, and numerous mechanical errors. In these cases, the auditors may have to perform extensive audit work to substantiate account balances. On occasion, the accounting records may be so inadequate that the auditors must deny an opinion on the financial statements.

Extent of testing. If the client's accounting records and procedures are well designed and efficiently maintained, it is reasonable to devote less audit time to verifying the mechanical accuracy of the records than would be required in audits in which less satisfactory conditions prevail. The extent to which the auditors test the accounting records depends upon three factors: (1) the general appearance of the records; (2) the auditors' preliminary appraisal of the client's system of internal control, developed from the flowcharts, written description, or questionnaire; and (3) the frequency and relative importance of any errors discovered during the actual testing. The first of these factors, the general appearance of the records, deserves some explanation. High-quality accounting records have basic characteristics which are readily apparent: journal entries include adequate written explanations, general journal entries are reviewed and approved by an officer before posting, and the records are legible and properly cross referenced. When records do not possess these characteristics, the existence of errors is a virtual certainty.

Testing of the accounting records may be done on a judgmental basis, or the auditors may use statistical sampling techniques. Estimation sampling for attributes, discussed in Chapter 8, is a statistical sampling plan which may be used to estimate error occurrence rates within specified precision and levels of confidence.

The general ledger

The function of the general ledger is to accumulate and classify the transaction data posted from the journals. To ascertain that the ledger is being properly maintained, the auditors should conduct tests to determine that (1) account balances are mathematically correct, (2) all entries in the ledger were posted from journal entries, and (3) all journal entries were properly posted.

To test the mathematical accuracy of account balances, the auditors should verify the footings of some or all of the ledger accounts. The term "footings" is used among practicing accountants to designate column totals. "To foot," on the other hand, means to verify the total by adding the column.

For the second group of tests, the auditors must satisfy themselves that all entries in the general ledger were posted from authentic sources; that is, from entries in the journals. This procedure is important because the financial statements are drawn from the general ledger balances, and these balances conceivably could be falsified through the recording of unsupported debits or credits in the general ledger. The auditors can determine that entries in the ledger are properly supported by *tracing a sample of ledger entries back into the journals.* Ledger entries included in this sample are normally selected at random from entries made throughout the year. Of course, the auditors may test most or all of the entries in excess of some specified dollar amount.

Finally, to test the accuracy of the client's posting procedures, the auditors should *trace entries from the journals into the general and subsidiary ledgers.* The sample used for this test usually includes all entries made during several randomly selected periods of time. The auditors may also test journal entries which, for any reason, appear unusual.

Direction of testing. In the two preceding paragraphs, two similar tests are described. In one test, ledger entries are traced back to the journals; in the other, journal entries are traced forward into the ledgers. The direction of the tracing is crucial to the effectiveness of the tests. The reasoning behind the direction of the tracing becomes apparent when we consider the nature of the errors for which the auditors are testing.

In the first test, the auditors are testing for unsupported entries in the ledger. Tracing ledger entries back to the journals may reveal the absence of supporting journal entries. On the other hand, the non-existence of journal entries cannot be disclosed by tracing existing journal entries into the ledger.

In the second test, the auditors are testing for posting errors. If a journal entry was never posted, this omission can be detected only by tracing from the journal into the ledger. If certain items have been improperly omitted from ledger accounts, these missing amounts cannot be brought to light by tracing existing ledger entries back to their sources. Of course, some posting errors, such as transposition errors and posting to the wrong account, may be discovered by tracing in either direction.

Each of these two tests should be conducted in connection with testing the quality of the general ledger. However, each test is suited to disclosing different types of errors. In the design of audit procedures, careful consideration must be given to the nature of the errors which may exist. Otherwise, the audit procedures are likely to be ineffective and inconclusive.

Computer-based systems. A client utilizing electronic data processing may not maintain a traditional general ledger. Instead, an updated daily trial balance, showing beginning account balances, debit and credit transactions entries, and ending balances, is printed out by the computer. The auditors may test footings for selected daily trial balances; in addition, they should trace beginning account balances in the selected trial balances to the ending account balances of the previous day.

Errors disclosed by the test of the general ledger should be summarized on a separate working paper. Each error listed should be carefully investigated to determine its significance and probable cause. Although most errors are the result of clerical inaccuracy, the possibility of fraud as a motive must always be considered. In many cases the chief significance of an error lies in the directing of the auditors' attention to inadequate internal control.

The general journal

The general journal is an accounting record used to record all transactions for which special journals have not been provided. In its simplest form, the general journal has only a single pair of columns for the recording of debit and credit entries, but many variations from this basic design are encountered. A third column may be added to provide for entries to subsidiary ledgers, or various multicolumn forms may be used. The addition of a number of debit and credit columns is intended to facilitate the recording of transactions which occur so frequently as to make individual postings undesirable but are not sufficiently numerous to warrant the establishment of a special journal. Special journals are frequently used for recording routine business transactions. The review and testing of the special journals will be discussed in later chapters in conjunction with the audit of the related assets, liabilities, and underlying transactions.

Some companies maintain a system of "journal vouchers." These are serially numbered documents, each containing a single general journal entry, with full supporting details, and bearing the signature of the controller or other officer authorized to approve the entry. A general journal in traditional form may be prepared from the journal vouchers, or that series of documents may be utilized in lieu of a general journal. Companies having electronic data processing equipment generally keypunch journal vouchers to serve as one of the transaction sources for the daily print-out of the trial balance described in the preceding section.

The auditors should conduct tests of compliance to determine that entries in the general journal are based upon actual transactions, and that these transactions have been properly recorded. Suggested procedures for testing the general journal follow:

1. *Foot column totals of the journal.*

The testing of footings in the general journal follows the pattern previously described for verification of ledger balances. A representative period for testing is selected, and all journal columns falling within that period are footed. Errors disclosed should be summarized on a working paper and investigated, and appropriate disposition should be made. With respect to the multicolumn form of general journal, it is necessary to cross-foot (add horizontally) the column totals and prove the equality of debits and credits. Discrepancies between the total of the debit columns and the total of the credit columns indicate either faulty addition or errors in individual entries.

2. Vouch selected entries to original documents.

"To vouch" a journal entry means to examine the original papers and documents supporting the entry. The term *voucher* is used to describe any type of supporting documentary evidence. For example, a journal entry recording the trade-in of a machine would be vouched by comparing it with a purchase order, supplier's invoice, sales contract, receiving report, and paid cheque—the vouchers for this entry. The auditors might not consider it necessary to examine all these documents if the evidence first examined appeared to provide adequate support for the entry. All general journal entries selected for compliance testing should be vouched.

Entries in the general journal should include clear, informative explanations; unfortunately, deviations from this principle are frequently encountered. The auditors should determine whether (1) the explanation is in agreement with the supporting documentation and (2) the entry reflects the transaction properly in the light of generally accepted accounting principles.

The supporting evidence to be examined during the review of general journal entries may include purchase orders, invoices, receiving reports, sales contracts, correspondence, the minutes book, and partnership contract. Journal vouchers represent an internal control device; however, they should not be considered as original source documents supporting entries in the general journal. Verification of journal entries requires that the auditors refer to original invoices and other evidence previously described.

3. Scan the general journal for unusual entries.

The importance of certain types of transactions which are recorded in the general journal makes it desirable for the auditors to scan this record for the entire period under audit, in addition to vouching all entries selected for testing. The following list is illustrative of the type of significant transactions for which the auditors should look in this scanning process:

a. The write-off of assets, particularly notes and accounts receivable: Collections from customers abstracted by employees and not recorded in the accounts may be permanently concealed if the accounts in question are written off as uncollectible. Any general journal entries containing credits to accounts and loans receivable from officers and employees require full investigation to provide assurance that such transactions are proper and have been authorized.

b. Assumption of liabilities: Transactions which create liabilities are normally recorded in special journals. Common examples of such transactions are the purchase of merchandise, materials, or equipment, and the receipt of cash. General journal entries which bring liabilities into the record warrant close investigation to determine that they have received proper authorization and are adequately supported.

c. Any debits or credits to cash accounts, other than for bank charges and other bank reconciliation items: Most transactions affecting cash are recorded in special journals.

d. Creation of revenue: Transactions affecting operating revenue accounts are usually recorded in special journals. Operating revenue would be recorded in the general journal only if the underlying transaction were of an unusual nature or, for some reason, was being processed in a special manner. In either case, the auditors should verify the authenticity of the transaction and the propriety of the entry.

e. Unexplained or fragmentary transactions, the purposes and nature of which are not apparent from the journal entry: General journal entries with inadequate or unintelligible explanations suggest that the person making the entry did not understand the issues involved or was unwilling to state the facts clearly. Entries of this type, and entries which affect seemingly unrelated accounts, should be fully investigated.

f. Related party transactions: Transactions between the client and affiliated companies, directors, officers, and principal owners and their immediate families are not at arm's length and should be investigated to determine that the substance of the transactions has been fairly recorded. These transactions, as discussed in Chapter 7, should be reviewed by the auditors as to reasonableness of amounts, business purpose, and adequacy of disclosure.

ILLUSTRATIVE CASE. In a widely publicized management fraud in the United States, the financial statements of Equity Funding Corporation of America were inflated over a period of years by more than $120 million in fictitious assets and revenue. Although falsified journal entries were prepared to record fictitious transactions, there was frequently no documentation to support the journal entries. Large amounts of revenue were also recognized in journal entries that involved debits and credits to an illogical combination of accounts. Thorough investigation of unusual revenue-creating journal entries could have alerted the company's independent auditors to the fraud long before it reached mammoth proportions.

4. Determine that all general journal entries have received the approval of an officer.

An adequate system of internal control includes procedures for regular review and written approval of all general journal entries by the controller or other appropriate executive. The auditors should determine that such procedures have been consistently followed. In those cases in which a client official does not regularly review and approve journal entries, the auditor may deem it desirable to review the general journal with the controller and request an approval signature on each page. In such cases the internal control report to the client should include a suggestion that the client undertake regular review and approval of journal entries.

5. *Trace selected transactions to general and subsidiary ledgers.*

This procedure will usually be combined with the verification of postings to general ledger accounts. It is listed here for the purpose of emphasizing that a review of postings from the general journal should include the tracing of entries to subsidiary ledgers as well as to general ledger control accounts.

In tracing general journal entries to the ledgers, inspection of the posting reference is not sufficient; the entry should be traced directly into the account. The tracing of postings should be preceded by sufficient study of the client's chart of accounts to minimize the work required in locating accounts. In addition to tracing the posting of selected transactions, the auditors should ascertain that the column totals of a multicolumn general journal have been posted to the appropriate accounts.

Audit working papers for the examination of accounting records

Upon completing the review and testing of the accounting records, the auditors should prepare a working paper describing the records in use, the compliance tests and other audit procedures followed, the nature and significance of errors discovered, any suggestions for improving the accounting system, and the auditors' conclusion as to the overall quality of the accounting records. This working paper summarizes an important part of the auditors' study and evaluation of internal control, and may serve as a reference for determining appropriate modifications in the audit program. At the beginning of the next annual audit, a review of this working paper will enable the auditors to concentrate upon the most significant aspects of the accounting records.

AUDIT PROGRAM DESIGN

The pattern of work in most audits is organized in terms of balance sheet topics, such as cash, marketable securities, inventories, and plant and equipment. In part, this method of organizing the work may be a carry-over from the days when the auditors' objective was the verification of the balance sheet alone. Even though present-day auditors are very much concerned with the verification of the income statement, they still find the balance sheet approach to be an effective method of organizing the audit work.

Assets usually are subject to direct verification by such procedures as physical observation, inspection of bank records, and confirmation by outside parties. Liabilities usually can be verified by externally created documents, and by inspecting paid cheques subsequent to the payment date. By substantiating the changes in the asset and liability accounts, the auditors indirectly verify revenue and expenses.

To understand why the income statement amounts are not the focal point of the verification procedures, it is important to remember the nature of revenue and expense in double-entry accounting. The entry to recognize revenue or expense has two parts: first, the recognition of revenue or expense; and second, the corresponding change in an asset or liability account. Revenue and expenses have no tangible form; they exist only as entries in the client's accounting records, purporting to represent changes in owners' equity. Consequently, the best evidence supporting the existence of revenue or expense is usually the verifiable change in the related asset or liability account.

The verification of a major balance sheet item ordinarily will involve several closely related balance sheet and income statement accounts. For example, the verification of marketable securities is inseparably linked with accrued interest receivable, interest earned, dividend revenue, and gains and losses on sale of securities. All of these accounts can be substantiated conveniently at the same time by the same set of audit procedures.

Similarly, depreciation expense, accumulated depreciation, and gains and losses on disposal of plant assets will be verified in conjunction with plant and equipment. Sales revenue, uncollectible accounts expense, and the allowance for uncollectible accounts will be substantiated together with accounts receivable.

Basic objectives of audit programs for asset accounts

In Chapter 4, an *audit program* was defined as the detailed outline of the auditing work to be performed during an engagement. In the next five chapters, we will consider the audit work to be done on the major asset categories, beginning with cash and concluding with plant assets and intangible assets. A sample audit program will be presented for each asset category to provide a framework for our discussion. It is important to remember that the audit programs presented in the test are merely illustrations of *typical* audit procedures. In actual practice, audit programs must be tailored to each client's business environment and system of internal control. The audit procedures comprising audit programs may vary substantially from one engagement to the next.

Each of the audit programs for an asset account will include from 10 to 20 specific audit procedures. Although the procedures differ in each program, it is useful to realize that each audit program follows basically the same approach to verifying the balance sheet items and related income statement amounts. The audit program for every asset category includes procedures designed to accomplish the following *general objectives:*

I.   Study and evaluate internal control.
   A.   Prepare a written description of the client's system of internal control.
   B.   Conduct tests of compliance to determine:
      1.   The "flow" of transaction data through the system (transactions tests).
      2.   The effectiveness of significant accounting controls procedures (functional tests).
   C.   Evaluate the strength of internal control and modify the remaining audit procedures as necessary.
II.   Substantiate account balances (substantive tests).
   A.   Establish the *existence* and *ownership* of the assets.
   B.   Determine the appropriate *valuation* of the assets.
   C.   Establish a proper *cutoff* of transactions to be included in the period under audit.
   D.   Verify the *related income statement amounts.*
   E.   Determine the appropriate *financial statement presentation.*

In some cases, one of the above general objectives may be accomplished by a single audit procedure; in others, several procedures may be necessary to accomplish a single objective. However, these general objectives are *common to all audit programs for asset accounts.* Changes in these audit objectives, with respect to audit programs for liability and owners' equity accounts, will be discussed in later chapters.

Substantiation of account balances

The central purpose of the auditors' study and evaluation of internal control is to determine the nature, extent, and timing of the audit work necessary to substantiate account balances. In previous chapters considerable attention has been given to the study and evaluation of internal control; let us now discuss the objectives of the auditors' substantiation procedures.

Existence and ownership of assets

The first step in substantiating the balance of an asset account is to verify the existence and ownership of the asset. For assets such as cash on hand, marketable securities, and inventories, existence of the asset usually may be verified by physical inspection. When assets are in the custody of others, such as cash in banks and inventory on consignment, the appropriate audit procedure may be direct confirmation with the outside party. The existence of accounts receivable normally is verified by confirming with customers the amounts receivable. Verifying the existence of intangibles is more difficult; the auditors must gather evidence that costs have been incurred and that these costs represent future economic benefits.

On occasion, the same procedures which verify existence may also establish ownership of the assets. For example, confirming cash balances in bank accounts establishes the existence, ownership, and appropriate valuation of the cash. Similarly, inspecting marketable securities verifies both existence and ownership because the registered owner's name usually appears on the face of the security certificate.

With other assets, such as plant and equipment, physical inspection establishes existence *but not ownership.* Plant and equipment may be rented or leased rather than owned. To verify the client's ownership of plant assets, the auditors must inspect documentary evidence such as purchase documents, deeds, and property tax bills.

Valuation of assets

Most assets are valued at cost. Therefore, a common audit procedure is to vouch the acquisition cost of assets to paid cheques and other documentary evidence. If the acquisition cost is subject to depreciation or amortization, the auditors must evaluate the reasonableness of the cost allocation program and verify the computation of the remaining unallocated cost. Assets valued at lower of cost or market necessitate an investigation of current market prices as well as acquisition costs.

Establishing a proper cutoff

A problem inherent in the preparation of periodic financial statements is making a proper *cutoff* of transactions to be included in the period. The financial statements should reflect all transactions occurring through the end of the period and none which occur subsequently.[1] The term "cutoff" refers to the process of determining that transactions occurring near the balance sheet date are assigned to the proper accounting period.

Making a proper cutoff is complicated by the fact that invoices for many purchases and expenses of the current period may not arrive for

---

[1] As discussed in Chapter 7, certain subsequent events may require adjustment to the financial statements. However, the financial statements are adjusted to reflect only those subsequent events which provide additional information regarding conditions existing on or before the balance sheet date.

several days or even weeks after the end of the period. For practical purposes, the preparation of financial statements cannot be delayed until all invoices have been received. Small items, such as utility bills, may be recorded in the period of payment rather than being accrued; as long as this method is followed consistently, no material error in the financial statements will result. Large items for which invoices have not been received should be recorded at estimated amounts. Two or three weeks are usually required for the accounting staff of a large company to complete the process of closing the accounts and preparing the financial statements.

The impact of cutoff errors upon the financial statements varies with the nature of the error. For example, a cutoff error in recording acquisitions of plant assets affects the balance sheet, but probably does not affect the income statement since depreciation usually is not recorded on assets acquired within a few days of year-end. On the other hand, a cutoff error in recording shipments of merchandise to customers affects both inventory and the cost of sales. In order to improve their financial picture, some clients may "hold their records open" to include in the current year cash receipts and revenue from the first part of the next period.

To verify the client's cutoff of transactions, the auditors should review transactions recorded shortly before and after the balance sheet date to ascertain that these transactions are assigned to the proper period. When such documents as cheques, receiving reports, and shipping documents are serially numbered, noting the last serial number issued during the period will assist the auditors in determining that a proper cutoff has been made in recording transactions.

Related income statement amounts

Income statement amounts often can be verified conveniently in conjunction with the substantiation of the related asset account. For example, after notes receivable have been verified, the related interest revenue can be substantiated by mathematically computing the interest applicable to the notes. In other cases, income statement amounts are determined by the same audit procedures used in determining the valuation of the related asset. Determining the undepreciated cost of plant assets, for example, necessitates computing (or testing) the depreciation expense for the period. Similarly, determining the net valuation of accounts receivable involves estimating the uncollectible accounts expense.

Some income statement items, such as sales revenue, do not lend themselves to verification by such *direct* audit procedures. However, when the auditors establish that accounts receivable are legitimate assets, and have been properly recorded, they have substantial *indirect* evidence that sales on account also have been properly measured.

Financial statement presentation

The concept of fair financial statement presentation embodies more than correct dollar amounts; the financial statements must also include adequate disclosure to enable users of the statements to interpret the information properly. Even after all dollar amounts have been substantiated, the auditors must perform procedures to assure that the financial statement presentation conforms to the requirements of authoritative accounting pronouncements and the general principle of adequate disclosure. Procedures falling into this category include the review of subsequent events; search for related party transactions; investigation of loss contingencies; review of disclosure of such items as leases, compensating balances, pledged assets, and inventory profits; and review of the statement of changes in financial position.

KEY TERMS INTRODUCED OR EMPHASIZED IN CHAPTER 10

articles of incorporation That part of the application to the provincial or federal government for a corporate charter which includes detailed information concerning the financial structure and other details of the business.

by-laws Rules adopted by the shareholders at the inception of a corporation to serve as general guidelines in the conduct of the business.

certificate of incorporation An official document issued by the government which shows the date on which a corporation comes into existence.

cutoff The process of determining that transactions occurring near the balance sheet date are assigned to the proper accounting period.

journal voucher A serially numbered document describing the details of a single journal entry and bearing the signature of the officer who approved the entry.

minutes book A formal record of the issues discussed and actions taken in meetings of shareholders and of the board of directors.

substantive tests Tests of account balances and transactions designed to detect any material errors in the financial statements.

trace To follow data from one accounting record to another.

vouch To verify the accuracy and authenticity of entries in the accounting records by examining the original source documents supporting the entries.

GROUP I
REVIEW QUESTIONS

10–1. Since an audit is an examination of financial statements, why need auditors be concerned with records of a non-financial nature?

10–2. During the first audit of a corporate client, the auditors will probably obtain a copy of the by-laws and review them carefully.

Required:

    a. What are by-laws of a corporation?

    b. What provisions of the by-laws are of interest to the independent auditors? Explain.

10–3. State five significant provisions for which an auditor should particularly look in examining the articles of incorporation of a company and any amendments thereto. (AICPA)

10–4. In connection with an annual audit of a corporation engaged in manufacturing operations, the auditors have regularly reviewed the minutes of the meetings of shareholders and of the board of directors. Name ten important items that might be found in the minutes of the meetings held during the period under review which would be of interest and significance to the auditors. (AICPA)

10–5. What should be the scope of an auditor's review of the corporate minutes book during the first audit of a client? During a repeat engagement?

10–6. Identify several federal and provincial laws with which the independent auditor should be familiar.

10–7. Should the auditors make a complete review of all correspondence in the client's files? Explain.

10–8. What are the purposes of the audit procedures of (*a*) tracing a sample of journal entries forward into the ledgers and (*b*) tracing a sample of ledger entries back into the journals?

10–9. Should the CAs expect to find a traditional type of general ledger in the audit of a client utilizing electronic data processing equipment? Explain.

10–10. List three types of general journal entries for which the auditors would search in scanning the general journal for unusual entries, and explain why the journal entries you list are unusual.

10–11. Charles Halstead, CA, has a number of clients who desire audits at the end of the calendar year. In an effort to spread his work load more uniformly throughout the year, he is preparing a list of audit procedures which could be performed satisfactorily prior to the year-end balance sheet date. What work, if any, might be done on the general records in advance of the balance sheet date?

10–12. What is the nature of the working papers used by the auditors to summarize the audit work performed on the accounting records?

10–13. Why is audit work usually organized around balance sheet topics rather than income statement items?

10–14. Identify the basic objectives of the auditors' substantiation procedures with respect to any major asset category.

10–15. What is meant by making a proper year-end *cutoff?* Explain the effects of errors in the cutoff of sales transactions in both the income statement and the balance sheet.

GROUP II
QUESTIONS REQUIRING ANALYSIS

10–16.   In a recent court case, the presiding judge criticized the work of a senior in charge of an audit in approximately the following language: "As to minutes, the senior read only what the secretary (of the company) gave him, which consisted only of the board of directors' minutes. He did not read such minutes as there were of the executive committee of the board. He did not know that there was an executive committee, hence he did not discover that the treasurer had notes of executive committee minutes which had not been written up."

Required:

How can the independent auditors be certain the client has provided them with minutes of all meetings of the board and committees thereof? Explain.

10–17.   Bonnie Cogan, CA, is a senior auditor assigned to the first examination of the financial statements of Pioneer Mfg. Company, Inc., for the current year ended December 31. In scanning the client's general journal, Cogan noted the following entry dated June 30 of the current year:

Cost of Sales 186,453		
Raw Materials	84,916	
Work in Process	24,518	
Finished Goods	77,019	

To adjust perpetual inventories to amounts of physical inventory taken this date.

The client-prepared income statement shows net sales and net income of approximately $5,500,000 and $600,000, respectively.

Required:

Do you think Cogan should investigate the above entry? Explain fully.

10–18.   Fred Murray, an assistant auditor, was instructed to use a discovery sampling plan to search for entries in the client's ledger which were not supported by entries in the journals. Murray defined the population as all journal entries made during the year. A statistical table for that size population indicated that a sample size of 300 was necessary to provide 95 percent confidence of finding at least one exception if the occurrence rate was 1 percent or greater. In conducting his test, Murray traced 300 randomly selected journal entries into the ledger and found no exceptions. Based upon this test, may Murray conclude with 95 percent confidence that at least 99 percent of the entries in the ledger are supported by journal entries? Explain fully.

10–19.   The partnership of Wheat Brothers operated successfully for many years until the death of one of the brothers. The business was reorganized as a corporation at the beginning of the current year with John Wheat, the surviving brother, elected to serve as president of the new entity, Wheat Corporation Limited. Mr. Wheat was also the largest shareholder.

To permit a cash settlement with the estate of the deceased partner, the organization of the corporation involved obtaining outside capital. This was readily accomplished by sale of capital stock to local residents who were familiar with the success and reputation of the business conducted by Wheat Brothers.

Near the close of the first year of operation as a corporation, John Wheat, president of the company, retained you to perform a year-end audit. Prior to the balance sheet date, you requested the secretary of Wheat Corporation Limited to provide you with the minutes books covering all meetings of the shareholders, the board of directors, and any committees of the board. The secretary had held a responsible position in the company throughout its years of operations as a partnership, during which time the company had never been audited. He expressed some reluctance to making available information which he regarded as highly confidential, but finally he offered to provide you with a certified copy of all resolutions relating to accounting matters which had been passed by the shareholders, the board of directors, and committees of the board. The secretary explained that some non-accounting matters of a highly confidential nature had been discussed in some of the board meetings, and that he considered it unwise for this confidential information to be made available to anyone other than directors of the company.

The secretary also informed you that he had discussed your request for the minutes book with Mr. Wheat, and that the president had suggested that you might be elected to the board of directors at an upcoming meeting. After such election, all records of the board and its committees would automatically be available to you.

Required:

a. What is the most likely explanation of the secretary's response to your request?

b. How would you respond to the statements by the secretary? Explain fully.

10–20. Select the best answer for each of the following and give the reasons for your choice.

a. An auditor should examine the minutes of board of directors' meetings:

  (1) Through the date of the financial statements.

  (2) Through the date of the audit report.

  (3) On a test basis.

  (4) Only at the beginning of the audit.

b. Which of the following statements most appropriately summarizes the auditor's responsibility for reviewing the client's correspondence files?

  (1) The auditor should review all correspondence for items relevant to the audit.

     (2)   The auditor should not review any correspondence; to do so would waste time more productively spent on gathering other evidence.

     (3)   The auditor should apply statistical selection techniques to draw a random sample of correspondence for review.

     (4)   The auditor should review correspondence with banks, other lending institutions, attorneys, and governmental agencies.

c. As one step in testing sales transactions, a CA traces a random sample of sales journal entries to debits in the accounts receivable subsidiary ledger. This test provides evidence as to whether:

     (1)   Each recorded sale represents a bona fide transaction.

     (2)   All sales have been recorded in the sales journal.

     (3)   All debit entries in the accounts receivable subsidiary ledger are properly supported by sales journal entries.

     (4)   Recorded sales have been properly posted to customer accounts.

d. Which of the following is not a basic objective of the audit procedures applied to any major asset category?

     (1)   Verifying the appropriate valuation of the asset.

     (2)   Determining that transactions affecting the asset were recorded in the proper accounting period.

     (3)   Determining that the asset is fully insured against possible loss.

     (4)   Verifying related income statement amounts. (AICPA, adapted)

GROUP III
PROBLEMS

10–21. Precision Industries Ltd. is a manufacturer of electronic components. When a purchase order is received from a customer, a salesclerk prepares a serially numbered sales order and sends copies to the shipping and accounting departments. When the merchandise is shipped to the customer, the shipping department prepares a serially numbered shipping advice and sends a copy to the accounting department. Upon receipt of the appropriate documents, the accounting department records the sale in the accounting records. All shipments are *f.o.b. shipping point.*

Required:

a. How can the auditors determine whether Precision Industries Ltd. has made a proper year-end cutoff of sales transactions?

b. Assume all shipments for the first five days of the following year were recorded as occurring in the current year. If not corrected, what effect will this cutoff error have upon the financial statements for the current year?

10–22. Kenneth J. Bryan, secretary of Jensen Corporation Limited, a federally incorporated company, has given you the minutes of the meetings of the board of directors. Summarize, in good form for the audit working papers, those contents of the following minutes which you consider to be of significance in the conduct of an annual audit.

Meeting of February 15, 1979

The meeting was called to order at 2:15 P.M. by Mr. H. R. Jensen, chairman of the board. The following directors were present:

John J. Savage	Harold Bruce Smith
Helen R. King	Ruth Andrews
Lee McCormick	Dale H. Lindberg
H. R. Coleman	Ralph Barker
George Anderson	H. R. Jensen
	Kenneth J. Bryan

Absent was Director J. B. Adams, who was in Vancouver on company business in connection with the opening of a sales office.

The minutes of the preceding meeting, December 15, 1978, were read by the secretary and duly approved as read.

President John J. Savage outlined the current status of negotiations leading toward the acquisition of a new factory site in Halifax, Nova Scotia, and recommended to the board the purchase of said property at a price not to exceed $200,000.

Mrs. King offered the following resolution, which was seconded by Mr. Smith, and unanimously carried:

Resolved: That Mr. Savage hereby is authorized to acquire in behalf of the company the factory site located at Donaldson Avenue, Halifax, Nova Scotia, at a price not in excess of $200,000, to be paid for in cash from the general funds of the corporation.

Upon a motion by Mr. Savage, seconded by Mrs. King and carried unanimously, the secretary was instructed to arrange for the purchase from the estate of J. B. Williams, former director, 100 shares of the company's own stock at a price not in excess of $110 per share.

Mr. Savage, after discussing the progress of the company in recent months and its current financial condition, submitted the following resolution, which was seconded by Mr. Coleman and unanimously passed:

Resolved: That the following cash dividends are hereby declared, payable April 10, 1979, to shareholders of record on March 31, 1979.

a. The regular quarterly dividend of $1 per share of capital stock.

b. A special dividend of $0.50 per share of capital stock.

There being no further business brought before the meeting, the meeting was adjourned at 4:00 P.M.

Kenneth J. Bryan
Secretary

Meeting of March 15, 1979

The meeting was called to order at 2:15 P.M. by Mr. H. R. Jensen, chairman of the board. The following directors were present:

John J. Savage	Ruth Andrews
Helen R. King	Dale H. Lindberg
Lee McCormick	J. B. Adams
H. R. Coleman	H. R. Jensen
George Anderson	Kenneth J. Bryan
Harold Bruce Smith	

Absent was Director Ralph Barker.

The minutes of the preceding meeting, February 15, 1979, were read by the secretary and duly approved as read.

Chairman H. R. Jensen stated that nominations for the coming year were in order for the positions of president, vice president in charge of sales, vice president in charge of manufacturing, treasurer, controller, and secretary.

The following nominations were made by Mrs. King, and there being no further nominations the nominations were declared closed:

President .... John J. Savage
Vice President—sales .... Otis Widener
Vice president—manufacturing .... Henry Pendleton
Treasurer .... Ruth Andrews
Controller .... Roger Dunn
Secretary .... Kenneth J. Bryan

The above nominees were duly elected.

Mr. McCormick then offered the following resolution, which was seconded by Mr. Coleman and unanimously carried:

Resolved: That the salaries of all officers be continued for the next year at the same rates currently in effect. These rates are as follows:

John J. Savage—president $120,000
Otis Widener—vice president—sales 70,000
Henry Pendleton—vice president—manufacturing 50,000
Ruth Andrews—treasurer 50,000
Roger Dunn—controller 50,000
Kenneth J. Bryan—secretary 30,000

Mr. Bryan offered the following resolution, which was seconded by Mrs. Andrews and unanimously carried:

Resolved: That the company establish a bank account at the United National Bank, Halifax, Nova Scotia, to be subject to cheque by either John J. Savage or Ruth Andrews.

There being no further business to come before the meeting, the meeting was adjourned at 4:00 P.M.

Kenneth J. Bryan
Secretary

10–23. Treefarm Ltd. is a closely held wholesale nursery which has never been audited. The business has been owned and operated by the same family for over 20 years. All shareholders in the company are family members and also serve as directors and officers of the corporation.

You are the senior auditor-in-charge of the first audit of Treefarm Ltd. for the year ended December 31, 1978. In your testing of the beginning account balances and review of the general journal, you encounter the following entries.

General Journal

June 9, 70   Accumulated Depreciation—
                  Equipment 2,154.80
                  Accounts Payable—Ace Garage ..   2,154.80
              Ted, vice president of operations,
              had tractor rebuilt; repairs will ex-
              tend useful life.

May 19, 74   Sales Returns and Allowances 6,422.00
                  Accounts Receivable—Valley
                      Construction Co. 6,422.00
              Return of trees not used in West-
              ridge housing development. See
              Credit Memo. No. 732

Jan. 10, 75	Office Equipment	42,809.30	
	Notes Payable		42,809.30
	Agreed to pay ten-year annuity to Mary Jean in exchange for hand-carved clock. Recorded at present value of annuity payments.		
Dec. 31, 75	Depreciation—Greenhouses	4,132.00	
	Accumulated Depreciation— Greenhouses		4,132.00
	Final year's depreciation on green-houses scheduled for demolition in two months.		
Dec. 31, 77	Retained Earnings	38,528.37	
	Office Equipment		38,528.37
	Adjustment per journal Voucher No. 1795		
Aug. 24, 78	Allowance for Uncollectible Accounts	12,710.00	
	Notes Receivable		12,710.00
	Notes receivable from Allan will not be collected in recognition of his promotion to treasurer.		

Required:

Which of the entries in the Treefarm Ltd. general journal would you investigate as being **unusual?** Explain fully.

10–24. A normal procedure in the audit of a corporate client consists of a careful reading of the minutes of meetings of the board of directors. One of the CAs' objectives in reading the minutes is to determine whether the transactions recorded in the accounting records are in agreement with actions approved by the board of directors.

Required:

a. What is the reasoning underlying this objective of reconciling transactions in the corporate accounting records with actions approved by the board of directors? Describe fully how the CAs achieve the stated objective after they have read the minutes of directors' meetings.

b. Discuss the effect each of the following situations would have on specific audit steps in the CAs examination and on the auditors' opinion:

(1) The minutes book does not show approval for the sale of an important manufacturing division which was consummated during the year.

(2) Some details of a contract negotiated during the year with the labour union are different from the outline of the contract included in the minutes of the board of directors.

(3) The minutes of a meeting of directors held after the balance sheet date have not yet been written, but the corporation's

secretary shows the CAs notes from which the minutes are to be prepared when the secretary has time.

c. What corporate actions should be approved by shareholders and recorded in the minutes of the shareholders' meetings? (AICPA, adapted)

11

Cash

What are auditors looking for?

In audit work on cash (and other assets), auditors are on guard against
overstatement of asset values. Assume, for example, that the client's balance sheet shows "Cash . . . . . $250,000." There is little chance that the
client has more cash than shown; the real danger is that the actual cash
is less than $250,000. If a cash shortage exists, it may have been concealed
merely by the insertion of a fictitious cheque in the cash on hand at year-
end, or by the omission of an outstanding cheque from the year-end bank
reconciliation. In this case the amount of cash on hand and on deposit is
actually less than the $250,000 amount shown in the balance sheet.

Auditors must also be alert for any understatement of cash receipts
or overstatement of cash disbursements. Either of these misstatements
can conceal a theft of cash by reducing the balance in the Cash account
to the amount remaining after the theft.

The auditors' objectives in examination of cash

In the examination of cash, the principal audit objectives are (*a*) to
study and evaluate the internal controls over cash transactions, and (*b*)
to determine that cash is fairly presented in the client's financial statements.

After preparing a working paper description of internal controls relating to cash, auditors conduct compliance tests of individual cash transactions and the related accounting records and control procedures. The size

of the audit samples and the areas selected for testing are determined according to the relative quality of internal control over the various phases of cash receipts, cash disbursements, and cash forecasting. Compliance tests of cash transactions indicate the extent to which controls purportedly in use are actually functioning in practice. The results of this testing provide the auditors with a basis for evaluating the validity of recorded cash transactions, the soundness of the methods used in handling and recording cash, and the general credibility of the accounting records.

The second objective—that of determining the fairness with which cash is presented as part of the client's overall financial position—is relatively simple, because cash, unlike other assets, poses virtually no problems of valuation. To substantiate the amount of cash shown on the balance sheet, auditors will conduct such substantive tests as confirming amounts on deposit by direct communication with banks, and counting cash on hand. Other important procedures to achieve the objective of fair presentation of cash include a review of the year-end cutoff of cash receipts and payments, and consideration of the reasonableness of the year-end cash balance in relation to the company's needs and any available cash forecasts. Ascertaining the existence of any restrictions on certain cash balances (such as loan agreements calling for the maintenance of compensating balances) is also an essential step in determining the fairness of the balance sheet presentation of cash.

In this discussion of major audit objectives the detection of fraud has purposely been omitted. Regardless of whether the asset under consideration is cash, inventory, plant and equipment, or some other category, the detection of fraud is relevant to overall fairness of the client's financial statements only if such fraud is material in amount. If fraud is material and widespread, normal auditing practices should lead to its disclosure.

How much audit time for cash?

The factor of materiality applies to audit work on cash as well as to other sections of the examination. The counting of a small petty cash fund, which is inconsequential in relation to the company's overall financial position, makes little contribution to achievement of the auditors' basic objective of expressing an independent opinion on the financial statements. Nevertheless, auditors do devote a much larger proportion of the total audit hours to cash than is indicated by the relative amount of cash shown on the balance sheet. This emphasis on cash transactions occurs despite the fact that scarcely any valuation problem exists for cash, whereas considerable audit time is expended on valuation problems in the work on inventories and accounts receivable.

There are several reasons for the auditors' traditional emphasis on cash transactions. Liabilities, revenue, expenses, and most other assets "flow through" the Cash account; that is, these items either stem from or result in cash transactions. Thus, the examination of cash transactions assists the auditors in the substantiation of many other items in the financial statements. If the auditors' study and evaluation of internal control over cash transactions discloses significant weaknesses, it is often necessary to extend the scope of audit work on cash and any other accounts which may be involved.

Another reason contributing to extensive auditing of cash is that cash is the most liquid of assets and offers the greatest temptation for theft, embezzlement, and misappropriation. Relative risk is high for liquid assets, and auditors tend to respond to high-risk situations with more detailed investigation. In some audit engagements, the client may have specific reasons to suspect the existence of employee fraud and may ask the auditors to stress the examination of cash transactions. In small business enterprises, some clients still cling to the outmoded notion that failure on the part of the auditors to detect a defalcation, even a small one, is evidence of incompetence. Such reasoning shows a lack of understanding of the objectives of an audit; but as long as clients react this way, some auditors may feel compelled to do extensive work on cash merely to protect themselves. The long-run answer to this, of course, is to educate clients as to the real benefits to be gained from an audit.

On occasion auditors may encounter evidence of small-scale employee fraud. After determining that such fraud could *not* have a material effect upon the financial statements, the auditors should discuss the situation with the client before investigating the matter further. This discussion will serve to alert the client to the situation, protect the auditors from charges of incompetence, and avoid wasting audit time on matters that are not material with respect to the financial statements and which may better be pursued by client personnel.

Internal control over cash transactions

The finance department, under the direction of the treasurer, usually is responsible for most of the functions relating to cash handling. These functions include credit approval; handling and depositing cash receipts; signing cheques; investing idle cash; and custody of cash, marketable securities, and other negotiable assets. In addition, the finance department participates actively in the process of forecasting cash requirements and makes both short-term and long-term financing arrangements.

Ideally, the functions of the finance department and the accounting department should be integrated in a manner which provides assurance that:

1. All cash which should have been received *was* in fact received and recorded promptly and accurately.
2. Cash disbursements have been made only for authorized purposes and have been properly recorded.

3. Cash on hand and in bank is accurately stated and subject to appropriate safeguards.
4. Cash balances are maintained at adequate but not excessive levels by forecasting expected cash receipts and payments related to normal operations. The need for obtaining loans or for investing excess cash is thus made known on a timely basis.

Independent auditors are often able to suggest changes in operating procedures which will strengthen controls over cash receipts and disbursements without imposing additional operating costs. Although a detailed study of the operating routines of the individual client is a necessary prelude to the development of the most efficient control procedures, there are some general guidelines useful to auditors in appraising the cash-handling practices of all types of business. These universal rules for achieving internal control over cash may be summarized as follows:

1. Do not permit any one employee to handle a transaction from beginning to end.
2. Separate cash handling from record keeping.
3. Centralize receiving of cash as much as possible.
4. Record cash receipts immediately.
5. Encourage customers to obtain receipts and observe cash register totals.
6. Deposit each day's cash receipts intact.
7. Make all disbursements by cheque, with the exception of expenditures from petty cash.
8. Have bank reconciliations performed by employees not responsible for the issuance of cheques or custody of cash.

Several good reasons exist for the rule that each day's cash receipts should be deposited intact. Daily deposits mean that less cash will be on hand to invite "borrowing"; moreover, the deposit of each day's receipts as a unit tends to prevent the substituting of later cash receipts to cover a shortage. If company policy permits the paying of expenses out of cash receipts, fictitious disbursements and overstatement of actual payments are much more easily concealed than when liabilities are paid by cheque after proper verification. Any delay in depositing cheques increases the risk that the cheques will be uncollectible. Furthermore, undeposited receipts represent idle cash, which is not a revenue-producing asset.

Internal control over cash sales

Control over cash sales is strongest when two or more employees (usually a salesclerk and a cashier) participate in each transaction with a customer. Restaurants and cafeterias often use a centrally located cashier who receives cash from the customer along with a sales ticket prepared by another employee. Theatres generally have a cashier selling prenumbered tickets which are collected by a doorman when the customer is admitted. If these tickets are serially numbered and all numbers accounted for, this separation of responsibility for the transaction is an effective means of preventing fraud.

Control features of cash registers. In many retail establishments the nature of the business is such that one employee must make over-the-counter sales, deliver the merchandise, receive cash, and record the transaction. In this situation, dishonesty may be discouraged by proper use of cash registers and form-writing machines with locked-in copies. The protective features of cash registers include (*a*) visual display of the amount of the sale in full view of the customer, (*b*) a printed receipt which the customer is urged to take with the merchandise, and (*c*) accumulation of a locked-in total of the day's sales. At the end of the day, the salesperson counts the cash in the drawer and turns in this amount without knowing the total sales recorded on the register. A supervisor inserts a key in the cash register, which permits a reading of the total sales for the day to be taken. Overages and shortages will inevitably occur from time to time, but a careful record of cash turned in and sales recorded by each salesperson will quickly disclose any unreasonable variations.

Electronic point-of-sale (POS) systems. Many retail stores use various types of electronic cash registers, including on-line computer terminals. With some of these registers, a "wand" or an electronic scanner is used to read the sales price and other data from specially prepared price tags. The salesperson need only pass the wand over the price tags (or merchandise over the scanner) and the register will automatically record the sale at the appropriate price. Thus, the risk of a salesperson recording sales at erroneous prices is substantially reduced. Besides providing strong control over cash sales, electronic registers often may be programmed to perform numerous other control functions. For example, online registers may verify the credit status of charge account customers, update accounts receivable and perpetual inventory records, and provide special printouts accumulating sales data by product line, salesperson, department, and type of sale.

Control features of form-writing machines. Many businesses making sales over the counter find that internal control is strengthened by use of a machine containing triplicate sales tickets. As each sales ticket is written, two copies are ejected by the machine and a third copy is retained in a locked compartment. The retention of the third copy which is not available to the salesclerk tends to prevent a dishonest employee from reducing the store's copy of the sales ticket to an amount less than that shown on the customer's copy.

Internal control over collections from customers

In many manufacturing and wholesale businesses, cash receipts consist principally of cheques received through the mail. This situation poses little threat of defalcation unless one employee is permitted to receive and deposit these cheques and also to record the credits to the customers' accounts. A typical system of internal control over cash received through the mail is described in the following paragraphs. Controls actually in use, of course, will vary from one client to the next.

Incoming mail usually is opened in the mailroom, where an employee prepares a *control listing* of the incoming cash receipts. This listing shows the amount received from each customer and identifies the customer by name or account number. Copies of the control listing are forwarded to the controller and to the employee responsible for the customers' accounts; cash receipts and customers' remittance advices are forwarded to the cashier.

What controls prevent the mailroom employee from abstracting the receipts from several customers, destroying the remittance advices, and omitting these receipts from the control listing? First, incoming cash receipts consist primarily of cheques made payable to the company. Second, if customers' accounts are not credited for payments made, the customers will complain to the company. If these customers can produce paid cheques supporting their claims of payment, and these cheques do not appear on the mailroom control listings, responsibility for the abstraction is quickly focused upon the mailroom employee.

Using the cheques and customers' remittance advices, the cashier records the cash received in the cash receipts journal and deposits the day's receipts intact in the bank. Control is exercised over the cashier by periodic reconciliation of the controller's copies of the mailroom control listings with the cash receipts journal and the detail of daily bank deposits.

After recording the cash receipts, the cashier forwards the remittance advices to the employee responsible for the customers' accounts ledger. This employee reconciles the remittance advices to his copy and of the control listing and, when satisfied that all remittance advices are accounted for, posts credits to the customers' accounts. Strong internal control requires that the accounts receivable clerk have no access to the cash receipts, and that the customers' accounts be periodically reconciled with the general ledger. When the nature of operations permits, different employees should be assigned responsibility for (a) preparation of sales invoices, (b) maintenance of customers' accounts, (c) reconciling customers' ledgers with controlling accounts, (d) initial listing of cash receipts, (e) custody and depositing of cash receipts, and (f) collection activity on past-due accounts.

The division of responsibilities, sequence of procedures, and internal controls over cash sales and collections from customers are illustrated in the systems flowchart in Figure 11–1.

"Lockbox" control over cash receipts. Businesses receiving a large volume of cash through the mail may use a "lockbox" system to strengthen internal control and hasten the depositing of cash receipts. The lockbox is actually a post office box controlled by the company's bank. The bank picks up mail at the post office box several times a day, credits the company's chequeing account for cash received, and sends the remittance advices to the company. Internal control is strengthened by the fact that the bank has no access to the company's accounting records.

Internal control over cash disbursements

The dangers inherent in making disbursements out of cash receipts have already been discussed. To state the issue in positive terms, all disbursements should be made by cheque, except for payment of minor items from petty cash funds. Although the issuance of cheques is somewhat more costly than making payments in cash, the advantages gained by use of cheques usually justify the expense involved. A principal advantage is the obtaining of a receipt from the payee in the form of an endorsement on the cheque. Other advantages include (*a*) the centralization of disbursement authority in the hands of a few designated officials —the only persons authorized to sign cheques, (*b*) a permanent record of disbursements, and (*c*) a reduction in the amount of cash kept on hand.

To secure in full the internal control benefits implicit in the use of cheques, it is essential that all cheques be prenumbered and all numbers in the series accounted for. Unissued prenumbered cheques should be adequately safeguarded against theft or misuse. Voided cheques should be defaced to eliminate any possibility of further use and filed in the regular sequence of paid cheques. Dollar amounts should be printed on all cheques by the computer or cheque-protecting machine. This practice prevents anyone from altering a cheque by raising its amount.

Officials authorized to sign cheques should review the documents supporting the payment and perforate these documents at the time of signing the cheque to prevent them from being submitted a second time. The official signing cheques should maintain control of the cheques until they are placed in the mail. Typically the cheque comes to the official complete except for signature. It is imperative that the signed cheques not be returned to the custody of the employee who prepared them for signature.

Most companies issuing a large volume of cheques use cheque-signing machines. These machines print the authorized signature, usually that of the treasurer, on each cheque by means of a facsimile signature plate. An item count of cheques signed is provided by the machine, and a key is required to retrieve the signed cheques. The facsimile signature plate

FIGURE 11–1

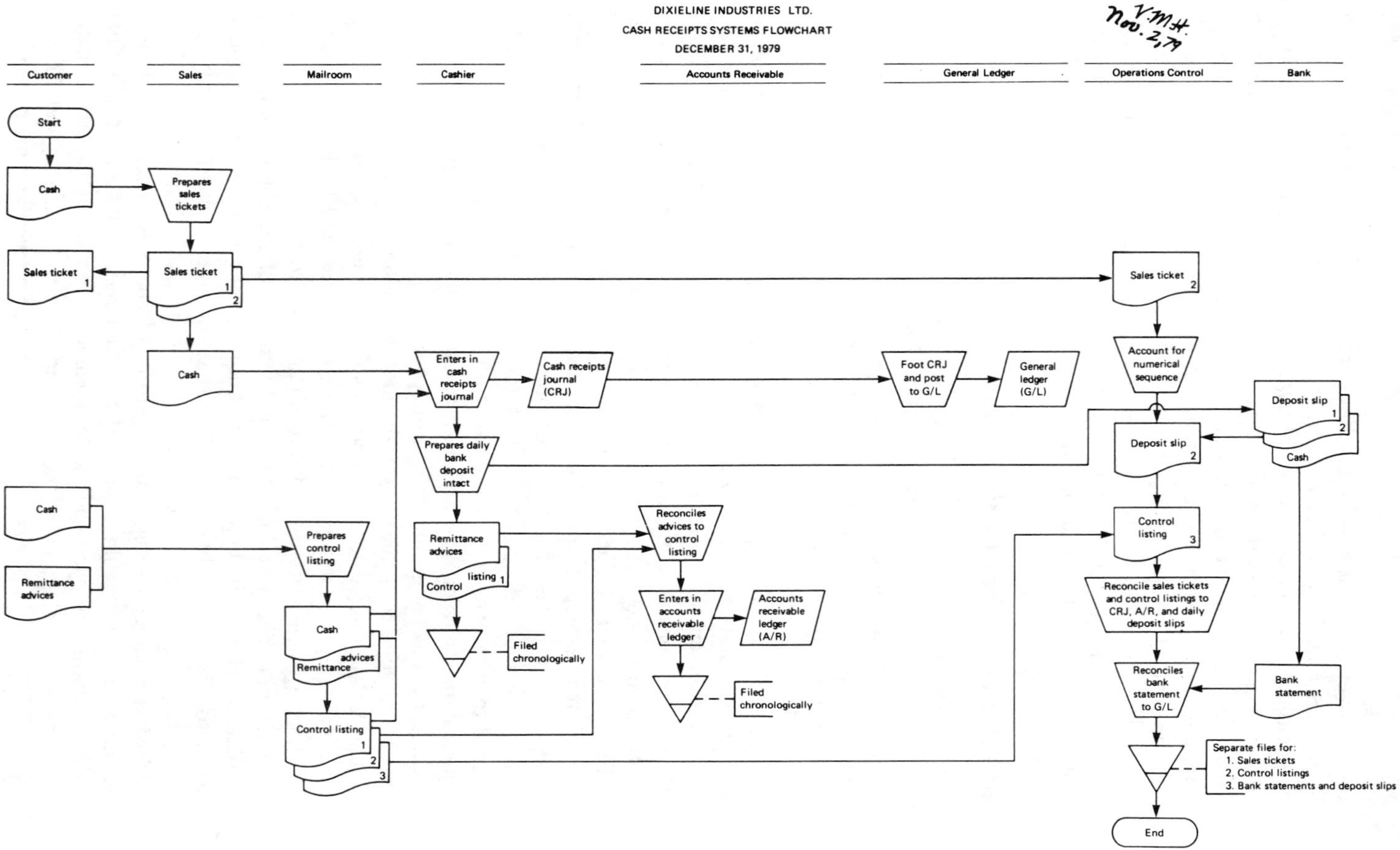
DIXIELINE INDUSTRIES LTD.
CASH RECEIPTS SYSTEMS FLOWCHART
DECEMBER 31, 1979
V.M.H.
Nov. 2, 79
Customer
Sales
Mailroom
Cashier
Accounts Receivable
General Ledger
Operations Control
Bank
Start
Cash
Prepares sales tickets
Sales ticket 1
Sales ticket 1 2
Sales ticket 2
Cash
Enters in cash receipts journal
Cash receipts journal (CRJ)
Foot CRJ and post to G/L
General ledger (G/L)
Account for numerical sequence
Deposit slip 1 2
Cash
Deposit slip 2
Prepares daily bank deposit intact
Cash
Remittance advices
Prepares control listing
Remittance advices
Control listing 1
Reconciles advices to control listing
Control listing 3
Cash
Remittance advices
Enters in accounts receivable ledger
Accounts receivable ledger (A/R)
Reconcile sales tickets and control listings to CRJ, A/R, and daily deposit slips
Filed chronologically
Filed chronologically
Reconciles bank statement to G/L
Bank statement
Control listing 1 2 3
Separate files for:
1. Sales tickets
2. Control listings
3. Bank statements and deposit slips
End

should be removed from the machine and safeguarded when the machine is not in use.

Reconciliation of monthly bank statements is essential to adequate internal control over cash receipts and disbursements. Bank statements should be reconciled by an employee having no part in authorizing or accounting for cash transactions, or in handling cash. Statements from the bank should come unopened to this employee.

ILLUSTRATIVE CASE. One large construction company ignored basic controls over cash disbursements. Unissued cheques were stored in an unlocked supply closet, along with styrofoam coffee cups. The company cheque-signing machine deposited signed cheques into a box which was equipped with a lock. Despite warnings from their independent auditors, company officials found it "too inconvenient" to keep the box locked or to pay attention to the cheque-counter built into the machine. The company maintained very large bank balances and did not bother to reconcile bank statements promptly.

A three-week-old bank statement and a group of paid cheques were given to an employee with instructions to prepare a bank reconciliation. The employee noticed that the group of paid cheques accompanying the bank statement was not complete. No paid cheques could be found to support over $700,000 in charges on the bank statement. Further investigation revealed that more than $1 million in unauthorized and unrecorded cheques had been paid from various company bank accounts. The cheques had been issued out-of-sequence and had been signed by the company cheque-signing machine. The company was unable to determine who was responsible for the theft, and the money was never recovered.

Control features of a voucher system. A voucher system is one method of achieving strong internal control over cash disbursements by providing assurance that all disbursements are properly authorized and reviewed before a cheque is issued. In a typical voucher system, the accounting department is responsible for assembling the appropriate documentation to support every cash disbursement. For example, before authorizing payment for merchandise purchased, the accounting department would assemble and determine agreement among copies of the purchase order, receiving report, and vendor's invoice. After determining that the transaction is properly supported, an accounting clerk prepares a voucher and cheque. However, this clerk *is not* authorized to sign the cheque. The voucher (including cheque and supporting documents) is filed in a "tickler" file according to the date upon which payment will be made.

A voucher, in this usage, is an authorization sheet which provides space for the initial of the employees performing various authorization functions. The cheque and supporting documents also are considered part of the voucher. Authorization functions include such procedures as extending and footing the vendor's invoice; determining the agreement of the invoice, purchase order, and receiving report; and recording the transaction in the accounts. Transactions are recorded in a *voucher register* by an entry debiting the appropriate asset, liability, or expense accounts, and crediting Vouchers Payable.

FIGURE 11–2
Flowchart of a voucher system

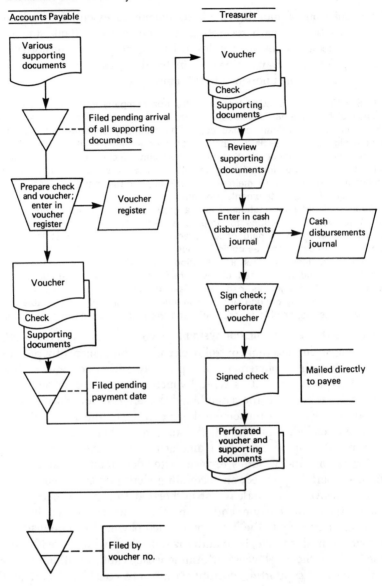

On the payment date, the voucher (including cheque and supporting documents) is removed from the tickler file and forwarded to the finance department. The treasurer reviews the voucher before signing the cheque; the cheque is then mailed directly to the payee, and the voucher and all supporting documents are perforated to prevent reuse. The cancelled vouchers are returned to the accounting department, where an entry is made to record the cash disbursement (a debit to Vouchers Payable and a credit to Cash). Paid vouchers usually are filed by voucher number in a paid voucher file.

Strong internal control is inherent in this system because every disbursement is authorized and reviewed before a cheque is used. Also, neither the accounting department nor the finance department is in a position to disburse cash without a review of the transaction by the other department. The operation of a voucher system is illustrated in the flowchart in Figure 11–2.

Internal control aspects of petty cash funds

An *imprest* system for petty cash requires that the cheques issued periodically to replenish the fund agree with the amount of disbursements from the fund. Consequently, an imprest petty cash fund remains at a fixed balance.

Payment of minor items can more conveniently be made in cash from an imprest fund than by going through the formal verification procedures required for issuance of a cheque. Internal control over payments from an imprest petty cash fund is achieved at the time the fund is replenished to its fixed balance, rather than at the time of handing out small amounts of cash. When the custodian of a petty cash fund requests replenishment of the fund, the documents supporting each disbursement should be reviewed for completeness and authenticity, and perforated to prevent reuse. Since the types and amounts of disbursements to be made from the fund are usually specifically limited, the opportunities for fraud of significant amount are not great.

Petty cash funds are sometimes kept in the form of separate bank accounts. The bank should be instructed in writing not to accept for deposit in such an account any cheques payable to the company. The deposits will be limited to cheques to replenish the fund and drawn payable to the bank or to the custodian of the fund. The prohibition against deposit of cheques payable to the company is designed to prevent the routing of cash receipts into petty cash, since this would violate the basic assumption of limited disbursements and review at time of replenishing the fund.

The petty cash fund should always be replenished at the end of the fiscal year so that expenses will be reflected in the proper accounting period. If the independent auditors find that the fund was not replenished at year-end, they may draft an adjusting entry for the unrecorded expenditures or they may decide against proposing an adjustment on the grounds that the amounts involved are not material.

Internal control over branch offices. Companies operating branch offices in which the branch managers are not subject to direct supervision must give particular attention to the maintenance of strong internal control. One protective device is to establish a "one-way" bank account into which each day's cash receipts are deposited intact by the branch manager. However, the branch manager is not authorized to write cheques on this account; only the home office can make withdrawals, and the bank is instructed to send bank statements and paid cheques directly to the home office. The home office makes frequent transfers from this bank account into its general account so that the balance of the branch account is kept quite low.

Even better control over branch receipts is achieved by the lockbox system in which customers of the branch mail remittances to a post office box controlled by the bank. The bank records and processes the remittances, and reports collections periodically to the home office.

A separate bank account operated on an imprest basis may be maintained by the branch for its disbursements. As this account becomes depleted, the branch manager sends a list of the disbursements to the home office with a request for replenishment. The home office, and not the branch manager, is authorized to make deposits in this account. The bank statements and paid cheques are sent to the home office for reconciliation. A variation of this procedure for controlling disbursements requires the branch manager to prepare each cheque in duplicate, with the carbon copy going immediately to the home office. The cheques are serially numbered, and all numbers in the series are accounted for by the home office.

This complete separation of cash receipts and disbursements at the branch, coupled with the prompt deposit of receipts, daily reporting of transactions, and use of an imprest fund for disbursements, leaves little opportunity for fraudulent handling of cash or for accidental errors. It also tends to conserve working capital by holding to a minimum the amount of idle cash held at branch locations. Other internal control practices relating to branch operation include daily reporting of key operating figures, continuous compilation of ratios and percentages, which will indicate any variation from forecast performance, and surprise counts of branch inventories by home office personnel.

Internal control and the computer

Processing cash transactions by computer can contribute substantially to strong internal control over cash. As previously discussed, control over cash sales may be strengthened by the use of online register terminals. Remittance advices or mailroom listings of customers' payments can be keypunched for processing by computer. Many companies use computers to issue cheques and, subsequently, to prepare bank reconciliations. The daily computer processing of cash receipts and cheques can provide management with a continually up-to-date cash receipts journal, cheque register, customers' accounts ledger, and cash balance. In addition to this, the computer can prepare reliable bank reconciliations even when thousands of cheques are outstanding, and can provide current information for cash planning and forecasting.

Audit working papers for cash

Auditors' working papers for cash should include a flowchart, a written description, and/or questionnaire describing the client's system of internal control for cash, working papers evidencing compliance tests of cash transactions, and an evaluation of internal control for cash. Additional cash working papers include a grouping sheet, cash counts, bank confirmations, confirmations of compensating balances, bank reconciliations, outstanding cheque lists, lists of cheques investigated, the auditors' written conclusions regarding the strength of internal control, recommendations to the client for improving internal control, and notes on a proper presentation of cash in the client's balance sheet.

AUDIT PROGRAM FOR CASH

The following audit program indicates the general pattern of work performed by the auditors in the verification of cash. Selection of the most appropriate procedures for a particular audit will be guided, of course, by the nature of the internal controls in force and by other circumstances of the engagement.

A.   Study and evaluation of internal control for cash

1.   Prepare a description of the internal control for cash.
2.   Trace a sample of each major type of cash transaction through the system.
3.   Prove footings of cash journals and trace postings to ledger accounts.
4.   Compare detail of cash receipts listings to cash receipts journal, accounts receivable postings, and authenticated deposit slips.
5.   Reconcile bank activity for one or more months with cash activity per the accounting records.
6.   Verify cash transactions in one or more selected expense accounts.
7.   Investigate any cheques payable to cash or to bearer.

8. Investigate any cheques representing large or unusual payments to related parties.
9. Evaluate internal control for cash.

B. Substantive tests of cash transactions and balances

10. Send confirmation letters to banks to verify amounts on deposit.
11. Count and list cash on hand.
12. Obtain or prepare reconciliations of bank accounts as of the balance sheet date.
    - a. Investigate N.S.F. cheques and other items charged back by bank.
    - b. Investigate any cheques outstanding for more than 30 days.
13. Verify the client's cutoff of cash receipts and cash disbursements.
14. Obtain a cutoff bank statement containing transactions of at least seven business days subsequent to balance sheet date.
15. Trace all bank transfers for last week of audit year and first week of following year.
16. Determine proper balance sheet presentation of cash.

A. Study and evaluation:

1. Prepare a description of the internal control for cash.

In the audit of a small business, auditors may prepare a written description of controls in force, based upon the questioning of owners and employees and upon first-hand observation. For larger companies, a flowchart or internal control questionnaire is usually employed to describe the system of internal control. An internal control questionnaire for cash receipts was illustrated in Chapter 5. Among the questions included in a questionnaire for cash disbursements are whether all disbursements (excepting those from petty cash) are made by prenumbered cheques and whether voided cheques are mutilated, preserved, and filed. The existence of these controls permits the auditors to determine that all disbursements have been recorded by accounting for the sequence of cheques issued or voided during the period.

Also, the questionnaire should determine the presence of such controls as cheque-signing authority being restricted to executives not having access to accounting records; vouchers and supporting documents being presented with cheques submitted for signature, these documents being stamped or perforated to prevent a second presentation; and cheques being mailed directly to the payee after being signed. Other sections of the internal control questionnaire, flowchart, or written description for cash cover cash disbursements for payroll and dividends, and bank reconciliation procedures. All questions on the internal control questionnaire are designed to require affirmative answers when satisfactory controls exist.

2. Trace a sample of each major type of cash transaction through the system.

One objective of compliance testing is to determine that the auditors' written description of internal control accurately describes the system in use. This objective is usually accomplished by following a small sample of each major type of transaction through the sequence of processing procedures applied by the client. For example, major types of cash receipts transactions may include cash received through the mail and cash sales. To test the handling of cash received through the mail, the auditors select a sample of mailroom control listings and trace the detail of specific cash receipts into the cash receipts journal, customers' accounts, filed remittance advices, and authenticated bank deposit slips. Cash sales are traced from cash register tapes into summary reports, entries in the cash receipts journal, and bank deposit slips.

Major categories of cash disbursements might include (*a*) invoices supported by purchase orders, (*b*) invoices not supported by purchase orders (such as utility bills), and (*c*) disbursements not supported by invoices (such as replenishing petty cash). Dividends and payroll transactions are discussed in Chapters 18 and 19, respectively. In conducting transactions tests of cash disbursements, the auditors select a sample of paid vouchers and note the appropriate authorization signatures; they also note the existence, agreement, and perforation of all supporting documents. In addition to this, the auditors trace the transactions through the accounting records, and examine the paid cheques to determine agreement as to amount and payee.

If these transactions tests indicate that the procedures and controls actually in effect differ from those contained in the auditors' description of internal control, the auditors should amend their working papers to describe the system actually in use.

3. Prove footings of cash journals and trace postings to ledger accounts.

Another objective of compliance tests is to determine the effectiveness of the clients' internal controls and the extent to which the auditors are justified in relying upon the client's accounting records. This is the objective of the next six audit procedures.

The purpose of proving footings of the cash receipts and cash disbursements journals is to verify the mechanical accuracy of the journals. The extent of the footings tests should be based upon the internal controls for cash described in the flowchart, questionnaire, or written description. For example, if one employee serves as both cashier and accountant, the auditors will generally test footings of most, if not all, of the journals. Cash embezzlements have been concealed by an understatement of the cash receipts journal "Cash-Debit" column or an overstatement of the "Cash-Credit" column of the cash disbursements journal. Generally, the "Sales Discounts" column total of the cash receipts journal will be overstated in the same amount as the cash column understatement, so that the journal will be in balance. In like manner, the "Purchase Discounts" column total of the cash disbursements journal may be understated to offset an overstatement of the Cash column total.

Closely associated with the proof of cash journal footings is the tracing of postings to the general ledger. Since there usually is only one posting per month from the cash receipts journal to the Cash account and one per month to the control accounts for receivables, it requires very little time to trace the posting of the Cash and Accounts Receivable columns for the entire year. Similar verification may readily be made for the totals posted from the cash payments journal to the Cash account and Accounts Payable account in the general ledger. With respect to other columns in the cash journals, particularly the "Miscellaneous" column, verification of postings for a judgment or statistical sample is usually deemed sufficient. If the testing of postings and footings discloses sloppy accounting work, with numerous errors and corrections, indistinct figures and ambiguous totals, the scope of the auditors' work should be increased, for these are often the hallmarks of fraudulent manipulation of the records.

4.   Compare detail of cash receipts listings to cash receipts journal, accounts receivable postings, and authenticated deposit slips.

Satisfactory internal control over cash receipts demands that each day's collections be deposited intact no later than the next banking day. Businesses that operate on weekends and holidays should segregate each day's receipts and prepare separate deposit tickets for each day. Thus, on Tuesday morning following a Labour Day weekend, three separate deposits should be made, each of which will consist of a single day's receipts. Rigid adherence to the rule of depositing each day's receipts intact will minimize the opportunity for employees handling cash to "borrow" from the funds in their custody. Moreover, this practice facilitates comparison by the auditors of the cash receipts record with the deposits per the bank.

To provide assurance that cash receipts have been deposited intact, the auditors should compare the detail of the original cash receipts listings (mailroom listings and register tapes) to the detail of the daily deposit tickets. The *detail* of cash receipts refers to a listing of the amount of each individual cheque and the total amount of currency comprising the day's receipts. In making a comparison of receipts and deposits, the auditors must emphasize the detail of cash receipts rather than relying upon daily or periodic totals. Agreement of total receipts and deposits for a period gives no assurance that worthless cheques have not been substituted for currency, or that shortages occurring early in the period have not been made up by subsequent deposits.

Comparison of daily entries in the cash receipts journal and postings to customers' accounts to the detail of mailroom listings and daily deposit slips may disclose a type of fraud known as *"lapping."* Lapping may be defined as the concealment of a shortage by delaying the recording of cash receipts. If cash collected from customer A is withheld by the cashier, a subsequent collection from customer B may be entered as a credit to A's account. B's account will not be shown as paid until a collection from customer C is recorded as a credit to B. Unless the money abstracted by the cashier is replaced, the accounts receivable as a group remain overstated; but judicious shifting of the overstatement from one account receivable to another may avert protests from customers receiving monthly statements. In companies in which the cashier has access to the general accounting records, shortages created in this manner have sometimes been transferred to inventory accounts or elsewhere in the records for temporary concealment.

If an employee who receives collections from customers is responsible for the posting of customers' accounts, lapping is most easily carried on. Familiarity with customers' accounts makes it relatively easy to lodge a shortage in an account that will not be currently questioned.

The best deterrent to lapping is the preparation of a control listing of cash receipts by a department which does not have access to the accounting records. However, even when no control listing is prepared, it is extremely difficult for an employee involved in lapping to maintain agreement between the detail of daily entries in the accounting records and daily bank deposits.

Duplicate deposit tickets in the possession of the client may be subject to alteration. If the auditors suspect that the duplicate slips have been altered, they should compare them with the originals on file at the bank. Most banks are willing to furnish auditors with copies of deposit tickets for comparison with the client's record of cash receipts.

5. *Reconcile bank activity for one or more months with cash activity per the accounting records.*

Reconciling the client's records of cash transactions with those of the bank is the most comprehensive compliance test of the client's controls over recording cash receipts and disbursements. This procedure, called a *proof of cash,* involves the detailed study of the cash transactions occurring with a specified test period. The starting point of this study is preparation of a four-column bank reconciliation for one or more months selected on a test basis. When internal control is weak, the auditors may decide to reconcile bank activity with the accounting records for the entire year under audit.

Satisfactory completion of the proof of cash will usually provide a clear indication as to whether cash receipts and disbursements are being properly handled and cash balances are accurately stated. In addition, this work will enable the auditors to learn whether prescribed internal controls are being effectively carried out in actual practice.

A proof of cash for the test period of September is illustrated in Figure 11–3. Notice that this working paper is so organized that the first and last columns reconcile the cash balance per bank and the balance per accounting records at the beginning of the test period (column 1) and at the end of this period (column 4). These outside columns are equivalent to typical monthly bank reconciliations. The two middle columns reconcile the bank's record of deposits with the client's record of cash receipts (column 2) and the bank's record of paid cheques with the client's record of cash disbursements (column 3).

Next let us consider the source of the figures used in this reconciliation. The amounts in column 1 (Balance, August 31) are taken from the client's bank reconciliation as of August 31. Similarly, the figures for column 4 (Balance, September 30) are taken from the client's bank reconciliation as of September 30. For column 2 (Deposits) the auditors arrive at the $46,001 of deposits per the bank by listing on an adding machine the deposits appearing on the September bank statement. The $45,338.50 of receipts per the books is obtained from the debits to Cash in Bank account in the general ledger. In column 3 the auditors compute the $40,362.90 of cheques paid by the bank by cross-footing the top line of the reconciliation and proving the figure by running an adding machine tape of the paid cheques. The bottom figure in column 3 represents the disbursements per the accounting records during September and is taken from the general ledger account. The reconciling items listed in columns 2 and 3 are computed by the auditors from analysis of the reconciling items at the beginning and end of September.

After completing the four-column bank reconciliation form, the auditors should prove the footings of all four columns and make a detailed verification of the figures used in the reconciliation. The balances taken from the client's bank reconciliations as of August 31 and September 30 should be traced to the bank statements and to the Cash in Bank account in the general ledger.

Verification of cash receipts and deposits during the test period. To verify receipts and deposits for the month being tested, an adding machine tape of deposits listed on the bank statement should be compared with the client's cash receipts record. This step will include not only a comparison of the total receipts with the total deposits but also a comparison of the date of each deposit with the date such funds were received by the company. Any failure to deposit each day's receipts intact should be investigated. For a few days of the period it may be desirable to perform the previously discussed procedure of comparing the detail of control listings and register tapes to entries in the accounting records and the authenticated deposit slips.

FIGURE 11–3

The Fairview Corporation Limited

Acct. No. 101 — Proof of Cash for September 1979 — E-4

Dec. 31, 79

	Balance Aug. 31, 79	Deposits	Cheques	Balance Sept. 30, 79
Per bank statement	39 236 40 z	46 001 00 # ②	40 362 90	44 874 50 z
Deposits in transit:				
At Aug. 31, 79	600 00 z	(600 00)		
At Sept. 30, 79		837 50		837 50
Outstanding cheques:				
At Aug. 31, 79	(1 241 00) x		(1 241 00)	
At Sept. 30, 79			3 402 00	(3 402 00) ✓
Bank service charge:				
August	4 60		4 60	
September			(2 80)	2 80
Cheque of customer A. G. Speeler charged back by bank Sept. 12, 79, redeposited Sept. 15, 79		(900 00)	(900 00)	
Per books	38 600 00 ч	45 338 50 ч	41 625 70 ч ①	42 312 80 ч E-1

z – Traced to client's Aug. 31, 79, bank reconciliation and/or to September 1979 bank statement.
\# – Per adding machine tape at E-4-1.
x – Per adding machine tape at E-4-2.
✓ – Per adding machine tape at E-4-3.
ч – Traced to general ledger.
① – Vouched all September 1979 disbursements to paid vouchers and other supporting documents.
② – Obtained authenticated deposit slips for September 1979 from bank and compared with cash receipts journal. Compared detail of 10 deposit slips with original control listings and postings to customers' accounts.

Footed cash receipts journal and cheque register for September 1979. Accounted for numerical sequence of all cheques issued September 1979 – nos. 610–792. No exceptions to tests.

Conclusion: Client's records of cash receipts and disbursements appear reliable.

V.M.H.
Oct. 16, 79

The misappropriation of cash receipts may sometimes be concealed by crediting the customers' accounts but debiting Sales Discounts rather than Cash. For this reason, auditors may verify all sales discounts recorded during the test period by computing the allowable discounts and noting the dates of invoices and customers' payments.

Verification of cash disbursements during the test period. In the verification of cash disbursements, the auditors' objectives are to determine that (*a*) all cash disbursements have been properly recorded, and (*b*) prescribed internal controls are operating effectively. The mechanical procedure of reconciling the client's record of cash disbursements to the bank's record of paid cheques provides the auditors with assurance that all disbursements clearing the bank during the test period have been recorded in the accounting records. To determine that the nature of these disbursements is properly reflected in the accounts, the auditors will vouch disbursements for the test period to such supporting evidence as vouchers, approved vendors' invoices, and payroll records.

While vouching these disbursements, the auditors have an opportunity to test many of the controls over cash disbursements. For example, they will notice whether all paid vouchers and supporting documents have been perforated or cancelled. Also, they will determine whether agreement exists among the supporting documents and note the presence of all required authorization signatures.

One of the most important procedures in the verification of cash disbursements is to account for the sequence of cheque numbers issued during the period. All cheques used should be paid, voided, or listed as outstanding on September 30. The auditors will examine any cheques voided during the period and may also obtain the October bank statement to examine cheques listed as outstanding on September 30.

Omitting an outstanding cheque from a bank reconciliation may conceal a cash shortage. Auditors should therefore determine that all cheque numbers not paid or voided during the test period are listed as outstanding on September 30. Another test of the client's bank reconciliation function is to determine that all cheques listed as outstanding on August 31 were either paid in September or listed as outstanding in the September 30 bank reconciliation.

6.   Verify cash transactions in one or more selected expense accounts.

Assume that an officer of an audit client has arranged for company cheques to be sent to a department store in payment of personal expenditures. What account would probably be charged with this transaction? Experience shows that such accounts as Miscellaneous Expense, Entertainment Expense, and Sales Promotion Expense are among the accounts *most likely to be charged with improper disbursements.* Analysis of the cash transactions in one or more of these accounts is a desirable auditing procedure—one which may focus considerable light on the adequacy of internal control over cash disbursements.

The extent to which cash disbursements are tested will be influenced by the number and nature of errors found. If auditors find that personal expenses of employees or officers have been treated as business expenses, they will propose an adjusting entry which transfers the charges to a drawings account or account receivable.

7. Investigate any cheques payable to cash or to bearer.

Drawing cheques payable to *cash* or *bearer* is a poor business practice that violates the fundamental control principle of providing adequate documentation. Such cheques do not require endorsement, hence there is no evidence as to who received the funds. Auditors may find that cheques payable to cash or bearer are used to replenish petty cash, to make expense advances to traveling employees, to reimburse officers for expenditures made in furtherance of company interests, to provide cash for personal drawings by officers, and to permit payment of wages in cash. In all of these cases, it is usually practicable for the cheque to be drawn payable to the individual who is authorized to receive the money; hence, the auditors should exert their influence against the issuance of cheques that are payable to cash.

Investigation of this category of cheques usually consists of an examination of supporting vouchers, analysis of the accounts to which the charges were made, and interrogation of officers. In some concerns, cheques drawn to cash or bearer have been used to provide funds for unethical commissions to buyers or to others who bestow favours on the concern. Such transactions usually are not explained or identified in the accounts or by supporting vouchers. The extent of the auditors' investigation of these disbursements must be determined tactfully and with professional judgment. One ever-present danger of such practices is that employees or officers familiar with the situation will abstract funds by drawing cheques payable to cash and utilizing the tradition of inadequate support for similar cheques as a cloak to avoid detection.

8. Investigate any cheques representing large or unusual payments to related parties.

All cheques payable to directors, officers, employees (other than payroll cheques and nominal expense reimbursements), or affiliates should be carefully reviewed by the auditors to determine whether the transactions (*a*) were properly authorized and recorded, and (*b*) are adequately disclosed in the financial statements.

To provide assurance that cash disbursements to related parties were authorized transactions and were properly recorded, the auditors should determine that each such transaction has been charged to the proper account, is supported by adequate vouchers or other records, and was specifically approved prior to payment by an officer other than the one receiving the funds. A cheque representing an advance to an officer but charged to miscellaneous expense will serve as an effective means of obtaining funds without the creation of a record to require repayment.

Misclassification of cheques issued to reimburse officers or employees for expenditures made in behalf of the company may open the door to duplicate reimbursement or to the concealment of improper expenditures. Most executives are anxious to have all payments to them supported and documented in a manner that will leave no room for doubt as to the propriety of the disbursement.

The need for financial statement disclosure of transactions with related parties was discussed in Chapter 7. To determine that such transactions are adequately disclosed, the auditors must obtain evidence concerning the relationship between the parties, the substance of each transaction (which may differ from its form), and the effect of each transaction upon the financial statements. Disclosure of related party transactions should include the nature of the relationships, a description of the transactions, and the dollar amounts involved.

9. Evaluate internal control for cash.

When the auditors have completed the procedures described in the preceding sections, they should evaluate the client's internal control for cash. As illustrated in Chapter 5, the internal control evaluation describes weaknesses and unusual strengths in internal control, related extensions or limitations of auditing procedures, and recommendations for inclusion in the internal control report to the client. The auditors then draft the portion of the audit program devoted to the substantive tests of cash transactions and balances.

B. Substantive tests:

10. Send confirmation letters to banks to verify amounts on deposit.

One of the objectives of the auditors' work on cash is to substantiate the existence and valuation of the amount of cash shown on the balance sheet. A direct approach to this objective is to confirm amounts on deposit, count the cash on hand, and obtain or prepare reconciliations between bank statements and the accounting records.

Confirmation of amounts on deposit by direct communication with bank officials is necessary in all cases, even when unopened bank statements are made available to the auditors. The confirmation letters are prepared by the client, but they must be mailed personally by the auditors, with return envelopes enclosed that are addressed to the auditors' office. A standard form of bank confirmation request agreed upon by the CICA and the Canadian Bankers' Association is widely used by the public accounting profession. This form is prepared in duplicate, the original to be retained by the bank and the duplicate to be returned to the auditors. An illustration of this form appears in Figure 11–4.

An important element of the confirmation letter is the request for disclosure of all indebtedness of the client to the bank. This request thus

FIGURE 11–4

<table>
<tr><td colspan="2" align="center">**BANK CONFIRMATION**</td><td>**DUPLICATE**
To be sent to accountant</td></tr>
</table>

Approved 1971 by
THE CANADIAN BANKERS' ASSOCIATION AND THE CANADIAN INSTITUTE OF CHARTERED ACCOUNTANTS

Dear Sirs: Date January 16, 1979

We shall be obliged if you will kindly complete this report and mail one copy in the enclosed addressed envelope direct to the accountants named below.

Report from   Yours truly,

(Bank) United National Bank   The Fairview Corporation Limited

(Branch) 1000 Greenview Avenue   By *Earl J. Forester*

Windsor, Ontario   Authorized Signature

Name of Accountants: Carter, Davis & Co.,
                           100 Ouellette Avenue,
                           Windsor, Ontario.

Dear Sirs: Re The Fairview Corporation Limited

We report that at the close of business on December 31, 1978 the records **of this branch** showed:

1. The following balance(s) at deposit (including savings accounts and particulars of any time deposits) or overdraft of the above mentioned customer:

	AMOUNT	DEPOSIT OR OVERDRAFT	ACCOUNT NUMBER	DESIGNATION OF ACCOUNT	INTEREST RATE IF ANY
E-1	$ 44,874.50	Deposit	123-5828	General Account	Nil
E-2	3,215.89	Deposit	123-6451	Payroll Account	Nil

2. The above mentioned customer was directly liable to this branch in respect of loans, except overdrafts noted in Section 1, in the total amount of $ 20,000.00 , as follows (**if none, so state**):

	AMOUNT OF LOAN	DUE DATE	INTEREST RATE	PAID TO	Nature of collateral lodged by customer, i.e., Section 88, Section 86, general assignment of book debts, hypothecation of collections, assignment of specified accounts and payments under contracts, stocks and bonds, etc. (Give full particulars of stocks, bonds or other negotiable securities lodged by customer.)
M-1	$ 20,000.00	April 1, 1979	6%	Dec. 31, 1978	Unsecured

3. The above mentioned customer was contingently liable as endorser of notes and drawer of drafts discounted at this branch and/or as guarantor in the total amount of $ none , as below (**if none, so state**):
If the number of items herein is substantial, the bank need report only the total unless the accountants submit a list of individual items for check by the bank.

AMOUNT	NAME OF MAKER	DATE OF NOTE	DUE DATE	REMARKS
$				

4. Other direct or contingent liabilities, open letters of credit and acceptances thereunder, forward exchange contracts and relative collateral lodged by customer (**if none, so state**):* none
Please list signing authorities:

Signing authorities: M.C. Beazley
                            Earl J. Forester

5. Securities held for account of customer, in addition to those reported in Sections 2 and 4 (**if none, so state**). If for other than safekeeping, state purpose. State whether bearer or registered and, if registered, in whose name.

None

(Bank)   United National Bank
(Branch)   1000 Greenview Avenue

Date January 20, 1979   By *Jannette Richards*
                                          Authorized Signature   Title

If the space provided is inadequate, please enter totals hereon and attach a statement giving full details as called for by the above headings.
*Note to accountant: If you require additional information, such as deposit totals on specified days, request it in the blank space in Section 4.

serves to bring to light any unrecorded liabilities to banks, as well as to confirm the existence of assets. Auditors should send confirmation letters to all banks in which the client has had deposits during the year, even though a deposit account may have been closed out during the period. It is entirely possible that a bank loan may continue after the closing of the deposit account. The same line of reasoning leads to the conclusion that confirmation letters are necessary even when the auditors obtain the bank statements and paid cheques directly from the bank.

Since every client maintains one or more bank accounts, the independent auditors will use bank confirmation requests on every audit engagement. Also, on some audits, a different form of confirmation letter will be sent to bank loan officers to enquire about requirements that the client maintain a specified minimum or average cash balance under the terms of a loan agreement. The principal significance of such *compensating balances* lies in the need for making proper balance sheet disclosure of them. The topic of compensating balances is therefore considered more fully under Procedure *16* of this audit program.

11.   Count and list cash on hand.

Cash on hand ordinarily consists of undeposited cash receipts, petty cash funds, and change funds. The petty cash funds and change funds may be counted at any time before or after the balance sheet date; many auditors prefer to make a surprise count of these funds. If the client's internal audit staff regularly performs surprise counts of petty cash and change funds, the CAs may review the internal auditors' working papers for these counts and conclude that it is unnecessary to include a count of petty cash and change funds among the procedures of the annual independent audit. If undeposited cash receipts constitute a material factor, a count at the balance sheet date is desirable; otherwise the auditors may verify the deposit in transit at year-end by referring to the date of deposit shown on the cutoff bank statement.

Whenever auditors make a cash count, they should insist that the *custodian of the funds be present throughout the count.* At the completion of the count, the auditors should obtain from the custodian a signed and dated acknowledgement that the funds were counted in the custodian's presence and were returned intact by the auditors. Such procedures avoid the possibility of an employee trying to explain a cash shortage by claiming that the funds were intact when turned over to the auditors. In some situations, the independent auditors may arrange for the client's internal auditing staff to assist under the CAs' supervision in the count of large amounts of cash on hand.

A first step in the verification of cash on hand is to establish control over all negotiable assets, such as cash funds, securities and other investments, notes receivable, and warehouse receipts. Unless all negotiable assets are verified at one time, an opportunity exists for a dishonest officer or employee to conceal a shortage by transferring it from one asset category to another.

ILLUSTRATIVE CASE.   John Sidell, a key office employee in a small business, misappropriated $10,000 by withholding cash collections and postponing the required credits to accounts receivable from customers. The accounting records were in balance; but Sidell was aware that when the independent auditors confirmed the balances due from customers, the shortage would be disclosed. He therefore "borrowed" negotiable securities from the office safe shortly before the annual audit and used them as collateral to obtain a short-term loan of $10,000. He intermingled the proceeds of this loan with the cash receipts on hand and credited the customers' accounts with all payments received to date. Mr. Sidell knew that unless the auditors insisted on verifying the securities owned by the business concurrently with their certification of cash, he would be able to abstract funds again after the cash had been counted, use these funds to pay off his loan, and return the "borrowed" securities to the safe before the auditors began their verification of investments. The defalcation was discovered when the auditors insisted on a simultaneous verification of all negotiable assets.

It is not uncommon to find included in cash on hand some personal cheques cashed for the convenience of officers, employees, and customers. Such cheques, of course, should not be entered in the cash receipts journal because they are merely substitutes for currency previously on hand. The auditors should determine that these cheques are valid and collectible, thus qualifying for inclusion in the balance sheet figure for cash. This may be accomplished by the auditors taking control of the last bank deposit for the period and determining that it includes all cheques received through year-end. The auditors will retain a validated deposit slip from this deposit for comparison to any cheques subsequently charged back by the bank.

Non-cash items included in cash on hand should receive the auditors' close attention. Such items as N.S.F. cheques held for redeposit, post-dated cheques, I.O.U's from employees, or expense vouchers included in the balance of cash per the accounting records should be reviewed with a member of management and definite disposition agreed upon. Adjusting entries normally will be necessary to exclude such items from the cash classification if the amounts are significant.

12. Obtain or prepare reconciliations of bank accounts as of the balance sheet date.

Determination of a company's cash position at the close of the period requires a reconciliation of the balance per the bank statement at that date with the balance per the company's accounting records. Even though the auditors may not be able to begin their field work for some time after the close of the year, they will prepare a bank reconciliation as of the balance sheet date or review the one prepared by the client.

If the year-end reconciliation has been made by the client prior to arrival of the auditors, there is no need for duplicating the work. However, the auditors should examine the reconciliation in detail to satisfy themselves that it has been properly prepared. Inspection of a reconciliation prepared by the client will include verifying the arithmetical accuracy, tracing balances to the bank statement and ledger account, and investigating the reconciling items. The total cheques drawn during the month according to the cash disbursements journal should be equal to the total of the paid cheques returned by the bank, plus the outstanding cheques at the end of the period and minus the outstanding cheques at the beginning of the period. The importance of a careful review of the client's reconciliation is indicated by the fact that a cash shortage may be concealed merely by omitting a cheque from the outstanding cheque list, or by purposely making an error in addition on the reconciliation.

There are many satisfactory forms of bank reconciliations. The form most frequently used by auditors begins with balance per bank and ends with unadjusted balance per the accounting records. This format permits the auditors to post adjusting entries affecting cash directly to the bank reconciliation working paper, so that the final balance can be cross referenced to the cash grouping sheet or to the working trial balance.

The mechanics of balancing the ledger account with the bank statement by no means complete the auditors' verification of cash on deposit. The authenticity of the individual items making up the reconciliation must be established by reference to their respective sources. The balance per the bank statement, for example, is not accepted at face value but is verified by direct confirmation with the bank, as described in the preceding pages. Other verification procedures associated with the reconciliation of the bank statement will now be discussed.

12a. Investigate N.S.F. cheques and other items charged back by bank. One of the traditional methods of attempting to conceal a cash shortage from auditors consists of inserting a fictitious cheque in the cash receipts, petty cash, or other cash on hand. If the auditors supervise the deposit of all cheques included in the cash count, the fictitious cheque will of course fail to clear the bank on which it is drawn and will be returned by the client's bank marked "N.S.F." (not sufficient funds), or "No such account," or with some similar term indicating its uncollectibility.

In addition to the problem of N.S.F. cheque included in cash at the audit date, there is often a weakness in the procedures for handling customers' cheques which have been deposited but returned by the bank as uncollectible. These should be immediately redeposited or charged back to the customer's account in the accounts receivable subsidiary ledger. Often the returned cheque will be paid if deposited a second time; this creates the danger of misuse of these cheques and concealment of such misuse by writing off the customer's account as worthless. Auditors should ascertain whether definite instructions have been issued to employees concerning the treatment of N.S.F. cheques, and whether these items receive the prompt attention of executives.

12b.   Investigate any cheques outstanding for more than 30 days. If cheques are permitted to remain outstanding for long periods, internal control over cash disbursements is weakened. Employees who become aware that certain cheques have long been outstanding and may never be presented have an opportunity to conceal a cash shortage merely by omitting the old outstanding cheque from the bank reconciliation. Such omissions will serve to increase the apparent balance of cash on deposit and may thus induce an employee to abstract a corresponding amount of cash on hand.

The auditors' investigation of old outstanding cheques will include examination of the voucher and other documents supporting the payment. Cheques outstanding for long periods should be called to the attention of the client, who customarily will contact the payee to learn why the cheque has not been cashed or deposited. Payroll and dividend cheques are the types most commonly misplaced or lost. It is good practice for the client to eliminate long-outstanding cheques of this nature by an entry debiting the Cash account and crediting Unclaimed Wages or another special liability account. This will reduce the work required in bank reconciliations, as well as lessen the opportunity for irregularities. Wherever outstanding cheques are reported as lost, a stop-payment order should be entered with the bank and a duplicate cheque then issued. Use of the stop-payment order will make the bank responsible if both the original and replacement cheques are subsequently paid.

13.   Verify the client's cutoff of cash receipts and cash disbursements. The balance sheet figure for cash should include all cash received on the final day of the year and none received subsequently. In other words, an accurate cutoff of cash receipts (and of cash disbursements) at year-end is essential to a proper statement of cash on the balance sheet. If the auditors can arrange to be present at the client's office at the close of business on the last day of the fiscal year, they will be able to verify the cutoff by counting the undeposited cash receipts. It will then be impossible for the client to include in the records any cash received after this cutoff point, without the auditor being aware of such actions.

All customers' cheques included in cash receipts should have been entered in the cash receipts journal before the auditors' cash count. The auditors should compare these cheques, both as to name and amount, with the cash journal entries. If cheques have been credited to accounts other than those of the drawers of the cheques, a likelihood of lapping or other fraudulent activity is indicated.

Of course auditors cannot visit every client's place of business on the last day of the fiscal year, nor is their presence at this time essential to a satisfactory verification of cash. As an alternative to a count on the balance sheet date, auditors can verify the cutoff of cash receipts by determining that deposits in transit as shown on the year-end bank reconciliation appear as credits on the bank statement on the first business day of the new year. Failure to make *immediate* deposit of the closing day's cash receipts would suggest that cash received at a later time might have been included in the deposit, thus overstating the cash balance at the balance sheet date.

To ensure an accurate cutoff of cash disbursements, the auditors should determine the serial number of the last cheque written on each bank account on the balance sheet date, and should enquire whether all cheques up to this number have been placed in the mail. Some companies, in an effort to improve the current ratio, will prepare cheques payable to creditors and enter these cheques as cash disbursements on the last day of the fiscal year, although there is no intention of mailing the cheques until several days or weeks later. When the auditors make a note of the number of the last cheque issued for the period, they are in a position to detect at once any additional cheques which the client might later issue and seek to show as disbursements of the year under audit.

An alternative means of verifying the accuracy of the cutoff of cash disbursements when the auditors are not on hand at the year-end consists of giving particular attention to the time period before cheques outstanding at year-end are presented to the bank for payment. This step is more fully considered in the next audit procedure.

14.   Obtain a cutoff bank statement containing transactions of at least seven business days subsequent to balance sheet date.

A *cutoff bank statement* is a statement covering a specified number of *business days* (usually seven to ten) following the end of the client's fiscal year. The client will request the bank to prepare such a statement and deliver it to the auditors. Most auditors do not actually prepare a second bank reconciliation but merely examine the cutoff statement closely to see that the year-end reconciling items such as deposits in transit and outstanding cheques have cleared the bank in the interval since the balance sheet date.

As previously mentioned, the verification of an accurate cutoff of cash disbursements is facilitated by observing the serial number of the last cheque issued on the final day of the year. Another approach to reviewing the accuracy of the cutoff involves examination of the cheques included in the cutoff bank statement. With respect to cheques which were shown as outstanding at year-end, the auditors should determine the dates on which these cheques were paid by the bank. By noting the dates of payment of these cheques, the auditors can determine whether the time intervals between the dates of the cheque and the time of payment by the bank were unreasonably long. Unreasonable delay in the presentation of these cheques for payment constitutes a strong implication that the cheques were not mailed by the client until some time after the close of the year. The appropriate adjusting entry in such cases consists of a debit to Cash and a credit to a liability account.

In studying the cutoff bank statement the auditors will also watch for any paid cheques issued on or before the balance sheet date but not listed as outstanding on the client's year-end bank reconciliation. Thus, the cutoff bank statement provides assurance that the amount of cash shown on the balance sheet was not overstated by omission of one or more cheques from the list of cheques outstanding.

15. Trace all bank transfers for last week of audit year and first week of following year.

The purpose of tracing bank transfers is to disclose overstatements of cash balances resulting from *kiting.* Many businesses maintain accounts with a number of banks and often find it necessary to transfer funds from one bank to another. When a cheque drawn on one bank is deposited in another, several days (called the "float" period) usually pass before the cheque clears the bank on which it is drawn. During this period, the amount of the cheque is included in the balance on deposit at both banks. Kiting refers to manipulations which utilize such temporarily overstated bank balances to overstate the results of operations, conceal a cash shortage, or meet short-term cash needs.

Auditors can easily detect manipulations of this type by preparing a schedule of bank transfers for a few days before and after the balance sheet date. This working paper lists all bank transfers and shows the dates that the receipt and disbursement of cash were recorded in the cash journals and on the bank statements. A partial illustration of a schedule of bank transfers is shown below.

| Cheque No. | Bank accounts | | Amount | Date of disbursement | | Date of receipt | |
	From	*To*		*Books*	*Bank*	*Books*	*Bank*
5897	General	Payroll	$30,620	Dec. 28	Jan. 3	Dec. 28	Dec. 28
6006	General	Branch #4	24,018	Jan. 2	Jan. 4	Dec. 30	Dec. 30
6029	Branch #2	General	10,000	Jan. 3	Jan. 5	Jan. 3	Dec. 31

Disclosure of kiting. By comparing the dates in this working paper, auditors can determine whether any manipulation of the cash balance has taken place. The increase in one bank account and decrease in the other bank account should be recorded in the cash journals in the same accounting period. Notice that Cheque No. 6006 in the transfer schedule was recorded in the cash journals as a receipt on December 30 and a disbursement of January 2. As a result of recording the debit and credit parts of the transaction in different accounting periods, cash is overstated on December 31. For the cash receipts journal to remain in balance, some account must have been credited on December 30 to offset the debit to Cash. If a revenue account were credited, the results of operations would be overstated along with cash. This type of kiting may indicate a deliberate management fraud.

Kiting may also be used to conceal a cash shortage. Assume, for example, that a financial executive misappropriates $10,000 from a company's general chequeing account. To conceal the shortage on December 31, the executive draws a cheque transferring $10,000 from the company's Halifax branch bank account to the general account. The executive deposits the transfer cheque in the general account on December 31 but records the transfer in the accounting records as occurring early in January. As of December 31, the shortage in the general account has been replaced, no reduction has yet been recorded in the branch account, and no shortage is apparent. Of course, the shortage will reappear in a few days when the transfer cheque is paid from the branch account.

A bank transfer schedule should disclose this type of kiting because the transfer deposit appears on the general account bank statement in December, while the transaction was not recorded in the cash journals until January. Cheque No. 6029 in the transfer schedule illustrates this discrepancy.

A third type of kiting uses the float period to meet short-term cash needs. For example, assume that a business does not have sufficient cash to meet the month-end payroll. The company might draw a cheque on its general account in one bank, deposit it in a payroll account in another bank, and rely upon subsequent deposits being made to the general account before the transfer cheque is presented for payment. If the transfer is properly recorded in the accounting records, this form of kiting will not cause a misstatement of the cash balance for financial reporting purposes (e.g., Cheque No. 5897). However, banks discourage this practice and may not allow the customer to draw against the deposit until the cheque has cleared the other account. In some deliberate schemes to defraud banks, this type of kiting has been used to create and conceal overdrafts of several hundred thousand dollars.

16. Determine proper balance sheet presentation of cash.

The balance sheet figure for cash should include only those amounts which are available for use in current operations. Most users of the balance sheet are not interested in the breakdown of cash by various bank accounts or in the distinction between cash on hand and on deposit. Consequently, all cash on hand and in banks which is available for general use is presented as a single amount on the balance sheet. Change funds and petty cash funds, although somewhat lacking in the "general availability" test, are usually not material in amount, and are included in the balance sheet figure for cash.

A bank deposit which is restricted to use in paying long-term debt should not be included in cash. Other types of restricted bank deposits, if material, are also generally excluded from cash and shown separately, as current or non-current assets, depending upon availability for liquidation of current liabilities. Certificates of deposit or time deposits are sometimes included in the figure for cash, but if material in amount, they should be listed separately.

Compensating balances. Long-term loan agreements or lines of credit carried with banks may require a borrower to maintain a minimum average bank balance of perhaps 20 percent or so of the loan or loan commitment. This compensating balance, by limiting the amount released by the lender and available to the borrower, results in increasing the effective rate of interest on the loan. The amount of any compensating balances should be disclosed in notes accompanying the financial statements.

Often the arrangement between the bank and the borrowing company as to maintenance of a compensating balance is an informal oral understanding and may not be strictly enforced. In effect, some banks expect, but do not demand, that the borrower maintain a compensating balance of perhaps 15 or 20 percent of the loan. In a few cases, however, the borrower may be legally restricted from withdrawing the compensating balance at any time during the period of the loan. Only in the event that compensating balances are legally restricted should they be excluded from cash and shown separately in the balance sheet. In all other situations, disclosure by footnote is sufficient.

In the United States the AICPA has developed a standard confirmation form to be used by the CPAs in confirming compensating balances, lines of credit, loan commitments, and other bank credit arrangements. Lending arrangements must be confirmed by the bank loan officer rather than by other bank employees. For this reason, the confirmation of lending arrangements is not combined with the form requesting confirmation of bank balances. As with all confirmations, the request should be prepared under the letterhead of the client and signed by the client, but should be mailed by the auditors and returned directly to the auditors' office.

Window dressing. The term *window dressing* refers to actions taken shortly before the balance sheet date to improve the cash position or in other ways to create an improved financial picture of the company. For example, if the cash receipts journal is "held open" for a few days after the close of the year, the balance sheet figure for cash is improperly increased to include cash collections actually received after the balance sheet date. Another approach to window dressing is found when a corporate officer who has borrowed money from the corporation repays the loan just before the end of the year and then promptly obtains the loan again after the balance sheet has been prepared. This second example is not an outright misrepresentation of the cash position (as in the case of holding the cash receipts journal open) but nevertheless creates misleading financial statements which fail to portray the underlying economic position and operations of the company.

Not all forms of window dressing require action by the auditors. Many companies make strenuous efforts at year-end to achieve an improved financial picture by rushing shipments to customers, by pressing for collection of receivables, and sometimes by paying liabilities down to an unusually low level. Such efforts to improve the financial picture to be reported are not improper. Before giving approval to the balance sheet presentation of cash, the auditors must exercise their professional judgment to determine whether the client has engaged in window dressing of a nature which causes the financial statements to be misleading.

Interim audit work on cash

In public accounting firms a question under continuous study is this: "How can we perform a larger share of our auditing work before the year-end?" In order to avoid a concentration of audit work within a few months of the year, public accountants sometimes divide an audit program into two portions: (a) procedures which can be performed on an interim basis during the year, and (b) procedures which cannot be carried out until the end of the year. The audit procedures illustrated in this chapter can be subdivided in this manner because the study and evaluation of internal control is ideally completed on an interim basis.

The extent to which other audit work can be performed prior to the balance sheet date will depend in large part upon the adequacy of internal control. The stronger the system of internal control, the greater the amount of audit work which can be satisfactorily performed in advance of the balance sheet date. If we assume an audit of a company having excellent internal control over cash transactions, the greater part of the audit program we have discussed in this chapter could be done prior to the year-end. Such procedures as compliance tests of cash transactions, reconciliation of bank activity with cash activity per accounting records, and counting of petty cash funds could be performed at any convenient time during the year.

At year-end the audit work on cash might be limited to such substantive tests as a review of the client's bank reconciliation, confirmation of year-end bank balances, procedures associated with the year-end cutoff of transactions, and a general review of cash transactions and changes in cash position during the interval between the interim work on cash and the end of the period. The point to emphasize is that much of the work suggested by the audit procedures discussed in this chapter could be done before the balance sheet date.

KEY TERMS INTRODUCED OR EMPHASIZED IN CHAPTER 11

cheque register   A journal used in a voucher system to record payment of vouchers. Since the cost distribution relating to voucher transactions is made in the voucher register, entries in the cheque register represent debits to Vouchers Payable and credits to Cash.

cheque-signing machine   A machine which signs cheques using a facsimile signature plate. The machine provides an automatic item count of cheques signed, and the signed cheques drop automatically into a locked box.

compensating balances   A requirement associated with a bank loan that the borrower maintain specified minimum or average balances on deposit with the bank. The compensating balance raises the effective interest rate by making less money available to the borrower.

confirmation letter (from bank)   Documentary evidence sent by the bank directly to the auditors confirming the client's bank account balances, outstanding loans, and other transactions involving the bank.

control listing   A detailed listing of cash receipts which may be compared to entries in the accounting records and to bank deposits to assure that cash receipts remain intact as they pass through the system.

cutoff bank statement   A bank statement covering a specified number of business days (usually seven to ten) after the client's balance sheet date. Auditors use this statement to determine that reconciling items shown on the year-end bank reconciliation have cleared the bank within a reasonable time.

kiting   Manipulations causing an amount of cash to simultaneously be included in the balance of two or more bank accounts. Kiting schemes are based on the "float" period—the time necessary for a cheque deposited in one bank to clear the bank on which it was drawn.

lockbox   A post office box controlled by a company's bank at which cash remittances from customers are received. The bank picks up the remittances, immediately credits the cash to the company's bank account, and forwards the remittance advices to the company.

proof of cash   An audit procedure which reconciles the bank's record of cash activity with the client's accounting records for a test period. The working paper used for the proof of cash is a four-column bank reconciliation.

remittance advice   A document which accompanies cash remittances from customers identifying the customer and the amount of the remittance.

voucher   A document authorizing a cash disbursement. A voucher usually provides space for employees performing various approval functions to initial. (The term "voucher" may also be applied to the group of documents that support a cash disbursement.)

voucher register   A special journal used to record the liabilities for payment originating in a voucher system. The debit entries are the cost distribution of the transaction, and the credits are to Vouchers Payable. Every transaction recorded in a voucher register corresponds to a voucher authorizing future payment of cash.

window dressing   Action taken by the client shortly before the balance sheet date to improve the financial picture presented in the financial statements.

GROUP I
REVIEW QUESTIONS

11-1.   What are the objectives of internal control over cash transactions?

11-2.   In what ways can the use of cash registers contribute to the effectiveness of internal control over receipts from cash sales? Explain. (AICPA)

11–3.   What prevents the person who opens incoming mail from being able to abstract cash collections from customers?

11–4.   Should an internal control questionnaire concerning cash receipts and disbursements be filled out for all audits? At what stage of an audit would you recommend use of the questionnaire?

11–5.   An internal control questionnaire includes the following items. For each item, explain what is accomplished by the existence of the controls involved:

   a.   Are each day's cash receipts deposited intact and without delay?
   b.   If an imprest fund is represented by a bank account, has the bank been notified that no cheques payable to the company should be accepted for deposit?
   c.   Are payroll disbursements made from an imprest bank account restricted to that purpose?
   d.   Are vouchers or other supporting documents stamped or perforated when cheques are signed? (AICPA, adapted)

11–6.   How can an auditor obtain assurance that cash receipts are being deposited intact?

11–7.   Prepare a simple illustration of "lapping" of cash receipts, showing actual transactions and the cash receipts journal entries. (AICPA)

11–8.   During the early months of the year, the cashier in a small company was engaged in lapping operations, but he was able to restore the amount of cash borrowed by March 31 and refrained from any fraudulent acts after that date. Will the year-end audit probably disclose his lapping activities? Explain.

11–9.   In the auditors' examination of paid cheques returned by the bank to the drawer, state the features of the cheque to be examined and the recorded data with which the cheque would be compared. Give a reason for each operation.

11–10.   In preparing a proof of cash, how does the auditor account for all cheques issued during the test period?

11–11.   An assistant auditor received the following instructions from her supervisor: "Here is a cutoff bank statement covering the first seven business days of January. Compare the paid cheques returned with the statement and dated December 31 or earlier with the list of cheques outstanding at December 31." What type of irregularity might this audit procedure bring to light? Explain.

11–12.   During your audit of a small manufacturing firm you find numerous cheques of large amount drawn payable to the treasurer and charged to the Miscellaneous Expense account. Does this require any action by the auditor? Explain.

11–13.   What information do CAs request from a bank in the Bank Confirmation?

11–14. What action should be taken by the auditors when the count of cash on hand discloses a shortage?

11–15. "The auditors should send confirmation requests to all banks with which the client has had deposits during the year, even though some of these accounts have been closed prior to the balance sheet date." Do you agree? Explain.

11–16. During your reconciliation of bank accounts in an audit, you find that a number of cheques of small amount have been outstanding for more than a year. Does this situation call for any action by the auditor? Explain.

11–17. Explain the objectives of each of the following audit procedures for cash:

   a.   Obtain a cutoff bank statement subsequent to the balance sheet date.

   b.   Compare paid cheques returned with bank statement to list of outstanding cheques in previous reconciliation.

   c.   Trace all bank transfers during the last week of the audit year and the first week of the following year.

   d.   Confirm compensating balance agreements with bank loan officers.

11–18. Explain two procedures by which auditors may verify the client's cutoff of cash receipts.

11–19. What is the meaning of the term "window dressing" when used in connection with year-end financial statements? How might the term be related to the making of loans by a corporation to one or more of its executives?

GROUP II
QUESTIONS REQUIRING ANALYSIS

11–20. You are retained on October 1 by Wilson Manufacturing Ltd. to perform an audit for the year ended December 31. Prior to the year-end you undertake a study of the new client's internal control over cash.

   Virtually all of the cash receipts consist of cheques received through the mail, but there is no prelisting of cash receipts before they are recorded in the accounts. You find that the incoming mail is opened either by the cashier or by the employee maintaining the accounts receivable subsidiary ledger, depending on which employee has time available. The controller stresses the necessity of flexibility in assignment of duties to the 20 employees comprising the office staff, in order to keep all employees busy and achieve maximum economy of operation.

   Required:

   a.   Explain how prelisting of cash receipts strengthens internal control over cash.

      b. List specific duties that should not be performed by an employee assigned to prelist the cash receipts in order to avoid any opportunity for that employee to conceal embezzlement of cash receipts. (AICPA, adapted)

11–21. Henry Mills is responsible for preparing cheques, recording cash disbursements, and preparing bank reconciliations for Signet Corporation Ltd. While reconciling the October bank statement, Mills noticed that several cheques totaling $937 had been outstanding for over one year. Concluding that these cheques would never be presented for payment, Mills prepared a cheque for $937 payable to himself, forged the treasurer's signature, and cashed the cheque. Mills made no entry in the accounts for this disbursement and attempted to conceal the theft by destroying the forged cheque and omitting the long-outstanding cheque from subsequent bank reconciliations.

Required:

    a. Identify the weaknesses in Signet's system of internal control.
    b. Explain several audit procedures which might disclose the fradulent disbursement.

11–22. Although the primary objective of an independent audit is not the discovery of fraud, the auditors in their work on cash take into consideration the high relative risk associated with this asset. One evidence of this attitude is evidenced by the CA's alertness for signs of "lapping."

Required:

    a. Define "lapping."
    b. Explain the audit procedures that CAs might utilize to uncover lapping.

11–23. During the examination of cash, the CAs are alert for any indications of "kiting."

Required:

    a. Define kiting.
    b. Explain the audit procedures that should enable the CAs to uncover kiting.

11–24. Explain how each of the following items would appear in a four-column proof of cash for the month of November 1978. Assume the format of the proof of cash begins with bank balances and ends with the unadjusted balances per the accounting records.
    a. Outstanding cheques at November 30, 1978.
    b. Deposits in transit at October 31, 1978.
    c. Cheque issued and paid in November, drawn payable to "Cash."
    d. The bank returned $1,800 in NSF cheques deposited by the client in November; the client redeposited $1,450 of these cheques in November and $350 in December, making no additional entries in the accounting records.

11–25. A new assistant on an audit staff asked why it was necessary to make any audit of petty cash when both the size of the fund and the total petty cash expenditures for the audit period appeared to be immaterial.

How would you answer the assistant's question? Give the reasons for your answer. (AICPA)

11–26. The CA obtains a July 10, 1979, bank statement directly from the bank. Explain how this cutoff bank statement will be used:

a. In the review of the June 30, 1979, bank reconciliation.

b. To obtain other audit information. (AICPA, adapted)

11–27. In the audit of Quadrasonic Corporation Ltd. for the year ended December 31, you discover the client had been drawing cheques as creditors' invoices became due but not necessarily mailing them. Because of a working capital shortage, some cheques have been held for two or three weeks.

The client's controller informs you that unmailed cheques totaling $48,500 were on hand at December 31 of the current year. He states these December-dated cheques had been entered in the cash disbursements journal and charged to the respective creditors' accounts in December because the cheques were prenumbered. However, these cheques were not actually mailed until early January. The controller wants to adjust the cash balance and accounts payable at December 31 by $48,500 because the Cash account had a credit balance. He objects to submitting to his bank your audit report showing an overdraft of cash.

Required:

a. Prepare a detailed audit program indicating the procedures you would use to satisfy yourself of the accuracy of the cash balance on the company's balance sheet.

b. Discuss the propriety of reversing the indicated amount of outstanding cheques. (AICPA, adapted)

11–28. Leeward Company obtained a three-year, 8 percent loan of $5,000,000 from its bank in order to finance its expanding volume of inventory and receivables. Terms of the borrowing agreement provided that Leeward Company must maintain a compensating balance equal to 15 percent of the amount of the loan throughout the period of the indebtedness.

a. What effect, if any, does the provision for a compensating balance have upon the effective rate of interest on the loan? Explain.

b. How can auditors determine the existence and terms of compensating balance agreements?

c. What disclosure, if any, is appropriate in the financial statements with respect to the compensating balance provision of the loan? Give reasons.

11–29. Select the best answer for each of the following questions and explain the reasons for your choice.

a. Operating control of the cheque-signing machine normally should be the responsibility of the—
    (1) General accounting function.
    (2) Treasury function.
    (3) Legal counsel.
    (4) Internal audit function.

b. A CA obtains a January 10 cutoff bank statement directly from the bank. Very few of the outstanding cheques listed on the client's December 31 bank reconciliation cleared during the cutoff period. A probable cause for this is that the client—
    (1) Is engaged in kiting.
    (2) Is engaged in lapping.
    (3) Transmitted cheques to payees after year-end.
    (4) Has overstated its year-end bank balance.

c. For good internal control, the monthly bank statements should be reconciled by someone under the direction of the—
    (1) Controller.
    (2) Cashier.
    (3) Credit manager.
    (4) Treasurer.

d. A CA learns that a client has paid a vendor twice for the same shipment, once based upon the original invoice and once based upon the monthly statement. A control procedure that should have prevented this duplicate payment is—
    (1) Cancellation of all paid vouchers.
    (2) Prenumbering of disbursement vouchers.
    (3) Attaching receiving reports to the disbursement support.
    (4) Prenumbering receiving reports. (AICPA, adapted)

GROUP III
PROBLEMS

11–30. During the audit of Sunset Building Supply Ltd., you are given the following year-end balance reconciliation prepared by the client:

SUNSET BUILDING SUPPLY LTD.
Bank Reconciliation
December 31

Balance per December 31 bank statement	$48,734
Add: Deposits in transit	4,467
	$53,201
Less: Cheques outstanding	20,758
Balance per ledger, December 31	32,443

According to the client's accounting records, cheques totaling $31,482 were issued between January 1 and January 14 of the following year. You have obtained a cutoff bank statement dated January 14 containing paid cheques amounting to $50,440. Of the cheques outstanding at December 31, $3,600 were not returned in the cutoff statement, and of those issued per the accounting records in January, $8,200 were not returned.

Required:

a. Prepare a working paper showing whether all cheques returned by the bank or still outstanding have been accounted for in the client's bank reconciliation and accounting records.

b. Suggest four possible explanations for the situation disclosed in your working paper. State what action you would take in each case, including any adjusting entry which you would propose.

11-31. Palmer Co. Ltd. is a nation-wide corporation with clearly defined regional sales divisions. Each sales division is responsible for the collection of its own accounts receivable. A separate local bank account is maintained by each division in which all cash receipts are deposited intact on a daily basis. Each Wednesday and Saturday these collections are transferred by cheque to the home office. No other cheques are drawn on these bank accounts. The sales division offices maintain no accounting records other than for accounts receivable, cash receipts, and cash disbursements. However, all cash records, such as paid cheques, bank statements, and remittance lists, are retained in the sales division offices. In planning your annual audit of Palmer you decide that members of your audit staff will visit the sales division offices in all regions and examine the cash transfers between the sales division and the home office.

Required:

a. List the specific objectives of the audit of cash transfers.

b. Design the specific audit steps your assistants should follow in auditing the cash transfers from the sales division to the home office. (Do not list other audit procedures relating to cash or receivables, as it is assumed that your assistants have adequate knowledge of such audit procedures.)

11-32. In connection with the audit of Brookhurst Limited for the year ended December 31, 1979, you are given the following working paper prepared by an employee of the client:

BROOKHURST LIMITED
Bank Reconciliation
December 31, 1979

Balance per ledger, December 31, 79		$51,524.58
Add:		
Deposit in transit, December 31, 79		7,986.75
Debit memo for customer's cheque returned un-paid (cheque is on hand but no entry has been made on the books)		600.00
Bank service charge for December		6.50
		$60,417.83
Deduct:		
Outstanding cheques, December 31, 79 (see detailed list below)	$6,803.25	
Credit memo for proceeds of a note receivable which had been left at the bank for collection but which has not been recorded as collected per books	1,190.00	
Cheque for an account payable entered on books as $722.70 but drawn by company and paid by bank as $1,257.00	534.30	8,527.55
Computed balance		$51,890.28
Unlocated difference		900.00
Balance per bank (agreed to confirmation)		$50,990.28

Outstanding cheques, December 31, 79

No.	Amount
573	$ 67.27
724	9.90
903	1,456.67
907	305.50
911	482.75
913	2,550.00
914	366.76
916	2,164.40
	$6,803.25

Required:

a. Prepare a corrected reconciliation for your working papers.

b. Prepare a journal entry for items which should be adjusted in the accounting records. (AICPA, adapted)

11–33. The cashier of Mission Corporation intercepted customer A's cheque, payable to the company in the amount of $500, and deposited it in a bank account which was part of the company petty cash fund, of which he was custodian. He then drew a $500 cheque on the petty cash fund bank account payable to himself, signed it, and cashed it. At the end of the month, while processing the monthly statements to customers, he was able to change the statement to customer A to show that A had received credit for the $500 cheque that had been intercepted. Ten days later he made an entry in the cash receipts journal which purported to record receipt of a remittance of $500 from customer A, thus restoring A's account to its proper balance but overstating cash in bank. He covered the overstatement by omitting from the list of outstanding cheques in the bank reconciliation two cheques, the aggregate amount of which was $500.

Required:

Discuss briefly what you regard as the more important deficiencies in the system of internal control in the above situation and in addition include what you consider a proper remedy for each deficiency. (AICPA, adapted)

11–34. You are the senior in charge of the July 31, 1979, audit of Reliable Auto Parts, Inc. Your newly hired staff assistant reports to you that she is unable to complete the four-column "proof of cash" for the month of April 1979 which you instructed her to do as part of the study of internal control for cash.

Your assistant shows you the following working paper which she has prepared:

RELIABLE AUTO PARTS, INC.
Proof of Cash for April 1979
July 31, 1979

	Balance March 31, 79	Deposits	Cheques	Balance April 30, 79
Per bank statement	71,682.84	61,488.19	68,119.40	65,051.63
Deposits in transit:				
At March 31, 79	2,118.18			(2,118.18)
At April 30, 79		4,918.16		4,918.16
Outstanding cheques:				
At March 31, 79	(14,888.16)		14,888.16	
At April 30, 79			(22,914.70)	22,914.70
Bank service charges:				
March 1979	(22.18)		22.18	
April 1979			(19.14)	19.14
Note receivable collected by bank, April 30, 79		18,180.00		18,180.00
N.S.F. cheque of customer L. G. Waite, charged back by bank March 31, 79, redeposited and cleared April 3, 79	(418.19)	418.19		
Balances as computed	58,472.49	85,004.54	60,095.90	108,965.45
Balances per books	59,353.23	45,689.98	76,148.98	28,894.23
Unlocated differene	(880.74)	39,314.56	(16,053.08)	80,071.22

Your review of your assistant's work reveals that the dollar amounts of all of the items in her working paper are correct. You learn that the accountant for Reliable Auto Parts, Inc., makes no journal entries for bank services charges or note collections until the month following the bank's recording of the item, and that Reliable's accountant makes no journal entries whatsoever for N.S.F. cheques which are redeposited and cleared.

Required:

Prepare a corrected four-column proof of cash in good form for Reliable Auto Parts, Inc., for the month of April 1979.

11–35.   John Axton recently acquired the financial controlling interest of Pacific Imports, Inc., importers and distributors of cutlery. In his review of the duties of employees, Axton became aware of loose practices in the signing of cheques and the operation of the petty cash fund.

You have been engaged as the company's CA, and Axton's first request is that you suggest a system of sound practices for the signing of cheques and the operation of the petty cash fund.

In addition to Axton, who is the company president, the company has 20 employees including four corporate officers. About 200 cheques are drawn each month. The petty cash fund has a working balance of about $200 and about $500 is expended by the fund each month.

Required:

Prepare a letter to Axton containing your recommendations for good internal control procedures for:

a.   Signing cheques. (Axton is unwilling to be drawn into routine cheque-signing duties.)

b.   Operation of the petty cash fund. (Where the effect of the control procedure is not evident, give the reason for the procedure.) (AICPA, adapted)

11–36.   You are the senior auditor in the examination of the financial statements of Home Products, Inc. Your flowcharts and internal control questionnaire provide the following information about the client's internal control over cash receipts:

All cash receipts are sent directly to the accounts receivable clerk with no processing by the mail department. The accounts receivable clerk maintains the cash receipts journal, prepares the bank deposit slips in duplicate, posts remittances to the accounts receivable subsidiary ledger, and mails the deposit to the bank.

The controller receives the validated deposit tickets directly from the bank. He also receives the monthly bank statement directly from the bank and promptly reconciles it. At the end of each month, the accounts receivable clerk notifies the general ledger clerk of the monthly totals of the cash receipts journal for posting to the general ledger. On occasion, the general ledger clerk makes debit entries to the Cash account from sources other than the cash receipts journal to record such transactions as long-term borrowing.

To date, assistant auditors have completed the following audit work on cash receipts: complete flowcharts and an internal control questionnaire, foot and cross-foot the cash receipts journal and trace the postings to the general ledger, and trace the detail of customer remittance advice into cash receipts journal.

Required:

List all other audit procedures that should be performed to obtain sufficient audit evidence regarding cash receipts. Opposite each procedure listed, explain your reason for including the procedure.

Organize your answer sheet as follows:

Other audit procedures	*Reason for other audit procedures*

(AICPA, adapted)

11–37. Diamond Pool Products had poor internal control over its cash transactions. Facts about its cash position at November 30, 1979, were as follows:

The accounting records showed a balance of $18,901.62, which included undeposited receipts. A credit of $100 on the bank's records did not appear in the accounting records of the company. The balance per bank statement was $15,550. Outstanding cheques were: No. 62 for $116.25, No. 183 for $150, No. 284 for $253.25, No. 8621 for $190.71, No. 8623 for $206.80, and No. 8632 for $145.28.

The cashier abstracted all undeposited receipts in excess of $3,794.41 and prepared the following reconciliation:

Balance per books, November 30, 1979		$18,901.62
Add: Outstanding cheques:		
8621	$190.71	
8623	206.80	
8632	145.28	442.79
		$19,344.41
Less: Undeposited receipts		3,794.41
Balance per bank, November 30, 1979		$15,550.00
Deduct: Unrecorded credit		100.00
True cash, November 30, 1979		$15,450.00

Required:

a. Prepare a working paper showing how much the cashier abstracted.

b. How did he attempt to conceal his theft?

c. Using only the information given, name two specific features of internal control which were apparently lacking. (AICPA, adapted)

11–38. You are auditing the Windsor Branch of Reed Distributing Company.

This branch has substantial annual sales which are billed and collected locally. As part of your audit you find that the procedures for handling cash receipts are as follows:

Cash collections on over-the-counter sales and C.O.D. sales are received by the cashier from the customer or delivery service. Upon receipt of cash the cashier stamps the sales ticket "paid" and files a copy for future reference. The only record of C.O.D. sales is a copy of the sales ticket, which is given to the cashier to hold until the cash is received from the delivery service.

Mail is opened by the secretary to the credit manager, and remittances are given to the credit manager for his review. The credit manager then places the remittances in a tray on the cashier's desk. At the daily deposit cutoff time, the cashier delivers the cheques and cash on hand to the assistant credit manager, who prepares remittance lists and makes up the bank deposit, which he also takes to the bank. The assistant credit manager also posts remittances to the accounts receivable subsidiary ledger cards and verifies the cash discount allowable.

You ascertain that the credit manager obtains approval from the executive office of Reed Distributing Company, located in Toronto, to write off uncollectible accounts, and that he has retained in his custody as of the end of the fiscal year some remittances that were received on various days during the last month.

Required:

a. Describe the irregularities that might occur under the procedures now in effect for handling cash collections and remittances.

b. Give procedures that you would recommend to strengthen internal control over cash collections and remittances.

GROUP IV
CASE STUDIES IN AUDITING

11–39.   SUNCRAFT APPLIANCE CORPORATION LIMITED

On October 21, Rand & Brink, a CA firm, was retained by Suncraft Appliance Corporation Limited to perform an audit for the year ended December 31. A month later James Minor, president of the corporation, invited the CA firm's partners, George Rand and Alice Brink, to attend a meeting of all officers of the corporation. Mr. Minor opened the meeting with the following statement:

"All of you know that we are not in a very liquid position and our October 31 balance sheet shows it. We need to raise some outside capital in January, and our December 31 financial statements (both balance sheet and income statement) must look reasonably good if we're going to make a favourable impression upon lenders or investors. I want every officer of this company to do everything possible during the next month to ensure that, at December 31, our financial statements look as strong as possible, especially our current position, and our earnings."

"I have invited our auditors to attend this meeting so they will understand the reason for some year-end transactions which might be a little unusual. It is essential that our financial statements carry the auditors' approval, or we'll never be able to get the financing we need. Now what suggestions can you offer?"

The vice president for sales was first to offer suggestions: "I can talk some of our large customers into placing some orders in December that they wouldn't ordinarily place until the first part of next year. If we get those extra orders shipped, it will increase this year's earnings and also increase our current assets."

The vice president in charge of production commented: "We can ship every order we have now and every order we get during December before the close of business on December 31. We'll have to pay some overtime in our shipping department, but we'll try not to have a single unshipped order on hand at year-end. Also we could overship some orders and the customers wouldn't make returns until January."

The controller spoke next: "If there are late December orders from customers which we can't actually ship, we can just label the merchandise as sold and bill the customers with December 31 sales invoices. Also, there are always some cheques from customers dated December 31 which don't reach us until January—some as late as January 10. We can record all those customers' cheques bearing dates of late December as part of our December 31 cash balance."

The treasurer offered the following suggestions: "I owe the company $50,000 on a call note I issued to buy some of our stock. I can borrow $50,000 from my mother-in-law about Christmas time and repay my note to the company. However, I'll have to borrow the money from the company again early in January, because my mother-in-law is buying an apartment building and will need the $50,000 back by January 15."

"Another thing we can do to improve our current ratio is to write cheques on December 31 to pay most of our current liabilities. We might even wait to mail the cheques for a few days or mail them to the wrong addresses. That will give time for the January cash receipts to cover the December 31 cheques."

The vice president of production made two final suggestions: "Some of our inventory, which we had tentatively identified as obsolete, does not represent an open and shut case of being unsalable. We could defer any write-down until next year. Another item is some machinery we have ordered for delivery in December. We could instruct the manufacturer not to ship the machines and not to bill us before January."

After listening to these suggestions, the president, James Minor, spoke directly to Rand and Brink, the auditors. "You can see I'm doing my best to give you full information and cooperation. If any of these suggested actions would prevent you from giving a clean bill of health to our year-end statements, I want to know about it now so we can avoid doing anything that would keep you from issuing an unqualified

audit report. I know you'll be doing a lot of preliminary work here before December 31, but I'd like for you not to bill us before January.
Will you please give us your reactions to what has been said in this
meeting?"

Required:

a. Put yourself in the role of Rand & Brink, CAs, and evaluate
    separately each suggestion made in the meeting. What general
    term is applicable to most of the suggested actions?
b. Could you assure the client that an unqualified audit report would
    be issued if your recommendations were followed on all the mat-
    ters discussed? Explain.
c. Would the discussion in this meeting cause you to withdraw from
    the engagement? Your answer on this point should be included as
    part of a statement to James Minor summarizing your firm's posi-
    tion as independent auditors.

12

Securities and other investments, and investment revenue

The most important group of investments, from the viewpoint of an auditor, consists of shares[1] and bonds, because they are found more frequently and usually are of greater dollar value than other kinds of investment holdings. Bank certificates of deposit, commercial paper issued by corporations, and the cash surrender value of life insurance policies are other types of investments often encountered. The greater part of this chapter is devoted to an audit program for securities; a brief discussion of audit procedures appropriate for other types of investments is presented in the latter part of the chapter.

Investments in securities are made by business concerns for a variety of reasons. In some lines of business, operations are highly seasonal and the cash required at the peak of operations would be idle and unproductive were it not invested during the slack season. Investment of temporarily idle cash in selected types of marketable securities is an element of good financial management. Such holdings are regarded as a secondary cash reserve, capable of quick conversion to cash at any time, although producing a steady, but modest, rate of return. Management may also choose to maintain some investments in marketable securities on a semi-permanent basis. The length of time such investments are held may be determined by the trend of the securities markets and by the company's income tax position, as well as by its cash requirements.

---

[1] Since the terms "share" and "stock" are both in common usage, they are used interchangeably in this text.

Investments in securities may also exist for the purpose of maintaining control or influence over affiliated companies. Although investment in common stock is the basic means of maintaining control over subsidiaries, the auditors often find that loans are extended by one affiliated company to another through the acquisition of bonds or notes.

The auditors' objectives in examination of securities

In the examination of investments in securities, the auditors attempt to determine that adequate internal control exists over the securities and the revenue from these investments. Other objectives include determining that the securities actually exist and are the property of the client, are fairly valued in accordance with generally accepted accounting principles, and are properly classified on the balance sheet. In addition to these objectives, the auditors' work is intended to determine that all revenue arising from the investments has been promptly collected and recorded. The verification of securities, therefore, may be considered as including the analysis of such related accounts as dividend revenue, interest earned, accrued interest, dividends receivable, and gain and loss on sale of securities. If the audit engagement includes the preparation of income tax returns, the procedures may be extended to obtain all necessary information, such as the dates of transactions.

Internal control for securities

Since most securities are readily negotiable, the problem of physical protection has an importance similar to that of safeguarding cash and notes receivable. The auditors' review of internal control will indicate the extent and direction of the auditing work required in a particular engagement. The review may also enable the auditors to suggest changes in records and procedures that will reduce the risk of loss through fraud or accidental error.

The major elements of an adequate system of internal control over securities include the following:

1. Separation of duties between the executive authorizing purchase and sale of securities, the custodian of the securities, and the person maintaining the record of investments.
2. Complete detailed records of all securities owned, and the related revenue from interest and dividends.
3. Authorization of all purchase and sale transactions by responsible officials.
4. Registration of securities in the name of the company.
5. Periodic physical inspection of securities by an internal auditor or an official having no responsibility for the authorization, custody, or record keeping of investments.

In many concerns, segregation of the functions of custody and record keeping is achieved by the use of an independent safekeeping agent, such as a stockbroker, bank, or trust company. Since the independent agent has no direct contact with the employee responsible for maintaining accounting records of the investments in securities, the possibilities of concealing fraud through falsification of the accounts are greatly reduced. The risks of physical loss or destruction are also minimized because the independent agent generally has fireproof vaults and other facilities especially designed to safeguard valuable documents. If securities are not placed in the custody of an independent agent, they should be kept in a bank safe-deposit box under the joint control of two or more of the company's officials. "Joint control" means that neither of the two custodians may have access to the securities except in the presence of the other. A list of securities in the box should be maintained there, and the deposit or withdrawal of securities should be recorded on this list along with the date and signatures of all persons present. The safe-deposit box rental should be in the name of the company, not in the name of an officer having custody of securities.

Complete detailed records of all securities owned, and of any securities held for others, are essential to a satisfactory system of internal control. These records frequently consist of a subsidiary record for each security, with such identifying data as the exact name, face amount or par value, certificate number, number of shares, date of acquisition, name of broker, cost, and any interest or dividends payments received. For securities providing regular revenue, it may be feasible to schedule in advance the payments to be received, thus providing a means of calling attention to any delay in receipt of revenue. Securities written off as worthless should be transferred to a separate memorandum account and periodically reviewed for possible recovery of value.

All purchases and sales of securities should be made only upon written authorization of an officer or committee of directors. The system of authorizations must not be so inflexible or cumbersome as to prevent the prompt action necessary to take advantage of security market movements and to minimize income tax liability. It is often convenient to entrust the purchase and sale of securities to a responsible financial executive, subject to frequent review by an investment committee of the board of directors.

The auditors may occasionally find that securities owned by the client are registered in the name of an officer or other individual rather than in the name of the company. Immediate registration in the company's name at date of purchase is the preferred practice, since this reduces the likelihood of fraudulent transfer or unauthorized use of the securities as collateral. Some bonds are payable to *bearer* and cannot be registered in the name of the owner. The registration of securities should not be considered as a substitute for the other control procedures described.

An internal auditor or other responsible employee should at frequent intervals inspect the securities on hand, compare the serial numbers and other identifying data for the securities examined with the accounting records, and reconcile the subsidiary record for securities with the control account. This procedure supplements the internal control inherent in the segregation of the functions of authorization, record keeping, and custodianship.

Internal control questionnaire

A questionnaire used by the auditors in studying and evaluating internal controls relating to securities will include such questions as the following. Are securities and similar instruments under the joint control of responsible officials? Are all persons having access to securities properly bonded? Is an independent safekeeping agent retained? Are all purchases and sales of securities authorized by a financial executive or by an investment committee of the board of directors?

Audit working papers for securities

Grouping sheets are rarely required for securities because a single ledger account, supported by subsidiary records, generally suffices for each balance sheet classification of securities. For marketable securities, the principal working paper is an analysis of the type illustrated in Figure 12–1.

AUDIT PROGRAM FOR SECURITIES

Listed below are procedures typically performed by auditors to achieve the objectives described earlier in this chapter. The procedures most appropriate for a particular audit depend upon the auditors' study and evaluation of the internal control over securities, and also upon other aspects of the engagement. For example, if the engagement includes preparation of the client's tax return, certain information concerning securities transactions will be compiled that might not be essential for audit purposes.

A.   Study and evaluation of internal control for securities

1.   Prepare a description of the internal control for securities.
2.   Trace transactions for purchases and sales of securities through the system.
3.   Review reports by internal auditors on their periodic inspection of securities.

FIGURE 12-1

Acct. No. 11a   F-1

Fairfield Corporation Limited
Marketable Securities
Dec. 31, 79

	Balance Dec. 31, 78 Shares or Face Amount	Cost	Purchases (Sales) Date	Shares or Face Amount	Cost	Balance Dec. 31, 79 Shares or Face Amount	Cost	Net Sales Proceeds	Gain (loss) on Sale Acct. No 414	Dividend Received	Market Value Per Share	Market Value Dec. 31, 79 Total
Bonds:												
L. Ltd. 4%/t 85 #8356-85	30,000.00	28,600.00				30,000.00	28,600.00			1,312.50	83 1/2	25,050.00
P. Ltd. 5 1/8/t 92 #4145-54	10,000.00	9,850.00				10,000.00	9,850.00			587.50	99 1/2	9,950.00
Q. Ltd. 7 3/4/t 2001 #376-475	100,000.00	94,600.00	July 15,79 / Oct. 1,79	(100,000.00) / 100,000.00	(94,400.00) / 99,800.00	100,000.00	99,800.00	102,500.00	7,900.00	2,302.00	87 3/8	87,150.00
Government of Canada 4s No #240-339										—	—	—
												347,175.00
Stocks:												
G.M. Std. Com. 2004	1,000	33,700.00		1,000		1,000	33,700.00			5,000.00	86	86,000.00
S.R. Std. Com. L4583	500	20,100.00		500		500	20,100.00			1,500.00	110 3/4	55,375.00
G.E. Std. Com. 1 DL475	2,000	54,400.00	Sept 21,79 / Dec. 1,79	(1,000) / 800	(27,200.00) / 40,560.00	1,000 / 800	27,200.00 / 40,560.00	45,000.00	17,800.00	2,000.00	59 1/4 / 51	59,250.00 / 40,800.00
Union Co. Std. Com. L4485								147,500.00	25,700.00	12,702.00		347,175.00
		247,250.00			18,560.00	259,810.00						

C-1

Less: Accrued at Dec. 31, 78   (1,495.00)
Plus: Accrued at Dec. 31, 79   1,670.00
   12,877.00
Q — A.G & 7 - G.M. Special Div.   1,200.00   Acct. No. 407
   14,077.00

A.G & 7
Dividends Received
Instructional Dividends
Q. account Special G.M. dividend of $1.20
per share declared Dec. 1, 79, payable
Jan. 15, 80, to shareholders of record Dec. 15, 79.

Abbreviations legend:

v — Footed and cross footed.

√ — Inspected certificates Jan. 12, 80, at Pacific United Bank. Bank records show no access to safe deposit box since Dec. 19, 79.

e — Computation verified.

ƒ — Traced to cash receipts record.

† — Actuals agreed to Dec. 31, 78, audit working papers.

ƒ — Per Jan. 1, 80, Financial Post.

Δ — Compared with dividend records published by Financial Post and Toronto Stock Exchange.

θ — Examined broker's advices and authorizations for purchases and sales by investment committee of board of directors.

▽ — Examined paid cheque.

Fairfield's policy is to accrue dividends as of the shareholders record date. A.G & 7 special div. was prepared in conformity with this policy.

Mr. G.B. Clark, Treasurer, stated that Fairfield's marketable securities are regarded as a secondary cash "reserve" and will be sold at any time the company's cash position makes such action advisable. Accordingly, Fairfield did not amortize premium or discount on bonds, and classifies these investments as current assets.

Our tests indicate that the client's established procedures have been followed consistently.

1,200.00

All our securities inspected in my presence and returned to me intact.
     G.B. Clark Jan. 12, 80

V.M.K.
Jan. 12, 80

4. Review monthly reports by officer of client company on securities owned, purchased and sold, and revenue earned.
5. Evaluate internal control for securities.

B. Substantive tests of securities transactions and year-end balances

6. Obtain or prepare analyses of security investment accounts and related revenue accounts.
7. Inspect securities on hand and compare serial numbers with those shown on previous examination.
8. Obtain confirmation of securities in the custody of others.
9. Verify purchases and sales of securities during the year and for a short period subsequent to the balance sheet date.
10. Verify gain or loss on securities transactions and obtain information for income tax returns.
11. Make an independent computation of revenue from securities by reference to dividend record books or other primary sources.
12. Investigate method of accounting for investments in subsidiary companies and investees other than subsidiaries.
13. Determine market value of securities at date of balance sheet.
14. Determine financial statement presentation for securities.

A. Study and evaluation

1. Prepare a description of the internal control for securities.

To acquire an understanding of the client's internal control system for securities the auditors may prepare a working paper describing the control measures purportedly in use. This description will include identification of (1) the officer or investment committee responsible for decisions to buy or sell securities, (2) the officials having custody of the securities and the location of the securities, and (3) the persons responsible for maintaining records of securities transactions. In the audit of small companies with relatively few securities transactions, the auditors may readily acquire this information by questioning officers and key employees. The information can conveniently be recorded in a written narrative. For larger clients a flowchart may be prepared to show clearly the separation of duties and the documentation required in authorizing, executing, and recording securities transactions. The use of an internal control questionnaire similar to the one illustrated on page 224 also will be especially helpful in pinpointing any weaknesses in internal control.

2. Trace transactions for purchases and sales of securities through the system.

Assume that the information gathered on internal control in Procedure 1 above indicated that all purchases and sales of securities were authorized in advance by an investment committee of the board of directors, that all transactions were executed by the treasurer through the brokerage firm of Hill, Gunn and Company, that all securities owned were kept in a safe-deposit box at First Provincial Bank, and that a subsidiary ledger was maintained showing all details of securities transactions.

The appropriate compliance tests by the auditors of the internal controls stated to be in use will include following selected transactions through the system to gather evidence that these control measures are actually being followed. For example, the auditors will determine for a selected purchase transaction whether minutes of the meetings of the investment committee show that an authorization to make the purchase was recorded prior to the transaction. They will examine documentary evidence of the placing of the purchase order with the broker by the client's treasurer, the written acknowledgment by the broker—Hill, Gunn and Company—of receipt of the order, and the brokerage firm's advice that the transaction had occurred. Other documents to be inspected will be the client's paid cheque issued for the security, the broker's month-end statement listing all transactions and delivery of securities, and the transmittal document accompanying the certificate when delivered to the client. The auditors will also trace the newly acquired security into the subsidiary ledger for securities and into the monthly report prepared by the treasurer summarizing all purchase, sales, revenue, and current holdings of securities.

3. *Review reports by internal auditors on their periodic inspection of securities.*

In large companies the internal auditors may, on a surprise basis, make a count of all securities in the bank safe-deposit box or other location of company-owned securities. The independent auditors, by examining the internal auditors' reports and discussing their findings with them, may obtain helpful supporting evidence indicating how fully the client is complying with the established internal control system. The extent of reliance to be placed by the independent auditors on the work of the client's internal auditing staff will depend upon the professional qualifications of the internal auditors, their placement in the organization, and the quality of their working papers and reports. Since the internal auditing activity is in itself an element of the system of internal control, as well as a device for enforcing other controls, the independent auditors must logically give careful consideration to the extent and quality of internal auditing work as part of their study and evaluation of internal control. The independent auditors may wish to reconcile the listing of securities at a given date, as prepared by the internal auditors, with the subsidiary ledger for securities and with the independent auditors' own working papers from the preceding year's audit.

4. *Review monthly reports by officer of client company on securities owned, purchased and sold, and revenue earned.*

Those situations in which independent auditors find serious accounting shortcomings, fraud, or violations of company policy relating to securities are usually encountered in client companies which do not regularly prepare monthly reports of all securities transactions, security holdings, and revenue earned. In other words, a requirement that the treasurer submit to the investment committee of the board of directors a report showing the company's securities investments at the beginning of the month, all purchases during the month, all sales and related gains and losses, all interest and dividends received during the month, and the month-end holdings of securities is a powerful internal control device. It serves as an incentive to follow authorization policies carefully, to maintain complete and current accounting records, and to review the results being achieved. Moreover, such required monthly reporting in a formal manner is a strong deterrent to any type of securities fraud.

5. *Evaluate internal control for securities.*

After preparing the description of internal control and performing the compliance tests described above, the auditors will *evaluate* the client's system of internal control for securities. This is the appropriate time to write recommendations for inclusion in the internal control letter to the client, suggesting improvements in internal control. At this point the auditors should be aware of the significant strengths and weaknesses in the system. Consequently, they are prepared to draft the audit procedures for substantive testing in the light of their evaluation of internal control. In the following sections we will suggest typical procedures for the substantive testing portion of the audit program for securities.

B. Substantive tests

6. *Obtain or prepare analysis of security investment accounts and related revenue accounts.*

The working paper in Figure 12–1 shows a client-prepared analysis of changes in the Marketable Securities account during the year, and the steps the auditors have taken to verify these changes and the closing balances. Similar analyses would be obtained or prepared for securities classified in the Investments section of the balance sheet. The starting point in the analysis is the beginning balance for each security; this balance is expressed in terms of cost, and also as a number of shares of stock or face value of bonds. The beginning balances are verified by comparison with the ending balances shown in the preceding year's audit working papers. Gains and losses for the year, as well as interest and dividends received, may also be listed on the same worksheet.

In proving the accuracy of the analysis the auditors foot and cross-foot the cost columns for beginning balances, purchases or sales, and ending balances. The column total for cost of securities sold plus the column total for gain or loss equals the column total showing the net proceeds of sale.

The total cost of all securities on hand at year-end should, of course, agree with the figure for marketable securities or investments in the working balance sheet or working trial balance.

Notice the tick marks and the explanatory legend used in the working paper to show the verification steps performed by the auditors. In this illustration the analysis of the Marketable Securities account has also been used in making an inspection of securities on hand, and includes the receipt from the custodian acknowledging return of the securities. If the company held a large number of securities, a separate "count sheet" would be more convenient.

The bonds held by the Fairfield Corporation Limited are shown at cost. This is a common practice among investors and, in general, an acceptable one, although amortization of discount or premium is preferable if the bonds are to be held to maturity.

7. Inspect securities on hand and compare serial numbers with those shown on previous examination.

The auditors inspect the securities (certificates) in the possession of the client to ascertain their existence and ownership. The inspection of securities on hand should be made at or near the balance sheet date whenever possible, and should be made concurrently with the count of cash and the verification of other negotiable assets. If the inspection of securities cannot be made until a later date, the count must first be reconciled with the accounting records at that later date and then an investigation made of any intervening securities transactions. As an alternative step, the auditors may seal the container for the securities and inspect these at the later, more convenient date. When securities are kept in a safe-deposit box, it is sometimes feasible for the client to instruct the bank on the balance sheet date that no one is to have access to the safe-deposit box unless accompanied by the auditors. A letter may then be obtained from the bank stating that the client's safe-deposit box was not opened between the balance sheet date and the auditors' arrival. Under this procedure, the securities found in the box may be considered as having been on hand at the close of the period. These precautions, of course, are intended to prevent the concealment of a shortage or other irregularity by substitution of one type of asset for another. The auditors should insist that a representative of the client be present throughout the inspection of securities.

The data to be noted when securities are inspected include:

a. Serial numbers.
b. Name of issuer.
c. Face value of bonds, par value of shares, and number of shares represented by each share certificate.
d. Name in which registered.
e. Maturity dates of bonds.

f. Interest dates and rates, and preferred dividend rates.

g. Maturity date of next succeeding coupon attached to bond.

The auditors may not be able to detect forged securities, but they should be alert for any obvious alterations on the face of the documents. Any irregularities observed, including deviations between the securities counted and the analysis prepared from the accounting records, should be recorded on the working paper, which must be rigidly controlled by the auditors throughout the examination.

Case histories of frauds involving securities sometimes show that securities have been removed by a dishonest officer or employee and other securities of the same issue and denomination placed in the vault or safe-deposit box before the audit date. The requirement that two persons be present at each opening of the safe-deposit box has already been mentioned as a control procedure designed to prevent unauthorized removal of securities. Substitution of similar securities can best be detected by a careful comparison of serial numbers of the securities inspected with those of the securities detail records, and also with the serial numbers listed on the auditors' working papers for the preceding examination.

8. *Obtain confirmation of securities in the custody of others.*

The use of a confirmation letter may be an acceptable alternative to first-hand inspection of securities. Before deciding to rely upon a confirmation letter as evidence of the existence and ownership of securities, the auditors should consider the financial strength and reputation of the entity to which the confirmation letter is to be sent. Securities belonging to the client may be in the possession of brokers, banks, or other parties for safekeeping, for transfer, or as collateral for loans. If the securities have been pledged as collateral, the confirmation letter should include confirmation of the amount of the notes or loans payable. Securities may also have been deposited in escrow for assurance of faithful performance under certain contracts or court orders.

A client-prepared confirmation request should be sent by the auditors directly to the holders of client-owned securities, requesting verification of all details of the securities held and the reason for which they are held. This letter should request that the reply be mailed direct to the auditors' office. Second and third confirmation requests may sometimes be necessary. If irregularities are indicated, the auditor may deem it desirable to visit the outside custodian. Careful investigation should be made of all instances where securities are not on hand and not in the custody of properly authorized persons. When such a condition exists, the auditors should not be satisfied with a confirmation; they should insist that the certificates be presented for their inspection, and should point out to the client the risks involved in such uncontrolled handling of negotiable assets.

Auditors are not ordinarily held responsible for the genuineness of stock and bond certificates; hence it is not common practice to obtain confirmation from the corporations issuing the securities. This type of confirmation might be desirable, however, if evidence of fraud in the handling of securities was discovered.

9. *Verify purchases and sales of securities during the year and for a short period subsequent to the balance sheet date.*

The auditors must determine that securities purchased during the period have been recorded at cost, determined in accordance with generally accepted accounting principles, and that the investment accounts have been credited with the cost or other carrying value of securities sold. The recording of the proceeds of sale must also be reviewed. By vouching all changes in the investment accounts during the year under audit, the auditors are assured of the validity of the ledger balances at the audit date.

The process of verifying purchases and sales during the year emphasizes the vouching of entries in the accounts to original documents, principally *brokers' advices* and *statements.* A typical form of brokers' advice is illustrated in Figure 12–2. Examination of these documents may be supplemented by inspection, on a test basis, of paid cheques issued in payment for securities purchased. Sales of securities may be vouched to brokers' advices of sale and receipts for delivery of securities. The pro-

FIGURE 12–2
Brokers' advice covering sale of securities

B. A. TRADER & COMPANY

INVESTMENT BROKERS

600 BAY STREET, TORONTO, ONTARIO

As agents, we have this day executed for your account and risk:

Settlement Date	Account Number						
June 12, 79	XL 9374	Adams Manufacturing Co. Ltd., Common Shares					
Trade Date	Bought	Sold	Price	Extension	Commission	Net Amount	
June 5, 79		100	20	2,000.00	38.00	1,962.00	

Account: The Rowell Company Limited
6930 Crucible Street
Toronto, Ontario

ceeds may also be traced to the cash receipts journal and to validated duplicate deposit slips. All transactions for the period may then be traced to the minutes of the board of directors or investment committee for approval authorizations. The ending balances computed as a result of these transactions should be compared with the general ledger and subsidiary records, and the internal reports prepared by the treasurer summarizing securities transactions during the period and the holdings at the end of the period.

The cost of a marketable security includes commissions, taxes on the transaction, and shipping charges. If securities are purchased on margin, the full cost should be charged to the investment account and a liability established for that portion of the cost not paid in cash. In recording a sale it is customary to enter the net proceeds—that is, the sale price reduced by the brokers' commission and any miscellaneous charges incurred. The cost of a bond does not include any accrued interest purchased; this element should be recorded in a separate Interest Receivable account.

Securities transactions occurring during a period of two or three weeks following the balance sheet date should be reviewed. The purpose of this procedure is to determine that a correct *cutoff* of transactions was made on the balance sheet date and that there have been no irregular transactions subsequent to this date which affect the audited period. Occasionally, securities may be sold before the balance sheet date but not recorded as sales until they are actually delivered some time early in the next period. Errors of this type are likely to go undiscovered unless the auditors examine transactions after the balance sheet date, comparing so-called "trade dates" on the brokers' advices with settlement dates. This review of transactions may be integrated with the reconciliation of the auditors' inspection of securities and the ledger balances in those engagements in which the inspection cannot be made until some time after the balance sheet date.

10. Verify gain or loss on securities transactions and obtain information for income tax returns.

The gain or loss on sales or exchanges of securities may be computed on the same working paper used to analyze security transactions. This working paper already contains information as to cost of securities sold, and columns may conveniently be added to show net proceeds and gain or loss.

Some accountants also add the necessary columns to show capital gains and losses under federal income tax rules, although this may not be considered part of the work of verifying securities. In some situations a separate working paper may be needed for income tax purposes. For example, if carrying value of securities and the interest or dividends received differ for income tax purposes from the amounts presented on financial statements, a separate working paper may be desirable. The dates of transactions are of prime importance because these will determine the percentage of gain or loss to be used on the return. Care should be given also to the basis of the securities sold, since the tax authorities may recognize a basis of cost determination quite different from the basis used by the client.

11.   Make an independent computation of revenue from securities by reference to dividend record books or other primary sources.

Dividend declarations, amounts, and payment dates on all listed stocks may be obtained from dividend record books published by various investment advisory services. The interest earned and collected on investments in bonds can be computed from the interest rates and payment dates shown on the bond certificates. From these sources the auditors can compute independently the revenue from investments for the year under audit. The total revenue as computed should be compared with the ledger balances for dividend and interest revenue, and any material discrepancies investigated.

The most frequent errors encountered in verifying revenue from investments include:

a.   Charging accrued interest purchased to the Bond Investment account and crediting Interest Earned with the full amount of bond interest collected.

b.   Recording ordinary stock dividends as revenue.

c.   Recording liquidating dividends, representing return of invested capital, as revenue.

d.   Inaccuracies in accruing bond interest at the balance sheet date.

The first three types of errors misstate the carrying value of the investment as well as the revenue for the period. Because of the misstatement of the cost basis, subsequently recorded gains and losses on sale of securities will be incorrect.

Revenue accounts showing interest and dividends earned on securities may occasionally reveal revenue from securities which are not recorded in the asset accounts. For this reason the analysis of these related revenue accounts is an integral part of the verification of securities: the revenue from securities is usually included in the working paper analyzing the Marketable Securities account as illustrated in Figure 12–1. Any reversing entries should be fully investigated, since the abstraction of dividend or interest cheques is sometimes camouflaged by fictitious reversing entries. Standard procedure for the analysis of all types of revenue accounts includes particular attention to any debit entries.

The auditors' work in verification of revenue from bonds should include analysis of the interest accrual accounts. Accrued revenue at the beginning of the period may be proved by comparison with the previous year's audit working papers. The computation of accrued interest on bond investments sold between interest dates should then be verified, along with the computation of accrued interest at the close of the year. Verification of accruals and tracing of interest collected to the cash receipts record will generally disclose the cause of any discrepancy between the year's interest earned as computed by the auditors and as reflected by the accounts.

The auditors should also review the propriety of any amortization of bond premium or discount. Many investors do not amortize the premium or the discount on bond investments, on the grounds that bonds are often sold prior to maturity and that the sales price is apt to be more influenced by other market considerations than by the approach of the maturity date. Auditors do not, as a rule, object to such practices.

The auditors' independent computation of revenue from securities may reveal that dividends declared and paid according to published dividend record books have not been received. This suggests the diversion of cash receipts and warrants detailed investigation. The fact that dividends are often not set up as receivables prior to collection may suggest to a dishonest employee the possibility of abstracting a dividend cheque without the need for concurrent falsification of the accounts.

12.   *Investigate method of accounting for investments in subsidiary companies and investees other than subsidiaries.*

The auditors must determine that the client's accounting for investments in subsidiary companies is in accordance with current financial accounting standards. If a subsidiary was acquired in a *pooling of interests,* the auditors will ascertain whether the rare circumstances for pooling as recommended by the CICA have been followed. A business combination recorded as a purchase must be recorded at cost at the date of acquisition and follow the recommendations of the *CICA Handbook.* A parent company is required by the *CICA Handbook* to use the equity method of accounting for investments in subsidiaries which, due to rare circumstances, are not consolidated with the parent.

Investments in common shares which give the investor company the ability to exercise effective control over operating and financial policies of the investee also require the use of the equity method of accounting. Some of the circumstances which determine whether a company (investee) is effectively controlled are:

1. continued ability to obtain proxies from other shareholders;
2. ownership of voting shares by officers, employees, nominees, or other persons having subordinated interests;
3. inactivity of minority shareholders who do not attend shareholders' meetings or do not give proxies;
4. possession of a lease or other contract which carries with it the virtual

ownership of assets without formal ownership of a majority of outstanding voting shares;

5.   holding of rights, options, warrants, convertible debt or convertible
preferred shares, the exercise of which is a reasonable possibility and
would result in a controlling interest in voting shares.[2]

Generally the auditors of a parent company will have examined the
financial statements of the subsidiaries, both at the date of the business
combination and for subsequent years. The reporting problems involved
when other independent auditors have examined the subsidiaries are discussed in Chapter 20.

If audited financial statements of an investee are not available for the
period covered by the independent auditors' report on the investor, the
auditors should perform sufficient auditing work on the investee's financial statements to determine the fairness of amounts recorded by the
investee.

13.   Determine market value of securities at date of balance sheet.

Marketable securities are shown on the balance sheet at the lower of
cost or market. In all cases, the market value of securities is to be *disclosed.* The auditors must therefore obtain current market quotations for
all marketable securities owned by the client. The current sales prices for
actively traded listed and over-the-counter securities can readily be obtained from the financial pages of daily newspapers; for less active securities, quotations are often obtainable from investment brokers. Closing
sales prices should be used whenever available. If there were no sales
on the last day of the period, the closing bid price may be used.

The current market price per share should be listed and extended
on the basic working paper described in the first section of this audit
program. The column showing total market value for each security
should then be footed, so that the present market value of all marketable
securities owned is available for comparison with the cost figures and for
use in the balance sheet.

14.   Determine financial statement presentation for securities.

Securities may be presented in financial statements either as temporary or long-term investments. Temporary investments are classified as
current assets and include those securities that are capable of reasonably
prompt liquidation such as marketable securities, treasury bills, investment certificates, and call loans. Long-term investments are classified as
non-current assets and include marketable securities and intercorporate
investments. Both the market value and the carrying value of temporary
and long-term investments should be disclosed in the balance sheet.

Since marketable securities may be presented in the financial statements either as current or long-term investments, it appears that manage-

---

[2] CICA, *CICA Handbook* (Toronto), p. 1112.

ment's intention is the primary if not the sole criterion for distinguishing which marketable securities are current assets and which marketable securities are long-term investments. As a practical matter, management is likely to show all marketable securities as current assets, regardless what the real intention is, because most companies prefer to have their balance sheets convey an impression of debt-paying ability and a strong financial position.

Moreover, management often has reached no decision as to the length of time its investments in marketable securities will be held. Such securities will be sold when and if cash is needed. Even in those cases in which management has a tentative holding period in mind, this intent is subject to change, depending upon such factors as changes in the direction of stock prices, in interest rates, and many other unpredictable matters. Consequently, we can say that management's intent as to the length of time that marketable securities will be held often is unsettled and is not a satisfactory criterion for deciding upon the proper classification of marketable securities.

The balance sheet classifications of current and non-current items exist largely as an aid in portraying the debt-paying ability of a company and are of particular interest to creditors. If a company has relatively large amounts of marketable securities which could be sold quickly if the need arose, such assets are highly liquid from the viewpoint of creditors. To exclude them from the current asset section does not appear reasonable.

The change needed in the method of valuation of marketable securities is simply a complete conversion to market value and away from cost. Objective evidence to support market valuation is readily available, and can as readily be verified by independent auditors. Market value is the most *relevant* information with respect to marketable securities, if financial statements are to be most useful to readers.

Accountants are now in agreement that marketable securities should not be carried at amounts in excess of net realizable value, and that current market price is the best indicator of net realizable value. Perhaps the next step in this chain of reasoning will be that current market value is the most meaningful value to emphasize in the presentation of marketable securities in financial statements.

ILLUSTRATIVE CASE.   Scotia Co. Ltd. owned large amounts of marketable securities that had increased greatly in market price. Late in December of the year under audit, the company sold those securities which had appreciated most in value and then repurchased them the same day. The sale and purchase transactions resulted in recording a large gain and in establishing a higher carrying value as the cost of the securities. Officers of the client company acknowledged this to be the purpose of the transactions and pointed out that, without the gain recorded from sale of the securities, the company would have reported a loss for the year. The sale and purchase transactions were at arm's length, executed by a stockbrokerage firm on the Toronto Stock Exchange. The old stock certificates were delivered to the broker and in due course of time new certificates were received. The transactions were authorized in advance by the board of directors.

The sale and immediate repurchase of the securities and the impact on the year's net income were fully disclosed in the financial statements and in a supporting note. The auditors therefore issued an unqualified report. This case illustrates how ineffective the existing rules for ignoring market price gains can be. It also raises the question as to why accountants have been reluctant to recognize gains which are supported by objective evidence in the form of published market prices from arm's-length trading on an organized stock exchange.

Other considerations in determining the most useful balance sheet presentation include the following:

1. The basis used by the client in valuation of securities should be stated in the balance sheet and followed consistently from year to year. An exception to the consistency rule occurs when the client no longer owns voting shares in an investee in an amount sufficient to influence the investee.
2. Investments in unconsolidated subsidiaries, joint ventures, and other investees in which control or effective control is exercised should be presented in the Long-term investments section of the balance sheet.
3. A note to financial statements should disclose the principles underlying consolidation of subsidiaries, or exclusion of subsidiaries from the consolidation. Subsidiary companies should be omitted from consolidation under rare circumstances. Investments in subsidiaries not consolidated should be accounted for under the equity method.
4. The name of each investee and percentage of common shares owned should be disclosed in the balance sheet or a note.
5. If the client's own securities are included in a sinking fund, or otherwise shown as an asset in the balance sheet, this fact should be disclosed.
6. Securities pledged to secure indebtedness should be identified and cross referenced to the related liability.

OTHER INVESTMENTS

A bank *certificate of deposit* is a receipt given by a bank for the deposit of funds for a specified time. Certificates of deposit are usually negotiable and bear an interest rate greater than that for ordinary bank savings accounts.

To verify a client's certificates of deposit, the auditors will use the standard bank confirmation form illustrated in Chapter 11, and will inspect the certificates in their count of cash and other negotiable assets.

The term *commercial paper* describes unsecured promissory notes issued by corporations for periods generally less than one year. The auditors should inspect the client's commercial paper and confirm it with the issuer. If the auditors have any doubt concerning the collectibility of the commercial paper, they should investigate the financial status of the issuer.

The use of life insurance policies by business concerns to compensate for the losses arising from the death of key members of the organization, and to provide cash for settlement with the estate of a deceased partner or shareholder, is described in most intermediate accounting textbooks. When the business is named as a beneficiary of a life insurance policy, an asset element is created in the form of the *cash surrender value,* which requires verification by the auditors during their examination of investments. Concurrently with the verification of cash surrender values, the auditors customarily review other aspects of agreements and transactions relating to life insurance policies which name the client company as beneficiary. These related matters include premiums paid, dividends received, loans on policies, and agreements for disposition of insurance proceeds.

The auditing procedures for verification of this form of investment may include the following:

1. Obtain or prepare a schedule of life insurance policies.
2. Obtain confirmation from insurance companies of cash surrender values, policy loans, and accumulated dividends.
3. Verify computation of insurance expense and prepaid insurance.
4. Review agreements for use of proceeds of policies.

Balance sheet presentation of other investments

As pointed out in Chapter 11, certificates of deposit which are material in amount are shown separately in the Current assets section of the balance sheet. Commercial paper also may be shown as a separate current asset, or may be combined with marketable securities included as current assets.

Although the cash surrender value of life insurance policies represents a source of immediately available funds, cash surrender values should not be included in current assets. Exclusion of cash surrender values from the current asset classification may be supported by the argument that the funds are obtainable through cancellation of the policy; and cancellation might violate collateral agreements with partners, shareholders, or others, and is generally not contemplated by management. Loans are sometimes obtained from insurance companies with the intention not of repayment but of ultimate liquidation by offset against the proceeds of the policy upon the death of the insured. Since there is no risk of loss, insurance companies are willing to carry such loans on a permanent basis.

Under these circumstances the loan may be excluded from current liabilities, and offset against the related cash surrender value in the investments section of the balance sheet.

KEY TERMS INTRODUCED OR EMPHASIZED IN CHAPTER 12

brokers' advice   A notification sent by a stockbrokerage firm to a customer reporting the terms of a purchase or sale of securities.

business combination   The bringing together into one accounting entity of a corporation and one or more incorporated or unincorporated businesses.

certificate of deposit   A receipt issued by a bank for a deposit of funds for a specified time. Usually in denomination of $100,000 or more and bearing interest at a higher rate than for most bank savings accounts.

commercial paper   Unsecured short-term notes issued by most large corporations for periods of one year or less.

confirmation request—securities   A letter prepared by the client and addressed to the broker, bank, or other holder of client-owned securities, requesting the holder to respond directly to the independent auditors giving full identification of the securities and the purpose for which held.

dividend record book   A reference book published monthly by investment advisory services reporting much detailed information concerning all listed and many unlisted securities. Includes dividend dates and amounts, current prices of securities, and other condenced financial data.

equity method   A method of accounting for a material investment in stock of another company. Requires that the investor recognize as investment income its proportionate share of the investee's net income, rather than considering dividends received as income.

investee   A company in which the client has invested. The investor may or may not be able to control or influence the investee.

pooling of interests   A business combination which is considered to be a combining of shareholder interests of the separate entities rather than an acquisition of assets.

valuation allowance—securities   A contra account used to reduce the carrying value of an investment in securities when market value is lower than cost.

GROUP I
REVIEW QUESTIONS

12–1.   Is a bank certificate of deposit the same as a bank savings account? Explain.

12–2.   How are cost, market value, and the equity method of accounting used in valuing securities?

12–3.   Under what conditions would CAs accept a confirmation of the securities in the possession of a custodian in lieu of inspecting the securities themselves? (AICPA)

12–4.   What are some of the kinds of errors sometimes encountered by auditors in examining revenue recorded on security investments?

12–5.   Should the auditors communicate directly with the issuing corporation to establish the authenticity of securities held as investments by a client? Explain.

12–6.   Much consideration has been given to a possible change from historical cost to current value accounting, and interest in this question has been increased by the U.S. SEC's action in requiring disclosure of replacement cost for inventories and plant and equipment. Would a change from cost (or lower of cost or market) to market value as the basis for valuation of investments in marketable securities be more or less difficult than for most types of assets? Explain.

12–7.   What documents should be examined in verifying the purchases and sales of securities made during the year under audit?

12–8.   A company which you are auditing carries $3 million of insurance on the lives of its officers. List the principal steps required in the verification of these policies and state how the transactions for the year and balances at the end of the year should be reflected in the financial statements. (AICPA)

12–9.   Should the inspection of securities on hand be correlated with any other specific phase of the audit? Explain.

12–10.   How can the auditors determine that all dividends applicable to marketable securities owned by the client have been received and recorded?

12–11.   What are the main objectives of the auditors in the examination of investments in securities?

12–12.   What information should be noted by the auditors during their inspection of securities on hand?

12–13.   What are the major considerations that induce manufacturing and merchandising concerns to invest in securities?

12–14.   Under what circumstances may securities owned by the client not be on hand at the balance sheet date?

12–15.   Are the auditors concerned with securities transactions subsequent to the balance sheet date? Explain.

12–16.   During your examination of a client's investments in corporate bonds, you note that premiums and discounts on these investments are not being amortized. Would you take exception to this practice? Explain.

12–17.   Assume that it is not possible for you to be present on the balance sheet date to inspect the securities owned by the client. What variation in audit procedures is appropriate if the inspection is not made until two weeks after the balance sheet date?

12–18.   One of your clients which has never before invested in securities recently acquired more than a million dollars in cash from the sale of real estate no longer used in operations. The president intends to invest this money in marketable securities until such time as the opportunity arises for advantageous acquisition of a new plant site. He asks you to enumerate the principal factors you would recommend to create a strong system of internal control over marketable securities.

GROUP II
QUESTIONS REQUIRING ANALYSIS

12–19. Your client, the Naylor Limited, is in strong financial condition and owns government bonds with a market value of $20 million which it classifies as current assets. There are no bank loans outstanding, and the company is dedicated to maintaining a liquid position. At the balance sheet date, the company has commitments for additions to plant and equipment in the amount of $12 million. Naylor expects to pay cash for the plant additions and not to assume any liabilities in connection with the expansion. It is possible that cash from some of the government bonds which will mature in the near future may be used to pay for the plan expansion program, but no bonds have been earmarked for this purpose. The company expects to continue to invest in government bonds as a means of maintaining a strong financial position and deriving some interest revenue from its liquid assets.

During a meeting of the independent auditors with the board of directors, one of the outside directors suggests that in view of the company's commitments and plans to spend $12 million for new plant during the next year or two, this amount of government bonds should be removed from the current asset classification and listed "below the line" as Long-term investments or Other assets. The director expresses the opinion that footnote disclosure of the expansion plans or mention of the matter in the auditors' report would not be a satisfactory alternative. Other members of the board disagree with this proposal for removing government bonds from the current asset section. The board asks you opinion.

Required:

Should the government bonds be removed from the current asset classification? How should the commitments and anticipated expenditures for plant expansion be presented, if at all, in the financial statements? Explain.

12–20. You are auditing the financial statements of Mason Co. Ltd., a new client, for the current year ended December 31. Mason's balance sheet shows an asset total of $10 million, including the following:

25% interest in Importers, Inc., at cost $2,000,000

You have inspected an Importers, Inc., stock certificate for 400 shares, dated April 1 of the current year and registered in the name of Mason Co. Ltd. In addition, you have inspected a paid Mason company cheque for $2,000,000 dated March 31 of the current year, payable to and endorsed by Importers, Inc.

Required:

Have you accumulated sufficient appropriate evidence for Mason company's investment in Importers, Inc.? Explain.

12–21. You are making your first audit of the financial statements of Judi Toguchi, an individual with large investments in marinas, motels, and apartments. In your review of the general ledger you notice an account entitled Davis Company, which has a debit balance of $150,000. Your investigation shows this to be the name of a local stockbrokerage firm with which your client had made a deposit for purchase of securities on margin. The only security transaction to date had been the purchase on December 10 of 3,000 shares of National Environmental Products Ltd. at a price per share of $80. The brokerage fee on the transaction had been $1,566. No entry had been made for this purchase.

Give the adjusting entry or entries that you consider necessary for a proper presentation of these facts in the balance sheet at December 31.

12–22. Select the best answer for each of the following situations and give reasons for your choice.

a. If securities belonging to the client are in the possession of others at the balance sheet date, an appropriate action to be taken by the independent auditors consists of—

(1) Disclosing in a footnote to the financial statements and also in the auditors' report that the securities were not inspected.

(2) Arranging for a confirmation request to be sent to the holder of the securities.

(3) A visit by the auditors to the location where the securities are being held, and inspection in the normal manner.

(4) Securing from management of the client company a written statement as to the ownership of the securities and the reasons for their not being on hand.

b. The marketable securities owned by the client were carried at the lower of cost or market. At the balance sheet date the auditors determined that current market value was above the client's cost. Two weeks later, before completion of the field work, a sharp drop occurred in the stock market and the auditors became aware that on the final day of field work the market value of the client's holdings of securities had fallen below cost.

(1) No change in the carrying value of the securities is required and no disclosure of the price decline need be made either in the financial statements or the auditors' report.

(2) A valuation allowance should be established to reduce the

securities to the lower carrying value indicated at the end of the field work.

(3) No change is required in the carrying value of the securities but disclosure of the reduced market value at the conclusion of field work should be made in a note to the financial statements.

(4) Disclosure of the excess of cost over market value as of the final date of field work should be made in a note to the financial statements and also in the auditors' report.

GROUP III
PROBLEMS

12–23. In connection with an examination of the financial statements of Morton, Inc., Jane Hill, CA, is considering the necessity of inspecting marketable securities on the balance sheet date, May 31, or at some other date. The marketable securities held by Morton include negotiable bearer bonds, which are kept in a safe in the treasurer's office, and miscellaneous stocks and bonds kept in a safe-deposit box at The Provincial Bank. Both the negotiable bearer bonds and the miscellaneous stocks and bonds are material to proper presentation of Morton's financial position.

Required:

a. What are the factors that Hill should consider in determining the necessity for inspecting these securities on May 31, as opposed to other dates?

b. Assume that Hill plans to send a member of her staff to Morton's office and The Provincial Bank on May 31 to make the security inspection. What instructions should she give to this staff member as to the conduct of the inspection and the evidence to be included in the audit working papers? (*Note:* Do not discuss the valuation of securities, the revenue from securities, or the examination of information contained in the accounting records of the company.)

c. Assume that Hill finds it impracticable to send a member of her staff to Morton's offices and The Provincial Bank on May 31. What alternative procedures may she employ to assure herself that the company had physical possession of its marketable securities on May 31 if the securities are inspected (1) May 28, (2) June 5? (AICPA, adapted)

12–24. CA has been appointed auditor of M Ltd. and its subsidiary companies for the year ended May 31, 1979, replacing another chartered accountant who had retired. No information is available from the former auditor.

The company's consolidated balance sheet as at May 31, 1979, contained the following account, amounting to about 8% of the net assets:

Investment in unconsolidated subsidiary (see Note) $612,478

    Note: The company acquired 57 percent of the common shares of B Ltd. on July 1, 1975, for $500,000. The investment is carried on an equity basis.

Required:

What procedures should CA carry out to form an opinion on the above item? Refer to the long-term intercorporation investments section of the *CICA Handbook,* if necessary. (CICA, adapted)

12–25.   A new client, Reyes Limited, has retained you to audit its financial statements for the year ended June 30, 1979. On May 1, 1979, Reyes Limited had borrowed $500,000 from Valley National Bank to finance plant expansion. The long-term note agreement provided for the annual payment of principal and interest over five years. The existing plant was pledged as security for the loan.

Because of unexpected difficulties in acquiring the building site, the plant expansion had not begun at June 30, 1979. To derive some revenue from the borrowed funds, management had decided to invest in stocks and bonds; and on May 16, 1979, the $500,000 had been invested in marketable securities.

Required:

a.   How could you verify the securities owned by Reyes at June 30, 1979?

b.   In your audit of marketable securities, how would you:
    (1)   Verify the dividend and interest revenue recorded?
    (2)   Determine market value?
    (3)   Establish the authority for securities purchases? (AICPA, adapted)

12–26.   In an audit at December 31, 1978, of a new client, Billings Limited, you find that the company owns only one security but that this investment is quite material in relation to other assets. The investment consists of $200,000 face value of a 6 percent bond issue listed on the Toronto Stock Exchange. The bonds were issued by one of the world's largest corporations, and you find by referring to published securities manuals that the entire bond issue totaled $100,000,000 and carried a very high rating. Market value of the bonds at year-end was $226,000.

The only entry in your client's accounting records pertaining to the investment was a debit to the general ledger account, Investment in Securities, and a credit to Cash, in the amount of $225,800. The journal entry for the investment was dated November 1, 1978, and carried an explanation that the $225,800 payment included a broker's commission of $1,000 and accrued interest of $2,000. The maturity date of the bonds was September 1, 1998.

The treasurer of Billings made the following comment to you: We have no plans for selling these bonds in the immediate future, but we will sell them at any time our cash position drops, which it probably will next summer."

Required:

a. The monthly balance sheets prepared by the company included the bond investment among the current assets. Would this classification be acceptable for the year-end audited financial statements? Give reasons for your answer.

b. What audit evidence would you need for verification of this investment, apart from examination of the ledger account and journal entry?

c. Draft the adjusting entry relating to the bond investment which Billings should make at December 31. (Amortization of the premium on the bonds owned is not required.)

12–27. You have been retained to make an examination of Fox Company Limited for the current year ended December 31. The company carries on a wholesale and retail business in lumber and building supplies; total assets amount to $1 million and shareholders' equity is $500,000.

The company's records show an investment of $100,000 for 100 shares of common stock of one of its customers, the Ozark Limited. You learn that Ozark Limited is closely held and that its capital stock, consisting of 1,000 shares of issued and outstanding common stock, has no published or quoted market value.

Examination of your client's cash disbursements record reveals an entry of a cheque of $100,000 drawn on January 23 of the current year to Fred Costello, who is said to be the former holder of the 100 shares of stock. Costello is president of Fox. Fox Company Limited has no other investments.

Required:

a. List the auditing procedures you would employ in connection with the $100,000 investment of your client in the capital stock of Ozark Limited.

b. Discuss the presentation of the investment on the balance sheet, including its valuation.

12–28.   You are in charge of the audit of the financial statements of Hawk Limited for the year ended December 31. The corporation has had the policy of investing its surplus cash in marketable securities. Its stock and bond certificates are kept in a safe-deposit box in a local bank. Only the president or the treasurer of the corporation has access to the box.

You were unable to obtain access to the safe-deposit box on December 31 because neither the president nor the treasurer was avaliable. Arrangements were made for your staff assistant to accompany the treasurer to the bank on January 11 to examine the securities. Your assistant has never examined securities that were being kept in a safe-deposit box and requires instructions. To inspect all the securities on hand should not require more than one hour.

Required:

a.   List the instructions that you would give to your assistant regarding the examination of the stock and bond certificates kept in the safe-deposit box. Include in your instructions the details of the securities to be examined and the reasons for examining these details.

b.   Upon returning from the bank your assistant reported that the treasurer had entered the box on January 4. The treasurer stated that the purpose of the January 4 visit to the safe-deposit box had been to remove an old photograph of the corporation's original building. The photograph was reportedly loaned to the local chamber of commerce for display purposes. List the additional audit procedures that are required because of the treasurer's action. (AICPA)

12–29.   The following is an excerpt from the "Statement of Assets and Liabilities" at March 31, 1979, of K Ltd., an investment company.

Assets		% of Net Assets
Marketable securities, at cost:		
Government of Canada securities		
(market value, $500,000)	$ 500,000	1.7
Corporate bonds and notes		
(market value $520,000)	500,000	1.7
Common stocks		
(market value, $30,000,000)	25,000,000	83.3
	$26,000,000	86.7
Cash at banks	500,000	1.7
Receivable for securities sold	3,300,000	11.0
Dividends and interest receivable	200,000	0.6
Total Assets	$30,000,000	100.0

Required:

Outline the audit procedures CA, the shareholders' auditor, should adopt to verify the marketable securities shown above before expressing an opinion. (CICA, adapted)

13

Accounts and notes receivable; and sales transactions

Sales transactions and receivables from customers are so closely related that the two can best be considered jointly in a discussion of auditing objectives and procedures. Receivables from customers include both accounts receivable and the various types of notes receivable. One of the traditional objectives of the auditors in the verification of receivables has been to determine the genuineness of customers' accounts and notes. A good approach to this objective consists of a study and evaluation of the internal controls over the issuance of sales invoices, shipping documents, and other evidences of claims against customers. Before discussing internal control over sales and receivables, however, it is desirable, first, to consider the nature of the various claims which may be grouped under the classification of accounts and notes receivable and, second, to state the major objectives of the auditors in this phase of their examination.

Meaning of accounts receivable

Accounts receivable in a broad sense include not only claims against customers arising from the sale of goods or services but also a great variety of miscellaneous claims, such as advances to officers or employees, loans to subsidiaries, uncollected share subscriptions, claims against railroads or other public carriers, claims for tax refunds, and advances to suppliers. Similar audit procedures are used in the verification of all these various types of receivables, although additional investigation may be required with respect to related party transactions which do not involve arm's-length bargaining—for example, loans to officers.

498

Meaning of notes receivable

Typically, notes and acceptances receivable are used for handling transactions of substantial amount; these negotiable documents are widely used by industrial and commercial concerns. In banks and finance companies, notes receivable usually constitute the most important single asset.

Notes receivable may be acquired in a variety of ways. In some lines of business, particularly the marketing of durable equipment of high unit cost, it is common practice to accept notes from customers in payment for the sale of merchandise. Installment notes are very widely used in the sale of industrial machinery, farm equipment, tractors, and automobiles. An installment note or contract is a negotiable instrument which grants possession of the goods to the purchaser but permits the seller to retain title as collateral until the final installment under the note has been received. Other transactions which may lead to the acquisition of notes receivable include: the disposal of equipment; the sale of divisions or subsidiary companies; and the making of loans to officers, employees, and affiliated companies.

The *trade acceptance* is a form of draft, defined as a "bill of exchange drawn by the seller on the purchaser of goods sold, and accepted by such purchaser." The purchaser or acceptor becomes primarily liable on the instrument, thus occupying a position similar to that of the maker of a note. The drawer of an acceptance is secondarily liable, as is an endorser on a note.

Regardless of the type or source of the notes on hand, however, the auditors' objectives and the procedures they employ to attain those objectives are sufficiently uniform that the following discussion may be considered applicable to virtually all types of notes receivables and to trade acceptances as well.

The auditors' objectives in examination of receivables and sales

The principal objectives of the auditors in their examination of receivables and sales are to determine (a) the adequacy of internal control for sales transactions and receivables, (b) the validity or genuineness of the recorded receivables, (c) the approximate realizable value of this group of assets, and (d) the propriety of the amounts recorded as sales and as interest revenue.

The most significant factor in selecting the audit procedures required for a particular engagement is the adequacy of the system of internal control. It is, therefore, appropriate to consider at this point the nature of internal control as applied to sales and receivable accounts, and the audit techniques for testing and appraising these controls.

Internal control of sales transactions and accounts receivable

Our discussion of internal control will be developed primarily in terms of the sales activities of manufacturing companies. When internal controls over sales on account are inadequate, large credit losses are almost inevitable. Merchandise may be shipped to customers whose credit standing has not been approved. Shipments may be made to customers without notice being given to the billing department—consequently no sales invoice is prepared. Sales invoices may contain errors in prices and quantities; and if sales invoices are not controlled by serial numbers, some may be lost and never recorded as accounts receivable. To avoid such difficulties, strong internal controls over credit sales are necessary. Usually internal control over credit sales is best achieved by a division of duties so that different departments or individuals are responsible for (1) preparation of the sales order, (2) credit approval, (3) issuance of merchandise from stock, (4) shipment, (5) billing, (6) invoice verification, (7) maintenance of control accounts, (8) maintenance of customers' ledgers, (9) approval of sales returns and allowances, and (10) authorization of write-offs of uncollectible accounts. When this degree of subdivision of duties is feasible, accidental errors are likely to be detected quickly through the comparison of documents and amounts emerging from independent units of the company, and the opportunity for fraud is reduced to a minimum. In an electronic data processing system, several of the functions described above may be performed by the computer. In these circumstances, internal controls of the type described in Chapter 6 should be in effect.

Controlling customers' orders. The controlling and processing of orders received from customers requires carefully designed operating procedures and numerous control devices if costly errors are to be avoided. Important initial steps include the registering of the customer's purchase order, a review of items and quantities to determine whether the order can be filled within a reasonable time, and the preparation of a sales order. The sales order is a translation of the terms of the customer's order into a set of specific instructions for the guidance of the factory, the shipping department, and the billing department. The action to be taken by the factory upon receipt of the sales order will depend upon whether the goods are standard products carried in stock or are to be produced to specifications set by the customer.

Credit approval. Before sales orders are processed, the credit department must determine whether goods may be shipped to the customer on open account. This department, supervised by a credit manager who reports to the treasurer or vice president of finance, monitors the financial condition of prospective and continuing customers by reference to the customers' periodic financial statements and published reports of credit agencies. Customers who do not meet standards for trade credit established by the finance committee of the board of directors are shipped goods on a cash-on-delivery (C.O.D.) basis.

Issuance of merchandise. Companies which carry standard products in stock maintain a finished goods storeroom supervised by a storeskeeper. The storeskeeper issues stock covered by a sales order to the shipping department only after the sales order has been approved by the credit department. Perpetual inventory records of finished goods are maintained in the accounting department, not by the storeskeeper.

The shipping function. When the goods are transmitted by the finished goods storeroom to the shipping department, this group must arrange for space in railroad cars, aircraft, or motor freight carriers. Shipping documents, such as bills of lading, are created at the time of loading the goods into cars or trucks. The shipping documents are numerically controlled and are entered in a shipping register before being forwarded to the billing department. When shipments are made by truck, some type of gate control is also needed to ensure that all goods leaving the plant have been recorded as shipments. This may require the surrender to the gatekeeper of special copies of shipping documents.

The billing function. Billing should be performed by a department not under the control of sales executives. The function is generally assigned to a separate section within the accounting, data processing, or finance departments. The billing section has the responsibility of (*a*) accounting for the serially numbered shipping documents, (*b*) comparing shipping documents with sales orders and customers' purchase orders and change notices, (*c*) entering pertinent data from these documents on the sales invoice, (*d*) applying prices and discounts from price lists to the invoice, (*e*) making the necessary extensions and footings, and (*f*) accumulating the total amounts billed. In the case of government contracts, the formal contract usually specifies prices, delivery procedures, inspection and acceptance routines, method of liquidating advances, and numerous other details, so that the contract is a most important source of information for preparation of the sales invoice.

Before invoices are mailed to customers, they should be reviewed to determine the propriety and accuracy of prices, credit terms, transportation charges, extensions, and footings. Daily totals of amounts invoiced should be transmitted directly to the general ledger accounting section for entry in control accounts. Copies of individual invoices should be transmitted to the accounts receivable section under control of transmittal letters, with a listing by serial number of all invoices being submitted.

In a company using an electronic data processing system, several of the billing and accounting processes described above are performed in a single processing "run" by the computer.

Collection of receivables. As receivables are collected, the cashier will retain customers' remittance advices or prepare a comparable form, listing the credit to each customer's account. These remittance advices will then be forwarded to the accounts receivable section or the data processing department, which will record them in the appropriate accounts in the customers' ledger. The total reduction in accounts receivable will be posted periodically to the general ledger control account from the total of the accounts receivable column in the cash receipts journal. Credit memoranda will be handled in a parallel manner.

An aged trial balance of customers' accounts should be prepared at regular intervals for use by the credit department in carrying out its collection program. Under this system the general ledger and the subsidiary ledger for accounts receivable are developed from separate data by employees working independently of each other, thus assuring detection of nearly all accidental errors. Fraud becomes unlikely except in the event of collusion of two or more employees. The subsidiary ledger should be balanced periodically with the control account by an employee from the operations control group.

Write-off receivables. Receivables judged by management to be uncollectible should be written off and transferred to a separate ledger and control account. This record may be of a memorandum nature rather than part of the regular accounting structure, but it is essential that the accounts which are written off be properly controlled. Otherwise any subsequent collections may be abstracted by employees without the necessity of any falsification of the records to conceal the theft.

Internal audit of receivables. In some large companies the internal auditors periodically take over the mailing of monthly statements to customers and investigate any discrepancies reported; or they may make extensive reviews of shipping reports, invoices, credit memoranda, and aged trial balances of receivables to determine whether authorized procedures are being consistently carried out.

The division of responsibility, sequence of procedures, and basic documentation of the handling of credit sales transactions are illustrated in the systems flowchart in Figure 13–1. Internal control over collections from customers is shown in the cash receipts systems flowchart on page 432 in Chapter 11.

Internal control of notes receivable

As previously stated, a basic element of internal control consists of the subdivision of duties. As applied to notes receivable, this principle requires that—

1. The custodian of notes receivable not have access to cash or to the general accounting records.

2. The acceptance and renewal of notes be authorized in writing by a responsible official who does not have custody of the notes.

3. The write-off of defaulted notes be approved in writing by responsible officials, and effective procedures adopted for subsequent follow-up of such defaulted notes.

These rules are obviously corollaries of the general proposition that the authorization and recording functions should be entirely separate from the custodial function, especially for cash and receivables.

If the acceptance of a note from a customer requires written approval of a responsible official, the likelihood of fictitious notes being created to offset a theft of cash is materially reduced. The same review and approval should be required for renewal of a note; otherwise, an opportunity is created for the withholding of cash when a note is collected and the concealment of the shortage by unauthorized "renewal" of the paid note. The protection given by this procedure for executive approval of the acceptance and renewal of notes will be greatly augmented if notes receivable are periodically confirmed directly with the makers by the internal auditing department.

The abstraction of cash receipts is sometimes concealed by failing to make any entry to record receipt of a partial payment on a note. Satisfactory control procedures for recording partial payments require that the date and amount of the payment and the new unpaid balance should be entered on the back of the instrument, with proper credit being given the debtor in the note register. Any notes written off as uncollectible should be kept under accounting control because occasionally debtors may attempt to re-establish their credit in later years by paying old dishonoured notes. Any credit memoranda or journal vouchers for partial payments, write-offs, or adjustment of disputed notes should be authorized by proper officials and kept under numerical control.

Adequate internal controls over notes receivable secured by mortgages and trust deeds must include follow-up procedures that assure prompt action on delinquent property taxes and insurance premiums, as well as for non-payment of interest and principal installments.

In many companies internal control is strengthened by the preparation of monthly reports summarizing note receivable transactions during the month and the details of notes owned at the end of the reporting period. These reports are often designed to focus executive attention immediately upon any delinquent notes, and to require advance approval for renewals of maturing notes. In addition, a monthly report on notes receivable ordinarily will show the amounts collected during the month, the new notes accepted, notes discounted, and interest earned. The person responsible for reporting on note transactions should be someone other than the custodian of the notes.

FIGURE 13–1

DIXIELINE INDUSTRIES LTD.

CREDIT SALES SYSTEMS FLOWCHART

DECEMBER 31, 1978

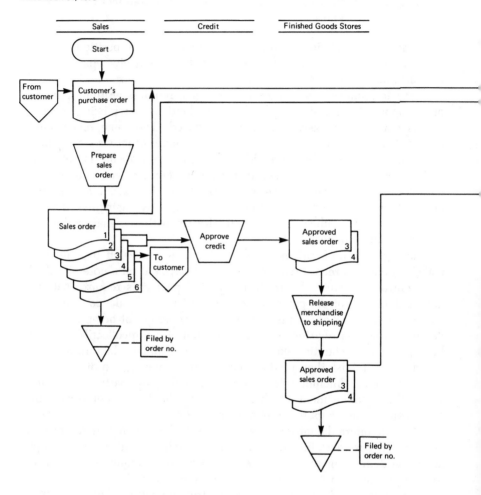

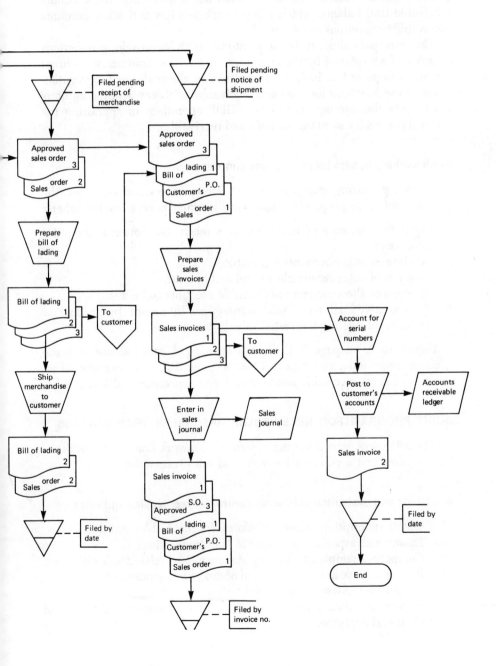

Internal control and the computer

The auditors whose client uses a computer may find sales and accounts receivable transactions processed by either a batch or an online, real-time system. Batch system print-outs usually include a daily sales journal (including sales returns and allowances) and a daily updated accounts receivable trial balance which reflects cash receipts and other accounts receivable transactions as well as sales.

The principal online, real-time print-outs are a log of sales transactions in order of acceptance by the computer, and a daily transactions journal for each computer terminal. In either situation, the traditional segregation of employee functions for sales and receivables is absent, and the auditors must study the internal control over EDP operations in appraising the internal control for sales transactions and receivables.

Audit working papers for receivables and sales

Besides preparing grouping sheets for receivables and net sales, the auditors obtain or prepare the following working papers, among others:

1. Aged trial balance of trade accounts receivable (often a computer print-out).
2. Analyses of other accounts receivable.
3. Analysis of notes receivable and related interest.
4. Analysis of allowance for uncollectible accounts and notes.
5. Comparative analyses of sales transactions by month, by product or territory, or relating forecasted sales to actual sales.

Figure 13–2, on page 513, illustrates an aged trial balance of trade accounts receivable, and Figure 13–3, on page 515, is an example of an analysis of notes receivable and related interest revenue and accruals.

AUDIT PROGRAM FOR RECEIVABLES AND SALES TRANSACTIONS

The following procedures are typical of the work done in the verification of notes and accounts receivable and sales transactions.

A. Study and evaluation of internal control for receivables and sales

1. Obtain description of internal control for receivables and sales.
2. Examine all aspects of a sample of sales transactions.
3. Compare a sample of shipping documents to related sales invoices.
4. Review the use and authorization of credit memoranda.
5. Review cash discounts and freight allowances.
6. Review accounting for sales taxes and proceeds from disposals of plant and equipment.

7. Reconcile selected cash register tapes and sales tickets with sales journals.
8. Review the basis for recognizing profit on installment sales.
9. Review and confirm notes and accounts written off as uncollectible.
10. Evaluate internal control for receivables and sales.

B. Substantive tests of receivables and sales transactions

11. Obtain or prepare an aged trial balance of trade accounts receivable and analyses of other accounts receivable.
12. Obtain or prepare an analysis of notes receivable and related interest.
13. Inspect notes on hand and confirm those not on hand by direct communication with holders.
14. Confirm notes and accounts receivable by direct communication with debtors.
15. Determine adequacy of allowance for uncollectible accounts and notes.
16. Review the year-end cutoff of sales transactions.
17. Verify interest earned on notes and accrued interest receivable.
18. Obtain or prepare a comparative analysis of sales and cost of goods sold.
19. Ascertain whether any receivables have been pledged.
20. Ascertain whether notes or accounts of "insiders" paid prior to the balance sheet date have since been renewed.
21. Determine proper balance sheet presentation of notes and accounts receivable and proper income statement presentation of sales.
22. Obtain from client a letter of representations concerning notes and accounts receivable and sales.

A. Study and evaluation:

1. Obtain description of internal control for receivables and sales.

The auditors' study and evaluation of internal controls over receivables and sales may begin with the preparation of a written description or flowchart or the filling in of an internal control questionnaire. Typical of the questions comprising an internal control questionnaire for receivables and sales are the following: Are orders from customers recorded and reviewed by a sales department? Are sales invoices prenumbered and all numbers accounted for? Are all sales approved by the credit department before shipment? The questionnaire should be viewed as an enumeration of matters to be investigated rather than as questions to be disposed of with "yes" or "no" answers.

2. Examine all aspects of a sample of sales transactions.

To determine that the internal control procedures for sales are being applied properly, the auditors select a sample of sales transactions for detailed compliance testing. The size of the sample and the transactions included therein may be determined by either statistical sampling or judgment sampling techniques. A generalized computer audit program is often used to select the invoices to be tested. To prove the extent of compliance with internal controls supposedly in force, the auditors should examine every aspect of the selected group of sales transactions.

In manufacturing companies the audit procedure for verification of a sales transaction which has been selected for compliance testing may begin with a comparison of the customer's purchase order, the client's sales order, and the duplicate copy of the sales invoice. The descriptions of items and the quantities are compared on these three documents and traced to the duplicate copy of the related shipping document. The credit manager's signature denoting approval of the customer's credit should appear on the sales order.

The extensions and footings on each invoice in the sample should be proved and the date of the invoice compared with the date on the shipping document and with the date of entry in the accounts receivable subsidiary ledger. Prices on the invoice may be compared with price lists, catalogs, or other official sources used in preparing invoices. If a block sample of invoices covering transactions of a week or a month has been selected, the sequence of invoice serial numbers should also be reviewed for any missing numbers. Bills of lading and freight bills may also be compared with invoices as a further test of validity of the invoices.

After proving the accuracy of selected individual invoices, the auditors next trace the invoices to the sales journal. The footing of the sales journal is proven, and the total is traced to the general ledger account for sales.

In summary, this process of testing selected sales transactions consists of tracing each transaction through the system from the receipt of the customer's order to the shipment of the goods and the subsequent collection of the account receivable. A converse technique may be used; entries in the sales journal may be selected for vouching to supporting invoices, customer purchase orders, and shipping documents. By these tests, the auditors should obtain evidence that all sales are being accurately and promptly billed, that billings do not include any anticipated sales or extraneous transactions, and that the amounts billed are accurately and promptly recorded in customers' ledgers and in control accounts. If these conditions prevail, the auditors are entitled to rely upon the charges appearing in customers' accounts.

During their compliance tests of sales transactions, the auditors should be alert for indications of consignment shipments treated as sales. Many concerns which dispose of only a small portion of their total output by consignment shipments fail to make any distinction between consignment shipments and regular sales.

If the subsidiary records for receivables include some accounts with large debit entries and more numerous small credit entries, this should suggest to the auditors that goods have been shipped on consignment and that payments are being received only as the consignee makes sales. Notations such as "Consignment shipment" or "On approval" are sometimes found in subsidiary ledgers or on the duplicate copies of sales invoices. Numerous large returns of merchandise are also suggestive of consignment shipments.

The auditors should also investigate the controls for sales to related parties. Effective control over intercompany or interbranch transfers of merchandise often requires the same kind of formal procedures for billing, shipping, and collection functions as for sales to outsiders; hence these movements of merchandise are often invoiced and recorded as sales. When the operations of the several organizational units are combined or consolidated into one income statement, however, it is apparent that any transactions not representing sales to outsiders should be eliminated from consolidated sales. In the examination of a client which operates subsidiaries or branches, the auditors should investigate the procedures for recording movements of merchandise between the various units of the company.

3. Compare a sample of shipping documents to related sales invoices.

The preceding step in the audit program called for an examination of selected invoices and a comparison of such invoices with sales records and shipping documents. That procedure would not, however, disclose orders which had been shipped but not billed. To assure that all shipments are billed, it is necessary for the auditors to obtain a sample of shipping documents issued during the year, and to compare these to sales invoices. In making this compliance test, particular emphasis should be placed upon accounting for all shipping documents by serial number. Any voided shipping documents should have been mutilated and retained in the files. The purposeful or accidental destruction of shipping documents prior to the creation of a sales invoice might go undetected if this type of test were not made. Correlation of serial numbers of sales orders, shipping advices, and sales invoices is highly desirable.

4. Review the use and authorization of credit memoranda.

All allowances to customers for returned or defective merchandise should be supported by serially numbered credit memoranda signed by an officer or responsible employee having no duties relating to cash handling or to the maintenance of customers' ledgers. Good internal control over credits for returned merchandise usually includes a requirement that the returned goods be received and examined before credit is given. The credit memoranda should then bear the date and serial number of the receiving report on the return shipment.

In addition to establishing that credit memoranda were properly authorized, the auditors should make tests of these documents similar to those suggested for sales invoices. Prices, extensions, and footings should be verified, and postings traced from the sales return journal or other accounting record to the customers' accounts in the subsidiary receivable ledgers.

5. Review cash discounts and freight allowances.

The auditors' review of internal control for cash discounts allowed should begin with a study of the client's established policy as to the rates of discounts for various classes of customers. The auditors then will scan the discounts column of the cash receipts journal, noting any deviations from the prescribed rates. This compliance test should be supplemented by selecting a number of customers' accounts in the accounts receivable subsidiary ledger, comparing the collections recorded therein with the credit terms shown on the duplicate sales invoices and tracing the entries to the cash records. Discounts allowed on payments beyond the discount period and any other variations should be reviewed with the controller or other appropriate executive.

Another approach in reviewing the property of recorded cash discounts is to analyze by months the dollar amount of collections on receivables, the dollar amount of cash discounts allowed, and the percentage relationship of discounts to collections. Any significant variations should be fully investigated. Comparison, period by period, of the ratio of cash discounts to net credit sales is also a useful step in bringing to light variations of substantial amount.

The review of freight allowances, trade discounts, and other reductions from invoice list prices may be begun by enquiry into the client's policies for such deductions from sales. It is customary for any such items to be deducted at the time of billing. The procedures employed should be investigated in detail and described in the audit working papers.

6. Review accounting for sales taxes and proceeds from disposals of plant and equipment.

Some companies responsible for collecting provincial and federal sales taxes on their products may credit tax collections to the Sales account. This is especially true for companies having substantial cash sales. The auditors should test the client's sales tax accounting procedures to ascertain that a liability account is credited for sales taxes payable, either at the time of sale or by adjusting entry at the end of the accounting period.

In compliance tests of sales transactions the auditors should be alert to detect any credits to sales representing the proceeds from disposal of items of plant and equipment. This type of error is most likely to occur when detailed subsidiary records are not maintained for plant and equipment. A similar type of error is crediting the Sales account for deposits on containers and for miscellaneous receipts, such as rental revenue, refunds of overpayments to vendors, and return of deposits. If the client sells products in returnable containers, the auditors should investigate the possibility that deposits on containers may have been treated as sales instead of liabilities.

7. Reconcile selected cash register tapes and sales tickets with sales journals.

In the audit of clients which make a substantial amount of sales for cash, the auditors may compare selected daily totals in the sales journal with cash register readings or tapes. The serial numbers of all sales tickets used during the selected periods should be accounted for, and the individual tickets examined for accuracy of calculations and traced to the sale summary or journal.

8. Review the basis for recognizing profit on installment sales.

If the client makes sales on the installment plan, the auditors should determine the basis used in recognizing profit on these transactions, and should prepare a memorandum for the working papers describing the method in use. For financial reporting purposes, the installment method of accounting for sales is acceptable only if collection of the sales price is substantially in doubt. In other words, revenue ordinarily should be recognized at the time of the sale, with appropriate provision for uncollectible receivables.

The client company's method of accounting for repossessed merchandise should also be covered in a memorandum, with particular attention being given to the procedures employed in placing valuations on repossessed goods.

9. Review and confirm notes and accounts written off as uncollectible.

The auditors should determine that proper authorization was obtained for all notes and accounts of significant amount written off as uncollectible during the year. Documentary evidence of aggressive collection efforts by the client will normally be available to support the classification of a note or an account receivable as uncollectible. In the absence of proper authorization procedures, a dishonest employee could permanently conceal an abstraction of cash by a charge to notes or accounts receivable and subsequent write-off.

A systematic review of the notes and accounts written off can conveniently be made by obtaining or preparing an analysis of the Allowance for Uncollectible Accounts and Notes. Debits to the allowance may be traced to the authorizing documents and to the control record of accounts and notes written off; confirmation requests should be mailed to these debtors to determine that the account or note was genuine when it was first recorded in the accounts. Credit entries should be compared with the charges to Uncollectible Accounts and Notes Expense. Any write-off which appears unreasonable should be fully investigated. Charge-off of a note or account receivable from an officer, shareholder, or director is unreasonable on its face and warrants the most searching investigation by the auditors.

The disposition of any collateral held on written-off notes or accounts should be ascertained; in the case of installment notes receivable written off, the disposition of any repossessed merchandise should be reviewed. The computation of percentages relating the year's write-offs to net credit sales, to the provision for uncollectible accounts and notes, and to the allowance for uncollectible accounts and notes may be useful in bringing to light any abnormal write-offs.

10. Evaluate internal control for receivables and sales.

After completion of the description of internal control for receivables and sales, and the compliance tests of sales transactions, the auditors will have accumulated sufficient evidence to evaluate internal control for receivables and sales. In their evaluation, the auditors will identify those weaknesses which require extension of auditing procedures and those strengths which permit curtailment of procedures. The evaluation is thus closely integrated with the audit program for substantive tests of receivables and sales transactions.

B. Substantive tests

11. Obtain or prepare an aged trial balance of trade accounts receivable and analyses of other accounts receivable.

An aged trial balance of trade accounts receivable at the audit date is commonly prepared for the auditors by employees of the client, often in the form of a computer print-out. The client-prepared schedule illustrated in Figure 13–2 is a multipurpose form designed for the aging of customers' accounts, the estimating of probable credit losses, and the controlling of confirmation requests. The inclusion of so many phases of the examination of receivables in a single working paper is practicable only for small concerns with a limited number of customers.

The auditors should also obtain from the client analyses of all types of accounts receivable other than trade accounts. Analyses of such accounts receivables are required because the transactions creating the receivables are between related parties rather than being at arm's length. Transactions not conducted at arm's length require more than ordinary attention from the auditors. Accounts with officers, directors, employees, shareholders, and affiliated enterprises are sometimes paid near the close of the fiscal year to avoid disclosure in the financial statements, but are reopened early in the succeeding period. Expense advances and various other types of receivable accounts have at times been used to disguise loans made to officers in violation of corporation laws or the client's by-laws. The nature of the transactions and the propriety of credits to the accounts should be studied.

Analyses of accounts receivable from branches or affiliated companies often disclose debit entries for transactions other than the sale of merchandise. The auditors should determine that the receivable balance

FIGURE 13–2

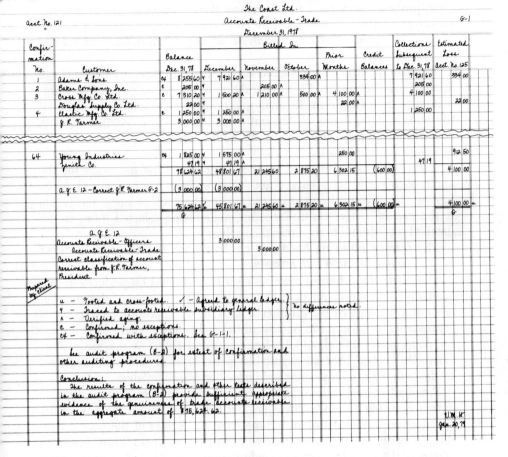

The Coast Ltd.
Accounts Receivable—Trade
December 31, 1978

agrees with the payable balance in the affiliate's accounting records. This can be accomplished by communication with the senior auditor in charge of the examination of the financial statements of the branch or affiliate. The elimination of intercompany accounts is, of course, essential to the preparation of combined or consolidated statements, and constitutes another reason for detailed analysis of such receivable accounts by the auditors.

When trial balances or analyses of accounts receivable are furnished to the auditors by the client's employees, some independent verification of the listing is essential. Determination of the proper extent of testing should be made in relation to the adequacy of the internal controls over receivables. The auditors should test footings, cross-footings and agings; compare totals with related control accounts; and trace selected individual accounts to the appropriate subsidiary ledger balances. In addition, the balances of the subsidiary ledger records should be verified by footing the debit and credit columns on a test basis. Generalized computer audit programs may be used to perform these tests when the client's accounts receivable are processed by an electronic data processing system.

12. Obtain or prepare an analysis of notes receivable and related interest.

An analysis of notes receivable supporting the general ledger control account may be prepared for the auditors by the client's staff. The information to be included in the analysis normally will include the name of the maker, date, maturity, amount, and interest rate. Additional data concerning interest earned often are added, as shown by the columnar headings in Figure 13–3.

If the analysis is prepared by the client, it will be necessary for the auditors to verify its accuracy and completeness by footing and cross-footing the analysis, comparing the ending balance of notes receivable to the general ledger control account, and tracing selected items to the detailed records and to the notes themselves.

13. Inspect notes on hand and confirm those not on hand by direct communication with holders.

The inspection of notes receivable on hand should be performed concurrently with the count of cash and securities to prevent the concealment of a shortage by substitution of cash for misappropriated negotiable instruments, or vice versa. Any securities held by the client as collateral for notes receivable should be inspected and listed at the same time. Complete control over all negotiable instruments should be maintained by the auditors until the count and inspection are completed.

Practical considerations often prevent the auditors from inspecting notes receivable owned by the client but held by others at the time of the examination. Confirmation in writing from the holder of the note is considered as an acceptable alternative to inspection; it does not, however, eliminate the need for securing confirmation from the maker of the note. The confirmation letter sent to a bank, collection agency, secured creditor, or other holder should contain a request for verification of the name of the maker, the balance of the note, the interest rate, and the due date.

Confirmation of notes receivable discounted or pledged as collateral with banks is obtained in connection with the verification of cash on deposit, since the standard form of bank confirmation request includes specific enquiry on these matters.

Printed note forms are readily available at any bank; an unscrupulous officer or employee of the client company desiring to create a fictitious note could do so by obtaining a blank note form and filling in the amount, date, maturity, and signature. The relative ease of creating a forged or fictitious note suggests that physical inspection by the auditors represents a less significant and conclusive audit procedure in verification of notes receivable than for cash or securities.

FIGURE 13–3

Acct. Nos. 124, 125, 453

The Cost Ltd.

Notes Receivable and Interest

December 31, 1978

6-4

Confirmation No.	Maker	Note Made	Due	Rate	Paid to	Face Amount	Acct. No. 124—Master Balance Dec. 31, 77	Additions	Payments	Balance Dec. 31, 78	Receivable Dec. 31, 77	Interest Earned Acct. No. 453	Received	Receivable Dec. 31, 78 Acct. No. 125
	A. Brandline, Inc.	July 1, 77	June 30, 78	6%	June 30, 78	10,000.00	10,000.00	– 0 –	10,000.00✓	– 0 –✓	300.00	300.00✓	600.00✓	– 0 –
	Brandmore Hotel Ltd.	Apr. 15, 78	Oct. 15, 78	5%	Oct. 15, 78	4,000.00	– 0 –	4,000.00	4,000.00✓	– 0 –✓	– 0 –	100.00✓	100.00✓	– 0 –
1	Moore Assn. Co. Ltd.	July 1, 78	July 1, 79	6%	–C	5,000.00	– 0 –	5,000.00	– 0 –	5,000.00✓	– 0 –	150.00✓	– 0 –	150.00
2	J. Blackburn & Co. Ltd.	July 1, 78	Demand	6%	–C	4,800.00	– 0 –	4,800.00	– 0 –	4,800.00✓	– 0 –	144.00✓	– 0 –	144.00
3	P. A. Lovett, Inc.	Sept. 1, 78	Sept. 1, 79	6%	–C	8,000.00	– 0 –	8,000.00	– 0 –	8,000.00✓	– 0 –	160.00✓	– 0 –	160.00
							10,000.00✗	21,800.00✗	14,000.00✗	17,800.00✗	300.00✗	854.00✗	700.00✗	454.00✗

✓ – Footed and cross-footed.
∧ – Agreed to general ledger.
✗ – Details of Brandline, Inc. note agree to Dec. 31, 77, working papers 6-5.
/ – Examined note Dec. 31, 78 during cash count and inspection of marketable securities.
e – Confirmed with maker; no exceptions.
4 – Traced to cash receipts journal and duplicate deposit slip.
u – Computation verified.

Conclusions:

The results of the confirmation and other procedures described in the audit program (6-2) provide sufficient appropriate evidence of the genuineness of notes receivable ($17,800.00), interest receivable ($454.00), and interest revenue ($854.00).

O.K. H.
Jan. 20, 79

14. *Confirm notes and accounts receivable by direct communication with debtors.*

Direct communication with debtors is generally considered to be the most essential and conclusive step in the verification of notes and accounts receivable. Written acknowledgment of the debt by the maker or customer serves the dual purposes of (*a*) establishing the existence and validity of the asset, and (*b*) providing some assurance that no lapping or other manipulations affecting receivables exists at the balance sheet date.

A better understanding of the emphasis placed on confirmation of receivables can be gained by a brief review of auditing history. Audit objectives and procedures were drastically revised in the late 1930s. Prior to that time the usual audit did not include procedures to assure that the receivables were genuine claims against existing companies, or that inventories actually existed and had been accurately counted. For the auditors to confirm receivables (or to observe the taking of physical inventory) was considered too expensive and not particularly important. Auditors generally relied in that early era upon a written statement by management concerning the validity of receivables and the existence of inventories.

Wide publicity given in 1938 to the spectacular *McKesson & Robbins* fraud case in the United States involving millions of dollars in fictitious receivables and inventories led to a thorough reconsideration of the auditors' responsibility for receivables and inventories. In October 1939, the membership of the AICPA in the United States voted that henceforth an examination must include both the confirmation of receivables and the observation of inventories if an unqualified audit report were to be issued. The resulting AICPA pronouncement, known as "Extensions of Auditing Procedure," was truly an important milestone in the movement toward enhancing the importance and value of the independent auditors' report on financial statements.

Some modifications of the requirements established in 1939 were made by the AICPA in *SAS No. 1* and *SAS No. 2*. In these publications the Auditing Standards Executive Committee of the AICPA reaffirmed the importance of confirming receivables, but deleted the requirement of disclosure in the audit report of omission of the confirmation procedure in some circumstances. The following quotations from *SAS No. 1* and *SAS No. 2* summarize the current status of the confirmation procedure.

> Confirmation of receivables . . . (is a) generally accepted auditing procedure. The independent auditor who issues an opinion when he has not employed . . . (confirmation) must bear in mind that he has the burden of justifying the opinion expressed.

❁   ❁   ❁   ❁   ❁

> Circumstances such as the timing of his work may make it *impracticable* or *impossible* for the auditor to accomplish . . . (confirmation of receiv-

ables). In such case, if he has been able to *satisfy himself as to . . . accounts receivable by applying alternative procedures*, there is no significant limitation on the scope of his work, and his report need not include a reference to the omission of . . . (confirmation) or to the use of alternative procedures. (Emphasis added.)

Similarly, Section 6020 of the *CICA Handbook* recommends the following:

> *Generally accepted auditing procedures in respect of accounts and notes receivable should include some form of direct confirmation of accounts and notes receivable by communication with debtors.*
>
> *In circumstances where direct confirmation would be impracticable or is deemed to be harmful to the client's business, auditors should substitute other acceptable procedures.*

As long as the auditors are satisfied that they have established the validity of the receivables by adequate alternative procedures, there is no need for them to refer to the omission of the confirmation procedures in their audit report when such procedures are impracticable in the circumstances.

Perhaps the most common example of a situation in which it is impracticable or impossible to confirm receivables arises when sales are made to governmental agencies. The operating records and procedures of these agencies will not ordinarily enable them to confirm the amounts payable under government contracts and purchase orders. The auditors will, therefore, resort to alternative methods of verification—such as the examination of contracts, purchase orders, shipping documents, sales invoices, subsequent payments, and other similar evidence—to satisfy themselves that the receivable resulted from an actual order and shipment.

Occasionally during the process of confirming receivables from commercial concerns the auditors may receive a reply from a customer stating that a voucher system is in use in place of an accounts payable ledger, and that consequently no record is available of the total liability to an individual supplier. When such replies are received, the auditors must resort to the alternative procedures for verification described above. In some cases, it may be possible to confirm one or more selected unpaid invoices comprising the major portion of the total receivable from the customer using a voucher system or confirm a specific list of payments made by the customer.

An important part of confirming notes and accounts receivable is determining the validity of the debtors' addresses. The auditors should investigate thoroughly if an excessive number of *individual* debtors have addresses which are post office boxes; the boxes may have been rented under fictitious debtors' names by employees of the client company engaged in accounts receivable fraud.

ILLUSTRATIVE CASE. In the Equity Funding Corporation of America fraud in the United States, fictitious receivables selected for confirmation by the auditors bore addresses of employees who were conspirators in the fraud. The fictitious confirmation requests were thus signed and returned to the auditors by the recipients.

All requests for confirmation of notes and accounts receivable should be mailed in envelopes bearing the CA firm's return address. A stamped or "business reply" envelope addressed to the office of the auditors should be enclosed with the request. The confirmation requests should be deposited personally by the auditors at the post office or in a government mailbox. These procedures are designed to prevent the client's employees from having any opportunity to alter or intercept a confirmation request or the customer's reply thereto. The entire process of confirming receivables will obviously contribute nothing toward the detection of overstated or fictitious accounts if the confirmation requests or replies from customers pass through the hands of the client. Requests returned as undeliverable by the post office may be of prime significance to the auditors and hence should be returned directly to their office.

Positive and negative confirmation requests.   There are two methods of confirming receivables by direct communication with the debtor. In each type of communication, the *client* makes the formal request for confirmation.

The *positive method* consists of a communication addressed to the debtor asking him to confirm *to the auditors* the accuracy of the balance shown. Thus, the essential characteristic of the positive method is that it calls for a reply in every case. An illustration of this form of request for an account receivable is shown in Figure 13–4. The form of positive confirmation request to be sent to the maker of a note includes the date of the note, the due date, the interest rate and date to which interest has been paid, the unpaid balance of the note, and a description of any collateral.

The *negative method* consists of a communication addressed to the debtor asking him to advise the auditors *only* if the balance shown is *incorrect.* This type of request may be made by applying a rubber stamp to the customer's regular monthly statement, or by affixing thereto a gummed label bearing the words shown in Figure 13–5.

Section 6020 of the *CICA Handbook* contains the following comments on the methods of confirming receivables:

> The positive and negative forms of confirmation each have certain applications, and the choice between them will depend on circumstances. The receipt of a positive confirmation provides better evidence of the correctness of an account than does failure to receive a protest under the negative form of circularization. The negative form, however, is simpler and less time consuming and consequently may permit coverage of a larger number of balances.
>
> Negative confirmation suffers from the fact that it does not always receive consideration from the debtor, and consequently a failure to reply does

FIGURE 13–4
Positive form of accounts receivable confirmation request

Smith & Co. Ltd.   ♦♦♦♦♦

1416 BAYVIEW STREET TORONTO, ONTARIO

December 31, 1978

Dear Sirs:

  Please advise our auditors, Adams and Barnes, Chartered Accountants, of the correctness of the balance in your account payable to us as shown on the enclosed statement dated December 31, 1978 or state any exception you may take thereto.

  The prompt return of the bottom portion of this form in the enclosed stamped envelope is essential to the completion of the auditors' examination of our financial statements and will be greatly appreciated.

                                    Smith & Co. Ltd.

                          By M. J. Crowley
                                    (Controller)

          THIS IS NOT A REQUEST FOR PAYMENT, BUT MERELY FOR
                CONFIRMATION OF YOUR ACCOUNT.

- -

                              Confirmation Request No. _83_

Adams and Barnes
Chartered Accountants
1000 Spring Street
Toronto, Ontario

Dear Sirs:

  The statement of our account showing a balance of $ _8,690.00_   as of
   Dec. 31, 78   is correct with the exceptions noted below.

                                    Very truly yours,

                                    Benson Brothers

Date_ January 16, 1979 _   By _R. J. Benson_

Exceptions:

 None

FIGURE 13–5
Negative form of accounts receivable confirmation request

Please examine this statement carefully
and advise our auditors

    Adams and Barnes
    Chartered Accountants
    1000 Spring Street, Toronto, Ontario

As to any exceptions.

A business reply envelope requiring no postage is
enclosed for your convenience.

THIS IS NOT A REQUEST FOR PAYMENT

not necessarily signify agreement. Positive confirmation will seldom produce replies to all requests, but it sometimes has the advantage of producing useful information in cases where the customer is not prepared to confirm or is unable to do so.

Positive confirmation would be preferred:

(a)   for individual balances of relatively large amounts; or
(b)   where there are few debtors; or
(c)   where there is evidence or suspicion of serious errors or irregularities.

For many audit engagements, a combination of positive requests for at least a sample of large accounts and negative requests for at least a sample of smaller accounts will provide a suitable coverage.

In the audit of companies with adequate systems of internal control, it is customary to limit the confirmation procedure to a sample of the accounts receivable. The sample should be sufficiently large to account for most of the dollar amount of the receivables, or it should be sufficiently representative to warrant the drawing of valid inferences about the entire population of receivables. Generalized computer audit programs are useful in stratifying computer-processed accounts receivable to facilitate the selection process described above.

It is not unusual for a client to request that certain accounts or notes not be confirmed. For example, the client may ask that confirmations not be sent to delinquent customers whom the client has sued for nonpayment because of the sensitive nature of the relationship with the customers. The auditors generally will honour legitimate client requests of this nature. A list of such accounts should be submitted to the client for written approval and made part of the audit working papers. Amounts receivable from officers, employees, directors, and shareholders should be confirmed in all cases.

Discrepancies in customers' replies. The auditors should resolve un-usual or significant differences reported by customers; other exceptions may be turned over to employees of the client with the request that in-vestigation be made and explanations furnished to the auditors. The majority of such reported discrepancies arise because of normal lags in the recording of cash receipts or sales transactions, or because of misun-derstanding on the part of the customer company as to the date of the balance it is asked to confirm. Some replies may state that the balance listed is incorrect because it does not reflect recent cash payments; in such instances the auditors may wish to trace the reported payments to the cash records.

The percentage of replies to be regarded as satisfactory when the positive form of confirmation request is used is a difficult point on which to generalize; however, it is safe to say that replies to less than 50 or 60 percent of the dollar amount of confirmations requested would seldom, if ever, be considered satisfactory. The percentage of replies to be expected will vary greatly according to the type of debtor. Second and third re-quests, the latter usually by registered mail or telegram, are often found necessary to produce replies. When replies are not received on notes or accounts with substantial balances, the auditors should verify the exist-ence, location, and credit standing of the debtor by reference to credit agencies or other sources independent of the client, as well as establish the authenticity of the underlying transactions by examination of sup-porting documents. Such documents include contracts, customer purchase orders, and copies of sales invoices and shipping advices.

It has sometimes been said that the best proof available to the auditors as to the validity of an account receivable is its collection during the course of their examination. But this statement requires qualification, as indicated by the following situation:

ILLUSTRATIVE CASE. During the first audit of a small manufacturing company the auditors sent confirmation requests to all customers whose accounts showed balances in excess of $1,000. Satisfactory replies were received from all but one account, which had a balance of approximately $10,000. A second confirmation request sent to this customer produced no response; but before the auditors could investigate further, they were informed by the cashier-accountant that the account has been paid in full. The auditors asked to examine the customer's cheque and the accompanying remittance advice, but were told that the cheque had been deposited and the remittance advice destroyed. Further questioning concerning transactions with this customer evoked such vague responses from the cashier-accountant that the auditors decided to discuss the account with the officers of the company. At this point the cashier-accountant confessed that the account in question was a fictitious one created to conceal a shortage and that to satisfy the auditors he had "collected" the account receivable by diverting current collections from other cus-tomers whose accounts had already been confirmed.

When all expected replies to confirmation requests have been received, a summary should be prepared outlining the extent and nature of the confirmation program and the overall results obtained. Such a summary is a highly important part of the audit working papers.

In any audit in which receivables are material but are not confirmed when it is practicable and possible to do so, the auditors should disclose in the scope paragraph of their report the omission of this generally accepted procedure. The auditors must qualify or deny, depending on the materiality of the receivables, an opinion when confirmation would have been practicable and possible but was not carried out. Whether or not they can express an unqualified opinion when confirmation was *not practicable or possible* will depend upon the ability of the auditors to satisfy themselves concerning the receivables by audit procedures other than confirmation.

15. Determine adequacy of allowance for uncollectible accounts and notes.

If the balance sheet is to reflect fairly the financial position of the business, the receivables must be stated at net realizable value, that is, face amount less an adequate allowance for uncollectible notes and accounts. Accurate measurement of income requires an impartial matching of expenses and revenue. Since one of the expenses involved is the charge for uncollectible notes and accounts, the auditors' review of doubtful receivables should be looked upon as the verification of both income statement and balance sheet accounts.

The auditors' best evidence of *collectibility* of accounts and notes receivable is payment in full by the debtors subsequent to the balance sheet date. The auditors should note in the working papers any such amounts paid; in the illustrated trial balance of trade accounts receivable (Figure 13–2) a special column has been provided for this purpose. Since one of the auditors' objectives in the examination of notes and accounts receivable is the determination of their collectibility, it is highly important for the auditors to be aware of any collections on past-due accounts or matured notes during the period subsequent to the balance sheet date.

A note receivable, especially one obtained in settlement of a past-due account receivable, may involve as much—or more—credit risk as an account receivable. Provision for loss may reasonably be made for notes which have been repeatedly renewed, for installment notes on which payments have been late and irregular, for notes received in consequence of past-due accounts receivable, for dishonoured notes, and for notes of concerns known to be in financial difficulties. To appraise the collectibility of notes receivable, the auditors may investigate the credit standing of the makers of any large or doubtful notes. Reports from credit-rating agencies and financial statements from the makers of notes should be available in the client's credit department.

Evaluation of any collateral supplied by the makers is another step in determining the collectibility of notes receivable. The auditors should determine current market value of securities held as collateral by the client by reference to market quotations or by enquiry from brokers. Attention of the client should be called to any cases in which the market value of the collateral is less than the note; the deficiency might have to be considered uncollectible.

A lender sometimes attempts to reduce the risk inherent in a large note receivable by insertion of restrictive provisions; for example, the lender may insist that the debtor agree not to pay dividends, not to purchase plant and equipment, and not to increase managerial salaries during the life of the note. Often the agreement permits these actions by the borrower, provided a specified amount of working capital and specified ratios are maintained. The auditors should ascertain if these restrictions have been observed by debtors of the client. Violations of the restrictions may indicate that a debtor will be unable to pay a note when it matures.

To provide a basis for estimating the necessary size of the allowance for uncollectible accounts receivable, the auditors may take the following steps:

a. Examine the past-due accounts receivable listed in the aging schedule which have not been paid subsequent to the balance sheet date, noting such factors as the size and recency of payments, settlement of old balances, and whether recent sales are on a cash or a credit basis. The client's correspondence file may furnish much of this information.

b. Investigate the credit ratings for delinquent and unusually large accounts. An account with a single customer may represent a major portion of the total receivables.

c. Review confirmation exceptions for indication of amounts in dispute or other clues as to possible uncollectible accounts.

d. Request the opinion of collection agents or attorneys as to prospects for collection of accounts which they are following up for the client.

e. Summarize in a working paper those accounts considered to be doubtful of collection based on the preceding procedures. List customer names, doubtful amounts, and reasons considered doubtful.

f. Review with the credit manager the current status of each doubtful account, ascertaining the collection action taken and the opinion of the credit manager as to ultimate collectibility. Indicate on the doubtful accounts working paper the credit manager's opinion as to the collectible portion of each account listed, and provide for the estimated losses on accounts considered by the auditors to be uncollectible.

g. Compute ratios expressing the relationship of the valuation allowance to (1) accounts receivable, (2) net credit sales, and (3) accounts written off during the year and compare to comparable ratios for prior years. Investigate any significant variations.

In determining the adequacy of the client's allowance for uncollectible accounts and notes, the auditors should avoid undue reliance on opinions of the credit manager or other client officials regarding the collectibility of specific accounts or notes receivable. Although the estimation of an adequate allowance is fraught with a great deal of uncertainty, the preceding discussion indicates that substantial evidence other than opinions of client personnel is available to support the adequacy of the allowance for uncollectible accounts and notes.

16.   Review the year-end cutoff of sales transactions.

One of the more common methods of falsifying accounting records is to inflate the sales for the year by holding open the sales journal beyond the balance sheet date. Shipments made in the first part of January may be covered by sales invoices bearing a December date and included in December sales. The purpose of such misleading entries is to present a more favourable financial picture than actually exists. Since sales are frequently used as the base for computation of bonuses and commissions, an additional incentive for padding the Sales account is often present. A related abuse affecting accounts receivable is the practice of holding the cash journals open beyond the balance sheet date; auditing procedures designed to detect this practice were described in connection with the audit of cash transactions in Chapter 11.

In addition to the intentional inflation of sales, the auditors often encounter accidental errors in the *cutoff* of the sales records. The auditors review the cutoff of sales transactions by comparing the sales recorded several days before and after the balance sheet date to the duplicate sales invoices and shipping documents.

The effectiveness of this step is largely dependent upon the degree of segregation of duties between the shipping, receiving, and billing functions. If warehousing, shipping, billing, and receiving are independently controlled, it is most unlikely that records in all these departments will be manipulated to disguise shipments of one period as sales of the preceding period. On the other hand, one individual who had control over both shipping records and billing documents could manipulate both sets of records if overstatement of the year's sales were attempted. Confirmation of accounts receivable by direct communication with customers will aid in disclosing any irregularities in the record of shipping and invoicing dates. In addition, the auditors' cutoff review in connection with the observation of physical inventory, described in Chapter 14, aids in the determination of an accurate sales cutoff.

Fictitious sales, as well as predated shipments, are occasionally recorded at year-end as a means of "window dressing" the financial statements. The merchandise in question may even be shipped to customers without their prior knowledge, and subsequently returned. To guard against such manipulation, the auditors should review carefully all substantial sales returns following the balance sheet date that may apply to receivables originating in the year under audit. Consideration should be given to reflecting these returns in the current year's business by means of adjusting entries. Confirmation of accounts receivable, if made at the balance sheet date, should also serve to bring any large unauthorized shipments to the attention of the auditors.

An exception to the rule that goods must be shipped before a sale is recorded may be found in some contracts. Goods ready for shipment under these "fixed-price" contracts may be accepted by customers on the client's premises. This acceptance constitutes passage of title to the goods to the customer, despite the fact that the goods have not been shipped.

The importance of the auditors' review of the sales cutoff cannot be stressed too greatly. This procedure is vital for determining if sales and cost of goods sold are fairly presented in the income statement. It is also essential for the verification of accounts receivable and inventories in the balance sheet.

17. Verify interest earned on notes and accrued interest receivable.

Before beginning a review of interest earned, the auditors should become familiar with the client's policy for the computation, accrual, and recording of interest. Variations in accounting policy relating to interest are often found, such as recording interest on a monthly basis, or at time of collection only. As long as the method used by the client gives reasonable results in the determination of income, most auditors raise no objections. Interest revenue is seldom material enough to justify an adjustment, even though the method used has some theoretical deficiencies.

The most effective verification of the Interest Earned account consists of an independent computation by the auditors of the interest earned during the year on notes receivable.

The independent computation of interest by the auditors may conveniently be handled on the same working paper (Figure 13–3) used to analyze notes receivable, since this working paper shows the interest rate and date of issuance of each note. The interest section of this working paper consists of four columns, which show for each note receivable owned during the year the following information:

a. Accrued interest receivable at the beginning of the year (taken from the preceding year's audit working papers).
b. Interest earned during the year (computed from the terms of the notes).
c. Interest received during the year (traced to cash receipts records).
d. Accrued interest receivable at the end of the year (computed by the auditors).

These four columns comprise a self-balancing set. The beginning balance of accrued interest receivable (first column) plus the interest earned during the year (second column) and minus the interest received (third column) should equal the accrued interest receivable at the end of the year (fourth column). The totals of the four columns should be cross-footed to ensure that they are in balance; in addition, the individual column totals should be traced to the balances in the general ledger.

If the interest earned for the year as computed by the auditors does not agree with interest earned as shown in the accounting records, the next step is an analysis of the ledger account. Any unaccounted-for credits in the Interest Earned account deserve particular attention because these credits may represent interest received on notes which have never been recorded.

ILLUSTRATIVE CASE. In an examination of a company which held numerous notes receivable, the auditors made an independent computation of the interest earned during the year. The amount of interest earned shown by the accounting records was somewhat larger than the amount computed by the auditors. Careful analysis of entries in the Interest Earned account revealed one credit entry not related to any of the notes shown in the Notes Receivable account. Further investigation of this entry disclosed that a note had been obtained from a customer who was delinquent in paying his account receivable. The note receivable had not been recorded as an asset, but the account receivable which was replaced by the note had been written off as uncollectible.

Because of this situation the auditors made a thorough investigation of all accounts written off in recent years. Several of the former customers when contacted stated that they had been asked to sign demand notes for the balances owed, and had been assured there would be no pressure for collection as long as interest was paid regularly. The existence of notes receivable totaling many thousands of dollars was brought to light; these notes were not recorded as assets and were not known to the officers of the client company. The note transactions had been arranged by a trusted employee who admitted having abstracted the interest payments received with the exception of one payment which, through oversight, he had permitted to be deposited and recorded as interest earned.

For financial institutions or other clients having numerous notes receivable, the auditors may verify interest computations on only a sample of the notes. In addition, they should test the reasonableness of total interest earned for the year by applying a weighted average rate of interest to the average balance of the Notes Receivable ledger account during the year.

18. _Obtain or prepare a comparative analysis of sales and cost of goods sold._

A key step used by the auditors to determine that all sales have been recorded and classified on a consistent basis is the comparison of monthly and annual sales of the current fiscal year with those of the prior period.

If the comparison of monthly or annual sales figures show a significant variation, the auditors should determine the cause. Perhaps the variation is the result of an error in recording sales invoices, or in making an accurate cutoff; perhaps it is the result of fraud involving purposeful omission of sales transactions from the records. In most cases the variation is readily accounted for as the result of price changes, strikes, new products, or other factors already known to management.

In manufacturing companies the comparison of monthly sales figures is most meaningful when the figures are classified by type of product. An expanding volume of sales for a new product may be offset by accidental or purposeful understatement of the sales of other products, with the net result that total sales for the month are unchanged from total sales of the same month a year ago. Unless the summary of monthly sales is classified by product, such irregularities may go unnoticed. In retail businesses, the classification of sales is often more conveniently made by department than by product.

Comparative summaries of sales are most useful when the related figures for cost of goods sold are included. The comparison may then show for each product the percentage of gross profit to sales. Any variation in profit margin is of course reason for more detailed investigation. Another comparative device available in the audit of some manufacturing companies is to calculate the pounds of product sold each month. By applying established prices to the pounds of material sold, the auditors may test the validity of the dollar amounts of sales. The point to be stressed is that *the auditors should be aware of any significant variation in sales and should determine the causes.*

19.   Ascertain whether any receivables have been pledged.

The auditors should enquire directly whether any notes or accounts receivable have been pledged or assigned. Evidence of the pledging of receivables may also be disclosed through the medium of bank confirmation requests, which specifically call for description of collateral securing bank loans. Analysis of the interest expense accounts may reflect charges from the pledging of receivables to finance companies.

Accounts receivable which have been pledged should, of course, be plainly labeled by stamping on the copy of the sales invoice a notice such as "Pledged to Scotia Bank under loan agreement of December 31, 1978," and by inserting an identifying code in the accounts receivable records. Accounts labeled in this manner would be identified by the auditors in their initial review of receivables, and confirmed by direct correspondence with the bank to which pledged. The auditors cannot, however, proceed on the assumption that all pledged receivables have been labeled to that effect, and they must be alert to detect any suggestions of an unrecorded pledging of accounts.

20.   Ascertain whether notes or accounts of "insiders" paid prior to the balance sheet date have since been renewed.

Loans by a corporation to its officers, directors, shareholders, or affiliates require particular attention from the auditors because these related party transactions are not the result of arm's-length bargaining by parties of opposing interests. Furthermore, such loans may be prohibited by the corporation's by-laws. It is somewhat difficult to reconcile substantial loans to insiders by a non-financial corporation with the avowed operating objectives of such an organization. The independent auditors have an obligation to shareholders, creditors, and others who rely upon audited statements to require disclosure of any self-dealing on the part of the management. It seems apparent that most loans to officers, directors, and shareholders are made for the convenience of the borrower rather than for the profit of the corporation. Because of the somewhat questionable character of such loans, they are sometimes paid off just prior to the balance sheet date and renewed shortly thereafter, in an effort to avoid disclosure in financial statements. Under these circumstances the renewed borrowing may be detected by the auditors through a scanning of notes and accounts receivable transactions subsequent to the balance sheet date.

21. ***Determine proper balance sheet presentation of notes and accounts receivable and proper income statement presentation of sales.***

The principal objective in presenting notes and accounts receivable in the current assets section of the balance sheet is adequate informative disclosure of the kinds or sources of the receivables, their estimated realizable value, their liquidity, and their availability. Good statement presentation requires that trade notes and accounts receivable be shown as a separate item and that other receivables be itemized if the amounts are material. Examples of these other kinds of receivables which may require separate listings include accounts with unconsolidated affiliated companies; loans to officers and employees; claims for refund of federal income taxes; advances to suppliers; and other items of accrued revenue. Receivables from consolidated subsidiaries are eliminated in consolidation.

Some types of receivables do not qualify as current assets. Prominent among these are advances to officers, directors, and unconsolidated affiliated companies; such related party transactions are more commonly made for the convenience of the borrower rather than in the interest of the lending company, and presumably will be collected only at the convenience of the borrower. It is a basic tenet of statement presentation that transactions not characterized by arm's-length bargaining be fully publicized.

Disclosure of pledged receivables, of course, is a first essential of proper statement presentation. When receivables are divided into several classifications, a question arises as to the position of the valuation allowance. If a valuation allowance relates exclusively to a given type of receivable, it should be deducted therefrom; otherwise, it should appear as a deduction from the group total.

Disclosure of the contingent liability arising from the discounting of notes receivable can be made most clearly and concisely in a footnote to the financial statements.

22. *Obtain from client a letter of representations concerning notes and accounts receivable and sales.*

Many accounting firms obtain from their clients written representations concerning accounts receivable, notes receivable, and sales, as well as various other items. A single letter of representations may be obtained with sections for inventories, receivables, and so on; or separate ones may be obtained for different financial statement categories. The client's letter of representations is not a substitute for any auditing procedure and does not reduce the auditors' responsibility. However, it may have a valuable psychological effect on management by emphasizing to executives that primary responsibility for accurate financial statements rests with them rather than with the auditors. A typical letter of representations covering receivables follows:

With respect to your examination of the financial statements of _____ Co. Ltd. I hereby make the following representations concerning accounts and notes receivable shown in the balance sheet at December 31, 19___, in the aggregate gross amount of $_____.

1. All accounts and notes receivable represent valid claims against debtors for sales or other charges arising on or before December 31, 19___.
2. The accounts and notes receivable are unencumbered assets of the company.
3. Merchandise shipped on consignment has been identified as such in the records and is not included in accounts receivable.
4. All known uncollectible accounts and notes receivable have been written off.
5. The amount of $_____ provided for doubtful receivables is, in my judgment, sufficient to cover losses which may be sustained in realization of the notes and accounts receivable.

Signature of officer

Client company

Interim audit work on receivables and sales

Much of the audit work on receivables and sales can be performed one or two months before the balance sheet date. This interim work may include the confirmation of accounts receivable as well as the study and evaluation of the internal controls. Receivables may be confirmed at an interim date only when internal controls for receivables are reasonably strong.

If interim audit work has been done on receivables and sales, the year-end audit work may be modified considerably. For example, if the confirmation of accounts receivable was performed at October 31, the year-end audit program would include preparation of a summary analysis of postings to the Accounts Receivable control account for the period from November 1 through December 31. This analysis would list the postings by month, showing the journal source of each. These postings would be traced to the respective journals, such as sales journal and cash receipts journal. The amounts of the postings would be compared with the amounts in preceding months and with the corresponding months in prior years. The purpose of this work is to bring to light any significant variations in receivables during the months between the interim audit work and the balance sheet date.

In addition to this analysis of the entries to the receivable account for the intervening period, the audit work at year-end would include obtaining the aging of the accounts receivable at December 31, confirmation of any large accounts in the year-end trial balance that are new or delinquent, and the usual investigation of the year-end cutoff of sales and cash receipts.

The comparison of current period sales with those for prior periods may be carried out in November for the first ten months of the year and later completed by entering figures for the final two months. Investigation of such problems as the handling of consignments and interbranch shipments can also largely be completed as preliminary work.

KEY TERMS INTRODUCED OR EMPHASIZED IN CHAPTER 13

bill of lading   A document issued by a common carrier acknowledging the receipt of goods and setting forth the provisions of the transportation agreement.

confirmation   A type of documentary evidence which is created outside the client organization and transmitted directly to the auditors.

consignment   A transfer of goods from the owner to another persons who acts as the sales agent of the owner.

mortgage   A document issued by a debtor to a creditor, to secure an obligation with a lien on real property.

negative confirmation   A confirmation request addressed to the debtor requesting a reply only if the balance shown on the request is incorrect.

positive confirmation   A confirmation request addressed to the debtor requesting a reply in all cases.

trade acceptance   A bill of exchange drawn by the seller on the purchaser of goods sold, and accepted by the purchaser.

trust deed   A document issued by a debtor to secure an obligation with a lien on real property, issued to a trustee for the benefit of the creditor.

GROUP I
REVIEW QUESTIONS

13–1.   Cite various procedures which the auditors employ that might lead to the detection of an inadequate allowance for doubtful accounts receivable. (AICPA, adapted)

13–2.   Describe the role of the credit department in a manufacturing company.

13–3.   In selecting accounts receivable for confirmation, the auditors discovered that the client company's records showed the addresses of several individual customers to be post office boxes. What should be the auditors' reaction to this situation?

13–4.   Why does a contingent liability result from a company's discounting of its notes receivable with a bank?

13–5.   A CA firm wishes to test the client's sales cutoff at June 30, 1978. Describe the steps that the auditors should include in this test. (AICPA, adapted)

13–6.   Several accounts receivable confirmations have been returned with notation that "verifications of vendors' statements are no longer possible because of our data processing system." What alternative auditing procedures could be used to verify these accounts receivable? (AICPA, adapted)

13–7.   *a.* What is an audit confirmation?
　　　b. What characteristics should an audit confirmation possess if a CA firm is to consider it as valid evidence?
　　　c. Distinguish between a positive confirmation and a negative confirmation in the auditors' examination of accounts receivable.
　　　d. In confirming a client's accounts receivable, what characteristics should be present in the accounts if the CA firm is to use negative confirmations? (AICPA, adapted)

13–8.   The confirmation of accounts receivable is an important auditing procedure. Should the formal request for confirmation be made by the client or by the auditors? Should the return envelope be addressed to the client, to the auditors in care of the client, or to the auditors' office? Explain.

13–9.   The controller of a new client operating a medium-sized manufacturing business complains to you that he believes the company has sustained significant losses on several occasions because certain sales invoices were misplaced and never recorded as accounts receivable. What internal control procedure can you suggest to guard against such problems?

13–10. In determining the propriety of cash discounts allowed, what overall test can the auditors make to determine the reasonableness of cash discounts taken by customers?

13–11. In the examination of credit memoranda covering allowances to customers for goods returned, how can the auditors ascertain whether the customer actually did return merchandise in each case in which accounts receivable were reduced?

13–12. Does the letter of representations obtained by the auditors from the client concerning accounts receivable usually include any representation as to collectibility? Explain.

13–13. What auditing procedures, if any, are necessary for notes receivable but are not required for accounts receivable?

13–14. During preliminary conversations with a new staff assistant you instruct her to send out confirmation requests for both accounts receivable and notes receivable. She asks whether the confirmation requests should go to the makers of the notes or to the holders of the notes in the case of notes which have been discounted. Give reasons for your answer.

13–15. In the examination of an automobile agency, you find that installment notes received from the purchasers of automobiles are promptly discounted with a bank. Would you consider it necessary to confirm these notes by communication with the bank? With the makers? Explain.

13–16. Your review of notes receivable from officers, directors, shareholders, and affiliated companies discloses that several notes of small amount were written off to the allowance for uncollectible notes during the year. Have these transactions any special significance? Explain.

13–17. Worthington Ltd. has requested you to conduct an audit so that it may support its application for a bank loan with audited financial statements. Worthington's president agrees that you shall have access to all records of the company and shall employ any audit procedures you deem necessary, except that you are not to communicate with customers. Under these circumstances will it be possible for you to issue an unqualified audit report? Explain.

13–18. Fair presentation of receivables in the balance sheet is achieved through observing a number of specific points, such as the segregation of material trade receivables, amounts due from officers, and any other special classes of receivables. List several other specific points to be observed.

13–19. Among specific procedures which contribute to good internal control over accounts receivable are (a) the approval of uncollectible account write-offs and credit memoranda by an executive, and (b) the sending of monthly statements to all customers. State three other procedures conducive to strong internal control. (AICPA)

13–20. What additional auditing procedures should be undertaken in connection with the confirmation of accounts receivable where customers having substantial balances fail to reply after second request forms have been mailed directly to them? (AICPA, adapted)

13–21. In your first examination of Hydro Manufacturing Company, a manufacturer of outboard motors, you discover that an unusually large number of sales transactions were recorded just prior to the end of the fiscal year. What significance would you attach to this unusual volume?

13–22. In connection with a regular annual audit, what are the purposes of a review of sales returns and allowances subsequent to the balance sheet date? (AICPA, adapted)

13–23. An inexperienced clerk assigned to the preparation of sales invoices in a manufacturing company became confused as to the nature of certain articles being shipped, with the result that the prices used on the invoices were far less than called for in the company's price lists. What internal control procedures could be established to guard against such errors? Would errors of this type be disclosed in the normal audit by independent public accountants? Explain.

13–24. The accounts receivable section of the accounting department in Annandale Products Ltd. maintains subsidiary ledgers which are posted from copies of the sales invoices transmitted daily from the billing department. How may the accounts receivable section be sure that it receives promptly a copy of each sales invoice prepared?

13–25. Edendale Co. Ltd., a dealer in new automobiles, had approximately the same volume of sales and earned approximately the same gross profit and the same net income for the years 1979 and 1978. The gross profit on new cars decreased in 1979 as compared with the preceding year, but this decrease was offset by increased gross profit from the sale of accessories attached to the new cars, particularly air-conditioning units. Would the normal examination by independent auditors disclose these changes in the sources of gross profit? Explain.

13–26. A company that ships goods to its customers must establish procedures to ensure that a sales invoice is prepared for every shipment. Describe procedures to meet this requirement.

GROUP II
QUESTIONS REQUIRING ANALYSIS

13–27. Joel Crane, the senior auditor-in-charge of examining the financial statements of Thorne Co. Ltd., a small manufacturing company, was busy writing the audit report for another engagement. Accordingly, he sent Martin Joseph, a recently hired staff assistant of the CA firm, to begin the audit of Thorne company, with the suggestion that Joseph start with the accounts receivable. Using the preceding year's audit working papers for Thorne company as a guide, Joseph prepared a trial balance of Thorne's trade accounts receivable, aged them, prepared and mailed positive confirmation requests, examined underlying documents plus other support for charges and credits to the Accounts Receivable ledger account, and performed such other work as he deemed necessary to assure the validity and collectibility of the accounts receivable. At the conclusion of Joseph's work, Crane traveled to Thorne company to review Joseph's working papers. Crane found that Joseph had carefully followed the prior-year audit working papers.

Required:

State how the three generally accepted auditing standards of field work were fulfilled, or were not fulfilled, in the audit of the accounts receivable of Thorne Co. Ltd. (AICPA, adapted)

13–28. Many CAs consider determining the adequacy of the allowance for uncollectible accounts and notes to be the most difficult procedure of an audit. Do you agree? Explain.

13–29.   *a.*   Why is confirmation of receivables a generally accepted auditing procedure where practicable and possible?

     b.   What is the auditors' course of action when they discover that confirmation of a significant account receivable from a government agency is not practicable or possible?

13–30.   You have been assigned to the audit of a wholesale grocery company which makes cash advances to affiliated retailers operating independently owned stores. The wholesale company receives for the cash advances non-interest-bearing notes receivable due in 60 monthly installments. In conjunction with the cash advances, the retailers contract in writing to purchase merchandise from the wholesaler, and to support a cooperative advertising program.

Required:

Assume that you have obtained sufficient appropriate audit evidence as to internal control for the notes receivable, existence and ownership of the notes, and collectibility of the notes. How would you resolve the problem of proper balance sheet presentation of the notes?

13–31.   Jean Ross, CA, has been assigned to the audit of D-T Bank. During the course of her interim work on mortgage notes receivable, Ross discovered that borrowing homeowners instruct the bank to remit proceeds of the loans direct to the contractors constructing the borrowers' homes. D-T Bank provides the borrowers with booklets containing coupons for equal monthly installment payments, including interest and the Bank's charges for county property tax bills. At the end of each calendar year, the bank furnishes each borrower with an itemized statement showing the allocation of equal monthly installment payments to mortgage note principal, interest, and property taxes.

Required:

Jean Ross is faced with a tight deadline after December 31 for delivery of the audit report to D-T Bank. Should Ross consider confirmation of mortgage notes receivable as of November 30? Discuss.

13–32.   *a.*   What are the implications to the auditors if during their examination of accounts receivable some of a client's customers do not respond to the auditor's request for positive confirmation of their accounts receivable?

     b.   What procedures should the auditors perform if there is no response to a second request for a positive confirmation? (AICPA, adapted)

13–33.   You are conducting an annual audit of Granite Corporation Ltd., which has total assets of approximately $1,000,000 and operates a wholesale merchandising business. The corporation is in good financial condition and maintains an adequate accounting system. Granite owns about 25 percent of the share capital of Desert Sun, Inc., which operates a dude ranch. This investment is regarded as a permanent one, and is accounted for by the equity method.

During your examination of accounts and notes receivable, you develop the information shown below concerning three short-term notes receivable due in the near future. All three of these notes receivable were discounted by Granite with its bank shortly before the balance sheet date.

1. An 8 percent, 60-day note for $50,000 received from a customer of unquestioned financial standing.
2. An 8 percent, six-month note for $60,000 received from the affiliated company, Desert Sun, Inc. The affiliated company is operating profitably, but is presently in a weak cash position because of recent additions to buildings and equipment. The president of Granite intends to make an $80,000 advance with a five-year maturity to Desert Sun, Inc. The proposed advance will enable Desert Sun, Inc. to pay the existing 8 percent, $60,000 note at maturity and to meet certain other obligations.
3. An 8 percent, $20,000 note from a former key executive of Granite whose employment had been terminated because of chronic alcoholism and excessive gambling. The maker of the note is presently unemployed and without personal resources.

Required:

Describe the proper balance sheet presentation with respect to these discounted notes receivable. Use a separate paragraph for each of the three notes, and state any assumptions you consider necessary.

13–34. You are considering using the services of a reputable outside mailing service for the confirmation of accounts receivable balances. The service would prepare and mail the confirmation requests and remove the returned confirmations from the envelopes and give them directly to you.

What reliance, if any, could you place on the services of the outside mailing service? Discuss and state the reasons in support of your answer. (AICPA)

13–35. An assistant auditor was instructed to "test the aging of accounts receivable as shown on the trial balance prepared by the client." In making this test, the assistant traced all past-due accounts shown on the trial balance to the ledger cards in the accounts receivable subsidiary ledger and recomputed the aging of these accounts. The assistant found no discrepancies and reported to the senior auditor that the aging work performed by the client was satisfactory.

Comment on the logic and adequacy of this test of the aging of accounts receivable.

13–36. During your annual examination of the financial statements of Wilshire Co. Ltd., you undertook the confirmation of accounts receivable, using the positive form of confirmation request. Satisfactory replies were received for all but one of the large accounts. You sent a second and third request to this customer, but received no reply. At this point an employee of the client company informed you that a cheque had been received for the full amount of the receivable. Would you regard this as a satisfactory disposition of the matter? Explain.

13–37. Milton Chambers, CA, was retained by Wall Corporation Ltd. to perform an audit of its financial statements for the year ending December 31. In a preliminary meeting with company officials, Chambers learned that the corporation customarily accepted numerous notes receivable from its customers. At December 31 the client company's controller provided Chambers with a list of the individual notes receivable owned at that date. The list showed for each note the date of the note, amount, interest rate, maturity date, and name and address of the maker. After a careful study and evaluation of the internal control relating to notes receivable, Chambers turned his attention to the list of notes receivable provided to him by the controller.

Chambers proved the footing of the list and determined that the total agreed with the general ledger control account for notes receivable and also with the amount shown in the balance sheet. Next he selected 20 of the larger amounts on the list of notes receivable for detailed investigation. This investigation consisted of confirming the amount, date, maturity, interest rate, and collateral, if any, by direct communication with the makers of the notes. By selection of the larger amounts, Chambers was able to verify 75 percent of the dollar amount of notes receivable by confirming only 20 percent of the notes. However, he also received a random sample of another 20 percent of the smaller notes on the list for confirmation with the makers. Satisfactory replies were received to all confirmation requests.

The president of Wall Corporation Ltd. informed Chambers that the company never required any collateral in support of the notes receivable; the replies to confirmation requests indicated no collateral had been pledged.

No notes were past due at the balance sheet date, and the credit manager stated that no losses were anticipated. Chambers verified the credit status of the makers of all the notes he had confirmed by reference to audited financial statements of the makers and Dun & Bradstreet credit ratings.

By independent computation of the interest accrued on the notes receivable at the balance sheet date, Chambers determined that the accrued interest receivable as shown on the balance sheet was correct.

Since Chambers found no deficiencies in any part of his examination, he issued an unqualified audit report. Some months later, Wall Corporation Ltd. became insolvent and the president fled the country. Chambers was sued by creditors of the company who charged that his audit was inadequate and failed to meet minimum professional standards. You are to comment on the audit program followed by Chambers with respects to notes receivable *only*.

13–38. Select the best answer for each of the questions below and explain fully the reason for your selection.

The following sales procedures were encountered during the regular annual audit of Marvel Wholesale Distributing Co. Ltd.

Customer orders are received by the sales order department. A clerk computes the dollar amount of the order and sends it to the credit department for approval. Credit approval is stamped on the order and returned to the sales order department. An invoice is prepared in two copies and the order is filed in the "customer order" file.

The "customer copy" of the invoice is sent to the billing department and held in the "pending" file awaiting notification that the order was shipped.

The "shipping copy" of the invoice is routed through the warehouse and the shipping department as authority for the respective departments to release and ship the merchandise. Shipping department personnel pack the order and prepare a three-copy bill of lading: the original copy is mailed to the customer, the second copy is sent with the shipment, and the other is filed in sequence in the "bill of lading" file. The invoice "shipping copy" is sent to the billing department.

The billing clerk matches the received "shipping copy" with the customer copy from the "pending" file. Both copies of the invoice are priced, extended, and footed. The customer copy is then mailed directly to the customer, and the "shipping copy" is sent to the accounts receivable clerk.

The accounts receivable clerk enters the invoice data in a sales–accounts receivable journal, posts the customer's account in the "subsidiary customer's accounts ledger," and files the "shipping copy" in the "sales invoice" file. The invoices are numbered and filed in sequence.

a. In order to gather audit evidence concerning the proper credit approval of sales, the auditors would select a sample of transaction documents from the population represented by the—
    (1) "Customer order" file.
    (2) "Bill of lading" file.
    (3) "Subsidiary customers' accounts ledger."
    (4) "Sales invoice" file.

b. In order to determine whether the system of internal control operated effectively to minimize errors of failure to post invoices to customers' accounts ledger, the auditors would select a sample of transactions from the population represented by the—
    (1) "Customer order" file.
    (2) "Bill of lading" file.
    (3) "Subsidiary customers' accounts ledger."
    (4) "Sales invoice" file.

c. In order to determine whether the system of internal control operated effectively to minimize errors of failure to invoice a shipment, the auditors would select a sample of transactions from the population represented by the—
    (1) "Customer order" file.
    (2) "Bill of lading" file.
    (3) "Subsidiary customers' accounts ledger."
    (4) "Sales invoice" file.

d. In order to gather audit evidence that uncollected items in customers' accounts represented valid trade receivables, the auditors

would select a sample of items from the population represented by the—
(1) "Customer order" file.
(2) "Bill of lading" file.
(3) "Subsidiary customers' accounts ledger."
(4) "Sales invoice" file. (AICPA, adapted)

GROUP III
PROBLEMS

13–39. Arthur Ross, CA, is auditing RCT Manufacturing Co. Ltd. as at February 28, 1979. One of Ross's initial procedures is to make analyses of the client's financial data by reviewing significant ratios and trends so that he has a better understanding of the business and can determine where to concentrate his audit efforts.

The financial statements prepared by the client with audited 1978 figures and preliminary 1979 figures are presented below in condensed form.

RCT MANUFACTURING CO. LTD.
Condensed Balance Sheets
February 28, 1979, and 1978

Assets	1979	1978
Cash	$ 12,000	$ 15,000
Accounts receivable, net	93,000	50,000
Inventories	72,000	67,000
Other current assets	5,000	6,000
Plan and equipment, net of depreciation	60,000	80,000
	$242,000	$218,000

Equities		
Accounts payable	$ 38,000	$ 41,000
Income taxes payable	30,000	14,400
Long-term liabilities	20,000	40,000
Common stock	70,000	70,000
Retained earnings	84,000	52,600
	$242,000	$218,000

RCT MANUFACTURING CO. LTD.
Condensed Income Statements
Years Ended February 28, 1979, and 1978

	1979	1978
Net sales	$1,684,000	$1,250,000
Cost of goods sold	927,000	710,000
Gross margin on sales	757,000	540,000
Selling and administrative expenses	682,000	504,000
Income before income taxes	75,000	36,000
Income taxes expense	30,000	14,400
Net Income	$ 45,000	$ 21,600

Additional information:

1. The company has an insignificant amount of cash sales.
2. The end of year figures are comparable to the averages for each respective year.

Required:

For each year compute the current ratio and a turnover ratio for accounts receivable. Based on these ratios, identify and discuss audit procedures that should be included in Ross's audit of accounts receivable. (AICPA, adapted)

13–40. As part of his examination of the financial statements of Marlborough Ltd. for the year ended March 31, 1979, Mark Wayne, CA, is reviewing the balance sheet presentation of a $1,200,000 advance to Franklin Olds, Marborough's president. The advance, which represents 50 percent of current assets and 10 percent of total assets, was made during the year ended March 31, 1979. It has been described in the balance sheet as "miscellaneous accounts receivable" and classified as a current asset.

Olds informs the CA that he has used the proceeds of the advance to purchase 35,000 shares of Marlborough's common stock in order to forestall a takeover raid on the company. He is reluctant to have his association with the advance described in the financial statements because he does not have voting control and fears that this will "just give the raiders ammunition."

Olds offers the following four-point program as an alternative to further disclosure:

1. Have the advance approved by the board of directors. (This can be done expeditiously because a majority of the board members are officers of the company.)
2. Prepare a demand note payable to the company with interest of 7½ percent (the average bank rate paid by the company).
3. Furnish an endorsement of the shares to the company as collateral for the loan. (During the year under audit, despite the fact that earnings did not increase, the market price of Marlborough common rose from $20 to $40 per share. The shares have maintained its $40 per share market price subsequent to year-end.)
4. Obtain a written opinion from the company attorney supporting the legality of the company's advance and the use of the proceeds.

Required:

a. Discuss the proper balance sheet classification of the advance to Olds and other appropriate disclosures in the financial statements and footnotes. (Ignore tax effects, creditors' restrictions on share repurchase, and the presentation of common stock dividends and interest revenue.)
b. Discuss each point of Olds' four-point program as to whether or

not it is desirable and as to whether or not it is an alternative to further disclosure.

c. If Olds refuses to permit further disclosure, what action should the CA take? Discuss.

d. In his discussion with the CA, Olds warns that the raiders, if successful, probably will appoint new auditors. What consideration should the CA give to this factor? Explain. (AICPA, adapted)

13–41. Lawrence Ltd. maintains its accounts on the basis of a fiscal year ending October 31. Assume that you were retained by the company in August 1979 to perform an audit for the fiscal year ending October 31, 1979. You decide to perform certain auditing procedures in advance of the balance sheet date. Among these interim procedures is the confirmation of accounts receivable, which you perform at September 30, 1979.

The accounts receivable at September 30, 1979, consisted of approximately 200 accounts with balances totaling $956,750. Seventy-five of these accounts with balances totaling $650,725 were selected for confirmation. All but 20 of the confirmation requests have been returned; 30 were signed without comments, 14 had minor differences which have been cleared satisfactorily, while 11 confirmations had the following comments:

1. We are sorry but we cannot answer your request for confirmation of our account as Moss Ltd. used a computerized accounts payable voucher system.
2. The balance of $1,050 was paid on September 23, 1979.
3. The above balance of $7,750 was paid on October 5, 1979.
4. The above balance has been paid.
5. We do not owe you anything at September 30, 1979, as the goods represented by your invoice dated September 30, 1979, Number 25,050, in the amount of $11,550, were received on October 5, 1979, on f.o.b. destination terms.
6. An advance payment of $2,500 made by us in August 1979 should cover the two invoices totaling $1,350 shown on the statement attached.
7. We never received these goods.
8. We are contesting the propriety of the $12,525 charge. We think the charge is excessive.
9. Amount okay. As the goods have been shipped to us on consignment, we will remit payment upon selling the goods.
10. The $10,000, representing a deposit under a lease, will be applied against the rent due to us during 1982, the last year of the lease.
11. Your credit dated September 5, 1979, in the amount of $440 cancels the above balance.

Required:

What steps would you take to clear satisfactorily each of the above 11 comments? (AICPA, adapted)

13–42.   You are performing your first examination of the financial statements of Havers Company, Inc., a closely held corporation. The balance sheet at June 30, 1979, drafted by the controller of Havers shows total assets of $9,500,000 and shareholders' equity of $4,000,000.

During the course of your examination of notes receivable, you discover that the corporation had loaned $1,200,000 on March 31, 1979, to the majority shareholder, on a 6 percent, unsecured note payable on demand. On June 30, 1979, Havers Company, Inc., sold this note without recourse to its depository bank. On July 1, 1979, Havers reacquired this note from the bank without recourse. The standard bank confirmation form returned to you by the bank shows no loss contingency at June 30, 1979, in connection with the $1,200,000 note.

Required:

Discuss the implications of the above transactions as they affect the client's June 30, 1979, statements and your audit report.

13–43.   The July 31, 1979, general ledger trial balance of Aerospace Contractors, Inc., reflects the following accounts associated with receivables. Balances of the accounts are after all adjusting journal entries proposed by the auditors and accepted by the client.

Accounts receivable—commercial	$ 595,000
Accounts receivable—government of Canada	3,182,000
Allowance for uncollectible accounts and notes	75,000 cr.
Claims receivable—public carries	7,000
Claims receivable—government of Canada terminated contracts	320,000
Due from Harwood Co. Ltd., investee	480,000
Notes receivable—trade	15,000

Required:

a.   Draft a partial balance sheet for Aerospace Contractors at July 31, 1979. In deciding upon which items deserve separate listing, consider materiality as well as the nature of the accounts.

b.   Write an explanation of the reasoning employed in your balance sheet presentation of these accounts.

13–44.   During your examination of the financial statements of Martin Mfg. Co. Ltd., a new client, for the year ended March 31, 1979, you note the following entry in the general journal dated March 31, 1979:

Notes Receivable	550,000	
Land		500,000
Gain on Sale of Land		50,000
To record sale of excess plan-site land to Ardmore Corp. for 4 percent note due March 31, 1984. No interest payment required until maturity of note.		

Your review of the contract for sale between Martin and Ardmore, your enquiries of Martin executives, and your study of minutes of Martin's directors' meetings develop the following facts:

1.   The land has been carried in your client's accounting records at its cost of $500,000.

2. Ardmore Limited is a land developer and plans to subdivide and resell the land acquired from Martin Mfg. Co. Ltd.

3. Martin had originally negotiated with Ardmore on the basis of an 8 percent interest rate on the note. This interest rate was established by Martin after a careful analysis of Ardmore's credit standing and current money market conditions.

4. Ardmore had rejected the 8 percent interest rate because the total outlay on an 8 percent note for $550,000 would amount to $770,000 at the end of five years; and Ardmore felt a total outlay of this amount would leave it with an inadequate return on the subdivision. Ardmore held out for a total cash outlay of $660,000, and Martin Mfg. Co. Ltd. finally agreed to this position.

Required:

Ignoring income tax considerations, is the journal entry recording Martin's sale of the land to Ardmore acceptable? Explain fully and draft an adjusting entry if you consider one to be necessary.

GROUP IV
CASE STUDIES IN AUDITING

13–45.   STAR FINANCE CO. LTD.

Star Finance Co. Ltd. is in the business of making small loans and investing in installment sales contracts purchased from dealers in automobiles, appliances, and other durable goods. Early in 1979, the company retained McGregor and Company, CAs, to make an examination of the financial statements for the fiscal year ended February 28, 1979. James Smith, one of the partners in the CA firm, went to the office of Star Finance to begin the audit. He took with him a senior auditor, Carol Brown, and spent some time explaining to Brown some of the differences between the handling of receivables in a finance company and in a merchandising concern. He stressed to Brown the importance in this business of obtaining bank loans and other capital, and of lending these funds to customers at higher interest rates. He added that a finance company usually was not anxious to have a customer pay an account in full because the company might then lose contact with him. On the contrary, Smith pointed out, the finance company would probably encourage its small-loan customers to obtain a new loan before the original one was paid off. If the customer could be developed into a more or less permanent borrower, the finance company would benefit from this relationship even though it never collected a loan in full. The important element, Smith commented, was to keep the customer in debt and paying interest charges.

One of the first steps taken by Smith and Brown was to obtain a trial balance of the general ledger. This trial balance showed installment loans receivable of $615,428. The allowance for uncollectible loans was $6,473.

Early in the audit, Brown made tests to determine that the detail of the receivables was in agreement with the control account, and she sent out requests for confirmation of the balances due from the borrowers. In addition she made enquiries into the collectibility of the receivables. She found that the installment receivables consisted of 1,706 loans, of which 18 were classified by the company as delinquent; these 18 loans had aggregate uncollected balances of $5,167. However, in reviewing the receivables, Brown noticed quite a number of loans that were rather slow in collection; as a matter of fact, some of them showed no recent collections of principal.

After having developed this information, Brown made enquiries of the president of Star Finance as to the company's basis of considering an installment receivable as delinquent. She was informed that the company defined a delinquent loan as one upon which no collection had been received on either principal or interest within the last 60 days, or generally, therefore, 30 days from the due date; conversely, loans on which collections of principal or interest were being received currently (although not necessarily the full monthly payment) were considered as current. Furthermore, the president pointed out, all loans defined by the company as delinquent 90 days or more (and which aggregated approximately $25,000) had been written off at February 28, 1979, by a charge against the allowance for uncollectible loans.

The number of loans which seemed to be slow in collection continued to disturb Brown, and she made a further study of installment receivables and the recent payments thereon. This study covered 169 other loans classified by the company as current and indicated the following status:

	Number	Amount
Paying interest only	29	$ 12,557
All other (including some accounts on which all interest had been waived)	140	88,112
	169	$100,669

After comparing the results of this test with the amount of the allowance for uncollectible loans which amounted to only $6,473, Brown became further concerned as to the adequacy of the allowance. She decided to make some further enquiries into the status of these loans; thus she requested the controller of Star Finance to compile the following information as to the 169 loans (which she then tested):

	Total	Paying interest only	All others
Balance, February 28, 1978	$106,299	$12,313	$ 93,986
Add additional loans made	9,907	249	9,658
Total	$116,206	$12,562	$103,644
Deduct collections received:			
Total collections	$ 34,180	$ 1,471	$ 32,709
Less amount applied to interest	18,643	1,465	17,178
Remainder—applied to principal	$ 15,537	$ 6	$ 15,531
Balance, February 28, 1979 (representing 169 accounts)	$100,669	$12,556	$ 88,113

Brown conferred with Smith, and they agreed that the allowance was insufficient. Both Smith and Brown then discussed the matter with the president of Star Finance, and it was decided that further studies should be made by the company. At the conclusion of these studies, the company increased its allowance for uncollectible loans from $6,473 to $34,182. This allowance, the company insisted, was sufficient to cover losses on collections of the receivables.

Brown was inclined first to think that the allowance of $34,182 would be sufficient; after all it did represent better than 5 percent of the receivables and, furthermore, the company would be receiving interest in the future on all of its loans, out of which further provision could be made if necessary; Smith, however, did not agree. On the other hand, Smith was not sure that he could indicate in the audit report the amount of allowance which should be necessary because (1) he did not regard himself as being qualified as an appraiser to evaluate the loans, and (2) the company had been in existence only a few years and hence did not have an extended background of credit experience.

The audit report, as finally issued by McGregor and Company, indicated that the client company was of the opinion its allowance for uncollectible loans was sufficient. In a middle paragraph, the report broke down the installment loans receivable as follows:

Loans being collected in substantial accordance with contract terms, $509,592 (less allowance for uncollectible loans $16,182)	$493,410
Loans not being collected in substantial accordance with contract terms, $105,836 (less allowance for uncollectible loans $18,000)	87,836
Total	$581,246

The audit report also contained the following:

As to the allowances for losses carried by the company against its loans receivable, we are of the opinion, based largely on the company's collection experience and in the light of present conditions, that—

1. The allowance of $16,182 carried against loans collected in substantial accordance with contract terms should be sufficient.
2. The allowance of $18,000 carried against loans not being collected in substantial accordance with contract terms is insufficient, and losses substantially in excess of $18,000 may be expected thereon. However, inasmuch as the company has been in existence only a relatively short period of years, and consequently does not have extensive experience as to losses and collections, and, further, since the ascertainment of adequate loss allowance in the absence of extensive loss experience is a technical matter for persons trained in small-loan operations and credits, we are unable to express an opinion as to the amount of loss allowance which should be required.

The opinion paragraph of the audit report stated: "In our opinion, except that the allowance for uncollectible loans receivable not being collected in substantial accordance with contract terms is inadequate, these financial statements present fairly the financial position of the company as at February 28, 1979 and the results of its operations and the changes in its financial position for the year then ended in conformity with generally accepted accounting principles applied on a basis consistent with that of the preceding year."

On review of the audit report, the president of Star Finance claimed that McGregor and Company was putting him out of business, and that the report would result in the bank (extending credit to the company) calling its line of credit; the president demanded that Smith change the report.

Required:

a. Do you agree with Smith's opinion that the allowance for uncollectible loans was insufficient?
b. Do you think that Smith should have specified the amount of allowance he deemed to be sufficient?
c. Do you think that Smith should have been swayed by the statement of the president of Star Finance that the audit report would put him out of business, and if so, what else should Smith have done?
d. Was there anything else which Smith could have done that he did not do?

14

Inventories and cost of goods sold

Although observing the taking of physical inventories is one of the generally accepted auditing procedures in Canada and the United States, its significance can be best understood by turning back to the time of the spectacular *McKesson & Robbins* fraud case in the United States. As mentioned in Chapter 13, the hearings conducted by the SEC in the United States in 1939 disclosed that the audited financial statements of Mc-Kesson & Robbins, Inc., a drug company listed on the New York Stock Exchange, contained $19,000,000 of fictitious assets, about one fourth of the total assets shown on the balance sheet. The fictitious assets included $10,000,000 of non-existent inventories. How was it possible for the independent auditors to have conducted an audit and to have issued an unqualified report without discovering the gigantic fraud? The audit program followed for inventories in this case was in accordance with customary auditing practice of the 1930s. The significant point is that in this period it was customary to limit the audit work on inventories to an examination of records only; the standards of that era did not require any observation, physical count, or other actual contact with the inventories.

Up to the time of the *McKesson & Robbins* case, auditors had avoided taking responsibility for verifying the accuracy of inventory quantities and the physical existence of the goods. With questionable logic, many auditors had argued that they were experts in handling figures and analyzing accounting records but were not qualified to identify and measure the great variety of raw materials and manufactured goods found in the factories, warehouses, and store buildings of their clients.

The *McKesson & Robbins* case brought a quick end to such limited views of the auditors' responsibility. The public accounting profession was faced with the necessity of accepting responsibility for verifying the physical existence of inventories or of confessing that its audit function offered no real protection to investors or other users of financial statements. The profession met the challenge by adopting new standards requiring the auditors to observe the taking of the physical inventory and to confirm accounts receivable.

Both Section 6030 of the *CICA Handbook* and *SAS No's. 1* and *2* of the AICPA now recommend the observation of the taking of physical inventories as one of the generally accepted auditing procedures. If such a procedure is not practicable or impossible in the circumstances, the auditors should substitute other satisfactory auditing procedures, which should include observing or making some physical counts of inventories at some time other than at the time of the clients inventory taking or stocktaking.[1] Where the auditors are able to obtain sufficient appropriate audit evidence through the use of other auditing procedures, they may issue an unqualified opinion without making any disclosure of the omission of an observation of the physical inventory.

It is also important to note that *SAS No. 1* made a distinction between companies which determine inventory quantities solely by an annual physical count and companies with well-kept perpetual inventory records. The latter companies often have strong internal control over inventories and many employ statistical sampling techniques to verify the records by occasional test counts rather than by a complete annual count of the entire inventory. For such clients the auditors' observation of physical inventory may be limited to such counts as they consider appropriate, and may occur during or after the end of the period being audited.

Critical importance of inventories to the auditors

Inventories have probably received more attention in auditing literature and in discussions among professional accountants than any other item to be found on financial statements. The reasons for the special significance attached to the verification of inventories are readily apparent:

1. Inventories usually constitute the largest current asset of an enterprise and are more susceptible to major errors and manipulation than any other asset category.
2. Numerous alternative methods for valuation of inventories are sanc-

---

[1] However, the AICPA's *SAS No. 1* stipulates that the use of alternative procedures must always include observing or making some physical counts of inventory even though this occurs after the balance sheet date.

tioned by the accounting profession and, in the United States, by the SEC, and the Internal Revenue Service—principally because of inflationary price changes over many years.

3. The determination of inventory value directly affects the cost of goods sold and has a major impact upon net income for the year.

4. The verification of inventory quantity, condition, and value is inherently a more complex and difficult task than is the verification of most elements of financial position.

The interrelationship of inventories and cost of goods sold makes it logical for the two topics to be considered together in an auditing textbook. In this chapter the term "inventories" is used to include (1) goods on hand ready for sale, either the merchandise of a trading concern or the finished goods of a manufacturer; (2) goods in the process of production; and (3) goods to be consumed directly or indirectly in production, consisting of raw materials, purchased parts, and supplies.

The auditors' objectives in examination of inventories and cost of goods sold

The principal objectives of the auditors in the examination of inventories and cost of goods sold are to determine (a) the adequacy of internal controls for inventories and cost of sales; (b) the existence and ownership of the inventories; (c) the quality or condition of the inventories; (d) the propriety of the valuation of inventories, including pricing, extensions, and footings; and (e) the fairness of the amount presented as cost of sales in the income statement.[2]

The auditors' approach to the verification of inventories and cost of goods sold should be one of awareness to the possibility of intentional misstatement, as well as to the prevalence of accidental error in the determination of inventory quantities and amounts. Purposeful misstatement of inventories has often been employed to evade income taxes, to conceal shortages arising from various irregularities, and to mislead shareholders or other inactive owners as to profits and financial position.

The very nature of entries in the Cost of Goods Sold ledger account makes it susceptible to misstatements, especially when perpetual inventories are maintained. For example, consider the variety of charges or credits that may be determinants of cost of sales for a manufacturing concern using perpetual inventories:

1. Amounts transferred from goods in process or finished goods inventory accounts.

---

[2] For those Canadian companies which are subject to the U.S. SEC *Accounting Series Release 190* reporting requirements, they must also determine the current replacement cost of inventories and cost of goods sold.

2. Proceeds from sales of scrap.
3. Charges for idle plant and equipment.
4. Underabsorbed or overabsorbed factory overhead.
5. Standard cost variances.
6. Inventory write-downs for shortages, obsolescence, and deterioration.
7. Losses on firm fixed-price contracts.

For a trading concern using the periodic method of determining inventories, the Cost of Goods Sold account is much less active. It is generally used only at the end of an accounting period when the ending inventory has been compiled. Nevertheless, a trading concern's cost of sales should be carefully examined to determine whether any significant inventory shrinkages are "buried" therein.

Internal control of inventories and cost of goods sold

The importance of adequate internal control over inventories and cost of goods sold from the viewpoint of both management and the auditors can scarcely be overemphasized. In some companies, management stresses internal controls over cash and securities but ignores the problem of control over inventories. This attitude may be based on the outmoded notion that the primary purpose of internal control is to prevent and detect fraud. Since many types of inventories are composed of items not particularly susceptible to theft, management may consider internal controls to be unnecessary in this area. Such thinking ignores the fact that internal control performs other functions even more important than fraud prevention.

Good internal control is a means of providing accurate cost data for inventories and cost of goods sold as well as accuracy in reporting physical quantities. Inadequate internal controls may cause losses by permitting erroneous cost data to be used by management in setting prices and in making other decisions based on reported profit margins. If the accounts do not furnish a realistic picture of the cost of inventories on hand, the cost of goods manufactured, and the cost of goods sold, the financial statements may be grossly misleading both as to earnings and as to financial position.

Internal control procedures for inventories and cost of goods sold affect nearly all the functions involved in producing and disposing of the company's products. Purchasing, receiving, storing, issuing, processing, and shipping are the physical functions directly connected with inventories; the cost accounting system and the perpetual inventory records comprise the recording functions. Since the auditors are interested in the final products of the recording functions, it is necessary for them to understand and appraise the cost accounting system and the perpetual inventory records, as well as the various procedures and original documents underlying the preparation of financial data.

The purchasing function. Adequate internal control over purchases requires, first of all, an organizational structure which delegates to a separate department of the company exclusive authority to make all purchases of materials and services. The purchasing, receiving, and recording functions should be clearly separated and lodged in separate departments. In small concerns, this type of departmentalized operation may not be possible; but even in very small enterprises, it is usually feasible to make one person responsible for all purchase transactions.

Serially numbered formal purchase orders should be prepared for all purchases, and copies forwarded to the accounting and receiving departments. The copy sent to receiving should have the quantities blacked out to assure that receiving personnel make independent counts of the merchandise received. Even though the buyer may actually place an order by telephone, the formal purchase order should be prepared and forwarded. In many large organizations, purchase orders are issued only after compliance with extensive procedures for (a) determining the need for the item, (b) obtaining of competitive bids, and (c) obtaining approval of the financial aspect of the commitment.

The receiving function. All goods received by the company—without exception—should be cleared through a receiving department which is independent of purchasing, storing, and shipping departments. This department is responsible for (1) the determination of quantities of goods received, (2) the detection of damaged or defective merchandise, (3) the preparation of a receiving report, and (4) the prompt transmittal of goods received to the stores department.

The storing function. As goods are delivered to stores, they are counted, inspected, and receipted for. The stores department will then notify the accounting department of the amount received and placed in stock. In performing these functions, the stores department makes an important contribution to overall control of inventories: by signing for the goods, it fixes its own responsibility; and by notifying the accounting department of actual goods stored, it provides verification of the receiving department's work.

The issuing function. The stores department, being responsible for all goods under its control, has reason to insist that for all items passing out of its hands it be given a prenumbered requisition accompanied by a signed receipt from the department accepting the goods. Requisitions are usually prepared in triplicate. One copy is retained by the department making the request; another acts as the stores department's receipt; and the third is a notice to the accounting department for cost distribution. To prevent the indiscriminate writing of requisitions for questionable purposes, some organizations establish policies requiring that requisitions be drawn only upon the authority of a bill of materials, an engineering order, or a sales order. In merchantile concerns, shipping orders rather than factory requisitions serve to authorize withdrawals from stores.

The processing function. Responsibility for the goods must be fixed, usually on foremen or superintendents. Thus, from the time materials are delivered to the factory until they are completed and routed to a finished goods storeroom, a designated supervisor should be in control and be prepared to answer for their location and disposition.

The system of internal control over goods in process may include regular inspection procedures to reveal defective work. This aids in disclosing inefficiencies in the productive system and also tends to prevent inflation of the goods in process inventory by the accumulation of cost for goods which will eventually be scrapped.

Control procedures should also assure that goods scrapped during the process of production are promptly reported to the accounting department so that the decrease in value of goods in process inventories may be recorded. Scrapped materials may have substantial salvage value, and this calls for segregation and control of scrap inventories.

The shipping function. Shipments of goods should be made only after proper authorization has been received. This authorization will normally be an order from the sales department, although the shipping function also includes the returning of defective goods to suppliers. In this latter case the authorization may take the form of a shipping advice from a purchasing department executive.

One copy of the shipping authorization will go to the stores department; a second copy will be retained by the shipping department as evidence of shipment; and a third copy will be enclosed as a packing slip with the goods when they are shipped. These forms should be prenumbered and kept under accounting control. The control aspect of this procedure is strengthened by the fact that an outsider, the customer, will inspect the packing slip and notify the company of any discrepancy between this list, the goods ordered, and the goods actually received.

When the goods have been shipped, the shipping department will attach to a fourth copy of each shipping order the related evidence of shipment: bills of lading, trucking bills, carriers' receipts, freight bills, and so on. This facilitates subsequent audit by grouping together the documents showing that shipments were properly authorized and carried out. The shipping advice, with supporting documents attached, is then sent to the billing department, where it is used as the basis for invoicing the customer.

Established shipping routines should be followed for all types of shipments, including the sale of scrap, return of defective goods, and forwarding of materials and parts to subcontractors.

The cost accounting system. To account for the usage of raw materials and supplies, to determine the content and value of goods in process inventories, and to compute the finished goods inventory, an adequate cost accounting system is necessary. This system comprises all the records, orders, requisitions, time tickets, and the like, needed in a proper accounting for the disposition of materials as they enter the flow of production and as they continue through the factory in the process of becoming finished goods. The cost accounting system also serves to accumulate labour costs and indirect costs which contribute to the goods in process and the finished goods inventories. The cost accounting system thus forms an integral part of the internal control for inventories.

The figures produced by the cost system should be controlled by general ledger accounts. Two general types of systems are widely used. Under one, all transactions in a factory are passed through a "factory ledger." The net balance of this ledger is represented by a "factory ledger control" in the general ledger. The other system records the cost of materials, labour, and factory overhead in individual goods in process accounts for each production order or process. These goods in process accounts are controlled by a single general ledger goods in process inventory account. In effect, a subsidiary goods in process ledger is produced by the cost system, which must at all times be represented in the general records.

Underlying this upper level of control between the factory records and the general ledger is found a system of production orders, material requisitions, job tickets or other labour distributions, and factory overhead distributions. Control is effected by having each production order properly authorized, recorded, and followed up. Payroll records are compiled only after all time tickets have been verified for accuracy. Indirect costs are distributed to the various job orders or processes through predetermined rates, which are adjusted to actual cost at the period's end. In addition, many cost systems have introduced methods of determining spoilage, idle labour, and idle machine time. These systems, known as "standard costing," provide for the prompt pricing of inventories and for a control over operations through a study of variances between actual and standard figures. All these various types of cost accounting systems are alike in that all are designed to contribute to effective internal control by tracing the execution of managerial directives in the factory, by providing reliable and accurate inventory figures, and by safeguarding company assets.

In the United States, companies having significant supply contracts with certain U.S. government agencies are subject to the pronouncements of the Cost Accounting Standards Board. This five-member board, chaired by the U.S. comptroller general, was established by the U.S. Congress to narrow the options in cost accounting which are available under generally accepted accounting principles. Cost accounting standards adopted by the board are published in the *Federal Register* (the daily publication of the U.S. National Archives and Records Service). Unless Congress objects to a proposed standard, the standard becomes effective shortly after its final publication in the *Federal Register*.

The perpetual inventory system.   Perpetual inventory records constitute a most important part of the system of internal control. These records, by showing at all times the quantity of goods on hand, provide information essential to intelligent purchasing, sales, and production-planning policies. With such a record it is possible to guide procurement by establishing points of minimum and maximum quantities for each standard item stocked.

The use of minimum-maximum stock quantities as a guide to reordering does not warrant placement of the ordering function in the hands of one employee, and does not eliminate the need for review of decisions to order goods. Good internal control requires a regular review of prospective purchases before final authority is given for placing the order.

ILLUSTRATIVE CASE. A large aircraft manufacturer planned to adopt the practice of an annual "Family Day," on which the families and friends of employees would be invited to visit the plant, go through the latest model airplanes, and view movies concerning aircraft of the future. In anticipation of a crowd of more than 100,000 people, the plant protection department decided to erect numerous rope lanes to guide the crowds along a designated route. The plan required enormous quantities of rope, so a supervisor called the material stores department to see how much rope was in stock and whether additional amounts might be borrowed from neighbouring plants. He was informed that through error the company had recently purchased 100,000 feet of rope when it had intended to buy only 10,000 feet. The plant protection department obtained the rope and used it in handling the Family Day crowds with the intention of returning it to the stores department in the next day or so. In the interim a stock clerk noticed that 100,000 feet of rope had been withdrawn from stores within the past week and that only a small quantity remained in stock. The stock clerk was accustomed to dealing in large quantities of various materials. Assuming that the withdrawal of 100,000 feet of rope during the past week was normal usage and that the company should have ten weeks' supply on hand, the stock clerk prepared a "Rush" request for an order of 1,000,000 feet of rope.

This colossal mistake was corrected through an internal control practice of requiring a supervisor to review and give written approval to all requests for orders of material before a purchase order was issued. The supervisor was puzzled why such quantities were needed and insisted upon a full investigation of the facts of the situation before he signed the request.

If perpetual inventory records are to produce the control implicit in their nature, it is desirable that the subsidiary records be maintained both in quantities and dollars for all stock, that the subsidiary records be controlled by the general ledger, that trial balances be prepared at reasonable intervals, and that both the detailed records and the general ledger control accounts be adjusted to agree with physical counts whenever taken.

Perpetual inventory records discourage inventory theft and waste, since storekeepers and other employees are aware of the accountability over goods established by this continuous record of goods received, issued, and on hand. The records, however, must be periodically verified through the physical counting of goods.

Internal control and the computer

Computers may be used for a number of inventory processes. Computer programs often provide for routine ordering of inventory items falling below established minimum quantities. The computer may also be programmed to print out periodically such information as slow-moving inventory items. An updated perpetual inventory listing can be provided by the computer as frequently as management requires it.

Audit working papers for inventories and cost of goods sold

A great variety of working papers may be prepared by the auditors in their verification of inventories and cost of goods sold. These papers will range in form from written comments on the manner in which the physical inventory was taken to elaborate analyses of production costs of finished goods and goods in process. Selected working papers will be illustrated in connection with the audit procedures to be described in succeeding sections of this chapter.

AUDIT PROGRAM FOR INVENTORIES AND COST OF GOODS SOLD

The following audit procedures for the verification of inventories and cost of goods sold will be discussed in detail in the succeeding pages. The program is appropriate for a manufacturing company which takes a complete physical inventory to verify the perpetual inventories at the close of each fiscal year.

A. Study and evaluation of internal control for inventories and cost of goods sold

1. Obtain description of internal control for inventories and cost of goods sold.
2. Examine a sample of purchase orders.
3. Test the cost accounting system.
4. Evaluate internal controls for inventories and cost of goods sold.

B. Substantive tests of inventories and cost of goods sold transactions

5. Participate in advance planning of physical inventory.
6. Observe the taking of physical inventory and make test counts.
7. Review the handling of goods held on consignment and determine that inventories do not include any items owned by others or properly chargeable to other asset accounts.

8. Verify existence of goods held by public warehouses and goods out on consignment.
9. Determine inventory quality and condition.
10. Obtain copy of the completed physical inventory, determine its clerical accuracy, and trace test counts.
11. Review the bases and methods of inventory pricing.
12. Test pricing of raw materials or purchased merchandise.
13. Determine reasonableness and accuracy of the pricing of finished goods and goods in process.
14. Apply "lower-of-cost-or-market" test to inventory prices.
15. Compare the completed physical inventory to perpetual inventory records.
16. Review the year-end cutoff of purchases and sales transactions.
17. Test the reasonableness of inventories by comparison with prior years, by application of the gross profit percentage method, by computing the rate of turnover, and by reference to capacity of production and storage facilities.
18. In the first audit of a new client, investigate beginning inventories.
19. Obtain and review an analysis of cost of goods sold.
20. Determine whether any inventories have been pledged and review purchase and sales commitments.
21. Review computations of replacement cost of inventories and cost of goods sold, as required by the U.S. SEC requirements for certain companies subject to its jurisdiction.
22. Determine proper balance sheet presentation of inventories and proper income statement presentation of cost of goods sold.
23. Obtain from client a letter of representations concerning inventories and cost of goods sold.

A. Study and evaluation

1. Obtain description of internal control for inventories and cost of goods sold.

As previously indicated, the study of internal controls may involve the filling out of a questionnaire, the writing of descriptive memoranda, and the preparation of flowcharts depicting organizational structure and the flow of materials and documents. All these approaches utilize the same basic investigative techniques of interview, study of reports and records, and the first-hand observation of employees' work.

During the review of internal controls over inventory, the auditors should become thoroughly conversant with the procedures for purchasing, receiving, storing, and issuing goods and for controlling production, as well as acquiring understanding of the cost accounting system and the perpetual inventory records.

The auditors should also give consideration to the physical protection for inventories. Any deficiencies in storage facilities, in guard service, or in physical handling which may lead to losses from weather, fire, flood, or theft may appropriately be called to the attention of management.

Should the auditors' study of internal control over inventories (or plant and equipment) include consideration of the client's insurance coverage? Management's policy as to the extent of insuring assets against fire, flood, earthquake, and other hazards will vary greatly from one company to another. The auditors' responsibility does not include a determination of what constitutes "adequate" insurance coverage. Consequently the auditors' report on financial statements need not contain any disclosure on the client's policies with respect to insurance coverage.

The matters to be investigated in the auditors' review of internal controls over inventory and cost of sales are fairly well indicated by the following questions: Are perpetual inventory records maintained for each class of inventory? Are the perpetual inventory records verified by physical inventories at least once each year? Do the procedures for physical inventories include the use of prenumbered tags, with all tag numbers accounted for? Are differences between physical inventory counts and perpetual inventory records investigated before the perpetual records are adjusted? Is a separate purchasing department responsible for purchasing all materials, supplies, and equipment? Are all incoming shipments, including returns by customers, processed by a separate receiving department? Are materials and supplies held in the custody of a stores department and issued only on properly approved requisitions?

2.   Examine a sample of purchase orders.

As part of the compliance tests of internal controls for inventories and cost of goods sold, the auditors should trace specific transactions through the entire system, noting the use of authorizations, transfers of responsibility, adequacy of documents and records, and degree of understanding by employees of the control procedures prescribed by management.

In most businesses, the purchasing function is inherently susceptible to fraud. Purchasing agents are beleaguered by salesmen of prospective vendors, and the possibility of conflicts of interest through "kick backs" and other fraudulent activities is often present. Although the auditors are not ordinarily responsible for discovering conflicts of interest, they should carefully test the purchasing procedures and make recommendations to the client for strengthening weak internal controls in the purchasing department.

The following procedures are typical of the compliance tests relating to purchase transactions. The principal objective is to ascertain whether the internal control procedures stated to be in use are actually functioning, and thereby to determine the degree of reliance to be placed upon purchases recorded in ledger accounts.

1. Select a sample of purchase orders from purchasing department files.
2. Examine the purchase requisition or other authorization for each purchase order in the sample.
3. Examine the related vendor's invoice, receiving report, and paid cheque copy for each purchase order in the sample. Trace transactions to the voucher register and cheque register.
4. Review invoices for approval of prices, extensions, footings, freight and credit terms, and account distribution.
5. Compare quantities and prices in invoice, purchase order, and receiving report.
6. Foot and cross-foot voucher register on a test basis.
7. Trace postings from voucher register to general ledger and any applicable subsidiary ledgers.
8. Select a sample of debit memoranda and perform procedures comparable to above. Also inspect shipping reports for goods returned to vendors.

The auditors' review of purchases will often include a comparison of the volume of transactions from perod to period. In this study the purchase transactions may be classified by vendor and also by type of product; comparisons made in this manner sometimes disclose unusual variations of quantities purchased or unusual concentration of purchases with particular vendors, indicating a possible conflict of interest.

3. Test the cost accounting system.

For a client in the manufacturing field, the auditors must become familiar with the cost accounting system in use, as a part of their study and evaluation of internal control. A wide variety of practices will be encountered for the costing of finished units. The cost accounting records may be controlled by general ledger accounts or operated independently of the general accounting system. In the latter case, the cost of completed units may be difficult or impossible to verify and may represent nothing more than a well-reasoned guess. Because cost accounting methods vary so widely, even among manufacturing concerns in the same industry, audit procedures for a cost accounting system must be designed to fit the specific circumstances encountered in each case.

In any cost accounting system, the three elements of manufacturing cost are direct materials costs, direct labour costs, and manufacturing overhead. Cost accounting systems may accumulate either actual costs or standard costs according to *processes* or *jobs.* The auditors' compliance tests of the client's cost accounting system must be designed to determine that costs allocated to specific jobs or processes are appropriately compiled.

To achieve this objective, the auditors must test the propriety of direct materials quantities and unit costs, direct labour hours and hourly rates, and overhead rates and allocation bases. Quantities of direct materials charged to jobs or processes are vouched to materials requisitions, while unit materials costs are traced to the raw materials perpetual inventory records. The auditors should examine job tickets or time summaries supporting direct labour hours accumulations, and should trace direct labour hourly rates to union contracts or individual employee personnel files.

The auditors must recognize that a variety of methods are generally accepted for the application of manufacturing overhead to inventories. A predetermined rate of factory overhead applied on the basis of machine-hours, direct labour dollars, direct labour hours, or some similar basis, is used by many manufacturing companies. The predetermined overhead rate is usually revised periodically, but nevertheless leads each year to some underabsorbed or overabsorbed overhead. The auditors will ordinarily insist that any significant amount of overabsorbed overhead be applied to a proportionate reduction in inventory and cost of sales. Underabsorbed overhead should generally be written off as a cost of the period; if material, it should be separately disclosed in the income statement.

A distinction between factory overhead, on the one hand, and overhead costs pertaining to selling or general administration of the business, on the other, must be made under generally accepted accounting principles, since selling expenses and general and administrative expenses usually are written off in the period incurred. The difference in the accounting treatment accorded to factory overhead and to "non-manufacturing" overhead implies a fundamental difference between these two types of cost. Nevertheless, as a practical matter it is often impossible to say with finality that a particular expenditure, such as the salary of a vice president in charge of production, should be classified as factory overhead, as general and administrative expense, or perhaps be divided between the two. Despite this difficulty, a vital procedure in the audit of cost of goods sold for a manufacturing concern is determining that factory overhead costs are reasonably allocated in the accounts. Failure to distribute factory costs to the correct accounts can cause significant distortions in the client's predetermined overhead rate and in over- or underapplied factory overhead. The auditors may find it necessary to obtain or prepare analyses of a number of the factory overhead subsidiary ledger accounts, and to verify the propriety of the charges thereto. Then, the auditors must determine the propriety of the total machine-hours, direct labour hours, or other aggregate allocation base used by the client company to predetermine the factory overhead rate.

If standard costs are in use, it is desirable to compare standard costs with actual costs for representative items, and to ascertain whether the standards reflect current materials and labour usage and unit costs. The composition of factory overhead, the basis for its distribution by department and product, and the effect of any change in basis during the year should be reviewed. The standard costs of selected products should be verified by testing computations, extensions, and footings, and by tracing charges for labour, material, and overhead to original sources.

The auditors' study of a manufacturing company's cost accounting system should give special attention to any changes in cost methods made during the year and the effect of such changes on the cost of sales. Close attention should also be given to the methods of summarizing costs of completed products and to the procedures for recording the cost of partial shipments.

4. Evaluate internal controls for inventories and cost of goods sold.

The description and compliance tests of the client's internal control for inventories and cost of goods sold provide the auditors with evidence as to weaknesses and strengths of the system. The auditors should appraise these weaknesses and strengths, and design the remainder of their audit program for substantive tests of inventories and cost of sales accordingly.

B. Substantive tests

5. Participate in advance planning of physical inventory.

Efficient and economical inventory taking requires careful planning in advance. Cooperation between the auditors and client personnel in formulating the procedures to be followed will prevent unnecessary confusion and will aid in securing a complete and well-controlled count. A first step in securing the desired elements of control and efficiency is the designation by the client management of an individual employee, often a representative of the controller, to assume responsibility for the physical inventory. This responsibility will begin with the drafting of procedures and will carry through to the final determination of the dollar value of all inventories.

Advance planning will include:

a. Selection of the most advantageous date or dates for inventory taking.
b. Scheduling operations to minimize amount of goods in process.
c. Determination of advisability of closing down entire plant or certain departments.
d. Segregation of obsolete and defective goods.
e. Designing of prenumbered inventory tags, summary sheets, and other necessary forms.
f. Preparation of written instruction for all persons who are to participate in the physical inventory.
g. Arranging for control of goods received while inventory is being taken.
h. Arranging for services of engineers or other specialists needed to determine quantity or condition of certain goods or materials.

i. Planning control over all inventory tags and other documents throughout the inventory taking, pricing, and summarizing.

Most important of all the preliminary work is that relating to the written procedures and instructions for the taking of the inventory. These instructions normally will be drafted by the client and reviewed by the auditors, who will judge their adequacy in the light of instructions used in previous years and the problems encountered in those years. If the instructions for taking inventory are adequate, then the auditors' responsibility during the count is largely a matter of seeing that the instructions are followed conscientiously.

Some companies prepare two sets of instructions for the physical inventory: one set for the supervisors who will direct the count and a second set for the employees who will perform the detailed work of counting and listing merchandise. A set of instructions prepared by the controller of a large clothing store for use by supervisors is illustrated in Figure 14–1.

Advance planning by the senior auditor-in-charge is also necessary to assure efficient use of audit staff members during the inventory taking. The auditor-in-charge should determine the dates of the counts, number of auditors needed at each location, and the estimated time required. The senior should then assign auditors to specific locations and provide them with a written statement of their duties. The senior may also wish to arrange for the cooperation of the client's internal auditing staff during the count, and possibly for the assistance of the company's engineers or independent specialists.

When written instructions are prepared by the auditing firm for use of its staff in a particular engagement, these instructions are not made available to the client. Their purpose is to make sure that all auditors understand their assignments and can therefore work efficiently during the physical inventory. An example of inventory instructions prepared by a public accounting firm for the use of its own staff members is presented in Figure 14–2; these instructions relate to the same audit engagement described in the client's instructions to supervisors illustrated in Figure 14–1. In every case, the audit staff members will have copies of the client's inventory instructions in their possession during the inventory observation.

6.   *Observe the taking of physical inventory and make test counts.*

It is not the auditors' function to *take* the inventory or to control or supervise the taking; this is the responsibility of management. The auditors *observe* the inventory taking in order to obtain sufficient appropriate evidence as to the *existence* and *ownership* of the client company's inventories. In brief, observation of inventory taking gives the auditors a basis for an opinion as to the credibility of representations by management as to inventory quantities.

FIGURE 14–1

GLEN HAVEN DEPARTMENT STORES LTD.

Instructions for Physical Inventory,
August 5, 1979

TO ALL SUPERVISORS:

A complete physical inventory of all departments in each store will be taken Sunday, August 5, 1979 beginning at 8:30 a.m. and continuing until completed. Employees are to report at 8:15 a.m. to receive your final briefing on their instructions, which are appended hereto.

Each count team should be assigned and started by a supervisor, and should be period-ically observed by that supervisor to assure that instructions are being complied with in the counting and listing processes.

A block of sequential prenumbered inventory sheets will be issued to each supervisor at 8:00 a.m. August 5, for later issuance to count teams. Each supervisor is to account for all sheets--used, unused, or voided. In addition, each supervisor will be furnished at that time with a listing of count teams under his supervision.

When a count team reports completion of a department, that team's supervisor should accompany a representative of the independent auditors, McDonald & Company, in per-forming test counts. A space is provided on each inventory sheet for the supervisor's signature as reviewer. When the independent auditors have "cleared" a department, the supervisor responsible should take possession of the count sheets. All completed count sheets are to be placed in numerical sequence and turned over to me when the entire inventory has been completed.

Before supervisors and employees leave the stores Saturday evening, August 4, they are to make certain that "housekeeping" is in order in each department, and that all merchandise bears a price ticket.

If you have any questions about these instructions or any other aspect of the physical inventory, please see me.

J. R. Adams

J. R. Adams
Controller
July 24, 1979

FIGURE 14–2

McDONALD and COMPANY

CHARTERED ACCOUNTANTS

Glen Haven Department Stores Ltd.
Inventory Observation--Instructions for Audit Staff
August 5, 1979

We will observe physical inventory taking at the following stores of Glen Haven Department Stores Ltd., on August 5, 1979:

Store	Store Manager	Our Staff
Wilshire	J. M. Baker	John Rodgers, Faye Arnold
Crenshaw	Roberta Bryan	Weldon Simpkins
Valley	Hugh Remington	Roger Dawson

Report to assigned stores promptly at 8:00 a.m. Attached are copies of the Company's detailed instructions to employees who are to take the physical inventories and to supervisors who are to be in charge. These instructions appear to be complete and adequate; we should satisfy ourselves by observation that the instructions are being followed.

All merchandise counted will be listed on prenumbered inventory sheets. We should make occasional test counts to ascertain the accuracy of the physical counts. Test counts are to be recorded in working papers, with the following information included:
Department number
Inventory sheet number
Stock number
Description of item, including season letter and year
Quantity
Selling price per price tag

We should ascertain that adequate control is maintained over the prenumbered inventory sheets issued. Also, we should prepare a listing of the last numbers used for transfers, markdowns, and markups in the various departments and stores. Inventory sheets are not to be removed from the departments until we have "cleared" them; we should not delay this operation.

Each staff member's working papers should include an opinion on the adequacy of the inventory taking. The papers should also include a summary of time incurred in the observation.

No cash or other cutoff procedures are to be performed as an adjunct to the inventory observation.

To observe the inventory taking, however, implies a much more active role than that of a mere spectator. Observation by the auditors also includes determining that all usable inventory owned by the client is included in the count and that the client's employees comply with the written inventory instructions. As part of the process of observing the physical inventory, the auditors will be alert to detect any obsolete or damaged merchandise included in inventory. Such merchandise should be segregated by the client and written down to net realizable value. In short, during the inventory observation the auditors are alert for, and follow up on, any unusual problems not anticipated in the client's written inventory instructions or improperly dealt with by the client's inventory teams.

The auditors will also make a record of the serial number of the final receiving and shipping documents issued before the taking of inventory so that the accuracy of the cutoff can be determined at a later date. Shipments or receipts of goods taking place during the counting process should be closely observed and any necessary reconciliations made. Observation of the physical inventory by the auditors also stresses determining that the client is controlling properly the inventory tags or sheets. These should be prenumbered so that all tags can be accounted for.

During their inventory observation, the auditors will make test counts of selected inventory items. The extent of the test counts will vary widely, dependent upon the circumstances of the individual case, but in general should cover a representative cross section of the stock on hand. All test counts should be recorded in the audit working papers for subsequent comparison with the completed inventory listing.

Serially numbered inventory count tags are usually attached to each lot of goods during the taking of a physical inventory. The design of the tag and the procedures for using it are intended to guard against two common pitfalls: (a) accidental omission of goods from the count and (b) double counting of goods.

Many companies use two-employee teams to count the inventories. Each team is charged with a sequence of the serially numbered tags and is required to turn in to the physical inventory supervisor any tags voided or not used.

The actual counting, the filing in of inventory tags, and the "pulling" of these tags are done by the client's employees. While the inventory tags are still attached to the goods, the auditors may make such test counts as they deem appropriate in the circumstances. The auditors will list in their working papers the tag numbers for which test counts were made. The client employees will ordinarily not collect ("pull") the inventory tags until the auditors indicate that they are satisfied with the accuracy of the count.

In comparing their test counts to the inventory tags, the auditors are alert for errors not only in quantities but also in part numbers, descriptions, units of measure, and all other aspects of the inventory item. For test counts of goods in process inventory, the auditors must ascertain that the percentage or stage of completion indicated on the inventory tag is appropriate.

If the test counts made by the auditors indicate discrepancies, the goods are recounted at once by the client's employees and the error corrected. If an excessive number of errors is found, the inventory for the entire department or even for the entire company should be recounted.

The information listed on the inventory tags is transferred by the client to serially numbered inventory sheets. These sheets are used in pricing the inventory and in summarizing the dollar amounts involved. After the inventory tags have been collected, the client employee supervising the inventory will ascertain that all tags are accounted for by serial number. The auditors should ascertain that numerical control is maintained over both inventory tags and inventory sheets.

The test counts and tag numbers listed by the auditors in their working papers will be traced later to the client's inventory summary sheets. A discrepancy will be regarded not as an error in counting but as a mistake in copying data from the tags, or as the result of a purposeful alteration of a tag, or creation of a fictitious tag.

ILLUSTRATIVE CASE. The auditors of Crown Aluminum Corporation in the United States did not adequately review the control of physical inventory tags, even though their firm's procedures required such a review. According to the SEC (*Accounting Series Release No. 157*), Crown personnel altered certain inventory tags and created other fictitious tags; the result was a $4.4 million overstatement of inventories with a carrying value of $9.2 million. In their review of Crown's physical inventory listing, the auditors did not discover that the fictitious and altered tags were listed in units of 50,000-pound aluminum coils; yet Crown did not manufacture or purchase aluminum coils in excess of 5,000 pounds. The public accounting firm paid $875,000 to the parent company of Crown Aluminum Corporation in reimbursement of expenses incurred in the subsequent discovery and investigation of the fraud.

The preceding discussion has assumed that inventory tags and summaries are prepared manually. Clients using electronic data processing equipment may facilitate inventory counting and summarizing through the use of punched cards and "machine-sensible" pencils. Tag numbers, part numbers, descriptions, and unit prices may be prepunched into cards used as inventory tags. Count teams then record counts with pencils that are computer-sensible. The computer extends quantity times unit price for each punched card and prints out a complete inventory summary.

Working papers will be prepared by each auditor participating in the observation of the inventory. These papers should indicate the extent of test counts, describe any deficiencies noted, and express an opinion as to whether the physical inventory appeared to have been properly taken in accordance with the client's instructions. The auditor-in-charge should prepare a concise summary memorandum indicating the overall extent of observation and the percentage of inventory value covered by quantity tests. The memorandum may also include comments on the consideration given to the factors of quality and condition of stock, the treatment of consigned goods on hand, and the control of shipments and receipts during the counting process. Figure 14–3 illustrates this type of memorandum.

Inventory verification when auditors are engaged after the end of the year. A company desiring an independent audit should engage the auditors well before the end of the year, so they can participate in advance planning of the physical inventory and be prepared to observe the actual counting process. Occasionally, however, auditors are not engaged until after the end of the year and therefore find it impossible to observe the taking of inventory at the close of the year. For example, the illness or death of a company's individual practitioner CA near the year-end might lead to the engagement of new auditors shortly after the balance sheet date.

Under these circumstances, the auditors may conclude that sufficient appropriate audit evidence cannot be obtained concerning inventories to permit them to express an opinion on the overall fairness of the financial statements. On the other hand, if circumstances are favourable, the auditors may be able to obtain satisfaction concerning the inventories by alternative auditing procedures. These favourable circumstances might include the existence of strong internal control, perpetual inventory records, availability of instructions and other records showing that the client had carried out a well-planned physical inventory at or near the year-end, and subsequent test counts made by the newly appointed auditors. If the auditors are to express an unqualified opinion, their investigation of inventories must include some physical contact with items of inventory and must be thorough enough to compensate for the fact that they were not present when the physical inventory was taken. Whether such alternative auditing procedures will be feasible and will enable the auditors to satisfy themselves depends upon the circumstances of the particular engagement.

7.   Review the handling of goods held on consignment and determine that inventories do not include any items owned by others or properly chargeable to other asset accounts.

During the observation of physical inventories the auditors should make enquiries to ascertain whether any of the materials or goods on hand are the property of others, such as goods held on consignment or customer-owned materials sent in for machine work or other processing.

Audit procedures applicable to goods held by the client on consignment may include a comparison of the physical inventory with the client's

FIGURE 14–3

THE WILSHIRE CORPORATION LIMITED
Comments on Observation of Physical Inventory   H–9

December 31, 1979

1. Advance Planning of Physical Inventory.

   A physical inventory was taken by the client on December 31, 1979. Two
weeks in advance of this date we reviewed the written inventory instructions
prepared by L. D. Frome, Controller. These instructions appeared entirely
adequate and reflected the experience gained during the counts of previous
years. The plan called for a complete closing down of the factory on December 31,
since the preceding year's count had been handicapped by movements of productive
material during the counting process. Training meetings were conducted by
Frome for all employees assigned to participate in the inventory; at these
meetings the written instructions were explained and discussed.

2. Observation of Physical Inventory.

   We were present throughout the taking of the physical inventory on December 31,
1979. Prior to the count, all materials had been neatly arranged, labeled, and
separated by type. Two-employee inventory teams were used: one employee counting and
calling quantities and descriptions; the other employee filling in data on the serially
numbered inventory tags. As the goods were counted, the counting team tore off
the "first count" portion of the inventory tag. A second count was made later by
another team working independently of the first; this second team recorded the
quantity of its count on the "second count" portion of the tag.
   We made test counts of the numerous items, covering approximately 30 percent
of the total inventory value. These counts were recorded on our working papers and
used as noted below. Our observation throughout the plant indicated that both the
first and second counts required by the inventory instructions were being performed
in a systematic and conscientious manner. The careful and alert attitude of employees
indicated that the training meetings preceding the count had been quite effective in
creating an understanding of the importance of an accurate count. Before the "second
count" portions of the tags were removed, we visited all departments in company with
Frome and satisfied ourselves that all goods had been tagged and counted.
   No goods were shipped on December 31. We ascertained that receiving reports
were prepared on all goods taken into the receiving department on this day. We
recorded the serial numbers of the last receiving report and the last shipping advice
for the year 1979. (See H–9–1.) We compared the quantities per the count with
perpetual inventory records and found no significant discrepancies.

3. Quality and Condition of Materials.

   Certain obsolete parts had been removed from stock prior to the count and reduced
to a scrap carrying value. On the basis of our personal observation and questions
addressed to supervisors, we have no reason to believe that any obsolete or defective
materials remained in inventory. During the course of inventory observation, we tested
the reasonableness of quantities of 10 items, representing 40 percent of the value
of the inventory, by comparing the quantity on hand with the quantity used in
recent months; in no case did we find that the quantity in inventory exceeded
three months' normal usage.

V.M.H.
Jan. 3, 80

records of consigned goods on hand, review of contracts and correspondence with consignors, and direct written communication with the consignors to confirm the quantity and value of goods held at the balance sheet date, and to disclose any client liability for unremitted sales proceeds or from inability to collect consignment accounts receivable.

8. *Verify existence of goods held by public warehouses and goods out on consignment.*

The examination of warehouse receipts is not a sufficient verification of goods stored in public warehouses. Section 6030 of the *CICA Handbook* suggests the examination of "independence documentary evidence." The AICPA in the United States has recommended direct confirmation in writing from outside custodians of inventories, and supplementary procedures when the amounts involved represent a significant proportion of the current assets or of the total assets of a concern. These supplementary procedures include, as a minimum, establishing the existence, independence, and financial responsibility of warehouses or other concerns holding substantial quantities of goods belonging to the client. The auditors may refer to a business directory to verify the existence of a bonded public warehouse, or if the amounts are quite material, or any reason for doubt exists, they may decide to visit the warehouse, accompanied by a representative of the client, and observe a physical inventory of the client's merchandise stored at the warehouse.

The verification of goods in the hands of consignees may conveniently be begun by obtaining from the client a list of all consignees and copies of the consignment contracts. Contract provisions concerning the payment of freight and other handling charges, the extension of credit, computation of commissions, and frequency of reports and remittances require close attention. After review of the contracts and the client's records of consignment shipments and collections, the auditors should communicate directly with the consignees and obtain full written information on consigned inventory, receivables, unremitted proceeds, and accrued expenses and commissions as of the balance sheet date.

Often, the client may own raw materials which are processed by a subcontractor before being used in the client's production process. The auditors should request the subcontractor to confirm quantities and descriptions of client-owned materials in the subcontractor's possession.

9. *Determine inventory quality and condition.*

The auditors' responsibility for determining quality or condition of inventories is less rigorous than their responsibility for determining existence and ownership of inventories, for auditors do not claim to be experts in detecting deterioration or obsolescence of goods. However, an awareness of the problem and an alert attitude to recognize and act upon any evidence of unsatisfactory condition of goods is expected of the auditors.

To discharge their responsibility for inventory quality and condition, the auditors may have to rely upon the advice of a specialist. For example, the auditors of a retail jeweler might request the client to hire an independent expert in jewelry to assist the auditors in identifying the precious stones and metals included in the client's inventory. Similarly, the auditors of a chemical producer might rely upon the expert opinion of an independent chemist as to the identity of components of the client's inventories. Guidelines for using the work of a specialist are in Chapter 7.

The auditors should also be alert during the course of their inventory observation for any inventory of questionable quality or condition. Excessive dust or rust on raw materials inventory items may be indicative of obsolescence or infrequent use. Goods in process inventories rejected by quality control inspectors are obviously of poor quality.

The auditors should also review perpetual inventory records for indications of slow-moving inventory items. Then, during the course of observing inventory taking, the auditors should examine these slow-moving items and determine that the client has identified the items as obsolete if appropriate.

10.   Obtain copy of the completed physical inventory, determine its clerical accuracy, and trace test counts.

The testing of inventory extensions and footings may disclose substantial misstatements of physical inventories. Often this test consists of "sight-footing" to the nearest hundred dollars or thousand dollars.

In testing extensions, the auditors should be alert for two sources of substantial errors—misplaced decimal points and incorrect extension of *count* units by *price* units. For example, an inventory listing that extends 1,000 units times $1.00C (per hundred) as $1,000 will be overstated $990. An inventory extension of 1,000 sheets of steel times $1 per pound will be substantially understated if each sheet of steel weighs more than one pound.

The auditors also should trace to the completed physical inventory their test counts made during the observation of physical inventory. During this tracing, the auditors should be alert for any indications that inventory tags had been altered, or that fictitious inventory tags had been created. The auditors may compare inventory tag number sequences in the physical inventory listing to tag numbers noted in their audit working papers for the inventory observation.

11.   Review the bases and methods of inventory pricing.

The auditors are responsible for determining that the bases and methods of pricing inventory are in accordance with generally accepted accounting principles. The investigation of inventory pricing often will emphasize the following three questions:

1.   What method of pricing does the client use?
2.   Is the method of pricing the same as that used in prior years?
3.   Has the method officially selected by the client been applied consistently and accurately in practice?

For the first question—a method of pricing—a long list of alternatives is possible, including such methods as cost; cost or market, whichever is lower; the retail method; and quoted market price (as for metals and staple commodities traded on organized exchanges). The "cost" method of course includes many diverse systems, such as last-in, first-out; first-in, first-out; specific identification; weighted average; and standard cost.

The second question raised in this section concerned a change in method of pricing inventory from one year to the next. For example, let us say that the client has changed from the first-in, first-out method to the last-in, first-out method. The nature and justification of the change in method of valuing inventory, and its effect on income, should be disclosed. In addition, the auditors must insert in the audit report a qualification concerning the lack of consistency in the two years.

The third question posed dealt with consistent accurate application in practice of the method of valuation officially adopted by the client. To answer this question the auditors must test the pricing of a representative number of inventory items.

12. Test pricing of raw materials or purchased merchandise.

The testing of prices applied to inventories of raw materials, purchased parts, and supplies by a manufacturing company is similar to the testing of prices of merchandise in a trading business. In both cases, cost of inventory items, whether last-in, first-out, first-in, first-out, weighted average, or specific identification, is readily verified by reference to purchase invoices. An illustration of a working paper prepared by an auditor in making price tests of an inventory of raw materials and purchased parts is presented in Figure 14–4.

13. Determine reasonableness and accuracy of the pricing of finished goods and goods in process.

Audit procedures for verification of the inventory values assigned to goods in process and finished goods are not so simple and conclusive as in the case of raw materials or merchandise for which purchase invoices are readily available. To determine whether the inventory valuation method used by the client has been properly applied, the auditors must make tests of the pricing of selected items of finished goods and goods in process. The items to be tested should be selected from the client's inventory summary sheets after the quantities established by the physical inventory have been priced and extended. Items of large total value may be selected for testing so that the tests will encompass a significant portion of the dollar amount of inventories. If statistical sampling is employed, the selection of items for testing will of course be on a random basis.

Let us assume that the client uses a job cost system and prices the inventory on a first-in, first-out basis. In this situation, the auditors may test the prices for finished goods by tracing the unit prices of selected products from the inventory sheets to the job cost records. The auditors

FIGURE 14–4

The Wilshire Corporation Limited

Test of Pricing – Raw Materials and Purchased Parts (Fifo)   K-5

December 31, 1978

Part No.	Description	Per Inventory Quantity	Price	Per Vendor's Invoice Vendor	Date	No.	Quantity	Price
8 Z 182	Aluminum 48 × 144 × 0.025	910 sheets	10.10	Hardy & Co. Ltd.	Dec. 18, 78	541 E	1,000	10.10 ✓
8 Z 195	Aluminum 45 × 72 × 0.032	804 sheets	9.01	Watson Mfg. Co. Ltd.	Nov. 28, 78	2815	500	9.01 ✓
					Dec. 22, 78	3207	500	9.01 ✓
K 1125	Stainless steel 0.025 × 23	80,625 Lbs.	0.80	Ajax Steel Co.	Dec. 3, 78	K 182	100,000	0.80 ✓
K 1382	Stainless steel 0.031 × 17	65,212 Lbs.	0.82	Ajax Steel Co.	Dec. 3, 78	K 182	75,000	0.82 ✓
XL 3925	10 H.P. Electronic motor	50 ea.	400.00	Cronyn Mfg. Co.	Nov. 18, 78	253	100	400.00 ✓
XJ 3821	3/4 H.P. Electronic motor	645 ea.	30.50	Long & Co.	Dec. 29, 78	E9821	650	30.50 ✓

Inventory value of raw materials and purchased parts selected for price testing — $301,825.56.

% of total raw materials and purchased parts selected for price testing — $\frac{\$301,825.56}{503,615.10} = 60\%$.

See audit program B-4 for method of selecting raw materials and purchased parts for price testing.

✓ – Inventory price appears reasonable.

Conclusion:
   Based on our tests, we are 95% confident that there are no material pricing errors in the pricing of raw materials and purchased parts.

U.M.H.
Jan. 20, 79

will already have determined during their study and evaluation of internal control the extent to which they may rely upon the client's job cost records. If the quantity of units on the most recently completed job covers the entire quantity in the year-end inventory, the cost per the job record should agree with the cost shown on the inventory sheet. If several completed jobs are included in the year-end inventory, it will be necessary to refer to additional job cost records.

Next let us assume that the client's cost accounting system is known to have some weakness in internal control. In this case the auditors should examine the documents supporting cost accumulations on the job records. For material cost, these documents will include material requisitions, perpetual inventory records for raw materials, and vendors' invoices. For the element of labour cost, the documents to be examined would include time reports showing hours worked on the job in question and pay rate authorizations from the personnel department for the workers involved.

Assuming that overhead has been allocated to the job cost records as a percentage of direct labour dollars, the auditors will compute the percentage relationship of overhead to labour cost on the job and compare this percentage with the overhead rate in use during the period. Of course, a predetermined overhead rate may vary significantly from the actual current level of overhead, and the auditors should verify the reasonableness of the overhead rate. The verification will consist of determining the total labour cost and total factory overhead for the current and preceding years. Attention should also be given to changes in the nature of items treated as overhead.

The auditors' approach to verifying items selected for testing from the goods in process inventory follows a pattern similar to that described for finished goods. The total of the labour and overhead costs required to complete a job currently in process is of course not definitely determinable, but as a rule the overall reasonableness of the charges to date can be appraised by making comparisons with the costs of similar jobs completed in the recent past.

14.   Apply "lower-of-cost-or-market" test to inventory prices.

Pricing the inventories at cost ordinarily leads to a satisfactory matching of costs and revenues. However, if evidence exists that the utility of goods when sold will be less than cost, the prospective loss should be recognized in the current period. There is no justification for carrying inventories at an amount in excess of replacement cost or net realizable value. The lower-of-cost-or-market rule is a common means of measuring any loss of utility in the inventories. Lower-of-cost-or-market valuation may be applied on an individual, group, or total inventory basis.

For raw materials and purchased parts, the client usually will obtain replacement cost data from vendors' price sheets or direct quotations. Replacement cost for in-process and finished goods may be determined by reference to costs of products completed subsequent to the balance sheet date, or from cost estimates compiled by the client's personnel. If the inventory includes any discontinued lines, obsolete, or damaged goods, the client should reduce these items to net realizable value, which is often scrap value.

ILLUSTRATIVE CASE. During the first audit of an automobile agency, the auditors were observing the taking of the physical inventory of repair parts. They noticed a large number of new fenders of a design and shape not used on the current model cars. Closer inspection revealed that the fenders (with a total inventory valuation of several thousand dollars) were for a model of automobile made seven years ago. The records showed that only one of this type of fender had been sold during the past two years. The automobile dealer explained that these fenders had been included in the parts inventory when he purchased the agency two years ago, and that he had no idea as to why such a large stock had originally been acquired. He agreed that few, if any, of this model of fender would ever be sold. It had not occurred to him to write down the carrying value of these obsolete parts, but he readily agreed with the auditors' suggestion that the fenders, being virtually unsalable, should be reduced to scrap value.

15. Compare the completed physical inventory to perpetual inventory records.

The auditors should compare the quantities and values of individual items per the physical inventory with the perpetual inventory records. The totals of various sections of inventory should also be compared with the corresponding control accounts. All substantial discrepancies should be fully investigated. The number, type, and cause of the discrepancies revealed by such comparisons are highly significant in appraising the adequacy of the system of internal control over inventories.

In the examination of concerns carrying on inventory counts continuously or at various times during the year, the auditors may gain considerable insight into the dependability of the records by a critical review of the adjustments arising from physical counts.

16. Review the year-end cutoff of purchases and sales transactions.

An accurate cutoff of purchases is one of the most important factors in verifying the amount of the year-end inventory. Assume that a shipment of goods costing $10,000 is received from a supplier on December 31, but the purchase invoice does not arrive until January 2 and is entered as a January transaction. If the goods are included in the December 31 physical inventory but there is no December entry to record the purchase and the liability, the result will be an overstatement of both net income for the year and retained earnings, and an understatement of accounts payable, each error being in the full amount of $10,000 (ignoring income taxes).

An opposite situation may arise if a purchase invoice is received and recorded on December 31, but the merchandise covered by the invoice is not received until several days later and is not included in the physical inventory taken at the year-end. The effect on the financial statements of recording a purchase without including the goods in the inventory will be to understate net income, retained earnings, and inventory.

How can the auditors determine that the liability to suppliers has been recorded for all goods included in inventory? Their approach is to examine on a test basis the purchase invoices and receiving reports for several days before and after the inventory date. Each purchase invoice in the files should have a receiving report attached; if an invoice recorded in late December is accompanied by a receiving report dated December 31 or earlier, the goods must have been on hand and included in the year-end physical inventory. However, if the receiving report carried a January date, the goods were not included in the physical count made on December 31.

A supplementary approach to the matching of purchase invoices and receiving reports is to examine the records of the receiving department. For each shipment received near the year-end, the auditors should determine that the related purchase invoice was recorded in the same period.

The effect on the financial statements of failing to include a year-end "in-transit purchase" as part of physical inventory is not a serious one, *provided* the related liability is not recorded until the following period. In other words, the primary point in effecting an accurate *cutoff of purchases is that both sides of a purchase transaction must be reflected in the same accounting period.* If a given shipment is included in the year-end physical inventory of the purchaser, the entry debiting Inventories and crediting Accounts Payable must be made. If the shipment is not included in the purchaser's year-end physical inventory, the purchase invoice must not be recorded until the following period.

Adjustments to achieve an accurate cutoff of purchases should of course be made by the client's staff; the function of the auditors should be to review the cutoff and determine that the necessary adjustments have been properly made.

Chapter 13 includes a detailed discussion of the audit procedures for determining the accuracy of the sales cutoff. The sales cutoff is mentioned again at this point to emphasize its importance in determining the fairness of the client's inventory and cost of goods sold as well as accounts receivable and sales.

17. *Test the reasonableness of inventories by comparison with prior years, by application of the gross profit percentage method, by computing the rate of turnover, and by reference to capacity of production and storage facilities.*

Gross errors in pricing, footings, and extensions of the physical inventory, as well as the recording of fictitious transactions, may be disclosed by overall tests designed to establish the general reasonableness of the inventory figures.

A comparative summary of inventories classified by major types, such as raw materials, goods in process, finished goods, and supplies, should be obtained or prepared. Explanations should be obtained for all major increases or decreases from the prior year's amounts.

In certain lines of business, particularly retail and wholesale concerns, gross profit margins may be quite uniform from year to year. Any major difference between the ending inventory estimated by the gross profit percentage method and the count of inventory at year-end should be investigated fully. The discrepancy may reflect theft of merchandise, or unrecorded or fictitious purchases or sales. On the other hand, it may be the result of changes in the basis of inventory valuation or of sharp changes in sales prices.

Another useful test is the computation of rates of inventory turnover, based on the relationship between the cost of goods sold for the year and the average inventory as shown on the monthly financial statements. These turnover rates should be compared with the rates prevailing in prior years. A decreasing rate of turnover suggests the possibility of obsolescence or of unnecessarily large inventories. Deliberate stockpiling in anticipation of higher prices or shortages of certain strategic materials will of course be reflected by a declining inventory turnover rate. Rates of turnover are most significant when computed for individual products or by departments; if compared on a company-wide basis, substantial declines in turnover in certain sections of the client company's operations may be obscured by compensating increases in the turnover rates for other units of the organization.

The auditors should also make certain that aggregate or unit inventories do not exceed the capacity of the client's production or storage facilities. For example, in the audit of a manufacturer of chemicals, the auditors should ascertain the total storage capacity of the client's containers, and determine that the aggregate quantity of chemicals in inventories does not exceed that capacity.

18. In the first audit of a new client, investigate beginning inventories.

The need for the auditors to be present to observe the taking of the ending inventory has been strongly emphasized in auditing literature. However, the figure for beginning inventory is equally significant in determining the cost of goods sold and the net income for the year. In the initial examination of a new client, the auditors obviously will not have been present to observe the taking of inventory at the beginning of the year. What procedures can they follow to obtain evidence that the beginning inventories are fairly stated?

The first factor to consider is whether the new client was audited by another firm of independent public accountants for the preceding year. If a review of the predecessor firm's working papers indicates compliance with generally accepted auditing standards, the new auditors can accept the beginning inventories with a minimum of investigation. That minimum might include the following steps: (*a*) study of the inventory valuation methods used; (*b*) review of the inventory records; (*c*) review of the inventory sheets used in taking the preceding year's physical inventory; and (*d*) comparison of the beginning and ending inventories, broken down by product classification.

If there had been no satisfactory audit for the preceding year, the investigation of the beginning inventories would include not only the procedures mentioned above but also the following steps: (*a*) discussion with the person in the client's organization who supervised the physical inventory at the preceding balance sheet date; (*b*) study of the written instructions used in planning the inventory; (*c*) tracing of numerous items from the inventory tags or count sheets to the final summary sheets; (*d*) tests of the perpetual inventory records for the preceding period by reference to supporting documents for receipts and withdrawals; and (*e*) tests of the overall reasonableness of the beginning inventories in relation to sales, gross profit, and rate of inventory turnover. An investigation along these lines will sometimes give the auditors definite assurance that the beginning inventory was carefully compiled and reasonable in amount; in other cases, these procedures may raise serious doubts as to the validity of the beginning inventory figure. In these latter cases, the auditors will not be able to issue an unqualified opinion *as to the income statement.* They may be able, however, to give an unqualified opinion on the *balance sheet* since this financial statement does not reflect the beginning inventories.

19.   Obtain and review an analysis of cost of goods sold.

Much of the audit work necessary to verify cost of goods sold in a trading business has already been suggested in Chapter 13, dealing with the audit of sales, and in the discussion of inventories in this chapter. Errors in cost of goods sold usually are caused by errors in beginning or ending inventories or from errors in accounting for purchases. The propriety of beginning and ending inventories is established in the verification of balance sheet items. The study and evaluation of internal controls for purchases were discussed earlier in this chapter.

In addition to the detailed testing of purchases and inventories, the auditors should review all general ledger accounts relating to cost of sales to make certain that they contain no apparent irregularities. Adjustments of substantial amount should be investigated to determine the propriety of their inclusion in the cost of goods sold. If this review of general ledger accounts were not made, the door would be left open for all types of gross errors to remain undetected—such obvious errors, for example, as closing miscellaneous revenue and expense into cost of goods sold.

In the audit of a manufacturing company the auditors must go beyond verification of the beginning and ending inventories of raw materials, goods in process, and finished goods in order to establish the validity of the figures for cost of goods manufactured and sold during the period. Since the determination of cost of goods manufactured involves all the ramifications of (*a*) raw material purchases and issuances, (*b*) direct labour costs, and (*c*) distribution of overhead costs, the review of cost of goods sold of a manufacturing company is clearly a more complex task than for a retail store or a wholesale business.

The auditors of a manufacturer client should obtain from the client or prepare an analysis of cost of sales by month, broken down into raw materials, direct labour, and factory overhead elements. The analysis should also include a description of all unusual and non-recurring charges or credits to cost of goods sold. Figure 14–5 illustrates an analysis of cost of goods sold for a manufacturing concern.

The extent of the auditors' verification of cost of sales for the year is largely dependent upon their evaluation of the client's cost accounting system. If the system is strong, the auditors may limit their substantive tests to verifying that perpetual inventory records have been relieved for the cost of goods sold and that the predetermined factory overhead rate is reasonable. These tests are illustrated in Figure 14–5. A weak cost accounting system will necessitate extensive tests to determine that all goods sold are costed in reasonable amounts.

20. *Determine whether any inventories have been pledged and review purchase and sales commitments.*

The verification of inventories includes a determination by the auditors as to whether any goods have been pledged or subjected to a lien of any kind. Pledging of inventories to secure bank loans should be brought to light when bank balances and indebtedness are confirmed.

A record of outstanding purchase commitments is usually readily available, since this information is essential to management in maintaining day-to-day control of the company's inventory position and cash flow.

In some lines of business it is customary to enter into firm contracts for the purchase of merchandise or materials well in advance of the scheduled delivery dates. Comparison by the auditors of the prices quoted in such commitments with the vendors' prices prevailing at the balance sheet date may indicate substantial losses if firm purchase commitments are not protected by firm sales contracts. Such losses should be reflected in the financial statements.

The quantities of purchase commitments should be reviewed in the light of current and prospective demand, as indicated by past operations, the backlog of sales orders, and current conditions within the industry. If quantities on order appear excessive by these standards, the auditors should seek full information on this phase of operations. As a general

FIGURE 14–5

The Constellation Limited
Cost of Goods Sold
Year Ended December 31, 1979

Acct. No. 501   R-1

| Month | Inventory Relief (4) | | | Scrap Sales Proceeds | Under-(Over-) absorbed Factory Overhead (2) | Total |
	Materials	Direct Labour	Factory Overhead (1)			
Jan.	15 160 28	42 815 70 ✗	64 223 55 ∧	(819 72) ч	1 214 68	122 594 49 ∧
Feb.	18 142 55 ✗	47 922 18	71 883 27	(947 55) ч	(881 14) ч	136 119 31 ∧
Mar.	17 655 95	45 814 00	68 721 00 ч	742 88	581 26	132 029 33 ∧
Apr.	20 944 16	50 222 16 ✗	75 333 24	(1 482 67)	(987 44) ч	144 029 45 ∧
May	19 446 82 ✗	48 144 76 ✗	72 217 14 ✗	(1 128 77) ч	(722 66)	137 957 29 ∧
June	22 814 70	52 581 22	78 871 83 ч	(1 222 14)	381 14	153 426 75 ∧
July	21 214 14	51 582 16 ✗	77 373 24 ✗	(998 82)	(701 28)	148 469 44 ∧
Aug.	20 844 27 ✗	51 018 00	76 527 00 ✗	(1 008 44) ч	914 68 ч	148 295 51 ∧
Sept.	19 842 10	49 827 14	74 740 71 ✗	(882 92)	(481 16)	143 045 87 ∧
Oct.	22 822 90	53 018 10 ✗	79 527 15 ∧	(1 871 28) ч	714 28 ч	154 211 15 ∧
Nov.	20 476 20 ✗	48 218 70	72 328 05	(1 347 19)	(422 19)	139 253 57 ∧
Dec.	21 807 14	50 976 10 ✗	76 464 15 ч	(1 548 02)	(781 16) ч	146 918 21 ∧
	241 171 21 ∧	592 140 22 ∧	888 210 33 ∧	(14 000 40) ∧	(1 170 99) ∧	1 706 350 37 ∧

Dec. 31 1979 Adjustment of perpetual inventory to physical inventory ③ { H-1   76 418 55
Write-off of loss on fixed price contract No. AF 219-716   { H-4   22 841 16

Prepared by client   1 805 610 08
                                                                      C-2

∧ — Footed and cross-footed.
ч — Computation tested — no exceptions.
✗ — Traced to relief of perpetual inventory accounts — no exceptions.
ч — Vouched proceeds to remittance advice from scrap dealer and to certified weight tickets — no exceptions.

① 150% of direct labour dollars. See R-1-1 for our satisfactory test of this predetermined rate.

② Net overabsorbed factory overhead is less than 1% of total factory overhead applied, hence immaterial.

③ See referenced working paper for satisfactory tests of these write-offs.

④ See H-3 for our satisfactory study of internal control for cost accounting system for year ended December 31, 1979.

Conclusion: In our opinion, cost of goods sold for the year ended December 31, 1979, is fairly stated at the amount of $1,805,610.   WM.H Jan 29, 80 rule, purchase commitments need not be mentioned in the financial statements unless significant losses are realized or the commitments are unusual in amount or nature.

Sales commitments are indicated by the client's *backlog* of unfilled sales orders. Losses inherent in firm sales commitments are generally recognized in the lower-of-cost-or-market valuation of inventories, with "market" being defined as the net realizable value of the goods in process or finished goods inventories applicable to the sales commitments. In addition, the backlog may include sales orders for which no production has been started as of the balance sheet date. The auditors must review the client's cost estimates for these sales orders. If estimated total costs to produce the goods ordered exceed fixed sales prices, the indicated loss and a related liability should be recorded in the client's financial statements for the current period.

21. Review computations of replacement cost of inventories and cost of goods sold, as required by the U.S. SEC requirements for certain companies subject to its jurisdiction.

Since Canadian companies listed in the United States stock exchanges are subject to the SEC regulations, it is important for auditors to be familiar with this reporting requirement. In *Accounting Series Release No. 190*, the U.S. SEC required certain companies subject to its jurisdiction to disclose *in reports to the Commission* the current replacement cost of inventories at the end of each year for which a balance sheet is required, and the approximate replacement cost valuation for cost of goods sold for the two most recent fiscal years. The replacement cost data may be designated as "unaudited," and may be presented either in a note to the financial statements or in a separate section of the financial statements following the notes. The disclosures must also include methods of determining the replacement cost data, and any additional information required to prevent the data from being misleading. In a related pronouncement, the Commission suggested that the companies' related *annual reports to shareholders* include in notes to financial statements only generalized descriptions of the impact of specific price changes on the companies' assets and earnings.

The SEC also urged the AICPA to develop guidelines for the independent auditors' *review* of the unaudited replacement cost data filed with the Commission or included in annual reports to shareholders.

22. Determine proper balance sheet presentation of inventories and proper income statement presentation of cost of goods sold.

Section 3030 of the *CICA Handbook* recommends the following statement presentation for inventories:

> *The basis of valuation of inventories should be clearly stated in the financial statements.*

If the method of determining cost has resulted in a figure which does not differ materially from recent cost, the simple term "cost" is considered to be suitable in describing the basis of valuation. Otherwise, the method of determining cost should be disclosed.

These recommendations are not entirely satisfactory because the disclosure of the method of determining inventory cost is not required in all cases.

One of the most important factors in proper presentation of inventories in the financial statements is disclosure of the inventory pricing method or methods in use. To say that inventories are stated at *cost* is not sufficient because cost may be determined under several alternative assumptions, each of which leads to a substantially different valuation.

From the standpoint of analyzing the current earnings of the company, it is extremely important to know whether the reported profits have been inflated by price changes, as has often been the case under first-in, first-out, or that the effect of price rises has been limited through the Lifo method of valuation. The users of the financial statements also need to know whether the carrying value of inventory approximates current cost (as with first-in, first-out) or whether inventories are stated at cost of an earlier period (as with the Lifo method).

In *Accounting Series Release No. 151,* the U.S. SEC urged companies to disclose the effects of *inventory profits* on net income reported in their financial statements filed with the Commission. *Inventory profits* are measured by the difference between the historical cost of an inventory item and its replacement cost at the time it is sold. The Commission considered disclosure of inventory profits essential for an assessment of the quality of a company's earnings.

Other important points in presenting inventories in the financial statements include the following:

a. Changes in methods of valuing inventory should be disclosed and the dollar effect and justification for the change reported. The auditors' report will contain a qualification in the opinion paragraph because of the lack of consistency between years.

b. Separate listing is desirable for the various classifications of inventory, such as finished goods, goods in process, and raw materials.

c. If any portion of the inventory has been pledged to secure liabilities, full disclosure of the arrangement should be made.

Examples of disclosures of inventory pricing methods. In many large companies the cost of certain portions of the inventory is determined on one basis, and other portions of inventory on some other basis. Typical of the disclosure of inventory pricing methods are the following examples taken from published financial statements:

CANADIAN REYNOLDS METALS CO., LTD.

Balance Sheet—current assets

Inventories (Note 2) $23,081,411

Notes to financial statements
1. Significant Accounting Policies (*in part*)
    Inventories
    Inventories are stated at the lower of cost and net realizable value; cost representing actual production cost (first-in, first-out method) for finished metal and average cost for raw materials and supplies.
2. Inventories
    The inventories used in the calculation of cost of products sold are classified as follows:

Finished metal	$ 5,555,265
Raw materials	13,916,249
Supplies	3,609,897
	$23,081,411

SKLAR MANUFACTURING LTD.

Balance Sheet—current assets

Inventories (note 3) $11,285,000

Notes to financial statements
1. SUMMARY OF SIGNIFICANT ACCOUNTING POLICIES
    c. Inventories—
    Inventories are valued at the lower of cost or net realizable value, with cost determined on a first-in first-out basis.
3. INVENTORIES
    At December 31, inventories consist of:

Raw materials	$ 6,467,000
Work in process	2,271,000
Finished goods	2,547,000
	$11,285,000

Cost of goods sold is reported as a deduction from net sales to arrive at gross profit on sales for a multiple-step income statement. In a single-step income statement, cost of goods sold is included among the "Costs and expenses" section of the income statement.

23. Obtain from client a letter of representations concerning inventories and cost of goods sold.

Public accounting firms generally obtain from clients a formal written statement concerning the overall accuracy of the inventories. The purpose of these representations is to emphasize to management that primary responsibility for the correctness of inventories and cost of sales and of the financial statements as a whole rests with the client rather than with the auditors. Officers or other executives asked to sign such representations are

FIGURE 14–6
Representations as to inventories and cost of goods sold

(Name of Accounting Firm)   Date_____
(Address)

Dear Sirs:
   In connection with your examination of the financial statements of the X Co. Ltd., for
the period ended December 31, 19--, we make the following statements and representations
concerning inventories and cost of goods sold:
   1. Inventories consisting of the following classifications:

Raw materials and purchased parts . . . . $ XXXX
Goods in process . . . . $ XXXX
Finished goods . . . . $ XXXX
Supplies . . . . $ XXXX

   Total . . . . $ XXXX

were on hand December 31, 19--, as determined by a physical inventory, taken
under our supervision in accordance with written instructions.
   2. All inventory quantities were determined by count, weight, or measurement.
   3. All inventories owned, and only inventories owned, are included in the above summary, and no inventories have been pledged or hypothecated.
   4. All liabilities for inventories have been recorded in the financial statements as of
the above balance sheet date.
   5. All raw materials, purchased parts, and supplies are stated at the lower of cost or
market, with cost determined by the first-in, first-out method after deduction of
all trade discounts, consistent with the basis employed in the preceding period.
   6. Finished goods and goods in process are stated at manufacturing cost, except for
items having a lower net realizable value after proper allowance for completion
and disposal costs, consistent with the basis employed in the preceding period.
   7. Proper provision has been made in cost of goods sold for obsolete, inactive,
and damaged goods.
   8. There are no purchase commitments in excess of current market price as of the
above balance sheet date.
   9. There are no sales commitments below inventory price and no purchase or sale
commitments in excess of normal operations.

                              Signed_____
                              Title _____

prone to attach greater significance to the process of taking, pricing, and summarizing the physical inventory than they otherwise would. The obtaining of the inventory representations does not in any way reduce the scope of the examination to be made by the auditors; nor does it lessen their responsibility.

The points usually covered in the inventory representations include quantities, titles, prices, commitments, and condition. An example of a form of inventories and cost of goods sold representations letter in common use is shown in Figure 14–6.

KEY TERMS INTRODUCED OR EMPHASIZED IN CHAPTER 14

bill of lading   A document issued by a common carrier acknowledging the receipt of goods and setting forth the provisions of the transportation agreement.

confirmation   A type of documentary evidence which is created outside the client organization and transmitted directly to the auditors.

consignment   A transfer of goods from the owner to another person who acts as the sales agent of the owner.

Cost Accounting Standards Board   A five-member board established by the U.S. Congress to narrow the options in cost accounting which are available under generally accepted accounting principles. Companies having significant supply contracts with certain U.S. government agencies are subject to the cost accounting standards established by the board.

inventory profits   The amount of net income represented by the difference between the historical cost of an inventory item and its replacement cost at the time it is sold.

observation   The auditors' evidence-gathering technique which provides physical evidence.

periodic inventory system   A method of accounting in which inventories are determined solely by means of a physical inventory at the end of the accounting period.

perpetual inventory system   A method of accounting for inventories in which control accounts and subsidiary ledgers are maintained to record receipts and issuances of goods, both in quantities and in dollar amounts. The accuracy of perpetual inventory records is tested periodically by phyiscal inventories.

purchase commitment   A contractual obligation to purchase goods at fixed prices, entered into well in advance of scheduled delivery dates.

replacement cost   The lowest amount that would have to be paid in the normal course of business to obtain a new asset of equivalent operating or productive capacity as an asset presently owned.

sales commitment   A contractual obligation to sell goods at fixed prices, entered into well in advance of scheduled delivery dates.

specialist   A person or firm possessing special skill or knowledge in a field other than accounting or auditing, such as an actuary.

GROUP I
REVIEW QUESTIONS

14–1. A client company wishes to conduct its physical inventory on a sampling basis. Many items will not be counted. Under what general conditions will this method of taking inventory be acceptable to the auditors?

14–2. What lessons did the Crown Aluminum Corporation case in the United States provide for independent auditors?

14–3. How do the independent auditors use the client's backlog of unfilled sales orders in the examination of inventories?

14–4. What are cost accounting standards?

14–5. What are general objectives or purposes of the auditors' observation of the taking of the physical inventory? (Do not discuss the procedures or techniques involved in making the observation.) (AICPA)

14–6. For what purposes do the auditors make and record test counts of inventory quantities during their observation of the taking of the physical inventory? Discuss. (AICPA)

14–7. What part, if any, do the independent auditors play in the planning for a client's physical inventory?

14–8. Once the auditors have completed their test counts of the physical inventory, will they have any reason to make later reference to the inventory tags used by the client's employees in the counting process? Explain.

14–9. The client's cost accounting system is often the focal point in the auditors' examination of the financial statements of a manufacturing company. For what purposes do the auditors review the cost accounting system? (AICPA)

14–10. What charges and credits may be disclosed in the auditors' analysis of the Cost of Goods Sold account of a manufacturing concern?

14–11. Explain the significance of the purchase order to adequate internal control over purchase transactions.

14–12. What segregation of duties would you recommend to attain maximum internal control over purchasing activities in a manufacturing concern?

14–13. Do you believe that the normal review of purchase transactions by the auditors should include examination of receiving reports? Explain.

14–14. Many auditors feel that the substantiation of the figure for inventory is a more difficult and challenging task than the verification of most other items on the balance sheet. List several specific factors which support this view.

14–15. "A well-prepared balance sheet usually includes a statement that the inventories are valued at cost." Evaluate this quotation.

14–16. Darnell Equipment Company use the last-in, first-out method of valuation for part of its inventories and weighted-average cost for another portion. Would you be willing to issue an unqualified opinion under these circumstances? Explain.

14–17. "If the auditors can determine that all goods in the physical inventory have been accurately counted and properly priced, they will have discharged fully their responsibility with respect to inventory." Evaluate this statement.

14–18. When perpetual inventory records are maintained, is it necessary for a physical inventory to be taken at the balance sheet date? Explain.

14–19. The controller of a new client company informs you that most of the inventories are stored in bonded public warehouses. He presents warehouse receipts to account for the inventories. Will careful examination of these warehouse receipts constitute adequate verification of these inventories? Explain.

14–20. Assume that a manufacturing company which has been among your clients for many years changes its methods of pricing inventories during the current year. What effect, if any, will the change in pricing method have upon your audit procedures and audit report?

14–21. Hana Ranch Ltd., which has never been audited, is asked on October 1 by its bank to arrange for a year-end audit. The company retains you to make this audit and asks what measures, if any, it should take to ensure a satisfactory year-end physical inventory. Perpetual inventories are not maintained. How would you answer this enquiry?

14–22. Enumerate specific steps to be taken by the auditors to ascertain that a client's inventories have not been pledged or subjected to a lien of any kind.

GROUP II
QUESTIONS REQUIRING ANALYSIS

14–23. During the March 31, 1979, audit of a new client, Electronics Co. Ltd., the auditors discovered that the client had acquired in a bulk purchase various raw materials used to produce parts for electronic data processing equipment. The bulk purchase had been completed more than a year previously, yet less than 10 percent of the raw materials had been used by Electronics since that time. The company's controller acknowledged that there might be some obsolete raw materials on hand from the bulk purchase; he claimed, however, that not enough time had elapsed to determine with assurance the complete degree of obsolescence. The controller therefore offered to write down to salvage value one third of the remaining raw materials from the bulk purchase. For the remainder, the controller offered to give the auditors a letter of representations stating that he believed the remaining materials to be not obsolete.

Will the controller's letter of representations provide sufficient, appropriate audit evidence for the auditors with respect to obsolescence of inventories? Discuss.

14-24. You are engaged in the audit of Reed Ltd., a new client, at the end of its first fiscal year, June 30, 1979. During your work on inventories, you discover that all of the mechandise remaining in stock on June 30, 1979, had been acquired July 1, 1978, from Andrew Reed, the sole shareholder and president of Reed Ltd., for an original selling price of $10,000 cash and a note payable due July 1, 1981, with interest at 10 percent, in the amount of $90,000. The merchandise had been used by the president when he operated a similar business as a single proprietor.

How can you verify the pricing of the June 30, 1979, inventory of Reed Ltd.? Explain.

14-25. The observation of a client's physical inventory is a mandatory auditing procedure when practicable and possible for the auditors to carry out, and inventories are material.

Required:

a. Why is the observation of physical inventory a mandatory auditing procedure? Explain.
b. Under what circumstances is observation of physical inventory impracticable or impossible?
c. Why is the auditor's review of the client's control for inventory tags important during the observation of physical inventory? Explain.

14-26. You have been asked to examine the financial statements of Wilson Ltd., a road-building contractor which has never before been audited by CAs. During your interim work, you learn that Wilson excludes a significant inventory item from its annual balance sheet. This inventory item, which Wilson management claims is approximately the same amount each year, is gravel which has been processed for use in road building and is placed at different road construction sites wherever it might be used. Wilson's controller states than any unused gravel at the completion of a construction contract is never moved to another job site; in fact, the gravel often disappears because of thefts during winter months when road construction is suspended.

Would you be able to issue an unqualified opinion on the financial statements of Wilson Ltd.? Explain.

14-27. Grandview Manufacturing Ltd. employs standard costs in its cost accounting system. List the audit procedures that you would apply to ascertain that Grandview's standard costs and related variance amounts are acceptable and have not distorted the financial statements. (Confine your audit procedures to those applicable to raw materials.) (AICPA, adapted)

14-28. At the beginning of your annual audit of Crestview Manufacturing Company's financial statements for the year ended December 31, 1979, the company president confides in you that Henry Ward, an employee, is living on a scale in excess of that which his salary would support. The employee has been a buyer in the purchasing department for six years and has charge of purchasing all general materials and supplies. He is authorized to sign purchase orders for amounts up to $500. Purchase orders in excess of $500 require the countersignature of the general purchasing agent.

The president understands that the usual examination of financial statements is not designed, and cannot be relied upon, to disclose fraud or conflicts of interest, although their discovery may result. The president authorizes you, however, to expand your regular audit procedures and to apply additional audit procedures to determine whether there is any evidence that the buyer has been misappropriating company funds or has been engaged in activities that were conflicts of interest.

Required:

List the audit procedures that you would apply to the company records and documents in an attempt to discover evidence within the purchasing department of defalcations being committed by the buyer. Give the purpose of each audit procedure. (AICPA, adapted)

14–29. A number of companies employ outside service companies which specialize in counting, pricing, extending and footing inventories. These service companies usually furnish a certificate attesting to the value of the physical inventory.

Assuming that the service company took the client company's inventory on the balance sheet date:

a. How much reliance, if any, can the auditors place on the inventory certificate of outside specialists? Discuss.

b. What effect, if any, would the inventory certificate of outside specialists have upon the type of report the auditors would render? Discuss.

c. What reference, if any, would the auditors make to the certificate of outside specialists in their audit report? (AICPA)

14–30. Santa Rosa Corporation Ltd. is a closely held furniture manufacturing company employing approximately 1,000 employees. On December 15, the corporation retained the firm of Warren and Wood, Chartered Accountants, to perform a December 31 year-end audit. The president of the corporation explained that perpetual inventory records were maintained and that every attention was given to maintaining a strong system of internal control. A complete count of inventories had been made at November 30 by the company's own employees; in addition, extensive test counts had been made in most departments at various intervals during the year. Although the company was not large, it employed an internal auditor and an assistant who had devoted their full time to analysis of internal control and appraisal of operations in the various organizational units of the company.

The chartered accountant who had audited Santa Rosa Corporation Ltd. for several years had died during the current year, and the company had decided to forego an annual audit. The physical inventory had therefore been taken at November 30 without being observed by an independent public accountant. Shortly thereafter, a major shareholder in the company had demanded that new auditors be retained. The president explained to Warren and Wood that the company was too far behind on its delivery schedules to take time out for another physical inventory, but that all the papers used in the recent count were available for their review. The auditors reviewed these papers, made a thorough analysis of the internal controls over inventory, and made test counts at December 31 of large items representing 10 percent of the total value of inventory. The items tested were traced to the perpetual inventory records, and no significant discrepancies were found. Inventories at December 31 amounted to $4,000,000 out of total assets of $9,000,000.

Required:

Assume that the auditors find no shortcomings in any aspect of the examination apart from the area of inventories. You are to prepare:

a. An argument setting forth the factors that indicate the issuance of an unqualified audit opinion.

b. An opposing argument setting forth the factors that indicate the auditors should not issue an unqualified opinion.

14–31. One of the problems faced by the auditors in their verification of inventory is the possibility that slow-moving and obsolete items may be included in the goods on hand at the balance sheet date. In the event that such items are identified in the physical inventory, their carrying value should be written down to an estimated scrap value or other recoverable amount.

Prepare a list of the auditing procedures that the auditors should employ to determine whether slow-moving or obsolete items are included in the physical inventory.

14–32. During your observation of the November 30, 1979, physical inventory of Jay Ltd., you note the following unusual items:

a. Electric motors in finished goods storeroom not tagged. Upon enquiry, you are informed that the motors are on consignment to Jay Ltd.

b. A cutting machine (one of Jay's principal products) in the receiving department, with the large "REWORK" tag attached.

c. A small, isolated storeroom with five types of dusty raw materials stored therein. Inventory tags are attached to all of the materials, and your test counts agree with the tags.

Required:

What additional procedures, if any, would you carry out for each of the above? Explain.

14–33. Nolan Manufacturing Ltd. retains you on April 1 to perform an audit for the fiscal year ending June 30. During the month of May you made extensive studies of the system of internal control over inventories.

All goods purchased pass through a receiving department under the direction of the chief purchasing agent. The duties of the receiving department are to unpack, count, and inspect the goods. The quantity received is compared with the quantity shown on the receiving department's copy of the purchase order. If there is no discrepancy, the purchase order is stamped "O.K.–Receiving Dept." and forwarded to the accounts payable section of the accounting department. Any discrepancies in quantity or variations from specifications are called to the attention of the buyer by returning the purchase order to him with an explanation of the circumstances. No records are maintained in the receiving department, and no reports originate there.

As soon as goods have been inspected and counted in the receiving department, they are sent to the factory production area and stored alongside the machines in which they are to be processed. Finished goods are moved from the assembly line to a storeroom in the custody of a stock clerk, who maintains a perpetual inventory record in terms of physical units but not in dollars.

What weaknesses, if any, do you see in the internal control over inventories?

14–34. Select the best answer for each of the following and explain fully the reason for your selection.

a. On June 15, 1979, Caldwell Ward, CA, accepted an engagement to perform an audit of Grant Company for the year ended December 31, 1979. Grant Company has not previously been audited by a CA and Ward has been unable to satisfy himself with respect to beginning inventories. How should Ward report on his examination?

(1) He would have to deny an opinion or qualify his opinion on the December 31, 1979, balance sheet, but could issue an unqualified opinion on the income statement and the statement of changes in financial position.

(2) He must deny an opinion on the financial statements taken as a whole.

(3) He could give an unqualified opinion on the financial statements taken as a whole so long as the change in the inventories from the beginning of the year to the end of the year was not material.

(4) He would have to deny an opinion or qualify his opinion on the income statement and the statement of changes in financial position, but could issue an unqualified opinion on the December 31, 1979, balance sheet.

b. McPherson Corporation does not make an annual physical count of year-end inventories, but instead makes weekly test counts on the basis of a statistical plan. During the year Sara Mullins, CA, observes such counts as she deems necessary and is able to satisfy herself as to the reliability of the client's procedures. In reporting on the results of her examination Mullins:

(1) Can issue an unqualified opinion without disclosing that she did not observe year-end inventories.

(2) Must comment in the scope paragraph as to her inability to observe year-end inventories, but can nevertheless issue an unqualified opinion.

(3) Is required, if the inventories were material, to deny an opinion on the financial statements taken as a whole.

(4) Must, if the inventories were material, qualify her opinion.

c. Ball Company, which has no perpetual inventory records, takes a monthly physical inventory and reorders any item which is less than its reorder point. On February 5, 1979, Ball ordered 5,000 units of item A. On February 6, 1979, Ball received 5,000 units of item A which had been ordered on January 3, 1979. To prevent this excess ordering, Ball should:

(1) Keep an adequate record of open purchase orders and review it before ordering.

(2) Use perpetual inventory records which indicate goods received, issued, and amounts on hand.

(3) Use prenumbered purchase orders.

(4) Prepare purchase orders only on the basis of purchase requisitions.

d. A CA is engaged in the annual audit of a client for the year ended December 31, 1979. The client took a complete physical inventory under the CA's observation on December 15 and adjusted its inventory control account and detailed perpetual inventory records to agree with the physical inventory. The client considers a sale to be made in the period that goods are shipped. Listed below are four items from the CA's sales-cutoff-test working paper. Which item does not require an adjusting entry in the client's accounting records?

Date (month/day)

	Shipped	Recorded as sale	Credited to inventory control
(1)	Dec. 10	Dec. 19	Dec. 12
(2)	Dec. 14	Dec. 16	Dec. 16
(3)	Dec. 31	Jan. 2	Dec. 31
(4)	Jan. 2	Dec. 31	Dec. 31

(AICPA, adapted)

GROUP III
PROBLEMS

14–35. David Anderson, CA, is engaged in the examination of the financial statements of Redondo Manufacturing Corporation Ltd. for the year ended June 30, 1979. Redondo's inventories at year-end include finished merchandise on consignment with consignees, and finished merchandise stored in public warehouses. The merchandise in public warehouses is pledged as collateral for outstanding debt.

Required:

Normal inventory and notes payable auditing procedures have been satisfactorily completed. Describe the specific additional auditing procedures that Anderson should undertake with respect to:

a. Consignments out.

b. Finished merchandise in public warehouses pledged as collateral for outstanding debt. (AICPA, adapted)

14–36. You have been engaged by the management of Alden, Inc., to review its internal control over the purchase, receipt, storage, and issue of raw materials. You have prepared the following comments which describe Alden's procedures.

1. Raw materials, which consist mainly of high-cost electronic components, are kept in a locked storeroom. Storeroom personnel include a supervisor and four clerks. All are well trained, competent, and adequately bonded. Raw materials are removed from the storeroom only upon written or oral authorization of one of the production foremen.

2. There are no perpetual inventory records; hence, the storeroom clerks do not keep records of goods received or issued. To compensate for the lack of perpetual records, a physical inventory count is taken monthly by the storeroom clerks who are well supervised. Appropriate procedures are followed in making the inventory count.

3. After the physical count, the storeroom supervisor matches quantities counted against a predetermined reorder level. If the count for a given part is below the reorder level, the supervisor enters the part number on a materials requisition list and sends this list to the accounts payable clerk. The accounts payable clerk prepares a purchase order for a predetermined reorder quantity for each part and mails the purchase order to the vendor from whom the part was last purchased.

4. When ordered materials arrive at Alden, they are received by the storeroom clerks. The clerks count the merchandise and agree the counts to the carrier's bill of lading. All bills of lading are initialed, dated, and filled in the storeroom to serve as receiving reports.

Required:

Describe the weaknesses in internal control and recommend improvements of Alden's procedures for the purchase, receipt, storage, and issue of raw materials. Organize your answer sheet as follows.

Weaknesses	*Recommended improvements*

(AICPA, adapted)

14–37. You are an audit manager of the rapidly growing CA firm of Raye and Coye. You have been placed in charge of three new audit clients which have the following inventory features:

1. Canyon Cattle Company, which maintains 15,000 head of cattle on a 1,000-square-mile ranch, mostly unfenced, near the south rim of the Grand Valley in a western province.
2. Rhoads Mfg. Co. Ltd., which has raw materials inventories consisting principally of pig iron loaded on gondola freight cars on a siding at the company's plant.
3. Strawser Ltd., which is in production around the clock on three shifts, and which cannot shut down production during the physical inventory.

Required:

What problems do you anticipate in the observation of physical inventories of the three new clients, and how would you deal with the problems?

14–38. Royal Meat Processing Ltd. buys and processes livestock for sale to supermarkets. In connection with the examination of the company's financial statements, you have prepared the following notes based on your review of inventory procedures:

1. Each livestock buyer submits a daily report of his purchases to the plant superintendent. This report shows the dates of purchase and expected delivery, the vendor and the number, weights and type of livestock purchased. As shipments are received, any available plant employee counts the number of each type received and places a check mark beside this quantity on the buyer's report. When all shipments listed on the report have been received, the report is returned to the buyer.
2. Vendor's invoices, after a clerical review, are sent to the appropriate buyer for approval and returned to the accounting department. A disbursement voucher and a cheque for the approved amount are prepared in the accounting department. Cheques are forwarded to the treasurer for signature. The treasurer's office sends signed cheques directly to the buyer for delivery to the vendor.
3. Livestock carcasses are processed by lots. Each lot is assigned a number. At the end of each day a tally sheet reporting the lots processed, the number and type of animals in each lot, and the carcass weight is sent to the accounting department, where a perpetual inventory record of processed carcasses and their weights is maintained.
4. Processed carcasses are stored in a refrigerated cooler located in a small building adjacent to the employee parking lot. The cooler is locked when the plant is not open, and a company guard is on duty when the employees report for work and leave at the end of their shifts. Supermarket truck drivers wishing to pick up their

orders have been instructed to contact someone in the plant if no one is in the cooler.

5. Substantial quantities of by-products are produced and stored, either in the cooler or elsewhere in the plant. By-products are initially accounted for as they are sold. At this time the sales manager prepares a two-part form: one copy serves as authorization to transfer the goods to the customer, and the other becomes the basis for billing the customer.

Required:

For each of the numbered notes 1 to 5 above, state the weaknesses, if any, in the present inventory procedures, and your suggestions, if any, for improvement. (AICPA, adapted)

14–39. Payne Press Ltd. is engaged in the manufacture of large-sized presses under specific contracts and in accordance with customers' specifications. Customers are required to advance 25 percent of the contract price. The company records sales on a shipment basis and accumulates costs by job orders. The normal profit margin over the past few years has been approximately 5 percent of sales, after provision for selling and administrative expenses of about 10 percent of sales. Inventories are valued at the lower of cost or market.

Among the jobs you are reviewing in the course of your annual examination the company's December 31 financial statements is Job No. 2357, calling for delivery of a three-colour press at a firm contract price of $50,000. Costs accumulated for the job at the year-end aggregated $30,250. The company's engineers estimated that the job was approximately 55 percent complete at December 31. Your audit procedures have been as follows:

1. Examined all contracts, noting pertinent provisions.
2. Observed physical inventory of jobs in process and reconciled details to job order accounts.
3. Compliance-tested input of labour, material, and overhead charges into the various jobs to determine that such charges were authentic and had been posted correctly.
4. Confirmed customers' advances at year-end.
5. Reconciled goods in process job ledger with control account.

Required:

With respect to Job No. 2357:

a. State what additional audit procedures, if any, you would follow and explain the purpose of the procedures.

b. Indicate the manner and the amount at which you would include Job No. 2357 in the balance sheet. (AICPA, adapted)

14–40. Late in December 1979 your CA firm accepted an audit engagement at Nash Jewelers, Inc., a corporation which deals largely in diamonds. The corporation has retail jewelry stores in several eastern cities and a diamond wholesale store in Toronto. The wholesale store also sets the diamonds in rings and other quality jewelry.

The retail stores place orders for diamond jewelry with the wholesale store in Toronto. A buyer employed by the wholesale store purchases diamonds in the Toronto diamond market; the wholesale store then fills orders from the retail stores and from independent customers, and maintains a substantial inventory of diamonds. The corporation values its inventory by the specific identification cost method.

Required:

Assume that at the inventory date you are satisfied that Nash Jewelers, Inc., has no items left by customers for repair or sale on consignment, and that no inventory owned by the corporation is in the possession of outsiders.

a. Discuss the problems the auditors should anticipate in planning for the observation of the physical inventory on this engagement because of the—
    (1) Different locations of the inventories.
    (2) Nature of the inventory.
b. Assume that a shipment of diamond rings was in transit by corporation messenger from the wholesale store to a retail store on the inventory date. What additional audit steps would you take to satisfy yourself as to the gems which were in transit from the wholesale store on the inventory date? (AICPA, adapted)

14–41. D Limited is a holding company with a number of subsidiaries. In 1978, D Limited incorporated a new wholly owned subsidiary, H Company Limited, for a specific project: the construction of a building and the operation of a venture utilizing the building up to August 31, 1980. The building will be sold at the end of the venture. The contract to construct the building was granted to an independent contractor on the basis of direct cost plus 20 percent. The direct costs were defined as material used and labour costs incurred on the construction site. The mark-up was intended to cover overhead and profit.

At August 31, 1979, the degree of completion was estimated at 75 percent. Mr A, president of D Limited, met with CA, the company's auditor. He mentioned that the latest estimates prepared by the controller forecasted a loss of at least $2,000,000 on the whole project (operation of the venture and the sale of the building). He expressed some doubts about the contractor's honesty and asked CA to conduct an investigation on costs billed by the contractor.

The president gave CA the following information:

Materials

The contractor can buy materials from suppliers of his choice as long as he conforms to specifications and submits bids to prove that he paid the lowest price for any material with a total cost over $50,000.

The materials are shipped directly to the construction site and the suppliers bill the contractor. The contractor sends monthly billings to H Company Limited with copies of suppliers' invoices.

Wages

Wage rates, specified in the contract, are based on the union contracts. The rates vary with every trade and with the worker's experience.

Employees are paid by the contractor. The payroll records are kept by an independent computer utility company. The contractor sends a monthly payroll summary, by employee, to H Company Limited to support his invoice.

Mr A explained that construction workers' mobility made it very difficult to verify that employees listed on the monthly summary actually worked on the site. He added that he had no confidence in the time-keeping system used on the site.

The contract provides H Company Limited with the right to examine the books of the contractor.

Required:

List the procedures that CA should perform to carry out the investigation requested by Mr. A. (CICA, adapted)

GROUP IV
CASE STUDIES IN AUDITING

14–42.   WESTERN TRADING COMPANY

Western Trading Company is a sole proprietorship engaged in the grain brokerage business. At December 31, 1979, the entire grain inventory of the company was stored in outside bonded warehouses. The company's procedure of pricing inventories in these warehouses included comparing the actual cost of each commodity in inventory with the market price as reported for transactions on the commodity exchanges at December 31. A write-down was made on commodities in which cost was in excess of market. During the course of the 1979 examination the auditors verified the company's computations. In addition to this, they compared the inventory prices with market prices at dates subsequent to the year-end. Before the end of the engagement the market declined sharply for one commodity until its market price was below the average inventory price. The auditors suggested that the inventory be written down to give effect to this decline in market price subsequent to December 31, 1979. The company agreed, and a write-down of $7,000 was made.

The auditors also examined the trading position of the company and found that there was a short position in grain trading; that is, the sales negotiated for future delivery exceeded the total of year-end inventory and purchase contracts. The indicated loss on these contracts was reflected in the financial statements. After the above adjustments, the final net income for 1979 amounted to $30,000.

At December 31, 1980, the auditors made a similar examination of the financial statements of Western Trading Company. They found that the company had priced the inventory in the same manner as in 1979. The auditors followed procedures similar to those used in 1979 and at the end of their field work on February 2, 1981, noted that the inventories were priced at an amount that was not in excess of the market at that time. The trading position had been examined; the short position at the end of 1980 had an indicated gain of $4,000. No adjustment was proposed for this amount. Subsequent to the completion of the field work, but prior to the issuance of the audit report, there was a sharp decline in the market price of one commodity. The inventory was repriced by the auditors on the basis of the new market price, and the inventory value at December 31, 1980, was found to be in excess of market by approximately $21,000. The auditors proposed that the inventories be written down by $17,000 to this new market value, net of the gains on the subsequent sales. The management protested this suggestion, stating that in their opinion the market decline was only temporary and that prices would recover in the near future. They refused to allow the write-down to be made. Accordingly, the auditors took an exception in their audit report dated February 16, 1981, and the opinion paragraph of their report read as follows:

"Except for the effect of the failure to record the market decline in grain inventories discussed in Note 2 to the financial statements, in our opinion, these financial statements present fairly the financial position of Western Trading Company at December 31, 1980, and the results of its operations and the changes in its financial position for the year then ended in accordance with generally accepted accounting principles. Except for the matter discussed in Note 2 to the financial statements, these accounting principles were applied on a basis consistent with that of the preceding year."

Note 2 stated:

"The company's grain inventories at December 31, 1979, were reduced by approximately $7,000 to reflect a decline in market value subsequent to that date. A similar market decline of approximately $21,000 subsequent to December 31, 1980, has not been recorded by the company. If this adjustment had been made as of December 31, 1980, the grain inventories shown on the accompanying balance sheet and the pretax accounting income for the year would have been reduced by $21,000.

"At December 31, 1980, the net short market position of the company was 20,000 bushels of wheat; a gain of some $4,000 applicable thereto, based on the year-end market prices, has not been reflected in the accompanying financial statements."

Net income for the year 1980 amounted to $37,000 as shown by the company's income statement. Subsequent to the issuance of the auditors' report, the market reversed its downward trend and regained the level prevailing at February 2, 1981.

Required:

a. Does the "lower-of-cost-or-market" method include recognition of price declines subsequent to the balance sheet date? Explain.

b. To what extent should financial statements disclose by footnotes events subsequent to the balance sheet date?

c. If "adequate disclosure" of facts is achieved in the financial statements and accompanying notes, is the position taken by the auditors in their report thereby justified?

d. Were the auditors justified in issuing a qualified opinion in this case? Discuss fully, including alternative courses of action.

e. Would the entry proposed by the auditors have eliminated the necessity for a qualification if it had been made?

f. Was it necessary to comment on lack of consistency in valuation of inventories?

15

Property, plant, and equipment; depreciation and depletion

The term *property, plant, and equipment* includes all tangible assets with a service life of more than one year which are used in the operation of the business. Three major groups of such assets are generally recognized:

1. *Land.* Land used in the operation of the business has the significant characteristic of not being subject to depreciation.
2. *Buildings, machinery, equipment,* and *land improvements* such as fences and parking lots. Properties in this classification have limited service lives and are subject to depreciation.
3. *Natural resources* (wasting assets) such as oil wells, coal mines, and tracts of timber. These assets are subject to depletion and should be presented on the balance sheet as a separate subgroup.

Closely related to the property, plant, and equipment category are *intangible assets* such as patents, franchises, and leaseholds. These assets are subject to amortization and should be shown as a separate subgroup on the balance sheet.

The auditors' objectives in examination of property, plant, and equipment

In the examination of property, plant, and equipment, the auditors try to determine (*a*) the adequacy of internal control; (*b*) the existence and ownership of the plant assets; (*c*) the propriety of the valuation methods used; (*d*) the reasonableness of the depreciation program; (*e*) the propriety of recorded revenue, gains and losses from plant assets; and (ƒ) the fairness of the presentation of plant assets in the balance sheet and depreciation in the income statement.

Contrast with audit of current assets

In many companies the investment in plant and equipment amounts to 50 percent or more of the total assets. However, the audit work required to verify these properties is usually a much smaller proportion of the total audit time spent on the engagement. The verification of plant and equipment is facilitated by several factors not applicable to audit work on current assets.

Typically a unit of property or equipment has a high dollar value, and relatively few transactions may lie behind a large balance sheet figure for plant and equipment. Secondly, there is usually little change in the property accounts from year to year. The Land account often remains unchanged for a long span of years. The durable nature of buildings and equipment also tends to hold accounting activity to a minimum for these accounts. By way of contrast, current assets such as accounts receivable and inventory may have a complete turnover several times a year.

In the discussion of inventories in Chapter 14, considerable attention was given to the problem of an accurate *cutoff* at the year-end. The auditors must make extensive tests to prove that the year-end cutoff of purchases and sales of merchandise is accurate, because an error in cutoff may cause an error of corresponding amount in the year's net income. Errors in making a cutoff of the year's transactions do not pose a comparable problem in the case of plant and equipment acquisitions; a cutoff error in recording the purchase or retirement of equipment will ordinarily not affect significantly the determination of net income for the year. Of course such errors could cause slight inaccuracies in depreciation, or in the timing of gains and losses on retirements.

The auditors' examination of property, plant, and equipment does not include a determination of the "adequacy" of insurance coverage for several reasons. The amount of insurance is logically related to current value of plant and equipment, and the auditors are not appraisers of property values. Furthermore, the auditors' opinion on financial statements concerns the consistent application of generally accepted accounting principles rather than an evaluation of management's wisdom in deciding whether or not to carry insurance against some of the many risks inherent in property ownership.

Cost as the basis of valuation

Accounting authorities have long held that cost is the proper basis for valuing plant and equipment. The cost basis is a highly satisfactory one during periods of stable price levels, for it gives a degree of objectivity to the process of income measurement not otherwise obtainable. During periods of drastic price changes, however, the computation of depreciation expense in terms of the original cost of long-lived assets leads to the reporting of operating profits of questionable validity. The tremendous pressures generated by inflation and by mounting tax rates create a demand that some type of current value be substituted for historical cost figures. The base for depreciation provisions would then be more in keeping with current replacement costs. Recognition of the inadequacies of conventional methods of computing depreciation has increased in recent years as the underlying assumption of stable price levels has become more and more unrealistic.

Under present standards, however, cost is normally the only accepted basis for valuing plant and equipment. Financial statements which presented property, equipment, and related depreciation on a basis other than cost would not be in conformity with generally accepted accounting principles, and therefore could not receive unqualified approval from the auditors. However, Section 3060 of the *CICA Handbook* recognizes that other valuation bases may be used in some circumstances such as appraisal values for fixed assets in reorganization.

Replacement cost

In *Accounting Series Release No. 190*, the U.S. SEC required certain companies subject to its jurisdiction to disclose in reports to the Commission the current replacement cost of *productive capacity* at the end of each year for which a balance sheet is required, and the approximate replacement cost valuation of depreciation for the two most recent fiscal years. *Productive capacity* was defined by the SEC as a measurement of a company's present ability to produce and distribute a specific number of units of its products within a particular time frame. Thus, *productive capacity* includes depreciable plant and equipment and assets used under financing leases, but excludes land other than land containing a natural resource which is depleted. The replacement cost data may be designated as "unaudited," and may be presented either in *a note to the financial statements or in a separate section of the financial statements following the notes.* The disclosures must also include methods of determining the replacement cost data, and any additional information required to prevent the data from being misleading. In a related pronouncement, the SEC suggested that annual reports to shareholders include in notes to financial statements only generalized descriptions of the impact of specific price changes on the companies' assets and earnings. The SEC's actions to date do not change the use of historical cost in the accounting records or in the body of the financial statements.

The SEC's action on replacement cost followed comparable actions or recommendations in two other industrialized countries suffering from inflation—the Netherlands and the United Kingdom. Further, the commission's preference for replacement cost accounting appeared to thwart an alternative position proposed by the U.S. Financial Accounting Standards Board—the presentation in annual reports of selected financial statement items valued in units of general purchasing power.

Internal controls over plant and equipment

The principal purpose of internal controls relating to plant and equipment *is to obtain maximum efficiency from the dollars invested in plant assets.*

The amounts invested in plant and equipment represent a major portion of the total assets of many industrial concerns. The expenses of maintenance, rearrangement, and depreciation of these assets are a major factor in the income statement. The sheer size of the amounts involved makes carefully devised internal controls essential to the production of reliable financial statements. Errors in measurement of income will be material if assets are scrapped without their cost being removed from the accounts, or if the distinction between capital and revenue expenditures is not maintained consistently. The losses which inevitably arise from uncontrolled methods of acquiring, maintaining, and retiring plant and equipment are often greater than the risks of fraud in cash handling.

The plant and equipment budget

In large corporate enterprises the auditors may expect to find an annual plant budget that is used to forecast and control acquisitions and retirements of plant and equipment. Many small concerns also forecast expenditures for plant assets. Successful utilization of a plant budget presupposes the existence of reliable and detailed accounting records for plant and equipment. A detailed knowledge of the kinds, quantities, and condition of existing equipment is an essential basis for intelligent forecasting of the need for replacements and additions to the plant.

If the auditors can ascertain that acquisitions of plant and equipment, whether by purchase or construction, are made in accordance with prior budgetary authorizations, and that any necessary expenditures not provided for in the budget are made only upon approval of a major executive, they will be able to minimize the routine testing of the year's acquisitions. Reference to the reports and working papers of the internal auditors is often a convenient method for the independent auditors to become familiar with the scope and dependability of the budgetary controls over plant and equipment.

Other major control devices

Other important internal controls applicable to plant and equipment are as follows:

1. A subsidiary ledger consisting of a separate record for each unit of property. An adequate plant and equipment ledger, usually on magnetic tape or punched cards in large concerns, facilitates the auditors' work in analyzing additions and retirements, in verifying the depreciation provision and maintenance expenses, and in comparing authorizations with actual expenditures.
2. A system of authorizations requiring advance executive approval of all plant and equipment acquisitions, whether by purchase, lease, or construction. Serially numbered capital work orders are a convenient means of recording authorizations.
3. A reporting procedure assuring prompt disclosure and analysis of variances between authorized expenditures and actual costs.
4. An authoritative written statement of company policy distinguishing between capital and revenue expenditures. A dollar minimum ordinarily will be established for capitalization; any expenditures of lesser amount automatically are classified as charges against current revenue.
5. A policy requiring all purchases of plant and equipment to be handled through the purchasing department and subjected to standard routines for receiving, inspection, and payment.
6. Periodic physical inventories, designed to verify the existence, location, and condition of all property listed in the accounts and to disclose the existence of any unrecorded units.
7. A system of retirement procedures, including serially numbered retirement work orders, stating reasons for retirement and bearing appropriate approvals.

Audit working papers for property, plant, and equipment

Apart from a grouping sheet, the key working paper obtained or prepared by the auditors for property, plant, and equipment is a summary analysis such as that illustrated in Figure 15–1.

The significant point to note in this working paper (Figure 15–1) is the emphasis upon *changes during the current period.* The analysis serves as a basis for completion of comparable forms in the client's federal and provincial income tax returns; it also is often presented in a long-form audit report.

Among the other working papers commonly prepared in the audit of property, plant, and equipment are analyses of plant asset additions and

FIGURE 15-1

The Mandeville Corporation Limited

Summary of Property, Plant and Equipment, and Accumulated Depreciation

December 31, 1979

Account No.	Description	Assets Balance Dec. 31, 78	Additions	Retirements	Balance Dec. 31, 79	Method	Rate	Accumulated Depreciation Balance Dec. 31, 78	Provision	Retirements	Balance Dec. 31, 79
151	Land	50 000 00	15 100 00		65 100 00 ✓						
152/3	Land Improvements	13 500 00	1 000 00		14 500 00 ✓	d.l	5%	1 350 00	700 00		2 050 00 ✓
154/5	Buildings	450 000 00	49 500 00		499 500 00 ✓	d.l	3%	29 200 00	14 242 00		43 442 00 ✓
156/7	Equipment	80 000 00	11 000 00	6 000 00	85 000 00 ✓	d.l	10%	23 500 00	7 060 00	5 040 00	25 520 00 ✓
		513 500 00	76 600 00	6 000 00	664 100 00 ✓			54 050 00	22 002 00	5 040 00	71 012 00 ✓
			K-1-1						K-1-2	K-1-1	

✓ — Footed plant and equipment subsidiary ledger. No exceptions.

Conclusions:

As a result of our audit procedures for plant and equipment and related depreciation, it is our opinion that the Dec. 31, 79, balances above are fairly stated.

V.M.H.
Jan. 9, 80

retirements, analyses of repairs and maintenance expense accounts, and tests of depreciation provisions. The analyses of plant additions and retirements and the tests of depreciation are cross-indexed to the summary analysis, as illustrated in Figure 15–1.

Initial audits and repeat engagements

The auditing procedures listed in subsequent pages are applicable to repeat engagements and therefore concern only transactions of the current year. In the auditors' first examination of a new client which has changed auditors, the beginning balances of plant and equipment may be substantiated by reference to the predecessor firm's working papers. If, in previous years, audits had been made by other reputable firms of public accountants, it is not customary to go beyond a general review of the past history of the plant and equipment as recorded in the accounts.

In a first audit of a concern for which audits by independent public accountants have not been made previously, the ideal approach is a complete historical analysis of the property accounts. By thorough review of all major charges and credits to the property accounts since their inception, the auditors can determine whether the company has consistently followed good accounting practices in recording capital additions and retirements, and in providing for periodic depreciation.

If the client has been in business for many years, the review of transactions in earlier years necessarily must be performed on a test basis in order to stay within reasonable time limits. However, the importance of an analysis of transactions of prior years deserves emphasis. Only by this approach can the auditors be in a sound position to express an opinion as to the propriety of the current period's depreciation. If repair and maintenance expenses have been capitalized, or asset additions have been recorded as operating expenses, or retirements of property have gone unrecorded, the entire depreciation program is invalidated regardless of the care taken in the selection of depreciation rates. The auditors should make clear to the client that the initial examination of plant and equipment requires procedures which need not be duplicated in subsequent engagements.

AUDIT PROGRAM FOR PROPERTY, PLANT, AND EQUIPMENT

The following procedures are typical of the work required in many engagements for the verification of property, plant, and equipment. The procedures for accumulated depreciation are covered in a separate program on pages 612–13.

A. Study and evaluation of internal control for property, plant, and equipment

1. Obtain description of internal control for property, plant, and equipment.
2. Test property, plant, and equipment transactions.
3. Evaluate internal control for property, plant, and equipment.

B. Substantive tests of property, plant, and equipment and related revenue and expenses

4. Determine that the plant and equipment ledger is in agreement with the control accounts.
5. Verify legal ownership of property, plant, and equipment.
6. Verify additions to property during the year.
7. Make physical inspection of substantial additions and consider the need for a complete physical inventory of plant and equipment.
8. Obtain or prepare analyses of repair and maintenance expense accounts.
9. Verify retirements of property during the year.
10. Investigate the status of property not in current use.
11. Obtain or prepare a summary analysis showing changes during the year in property owned.
12. Review rental revenue from land, buildings, and equipment.
13. Verify property taxes expense by inspection of property tax bills and paid cheques.
14. Determine proper balance sheet presentation.

A. Study and evaluation

1. Obtain description of internal control for property, plant, and equipment.

In the study of internal control for plant and equipment, the auditors may utilize a written description, flowcharts, or an internal control questionnaire. The following are typical of the questions included in a questionnaire: Are plant ledgers regularly reconciled with general ledger control accounts? Are periodic physical inventories of plant assets compared with the plant ledgers? Are variances between plant budgets and actual expenditures for plant assets subject to review and approval of executives? Does the sale, transfer, or dismantling of equipment require written executive approval on a serially numbered retirement work order? Is there a written policy for distinguishing between capital expenditures and revenue expenditures?

2. Test property, plant, and equipment transactions.

The purpose of the compliance tests for property, plant, and equipment is to determine whether the internal controls established by the client are being followed consistently in practice. The auditors should be alert for any indications that the client's policy for distinguishing between capital expenditures and revenue expenditures has been violated.

3. Evaluate internal control for property, plant, and equipment.

The evaluation of internal control for plant assets includes an identification of weaknesses and unusual strengths in controls. The auditors then select the substantice tests necessary to provide sufficient appropriate evidence as to existence, ownership, and valuation of the client's property, plant, and equipment, given the quality of the internal control for plant assets.

B. Substantive tests

4. Determine that the plant and equipment ledger is in agreement with the control accounts.

Before a detailed analysis of changes in property accounts during the year is made, it is necessary to determine that the individual plant asset records in the subsidiary ledger agree in total with the balances in the general ledger control accounts. This is also a desirable prerequisite to any tests of the ledger by observation of plant and equipment. Computer print-outs or adding machine tapes prepared from the subsidiary property ledger should also be compared with the ending balances shown on the summary analysis obtained in Procedure 11.

5. Verify legal ownership of property, plant, and equipment.

To determine that plant assets are the property of the client, the auditors look for such evidence as a deed, property tax bills, receipts for payments to mortgagee, and fire insurance policies. Additionally, the fact that rental payments are not being made is supporting evidence of ownership.

It is sometimes suggested that the auditors may verify ownership of real property and the absence of liens by examination of public records. Inspection of the documentary evidence listed above usually provides adequate proof of ownership. If some doubt exists as to whether the client has clear title to property, the auditors should obtain the opinion of the client's legal counsel.

In the first audit of a company, the auditors should obtain a copy of the deed for inclusion in the permanent file. The legal description in the deed should be compared with that in the abstract of title. Possession of a deed is not proof of present ownership because in the sale of real property a new deed is usually prepared and the seller may retain the old one. Better evidence of continuing ownership is found in tax bills made out in the name of the client, and in fire insurance policies, rent receipts from lessees, and regular principal and interest payments to a mortgagee or trustee.

The disclosure of liens on property will usually be made during the examination of liabilities, but in the audit work on plant and equipment the auditors should be alert for evidence indicating the existence of liens. Purchase contracts examined in verifying the cost of property may reveal unpaid balances. Insurance policies may contain "loss payable" endorsements in favour of a secured party.

The ownership of automobiles and trucks can readily be ascertained by the auditors by reference to certificates of title and registration documents. The ease of transfer of title to automotive equipment, plus the fact that it is often used as collateral for loans, makes it important that the auditors verify title to such property.

6. Verify additions to property during the year.

The vouching of additions to the property accounts during the period under audit is one of the most important substantive tests of plant and equipment. The extent of the vouching is dependent upon the auditors' evaluation of internal control for plant and equipment expenditures. The vouching process utilizes a working paper analysis of the general ledger control accounts and will include the tracing of entries through the journals to the original documents, such as contracts, deeds, construction work orders, invoices, and authorization by directors.

The specific steps to be taken in investigating the year's property additions usually will include the following:

a. Examine authorizations for all major additions, including assets both purchased and constructed.

b. Review changes during the year in construction in progress and examine supporting work orders, both incomplete and closed.

c. Trace transfers from the Construction in Progress account to the property accounts, observing propriety of classification. Determine that all completed items have been transferred.

d. On a test basis, vouch purchases of plant and equipment assets to invoices, deeds, contracts, or other supporting documents. Test extensions, footings, and treatment of discounts. Make certain revenue expenditures were not improperly capitalized.

e. Investigate all instances in which the actual cost of acquisitions substantially exceeded authorized amounts. Determine whether such excess expenditures were analyzed and approved by appropriate officials.

f. Investigate fully any debits to property accounts not arising from acquisition of physical assets.

g. Determine that the total cost of any plant and equipment assets purchased on the installment plan is reflected in the asset accounts and
that the unpaid installments are set up as liabilities. Ascertain that all
plant and equipment leases that in effect are installment purchases
are accounted for in a similar fashion. Interest charges should not be
capitalized as a cost of the asset acquired.

The accounting for plant assets acquired in a trade-in or other exchange is specified by *APB Opinion No. 29* of the AICPA in the United
States, "Accounting for Nonmonetary Transactions." No gain is recognized when a plant asset is exchanged for a similar plant asset. The asset
acquired in the exchange is valued at the carrying amount of the asset
given up plus any additional cash paid or amount owed. This is also an
acceptable practice in Canada even though the CICA has no pronouncement on this matter.

Assets constructed by a company for its own use should be recorded
at the cost of direct material, direct labour, and applicable overhead cost.
However, auditors usually apply the additional test of comparing the total
cost of self-constructed equipment with bids or estimated purchase prices
for similar equipment from outside suppliers, and they take exception to
the capitalization of costs substantially in excess of the amount for which
the asset could have been purchased and installed.

Related party transactions. Assets acquired from affiliated corporations, from promoters or shareholders, or by any other type of related
party transaction not involving arm's-length bargaining between buyer
and seller, have often been recorded at inflated amounts. The auditors
should enquire into the methods by which the sales price was determined,
the cost of the property to the vendor, length of ownership by vendor,
and any other available evidence which might indicate an arbitrarily
determined valuation. When vendor and vendee are under common
control, or for any reason arm's-length bargaining does not appear to
have been present in the acquisition of plant and equipment, the notes to
financial statements should contain full disclosure of the transaction.

**7. Make physical inspection of substantial additions and consider the
need for a complete physical inventory of plant and equipment.**

It is customary for the auditors to make a physical inspection of any
major items of plant and equipment *acquired* during the period under
audit, but not to undertake the observation of a complete physical inventory of plant and equipment. At first thought, it may appear that verification of the existence of *all* plant and equipment listed in the financial
statements and accounting records could best be accomplished through
physical inspection by the auditors. Auditing procedures with respect to
merchandise inventories and other current assets call for observation,
inspection or confirmation; and the Securities and Exchange Commission

in the United States has in *Accounting Series Release No. 19* expressed the opinion that audit procedures should include physical inspection of plant and equipment to supplement the examination of entries in the accounting records. Current practice, however, does not include physical inspection as a standard procedure of verification, and casual inspection as part of a conducted plant tour can hardly be considered as verification. The omission of physical inspection from verification work in this area of the examination appears to be the result of several factors:

a. The risk of loss from theft or disappearance is slight, as compared with cash or other current assets.

b. Management, in general, has been reluctant to authorize frequent physical inventories of plant and equipment. This attitude is attributable to the cost and effort required for a physical inventory, and also may be based upon the outmoded notion that internal controls are applicable only to current assets.

c. The variety, quantity, and location of plant and equipment in large enterprises make a physical inventory thereof difficult and time consuming. It can be performed more satisfactorily by the internal auditing staff than by outside auditors.

In certain lines of business—as, for example, in construction work, where costly mobile equipment is often scrapped or sold upon authorization of a field supervisor—good audit practice would call for physical inspection as part of the verification procedures. In the audit of concerns owning substantial numbers of automobiles and trucks, physical inspection and verification of legal title are practicable and desirable measures.

8. Obtain or prepare analyses of repair and maintenance expense accounts.

The auditors' principal objective in analyzing repair and maintenance expense accounts is to discover items which should have been capitalized. Large concerns often have a written policy setting the minimum expenditure to be capitalized. For example, company policy may prescribe that no expenditure for less than $500 shall be capitalized regardless of the service life of the item purchased. In such cases the auditors will analyze the repair and maintenance accounts with a view toward determining the consistency of application of this policy as well as compliance with generally accepted accounting principles. To determine that the accounts contain only bona fide repair and maintenance charges, the auditors will trace the larger expenditures to written authorizations for the transaction. Correctness of the amounts involved may be verified by reference to vendors' invoices, to material requisitions, and to labour time records.

One particularly useful means of identifying capital expenditures buried in the repair and maintenance accounts is to obtain or prepare an analysis of the monthly amounts of expense with corresponding amounts listed for the preceding year. Any significant variations from month to month or between corresponding months of the two years should be fully investigated. If maintenance expense is classified by the departments serviced, the variations are especially noticeable.

9. Verify retirements of property during the year.

The principal purpose of this procedure is to determine whether any property has been replaced, sold, dismantled, or abandoned without having been reflected properly in the accounting records. Nearly every thorough physical inventory of plant and equipment reveals missing units of property: units disposed of without a corresponding reduction of the accounts.

It is not unusual for a factory supervisor to order that a machine be scrapped, without realizing that the accounting department has an interest in such action. How is the accounting department expected to know when a factory asset is retired? If a machine is sold for cash or traded in on a new machine, the transaction will presumably involve the use of documents, such as a cash receipts form or a purchase order; the processing of these documents may bring the retirement to the attention of alert accounting personnel. Not all employees are alert, however, and some are not sufficiently trained to recognize a clue to the retirement of a plant asset. Moreover, many plant assets are scrapped rather than being sold or traded in on new equipment; consequently, there may be no paper work to evidence the disappearance of the machine.

One method of guarding against unrecorded retirements is enforcement of a company-wide policy that no plant asset shall be retired from use without prior approval on a special type of serially numbered work order. A copy of the retirement work order is routed to the accounting department. To supplement this policy, a physical inventory of plant and equipment should be taken on a test basis by the client at regular intervals. Together, these two measures provide reasonable assurance that retirements will be reflected in the accounting records.

What specific steps should the auditors take to discover any unrecorded retirements? The following measures often are effective:

a. If major additions of plant and equipment have been made during the year, ascertain whether old equipment was traded in or superseded by the new units.

b. Analyze the Miscellaneous Revenue account to locate any cash proceeds from sale of plant assets.

c. If any of the company's products have been discontinued during the year, investigate the disposition of plant facilities formerly used in manufacturing such products.

d. Enquire of executives and supervisors whether any plant assets have been retired during the year.

e. Examine retirement work orders or other source documents for authorization by the appropriate official or committee.

f. Investigate any reduction of insurance coverage to determine whether this was caused by retirement of plant assets.

10. Investigate the status of property not in current use.

Land, buildings, and equipment not in current use should be investigated thoroughly to determine the prospects for their future use in operations. Plant assets which are temporarily idle need not be reclassified, and depreciation may be continued at normal rates. On the other hand, idle equipment which has been dismantled, or for any reason appears unsuitable for future operating use, should generally be written down to an estimated realizable value and excluded from the plant and equipment classification. In the case of stand-by equipment and other property not needed at present or prospective levels of operation, the auditors should consider whether the carrying value is recoverable through future use in operations.

11. Obtain or prepare a summary analysis showing changes during the year in property owned.

At this point in the audit, the auditors have verified the beginning balances of plant and equipment assets by reference to the prior year's working papers or by carrying out procedures necessary in the audit of a new client. In addition to this, they have tested the additions and retirements of plant and equipment during the year. The auditors may now obtain or prepare the summary analysis illustrated in Figure 15–1, and cross-index it to the analyses of additions and disposals.

12. Review rental revenue from land, buildings, and equipment.

In verifying rental revenue from land and buildings it is often desirable for the auditors to obtain or to sketch a map of the property and to make a physical inspection of each unit. This may disclose that premises reported as vacant are in fact occupied by lessees and are producing revenue not reflected in the accounting records. If the client's property includes an office or apartment building, the auditors should obtain a floor plan of the building as well as copies of all lease contracts. In this way they can account for all available rental space as revenue producing or vacant under terms of lease agreements, and can verify reported vacancies by physical inspection at the balance sheet date. If interim audit work is being performed, vacancies should also be verified by inspection and discussion with management during each visit by the auditors during the year.

Examination of leases will indicate whether tenants are responsible for the cost of electricity, water, gas, and telephone service. These provisions should be reconciled with the handling of utility expense accounts. Rental revenue accounts should be analyzed in all cases, and the amounts compared with lease agreements and cash records.

13. *Verify property taxes expense by inspection of property tax bills and paid cheques.*

The client's property taxes expense may be verified conveniently during the audit of the related plant assets. The auditors should obtain or prepare an analysis of prepaid taxes, taxes expense, and taxes payable, and should vouch property tax payments to tax bills and paid cheques.

14. *Determine proper balance sheet presentation.*

Section 3060 of the *CICA Handbook* recommends that the basis of valuation and accumulated depreciation be disclosed in the balance sheet. Adequate and proper balance sheet presentation will normally include the following:

a. Property, plant, and equipment can usually be summarized by the following major classes: Land and Land Improvements; Buildings and Leasehold Improvements; Machinery and Equipment; Furniture and Fixtures; and Construction in Progress.

b. Property not in current use should be segregated in the balance sheet.

c. Property pledged to secure loans should be clearly identified.

d. The basis of valuation should be explicitly stated. At present, cost is the generally accepted basis of valuation for plant and equipment; property not in use should be valued at estimated realizable value.

Depreciation

The technical knowledge needed by the auditors includes a thorough understanding of the various alternative methods of computing depreciation. Only a brief general review of depreciation methods is appropriate, however, in an auditing text; the reader who desires comprehensive coverage should refer to textbooks in accounting theory.

Computation of depreciation charges. Among the methods of computing depreciation charges most frequently encountered by the auditors are the straight-line method and the declining-balance methods. Far less common, although quite acceptable, are methods based on units of output or hours of service. The fixed-percentage-of-declining-balance method of depreciation is permitted by the income tax regulations and is often used by many concerns for both accounting and taxation purposes. This method provides the immediate advantage of deferring tax payments and thereby conserving working capital because depreciation under this method is greatest in the first year and becomes smaller in succeeding years.

The use of this or other accelerated methods for income tax purposes does not necessarily mean that this method should also be used for general accounting purposes. Many accountants, however, believe that accelerated methods constitute a logical and reasonable basis for allocating cost of property to operating periods because, in general, plant assets render services of greater value in the earlier years of their useful lives. There is the additional argument that repairs and maintenance tend to be greater in later years, plus the factor of convenience in maintaining the accounting records on the same basis used for income tax purposes.

Review of depreciation rates. In reviewing the client's depreciation rates, the auditors must determine that the estimates of service lives are reasonable.

The auditors' objectives in review of depreciation

The principal objectives of the auditors in reviewing depreciation methods and amounts are to determine (a) that the method in use is a reasonable one, (b) that it is being followed consistently, and (c) that the computations required by the chosen method are accurately made. A more detailed picture of the auditors' objectives is conveyed by the audit program in the following section.

Audit program—depreciation expense and accumulated depreciation

The following outline of substantive tests to be performed by the auditors in reviewing depreciation is stated in sufficient detail to be largely self-explanatory. Consequently, no point-by-point discussion will be presented. Techniques for testing the client's provision of depreciation for the year and for analyzing the accumulated depreciation accounts are, however, discussed immediately following the audit program.

1. Review the depreciation policies set forth in company manuals or other management directives. Determine whether the methods in use are carefully designed and intended to allocate costs of plant and equipment assets equitable over their service lives.
    a. Enquire whether any extra working shifts or other conditions of accelerated production are present which might warrant adjustment of normal depreciation rates.
    b. Discuss with executives the possible need for recognition of obsolescence resulting from inventions, design changes, or economic developments.
2. Obtain or prepare a summary analysis (see Figure 15–1) of accumulated depreciation for the major property classifications as shown by the general ledger control accounts, listing beginning balances, provisions for depreciation during the year, retirements, and ending balances.
    a. Compare beginning balances with the audited amounts in last year's working papers.

    b. Determine that the totals of accumulated depreciation recorded in the plant and equipment subsidiary records agree with the applicable general ledger control accounts.

3. Verify the provisions for depreciation.

    a. Compare rates used in current year with those employed in prior year and investigate any variances.

    b. Test computations of depreciation provisions for a representative number of units and trace to individual records in property ledger. Be alert for excessive depreciation on fully depreciated assets.

    c. Compare credits to accumulated depreciation accounts for year's depreciation provisions with debit entries in related depreciation expense accounts.

4. Verify deductions from accumulated depreciation for assets retired.

    a. Trace deductions to the working paper analyzing retirements of assets during year.

    b. Test accuracy of accumulated depreciation to date of retirement.

5. Review the most recent assessment notice on depreciation made by the Department of National Revenue. Determine whether provisions and rates have been adjusted, when necessary, to agree with the findings of the Department of National Revenue.

6. Compare the percentage relationships between accumulated depreciation and related property accounts with that prevailing in prior years, and discuss significant variations from the normal depreciation program with appropriate members of management.

Testing the client's provision for depreciation

An *overall* test of the annual provision for depreciation requires the auditors to perform the following steps:

a. List the balances in the various asset accounts at the beginning of the year.

b. Deduct any fully depreciated assets, since these items should no longer be subject to depreciation.

c. Add one half of the asset additions for the year.

d. Deduct one half of the asset retirements for the year (exclusive of any fully depreciated assets).

These four steps produce average amounts subject to depreciation at the regular rates in each of the major asset categories. By applying the appropriate rates to these amounts, the auditors determine on an overall average basis the amount of the provision for depreciation and compare their computation with the client's figures. Any significant discrepancy between the depreciation expense computed in this manner and the amounts set up by the client should be fully investigated.

Verification of natural resources

In the examination of companies operating properties subject to depletion (mines, oil and gas deposits, timberlands, and other natural resources), the auditors follow a pattern similar to that used in evaluating the provision for depreciation expense and accumulated depreciation. They seek to determine whether depletion has been recorded consistently and in accordance with generally accepted accounting principles, and they test the mathematical accuracy of the client's computations.

The depletion of timberlands is usually based on physical quantities established by cruising. The determination of physical quantities to use as a basis for depletion is more difficult in many mining ventures and for oil and gas deposits. The auditors often rely upon the opinions of such specialists as mining engineers and geologists about the reasonableness of the depletion rates being used for such resources.

If the number of tons of ore in a mining property could be accurately determined in advance, an exact depletion cost per ton could be computed by dividing the cost of the mine by the number of tons available for extraction. In reality the contents of the mine can only be estimated, and the estimates may require drastic revision as mining operations progress.

The auditors verify the ownership and the cost of mining properties by examining deeds, leases, tax bills, vouchers, paid cheques, and other records in the same manner that they verify the plant and equipment of a manufacturing or trading concern. The costs of exploration and development work in a mine customarily are capitalized until such time as commercial production begins. After that date additional development work generally is treated as expense. The costs of drilling oil wells usually are capitalized. When an oil company leases land, it often makes an immediate payment followed by annual rental payments until production begins, after which time the landowner receives payment in the form of royalties. In the records of the oil company, the lease may be carried at the total of the payments made, including the cost of developmental work, with this total becoming the basis for depletion, or being written off if the property proves to be non-productive. As an alternative some oil companies capitalize the bonus paid for a lease but treat rental payments as an immediate charge to expense.

For some extractive companies the cost of the mine or oil deposit is negligible, and a "discovery" value or appraised value is substituted as the basis for computing depletion. The auditors' responsibility in this situation is the same as when they encounter appraised values in the accounting records of a manufacturing or mercantile business; the auditors must investigate the appraisal report, determine the basis of the appraisal values, trace the amounts from the report into the records, and insist upon appropriate disclosure in the financial statements.

It is important to emphasize that *cost* of natural resources is the usual basis for the computation of depletion for financial reporting. The method of computing depletion for income tax purposes may not be relevant for financial accounting purposes.

Verification of intangible assets

The balance sheet caption, *Intangible Assets,* include a variety of assets. All intangible assets are characterized by a lack of physical substance. Furthermore, they do not qualify as current assets, and they are non-monetary—that is, they do not represent fixed claims to cash.

Among the more prominent intangible assets are goodwill, patents, trademarks, franchises, and leaseholds. Notice that investment in securities is *not* included in our list of intangibles. Since intangible assets are lacking in physical substance, their value lies in the rights or economic advantages afforded in their ownership. Because of their intangible nature, these assets may be more difficult to identify than units of plant and equipment. When a client treats an expenditure as creating an intangible asset, the auditors must look for objective evidence that a genuine asset has come into existence.

The auditors' substantiation of intangible assets is begun with an analysis of the ledger accounts for these assets. Charges to the accounts should be traced to evidence of payment having been made and to documentary evidence of the rights or benefits acquired. Credits to the accounts should be reconciled with the client's program of amortization or traced to appropriate authorization for the write-off of the asset.

Research and development costs may be classified as a deferred charge or as an intangible asset. Section 3070 of the *CICA Handbook* does not stipulate whether amortization should be made; it only recommends that where amortization is provided, this fact should be disclosed. However, in the United States, FASB's *Statement No. 2* recommends that research and development costs generally must be expensed within the current period.

Other intangibles such as patents and trademarks do not pose audit problems comparable to those raised by the capitalization of large expenditures for research and development. The cost of patents and other similar intangibles is relatively small; furthermore, documentary evidence usually exists to substantiate the existence of the future legal rights stemming from the expenditures.

One intangible asset which may still be large in amount yet of questionable future economic benefit is *goodwill.* Goodwill frequently arises in accounting for business combinations in which the price paid to acquire another company exceeds the fair value of the identifiable net assets acquired. When business combinations result in the recording of goodwill, the auditors should review the allocation of the lump-sum acquisition cost among tangible assets, identifiable intangible assets, and goodwill. Any allocation of total acquisition cost to goodwill should be considered for reasonableness, and also traced to the authorization and subsequent approval in the minutes of the directors' meetings.

In conjunction with an analysis of intangible asset accounts, the auditors should review the reasonableness of the client's amortization program. Since the *CICA Handbook* does not provide any clear guidance in this area, the auditors must exercise their professional judgment to ensure the reasonableness of the client's amortization charges. *APB Opinion No. 17* recommends that all intangible assets should be amortized over a period not exceeding 40 years. Generally, intangible assets should be amortized by the straight-line method unless another method can be clearly shown to produce more meaningful results.

Examination of plant and equipment in advance of the balance sheet date

Most of the audit work on plant and equipment can be done in advance of the balance sheet date. For the initial audit of a new client, the time-consuming task of reviewing the records of prior years and establishing the beginning balances in the plant accounts for the current period should be completed before the year-end.

In repeat engagements, as well as in first examinations, the study and evaluation of internal control can be carried out at any convenient time during the year. Many auditing firms lighten their year-end work loads by performing interim work during October and November, including the analysis of the plant and equipment ledger accounts for the first nine or ten months of the year. After the balance sheet date, the work necessary on property accounts is then limited to the final two or three months' transactions. One of the major problems in managing an accounting practice is arranging a uniform work load for the staff throughout the year. A step toward the solution of this problem lies in performing most of the work on plant and equipment in advance of the balance sheet date.

KEY TERMS INTRODUCED OR EMPHASIZED IN CHAPTER 15

capital expenditure An expenditure for property, plant, and equipment which is properly charged to an asset account.

cruising The inspection of a tract of forest land for the purpose of estimating the total lumber yield.

loss payable endorsement   A clause in a fire or other casualty insurance policy providing for payments to lienholders of the insured property to the extent of their unpaid loans or the face amount of the insurance, whichever is less.

revenue expenditure   An expenditure for property, plant, and equipment which is properly charged to an expense account.

work order   An accounting record to record the cost of raw materials, direct labour, and overhead incurred in the acquisition, retirement, repair, or maintenance of a plant asset.

GROUP I
REVIEW QUESTIONS

15–1.   Identify at least three elements of a strong system of internal control for property, plant, and equipment.

15–2.   In the first audit of Newmark Ltd., Ralph James, CA, discovered that several capital expenditures had been erroneously treated as revenue expenditures during the three-year history of the company. Describe the effects of these accounting errors on Newmark's financial statements for the current year, prior to correction of the errors.

15–3.   Under what circumstances might the auditors use the work of a specialist during their audit of property, plant, and equipment? Explain.

15–4.   Do the auditors question the service lives adopted by the client for plant assets, or do they accept the service lives without investigation? Explain.

15–5.   Should the independent auditors observe a physical inventory of property and equipment in every audit engagement? Discuss.

15–6.   Hamlin Metals Ltd. has sales representatives covering several provinces and provides automobiles for them and for its executives. Describe any substantive tests you would consider appropriate for the company's fleet of over 100 automobiles, other than the verification procedures generally applicable to all property and equipment.

15–7.   Explain the use of a "system of authorizations" for property and equipment additions.

15–8.   What is the principal objective of the auditors in analyzing a Maintenance and Repairs expense account?

15.9.   Gibson Manufacturing Ltd. acquired new factory machinery this year and ceased using the old machinery. The old equipment was retained, however, and is capable of being used if the demand for the company's products warrants additional production. How should the old machinery be handled in the accounting records and on the financial statements?

15–10.   What objections do business executives have to the traditional practice of basing depreciation charges on original cost?

15–11.   Moultrie Ltd. discovered recently that a number of its property and equipment assets had been retired from use several years ago without any entries made in the accounting records. The company asks you to suggest procedures which will prevent unrecorded retirement of assets.

15–12. Does a failure to record the retirement of machinery affect net income? Explain.

15–13. What documentary evidence is usually available to the auditors in the client's office to substantiate the ownership of property, plant, and equipment?

15–14. The auditors' verification of current assets such as cash, securities, and inventories emphasizes observation, inspection, and confirmation to determine the physical existence of these assets. Should the auditors take a similar approach to establish the existence of the recorded plan assests? Explain fully.

15–15. The current assets of Miller Manufacturing, Inc., amount to $2,500,-000, and are approximately equal in amount to the plant and equipment. You have audited the company for several years. Which group of assets should require more audit time? Give reasons.

15–16. You are making your first examination of Clarke Manufacturing Ltd. Plant and equipment represent a very substantial portion of the total assets. What verification, if any, will you make of the balances of the ledger accounts for Plan and Equipment as of the beginning of the period under audit?

15–17. Should the auditors examine public records to determine the legal title of property apparently owned by the client?

15–18. Cite various substantive tests that the auditors employ that might detect unrecorded retirements of property, plant, and equipment. (AICPA, adapted)

GROUP II
QUESTIONS REQUIRING ANALYSIS

15–19. Give the purposes of each of the following procedures that may be included in a system of internal control, and explain how each procedure contributes to strong internal control:
  a. Forecasting of expenditures for property, plant, and equipment.
  b. Maintaining a plant ledger for property, plant, and equipment. (AICPA, adapted)

15–20. During your audit of Pioneer Ltd., a new client in its first year of operations in Madison City, you find that the company has charged to the Rent Expense account all its payments for its land and building, which are leased from Madison City. The lease, which is for a ten-year term, provides for monthly rental payments sufficient to retire the principal and interest on an issue of 8 percent, ten-year serial general obligation bonds which Madison City issued to purchase the land and finance construction of the building. The lease provides that title to the real property will be transferred to Pioneer when the entire bond issue has been retired. The building has an estimated service life of 25 years.

Do you agree with Pioneer's accounting for lease rental payments? Explain.

15–21.   During the year ended April 30, 1979, Metropole Ltd., your long-time audit client, changed the estimated service lives of its machinery and equipment to ten years from eight years. The company included the cumulative effect of the accounting change, net of applicable income taxes, in its income statement for the year which you are examining. Would you recommend a change in the company's accounting for the change in estimated service lives of machinery and equipment? Explain.

15–22.   Your new client, Ross Products, Inc., completed its first fiscal year March 31, 1979. During the course of your examination you discover the following entry in the general journal, dated April 1, 1978:

```
Building  ...........................  2,400,000
    Mortgage Note Payable .............             1,400,000
    Common Stock ....................             1,000,000
    To record (1) acquisition of building con-
    structed by J. A. Ross Construction Co.
    (a sole proprietorship); (2) assumption of
    Ross Construction Co. mortgage loan for
    construction of the building; and (3)
    issuance of entire authorized common
    stock (10,000 shares, $100 par value) to
    J. A. Ross.
```

During your investigation, you learn that the entire authorized preferred stock of Ross Products, Inc.—10,000 shares, $50 par value, had been issued to J. A. Ross for $500,000 cash. The cash was used to purchase the land for the building site from an unrelated party.

Required:

Explain how you would accomplish the following objective relating to audit of this client's plant and equipment: "Determine the propriety of the valuation methods used."

15–23.   Ashton Manufacturing Ltd., a closely held corporation, has operated since 1970 but has not had its financial statements audited. The company now plans to issue additional share capital expected to be sold to outsiders and wishes to engage you to examine its 1979 transactions and render an opinion on the financial statements for the year ended December 31, 1979.

The company has expanded from one plant to three plants and has frequently acquired, modified, and disposed of all types of equipment. Plant assets have a net depreciated value of 70 percent of total assets and consist of land and buildings, diversified machinery and equipment, and furniture and fixtures. Some property was acquired by donation from shareholders. Depreciation was recorded by several methods using various estimated service lives.

Required:

a. May you confine your examination solely to 1979 transactions as requested by this prospective client whose financial statements have not previously been examined? Explain.

b. Prepare an audit program for the January 1, 1979, balances of the Land, Building, and Equipment and Accumulated Depreciation accounts of Ashton Manufacturing Ltd. You need not include substantive tests of 1979 transactions in your program. (AICPA, adapted)

15–24. An executive of a manufacturing company informs you that no formal procedures have been followed to control the retirement of machinery and equipment. A physical inventory of plant assets has just been completed. It revealed that 25 percent of the assets carried in the ledger were not on hand and had presumably been scrapped. The accounting records have been adjusted to agree with the physical inventory. You are asked to outline internal control practices to govern future retirements.

15–25. List and state the purpose of all audit procedures which might reasonably be applied by the auditors to determine that all property and equipment retirements have been recorded in the accounting records. (AICPA)

15–26. Allen Fraser was president of three corporations: Mouri Metals Corporation Ltd., Kansan Metals Corporation Ltd., and Hamton Metals Corporation Ltd. Each of the three corporations owned land and buildings acquired for approximately $20,000. An appraiser retained by Fraser in 1979 estimated the current value of the land and buildings in each corporation at approximately $200,000. The appraisals were recorded in the accounts. A new corporation, called Midland Corporation Ltd., was then formed, and Fraser became its president. The new corporation purchased the assets of the three predecessor corporations, making payment in share capital. The balance sheet of Midland Corporation Ltd. shows land and buildings "valued at cost" in the amount of $600,000, the carrying values to the vendor companies at the time of transfer to Midland Corporation Ltd. Do you consider this treatment acceptable? Explain.

15–27. Shortly after you were retained to examine the financial statements of Case Corporation Ltd., you learned from a preliminary discussion with management that the corporation had recently acquired a competing business, the Mall Ltd. In your study of the terms of the acquisition, you find that the total purchase price was paid in cash and that the transaction was authorized by the board of directors and fully described in the minutes of the directors' meetings. The only aspect of the acquisition of the Mall Ltd. which raises any doubts in your mind is the allocation of the total purchase price among the several kinds of assets acquired. This allocation, which had been specifically approved by the board of directors of Case Corporation Ltd., placed very high values on the tangible assets acquired and allowed nothing for goodwill.

You are inclined to believe that the allocation of the lump-sum price to the several types of assets was somewhat unreasonable, because the total price for the business was as much or more than the current replacement cost of the tangible assets acquired. However, as an auditor, you do not claim to be an expert in property values. Would you question the property of the directors' allocation of the lump-sum purchase price? Explain fully.

GROUP III
PROBLEMS

15–28. In connection with the annual examination of Johnson Corporation Ltd., a manufacturer of janitorial supplies, you have been assigned to audit the plant assets. The company maintains a detailed property ledger for all plant assets. You prepared an audit program for the property, plant, and equipment asset accounts but have yet to prepare one for accumulated depreciation and depreciation expense.

Required:

Prepare an audit program for the accumulated depreciation and depreciation expense accounts. (AICPA, adapted)

15–29. During your examination of the financial statements of Scope Ltd. for the year ended April 30, 1979, you reviewed the following journal entries, which represent the only additions to the Equipment ledger account for the year:

| Mar. 31, 79 | Equipment .... | | 2,147 | |
| | Cash .... | | | 2,147 |

To record down payment for new equipment under installment contract with the following terms:

List price	$13,000
Sale tax	780
Total	$13,780
Down payment	2,147
Balance	$11,633
13.47% interest, one year ..	1,567
Contract balance (12 × $1,100)	$13,200

| Apr. 30, 79 | Equipment .... | | 1,100 | |
| | Cash .... | | | 1,100 |

To record first monthly payment under installment contract for equipment.

The company uses straight-line depreciation, ten-year service life, and 10 percent residual value for all its equipment. The company takes a full-year's depreciation on all additions to equipment during the fiscal year, and you may treat this policy as a satisfactory one for the purpose of this problem. The company has recorded depreciation for the fiscal year ended April 30, 1979.

Required:

Assume that you have examined the contract described in the explanation for the March 31, 1979, journal entry, and have found that the description was accurate. Prepare the proposed adjusting journal entry or entries for Scope Ltd. with respect to the equipment and related depreciation accounts at April 30, 1979. Relevant data from compound interest tables for $n = 12$ are as follows:

i	$a_{\overline{n}|i}$	$p_{\overline{n}|i}$	$A_{\overline{n}|i}$	$P_{\overline{n}|i}$
½%	1.062	0.942	12.336	11.619
1	1.127	0.887	12.683	11.255
1½	1.196	0.836	13.041	10.908
2	1.268	0.788	13.412	10.575
2½	1.345	0.744	13.796	10.258
3	1.426	0.701	14.192	9.954

15–30. Nova Land Development Corporation is a closely held corporation engaged in purchasing large tracts of land, subdividing the tracts, and installing paved streets and utilities. The corporation does not construct buildings for the buyers of the land and does not have any affiliated construction companies. Undeveloped land usually is leased for farming until the corporation is ready to begin developing it.

The corporation finances its land acquisitions by mortgages; the mortgagees require audited financial statements. This is your first audit of the company and you have now begun the examination of the financial statements for the year ended December 31, 1979.

Required:

The corporation has three tracts of land in various stages of development. List the audit procedures to be employed in the verification of the physical existence and title to the corporation's three landholdings. (AICPA, adapted)

15–31. You are engaged in the examination of the financial statements of Holman Corporation Ltd. for the year ended December 31, 1979. The accompanying analyses of the Property, Plant, and Equipment, and related Accumulated Depreciation accounts have been prepared by the chief accountant of the client. You have traced the beginning balances to your prior year's audit working papers.

HOLMAN CORPORATION LTD.
Analysis of Property, Plant, and Equipment, and
Related Accumulated Depreciation Accounts
Year Ended December 31, 1979

Assets

Description	Final Dec. 31, 78	Additions	Retirements	Per ledger Dec. 31, 79
Land	$ 22,500	$ 5,000		$ 27,500
Buildings	120,000	17,500		137,500
Machinery and equipment	385,000	40,400	$26,000	399,400
	$527,500	$62,900	$26,000	$564,400

Accumulated Depreciation

Description	Final Dec. 31, 78	Additions°	Retirements	Per ledger Dec. 31, 79
Buildings	$ 60,000	$ 5,150		$ 65,150
Machinery and equipment	173,250	$39,220		212,470
	$233,250	$44,370		$277,620

° Depreciation expense for the year.

All plant assets are depreciated on the straight-line basis (no residual value taken in consideration) based on the following estimated service lives: building, 25 years; and all other items, 10 years. The company's policy is to take one half-year's depreciation on all asset additions and disposals during the year.

Your examination revealed the following information:

1. On April 1 the company entered into a ten-year lease contract for a die casting machine, with annual rentals of $5,000 payable in advance every April 1. The lease is cancellable by either party (60 days' written notice is required), and there is no option to renew the lease or buy the equipment at the end of the lease. The estimated service life of the machine is ten years with no residual value. The company recorded the die casting machine in the Machinery and Equipment account at $40,400, the present value at the date of the lease, and $2,020 applicable to the machine has been included in depreciation expense for the year.

2. The company completed the construction of a wing on the plant building on June 30. The service life of the building was not extended by this addition. The lowest construction bid received was $17,500, the amount recorded in the Buildings account. Company personnel constructed the addition at a cost of $16,000 (materials, $7,000; labour, $5,500; and overhead, $3,000).

3. On August 18, $5,000 was paid for paving and fencing a portion of land owned by the company and used as a parking lot for employees. The expenditure was charged to the Land account.

4. The amount shown in the machinery and equipment asset retirement column represents cash received on September 5 upon disposal of a machine purchased in July 1975 for $48,000. The chief accountant recorded depreciation expense of $3,500 on this machine in 1979.

5. Harbor City donated land and bulding appraised at $10,000 and $40,000, respectively, to Holman Corporation Ltd. for a plant. On September 1, the company began operating the plant. Since no costs were involved, the chief acocuntant made no entry for the above transaction.

Required:

Prepare the adjusting journal entries that you would propose at December 31, 1979, to adjust the accounts for the above transactions. Disregard income tax implications. The accounts have not been closed.

Computations should be rounded off to the nearest dollar. (AICPA, adapted)

15–32. You are the senior accountant in the audit of Granger Grain Corporation Ltd., whose business primarily involves the purchase, storage, and sale of grain products. The corporation owns several elevators located along navigable water routes and transports its grain by barge and rail. Your staff assistant submitted the following working paper analysis for your review.

GRANGER GRAIN CORPORATION LTD.
Advances Paid on Barges under Construction—a/c 210
December 31, 1979

Advances made:

Jan. 15, 79—Ch. No. 3463—Jones Barge Construction Co. Ltd..		$100,000[1]
Apr. 13, 79—Ch. No. 4129—Jones Barge Construction Co. Ltd..		25,000[1]
June 19, 79—Ch. No. 5396—Jones Barge Construction Co. Ltd..		63,000[1]
Total payments		$188,000
Deduct cash received Sept. 1, 79 from City Insurance Co. Ltd...		188,000[2]
Balance per general ledger—Dec. 31, 79....................		-0-

[1] Examined approved cheque request and paid cheque and traced to cash disbursements journal.
[2] Traced to cash receipts journal and to duplicate deposit ticket.

Required:

a. In what respects is the analysis incomplete for audit purposes? (Do not include any discussion of specific auditing procedures.)
b. What two different types of contractual arrangements may be inferred from your assistant's analysis?
c. What additional auditing procedures would you suggest that your staff assistant perform before you accept the working paper as being complete? (AICPA, adapted)

15–33. CA has been the auditor of W Ltd. for many years. The company is a large manufacturer with 11 factories located across Canada; the factories maintain their own accounting records. Three years ago the company appointed an internal auditor, R, who works out of the corporate head office and is independent of any factory. CA's practice has been to examine R's audit programs, discuss them with him, and review the results of his work.

R visits each factory at least once annually; until now, he has never concerned himself with fixed assets. This year, however, he intends to carry out the following procedures at all factories:

1. Obtain listings of fixed asset additions and disposals from the beginning of the fiscal year to the date of his visit.
2. Trace all additions to the head office "Authorization for Capital Expenditure" forms, and to "Supplementary Authorizations" if the expenditures exceed original estimates.
3. Ensure that additions for each factory are within the limits of authorized capital budgets.

4. See that the additions are charged to the proper general ledger accounts.
5. Check repair and maintenance control records to ensure that assets are maintained in good condition.
6. Ascertain that assets are adequately insured.
7. Enquire as to possible obsolescence of any machinery that the machine-hour records show to be idle for extended periods.

Required:

State the alterations or additions to R's proposed audit program covering factory fixed assets that CA might suggest to increase the program's effectiveness. (CICA)

16

Accounts payable and other liabilities

Now that the several chapters dealing with the verification of assets have been completed and we are ready to consider the examination of liability accounts, it is appropriate to compare and contrast the auditors' work on assets with the work to be done on liabilities. In the verification of every asset the auditors are constantly on guard against *overstated* asset values. Accounting records which overstate the amount of cash on hand or on deposit are usually suggestive of fraud, and the auditors' approach to this danger is a careful count of cash on hand and confirmation of amounts shown as on deposit with banks. Similarly, the threat of an overstated or fictitious account receivable necessitates direct communication with customers. The possibility of an overstated inventory requires that the auditors observe the physical count of goods. In carrying out these audit procedures the auditors are, of course, on the alert for all types of errors, but they are particularly aware of the dangers of overstatement of asset accounts.

The auditors' concern with possible overstatement of asset values arises from the fact that creditors and investors may sustain serious losses if they extend credit in reliance upon financial statements with inflated asset valuations. Second, any theft from the company by dishonest employees usually involves the abstraction of cash and improper entries in the accounts to conceal the theft. The question of legal liability on the part of public accountants is usually illustrated by cases in which auditors failed to detect material overstatement of assets and earnings.

In the study of audit work on liabilities, the point to be emphasized is this: An *understatement of liabilities* will exaggerate financial strength of a company and conceal fraud just as effectively as *overstatement of assets*. Furthermore, the understatement of liabilities is usually accompanied by understatement of expenses and overstatement of net income. For example, dishonest management of a company could inflate net income for the year ended December 31, 1979 (and understate liabilities and overstate shareholders' equity at that date), merely by delaying the recording of bills for December 1979 operating expenses until they were paid in January 1980. Audit procedures for liabilities should be designed to detect understatement, just as audit procedures for assets are designed to detect overstatement.

To overstate an asset account usually requires an improper entry in the accounting records, as by the recording of a fictitious transaction. Such improper entries can be detected by the auditors through verification of the individual items making up the balance of an asset account. Once a fictitious entry is detected, the individual responsible for the fraud has little alternative but to admit his acts. By way of contrast, it is possible to understate a liability account merely by *failing to make an entry* for a transaction creating a liability. The omission of an entry is less susceptible of detection than is a fictitious entry. If the omission is detected, there is at least a possibility of passing it off as an accidental error. Auditors have long recognized that the most difficult type of fraud to detect is fraud based on the non-recording of transactions. Once transactions are entered in the records, there are many verification techniques available.

ILLUSTRATIVE CASE.   The audited 1963 financial statements of Yale Express System, Inc., a trucking and freight forwarding concern in the United States, reported **net income** of $1.1 million. In 1965, Yale's 1963 operating results were restated to a **net loss** of $1.9 million. A significant part of the original overstatement of Yale's 1963 earnings was reportedly caused by unrecorded accounts payable for railroad freight bills and for loss, injury, and damage claims. The company admitted that documentary evidence supporting these liabilities was withheld from the independent auditors.

Another point of difference between the auditors' work on assets and liabilities is that liabilities generally do not present a problem of valuation. The amount of a liability is usually a matter of fact, whereas the proper valuation of an asset is a matter of opinion. (Income taxes payable and liabilities for pensions represent prominent exceptions to this generalization; the use of present values for long-term notes payable is another exception.) Much of the audit time devoted to assets is concerned with the propriety of the valuation methods used by the client. Consequently, the audit time required for verification of liability accounts may be considerably shorter than for verification of corresponding dollar amounts in asset accounts.

Meaning of accounts payable

In a broad sense, accounts payable include not only amounts owing for merchandise and materials but all obligations of a business except those evidenced by bonds and notes. Apart from the purchase of materials and merchandise, other transactions giving rise to accounts payable include the acquisition of plant and equipment and the incurring of various types of production costs, as well as selling, general, and administrative expenses. Taxes, wages, salaries, light, power, rent, and a host of other items all result in liabilities which must be verified, classified, recorded, and paid by the client. The auditors' verification of these liabilities will ordinarily be broken down into separate phases corresponding to balance sheet captions, such as "Accounts payable—trade," "Accounts payable—officers and employees," and "Accrued liabilities."

Trade accounts payable are those current liabilities arising from the purchase of goods and services from trade creditors, and generally are evidenced by invoices or statements received from the creditors. Other types of accounts payable are those current liabilities for which the company acts as fiduciary, such as taxes withheld from employees' salaries, unclaimed wages, and customers' deposits. *Accrued liabilities* generally accumulate as a result of the company's contractual or legal obligation to pay salaries, pensions, interest, rent, taxes chargeable to expense, and obligations under product warranties. The company seldom receives invoices or statements for accrued liabilities.

In terms of auditing procedures, liabilities arising from transactions with outside suppliers differ significantly from payroll and other obligations originating within the company. Moreover, purchases of merchandise and materials make up the major portion of accounts payable transactions and require a corresponding amount of auditing activity. For these reasons, it is convenient to centre the discussion at present on trade accounts payable and to deal separately with other current liabilities, such as accrued expenses, taxes, and deferred credits to revenue.

The auditors' objectives in examination of accounts payable

The principal objectives of the auditors in the examination of accounts payable are to (*a*) determine the adequacy of internal controls for the processing and payment of vendors' invoices; (*b*) prove that the amount shown on the balance sheet is in agreement with the supporting accounting records; and (*c*) determine that all liabilities existing at the balance sheet date have been recorded.

Internal control over accounts payable

In thinking about internal control for accounts payable, it is important to recognize that the accounts payable of one company are the accounts receivable of other companies. It follows that there is little danger of a client permanently overlooking or misplacing a liability because creditors will naturally maintain complete records of their receivables and will speak up if payment is not received. A company, therefore, may choose to minimize its record keeping of liabilities and to rely on creditors to call attention to any delay in making payment. This viewpoint is not an endorsement of inaccurate or incomplete records of accounts payable, but merely a recognition that the self-interest of creditors constitutes a protective feature of accounting for payables which is not present in the case of accounts receivable.

Discussions of internal control applicable to accounts payable are often extended to cover the functions of purchasing and receiving, as well as the activities of the accounts payable department. This is not surprising, for the end objective of controls in this area of operations is to provide assurance that the company receives value for all payments made; and this, in turn, requires proof that goods have been received in proper quantity and condition before vendors' invoices are approved. A first essential of adequate control is the segregation of duties so that a cash disbursement to a creditor will be made only upon approval of the purchasing, receiving, accounting, and finance departments. All purchase transactions should be evidenced by serially numbered purchase orders, copies of which are sent to the accounts payable department for comparison with vendors' invoices and receiving reports.

The receiving department should be independent of the purchasing department. Receiving reports should be prepared for all goods received. These documents should be serially numbered and prepared in a sufficient number of copies to permit prompt notification of receipts to the accounts payable department, purchasing department, and stores department. In smaller companies, vendors' packing slips often are utilized as receiving reports.

Within the accounts payable department, all forms should be stamped with the date and hour received. Vouchers and other documents originating within the department can be controlled through the use of serial numbers. Each step in the verification of an invoice should be evidenced by the entering of a date and signature on the voucher. The most effective means of assuring that routine procedures, such as the proof of extensions and footings and the review of the propriety of discounts taken, are carried out consistently is the requirement that a designated employee sign the voucher as each step in verification is completed. Comparison of the quantities listed on the invoice with those shown on the receiving report and purchase order, if carefully made, will prevent the payment of charges for goods in excess of those ordered and received. Comparison of the prices, discounts, and terms of shipment as shown on the purchase order and on the vendor's invoice provides a safeguard against the payment of excessive prices.

Separation of the function of invoice verification and approval from that of cash disbursement is another step which tends to prevent error or fraud. Before invoices are approved for payment, written evidence must be presented to show that all aspects of the transaction have been verified.

Another control procedure which the auditors may expect to find in a well-managed accounts payable department is regular monthly balancing of the detailed records of accounts payable to the general ledger control. These trial balances should be preserved as evidence of the performance of this procedure and as an aid in localizing any subsequent errors.

Monthly statements from vendors should be reconciled with the accounts payable ledger or list of open vouchers, and any discrepancies fully investigated. In some industries it is common practice to make advances to vendors which are recovered by making percentage deductions from invoices. When such advances are in use, the auditors should ascertain what procedures are followed to assure that deductions from the invoices are made in accordance with the agreement.

Internal control and the computer

The substantial volume of accounts payable transactions of a company makes processing of payables an effective application of a computer. The traditional accounts payable subsidiary ledger is seldom found in a computerized payables system; instead, invoices are processed by a voucher system for payment within the discount or credit period. Periodically, a computer print-out of purchasing volume from each vendor is provided for use by the purchasing department. In addition, the computer may be programmed to print out unpaid accounts payable vouchers for each vendor, for use by internal auditors or independent auditors.

With the increased utilization of electronic computers, some changes in the traditional procedures for accounts payable have become desirable. Some companies, for example, have overcome the difficulties of converting the variety of invoices and statements received from vendors to computer input form by dispensing with these documents entirely. Instead, the company's own purchase orders, supported by comparable receiving reports, serve as the source data for credits to accounts payable.

Audit working papers for accounts payable

Besides the grouping sheet for accounts payable, the principal working papers are schedules or trial balances of the various types of accounts payable at the balance sheet date. The trial balances are often in the form of computer print-outs. In addition, the auditors usually prepare a listing of unrecorded accounts payable discovered during the course of the audit, as illustrated in Figure 16–1.

AUDIT PROGRAM FOR ACCOUNTS PAYABLE

The examination of trade accounts payable usually requires audit work along the following lines. The first five procedures are performed as a part of the study and evaluation of internal control for accounts payable. The remainder of the audit program is performed on or subsequent to the balance sheet date.

A. Study and evaluation of internal control for accounts payable

1. Prepare a description of the internal control for accounts payable.
2. Verify postings to Accounts Payable control account for a test period.
3. Vouch to supporting documents all postings in selected accounts of the accounts payable subsidiary ledger.
4. Review cash discounts.
5. Evaluate internal control for accounts payable.

B. Substantive tests of accounts payable transactions and balances

6. Obtain or prepare a trial balance of accounts payable as of the balance sheet date and reconcile with the general ledger.
7. Vouch balances payable to selected creditors to supporting documents.
8. Reconcile liabilities with monthly statements from creditors.
9. Consider confirming accounts by direct correspondence if statements from creditors are not available.
10. Investigate debit balances for collectibility and reclassify if substantial in amount.
11. Ascertain that liability to consignors for merchandise sold has been recorded.
12. Trace balances owing to affiliated companies to accounting records of respective companies, or confirm if accounting records are not available.
13. Compare cash disbursements subsequent to the balance sheet date with the accounts payable trial balance.
14. Search for unrecorded accounts payable.
15. Determine proper balance sheet presentation of accounts payable.
16. Obtain from client a letter of representations concerning liabilities.

A. Study and evaluation

1. Prepare a description of the internal control for accounts payable.

One approach used by auditors in becoming familiar with a client's system of internal control for accounts payable is to prepare a flowchart or to use flowcharts prepared by the client. In some engagements the auditors may choose to prepare a narrative description covering such matters as the independence of the accounts payable department and the receiving department from the purchasing department. The auditors might also use a questionnaire to obtain a description of accounts payable controls. Typical of the questions are the following: Is an accounts payable trial balance prepared monthly and reconciled to the general ledger control account? Are monthly statements from vendors reconciled with accounts payable ledgers or unpaid vouchers? Are advance payments to vendors recorded as receivables and controlled in a manner which assures that they will be recovered by offset against vendors' invoices? Are debit memos issued to vendors for discrepancies in invoice prices, quantities, or computations? Are debit balances in vendors' accounts brought to the attention of the credit and purchasing departments?

2. Verify postings to Accounts Payable control account for a test period.

A procedure necessary to establish the validity of the balance shown by the general ledger control account for accounts payable consists of tracing postings for one or more months to the voucher register and cash disbursements journal. Any postings to the control account from the general journal during this test period should also be traced. This work is performed prior to the audit date as part of a general compliance test of postings to all records. At the same time, the auditors should scrutinize all entries to the control account for the entire period under audit and should investigate any unusual entries.

3. Vouch to supporting documents all postings in selected accounts of the accounts payable subsidiary ledger.

Testing the accuracy of the voucher register or the accounts payable ledgers by tracing specific items back through the cash payments journal, purchases journal, and other journals to original documents, such as purchase orders, receiving reports, invoices, and paid cheques, is necessary to determine the adequacy of the system of internal control. If the functions of purchasing, receiving, invoice verification, and cash disbursement are delegated to separate departments and internal controls appear adequate, the tracing of individual items from the ledgers to the original records may be undertaken only to the extent necessary to determine that the system is operating properly.

The auditors may also make tests by following the audit trail in the opposite direction. By tracing a representative sample of entries from the journals to the accounts payable ledger, the auditors can verify that journal entries have been posted consistently to the subsidiary ledger.

4. Review cash discounts.

Some concerns record purchase invoices in the voucher register at the net amount after deduction of any available cash discounts. It is also acceptable practice to record invoices at the gross amount before deduction of cash discounts.

The auditors' concern with purchase discounts is based on the possibility of fraudulent manipulation by employees and also on the possibility of accidental loss through failure to take discounts. Numerous case histories of fraud relating to cash disbursements have involved the drawing of cheques for the gross amount of an invoice paid within the discount period. The dishonest employee was then in a position to request a refund from the creditor, to substitute the refund cheque for currency, and to abstract cash in this amount without any further manipulation of the records.

The most convenient test of discounts when these are recorded separately is to compute the ratio of cash discounts earned to total purchases during the period and to compare this ratio from period to period. Any significant decrease in the ratio indicates a change in terms of purchases, failure to take discounts, or fraudulent manipulation.

5. Evaluate internal control for accounts payable.

Completion of the preceding audit procedures enables the auditors to evaluate internal control for accounts payable. The internal control evaluation provides the basis for selecting the necessary substantive tests for verification of accounts payable at the balance sheet date.

B. Substantive tests:

6. Obtain or prepare a trial balance of accounts payable as of the balance sheet date and reconcile with the general ledger.

One purpose of this procedure is to prove that the liability figure appearing in the balance sheet is in agreement with the individual items comprising the detail records. A second purpose is to provide a starting point for substantive testing procedures: from the list of vouchers or accounts payable the auditors will select a representative group of items for careful examination.

Large companies with numerous accounts payable usually furnish the auditors with a computer-prepared trial balance. For a lesser volume of accounts, a manually completed listing may be used. In either case, the auditors should verify the footing and the accuracy of individual amounts of the trial balance.

If the schedule of individual items does not agree in total with the control account, the cause of the discrepancy must be investigated. In most situations the auditors will arrange for the client's staff to locate such errors and make the necessary adjustments. Agreement of the control account and the list of individual account balances is not absolute proof of the total indebtedness; invoices received near the close of the period may not be reflected in either the control account or the subsidiary records, and other similar errors may exist without causing the accounts to be out of balance.

7. Vouch balances payable to selected creditors to supporting documents.

Another substantive test for establishing the validity of the client-prepared trial balance of accounts payable is the vouching of selected creditors' balances to supporting vouchers, invoices, purchase orders, and receiving documents. This work, generally performed on a test basis, also establishes additional evidence as to the status of internal control for accounts payable.

Many companies use a voucher system; and in this case, the verification of the individual vouchers is made most conveniently at the balance sheet date, when they will all be together in the unpaid voucher file. The content of the unpaid voucher file changes daily; as vouchers are paid, they are removed from the file and filed alphabetically by vendor. Consequently, it is very difficult to determine at a later date what vouchers were outstanding at the year-end.

If the auditors cannot be present at the balance sheet date, they should ask the client to prepare a list of vouchers at that date with sufficient identifying data for each voucher to permit its being located some weeks later. This listing of vouchers payable at the end of the year should show the names of vendors, voucher numbers, dates, and amounts.

8. Reconcile liabilities with monthly statements from creditors.

In some companies it is a regular practice each month to reconcile vendors' statements with the detailed records of payables. If the auditors find that this reconciliation is regularly performed by the client's staff, they may limit their review of vendors' statements to establishing that the reconciliation work has been satisfactory.

If the client's staff has not reconciled vendors' statements and accounts payable, the auditors generally will do so. If internal control for accounts payable is weak, the auditors may control incoming mail to assure that all vendors' statements received by the client are made available to the auditors. Among the discrepancies often revealed by reconciliation of vendors' statements are charges by the vendor for shipments not yet received or recorded by the client. Normal accounting procedures do not provide for recording invoices as liabilities until the merchandise has been received. These in-transit shipments should be listed and a decision reached as to whether they are sufficiently material to warrant being recorded.

In judging the materiality of unrecorded liabilities, the auditors should consider the related unrecorded debits. If recording the transaction would mean adding an asset as well as a liability, the effect on the financial statements would be less significant than recording an invoice of like amount for which the debit belonged in an expense account. The auditors must be sure, however, that invoices have been recorded as liabilities for all goods received and included in the year-end physical inventory.

9. Consider confirming accounts by direct correspondence if statements from creditors are not available.

Confirmation of accounts payable by direct correspondence with creditors is not a universal or mandatory procedure, as is the confirmation of accounts receivable. However, in many engagements the confirmation of at least a few accounts with creditors is advisable.

If confirmation of accounts payable is undertaken, confirmation requests should be mailed to suppliers from whom substantial purchases have been made during the year, regardless of the balances of their accounts at the balance sheet date. These suppliers can be identified by reference to the accounts payable subsidiary ledger, to computer printouts of purchase volume for individual vendors, or by enquiry of purchasing department personnel. Other accounts warranting circularization by the auditors include those for which monthly statements are not available, accounts reflecting unusual transactions, accounts with parent or subsidiary corporations, and accounts secured by pledged assets. The confirmation letter affords an opportunity to enquire into purchase commitments as well as to establish the facts concerning completed transactions.

Why is confirmation of accounts payable not a mandatory procedure as is the confirmation of receivables? One reason is that the greatest hazard in the verification of liabilities is the existence of unrecorded liabilities. To confirm the *recorded accounts payable* contributes little or nothing to determining whether any *unrecorded accounts payable* exist. Secondly, the auditors will find in the client's possession externally created evidence such as vendors' invoices and statements which substantiate the accounts payable. No such external evidence is on hand to support accounts receivable. Finally, many of the recorded liabilities as of the balance sheet date will be paid before the auditors complete their examination. The act of payment serves further to substantiate the authenticity of recorded liabilities. Of course, some accounts receivable are also collected during the course of an audit, but often the receivables of greatest significance to the auditors will not be promptly collected, and confirmation is the only external evidence of their validity. For all these reasons, the audit procedure of confirmation is of less importance for accounts payable than for accounts receivable.

10. Investigate debit balances for collectibility and reclassify if substantial in amount.

Debit balances in accounts payable arise from a variety of sources, including the return of merchandise after payment has been made, duplicate payments, payment of excessive amounts, advances to suppliers, outright loans, and incorrect postings. Old debit balances may reflect disputed items for which collection is doubtful. The auditors should make sufficient investigation to obtain evidence as to the nature and collectibility of any substantial amounts. If collectible, these should be reclassified as assets for statement purposes rather than offset against accounts with credit balances.

If a vendor company is also a customer, a single ledger account is sometimes used to record both purchase and sales transactions. Such an account should be divided into the receivable and payable elements for balance sheet presentation.

11. Ascertain that liability to consignors for merchandise sold has been recorded.

A review of the contracts with consignors is a prerequisite to the analysis of consignment transactions. The terms of these contracts often call for the rendering of "account sales" and the remittance of sales proceeds on a weekly or monthly basis. Sales of consigned goods shortly before the close of the period may not have been set up as a liability to the consignor; this is the central point of the auditors' enquiry. To determine that the liability to the consignor is correctly stated as of the balance sheet date will usually require these steps: tracing sales invoices to the liability account, a review of the computation of commissions, and determining the disposition of freight and handling charges applicable to the consigned goods.

12. Trace balances owing to affiliated companies to accounting records of respective companies, or confirm if accounting records are not available.

Transactions with parent or subsidiary corporations are *related party transactions.* They are often not conducted on the same basis as transactions with outsiders; consequently, they deserve special attention from the independent auditors. Unusual items, such as charges for machinery and equipment borrowed from an affiliated company, may be intermingled with outright purchase transactions. One ledger account is often used to record all transactions between two related concerns. Such an account may have either a debit or credit balance and must be analyzed to determine the proper presentation in the balance sheet. Whenever feasible, reconciliation of the account by reference to both sets of accounting records is desirable. If this cannot be done, confirmation of the balance is essential.

13. *Compare cash disbursements subsequent to the balance sheet date with the accounts payable trial balance.*

The comparison of cash disbursements occurring after the balance sheet date with the accounts payable trial balance is an excellent means of disclosing any unrecorded accounts payable. All liabilities must eventually be paid, and will, therefore, be reflected in the accounts when paid if not when incurred. By close study of payments made subsequent to the balance sheet date, the auditors may find some items that should have appeared as liabilities on the balance sheet. Regular monthly expenses, such as rent and utilities, are often posted to the ledger accounts directly from the cash disbursements journal without any account payable or other liability having been set up. After having located such items the auditors might decide against proposing any adjusting entry, but it is still essential that they have all the facts about omitted liabilities before they reach a decision as to the materiality of these items.

The auditors' comparison of cash disbursements occurring after the balance sheet date with the accounts payable trial balance also furnishes evidence of the validity of the recorded payables. Some clients retain copies of all cheques issued; other clients maintain a cash disbursements journal only. In either case, the auditors should account for the numerical sequence of all cheques issued subsequent to the balance sheet date, through the date of completion of field work.

14. *Search for unrecorded accounts payable.*

Throughout the examination of accounts payable, the auditors are alert for any indication that liabilities may have been omitted from the records. The six preceding audit procedures are directly or indirectly concerned with bringing unrecorded accounts payable to light. The auditors should also consider such sources of potential unrecorded accounts payable as the following:

a. Unmatched invoices and unbilled receiving reports. These documents are "work in process" in a voucher system. The auditors should review such unprocessed documents at the balance sheet date to ascertain that the client has recorded an account payable where appropriate.

b. Unpaid vouchers entered in the voucher register subsequent to the balance sheet date. Inspection of these records may uncover an item which should have been recorded as of the balance sheet date.

c. Invoices received by the client after the balance sheet date. Not all vendors bill promptly when goods are shipped or services are rendered. Accordingly, the auditors' review of invoices received by the client in the subsequent period may disclose unrecorded accounts payable as of the balance sheet date.

d. Other audit areas. A variety of unrecorded accounts payable may be discovered during the course of the entire audit. Examples are customers' deposits recorded as credits to accounts receivable; obligations for securities purchased but not "settled" at the balance sheet date; unbilled contractor or architect fees for a building under construction at the audit date; and unpaid attorney or insurance broker fees. In all areas of the audit, the auditors should be alert for unrecorded payables.

A form of audit working paper used to summarize unrecorded accounts payable discovered by the auditors is illustrated in Figure 16–1.

When unrecorded liabilities are discovered by the auditors, the next question is whether the omissions are sufficiently material to warrant proposing an adjusting entry. Will the adjustment cause a sufficient change in the financial statements to give a different impression of the company's current position or of its earning power? As previously indicated in the discussion of the reconciliation of vendors' statements with accounts payable, auditors seldom propose adjustments for the purpose of adding shipments in transit to the year-end inventory unless the shipments are unusually large.

As a further illustration of the factors to be considered in deciding upon the materiality of an unrecorded transaction, let us use as an example the December 31 annual audit of a small manufacturing company in good financial condition with total assets of $1 million and preadjustment net income of $100,000. The auditors' procedures bring to light the following unrecorded liabilities:

a. An invoice for $1,400, dated December 30, and bearing terms of f.o.b. shipping point. The goods were shipped on December 30 but were not received until January 4. The invoice was also received and recorded on January 4.

   In considering the materiality of this omission, the first point is that net income is not affected. The adjusting entry, if made, would add equal amounts to current assets (inventories) and to current liabilities, hence would not change the amount of working capital. The omission does affect the current ratio very slightly. The auditor would probably consider this transaction as not sufficiently material to warrant adjustment.

b. Another invoice for $4,000 dated December 30, and bearing terms of f.o.b. shipping point. The goods arrived on December 31 and were included in the physical inventory taken that day. The invoice was not received until January 8 and was entered as a January transaction.

   This error should be corrected because the inclusion of the goods in the physical inventory without recognition of the liability has caused an error of $4,000 in pretax income for the year. Since the current liabilities are understated, both the amount of working capital and the current ratio are exaggerated. The owners' equity is also over-

FIGURE 16–1

The Palermo Company Limited
Unrecorded Accounts Payable   M-1-1
December 31, 1979

Invoice Date	No.	Vendor and Description	Account Charged	Amount
Dec. 31, 79	2851	Hayes Mfg. Co. Ltd. – invoice & shipment in transit	Inventories	10 650 00
—	—	Fox & Williams – unpaid legal fees – see M-4	Legal Expense	1 000 00
Dec. 28, 79	428	Hart & Co. Ltd. – machinery repairs (paid Jan. 18, 80)	Repairs Exp.	12 600 00
Dec. 31, 79	—	Allen Enterprises – Dec. 1979 account sales for consigned goods	Sales	25 680 00
—	—	Grant Co. Ltd. – shipment received Dec. 31, 79 per receiver no. 2907; invoice not yet received	Inventories	15 820 00
—	—	Arthur & Baker – earned but unpaid architect's fee for building under construction – see K-5	Construction in Progress	23 370 00
				89 120 00
				M-1

A.J.E. 8	131	Inventories	26 470 00	
	156	Construction in Progress	23 370 00	
	401	Sales	25 680 00	
	518	Legal Expense	1 000 00	
	527	Repairs Expense	12 600 00	
	203	Accounts Payable – Trade		89 120 00

To record unrecorded accounts payable at Dec. 31, 79.

Above payables were developed principally in the audit of accounts payable. See audit program B-4 for procedures employed. In my opinion, the $89,120 adjustment includes all material unrecorded accounts payable.

V.M.H.
Jan. 28, 80

stated. These facts point to the materiality of the omission and constitute strong arguments for an adjusting entry.

c. An invoice for $1,500 dated December 31 for a new office safe. The safe was installed on December 31, but the invoice was not recorded until paid on January 15. Since the transaction involved only asset and liability accounts, the omission of an entry did not affect net income. However, working capital and the current ratio are affected by the error since the debit affects a non-current asset and the credit affects a current liability. Most auditors would probably not propose an adjusting entry for this item.

d. An invoice for $3,000 dated December 31 for advertising services rendered during October, November, and December. The invoice was not recorded until paid on January 15.

   The argument for treating this item as sufficiently material to warrant adjustment is based on the fact that net income is affected, as well as the amount of working capital and the current ratio. The adjusting entry should probably be recommended in these circumstances.

The preceding examples suggest that a decision as to the materiality of an unrecorded transaction hinges to an important extent on whether the transaction affects net income. Assuming that an omitted transaction does affect net income and there is doubt as to whether the dollar amount is large enough to warrant adjustment, the auditors should bear in mind that approximately half of the effect of the error on net income is eliminated by the present high level of corporate income taxes. In other words, an adjusting entry to record an omitted expense item of $1,000 will reduce net income after income taxes by approximately $500. If the adjusting entry is not made, the only ultimate effect is a shift of $500 between the net income of two successive years. As a general rule, the auditors should avoid proposing adjusting entries for errors in the year-end cutoff of transactions unless the effect on the statements is clearly significant. However, it should be borne in mind that a number of insignificant individual errors may be material in their *cumulative* effect on the financial statements.

15. Determine proper balance sheet presentation of accounts payable.
Proper balance sheet presentation of accounts payable requires segregation of the following groups, if material:

a. Accounts payable to trade creditors.
b. Accounts payable to affiliates.
c. Accounts payable to directors, principal shareholders, officers, and employees.

Accounts payable secured by pledged assets should be disclosed in the balance sheet or a note thereto, and cross referenced to the pledged assets.

16.   *Obtain from client a letter of representations concerning liabilities.*
Most public accounting firms obtain written representations from clients concerning nearly all financial statement items. Although some accountants do not utilize representations by clients to this extent, it is standard practice to obtain a *liability representation* signed by responsible officers that all liabilities and contingent liabilities known to them are disclosed in the financial statements. Such a representation does not reduce the auditors' responsibility, but it often serves as an effective reminder to executives that management is primarily responsible for the fairness of financial statements.

OTHER LIABILITIES

Notes payable are discussed in the next chapter. In addition to the accounts payable previously considered, other important items in the current liability section of the balance sheet include:

a.   Amounts withheld from employees' pay.
b.   Sales taxes payable.
c.   Unclaimed wages.
d.   Customers' deposits.
e.   Liabilities for fines or other penalties.
f.   Accrued liabilities.

Amounts withheld from employees' pay

Payroll deductions are notoriously numerous; among the more important are unemployment insurance premiums and individual income taxes. Although the federal and provincial governments do not specify the exact form of records to be maintained, they do require that records of amounts earned and withheld be adequate to permit a determination of compliance with tax laws.

Income taxes withheld from employees' pay and not remitted as of the balance sheet date constitute a liability to be verified by the auditors. Accrued employer payroll taxes may be audited at the same time. This verification usually consists of tracing the amounts withheld to the payroll summary sheets, testing computations of taxes withheld and accrued, determining that taxes have been deposited or paid in accordance with the federal and provincial laws and regulations, and reviewing quarterly tax returns.

Payroll deductions also are often made for union dues, charitable contributions, retirement plans, insurance, savings bonds, and other purposes. Besides verifying the liability for any such amounts withheld from employees and not remitted as of the balance sheet date, the auditors should review the adequacy of the withholding procedures and determine that payroll deductions have been properly authorized and accurately computed.

Sales taxes payable

Business concerns are required to collect sales taxes imposed by federal and provincial governments. These taxes do not represent an expense to the business; the wholesaler and retailer merely act as collecting agents. Until the amounts collected from customers are remitted to the taxing authority, they constitute current liabilities of the business. The auditors' verification of this liability includes a review of the client's periodic tax returns. The reasonableness of the liability is also tested by a computation applying the tax rate to total taxable sales. In addition, the auditors should examine a number of sales invoices to ascertain that customers are being charged the correct amount of tax. Debits to the liability account for remittances to the taxing authority should be traced to copies of the tax returns and should be vouched to the paid cheques.

Unclaimed wages

Unclaimed wages are, by their very nature, subject to misappropriation. The auditors, therefore, are particularly concerned with the adequacy of internal control over this item. A list of unpaid wages should be prepared after each payroll distribution and recorded in the accounts. The payroll cheques should not be left for more than a few days in the payroll department. Prompt deposit in a special bank account provides much improved control. The auditors will analyze the Unclaimed Wages account for the purpose of determining that (1) the credits represent all unclaimed wages after each payroll distribution, and (2) the debits represent only authorized payments to employees, remittances to the government under unclaimed property laws, or transfers back to general cash funds through approved procedures.

Customers' deposits

Many business concerns require that customers make deposits on returnable containers, and public utilities and common carriers may require deposits to guarantee payments of bills or to cover equipment on loan to the customer. A review of the procedures followed in accepting and returning deposits should be made by the auditors with a view to disclosing any shortcomings in internal control. In some instances deposits shown by the records as refunded to customers may have been in fact abstracted by employees.

The verification, in addition to a review of procedures, should include obtaining a list of the individual deposits and a comparison of the total with the general ledger control account. If deposits are interest bearing, the amount of accrued interest should also be verified. As a general rule, the auditors do not attempt to confirm deposits by direct communication with customers; but this procedure is desirable if the amounts involved are substantial or the internal control procedures are considered to be deficient.

Liabilities for fines or other penalties

In Chapter 10 the point was made that the auditors must be familiar with federal and provincial laws and regulations that affect the client's financial statements. If the auditors discover that the client has apparently violated a law or regulation, they should discuss the matter with management and legal counsel of the client company and consider the possibility of a liability for a fine or penalty.

Penalties known as *liquidated damages* are often specified in a production contract in the event that scheduled delivery dates or performance specifications are not met for the product. The auditors should determine if the client is, or obviously will be, in violation of such contractual provisions; if so, the client should record a liability for the liquidated damages.

Accrued liabilities

Most accrued liabilities represent obligations payable sometime during the succeeding period for services or privileges received prior to the balance sheet date. Examples include interest payable, accrued property taxes, accrued payrolls and payroll taxes, income taxes payable, and amounts accrued under service guarantees.

Unlike accounts payable, which result from executed contracts, accrued liabilities pertain to services of a continuing nature, with the related expense often measured on a time basis. The basic auditing steps for accrued liabilities are:

1. Examine any contracts or other documents on hand which provide the basis for the accrual.
2. Appraise the accuracy of the detailed accounting records maintained for this category of liability.
3. Test the computations made by the client in setting up the accrual.
4. Determine that accrued liabilities have been treated consistently at the beginning and end of the period.

If the accounting records are well maintained and internal control is reasonably satisfactory, there is no need for the auditors to make an independent computation of accrued liabilities. They should merely review the methods employed in setting up the accruals and test the arithmetical accuracy of the computations made by the employees of the company.

Accrued property taxes. Property tax payments are usually few in number and substantial in amount. It is, therefore, feasible for the audit working papers to include an analysis showing all of the year's property tax transactions. Tax payments should be verified by inspection of the tax bills issued by governmental units and by reference to the related paid cheques. If the tax accruals at the balance sheet date differ significantly from those of prior years, an explanation of the variation should be obtained. It is of utmost importance that the auditors verify that tax bills have been received on all taxable property, or that an estimated tax has been accrued.

Accrued payrolls. The examination of payrolls from the standpoint of appraising the adequacy of internal controls and substantiating the expenditures for the period under audit is considered in Chapter 19. The present consideration of payrolls is limited to the procedures required for the verification of accrued payrolls at the balance sheet date.

Accrued gross salaries and wages appear on the balance sheets of virtually all concerns. The correctness of the amount accrued is significant in the determination of total liabilities and also in the proper matching of costs and revenue. The verification procedure consists principally of comparing the amounts accrued to the actual payroll of the subsequent period and reviewing the method of allocation at the balance sheet date. Payments made at the first payroll dates of the subsequent period are reviewed to determine that no unrecorded payroll liability existed as of the balance sheet date.

Pension plan accruals. Accounting for the cost of pension plans is highly complex. The auditors reviewing a client's pension costs and accruals should be familiar with the pronouncements on the subject in Section 3460 of the *CICA Handbook*.

Auditing procedures for the accrued liability for pension costs include a review of the pension plan copy in the permanent file, confirmation of the client's pension cost for the period by direct correspondence with the client's actuary, and analysis of the related liability account, including confirmation of payments to the trustee, if appropriate.

Accrued vacation pay. Closely related to accrued salaries and wages is the liability which may exist for accrued vacation pay. This type of liability arises from two situations: (1) an employee entitled by contract to a vacation during the past year may have been prevented from taking it by an emergency work schedule, and (2) an employee may be entitled to a future vacation of which part of the cost must be accrued to achieve a proper matching of costs and revenue.

The auditors' verification of accrued vacation pay may begin with a review of the permanent file copy of the employment contract or agreement stipulating vacation terms. The computation of the accrual should then be verified both as to arithmetical accuracy and for agreement with the terms of the company's vacation policy. The auditors should also ascertain whether the expense provision offsetting the vacation accrual qualifies as an income tax deduction. If not, income tax allocation will be required.

Service guarantees. The products of many companies are sold with a guarantee of free service or replacement during a rather extended warranty period. The costs of rendering such services should be recognized as expense in the year the product is sold rather than in a later year in which the replacement is made or repair service performed. If this policy is followed, the company will make an annual charge to expense and credit to a liability account based on the amount of the year's sales and the estimated future service or replacement. As repairs and replacements take place the costs will be charged to the liability account.

The auditors should review the client's annual provision for estimated future expenditures and compute the percentage relationship between the amount in the liability account and the amount of the year's sales. If this relationship varies sharply from year to year, the client should be asked for an explanation. The auditors should also review the charges month by month to the liability account and be alert for the "burial" of other expenses in this account. Sudden variations in the monthly charges to the liability account require investigation. In general, the auditors should determine that the balance in the liability account for service guarantees moves in reasonable relationship with the trend of sales and is properly segregated into current and long-term portions in the balance sheet.

Accrued commissions and bonuses. Accrued commissions to salesmen and bonuses payable to managerial personnel also require verification. The essential step in this case is reference to the authority for the commission or bonus. The basic contracts should be examined and traced to minutes of directors' meetings. If the bonus or commission is based on the total volume of sales or some other objective measure, the auditors should verify the computation of the accrual by applying the prescribed rate to the amount used as a base.

Income taxes payable. Federal, provincial, and foreign income taxes on corporations represent a material factor in determining both net income and financial position. The auditors cannot express an opinion on either the balance sheet or income statement of a corporation without first obtaining evidence that the provision for income taxes has been properly computed. In the audit of small- and medium-sized companies, it is customary for the audit engagement to include the preparation of the client's tax returns. If the income tax returns have been prepared by the client's staff or other persons, the auditors must nevertheless verify the reasonableness of the tax liability if they are to express an opinion on the fairness of the financial statements. In performing such a review of a tax return prepared by the client's staff or by others, the auditors may sometimes discover an opportunity for a tax saving which has been overlooked; obviously such a discovery tends to enhance the client's appreciation of the services rendered by the auditors. For businesses organized as single proprietorships or partnerships, no provision for income taxes appears on the income statement because taxes on the profits of these enterprises are payable by the individual owner or owners.

Taxable income often differs from pretax accounting income presented in the financial statements. If the difference between income as determined for tax purposes and income as determined by applying generally accepted accounting principles is substantial, allocation of income taxes is necessary to avoid a distortion of net income.

The auditors should analyze the Income Taxes Payable account and vouch all amounts to paid cheques, income tax returns, or other supporting documents. The final balance in the Income Taxes Payable account will ordinarily equal the computed federal, provincial, and foreign taxes on the current year's income tax returns, less any payments thereon.

Besides reviewing the computation of the income tax liability for the current year, the auditors should determine the date to which returns for prior years have been examined by taxing authorities, and the particulars of any disputes or additional assessments. Review of the income tax assessment notice is also an essential step. In the first audit of a new client, the auditors should review any prior years' tax returns not yet examined by the Department of National Revenue to make sure that there has been no substantial underpayment of taxes which would warrant presentation as a liability.

Accrued professional fees. Fees of professional firms include charges for the services of attorneys, public accountants, consulting engineers, and other specialists who often render services of a continuing nature but present bills only at infrequent intervals. By enquiry of officers and by review of corporate minutes, the auditors may learn of professional services received for which no liability has yet been reflected in the accounts. Review of the expense account for legal fees is always mandatory because it may reveal damage suits, tax disputes, or other litigation warranting disclosure in the financial statements. Fees of public accountants for periodic audits are properly reflected in the accounts of the year subsequent to the period under audit. Accruals are desirable, however, for any other accounting services completed but unbilled as of the balance sheet date.

Balance sheet presentation

Accrued expenses—interest, taxes, rent, and wages—are included in the current liability section of the balance sheet. These items are generally combined into one figure. However, any liability of material amount should be separately listed.

Federal, provincial, and foreign income taxes payable usually are material in amount and should be listed as a separate item. Although the tax liability usually is an estimated amount rather than a final determination, there is little justification for including the word "reserve" in the title of the income tax liability, or in any other liability of estimated amount. Neither is there any justification for placing so-called "liability reserves" midway between the liability and owners' equity sections, as has been done in some published financial statements. In short, liabilities should be clearly identified as such, regardless of whether the amount is precisely determined or merely estimated.

Deferred income taxes resulting from tax allocations should be classified as current liabilities if they relate to current assets. Otherwise, deferred income taxes are classified as long term.

Deferred credits to revenue for such items as rent or interest collected in advance that will be taken into earnings in the succeeding period are customarily included in current liabilities. Deposits on contracts and similar advances from customers also are accorded the status of current liabilities because the receipt of an advance increases the current assets total, and because the goods to be used in liquidating the advance are generally included in current assets.

Time of examination

The nature and amount of trade accounts payable may change greatly within a few weeks' time; consequently, the auditors' verification of these rapidly changing liabilities is most effective when performed immediately after the balance sheet date. As stressed at the beginning of this chapter, failure to record a liability will cause an overstatement of financial position; if audit work on accounts payable is performed prior to the balance sheet date, the possibility exists that the client may fail to record important liabilities coming into existence during the remaining weeks of the year under audit. For this reason many auditors believe that most of the audit work on accounts payable should be performed after the balance sheet date. Certainly, the auditors' search for unrecorded liabilities must be made after the balance sheet date, because this search is concentrated on the transactions occurring during the first few weeks of the new year.

Some current liability accounts other than accounts payable are more suitable for preliminary audit work. The documents relating to accrued property taxes, for example, may be available in advance of the balance sheet date. Amounts withheld from employees' pay can be reviewed before the end of the year. The propriety of amounts withheld and of amounts remitted to the tax authorities during the year can be verified before the pressure of year-end work begins. The working papers relating to such liability accounts then may be completed very quickly after the end of the accounting period.

KEY TERMS INTRODUCED OR EMPHASIZED IN CHAPTER 16

confirmation   A type of documentary evidence which is created outside the client organization and transmitted directly to the auditors.

consignment   A transfer of goods from the owner to another person who acts as the sales agent of the owner.

liquidated damages   Penalties specified in a production contract in the event that scheduled delivery dates or performance specifications are not met for the product.

subsequent period   The time extending from the balance sheet date to the date of the auditors' report.

trade accounts payable   Current liabilities arising from the purchase of goods and services from trade creditors, generally evidenced by invoices or statements received from the creditors.

voucher   A document authorizing a cash disbursement. A voucher usually provides space for employees performing various approval functions to initial. The term "voucher" may also be applied to the group of supporting documents used as a basis for recording liabilities or for making cash disbursements.

voucher register   A special journal used in a voucher system to record liabilities requiring cash payment in the near future. Every liability recorded in a voucher register corresponds to a voucher authorizing future payment.

GROUP I
REVIEW QUESTIONS

16–1.   Identify at least three audit procedures (other than "Search for unrecorded accounts payable") which are concerned directly or indirectly with disclosing unrecorded accounts payable.

16–2.   What use should be made of monthly statements for vendors by personnel in the accounts payable department?

16–3.   Is the confirmation of accounts payable by direct communication with vendors as useful and important an audit procedure as is the confirmation of accounts receivable? Explain fully. (AICPA)

16–4.   During the verification of the individual invoices comprising the total of accounts payable at the balance sheet date, the auditors discovered some receiving reports indicating that the merchandise covered by several of these invoices was not received until after the balance sheet date. What action should the auditors take?

16–5.   What do you consider to be the most important single procedure in the auditors' search for unrecorded accounts payable? Explain.

16–6.   Whitehall Co. Ltd. records its liabilities in accounts payable subsidiary ledgers. The auditors decided to select some of the accounts for confirmation by direct communication with vendors. The largest volume of purchases during the year had been made from Ranchero Ltd., but at the balance sheet date this account had a zero balance. Under these circumstances should the auditors send a confirmation request to Ranchero Ltd. or would they accomplish more by limiting their confirmation program to accounts with large year-end balances?

16–7.   What audit procedure would you recommend for the verification of balances owed to affiliated companies?

16–8.   During an audit, is a CA firm concerned with invoices and debit memoranda recorded during the period subsequent to the balance sheet date? Explain.

16–9.   Outline a procedure by which the auditors may determine the accuracy of any amounts owed to consignors.

16–10.   Outline the procedure you would follow in verifying accrued tax liabilities relating to payrolls.

16–11.   Compare the auditors' approach to the verification of liabilities with their approach to the verification of assets.

16–12.   What are "liquidated damages"?

16–13.   Describe two changes in the traditional processing procedures for accounts payable which have been brought about by the increased use of electronic computers.

16–14.   Most auditors are interested in performing as many phases of an examination as possible in advance of the balance sheet date. The verification of accounts payable, however, generally is regarded as something to be done after the balance sheet date. What specific factors can you suggest that make the verification of accounts payable less suitable than many other accounts for interim work?

16–15.   If accounts with a few creditors represent the major portion of the total outstanding accounts payable, what special verification would you suggest for these accounts?

16–16.   The operating procedures of a well-managed accounts payable department will provide for the verification of several specific points before a vendor's invoice is recorded as an approved liability. What are the points requiring verification?

16–17. List the major responsibilities of an accounts payable department.

16–18. Would you, as an auditor, take exception to the practice followed by some small businesses of not recording invoices until the time of payment?

16–19. In achieving adequate internal control over operations of the accounts payable department, a company should establish procedures that will ensure that extensions and footings are proved on all invoices, and that the propriety of prices is reviewed. What is the most effective means of assuring consistent performance of these duties?

16–20. Which do you consider the more significant step in establishing strong internal control over accounts payable transactions: the approval of an invoice for payment, or the issuance of a cheque in payment of an invoice? Explain.

16–21. Outline a method by which the auditors may test the propriety of cash discounts taken on accounts payable.

16–22. For what documents relating to the accounts payable operation would you recommend the use of serial numbers as an internal control procedure?

16–23. What internal control procedure would you recommend to call attention to failure to pay invoices within the discount period?

16–24. As part of the investigation of accounts payable, auditors sometimes vouch entries in selected creditors' accounts back through the journals to original documents, such as purchase orders, receiving reports, invoices, and paid cheques. What is the principal purpose of this procedure?

GROUP II
QUESTIONS REQUIRING ANALYSIS

16–25. The *subsequent period* in an audit is the time extending from the balance sheet date to the date of the auditors' report.

Required:

Discuss the importance of the subsequent period in the audit of trade accounts payable.

16–26. Danville Ltd., your new audit client, purchases the bulk of its stock in trade from Maryville Ltd. Under a contractual agreement with Maryville, Danville's accounts payable to Maryville are deferred indefinitely so long as Danville maintains inventories of at least $100,000; however, title to all merchandise passes to Danville at the date Maryville ships the goods. May you express an unqualified opinion on Danville's balance sheet which includes inventories of $150,000 among current assets and accounts payable to Maryville Ltd. of $50,000 among long-term liabilities? Explain.

16–27. The partnership of Riggs and Baker has followed the policy of paying pensions to selected employees who retire after long service with the company. The amount of the pension has in most cases been approximately half the salary rate of the employee at the date of retirement, but the partners have varied this method of computation in accordance with the personal circumstances of the retiring employee and the overall value of the employee's services to the company. At present there are 35 employees who have been with the company for more than 15 years, and who will presumably continue until they reach retirement age. One of the partners asks you whether the balance sheet of the company should include a liability for the estimated amount to be paid to these employees as pensions.

16–28. CA has been the auditor of X Ltd., a medium-sized clothing retailer with six stores, for several years. Each store has its own inventory and the inventories at the stores comprise all of X Ltd.'s inventory. Invoices for inventory purchases are paid by a central office and are approved for payment only after they are matched with receiving slips sent in from the stores.

Every year, CA has verified X Ltd.'s accounts receivable by direct communication with debtors. However, accounts payable (which consists of about 200 accounts) have been verified by checking creditors' statements to the records rather than by direct communication with creditors.

This year, on reviewing his audit program, CA decided that he should use direct communication in verifying accounts payable. He conveyed this decision to X, the manager and principal shareholder of X Ltd., when they were making arrangements for the annual visit of CA's staff. X has never been happy about CA's direct communication with debtors but over the years had gradually accepted the need for it. When he learned that CA now planned to communicate directly with creditors, he was furious. "Why," he said, "would you want to communicate with creditors when you have statements from them for almost all of the accounts and certainly all of the larger ones? You've asked us to keep the statements that come in and we've gone out of our way to do so but now you're saying they're not good enough. I've gone along with you writing to our debtors because they don't send out statements, but our creditors do. What you're proposing would only serve to remind our creditors that we owe them money and there are some I don't want to remind because then we'll have to pay them faster. Anyway, I understand your main purpose in verifying accounts payable is to detect unrecorded liabilities, not that there would be any, and surely communicating with existing creditors is not going to help you do that. I can see why you have to verify acounts receivable this way, but accounts payable are completely different. Besides, it'll cost me more money because it will take you more time to do the audit."

Required:

The points CA would make in replying to X. Cover both *theoretical* and *practical* points. (CICA)

16–29. Overland Ltd. engaged you to perform a year-end audit for the year 1979. The pretax income for the year was approximately $800,000 and retained earnings on December 31, 1979, amounted to $610,000. The company has filed a federal income tax return for 1979 indicating a total tax of $400,000, of which $320,000 had been paid on an "estimated tax" basis prior to the end of 1979. In addition, you find that the tax department has disallowed part of the depreciation deductions claimed in 1976 and 1977 on certain equipment. The additional income tax liability resulting from the disallowances in 1976 and 1977 amounts to $50,000. The depreciation claimed in returns filed for 1976 through 1979 was on a consistent basis. Upon examination by the tax department of the years 1978 and 1979, the anticipated disallowances will result in a further additional income tax liability for each year of $20,000. Your examination disclosed no questionable items other than depreciation deductions.

Required:

Give the balance sheet presentation of the federal income taxes payable in the following situation:

a. The company has agreed to the disallowances and has accepted but not paid the tax department assessment of $50,000.
b. The company has been advised by its counsel that the disallowances are improper and has notified the tax department that the disallowances will be contested. (AICPA, adapted)

16–30. Compare the confirmation of accounts receivable with the confirmation of accounts payable under the following headings:

a. Generally accepted auditing procedures. (Justify the differences revealed by your comparison.)
b. Selection of accounts to be confirmed. (AICPA, adapted)

16–31. In connection with their examination of the financial statements of Davis Ltd., the auditors reviewed the Federal Income Taxes Payable account.

Required:

a. Discuss reasons why the auditors should review the federal income tax returns for prior years and the assessment notices.
b. What information will these reviews provide? (Do not discuss specific tax return items.) (AICPA, adapted)

16–32. During the course of any audit, the auditors are always alert for unrecorded accounts payable or other unrecorded liabilities.

Required:

For each of the following audit areas, (1) describe an unrecorded liability which might be discovered, and (2) state what auditing procedure(s) might bring it to light.

a. Construction in progress (property, plant, and equipment).
b. Prepaid insurance.
c. License authorizing the client to produce a product patented by another company.
d. Minutes of directors' meetings.

16–33. Describe the audit steps that generally would be followed in establishing the propriety of the recorded liability for federal income taxes of a corporation which you are auditing for the first time. Consideration should be given the status of (a) the liability for prior years and (b) the liability arising from the current year's taxable income. (AICPA)

16–34. In the course of your initial examination of the financial statements of Sylvan Ltd., you ascertain that of the substantial amount of accounts payable outstanding at the close of the period, approximately 75 percent is owing to six creditors. You have requested that you be permitted to confirm the balances owing to these six creditors by communicating with the creditors, but the president of the company is unwilling to approve your request on the grounds that correspondence in regard to the balances—all of which contain some overdue items—might give rise to demands on the part of the creditors for immediate payment of the overdue items and thereby embarrass Sylvan.

In the circumstances, what alternative procedure would you adopt in an effort to satisfy yourself that the accounting records show the correct amounts payable to these creditors? (AICPA, adapted)

16–35. Select the best answer for each of the following and explain fully the reason for selection.

a. Bell Company's accounts payable clerk has a brother who is one of Bell's vendors. The brother will often invoice Bell twice for the same delivery. The accounts payable clerk removes the receiving report for the first invoice from the paid voucher file and uses it for support of payment for the duplicate invoice. The most effective procedure for preventing this activity is to—

(1) Use prenumbered receiving reports.

(2) Mail signed cheques without allowing them to be returned to the accounts payable clerk.

(3) Cancel vouchers and supporting papers when payment is made.

(4) Use dual signatures on cheques.

b. Only one of the following four statements, which compare confirmation of accounts payable with suppliers and confirmation of accounts receivable with debtors, is true. The true statement is that—

(1) Confirmation of accounts payable with suppliers is a more widely accepted auditing procedure than is confirmation of accounts receivable with debtors.

(2) Statistical sampling techniques are more widely accepted in the confirmation of accounts payable than in the confirmation of accounts receivable.

(3) As compared to the confirmation of accounts payable, the confirmation of accounts receivable will tend to emphasize accounts with zero balances at balance sheet date.

(4) It is less likely that the confirmation request sent to the sup-

plier company will show the amount owed it than that the request sent to the debtor company will show the amount due from it.

c. As part of the search for unrecorded liabilities, the auditors examine invoices and accounts payable vouchers. In general this examination may be limited to—

    (1) Unpaid accounts payable vouchers and unvouched invoices on hand at the balance sheet date.

    (2) Accounts payable vouchers prepared during the subsequent period and unvouchered invoices received through the last day of field work whose dollar values exceed reasonable amounts.

    (3) Invoices received through the last day of field work (whether or not accounts payable vouchers have been prepared), but must include all invoices of any amount received during this period.

    (4) A reasonable period following the balance sheet date, normally the same period used for the cutoff bank statement.

d. The auditors learn that the client has paid a vendor twice for the same shipment—once based upon the original invoice and once based upon the monthly statement. A control procedure that should have prevented this duplicate payment is:

    (1) Attachment of the receiving report of the disbursement support.

    (2) Prenumbering of disbursement vouchers.

    (3) Use of a limit or reasonable test.

    (4) Prenumbering of receiving reports. (AICPA, adapted)

GROUP III PROBLEMS

16–36. James Rowe, CA, is the independent auditor of Raleigh Corporation Ltd. Rowe is considering the audit work to be performed in the accounts payable area for the current year's engagement.

    The prior-year's working papers show that confirmation requests were mailed to 100 of Raleigh's 1,000 suppliers. The selected suppliers were based on Rowe's sample that was designed to select accounts with large dollar balances. A substantial number of hours was spent by Raleigh employees and by Rowe resolving relatively minor differences between the confirmation replies and Raleigh's accounting records. Alternate audit procedures were used for those suppliers that did not respond to the confirmation requests.

Required:

a. Identify the accounts payable audit objectives that Rowe must consider in determining the audit procedures to be followed.

b. Identify situations when Rowe should use accounts payable confirmations and discuss whether Rowe is required to use them.

c. Discuss why the use of large dollar balances as the basis for selecting accounts payable for confirmation might not be the most efficient approach, and indicate what more efficient procedures could be followed when selecting accounts payable for confirmation. (AICPA, adapted)

16–37. Nancy Howe, your staff assistant on the April 30, 1979, audit of Wilcox Ltd., has been transferred to another audit engagement before she could complete the audit of unrecorded accounts payable. Her working paper, which you have reviewed and are satisfied is complete, is on page 656.

Required:

Prepare a proposed adjusting journal entry for the unrecorded accounts payable of Wilcox at April 30, 1979. The amounts are material. (Do not deal with income taxes.)

16–38. In 1979 your client, Video Corporation Ltd., was licensed to manufacture a patented type of television tube. The licensing agreement called for royalty payments of 10 cents for each tube manufactured. What procedures would you follow in connection with your regular annual audit as of December 31, 1979, to obtain evidence that the liability for royalties is correctly stated? (AICPA, adapted)

16–39. You are engaged in auditing the financial statements of Bay Ltd., a large independent contractor. All employees are paid in cash because Bay's controller believes this arrangement reduces clerical expenses and is preferred by the employees.

During the audit you find in the petty cash fund approximately $500, of which $485 is stated to be unclaimed wages. Further investigation reveals that the controller has installed the procedure of putting any unclaimed wages in the petty cash fund so that the cash can be used for disbursements. When the claimant to the wages appears, he is paid from the petty cash fund. The controller contends that this procedure reduces the number of cheques drawn to replenish the petty cash fund and centres the responsibility for all cash on hand in one person, inasmuch as the petty cash custodian distributes the pay envelopes.

Required:

a. Does Bay Ltd.'s system provide proper internal control of unclaimed wages? Explain fully.

b. Because Bay's controller insists on paying salaries in cash, what procedures would you recommend to provide better internal control over unclaimed wages? (AICPA, adapted)

16–40. You were in the final stages of your examination of the financial statements of Scott Corporation Ltd. for the year ended December 31, 1979, when you were consulted by the corporation's president, who believes there is no point to your examining the 1980 voucher register and testing data in support of 1979 entries. He stated that (a) bills

Wilcox Ltd.

Unrecorded Accounts Payable   M-1-1

April 30, 1979

Invoice Date	Vendor and Description	Amount
	Hill & Harper – unpaid legal fees at Apr. 30, 79 (see attorney letter at M-4)	1 000 – ↵
Apr. 1, 79	Drew Insurance Agency – unpaid premium on fire insurance for period Apr. 1, 79 – Mar. 31, 82 (see insurance broker letter at J-1-1)	1 800 – ↵
Apr. 30, 79	Mays and Sage, Stockbrokers – advice for 100 shares of Madison Ltd. common stock (settlement date May 7, 79)	2 125 – ↵
	Lane Ltd. – shipment received Apr. 30, 79 per receiver no. 3361 and included in Apr. 30, 79 physical inventory; invoice not yet received (amount is per purchase order)	5 863 – ↵
		10 788 –

↵ – Examined document described.

    In my opinion, the $10,788 adjustment includes all material unrecorded accounts payable.

                                                n. a. w.
                                            May 29, 79

pertaining to 1979 which were received too late to be included in the December voucher register were recorded as of the year-end by the corporation by journal entry, (*b*) the internal auditors made tests after the year-end, and (*c*) he would furnish you with a letter representing that there were no unrecorded liabilities.

Required:

a. Should the independent auditors' test for unrecorded liabilities be affected by the fact that the client made a journal entry to record 1979 bills which were received late? Explain.

b. Should the independent auditors' test for unrecorded liabilities be affected by the fact that a letter is obtained in which a responsible management official represents that to the best of his knowledge all liabilities have been recorded? Explain.

c. Should the independent auditors' test for unrecorded liabilities be eliminated or reduced because of the internal audit tests? Explain.

d. Assume that the client company, which handled some government contracts, had no internal auditors but that auditors for a federal agency spent three weeks auditing the records and were just completing their work at this time. How would the independent auditors' unrecorded liability test be affected by the work of the auditors for a federal agency?

e. What sources in addition to the 1980 voucher register should the independent auditors consider to locate possible unrecorded liabilities? (AICPA, adapted)

17

Interest-bearing debt and interest expense; disclosure of contingencies

Business enterprises obtain substantial amounts of their financial resources by borrowing. Short-term bank loans, evidenced by notes payable, commonly are used to finance inventories and other short-term working capital requirements; commercial paper also may be used for this purpose. Closely held companies also may borrow on a short-term basis from shareholders, directors, or officers. Purchases of small components of plant assets may be financed on an installment credit basis, including a lease which is in substance an installment purchase. Long-term debt, issued either to the public or to an institutional investor in a *private placement*, often is incurred to finance the purchase of another company or of substantial amounts of plant and equipment. The judicious use of debt financing in conjunction with equity financing and resources provided by profitable operations enables a business to maximize the return on its assets.

A business with an excellent credit reputation may find it possible to borrow from a bank on a simple unsecured note. A business of lesser financial standing may find that the obtaining of bank credit requires the pledging of specific assets as collateral; or that it must agree to certain restrictive covenants, such as the suspension of dividends and other protective provisions during the term of the loan; or that a loan is obtainable only if the signature of a cosigner of greater financial strength can be obtained on the note. The issuance of notes payable in the settlement of past-due accounts payable obviously is an indication of serious financial weakness.

Long-term debt usually is substantial in amount and often extends for periods of 30 years or more. Debentures, secured bonds, and notes payable (sometimes secured by mortgages or trust deeds) are the principal types of long-term debt. Debentures are backed only by the general credit of the issuing corporation and not by liens on specific assets. Since in most respects debentures have the characteristics of other corporate bonds, we shall use the term *bonds* to include both debentures and secured bonds payable.

The formal document creating bonded indebtedness is called the *indenture* or *trust indenture*. When creditors supply capital on a long-term basis, they often insist upon placing certain restrictions on the company. For example, the indenture often provides that a company may not declare dividends unless the amount of working capital is maintained above a specified amount. The acquisition of plant and equipment, or the increase of managerial salaries, may be permitted only if the current ratio is maintained at a specified level and if net income reaches a designated amount. Another device for protecting the long-term creditor is the requirement of a sinking fund or redemption fund to be held by a trustee. If these restrictions are violated, the indenture may provide that the entire debt is due on demand.

Fashions change in securities as for merchandise and services. For example, in some years convertible subordinate debentures have been popular; in other years, few convertible securities have been issued. These securities are subordinate to other types of creditors' claims and may be converted into common stock in a specified ratio at the option of the holder. A full description of these special features, such as the conversion privilege, should be presented in the notes accompanying the financial statements.

The auditors' objectives in examination of interest-bearing debt

The objectives of the auditors in their examination of interest-bearing debt are to determine that (*a*) internal controls are adequate; (*b*) all interest-bearing debt of the client has been recorded and represents bona fide obligations issued in accordance with federal and provincial laws; (*c*) interest payable and interest expense have been accurately computed, including the amortization of bond discount or premium; (*d*) the client company has met all requirements and restrictions imposed upon it by debt contracts; and (*e*) the interest-bearing debt and related expenses are properly presented in the financial statements and adequate informative disclosure is achieved.

Internal control over interest-bearing debt

Authorization by the board of directors. Effective internal control over interest-bearing debt begins with the authorization to incur the debt.

The by-laws of a corporation usually require that borrowing be approved by the board of directors. The treasurer of the corporation will prepare a report on any proposed financing, explaining the need for funds, the estimated effect of borrowing upon future earnings, the estimated financial position of the company in comparison with others in the industry both before and after the borrowing, and alternative methods of raising the amount desired. Authorization by the board of directors will include review and approval of such matters as the choice of a bank, the type of security, the choice of a trustee, registration with the securities commission, agreements with investment bankers, compliance with requirements of the laws of incorporation, and listing of bonds on a securities exchange. After the issuance of long-term debt, the board of directors should receive a report stating the net amount received and its disposition, as for acquisition of plant assets, addition to working capital, or other purposes.

Use of an independent trustee.   Bond issues are always for large amounts—usually many millions of dollars. Therefore, only large companies issue bonds; small companies obtain long-term capital through mortgage loans or other sources. Any company large enough to issue bonds and find a ready market for the securities will almost always utilize the services of a large bank as an independent trustee.

The trustee is charged with the protection of the creditors' interests and must continually review the issuing company's compliance with the provisions of the indenture. Besides, the trustee maintains detailed records of the names and addresses of the registered owners of the bonds, cancels old bond certificates and issues new ones when bonds change ownership, follows procedures to prevent over issuance of bond certificates, distributes interest payments, and distributes principal payments when the bonds mature. Each individual bond issued bears a "certificate of authentication" signed by the trustee. Use of an independent trustee thus largely eliminates the problem of internal control over bonds payable. Internal control is strengthened by the fact that the trustee does not have access to the issuing company's assets or accounting records, and because the trustee is always a large financial institution of unquestionable integrity with legal responsibility for its activities.

In the rare instances that a trustee is not employed, bonds should be serially numbered by the printer and kept in the custody of an officer of the corporation. At least two specified corporate officers should be required to sign each bond certificate before it becomes a negotiable instrument; signing and countersigning should not take place until the time for issuance.

An official of the corporation who does not have access to bond certificates should be given direct responsibility for maintaining the required accounting records of bond transactions and bond ownership. Even though the services of an independent trustee are employed, the issuing company usually will maintain a bond or note register to show the amount of the indebtedness issued, cancelled, and currently outstanding. If the loan is obtained directly from a bank, insurance company, or other single creditor, there is, of course, no need for such subsidiary records; the original amount of the loan and any subsequent reductions can be recorded in a general ledger account.

Proper authorization procedures are important for the redemption or cancellation of bonds, as well as for the original issuance of the securities. If the company employs a trustee, the reacquired certificates may be destroyed by the trustee and a cremation certificate issued to the company. If bonds are reacquired directly by the issuing company, they should be cancelled and attached to the stubs in the certificate book. All certificate numbers should be accounted for periodically and at the final redemption of the issue. The authorization procedures should also provide for bonds reacquired for a sinking fund. These customarily are turned over to the trustee; but in any event, the acquisition should be reflected in the accounts of the issuing company.

Interest payments on bonds, notes, and mortgages or trust deeds. The auditors' appraisal of internal controls relating to bonds, notes, and mortgages or trust deeds also must extend to the handling of interest payments. In the case of a note, mortgage, or trust deed, there may be only one recipient of interest, and the disbursement may be controlled in the same manner as other cash payments. For widely distributed issues of ***registered bonds,*** the issuing company (or trustee) maintains records of the names and addresses of all bondholders. Interest cheques may then be prepared and addressed by a computer master file. The custody, use, and making of changes in such a master file should be controlled carefully.

In the case of ***bearer bonds,*** interest coupons attached to the bonds provide an effective means of control. As the coupons are presented for payment, they are cancelled and preserved in a specially designed book. The total cash disbursements for interest then may be reconciled to the number of coupons collected. This approach should be supplemented by the maintenance of standard controls over the signing and issuance of interest cheques.

Many corporations assign the entire problem of paying interest to the trustee. Highly effective control is then achieved, since the company will issue a single cheque for the full amount of the periodic interest payment. Upon receipt of this cheque the trustee will make payment for coupons presented, cancel the coupons, and file them numerically. A second count of the coupons is made at a later date; the coupons then are destroyed and a cremation certificate delivered to the issuing company. The trustee does not attempt to maintain a list of the holders of coupon bonds, since these securities are transferable by the mere act of delivery. If certain coupons are not presented for payment, the trustee will hold the funds corresponding to such coupons for the length of time prescribed by statute. In the case of registered bonds, the trustee will maintain a current list of holders and will remit interest cheques to them in the same manner as dividend cheques are distributed to shareholders.

Audit working papers for interest-bearing debt

A copy of the indenture relating to a bond issued should be placed in the permanent file. Analyses of ledger accounts for notes and bonds payable, and the related accounts for interest and discount or premium, should be obtained for the current working papers file or the permanent file. A grouping sheet is seldom required for short-term notes payable or for long-term debt.

AUDIT PROGRAM FOR INTEREST-BEARING DEBT

This audit program does not provide for the usual distinction between substantive testing and the study and evaluation of internal control. After the auditors have obtained a description of the client's system of internal control over interest-bearing debt, they usually do not conduct tests of compliance. Rather, since transactions are few in number but large in dollar amount, the auditors may follow the approach of substantiating the individual transactions. Thus, the audit program for interest-bearing debt consists primarily of substantive tests.

Audit procedures appropriate for the verification of interest-bearing debt include the following:

1. Obtain or prepare a description of internal control over interest-bearing debt.
2. Obtain or prepare analyses of interest-bearing debt accounts and related interest, premium, and discount accounts.
3. Examine copies of notes and mortgages or trust deeds payable.
4. Obtain copy of indenture for bonds payable and review its important provisions.
5. Trace authority for issuance of interest-bearing debt to the corporate minutes.
6. Vouch interest-bearing debt transactions for the year to supporting documents.
7. Confirm interest-bearing debt with appropriate third parties.
8. Examine treasury bonds and reconcile to the general ledger.
9. Verify computation of interest expense, interest payable, and amortization of discount or premium.
10. Determinine that all provisions of the indenture have been met.

11. Determine that debt issuance is in accordance with applicable securities laws.
12. Review notes paid or renewed since the balance sheet date.
13. Determine proper financial statement presentation of interest-bearing debt and related transactions.

1. Obtain or prepare a description of internal control over interest-bearing debt.

The study and evaluation of the client's internal control over interest-bearing debt often will involve the preparation of a written description and a flowchart, as well as the filling in of an internal control questionnaire. Some of the typical questions in this questionnaire are the following: Are interest-bearing liabilities incurred only under authorization of the board of directors? Is an independent trustee retained to account for all bond issuances, cancellations, and interest payments? Has the board of directors specified banks from which loans may be obtained? The questionnaire serves to remind the auditors of matters which should be investigated fully; the filling in of yes and no answers to the questions in itself is not a significant audit procedure.

2. Obtain or prepare analyses of interest-bearing debt accounts and related interest, premium, and discount accounts.

A working paper analysis for notes payable is very similar to the analysis of notes receivable illustrated in Chapter 13 (Figure 13–3). A notes payable analysis shows the beginning balance, if any, of each individual notes; additional notes issued and payments on notes during the year; and the ending balance of each note. In addition, the beginning balances of interest payable or prepaid interest, interest expense, interest paid, and ending balances of interest payable or prepaid interest, are presented in the analysis working paper.

An analysis of the Notes Payable account will serve a number of purposes: (a) the payment or other disposition of notes listed as outstanding in the previous year's audit can be verified; (b) the propriety of individual debits and credits can be established; and (c) the validity of the year-end balance of the account is proved through the step-by-step verification of all changes in the account during the year. Such a detailed analysis of notes payable is feasible and justified because normally there are not very many transactions and the dollar amounts are relatively large. Analysis of the Notes Payable account also will give the auditors an understanding of the purposes for which the company utilizes notes payable, and will enable them to form an opinion as to the quality of the accounting routines followed.

In the first audit of a client, the auditor will analyze the ledger accounts for Bonds Payable, Bond Issue Costs, and Bond Discount (or Bond Premium) for the entire period since the bonds were issued. A working

FIGURE 17–1

Bonds Payable, Bond Issue Costs, and Bond Discount   U-6

9%, 20-Year Debenture due July 1, 97   December 31, 1978

Date				Bonds Payable Acct. No. 220	Bond Issue Costs Acct. No. 185	Bond Discount Acct. No. 221
July 1, 77	Issue at 98 to underwriting syndicate	X		10 000 000 — ⁴		200 000 — ⁴
July 2, 77	Bond issue costs paid:					
	Printing charges				3 500 — ⁴	
	Legal fees				5 000 — ⁴	
	Audit fees				5 500 — ⁴	
	Securities Commission registration fee				2 000 —	
				10 000 000 —	16 000 —	200 000 —
July 1 – Dec. 31, 77	"Interest method" amortization of discount – at 3.088% semiannual rate					(2 624 —) ⁴
	Straight-line amortization of issue costs				(400 —) ⁴	
	Balances Dec. 31, 77	C-1		10 000 000 — C	15 600 —	197 376 —
Jan. 1 – Dec. 31, 78	Amortization as above				(800 —) ⁴	(5 494 —) ⁴
	Balances Dec. 31, 78	C-1		10 000 000 — C	14 800 —	191 882 —

⁴ — Traced net proceeds to cash receipts records.
X — Traced authorization to minutes of May 22, 77, directors'
    meeting (U-3); see U-6-1 for copy of Prospectus filed
    with the Securities Commission.
⁴ — Vouched to paid cheque and invoice or statement.
⁴ — Computation verified (amortization methods are in
    accordance with directors' resolution of July 22, 77).
C — Confirmed.

U. M. H.
Jan. 5, 78
Jan. 3, 79

paper used in analyzing the Bonds Payable, Bond Issue Costs, and Bond Discount accounts is illustrated in Figure 17–1. This working paper is placed in the auditors' permanent file; in subsequent examinations any further entries in the accounts may be added to the analysis. In this way the preparation of detailed analyses of these accounts during each repeat engagement is avoided. This practice is appropriate because these accounts usually change very little over a period of years. On the other hand, Interest Expense and Interest Payable are more active accounts which should, therefore, be analyzed separately during each engagement.

An analysis of the Mortgages Payable account also should be designed in a form permitting the addition of information in subsequent years, and should be made part of the permanent audit file. The analysis should include a detailed description of the mortgage or trust deed, the total initial amount, installment payments, and the balance outstanding.

If the analysis of interest-bearing debt is prepared by the client's employees, the auditors should compare the individual items listed with entries in the detailed records. The footings of the analyses should be proved and compared with the balances of the control accounts in the general ledger. In addition, the footings of the control accounts should be tested. Any discrepancy between the auditors' analysis and the balances of the control accounts must be investigated, of course. Common causes of such discrepancies include failure to enter installment payments in the detailed records and making credit entries to the control account for the net proceeds, rather than for the face amount, when notes are issued with interest included in the face amount.

3. Examine copies of notes and mortgages or trust deeds payable.

The auditors should examine the client's copies of notes payable and mortgages and trust deeds payable as of the balance sheet date. The original documents will of course be in the possession of the respective payees; but the auditors should make certain that the client has retained copies of the debt instruments, and that their details correspond to the analyses obtained in the second procedure of this audit program.

4. Obtain copy of indenture for bonds payable and review its important provisions.

In the first audit of a client or upon the issuance of a new bond issue, the auditors will obtain a copy of the bond indenture for the permanent file. The indenture should be carefully studied, with particular attention to such points as the amount of bonds authorized, interest rates and dates, maturity dates, descriptions of property pledged as collateral, provisions for retirement or conversion, duties and responsibilities of the trustee, and any restrictions imposed on the borrowing company.

5. Trace authority for issuance of interest-bearing debt to the corporate minutes.

The authority to issue interest-bearing debt generally lies in the board of directors. To determine that the bonds outstanding were properly authorized, the auditors should read the passages in the minutes of directors' (and shareholders') meetings concerning the issuance of debt. The minutes usually will cite the applicable sections of the corporate by-laws permitting the issuance of debt instruments, and may also contain reference to the opinion of the company's counsel concerning the legality of the issue. Such information should then be traced by the auditors to the original sources. Adequate comments should be prepared for the audit working papers showing the extent of the auditors' investigation of authorization for the debt issue.

6.   Vouch interest-bearing debt transactions for the year to supporting documents.

The auditors must obtain evidence that transactions in interest-bearing debt accounts were valid. To accomplish this objective, the auditors trace the cash received from the issuance of notes, bonds, or mortgages to the validated copy of the bank deposit slip and to the bank statement. Any remittance advices supporting these cash receipts are also examined.

The auditors can find further support for the net proceeds of a bond issue by reference to the underwriting contract and to the prospectus filed with the securities commission. In a private placement of a debt issue, the principal supporting document usually is a contract between the issuer and the institutional investor. In either a public or private offering of debt, where the issuing costs are paid separately the difference between the net proceeds and the face amount of the debt represents the discount or premium on the debt. The auditors vouch bond issue costs to supporting paid cheques and to invoices or statements from attorneys, CAs, printers, and the securities commission.

Debits to a Notes Payable or a Mortgages Payable account generally represent payments in full or in installments. The auditors should examine paid cheques for these payments; in so doing, they also will account for payments of accrued interest. The propriety of installment payments should be verified by reference to the repayment schedule set forth in the note or mortgage copy in the client's possession.

A comparison of cancelled notes payable with the debit entries in the Notes Payable account provides further assurance that notes indicated as paid during the year have, in fact, been retired. The auditors' inspection of these notes should include a comparison of the maturity date of the note with the date of cash disbursement. Failure to pay notes promptly at maturity is suggestive of serious financial weakness. Payment prior to maturity, on the other hand, may be accompanied by a reduction in the amount of the liability on non-interest-bearing notes. The auditors should ascertain whether any such saving of interest by early payment has been properly recorded. Other points to be verified include the authenticity of the signatures and the unmistakable evidence of cancellation.

There is seldom any justification for a paid note to be missing from the files; a receipt for payment from the payee of the note is not a satisfactory substitute. If, for any reason, a paid note is not available for inspection, the auditors should review the request for a cheque or other vouchers supporting the disbursement, and should discuss the transaction with an appropriate official.

In examining the cancelled notes the auditors should also trace the disposition of any collateral used to secure these notes. A convenient opportunity for diversion of pledged securities or other assets to an unauthorized use may be created at the time these assets are regained from a secured creditor.

Debit entries in a Bonds Payable account are best verified by direct communication with the trustee, as described in the next portion of this audit program.

7. Confirm interest-bearing debt with appropriate third parties.

Notes payable to banks are confirmed as part of the confirmation of bank balances. The standard bank confirmation form illustrated in the chapter on cash includes a request that the bank prepare a list of all borrowings by the depositor. The primary objective of this enquiry is to bring to light any unrecorded notes. As mentioned previously in the discussion of bank accounts, confirmation requests should be sent to all banks with which the client has done business during the year, since a note payable to a bank may be outstanding long after a deposit account has been closed.

Confirmation requests for notes payable to payees other than banks should be drafted on the client's letterhead stationery, signed by the controller or other appropriate executive, and mailed by the auditors. Payees should be requested to confirm dates of origin, due dates, unpaid balances of notes, interest rates and dates to which paid, and collateral for the notes. If any notes payable have been subordinated—that is, made subject to prior settlement of some other obligation—the holders of the notes should be requested to acknowledge such agreement.

The auditors may also substantiate the existence and amount of a mortgage or trust deed liability outstanding by direct confirmation with the mortgage or trustee. The information received should be compared with the client's records and the audit working papers. When no change in the liability account has occurred in the period under audit, the only major procedure necessary will be this confirmation with the creditor. At the same time that the mortgagee or trustee is asked to confirm the debt, he may be requested for an opinion as to the company's compliance with the mortgage or trust deed agreement.

Bond transactions usually can be confirmed directly with the trustee. The trustee's reply should include an exact description of the bonds, including maturity dates and interest rates; bonds retired, purchased for the treasury, or converted into shares during the year; bonds outstanding

FIGURE 17–2
Trustee's reply to confirmation request

THE LAKESIDE TRUST COMPANY LIMITED

123 BAY STREET,   TORONTO, ONTARIO

McArthur and Company
Chartered Accountants   January 12, 1979
97 Green Street
Toronto, Ontario

Dear Sirs:

    In reply to the request of The Torino Corporation Ltd., concerning their 9 percent, 20-year, Debenture Bonds, we are pleased to provide the following information based on our records as of December 31, 1979:

    Issued and outstanding at December 31, 1978 . . . . $10,000,000

    There were no acquisitions or issuances of bonds of this issue during the year ended December 31, 1978. The bonds are not convertible, and no sinking fund is required under the indenture. Our fees billed during the year ended December 31, 1978 totaled $6,240, none of which remained unpaid at December 31, 1978.

Very truly yours,
The Lakeside Trust Company Limited

Vice President

at the balance sheet date; and sinking fund transactions and balances. The trustee also may be asked to confirm the trustee's fees billed during the year, and any amount unpaid at year-end.

An example of a confirmation statement obtained from the trustee of a bond issue is presented in Figure 17–2. The information obtained is used to verify the data shown in the account analysis of bonds payable, bond issue costs, and unamortized discount illustrated in Figure 17–1.

When the trustee reports any conversions, cancellations or redemptions during the period under audit, the auditors will inspect the cancelled certificates or the trustee's cremation certificate to determine that proper evidence exists for the reduction in bonds outstanding. This objective may also require tracing the reported cash outlays to the cash records. When bonds are cancelled, it is important to note that any coupons which had not been redeemed are cancelled or cremated. On the other hand, if the trustee reports additional issuances of bonds during the period, the CAs will trace the proceeds to the cash records to ascertain that the issuing corporation has received proper payment for these additional sales. In this case the auditors should determine that any coupons for interest prior to the date the bonds were sold have been retained by the issuing corporation and mutilated to prevent their being redeemed.

Alternative procedures in the absence of a trustee. In the unlikely event that the indenture does not provide for the services of a trustee, the auditors may direct their substantive tests along the following lines:

a. Inspect unissued bonds on hand to determine that all numbers are accounted for.
b. Verify all sales and purchases of bonds to cash journals, bank statements, and vouchers.
c. Reconcile subsidiary records for bonds payable with the general ledger control account.
d. Confirm registered bonds with the holders.

These procedures are intended to provide the same assurances as the steps previously described for companies utilizing the services of an independent trustee.

8. Examine treasury bonds and reconcile to the general ledger.

Some companies reacquire their own bonds in the open market or directly from bondholders for the purpose of reissuing them at a later date. These bonds are usually carried in a Treasury Bonds account. To verify this item, the auditors will trace all debits for treasury bonds reacquired (and all credits for reissuances) directly to the minutes authorizing these transactions and to the cash records. They will inspect and count the bonds in the treasury and reconcile the total amount to the general ledger account. At the same time the auditors can conveniently review any gains or losses from dealings in treasury bonds, and the effect of these transactions on unamortized issue costs, discount, or premium.

Occasionally, a corporation may elect to deliver treasury bonds or unissued bonds to creditors as collateral for other loans. One supplementary objective of the inspection of treasury bonds and unissued bonds is to disclose the existence of any such loans which the client might have obtained but failed to record. The auditors may also make direct enquiries as to whether treasury bonds have been used as collateral, and whether at the balance sheet date there were any loans so secured.

9. Verify computation of interest expense, interest payable, and amortization of discount or premium.

Interest expense is of special significance to auditors because it indicates the amount of outstanding liabilities. In other words, close study of interest payments is a means of bringing to light any unrecorded interest-bearing liabilities.

Verification of interest expense and interest payable for notes, mortgages, or trust deeds payable usually is a simple matter. The auditors test the propriety of the client's interest expense and interest payable computations, which are set forth in the working paper analyses of the related notes or mortgages obtained in the second procedure of this audit program. In addition to this, the auditors should examine paid cheques supporting interest payments and review confirmations received from note payees or mortgages to verify the dates to which interest on each note or mortgage has been paid.

In their review of vouchers payable and cash records for the period between the balance sheet date and the completion of the audit field work, the auditors should also be alert for any interest payments which do not correspond to notes shown as outstanding at the balance sheet date. This is one more step in the auditors' search for unrecorded liabilities.

If bonds were issued at face amount and the interest payment dates coincided with the company's fiscal year, the proof of bond interest expense would be simple indeed. The auditors would need only to multiply the stated interest rate times the face value of bonds outstanding. Such a simplified situation is of course seldom found in practice. The total bond interest expense for the period usually reflects not only the interest actually paid and accrued but also amortization of bond premium or discount and costs of issuance. Current fees of the trustee may also be included.

The nominal interest on the bonds should be verified by computation (interest rate times face value). Cheques drawn in payment of interest are traced to the cash records. Any balance of interest expense which remains unpaid at the balance sheet date is traced to an accrued liability account. Cancelled coupons (or the trustee's cremation certificate covering such coupons) are examined and reconciled with the cash interest payments. If the payment of interest to bondholders is handled through the independent trustee, a direct confirmation of the trustee's transactions for the period under review should be obtained. All cash transactions will be vouched to the underlying documents showing authority for interest payments.

The amortization of bond issue costs and premium or discount is verified by computation. In making these computations the auditors should give attention to any charges arising because of refunding or the acquisition by the company of its own bonds. If the current fees of the trustee are charged to the Interest Expense account, these expenses should be traced to the trustee's statements and to the confirmation letter.

10. *Determine that all provisions of the indenture have been met.*

Bond issues generally impose upon the borrowing company a number of restrictions and prohibitions—all designed to protect the interests of the bondholders. Indenture provisions frequently require maintenance of a sinking fund; maintenance of stipulated minimum levels of working capital; and repair, maintenance, and insurance of pledged property. The indenture may also restrict dividends to a specified proportion of earnings and prohibit additional long-term borrowing, except under stipulated conditions.

The auditors will already have accumulated information bearing on many of these points. Adequate comments should be included in the audit working papers as to the company's compliance with the provisions of the indenture. If the company has not complied fully with the requirements, the auditors should inform both the client and the client's legal counsel of the violation; explanation of the extent of non-compliance should also be included in the client's financial statements and possibly in the audit report. In some cases of violation the entire bond issue may be due and payable on demand, and hence a current liability.

ILLUSTRATIVE CASE. In the audit of a large construction company, the auditors found the client's working capital to be far below the minimum level stipulated in the indenture of long-term secured bonds payable. In addition to this, the client had allowed the required insurance coverage of pledged assets to lapse. These violations of the indenture were sufficient to cause the bond issue to become payable on demand.

Although the client agreed to reclassify the bond issue as a current liability, the auditors were unable to satisfy themselves that the client could meet the obligation if the bondholders demanded payment. Also, if the bondholders foreclosed on the pledged assets, the ability of the client to continue as a going concern would be questionable. Thus, even after the liability was reclassified as current, the auditors had to qualify their report as being subject to the client company's ability to meet its obligations and remain a going concern.

11. *Determine that debt issuance is in accordance with applicable securities laws.*

Auditors are not qualified to pass on the legality of a bond issue; this is a problem for the client's attorneys. The auditors should be familiar, however, with the principal provisions of the securities laws applicable to the clients' debt issues. They should ascertain that the client has obtained an attorney's opinion on the legality of the bond issuance. In doubtful cases they should consult the client's legal counsel.

12. *Review notes paid or renewed since the balance sheet date.*

If any of the notes payable outstanding at the balance sheet date are paid before completion of the audit engagement, the auditors are provided with an opportunity for verification of these items. Renewal of notes maturing shortly after the balance sheet date may alter the auditors' thinking as to the proper classification of these liabilities. The classification of maturing obligations refinanced or expected to be refinanced on a long-term basis is discussed further in the following section of this chapter.

In the discussion of notes receivable in Chapter 13, emphasis was placed on the necessity of close scrutiny of loans to officers, directors, and affiliates because of the absence of arm's-length bargaining in these related party transactions. Similar emphasis should be placed on the examination of notes payable to insiders or affiliates, although the opportunities for self-dealing are more limited than with receivables. The auditors should scan the notes payable records for the period between the balance sheet date and the completion of examination so that they may be aware of any unusual transactions, such as the re-establishment of an "insider" note which had been paid just prior to the balance sheet date.

13. Determine proper financial statement presentation of interest-bearing debt and related transactions.

Bankers and other prospective creditors study the current liability section of a balance sheet very closely for clues to a company's credit status. The presence of unsecured bank loans indicates financial strength and good credit standing. In the evaluation of secured bank loans, the nature of the assets pledged is of great significance. The pledging of government bonds, for example, indicates a strong financial position coupled with a policy decision to retain the bonds and borrow money rather than to sell the bonds. The pledging of inventories or of accounts receivable as security for loans is quite another matter and suggests a hard-pressed financial situation.

Because of the interest of creditors in the current liability section of the balance sheet and the inferences which may be drawn from various uses of notes payable, adequate informative disclosure is extremely important. Classification of notes by types of payees, as well as by current or long-term maturity, is desirable. Separate listing is needed for notes payable to banks, notes payable to trade creditors, and notes payable to officers, directors, shareholders, and affiliates.

Secured liabilities and pledged assets should be cross referenced to one another with an explanation in the footnotes to the financial statements. In the event of financial difficulties and dissolution, creditors expect to share in the assets in proportion to their respective claims; and if choice assets, such as currrent receivables, have been pledged to one creditor, the risk to unsecured creditors is increased. Current liabilities should include not only those notes maturing within a period of 12 months (or a longer operating cycle) but also any installments currently payable on long-term obligations, such as mortgages. If notes bear the personal endorsement or guarantee of officers or directors, this fact should also be disclosed as a significant element in the appraisal of financial position.

The essential point in balance sheet presentation of long-term liabilities is that they be adequately and fully described. Each category of long-term debt should be stated under a separate title, which describes the type of debt, amounts authorized and issued, interest rate, maturity date, and any conversion or subordination features.

Long-term debt payable in the current period. It is general practice to include under long-term liabilities all debts which will not mature within the ensuing operating cycle, and any debt which will mature but which will not be liquidated from current assets. In other words, any bonds or notes falling due in the coming operating cycle which are to be paid from special funds or refinanced will be classified as long-term obligations regardless of maturity date. Before approving a long-term classification for maturing obligations, auditors must satisfy themselves that the client has both the *intent* and the *ability* to refinance the obligation on a long-term basis. Intent and ability to refinance are demonstrated by the client through either (1) refinancing the obligation on a long-term basis prior to the issuance of the audit report, or (2) entering into a financing agreement by that date which clearly permits such refinancing. Any debt maturing currently and payable from current assets will be a current liability. This distinction is necessary to present a picture of the working capital showing clearly the amount of current funds and the liabilities payable therefrom.

Gains and losses on the retirement of debt. When long-term debt is retired prior to its maturity date, the transaction usually results in either a gain or a loss. If these gains or losses are material in amount, they should be presented in the income statement as extraordinary items, net of the income tax effect. This treatment does not apply to the repurchase of debt to satisfy sinking fund or similar indenture requirements. Such a practice is recommended by *Statement No. 4* of FASB in the United States.

Restrictions imposed by long-term debt agreements. Most long-term debt agreements contain clauses limiting the borrowing company's right to pay dividends. Such a restriction is vitally significant to investors in common stocks. Consequently, the nature of the restriction should be clearly set forth in a footnote to the financial statement. An example adapted from a published financial statement follows:

> The long-term notes payable contain restrictions on the payment of common stock dividends. The notes provide that the company may not pay dividends (except in common stock of the company) if, since July 31, 1970, the aggregate thereof, plus dividends paid on preferred stock and net expenditures for the reacquisition of common stock, will exceed consolidated net income (as defined) since that date plus $5,000,000. Approximately $12,000,000 of consolidated earnings retained in the business at July 31, 1979, is free of this restriction.

Unamortized bond issue costs and premium or discount. Section 3070 of the *CICA Handbook* recommends that unamortized bond discounts and issue costs be treated as deferred charges. Unamortized premium should, based on the same reasoning, be treated as deferred credits. However, it is more appropriate to show unamortized bond discounts and premiums by grouping them together with the face amount of the bonds or debentures. This presentation is sanctioned by *APB Opinion No. 21* of the AICPA in the United States.

APB Opinion No. 21 also requires the imputation of an appropriate interest rate to a long-term liability which either is non-interest-bearing on its face or has an interest rate clearly out of line with prevailing rates for comparable debt instruments. Such an interest imputation results in the recording of a discount to be amortized over the life of the liability.

Treasury bonds. Some accountants have argued that treasury bonds being held for reissuance constitute a valid asset. In theory, however, a bond payable reacquired by the issuing company in advance of the maturity date is little different from a promissory note paid prior to maturity. Both constitute evidence that former indebtedness has been liquidated; neither represents anything of value owned. Treasury bonds need not be distinguished from unissued bonds in the balance sheet, and are properly shown as a deduction from the amount of bonds authorized in arriving at the amount outstanding.

Time of examination

The review of internal control over interest-bearing debt may be carried out in advance of the balance sheet date. Analysis of the ledger accounts for interest-bearing debt and interest expense takes very little time in most audits because of the small number of entries. Consequently, most auditors prefer to wait until the end of the year before analyzing these accounts.

Throughout this chapter, emphasis has been placed on the auditors' concern over a possible understatement of liabilities; audit procedures intended to bring to light any unrecorded liabilities cannot very well be performed in advance of the balance sheet date. Such steps as the confirmation of outstanding interest-bearing debt, the verification of accrued interest, and the investigation of notes paid or renewed shortly after the balance sheet date must necessarily await the close of the period being audited. We must conclude, therefore, that the opportunities for performing audit work in advance of the balance sheet date are much more limited in the case of interest-bearing debt than for most of the asset groups previously discussed.

DISCLOSURE OF CONTINGENCIES

A *loss contingency* may be defined as a *possible* loss, stemming from past events, that will be resolved as to existence and amount by some future event. Central to the concept of a contingent loss is the idea of uncertainty—uncertainty both as to the amount of loss and whether, in fact, any loss has been incurred. This uncertainty is resolved when some future event occurs or fails to occur.

Most loss contingencies may also appropriately be called *contingent liabilities.* "Loss contingencies," however, is a broader term, encompassing the possible impairment of assets as well as the possible existence of liabilities.

The treatment accorded to loss contingencies in financial statements varies depending upon the nature of the contingency and the probability that a loss has been sustained. Thus, the audit problem with respect to loss contingencies is twofold. First, the auditors must determine the existence of the loss contingencies. Because of the uncertainty factor, most loss contingencies do not appear in the accounting records, and a systematic search is required if the auditors are to have reasonable assurance that no important loss contingencies have been overlooked. Second, the auditors must appraise the probability that a loss has been incurred. This is made difficult both by the uncertainty factor and also by the tendency of the client management to maintain at least an outward appearance of optimism.

In *Statement No. 5,* the Financial Accounting Standards Board in the United States set forth the criteria for accounting for loss contingencies. Such losses should be reflected in the accounting records when both of the following conditions are met: (1) information available prior to the issuance of the financial statements indicates that it is *probable* that a loss had been sustained prior to the balance sheet date, *and* (2) the amount of the loss can be *reasonably estimated.* Recognition of the loss may involve either recognition of a liability or reduction of an asset. When a loss contingency has been accrued in the accounts, it is usually desirable to explain the nature of the contingency in a footnote to the financial statements and to disclose any exposure to loss in excess of the amount accrued.

Loss contingencies that do not meet both of the above criteria should still be disclosed when there is at least a *reasonable possibility* that a loss has been incurred. This disclosure should describe the nature of the contingency and, if possible, provide an estimate of the possible loss. If the amount of possible loss cannot be reasonably estimated, the disclosure should include either a range of loss or a statement that an estimate cannot be made.

Certain contingent liabilities traditionally have been disclosed in financial statements even though the possibility that a loss has occurred is remote. Such items include notes receivable discounted and guarantee endorsements. With the exception of those items for which disclosure is traditional, disclosure need not be made of loss contingencies when the possibility of loss is *remote.*

The procedures undertaken by auditors to ascertain the existence of loss contingencies, and to assess the probability of loss, vary with the nature of the contingent item. To illustrate these types of procedures, we will discuss several of the more frequent types of contingencies warranting financial statement disclosure.

1. Pending litigation.

Perhaps the most common loss contingency appearing in financial statements is that stemming from pending or threatened litigation. An *enquiry letter* (or *lawyer's letter*) to the client's legal counsel is the auditors' primary means of obtaining evidence regarding pending and threatened litigation. In the past, many attorneys were reluctant to disclose information about such issues to auditors. They believed that such disclosure was a violation of their confidential relationship with their client and that it might adversely affect the outcome of the litigation. Auditors, on the other hand, felt that they could not issue an unqualified opinion on the financial statements of a client if they were not fully informed as to potential loss contingencies.

To resolve this conflict, a proposed *Joint Policy Statement* has been issued by the Canadian Bar Association and the CICA. Also, the CICA's Auditing Standards Committee has issued an exposure draft on *Communications with Lawyers Regarding Claims and Possible Claims in Connection with the Preparation and Audit of Financial Statements.* Some of the main proposed recommendations are:

1. The client lists and evaluates outstanding legal matters in a letter which is sent to the lawyer.
2. The lawyer advises the client in writing, with a copy to the auditor, if he agrees with the evaluations and indicates any claims which have been omitted by the client.
3. Where the lawyer disagrees with an evaluation, he requests a conference with the client and the auditor.
4. Where a legal matter which has not yet resulted in a claim is omitted from the client's list, the lawyer is requested to discuss the matter with the client but he is not required to disclose it to the auditor.
5. The auditor should obtain a written representation from the client that he has disclosed to the auditor all outstanding claims and possible claims, whether or not discussed with the lawyer.

The position of the AICPA in the United States is somewhat different. Its *SAS No. 12* requires that auditors obtain a list from management describing and evaluating threatened or pending litigation. The auditors then should request the client's attorneys to comment on those areas where their views differ from those of management, or to provide an independent description of each item. The attorneys should also be requested to identify any pending or threatened litigation omitted from management's list. Auditors must also enquire into the possibility of unasserted claims. Even though no potential claimant has exhibited an awareness of a claim, a loss contingency should be disclosed if it is (1) *probable* that a claim will be asserted, and (2) *reasonably possible* that the outcome will be adverse. Thus, management and legal counsel should be asked to disclose any unasserted actions which meet these criteria.

Illustration of disclosure. The following footnote to the financial statements of an aircraft manufacturer illustrates the disclosure of the contingent liability associated with pending litigation:

> A number of suits are pending against the company as the result of accidents in prior years involving airplanes manufactured by the company. It is believed that insurance carried by the company is sufficient to protect it against loss by reason of suits involving the lives of passengers and damage to aircraft. Other litigation pending against the company involves no substantial amount or is covered by insurance.

The balance sheet of another large corporation contained the following note concerning such contingent liabilities:

> The company has suits pending against it, some of which are for large amounts. The company is advised by counsel that, while it is impossible to ascertain the ultimate legal and financial responsibility in respect to such litigation as of December 31, 1978, it is their opinion that the ultimate liability will not be materially important in relation to the total assets of the company.

The refusal of a lawyer to furnish the information requested in the auditors' enquiry letter would be a limitation of the scope of the auditors' examination and would necessitate qualification of the audit report. Even when all of the requested information is provided to the auditors and adequately disclosed in the financial statements, the uncertainty of the outcome of litigation may require the auditors to qualify their report. In such a situation, their report would be qualified as being subject to any adjustment necessary to reflect the resolution of the litigation. Various types of qualifications of audit reports are discussed further in Chapter 20.

2. Income tax disputes.

The necessity of estimating the income tax liability applicable to the year under audit was discussed in Chapter 16. In addition to the taxes relating to the current year's income, uncertainty often exists concerning the amount ultimately payable for prior years. A lag of two or three years often exists between the filing of income tax returns and the final settlement after review by the Department of National Revenue. Disputes between the taxpayer and the Department may create contingent liabilities not settled for several more years. The auditors should determine whether the Department has examined any returns of the client since the preceding audit, and if so, whether any additional taxes have been assessed.

3. Notes receivable discounted.

The determination of the loss contingency for notes receivable discounted is one of the essential steps in the verification of notes receivable and was discussed in Chapter 13.

The auditors' determination of the contingent liability existing at the balance sheet date may be begun by obtaining or preparing a schedule of notes receivable discounted. These should be verified by confirmation from the bank or other holders. The usual form of confirmation request used in verifying bank balances contains a section for the listing of contingent liabilities.

In addition to enquiring from banks as to the existence of contingent liabilities, the auditors should review the credits to the Notes Receivable account to see whether any of these entries represent discounting transactions rather than collections of maturing notes. Other desirable procedures include making enquiry of officers and reviewing the minutes of directors' meetings for resolutions authorizing the discounting of receivables.

4. Accommodation endorsements and other guarantees of indebtedness.

The endorsement of notes of other concerns or individuals is very seldom recorded in the accounts but may be reflected in the minutes of directors' meetings. The practice is more common among small concerns—particularly when one person has a proprietary interest in several companies. Officers, partners, and sole proprietors of small organizations should be questioned as to the existence of any contingent liability from this source. Enquiry should also be made as to whether any collateral has been received to protect the company. The auditors may suggest the desirability of maintaining a record of any accommodation endorsements by inclusion of a pair of memorandum accounts in the general ledger.

A corporation sometimes guarantees the payment of principal and/or interest on bonds or notes issued by affiliated companies. Information concerning such guarantees usually is presented in detail in the minutes of directors' meetings. A company cannot guarantee its own obligations, for it is already fully committed to pay its debts. The following note illustrates the disclosure of a contingent liability arising from guaranteeing securities of affiliates:

> The company has guaranteed payment of liabilities of affiliates in the amount of $2,500,000. Additional loans by insurance companies to affili-

ates in the amount of $2,000,000 are to be guaranteed by the company under an existing agreement.

5. Accounts receivable sold or assigned with recourse.

When accounts receivable are sold or assigned *with recourse,* a guarantee of collectibility is given. Authorization of such a transaction should be revealed during the auditors' reading of the minutes, and a clue also may be found during the examination of transactions and correspondence with financial institutions. Confirmation by direct communication with the purchaser or assignee is necessary for any receivables sold or assigned.

Commitments

Closely related to contingent liabilities are obligations termed *commitments.* The auditors may discover during their examination many of the following commitments: inventory purchase commitments, commitments to sell merchandise at specified prices, contracts for the construction of plant and equipment, pension or profit-sharing plans, long-term operating leases of plant and equipment, employee stock option plans, and employment contracts with key officers. A common characteristic of these commitments is the contractual obligation to enter into transactions *in the future.* All classes of material commitments may be described in a single note to financial statements; or they may be included in a "Contingencies and Commitments" footnote.

General risk contingencies

In addition to loss contingencies and commitments, all businesses face the risk of loss from numerous factors called *general risk contingencies.* A general risk contingency represents a loss that *might occur in the future,* as opposed to a loss contingency that *might have occurred in the past.* Examples of general risk contingencies are threat of a strike or consumer boycott, risk of price increases in essential raw materials, and risk of catastrophe.

General risk contingencies should not be disclosed in financial statements. Such disclosure would be confusing to investors, since the events which might produce a loss actually have not occurred, and since these risks are part of the general business environment. The lack of insurance coverage is a general risk contingency. While auditors may review the extent of insurance coverage for purposes of making recommendations to the client, they do not require financial statement disclosure of the adequacy or lack of insurance coverage.

General audit procedures

Although audit procedures vary with the individual type of loss contingency, the following steps are taken in most audits as a means of discovering these conditions.

1. Review the minutes of directors' and shareholders' meetings to the date of completion of field work. Important contracts, lawsuits, and dealings with subsidiaries are typical of matters discussed in board meetings which may involve loss contingencies.
2. Request the client to send an enquiry letter to its lawyers asking for their evaluation of the completeness of the claims listed and the correctness of the description of the claims and possible claims. A copy of this letter and the lawyers' response to it will be sent to the auditors.
3. Examine the client's legal correspondence files.
4. Send standard bank confirmation request to all banks with which the client has done business during the year. This standard form includes a request for information on any indirect or contingent liabilities of the client.
5. Review correspondence with financial institutions for evidence of accommodation endorsements, guarantees of indebtedness, or sales or assignments of accounts receivable.
6. Analyze amounts recorded as legal expenses.

Liability representations

Since contingent liabilities often are not entered in the accounting records, the officers of the company may be the only persons aware of the contingencies. It is therefore important that the auditors should ask the officers to disclose all liabilities and contingencies of which they have knowledge. To emphasize the importance of the request and to guard against any possible misunderstanding, the officers should be asked to sign a written liability representation, stating that all liabilities known to them are reflected in the accounts or otherwise disclosed in the financial statements.

Financial statement presentation

Current practice almost universally relies upon supporting footnotes as a means of disclosure of loss contingencies. This permits presentation of the pertinent facts in some detail. It is customary to include in the balance sheet proper a reference to the footnote so that all readers will be made aware of the existence of the contingent liabilities.

Some concerns have listed so-called "reserves for contingencies" on the balance sheet midway between the liability and shareholders' equity sections. This practice creates confusion as to whether the reserve was created by a charge against revenue or by appropriation of retained earnings. It also leaves room for doubt as to what amount is intended to represent the total shareholders equity of the company. In some cases it appears that management has created reserves for the purpose of arbitrarily shifting income from one period to another. Such practices do untold harm by destroying public confidence in financial statements and in the integrity of the accounting profession. It is doubtful whether reserves for contingencies serve any constructive purpose; if used at all, they should be included in the shareholders' equity section and be clearly labeled as part of retained earnings. Presentation of information concerning loss contingencies should be limited to specific factual situations, such as accommodation endorsements, guarantees, and pending lawsuits. To fill the financial statements with vague generalities about the uncertainties of the future is more akin to fortunetelling than financial reporting.

KEY TERMS INTRODUCED OR EMPHASIZED IN CHAPTER 17

commitment A contractual obligation to carry out a transaction at specified terms in the future. Material commitments should be disclosed in the financial statements.

contingent liability A possible liability, stemming from past events, that will be resolved as to existence and amount by some future event.

debenture bond An unsecured bond, dependent upon the general credit of the issuer.

general risk contingency An element of the business environment that involves some risk of a future loss. Examples include the risk of accident, strike, price fluctuations, or natural catastrophe. General risk contingencies should not be disclosed in financial statements.

indenture The formal agreement between bondholders and the issuer as to the terms of the debt.

lawyer's letter An enquiry letter sent by the client to its legal counsel, regarding outstanding legal matters, including claims and possible claims against the client.

liability representation A written representation provided by key officers of the client that all liabilities and loss contingencies known to them are disclosed in the financial statements.

loss contingency A possible loss, stemming from past events, that will be resolved as to existence and amount by some future event. Loss contingencies should be disclosed in footnotes to the financial statements if there is a reasonable possibility that a loss has been incurred. In some instances, loss contingencies should be accrued in the accounts.

nominal interest rate The contractual rate of interest that is applied to the face amount of the debt.

registered bonds   Bonds providing for the payment of principal and interest only to the person whose name is recorded in the accounts of the debtor or trustee.

sinking fund   Cash or other assets set aside for the retirement of a debt.

treasury bonds   Bonds which have been repurchased by the issuer for the purpose of being reissued at a later date or retired.

GROUP I
REVIEW QUESTIONS

17-1.   In addition to verifying the recorded liabilities of a company, the auditors must also give consideration to the possibility that other unrecorded liabilities exist. What specific steps may be taken by the auditors to determine that all of their client's interest-bearing liabilities are recorded?

17-2.   An assistant auditor was assigned by the auditor-in-charge to the verification of long-term liabilities. Some time later he reported to the auditor-in-charge that he had determined that all long-term liabilities were properly recorded and that all recorded long-term liabilities were genuine obligations. Does this determination constitute a sufficient examination of long-term liabilities? Explain.

17-3.   Explain the meaning of the term "liability representation."

17-4.   Palmer Ltd. has issued a number of notes payable during the year, and several of these notes are outstanding at the balance sheet date. What source of information should the auditors use in preparing a working paper analysis of the notes payable?

17-5.   What is the principal reason for verifying the Interest Expense account in conjunction with the verification of notes payable?

17-6.   Suggest two important audit procedures commonly used to verify the contingent liability from discounting of notes receivable.

17-7.   What are *loss contingencies?* How are such items presented in the financial statements? Explain.

17-8.   If the federal income tax returns for prior years have not as yet been reviewed by federal tax authorities, would you consider it necessary for the client to disclose this situation in footnotes to the financial statements? Explain.

17-9.   Audit programs for verification of accounts receivable and notes receivable often include investigation of selected transactions occurring after the balance sheet date as well as transactions during the year under audit. Are the auditors concerned with note payable transactions subsequent to the balance sheet date? Explain.

17-10.   Is the confirmation of notes payable usually correlated with other specific phase of the audit? Explain.

17-11.   What is the meaning of the term *commitment* as used in accounting?

17-12.   What constitutes adequate informative disclosure for long-term liabilities in the balance sheet?

17-13. Long-term creditors often insist upon placing certain restrictions upon the borrowing company for the term of the loan. Give three examples of such restrictions and indicate how each restriction protects the long term creditor.

17-14. Most corporations with bonds payable outstanding utilize the services of a trustee. What relation, if any, does this practice have to the maintenance of adequate internal control?

17-15. "Auditors are not qualified to pass on the legality of a bond issue; this is a problem for the company's attorneys. It is therefore unnecessary for the auditors to inspect the bond indenture." Criticize this quotation.

17-16. Should the audit working papers for debentures payable be placed in the permanent file or in the file of working papers for the current audit? Why?

17-17. Schofield Corporation Ltd. has recently issued a large amount of bonds payable and is required to make semiannual contributions to a sinking fund under the control of an independent trustee. What audit procedures are appropriate in connection with the sinking fund?

17-18. What information should be requested by the auditors from the trustee responsible for an issue of debentures payable?

17-19. What are general risk contingencies? Do such items require disclosure in the financial statements?

GROUP II
QUESTIONS REQUIRING ANALYSIS

17-20. You are the audit manager in the examination of the financial statements of Western Grain Storage, Inc., a new client. The company's records show that as of the balance sheet date, approximately 15 million bushels of various grains are in storage for the Commodity Credit Corporation.

In your review of the audit senior's working papers, you ascertain the following facts:

1. All grain is stored under an agreement which holds Western responsible for the quantity and quality of the grain.
2. Losses due to shrinkage, spoilage, and so forth are inherent in the storage of grain. Western's losses, however, have been negligible due to the excellence of its storage facilities.
3. Western carries a warehouseman's bond covering approximately 20 percent of the value of the stored grain.

In the "loss contingencies" section of the working papers, the senior auditor has made the following notation: "I propose recommending to Western's controller that the contingent liability for grain spoilage and shrinkage be disclosed in a note to the financial statements."

Required:

Do you concur with the senior's proposal? Explain.

17–21. You are engaged in the examination of the financial statements of Armada Corporation Ltd., a publicly owned company, for the year ended August 31, 1978. The balance sheet, reflecting all of your audit adjustments accepted by the client to date, shows total current assets, $5,000,000; total current liabilities, $2,000,000; and shareholders' equity, $3,500,000. Included in current liabilities are two unsecured, 8 percent notes payable—one payable to United Provincial Bank in the amount of $400,000 due October 31, 1978, the other payable to First Dominion Bank in the amount of $300,000 due September 30, 1978. On September 30, the last scheduled date for your audit field work, you learn that Armada Corporation Ltd. is unable to pay the $312,000 maturity value of the First Dominion Bank note; that Armada executives are negotiating with First Dominion Bank for an extension of the due date of the note; and that nothing definite has been decided as to the extension.

Required:

a. Should this situation be disclosed in footnotes to Armada Corporation Ltd.'s August 31, 1978, financial statements?

b. After the question of financial statement disclosure has been resolved to the auditor's satisfaction, might this situation have any effect upon the audit report?

17–22. Linda Reeves, CA, receives a telephone call from her client, Lane Ltd. The company's controller states that the board of directors of Lane has entered into two contractual arrangements with Ted Forbes, the company's former president, who has recently retired. Under one agreement, Lane will pay the ex-president $900 per month for five years if he does not compete with the company during that time in a rival business. Under the other agreement, the company will pay the ex-president $600 per month for five years for such advisory services as the company may request from the ex-president.

Lane's controller asks Reeves whether the balance sheet as of the date the two agreements were signed should show $18,000 in current liabilities and $72,000 in long-term liabilities, or whether the two agreements should be disclosed in a "contingencies" note to the financial statements.

Required:

How should Linda Reeves reply to the controller's questions? Explain.

17–23. Wilson Hall, CA, is engaged in the examination of Garrett Ltd.'s financial statements for the year ended December 31, 1978. During the course of his field work, Hall accumulates the following audit evidence for a $100,000 note receivable from Memphis Mfg. Co., Inc., a customer of Garrett Ltd.:

Date of note: November 1, 1978
Due date: May 1, 1979
Interest: 6 percent payable in full at maturity of note
Discounting: December 1, 1978, with First Eastern Bank, discount rate 8 percent

A Dun & Bradstreet credit report in Hall's working papers dated January 22, 1979, reports that Memphis Mfg. Co., Inc., is in the process of liquidation and that Memphis's management estimates that creditors will receive 25 cents on the dollar.

How should Hall advise Garrett to present the note receivable from Memphis Mfg. Co., Inc., in the balance sheet for December 31, 1978? Explain.

17–24. The only long-term liability of Mesa Corporation Ltd. is a note payable for $100,000 secured by a mortgage on the company's plant and equipment. You have audited the company annually for the last three years, during which time there has been no change in the principal amount of the note. The maturity date is ten years from the current balance sheet date. All interest payments have been made promptly in accordance with the terms of the note. Under these circumstances, what audit work, if any, is necessary with respect to this long-term liability during your present year-end audit?

17–25. During your annual audit of Walker Distributing Ltd., your assistant reports to you that although a number of entries were made during the year in the general ledger account, Notes Payable to Officers, she decided that it was not necessary to audit the account because it had a zero balance at year-end.

Required:

Do you agree with your assistant's decision? Discuss. (AICPA)

17–26. In an audit of a corporation that has a bond issue outstanding, the trust indenture is reviewed and confirmation as to the issue is obtained from the trustee. List eight matters of importance to the auditors that might be found either in the indenture or in the confirmation obtained from the trustee. Explain briefly the reason for the auditors' interest in each of the items. (AICPA)

17–27. You are retained by Columbia Corporation Ltd. to make an examination of its financial statements for the fiscal year ended June 30, and you begin work on July 15. Your survey of internal control indicates a fairly satisfactory condition, although there are not enough employees to permit extensive subdivision of duties. The company is one of the smaller units in the industry but has realized net income of about $300,000 in each of the last three years.

Near the end of your field work you overhear a telephone call received by the president of the company while you are discussing the audit with him. The telephone conversation indicates that on May 15 of the current year the Columbia Corporation Ltd. made an accommodation endorsement of a 60-day, $130,000 note issued by a major customer, Brill Corporation Ltd., to its bank. The purpose of the telephone call from Brill was to inform your client that the note had been paid at the maturity date. You had not been aware of the existence of the note prior to overhearing the telephone call.

Required:

a. Do you think the auditors would be justified from an ethical standpoint in acting on information acquired in this manner?

b. Should the balance sheet as of June 30 disclose the contingent liability? Give reasons for your answer.

c. Prepare a list of auditing procedures which might have brought the contingency to light. Explain fully the likelihood of detection of the accommodation endorsement by each procedure listed.

17–28. Select the best answer choice for each of the following and justify your selection in a brief statement.

a. A covenant in Milton Ltd.'s indenture for an outstanding issue of mortgage bonds requires the maintenance at all times of a current ratio in excess of 2 to 1. The indenture also provides that should any covenant be violated, the bond trustee has the option of requiring immediate payment of the principal due.

A CA firm is engaged in the initial examination of the financial statements of Milton for the year ended December 31, 1979. The auditors note that the current ratio has not met indenture requirements since 1974 and is 1.7 to 1 at December 31, 1979. The bond trustee has been furnished financial statements yearly and has not questioned the failure to comply with the covenant; in response to a standard confirmation letter the trustee indicated that to the best of his knowledge there had been no covenant violation to December 31, 1979. Under the circumstances the CAs should—

(1) Rely upon the bond trustee's confirmation and require no reclassification or further enquiry.

(2) Require reclassification of the bonds payable as a current liability.

(3) Request that the management letter of representations explicitly refer to the non-compliance with the covenant and management's expectation that the trustee will take no action.

(4) Request that Milton Ltd. obtain a waiver of the requirement from the bond trustee.

b. A CA analyzes the accrued interest payable account for the year, recomputes the amounts of payments and beginning and ending balances, and reconciles to the interest expense account. Which of the following errors or questionable practices has the best chance of being detected by the CA's audit procedures?

(1) Interest revenue of $520 on a note receivable was credited against miscellaneous expense.

(2) A provision of the company's loan agreement was violated. Common dividends are prohibited if income available for

interest and dividends is not three times interest requirements.

(3) Interest paid on an account payable was charged to the Raw Material Purchases account.

(4) A note payable had not been recorded. Interest of $1,500 on the note was properly paid and was charged to the Interest Expense account.

c. Which of the following transactions or events does not result in a loss contingency?

(1) Termination of fire insurance coverage of certain plant assets.

(2) Sale of products to a government agency under a contract subject to renegotiation.

(3) Sale of accounts receivable with recourse.

(4) Client named as a defendant in a lawsuit claiming damages for patent infringement.

d. The audit procedure most likely to reveal the existence of a contingent liability is:

(1) A review of vouchers paid during the month following year-end.

(2) Confirmation of outstanding debt from third parties.

(3) An enquiry directed to client's legal counsel.

(4) An enquiry directed to the independent trustee for a bond issue. (AICPA, adapted)

GROUP III
PROBLEMS

17–29. You were engaged to examine the financial statements of King Corporation Ltd. for the year ended June 30.

On May 1, of the current year, the corporation borrowed $500,000 from Scotia Valley Bank to finance plant expansion. The long-term note agreement provided for the annual payment of principal and interest over five years. The existing plant was pledged as security for the loan.

Required:

a. What are the audit objectives in the examination of long-term debt?

b. Prepare an audit program for the examination of the long-term note agreement between King and Scotia Valley Bank. (AICPA, adapted)

17–30. In your first audit of Hydrafoil Ltd., a manufacturer of specially designed boats capable of transporting passengers over water at very high speeds, you find that sales are made to commercial transportation companies. The sales price per unit is $200,000; and with each unit sold, the client gives the purchasing company a certificate reading as follows:

Hydrafoil Ltd. promises to pay to _____ the sum of $12,000 when the boat designated as Serial No. _____ is permanently retired from service and evidence of such retirement is submitted.

The president of Hydrafoil Ltd. explains to you that the purpose of issuing the certificates is to ensure contact with customers when they are in the market for new equipment. You also learn that the company makes no journal entry to record a certificate when it is issued. Instead, the company charges an expense account and credits a liability account $100 per month for each outstanding certificate, based on the company's experience that its hydrafoil boats will be rendered obsolete by new, more efficient models in approximately ten years from the date of sale.

Required:

Do you concur with Hydrafoil Ltd.'s accounting for the certificates? You may assume that the ten-year service life of the product (and therefore of the certificates) is an accurate determination. Explain your position clearly.

17–31. Prepare an audit program which would bring to light various types of loss contingencies and commitments. (The program should be in general terms for each area covered and should describe briefly the type of contingent item which might be found under each step. Ignore the fact that several of the steps in the program might normally be included in programs for other parts of your examination.) (AICPA)

17–32. The following covenants are extracted from the indenture of a bond issue of Case Ltd. The indenture provides that failure to comply with its terms in any respect automatically advances the due date of the loan to the date of non-compliance (the regular due date is 20 years hence). Give any audit procedures or reporting requirements you feel should be taken or recognized in connection with each one of the following:

1. "The debtor company shall endeavour to maintain a working capital ratio of 2 to 1 at all times; and in any fiscal year following a failure to maintain said ratio, the company shall restrict compensation of officers to a total of $500,000. Officers for this purpose shall include chairman of the board of directors, president, all vice presidents, secretary, controller, and treasurer."

2. "The debtor company shall keep all property which is security for this debt insured against loss by fire to the extent of 100 percent of its actual value. Policies of insurance comprising this protection shall be filed with the trustee."

3. "The debtor company shall pay all taxes legally assessed against property which is security for this debt within the time provided by law for payment without penalty, and shall deposit receipted tax bills or equally acceptable evidence of payment of same with the trustee."

4. "A sinking fund shall be deposited with the trustee by semiannual

payments of $300,000, from which the trustee shall, in its discretion, purchase bonds of this issue." (AICPA, adapted)

17–33.   In an examination of the Ludlow Corporation Ltd. at December 31, 1978, you have learned that the following situations exist. No entries in respect thereto have been made in the accounting records. What *entries* would you recommend and what *disclosures,* if any, would you suggest for these situations in the financial statements for December 31, 1978?

1.   The Ludlow Corporation Ltd. has guaranteed the payment of interest on the ten-year, first-mortgage bonds of the Kipling Ltd., an unconsolidated affiliate. Outstanding bonds of Kipling amount to $1,500,000 with interest payable at 5 percent per annum, due June 1 and December 1 of each year. The bonds were issued by Kipling on December 1, 1976, and all interest payments have been met by that company with the exception of the payment due December 1, 1978. The Ludlow Corporation Ltd. states that it will pay the defaulted interest to the bondholders on January 15, 1979.

2.   During the year 1978, the Ludlow Corporation Ltd. was named as defendant in a suit for damages by the Dalton Company for breach of contract. An adverse decision to the Ludlow Corporation Ltd. was rendered, and the Dalton Company was awarded $400,000 damages. At the time of the audit, the case was under appeal to a higher court.

3.   On December 23, 1978, the Ludlow Corporation Ltd. declared a common stock dividend of 1,000 shares, par $100,000, of its common stock, payable February 2, 1979, to the common shareholders of record December 30, 1978. (AICPA, adapted)

17–34.   Palmdale Ltd. issued bonds of the face amount of $10,000,000 on January 1, 1978, to an underwriting syndicate at 100. The bonds were due serially $1,000,000 on December 31, 1978, and annually thereafter. Interest at the rate of 5 percent is payable semiannually on June 30, and December 31 of each year. The bonds refer to a trust indenture naming Lancaster Trust Company as trustee. All principal and interest payments to the bondholders are specified to be made by the trust company, and the indenture also states that Palmdale Ltd. shall pay all maturing principal and interest amounts to the trustee on the due dates.

On June 30, 1978, the company paid $250,000 to the trustee and charged this amount to interest expense. On December 31, 1978, the company paid $1,250,000 to the trustee and charged $1,000,000 to the Bonds Payable account and $250,000 to the Interest Expense account.

You are the auditor of Palmdale and have received confirmation from the trustee as of December 31, 1978, stating that interest coupons maturing June 30, 1978, have been paid in the amount of $239,000, and that interest coupons maturing December 31, 1978, have been paid in the amount of $8,000; also, that bonds maturing December 31 have been paid in the amount of $130,000. The trustee also reports that it has on hand a cash balance of $1,123,000 in favour of Palmdale. The paid bonds and coupons referred to by the trustee had been returned to the company and were inspected by you.

How should Palmdale treat the outstanding bonds, interest coupons, and cash balance in the hands of the trustee in the company's balance sheet of December 31, 1978? (AICPA, adapted)

17–35. Robert Hopkins was the senior office employee in Griffin Equipment Ltd. and enjoyed the complete confidence of the owner, William Barton, who devoted most of his attention to sales, engineering, and production problems. All financial and accounting matters were entrusted to Hopkins, whose title was office manager. Hopkins had two assistants, but their only experience in accounting and financial work had been gained under Hopkins's supervision. Barton had informed Hopkins that it was his responsibility to keep him (Barton) informed on financial position and operating results of the company but not to bother him with details.

The company was short of working capital and would occasionally issue notes payable in settlement of past-due open accounts to suppliers. The situations warranting issuance of notes were decided upon by Hopkins, and the notes were drawn by him for signature by Barton. Hopkins was aware of the weakness in internal control and finally devised a scheme for defrauding the company through understating the amount of notes payable outstanding. He prepared a note in the amount of $24,000 payable to a supplier to whom several invoices were past due. After securing Barton's signature on the note and mailing it to the creditor, Hopkins entered the note in the Notes Payable account of the general ledger as $4,000, with an offsetting debit of $4,000 to the creditor's account payable.

Several months later when the note matured, a cheque for $24,000 plus interest was issued and properly recorded, including a debit of $24,000 to the Notes Payable account. Hopkins then altered the original credit in the account by changing the figure from $4,000 to $24,-000. He also changed the original debit to Accounts Payable from $4,000 to $24,000. This alteration caused the Notes Payable account to have a balance in agreement with the total of other notes outstanding. To complete the fraud, Hopkins called the supplier to whom the cheque had been sent and explained that the cheque should have been for only $4,000 plus interest.

Hopkins explained to the supplier that the note for $24,000 originally had been issued in settlement of a number of past-due invoices, but that while the note was outstanding, cheques had been sent in payment of all the invoices. "In other words," said Hopkins over the telephone, "we made the mistake of giving you a note for those invoices and then going ahead and sending you cheques for them as soon as our cash position had improved. Then we paid the note at maturity. So please excuse our mistakes and return the overpayment." After reviewing the record of invoices and cheques received, the supplier agreed he had been overpaid by $20,000 plus interest and promptly sent a refund, which Hopkins abstracted without making any entry in the accounts.

Required:

a. Assuming that an audit by independent CAs was made while the note was outstanding, do you think that the $20,000 understatement of the Notes Payable account would have been detected? Explain fully the reasoning underlying your answer.

b. If the irregularity was not discovered while the note was outstanding, do you think that an audit subsequent to the payment of the note would have disclosed the fraud? Explain.

c. What internal control procedures would you recommend for Griffin Equipment Ltd. to avoid fraud of this type?

GROUP IV
CASE STUDY IN AUDITING

17–36.   BROWN CONSTRUCTION CORPORATION LTD.

Jones and Miller, CAs, have been assisting Brown Construction Corportation Ltd., a contractor, in its accounting problems. In the summer of 1978, Herbert Brown, president of Brown Construction Corporation Ltd., called George Jones, senior partner of Jones and Miller, and requested a complete audit of the company's financial statements for the year ended June 30, 1978, since the bank had requested audited statements.

Jones discussed the outlines of an audit plan with Susan Black, the senior accountant familiar with the corporation's affairs, and sent her out to start the audit.

As part of the examination, Black reviewed all expense accounts for items which should possibly have been capitalized. One recurring charge of $5,140, appearing in the May and June entries in the Equipment Rental account, attracted Black's attention. The invoices supporting the charges bore the name of a local firm of construction equipment dealers. The body of the invoices read, "For equipment leased to you per our agreement, $5,140."

Black asked to see the agreement and any other correspondence related to the transaction. The agreement was in the form of a lease, stating that the dealers had leased to Brown Construction Corporation Ltd. six pieces of equipment for a period of ten months, at a monthly rental of $5,140. The lease specified that the lessors retained all property rights, title, and so forth, to the equipment and that Brown Construction Corporation Ltd. was to return the equipment at the end of the ten months. It also required the corporation to pay all expenses of maintenance and licenses, if any, and to insure the equipment loss in the amount of $53,000, in favour of the lessors.

The correspondence covering this transaction included several printed prospectuses of the equipment covered by the lease agreement, pencil notes, and a typed letter from the lessor, listing the equipment and its sales price, a financing charge, and sales tax in the total amount of $53,600. There was also a notation on the margin of the letter, showing the total of $53,600, deducting ten payments of $5,140 each, and a remainder of $2,200.

Black made careful and extensive working paper notes on her findings and discussed them with Jones. They both felt that the transaction was more in the nature of a purchase than a lease, especially in view of the size of the monthly "rental" in relation to the value of the equipment rented. Jones called the president of Brown Construction Corporation Ltd., who told him that the corporation was renting the equipment but that there was a verbal understanding that it could buy the equipment at the end of the ten-month lease by paying $2,200. The president insisted, however, that he did not believe the corporation would buy the equipment, although to date, rental payments aggregating $20,560 had been made.

Black drafted a proposed adjusting entry to reflect a purchase of equipment of $53,000, a current liability of $42,720, and depreciation for two months. When Black submitted the proposed adjusting entry to the president of Brown Construction Corporation Ltd. for his approval, Brown protested strongly against the conversion, as he called it, of a simple equipment lease into a purchase arrangement.

Required:

a. Was Jones justified in considering the transaction to be a purchase? Explain.

b. Could the auditors express an unqualified opinion if Brown refused to record Black's proposed adjustment?

c. Assume that Brown Construction Corporation Ltd. had current assets of $100,000 and a current ratio of 2 to 1 before the audit adjustment on the equipment. Would the treatment of the transaction have a material effect on the financial picture of the corporation?

d. What effect, if any, will a decision either way have on the current and future income statements?

e. If you had to argue either side, what additional steps would you take to support your reasoning?

   (1) As the corporation's president.

   (2) As the independent auditors.

18

Owners' equity

Most of this chapter is concerned with the audit of the shareholders' equity accounts of corporate clients; the audit of owners' equity in partnerships and sole proprietorships is discussed briefly near the end of the chapter.

The examination of owners' equity differs from the audit of assets and current liabilities in that transactions are generally few in number but material in amount. Consequently, each transaction requires careful attention. In many respects, the audit of owners' equity is similar to that of long-term debt. The auditors will find in many audit engagements that no change has occurred during the current year in the Capital Stock[1] account and perhaps only one or two entries have been made in the Retained Earnings account. Under these circumstances, the audit time required will be very small in relation to the dollar amounts in these accounts. The Capital Stock account often has a larger balance than the Cash account, but the audit work required for capital stock is usually far less.

The auditors' objectives in examination of owners' equity

The auditors' principal objectives in their examination of owners' equity are (a) to evaluate the internal control over stock certificates, stock

---

[1] According to the CICA's *Financial Reporting in Canada*, 12th ed., 1977, the term "capital stock" is more commonly used than "share capital;" thus, the term "capital stock" is used here.

transactions, and dividend payments; (*b*) to determine that all transactions during the year affecting owners' equity accounts were properly authorized and recorded; (*c*) to determine that legal requirements relating to corporate capital have been met; and (*d*) to determine that owners' equity is presented properly in the financial statements.

To accomplish these objectives, auditors need some familiarity with federal and provincial laws concerning securities and also with the rules and regulations of the securities commissions.

Internal control for owners' equity

There are three principal elements of strong internal control over capital stock and dividends. These three elements are (1) the proper authorization of transactions by the board of directors and corporate officers; (2) the segregation of duties in handling these transactions (especially the use of independent agents for stock registration and transfer and dividend payments); and (3) the maintenance of adequate records. These elements closely parallel the methods of achieving internal control over long-term debt and interest.

Control of capital stock transactions by board of directors

All capital stock transactions should receive formal advance approval by the board of directors. The substantive tests for verifying an entry in a Capital Stock account, therefore, should include tracing the entry to an authorization in the minutes of directors' meetings.

Let us consider for a moment some of the specific steps relating to capital stock transactions which require authorization by directors. The board of directors must determine the number of shares to be issued and the price per share; if an installment plan of payment is to be used, the terms must be prescribed by the board. If plant and equipment, services, or any considerations other than cash are to be accepted in payment for shares, the board of directors must set the valuation on the noncash assets received. Many growth-oriented companies acquire other companies by issuing convertible preferred shares and other securities in exchange for the outstanding stock of the companies being acquired. The terms of such business combinations naturally require approval of the board of directors prior to the making of the acquisition offer. Transfers from retained earnings to the Capital Stock and contributed surplus accounts, as in the case of stock dividends, are initiated by action of the board. Stock splits and changes in par or stated value of shares also require formal authorization by the board.

Authority for all dividend actions rests with the directors. The declaration of a dividend must specify not only the amount per share but also the date of record and the date of payment.

If a corporation handles its own capital stock transactions rather than utilizing the services of an independent registrar and stock transfer agent, the board of directors should pass a resolution designating those officers who are authorized to (a) sign stock certificates, (b) maintain records of shareholders, (c) have custody of unissued certificates, and (d) sign dividend cheques. The signatures of two officers are generally required on stock certificates.

Independent registrar and stock transfer agent

In appraising the adequacy of internal controls over capital stock, the first question that the auditors consider is whether the corporation employs the services of an independent stock registrar and a stock transfer agent or handles its own capital stock transactions. Internal control is far stronger when the services of an independent stock registrar and a stock transfer agent are utilized because the banks or trust companies acting in these capacities will have the necessary experience, the specialized facilities, and the trained personnel to perform the work in an expert manner. Moreover, by placing the responsibility for handling capital stock certificates in separate and independent organizations, the corporation achieves to the fullest extent the internal control concept of separation of duties.

The primary responsibility of the stock registrar is to avoid any over-issuance of stock. The danger of overissuance is illustrated by the old story of a promoter who sold a 25 percent interest in a new corporation to each of ten investors. To prevent such irregularities, the registrar must verify that stock certificates are issued in accordance with the articles of incorporation (letters patent or memorandum of association) and the formal authorizations by the board of directors. The registrar obtains copies of the documents authorizing the total shares to be issued and maintains records of total shares issued and cancelled. Each new certificate must be presented to the registrar for examination and registration before it is issued to shareholders. The dangers of fraud and accidental error relating to improper issuance of stock certificates are obviously greatly reduced when an independent registrar is employed.

Corporations with actively traded securities employ independent stock transfer agents. Although the stock transfer agent maintains a record of the total shares outstanding, its primary responsibility is the task of maintaining detail shareholder records and carrying out transfers of stock ownership. The appointment of an independent transfer agent requires a formal resolution by the board of directors.

The procedures for transfer of stock are governed by provisions of the provincial securities acts, the business corporations acts, and also by the regulations of the stock exchanges. The objectives of these procedures are to ensure that forged or altered certificates are not negotiated, that "stop orders" are placed in effect for lost certificates, and that up-to-date records are maintained showing the name and address of each shareholder and the number of shares owned. The rights of a shareholder—to receive dividends when declared, to vote, to subscribe to new issues in proportion to present holdings, and to share in the proceeds of liquidation—obviously cannot be observed if the records of shareholders are inaccurate or incomplete. Moreover, the laws have placed the responsibility for propriety of stock transfers upon the officers of the corporation.

The stock certificate book

If the corporation does not utilize the services of an independent registrar and stock transfer agent, these functions usually are assigned by the board of directors to the secretary of the company. The stock certificates should be serially numbered by the printer; and from the time of delivery to the company until issuance, they should be in the exclusive custody of the designated officer. The internal auditing staff of the corporation may periodically examine the unissued stock certificates and review the procedures being followed to determine their effectiveness and the extent of compliance with established policies.

The certificates often are prepared in bound books, with attached stubs similar to those in a cheque book. Each stub shows the certificate number and contains blank spaces for entering the number of shares represented by the certificate, the name of the shareholder, and the serial number of any previously issued certificate surrendered in exchange for the new one. Certificates should be issued in numerical sequence and not signed or countersigned until the time of issuance. When outstanding shares are transferred from one holder to another, the old certificate is surrendered to the company. After careful inspection of the signature of the transferer and other details, the designated officer cancels the old certificate by perforation and attaches it to the corresponding stub in the certificate book.

The shareholders' ledger

The stock certificate book is not in itself an adequate record of the capital stock outstanding. The certificates appear in the book in serial number order, and a single shareholder may own several certificates listed as various places in the certificate book.

A shareholders' ledger provides a separate record for each shareholder, thus making it possible to determine at a glance the total number of shares owned by any one person. This record may be used in compiling the list of dividend cheques or for any other communication with shareholders. The shareholders' ledger may be maintained by the secretary of the corporation, by a stock transfer department, or in the accounting department. For corporations with numerous shareholders, this record usually is maintained in the form of a computer master file.

Other records significant in the maintenance of adequate internal control for capital stock include transfer journals, files of receipts for certificates delivered, and records of the signatures of shareholders. These records should be under the control of an officer of the corporation and not accessible to employees.

The acquisition of treasury stock by a corporation requires authorization by the board of directors. If reacquired shares are to be held for possible reissuance, they should be registered in the name of the corporation and kept under the same type of control applicable to investments in securities of other companies. Reissuance of treasury shares also requires authorization by the board of directors.

Internal control over contributed surplus and retained earnings

The major consideration in the internal control over contributed surplus and retained earnings is that all entries be made only after proper approval of an officer. In many cases the board of directors will provide the authorization for entries in these accounts. As an additional control, periodically, the controller should review all entries to retained earnings and other capital accounts to determine their propriety.

Internal control over dividends

The nature of internal control over the payment of dividends, as in the case of stock issuance, depends primarily upon whether the company performs the function of dividend payment itself or utilizes the services of an independent dividend-paying agent. If an independent dividend-disbursing agent is used, the corporation will provide the agent with a certified copy of the dividend declaration and with a cheque for the full amount of the dividend. The bank or trust company serving as stock transfer agent is usually appointed to distribute the dividend, since it maintains the detailed records of shareholders. The agent issues dividend cheque to the individual shareholder and sends the corporation a detailed list of the payments made. The use of an independent agent is to be recommended from the standpoint of internal control, for it materially reduces the possibility of fraud or error arising in connection with the distribution of dividends.

In a small corporation not utilizing the services of a dividend-paying agent, the responsibility for payment of dividends is usually lodged with the treasurer and the secretary. After declaration of a dividend by the board of directors, the secretary prepares a list of shareholders as of the date of record, the number of shares held by each, and the amount of the dividend each is to receive. The total of these individual amounts is proved by multiplying the dividend per share by the total number of outstanding shares.

Dividend cheques controlled by serial numbers are drawn payable to individual shareholders in the amounts shown on the list described above. If the shareholders' ledger is maintained on a computer master file, the dividend cheques may be prepared by the computer directly from this record. The shareholder list and dividend cheques are submitted to the treasurer for approval and signature. The cheques should be reconciled by the treasurer with the total shares outstanding and mailed without again coming under control of the officer who prepared them.

A separate dividend bank account is then opened by the deposit of a cheque drawn for the total amount of the dividend. As the individual dividend cheques are paid from this account and returned by the bank, they should be matched with the cheque stubs or marked *paid* in the dividend cheque register. A list of outstanding cheques should be prepared monthly from the open stubs or open items in the cheque register. This list should agree in total with the balance remaining in the dividend bank account. Companies with numerous shareholders prepare dividend cheques in machine-sensible form, so that the reconciliation of outstanding cheques may be done by computer.

It is to be expected that some dividend cheques will be long outstanding. Eventually, unclaimed dividends may be returned to retained earnings if this is permitted by corporation laws.

Audit working papers for owners' equity

In addition to the grouping sheet for owners' equity accounts, an analysis of each equity account is prepared by the auditors for the permanent file. A detailed analysis is essential for all aspects of a stock option plan: options authorized, issued, and outstanding. For a closely held corporation not served by a transfer agent, the auditors will often prepare for the permanent file a list of shareholders and the number of shares owned by each.

AUDIT PROGRAM—CAPITAL STOCK

The following procedures are typical of the work required in many engagements for the verification of capital stock:

1. Obtain or prepare a description of internal control over capital stock transactions.
2. Review articles of incorporation (letters patent or memorandum of association), by-laws, and minutes for provisions relating to capital stock.

3. Obtain or prepare an analysis of the Capital Stock account.
4. Account for all proceeds from stock issues.
5. Obtain or prepare an analysis of the Treasury Stock account and examine treasury shares on hand.
6. Confirm shares outstanding with the independent registrar and stock transfer agent.
7. Account for all certificate numbers.
8. Examine all cancelled certificates.
9. Reconcile shareholder records and stock certificate book with general ledger control account.
10. Determine compliance with stock option plans and with other restrictions and preferences pertaining to capital stock.

Compliance tests usually are unnecessary in the audit of capital stock. Since transactions are so few in number, the auditors usually substantiate all transactions rather than rely upon the client's system of internal control. In addition to the preceding steps, the auditors must determine the appropriate financial statement presentation of capital stock. This topic will be discussed later in this chapter, along with the financial statement presentation of other elements of owners' equity.

1. *Obtain or prepare a description of internal control over capital stock transactions.*

Even though the examination of capital stock consists primarily of substantive tests, the auditors must acquire an understanding of the client's procedures for authorizing, executing, and recording capital stock transactions. This may be achieved by preparing a written description or flowchart of the system, or by filling in an internal control questionnaire. If the questionnaire approach is employed, typical questions to be answered might include: Does the company utilize the services of an independent registrar and stock transfer agent? Are issues and retirements made only on proper authority? Are shareholders' ledger and transfer journals maintained? Are entries in owners' equity accounts reviewed periodically by the controller? These questions should be regarded as identifying the areas to be investigated, rather than as items requiring simple yes or no answers.

2. *Review articles of incorporation (letters patent or memorandum of association), by-laws, and minutes for provisions relating to capital stock.*

In a first audit, copies of the articles of incorporation, by-laws, and minutes of the meetings of directors and shareholders obtained for the permanent file should be carefully read. All provisions of significance from an accounting standpoint should be underscored or otherwise highlighted for follow-up during the audit.

The information required by the auditors for each issue of capital stock includes the number of shares authorized and issued, par or stated value if any, dividend rates, call and conversion provisions, stock splits, and stock options. By gathering evidence on these points, the auditors will have some assurance that capital stock transactions and dividend payments have been in accordance with legal requirements and specific authorizations by shareholders and directors. Also, they will be able to judge whether the balance sheet contains all necessary information to describe adequately the various stock issues and other elements of corporate capital.

3. Obtain or prepare an analysis of the Capital Stock account.

In an initial audit engagement, Capital Stock accounts should be analyzed from the beginning of the corporation to provide the auditors with a complete historical picture of corporate capital. This approach is comparable to that employed for plant and equipment; in both cases the auditors require assurance as to the propriety of the balances at the beginning of the period under audit. Analysis of capital stock includes an appraisal of the nature of all changes, and the vouching of these changes to the supporting documents and records. All journal entries should be inspected to determine that they represent bona fide charges or credits to the accounts, and that they were properly authorized. Special attention should be given to the capitalization of retained earnings when stock dividends are issued, and the reduction of stated or par values in quasi reorganizations. All capital stock transactions should bear the authority of the board. In addition, the auditors may obtain from the clients' legal counsel an opinion as to the legality of all prior stock issuances.

The analysis of Capital Stock accounts may be prepared in such a manner as to permit additions during subsequent audit engagements. After the initial audit, if the analysis is kept in a permanent file, all that will be necessary is to record the current period's increases and decreases and to vouch these transactions. The auditors then will have a working paper showing all changes in capital stock from the inception of the corporation.

4. Account for all proceeds from stock issues.

Closely related to the analysis of Capital Stock accounts is the audit procedure of accounting for the receipt and proper disposition of all funds derived from the issuance of capital stock. The proceeds should be traced to the cash records and bank statements. In this connection, it is essential that the auditors be familiar with any underwriting contracts and securities commission registration statements so that they can determine the propriety of amounts reported as receipts from stock issues. These documents provide necessary information as to issuance prices, the net cash consideration to be received by the corporation, and the use of the proceeds.

When assets other than cash are received as consideration for the issuance of capital stock, the entire transaction requires the most careful study. Generally the value of assets and services received in exchange for capital shares depends upon the decision of the board of directors. Business corporation laws frequently provide that in the absence of fraud this valuation must be accepted as valid.

While tracing the proceeds of capital stock issues, the auditors will determine the propriety of all allocations between amounts credited to Capital Stock accounts and amounts applicable to Contributed Surplus accounts. If the stock carries no par value, the amount to be credited to the capital stock account depends upon appropriate business corporation laws. The amount of the credit may be (1) the total consideration received, (2) the declared or stated value, or (3) a prescribed minimum amount. In all examinations, the auditors are interested in determining that the capital stock is fairly stated in accordance with accepted legal and accounting requirements.

5. *Obtain or prepare an analysis of the Treasury Stock account and examine treasury shares on hand.*

Treasury stock is capital stock originally issued as fully paid and subsequently reacquired, but not retired, by the issuing corporation. These shares may be acquired by purchase on the open market, by acceptance for the cancellation of a debt, in exchange for assets, or possibly by donation from shareholders. Corporations often purchase their own shares in order to make required distributions of shares under employee stock purchase plans or executive stock option plans.

The auditors should analyze the Treasury Stock account and prepare a list showing the number of shares of treasury stock on hand. All certificates on hand then may be inspected. If the certificates are not on hand, they should be confirmed directly with the custodian.

In their review of treasury stock transactions, the auditors should refer to permanent file copies of the minutes of directors' meetings to determine that (a) the acquisition or reissuance of treasury stock was authorized by directors, and (b) the price paid or received was in accordance with prices specified by the board. Also, the auditors should ensure that these transactions are legal under the relevant statutes.

In verifying the cost of treasury stock acquired, the auditors will also examine the paid cheques. Reissuances of treasury stock should be verified in a parallel manner, including the tracing of the proceeds of reissuance into the bank account.

Gains on reissuance of treasury stock represent an increase in contributed capital and should be credited to a Contributed Surplus account, not to Retained Earnings or to current income.

In summary, the auditors' review of treasury stock transactions will make clear whether these transactions were properly authorized by the board of directors, and also will determine that the recording methods used were in conformity with generally accepted accounting principles and with business corporation laws.

6. Confirm shares outstanding with the independent registrar and stock transfer agent.

The number of shares issued and outstanding on the balance sheet date may be confirmed by direct communication with the independent registrar and stock transfer agent. The confirmation request should be written by the client under the client's letterhead, but should be mailed by the auditors. Confirmation replies should be sent directly to the auditors, not to the client. All information contained in these replies should be traced to the corporate records, and a reconciliation made between the records and confirmations, if necessary. It is essential that the general ledger control accounts agree with the amount of stock issued as reported by the independent registrar and stock transfer agent. Because of the strong internal controls usually maintained over stock certificates, it is not customary to communicate with individual shareholders in establishing the number of shares outstanding.

When a corporation acts as its own transfer agent and registrar, the auditors must adopt alternative procedures as nearly as possible equivalent to direct confirmation with outside parties. These procedures are described in subsequent steps in this audit program.

7. Account for all certificate numbers.

The audit working papers should include a record of the last certificate number issued during the year. Reference to the working papers for the preceding audit, combined with the verification of certificate numbers issued during the current period, will enable the auditors to account for all certificates by serial number.

A working paper prepared during the auditors' examination of the stock certificate book of a small closely held corporation is designed to be utilized during several audits; it may be retained in the permanent file or forwarded to successive current files. Additionally, it is desirable for the auditors to inspect the unissued certificates to determine that all certificates purported to be unissued are actually on hand and blank. In this connection it is sometimes advocated that the auditors confirm directly with the printer the number of certificates printed and delivered, and the serial numbers used.

8. Examine all cancelled certificates.

An adequate system of internal control for corporations not utilizing the services of an independent registrar and stock transfer agent requires that all cancelled stock certificates be perforated or marked in a manner precluding the possibility of further use. Cancelled certificates should be attached to the corresponding stubs in the stock certificate book and permanently preserved. If reacquired certificates are not properly cancelled, the danger exists that they may be fraudulently reissued by officers or employees. Such unauthorized reissuance would create an excess of capital stock outstanding over the amount properly issued and reflected in the accounts. Auditors, therefore, will examine all cancelled stock certificates on hand, noting in particular that these have been effectively voided.

9. Reconcile shareholder records and stock certificate book with general ledger control account.

The general ledger account for capital stock shows the total par value or stated value of all shares outstanding, plus any treasury shares. The subsidiary records for capital stock contains an account for each shareholder. The stock certificate book contains all cancelled certificates, and also open stubs for outstanding certificates. These three records must be reconciled by the auditors to establish the amount of outstanding stock, and to rule out the possibility of an overissuance of shares. If this verification were not made, it would be possible for a dishonest official to issue unlimited amounts of stock and to withhold the proceeds from such sales.

A trial balance of the subsidiary shareholder records may be obtained from the client or prepared by the auditors, and compared with the general ledger control account. In conjunction with this procedure, the total shares outstanding, as shown by the stock certificate book stubs, should also be reconciled with the control account and with the subsidiary trial balance. These procedures assure the auditors of the accuracy of the ledger account balances for capital stock.

10. Determine compliance with stock option plans and with other restrictions and preferences pertaining to capital stock.

Many corporations grant stock options to officers and key employees as an incentive-type compensation plan. For example, a corporation with stock selling in the open market for $30 a share on December 31, 1979, might agree to sell 50,000 additional shares to its management group at a price of $30 at any time during the next five years. Any rise in the market price of the stock will obviously benefit the holders of stock options. When stock options are granted, a portion of the authorized but unissued stock must be held in reserve by the corporation so that it will be in a position to fulfill the option agreements. Similarly, corporations with convertible debentures or convertible preferred stocks outstanding must hold in reserve a sufficient number of common shares to meet the demands of preferred shareholders and debenture holders who may elect to convert their securities into common stock.

The auditors must become thoroughly familiar with the terms of any stock options and stock purchase plans and with the conversion features in debenture bonds and preferred stock, so that they can determine whether the financial statements make adequate disclosure of these agreements. They must also verify the shares issued during the year through conversion or exercise of stock options, and must ascertain that the number of shares held in reserve at the balance sheet date does not exceed the corporation's authorized but unissued stock. The following footnote to a corporate balance sheet is suggestive of the work done by the auditors along these lines:

> At December 31, 1979, 2,033,982 shares of Common Stock were reserved for the following purposes: (*a*) 228,079 shares for conversion of 4 percent Convertible Subordinated Debentures; (*b*) 1,293,103 shares for conversion of 5 percent Convertible Subordinated Debentures; (*c*) 512,-800 shares for Qualified Stock Option Plans.
>
> Of the 512,800 shares reserved for Qualified Stock Option Plans, options for 71,763 shares, including options presently exercisable for 9,943 shares, are outstanding at prices ranging from $12 to $16.51 a share under two 1974 Plans, and options for 391,013 shares are outstanding at prices ranging from $19.02 to $26.72 a share under the 1978 Plan. These prices are 100 percent of the market prices on the dates the options were granted or accepted, adjusted to give effect to stock dividends paid subsequent to those dates.

Business combination agreements sometimes provide for the issuance of additional shares of stock contingent upon specified future events, such as earnings performance or changes in stock prices. The terms of such contingent issuances of shares should be disclosed in footnotes to the financial statements, but the contingent shares generally should not be recorded as outstanding until they are actually issued.

Other restrictions and preferences pertaining to capital stock include the callable and cumulative provisions frequently attached to preferred stock. Most preferred stocks are callable at specified prices slightly above par; and the auditors must ascertain that any program of reacquiring shares accurately carries out the call provisions of the issue. The cumulative provision found in many preferred stocks must be considered by the auditors in reviewing the propriety of dividend payments and in determining the disclosure to be made of any arrearage of preferred dividends.

Audit procedures—contributed surplus

The auditors' objective is to determine that all entries in the Contributed Surplus accounts represent properly authorized transactions, recorded in accordance with generally accepted accounting principles. To achieve this objective the auditors obtain or prepare an analysis of the Contributed Surplus accounts. In the initial audit of a client, this analysis must begin with the very first entries in these accounts—which often means the date of organization of the corporation. Since this analysis consists mainly of identifying credit entries arising from capital stock transactions, the work is most conveniently done as part of the examination of capital stock.

Credits from other sources, such as the declaration of stock dividends and from treasury stock transactions, should be verified by reference to the original documents and authorizations. Debit entries to Contributed Surplus accounts are not frequent in most companies; one basis for debit entries is the redemption of preferred stock at a price in excess of par value.

The work required in an initial examination with respect to analysis of Contributed Surplus accounts for prior years may be considerably reduced if audits have been made in the past by other chartered accountants. However, there is seldom enough activity in accounts of this type to make the analysis a difficult task.

The process of analyzing the Contributed Surplus accounts usually will lead to the auditors to authorizations in the minutes of directors and shareholders. Conversely, a reading of the minutes may bring to light the authorization of other transactions which should have resulted in entries in the Contributed Surplus accounts, but which were improperly placed in other accounts.

AUDIT PROGRAM—RETAINED EARNINGS AND DIVIDENDS

A suggested audit program for retained earnings and dividends includes the following steps:

1. Analyze retained earnings and appropriations of retained earnings.
2. Investigate any prior-period adjustments to retained earnings.
3. Review dividend procedures for both cash and stock dividends.

1. Analyze retained earnings and appropriations of retained earnings.

The analysis of retained earnings and any appropriations of retained earnings should cover the entire history of these accounts. Such an analysis is prepared for the permanent file and added to each year.

Credits to the Retained Earnings account ordinarily represent amounts of net income transferred from the Income Summary account. In addition, the account may contain credits derived from appropriations which have been discontinued and restored to retained earnings.

Debits to the Retained Earnings account may include entries for net losses, cash and stock dividends, and for the creation or enlargement of appropriations. Appropriations of retained earnings require specific authorization by the board of directors. The only verification necessary for these entries is to ascertain that the dates and amounts correspond to the actions of the board.

Appropriations of retained earnings appear to be made less commonly now than they were a few years ago. The decline in use of these appropriations from retained earnings may reflect a growing awareness that such segregations of retained earnings seldom serve any constructive purpose and may create confusion and misunderstanding on the part of some readers of the financial statements.

Under no circumstances should operating expenses or losses be absorbed against appropriations of retained earnings. Such misuse of appropriations would cause operating expenses to be entirely omitted from the determination of net income and consequently would cause an overstatement of that highly significant figure.

2. Investigate any prior-period adjustments to retained earnings.

In single-year financial statements, prior-period adjustments are treated as restatements of the beginning retained earnings balance. The adjustment amounts are presented net of applicable income taxes. The auditors should investigate any charges or credits to retained earnings which the client has labeled as prior-period adjustments, to determine that the criteria of the *CICA Handbook* have been met.

3. Review dividend procedures for both cash and stock dividends.

In the verification of cash dividends the auditors usually will perform the following steps:

a.   Determine the dates and amounts of dividends authorized.
b.   Verify the amounts paid.
c.   Determine the amount of any preferred dividends in arrears.
d.   Review the treatment of unclaimed dividend cheques.

When reviewing minutes of the directors' meetings, the auditors should note the date and amount of each dividend declaration. This serves to establish the authority for dividend disbursements. The dividend payments may then be verified by obtaining the list of shareholders as of the dividend date and multiplying the total number of shares by the dividend rate per share set forth in the minutes. The accuracy of these dividend lists may be verified by tracing them to the shareholders' ledger on a test basis. The total dividend payment may also be verified by multiplying the number of shares in the general ledger control account by the amount per share. In special situations the auditors may request the client's legal counsel for an opinion as to the legality of dividends declared.

The auditors' review of dividend declarations may reveal the existence of cash dividends declared but not paid. These declared but unpaid dividends must be shown as liabilities in the balance sheet. The auditors also may review the procedures for handling unclaimed dividends and ascertain that these items are recognized as liabilities. The amount of any accumulated dividends in arrears on preferred stock should be computed and disclosed.

In the verification of stock dividends there is the additional problem of determining that the proper amount has been transferred from the Retained Earnings account to the Capital Stock and Contributed Surplus accounts. The auditors should ensure that the accounting for stock dividend is in accordance with both business corporation laws and generally accepted accounting principles. The Canada Business Corporations

Act stipulates that in the case of stock dividends, "the value of the dividend stated as an amount of money shall be added to the stated capital account."

Donated capital

Donated capital represents the fair value of any assets contributed to a corporation by shareholders and other parties. For example, a city may donate a building site to a manufacturing concern as a means of attracting new enterprises to the community.

In the audit of the Donated Capital account, the objectives of the auditors are (a) to establish the propriety of the amounts originally entered in the account; (b) to determine the nature of any changes which have been recorded; and (c) to determine that any restrictions imposed by the donor are being observed. The logical starting point is to analyze the account. Credit entries should be vouched to the gift contract or to the appraiser's report. This will serve to establish the beginning balances and any additions. Any debits to the account should be carefully investigated. Perhaps the only charges properly made against donated capital are for the costs of acquiring the gift; these costs may be vouched to the cash records.

Time of examination

The ledger accounts for capital stock, contributed surplus, and retained earnings ordinarily receive very few entries during the year. Consequently, most auditors feel that nothing can be gained by making a preliminary analysis of these accounts for a fraction of the year. It usually is more efficient to make the analysis in one step after the close of the period. Other audit procedures, such as the examination of the stock certificate book or the confirmation of outstanding shares with the independent registrar and stock transfer agent, also are performed at the year-end. In the first audit of a new client, some preliminary work can be done advantageously in obtaining and reviewing copies of the articles of incorporation and by-laws, and in analyzing the capital accounts. For repeat engagements, however, there is usually little opportunity to perform audit work on owners' equity accounts before the end of the period.

FINANCIAL STATEMENT PRESENTATION

Adequate informative disclosure is a critical requirement for shareholders' equity. All changes during the year in each of the equity accounts must be disclosed. If many transactions have affected these accounts, a statement of shareholders' equity is appropriate. A statement of shareholders' equity is an expanded statement of retained earnings, showing the changes over the year in all of the equity accounts. Although a statement of shareholders' equity generally is not a required financial statement, many corporations include it in their annual reports. Alternatively, a statement of retained earnings, together with footnote disclosure of any changes in contributed capital, may be presented.

Capital stock

The presentation of capital stock on the balance sheet should include a complete description of each issue. To enable the investor or financial analyst to make a close appraisal of a stock issue, the following data should be provided in the shareholders' equity section, or in notes to the financial statements:

1. Exact title of the issue; par or stated value; dividend rate, if any.
2. For preferred stock, the extent of dividend preference, call provisions, conversion privileges, and aggregate liquidation rights.
3. Number of shares authorized, issued, in treasury, and outstanding.
4. Per share and aggregate amounts of cumulative preferred dividends in arrears.
5. Information as to shares reserved for stock option plans and for conversion of bonds or preferred stock. The number of shares reserved for outstanding stock warrants, subscribed but unissued stock, stock dividends declared but undistributed, and stock to be issued in completion of a business combination, should also be disclosed.

Treasury stock

Treasury stock preferably is shown in the shareholders' equity section, at cost, as a deduction from the combined total of contributed capital and retained earnings. The presentation of treasury stock as an asset is still encountered on a few published financial statements. Such treatment is to be discouraged; if the auditors accept such classification, they should at least insist upon clear-cut identification of the "asset" as the company's own shares. Dividends are not to be paid on treasury shares; to do so would lead to an overstatement of the company's revenue.

Various business corporation laws have specific regulations regarding the acquisition of treasury stock, and the auditors should be familiar with these laws.

The restriction of retained earnings is intended for the protection of creditors. When a corporation reacquires shares of its own stock by purchase, it is paying cash to shareholders, just as when a cash dividend is paid. Total cash payments to shareholders should not exceed total earnings or an impairment of the original contributed capital will result. This original contributed capital is intended to stand as a permanent buffer between corporate creditors and any operating losses which the company may incur. Consequently, a corporation is not permitted to impair its permanent contributed capital by handing out cash to its shareholders in excess of earnings, regardless of whether these cash payouts are in the form of dividends or in payments for reacquired shares. The balance sheet or notes to the financial statements should disclose retained earnings restricted under business corporation law because of treasury stock acquisitions.

Retained earnings

The term "Retained Earnings" has generally displaced "Earned Surplus" in published financial statements. Other terms enjoying a significant degree of use include "Earnings Retained for Use in the Business," and "Earnings Reinvested in the Business."

Changes in retained earnings during the year may be shown in a separate statement or combined with the income statement. The combined statement of income and retained earnings appears to be continuing in popularity. In this form of presentation the amount of retained earnings at the beginning of the year is added to the net income figure, dividends paid are subtracted from the subtotal, and the final figure represents the new balance of retained earnings.

Amounts placed in reserve accounts by appropriation of retained earnings are still part of total retained earnings. They should be presented as separate items, but in a position where they may be added to the portion of retained earnings presently available for dividends. The term "reserve" should not be used in any sense other than for appropriations of retained earnings. This usage has been recommended by the CICA; if it is observed, the term "reserve" will appear only in the shareholders' equity section of the balance sheet.

One of the most significant points to consider in determining the presentation of retained earnings in the balance sheet is the existence of any restriction on the use of this retained income. Agreements with banks, bondholders, and other creditors very commonly impose limitations on the payment of dividends. These restrictions must be fully disclosed in the notes to financial statements.

AUDIT OF SOLE PROPRIETORSHIPS AND PARTNERSHIPS

We have discussed the pressures which cause large corporations to have regular annual audits; these pressures generally do not exist for small companies. However, many small businesses may feel the need for an occasional audit if not an annual one. The owner of a small business may feel audits are worthwhile because they tend to discourage fraud, bring irregularities to light, and are very useful in the event that the company's income tax returns are questioned by the Department of National Revenue. Additionally, managements of many small businesses feel that they have much to gain from an analysis of their accounting and financial operations by an independent expert. Perhaps the most important reason for a small business to arrange for an audit, however, is the need for audited financial statements in order to obtain bank loans. Typically, a banker when approached by the owner of a small business applying for a loan will request audited financial statements as an aid to reaching a decision on the loan application.

It is perfectly natural for the owner of a business being audited for the first time to be concerned about the auditors' fee and to question whether all the procedures performed by the auditors are really necessary. The CA retained to audit a small business, of course, will enquire as to the reason for the audit. If a bank loan is involved, the CA may find it useful to arrange a joint meeting in which the owner, the banker, and the CA discuss the objectives and scope of the examination. Such a meeting is helpful in making the small business owner aware that the CAs must have unlimited access to all information about the business. The owner then is more likely to cooperate fully with respect to such audit procedures as confirmation of receivables and observation of inventories.

In general, the same principles described for the audit of corporate capital are applicable to the examination of the capital accounts and drawing accounts of a sole proprietorship or partnership. Analyses are made of all proprietorship accounts from the beginning of the business; the initial capital investment and any additions are traced to the cash and asset records; and the net income or loss for the period and any withdrawals are verified. In the case of a sole proprietorship, a common source of difficulty is the practice of intermingling business and personal transactions, making it necessary for the auditors to segregate personal net worth from business capital.

Intermingling of business and personal transactions.   In the audit of a sole proprietorship the auditors often find that personal expenses of the owner have been paid with business funds and charged as business expenses. It is extremely difficult to segregate many types of expenditures between business and personal because the business and social activities of the proprietor of a small business are likely to be very closely interwoven. Moreover, a tendency exists to classify borderline or doubtful items as business expense, since this classification makes them deductible in the determination of the owner's taxable income. On the other hand, the auditors may occasionally find that expenses of the business have been paid from the proprietor's personal funds without any reflection in the proprietorship accounting records. In some cases, business and personal funds and transactions may be intermingled continually without any effort by the proprietor to make a distinction.

A theoretical answer to this problem, of course, would require that the auditors insist that all personal expenditures be excluded from the proprietorship expense accounts. Any such expenditures paid with company funds should, by means of adjusting entries, be transferred from expense accounts to the owner's drawing account.

As a practical matter, however, it may as well be recognized that the auditors' work in this area is necessarily quite limited. In many sole proprietorships there is little internal control, and consequently there is limited assurance of the dependability of the accounting records. The auditors can, and should, question any substantial expenditures which do not appear to be of a business nature; but unless the facts are quite apparent, they are seldom in a position to challenge any explanation offered by the proprietor. Moreover, it would not serve the primary purposes of the audit to expend a large amount of time in seeking to make precise distinctions between business and non-business expenditures if the amounts involved are comparatively small.

Procedures for audit of partners' accounts. A most significant document underlying the partnership form of organization is the partnership contract. The auditors are particularly interested in determining that the distribution of net income has been carried out in accordance with the profit-sharing provisions of the partnership contract. Maintenance of partners' capital accounts at prescribed levels and restriction of drawings by partners to specified amounts are other points often covered in the contract; compliance with these clauses should be verified by the auditors in determining the propriety of the year's entries in the capital accounts. Partners' loan accounts also require reference to the partnership contract to determine the treatment intended by the partners.

Occasionally auditors may find that a partnership is operating without any written agreement of partnership. This situation raises a question of whether profits have been divided in accordance with the understanding existing between the partners. The auditors may appropriately suggest that the firm develop a written partnership contract; for their own protection the auditors may wish to obtain from each partner a written statement confirming the balance in his or her capital account and approval of the method used in dividing the year's earnings.

KEY TERMS INTRODUCED OR EMPHASIZED IN CHAPTER 18

contributed surplus Capital contributed by shareholders in excess of the par or stated value of the shares issued or donated by shareholders or others.

donated capital The fair value of assets contributed to a corporation by shareholders and other parties.

permanent file A file of audit working papers applicable to all (or several successive) audits of a specific client.

shareholders' ledger A record showing the number of shares owned by each shareholder. This is the basic record used for preparing dividend payments and other communications with shareholders.

stock certificate   A certificate representing ownership of shares of stock. To be valid, the certificate usually must be signed by appropriate company officers, countersigned by the stock transfer agent, and registered by the stock registrar.

stock certificate book   A book of serially numbered certificates with attached stubs. Each stub shows the corresponding certificate number and provides space for entering the number of shares represented by the certificate, name of the shareholder, and serial number of the certificate surrendered in exchange for the new one. Surrendered certificates are cancelled and replaced in the certificate book.

stock option plan   A formal plan granting the right to buy a specified number of shares at a stipulated price during a specified time. Stock option plans are frequently used as a form of executive compensation. The terms of such plans should be disclosed in financial statements.

stock registrar   An institution charged with responsibility for avoiding over-issuance of a corporation's stock. Every new certificate must be presented to the registrar for examination and registration before it is issued to a shareholder.

stock transfer agent   An institution responsible for maintaining detailed records of shareholders and handling transfers of stock ownership.

treasury stock   Shares of its own stock acquired by a corporation for the purpose of begin reissued or cancelled at a later date.

GROUP I
REVIEW QUESTIONS

18–1.   Compare the auditors' examination of owners' equity with their work on assets and current liabilities. Among other factors to be considered are the relative amounts of time involved and the character of the transactions to be reviewed.

18–2.   What do you consider to be the most important internal control device which a corporation can adopt with respect to capital stock transactions?

18–3.   What working papers, if any, should be prepared for the auditors' permanent file in connection with the examination of Capital Stock accounts or Partners' Capital accounts?

18–4.   With respect to the examination of the Capital Stock account, how does the work in an initial audit differ from that required in a repeat engagement?

18–5.   Comment on the desirability of audit work on the owners' equity accounts prior to the balance sheet date.

18–6.   Name three situations which might place a restriction on retained earnings limiting or preventing dividend payments. Explain how the auditors might become aware of each such restricting factor.

18-7. Delta Ltd. has issued stock options to four of its officers permitting them to purchase 5,000 shares each of common stock at a price of $25 per share at any time during the next five years. The president asks you what effect, if any, the granting of the options will have upon the balance sheet presentation of the shareholders' equity accounts.

18-8. Describe the significant features of a stock certificate book, its purpose, and the method of using it.

18-9. What use is made of the stock certificate book by the auditors?

18-10. Are the procedures for transfer of capital stock prescribed by statute or devised by the issuing corporation? Explain.

18-11. What is the primary responsibility of an independent registrar?

18-12. Some corporations use a separate bank account for the payment of dividends. What advantages are gained by this practice?

18-13. In their first examination of Wright Corporation Ltd., the auditors verified all items on the balance sheet other than retained earnings; they also noted that the figure for retained earnings was the proper amount to put the statement in balance. Is any additional verification of the retained earnings figure necessary? Explain.

18-14. What errors are commonly encountered by the auditors in their examination of the capital and drawing accounts of a sole proprietorship?

18-15. In your examination of Kelley Corporation Ltd. you find that two 10 percent stock dividends were distributed during the year. On what basis would you expect the charges to Retained Earnings to be computed?

18-16. How are changes in contributed capital during a period disclosed in the financial statements?

18-17. The CAs' examination normally would not include (select one):
   a. Determining that dividend declarations have been in compliance with debt agreements.
   b. Tracing the authorization of the dividend to the directors' minutes
   c. Detail tracing from the dividend payment list to the capital stock records.
   d. Reviewing the bank reconciliation for the imprest dividend account. (AICPA, adapted)

18-18. How can the independent auditors determine the propriety of charges or credits to retained earnings which the client has identified as prior-period adjustments?

18-19. Contrast the auditors' responsibility in the examination of the capital and drawing accounts of a partnership with their responsibility relating to the shareholders' equity accounts of a corporation.

18-20. Corporations sometimes issue their own capital stock in exchange for services and various assets other than cash. As an auditor, what evidence would you look for to determine the propriety of the values used in recording such transactions?

18-21. In your second annual examination of a corporate client you find a new account in the general ledger, "Treasury Stock," with a balance of $10,500. Describe the procedures you would follow to verify this item.

18–22.   In examining the financial statements of Foster Ltd., you observe a debit entry for $20,000 labeled as "Dividends" in the Retained Earnings account. Explain in detail how you would verify this entry.

18–23.   A staff assistant reported to the auditor in charge that the Retained Earnings account of the Olympic Corporation Ltd. contained a debit entry on December 15 for $100,000, representing a dividend. In reviewing cash disbursements, however, the assistant had found the total of dividend cheques issued to be less than half this amount. What is the most probable explanation of this situation?

GROUP II
QUESTIONS REQUIRING ANALYSIS

18–24.   In your first examination of Farber Corporation Ltd., you find a credit to the Capital Stock account offset by a debit to Goodwill. Upon investigating the transaction further, you learn that the corporation issued small amounts of stock to several prominent citizens in the area as a "good-will gesture." No consideration was received by the corporation in exchange for these shares. The transaction had been recorded at the par value of the shares issued.

Required:

Would you take exception to the manner in which Farber Corporation Ltd. has recorded this transaction? Discuss.

18–25.   Denton Corporation Ltd., a closely held manufacturing company, was short of cash when a large note payable became due. To prevent the corporation from becoming insolvent, several shareholders paid the note upon maturity from their personal funds. The shareholders do not expect to be repaid by Denton Corporation Ltd.

Required:

What effect does the shareholders' payment of this corporate liability have upon the financial statements of Denton Corporation Ltd.? Explain.

18–26.   Tower Ltd. was incorporated July 10, 1979, with authorized capital as follows:

Common stock, Class A, 20,000 shares, par value $25 per share
Common stock, Class B, 100,000 shares, par value $5 per share

The Capital Stock account in the general ledger is credited with only one item in the year, 1979, representing capital stock sold for cash, at par, as follows:

Class A, 12,000 shares
Class B, 60,000 shares

The sum of open certificate stubs in the stock certificate books at December 31, 1979, indicates that 82,000 shares of stock were outstanding.

Required:

a. State possible explanations for this apparent discrepancy.

b. State the steps you would take to determine the cause of the discrepancy. (AICPA, adapted)

18–27. Hilliard Ltd. found itself short of cash in 1979 and decided to forego cash dividends in favour of a 4 percent stock dividend. The dividend was declared on April 30, at which time the company's stock was selling at $25 a share. The date of record was May 15, and the date of distribution June 10. The outstanding shares prior to the dividend numbered 800,000 with a par value of $10 each; the original issuance price of these shares had been $15. In your first examination of the company at December 31, 1979, you observed that the only effects of the stock dividend had been transfer of $320,000 from the Retained Earnings account to the Capital Stock account and an increase in the number of outstanding shares to 832,000. Was the stock dividend properly recorded? Explain fully.

18–28. Several years ago the board of directors of Dayton Labs, Inc., authorized the creation of a Reserve for Development of New Products by a charge to the Retained Earnings account. Until the present year, expenditures for research and development had been fairly consistent at about 5 percent of sales and had been treated as operating expense. In the present year, however, the corporation increased its research and development program substantially, and it is estimated that expenditures for the program will approximate 12 percent of the current year's sales. The directors propose to charge the portion in excess of 5 percent of sales to the Reserve for Development of New Products. Would you as an auditor take exception to the action proposed by the board of directors?

18–29. What would be the course of action in an audit of a partnership if the examination disclosed that—

a. The division of profits and the capital contributed by each partner does not agree with the partnership contract?

b. A partner had died in the year under examination but no recognition of this fact was shown in the account records?

c. A partner had sold his share during the year to one of his co-partners, but this sale was not reflected in the accounts?

d. A new partner was admitted during the year? (AICPA)

GROUP III
PROBLEMS

18–30. You are engaged in the first audit of a corporation. The corporation has both a stock transfer agent and an independent registrar for its capital stock. The transfer agent maintains the record of shareholders, and the registrar determines that there is no overissue of stock. Signatures of both are required to validate stock certificates.

It has been proposed that confirmations be obtained from both the transfer agent and the registrar as to the stock outstanding at balance sheet date. If such confirmations agree with the accounting records, no additional work in to be performed as to capital stock.

If you agree that obtaining the confirmations as suggested would be sufficient in this case, give the justification for your position. If you do not agree, state specifically all additional steps you would take and explain your reasons for taking them. (AICPA, adapted)

18–31. You are engaged in the audit of Phoenix Corporation Ltd., a new client, at the close of its first fiscal year, April 30, 1979. The accounts had been closed prior to the time you began your year-end field work.

You review the following shareholders' equity accounts in the general ledger.

Capital stock

	May 1, 78 CR1 500,000
	Apr. 28, 79 J12–5 50,000

Premium on Capital Stock

	May 1, 79 CR1 250,000
	Feb. 2, 79 CR10 2,500

Retained Earnings

Apr. 28, 79 J12–5 50,000	Apr. 30, 79 J12–14 800,000

Treasury Stock

Sept. 14, 78 CD5 80,000	Feb. 2, 79 CR10 40,000

Income Summary

Apr. 30, 79 J12–13 5,200,000	Apr. 30, 79 J12–12 6,000,000
Apr. 30, 79 J12–14 800,000	

Other information in your working papers includes the following:

1. Phoenix's articles of incorporation filed April 17, 1978, authorize 100,000 shares of no-par value capital stock. Phoenix was incorporated under the Canada Business Corporations Act.

2. Directors' minutes include the following resolutions:

    Apr. 30, 78   Authorized issue of 10,000 shares to an underwriting syndicate for $75 per share.
    Sept. 13, 78 Authorized acquisition of 1,000 shares from a dissident holder at $80 per share.
    Feb. 1, 79   Authorized reissue of 500 treasury shares at $85 per share.
    Apr. 28, 79   Declared 10 percent stock dividend, payable May 18, 1979, to shareholders of record May 4, 1979.

3. The following costs of the May 1, 1978, and February 2, 1979, stock issuances were charged to the named expense accounts: Printing Expense, $2,500; Legal Fees, $17,350; Accounting Fees, $12,000; Securities Commission Filing and Other Fees, $150.

4. Market values for Phoenix Corporation Ltd. capital stock on various dates were:

Sept. 13, 78	$78.50
Sept. 14, 78	79.00
Feb. 2, 79	85.00
Apr. 28, 79	90.00

5. Phoenix Corporation Ltd.'s combined federal and provincial income tax rates total 50 percent.

Required:

a. Adjusting journal entries at April 30, 1979.
b. Shareholders' equity section of Phoenix Corporation Ltd.'s April 30, 1979, balance sheet.

18–32. You were engaged on May 1, 1979, by a committee of shareholders to perform a special audit as of December 31, 1978, of the shareholders' equity of McCoy Corporation Ltd. The stock is actively traded on a stock exchange. The group of shareholders who engaged you believe that the information contained in the shareholders' equity section of the published annual report for the year ended December 31, 1978, is not correct. If your examination substantiates their suspicions, they intend to use your report in a proxy fight to gain control of McCoy Corporation Ltd.

Management agrees to permit your audit but refuses to permit any direct confirmation with shareholders. To secure management's cooperation in the audit, the committee of shareholders has agreed to this limitation and you have been instructed by the committee to limit your audit procedure in this respect. You have also been instructed to exclude the audit of revenue and expense accounts for 1978.

Required:

a. Prepare an audit program for the usual examination of the share-holders equity section of a corporation's balance sheet, assuming no limitation upon the scope of your examination. Exclude the audit of revenue and expense accounts.

b. Describe any special auditing procedures you would undertake in view of the limitations and other special circumstances of your examination of McCoy Corporation Ltd.'s shareholders' equity accounts. (AICPA, adapted)

18–33. You are engaged in the audit of the financial statements of Glasco Mfg. Co., Inc., for its second year of operations. Financial statements for the preceding year, which included net income of $92,500, were not examined by independent CAs. Your engagement includes preparation of the company's federal and provincial income tax returns for the year under audit.

The company's income statement, prepared by the controller, is as follows:

GLASCO MFG. CO., INC.
Income Statement
Year Ended September 30, 1979

Net sales	$2,000,000
Cost and expenses:	
Cost of sales	1,300,000
Selling, general and administrative	400,000
Interest	30,000
Federal and Provincial income taxes	148,500
	$1,878,500
Net Income	$ 121,500

During the course of your examination you learn that manufacturing overhead had been excluded from the valuation of Glasco's inventories at first-in, first-out cost. Overhead thus excluded amounted to $100,000 at September 30, 1978, and $160,000 at September 30, 1979. Glasco's federal and provincial income tax returns for the year ended September 30, 1978, were prepared by Glasco's controller on the same basis as the financial statements for that year. The company's combined federal and provincial income tax rates total 55 percent. And deficiency in income taxes paid for the fiscal year ended September 30, 1978, would be subject to an annual interest rate of 6 percent, computed from the due date (December 15, 1978) to September 30, 1979.

Required:

a. Draft proposed adjusting journal entries to correct the exclusion of manufacturing overhead from inventories. (Show your adjustments to Glasco's 1978 operating results in one adjusting entry, and your adjustment to its 1979 operating results in another.)

b. How should you advise Glasco Mfg. Co., Inc., regarding the income tax return for the year ended September 30, 1978?

GROUP IV
CASE STUDIES IN AUDITING

18–34.   CONTRACTOR'S INSPECTION &
                         DISBURSEMENT SERVICE, INC.

Contractor's Inspection & Disbursement Service, Inc., furnishes a control service for building contractors. Contractors of limited financial standing are required by certain lending institutions to engage such a service to make regular progress inspections of their projects and to control the disbursement of funds advanced to the contractor by the lenders. The funds are advanced by the bank and deposited in a separate bank account for each contractor; the service controls these accounts. Disbursements are made on the basis of approved invoices supported by release and lien waivers where necessary.

One of the larger financial institutions has become apprehensive over the financial condition of Contractor's Inspection & Disbursements Service, Inc., and has threatened to discontinue referrals of its borrowers to this service unless the shareholders' equity of the corporation can be increased to at least $150,000. The financial position of the service at present is as follows:

Assets

Cash	$ 25,000
Acounts receivable	200,000
Other assets	25,000
Total	$250,000

Liabilities and Shareholders' Equity

Accounts payable	$ 50,000
Deferred revenue	125,000
Shareholders' equity	75,000
Total	$250,000

Note: This statement does not include any funds held for account of contractors.

The present billing procedure of the service is to bill the contractor as soon as construction begins and the first funds are received from the bank. In most cases the fee is payable out of the first advance from the bank, so that accounts receivable generally are collected promptly; in some agreeemnts the fee is not payable until the construction is completed. At the time the fee is billed, deferred revenue is credited, and this deferred revenue subsequently is taken into income pro rata over the period of construction. Therefore, there is always a substantial balance of deferred revenue representing the advance charges for control services that have not been rendered.

The shareholders of the company either do not have the necessary additional capital required by the lending institution or they are reluctant to transfer such capital from other investments. Therefore, the controller has proposed the following:

A new corporation, called "Contractor's Inspection & Disbursement

Ltd.," will be formed. To it will be transferred all collectible accounts receivable, as well as cash and other assets, and all liabilities except the deferred revenue. After this transfer the balance sheet of the new company will appear as follows:

Assets

Cash	$ 25,000
Accounts receivable	150,000
Other assets	25,000
Total	$200,000

Liabilities and Shareholders' Equity

Accounts payable	$ 50,000
Capital stock	150,000
Total	$200,000

The balance sheet of Contractor's Inspection & Disbursement Service, Inc. (the old company), will appear as follows:

Assets

Cash	-0-
Accounts receivable	$ 50,000
Other assets	-0-
Investment in Contractor's Inspection & Disbursement Company	150,000
Total	$200,000

Liabilities and Shareholders' Equity

Deferred revenue	$125,000
Shareholders' equity	75,000
Total	$200,000

To compensate for the failure to transfer the deferred revenue to the new company, the old company will sign an agreement guaranteeing to complete any control contracts which the new company may be financially unable to carry out, and to take over certain problem jobs when they arise. (In the past the old company frequently has had to take over a contractor's work and finish the job when the contractor became hopelessly delinquent.) Through this agreement, the old company intends to indemnify the new company for any such occurrences. The old company will adjust the balance of deferred revenue in its accounting records at the end of each year to show the correct amount of deferred revenue.

In establishing accounting policies for the new company, the controller proposes to take all fees into income as they are billed, without any deferral. He says he is justified in doing this because many companies operate on a cash basis, and he feels such a procedure is in order if it helps accomplish the objective of increasing the shareholders' equity of the organization to the level of $150,000, as required by the bank.

The controller has outlined this procedure to the bank official handling the case, and this official has agreed that the proposed reorganization will be satisfactory to the bank. However, you were not present during the conference, and there is nothing in writing to assure you that the bank official fully understood just what was being done. It is understood that the bank will be given financial statements of only the new company and that it no longer will be interested in the old company.

You were asked to perform an examination and submit an opinion as to the balance sheet of the new company in a report to the bank. Your engagement also contemplates making annual audits of the new company.

Required:

a. What kind of an opinion would you give on the beginning balance sheet?

b. In your report at the end of the first year, can you give an opinion that the income statement presents fairly the results of operations for the year? Explain fully.

19

Further verification of revenue and expenses

Today, with greater and greater emphasis being placed upon corporate earnings as an indicator of the health and well-being of our industrialized economy, the income statement is of fundamental importance to management, shareholders, creditors, employees, and government. The relative level of corporate earnings is now a key factor in the determination of such issues as wage negotiations, income tax rates, price controls, subsidies, and government fiscal policy. It must be remembered that the function of the independent public accountants is to give integrity to financial statements—to give assurance to all who use these statements that the net earnings reported each year have been determined in accordance with generally accepted accounting principles, in an unbiased manner, and on a basis consistent with that of the preceding year. Acceptance of this responsibility is the best evidence that public accounting has reached the status of a profession. The development of the profession is most apparent when we recall that not long ago auditors were largely concerned with protecting creditors against overstatement of asset values, rather than serving the needs of all the varied groups that play a part in our economy.

The auditors' approach to verification of income

Accountants generally agree that the measurement of income is the most important single function of accounting. A fair and informative income statement is then surely as important as, if not more important than, the balance sheet. Nevertheless, audits continue to be organized in terms of balance sheet topics. The reasons for organizing audit work in this manner were discussed in Chapter 10.

As the significance of the income statement increased, auditors began to verify income statement accounts concurrently with related balance sheet accounts. Depreciation expense, for example, is most conveniently verified along with the plant and equipment accounts; once the existence and cost of depreciable assets is established, the verification of depreciation expense is merely an additional step. On the other hand, to verify depreciation expense without first establishing the nature and amount of assets owned and subject to depreciation would obviously be a cart-before-the-horse approach. The same line of reasoning tells us that the auditors' work on inventories, especially in determining that inventory transactions were accurately cut off at the end of the period, is a major step toward the verification of the income statement figures for sales and cost of goods sold. Much of the material in the preceding eight chapters of this book has related to income statement accounts, although the sequence of topics has followed a balance sheet arrangement.

When the balance sheets at the beginning and end of an accounting period have been fully verified, the net income for the year is fairly well established, although considerable additional work remains to be done before the auditors can express a professional opinion that the income statement "presents fairly" the results of operations.

Let us emphasize the fact that the auditors' review of revenue and expense transactions should be much more than an incidental by-product of the examination of assets and liabilities. Critical examination of revenue and expense accounts may bring to light errors, omissions, and inconsistencies not disclosed in the examination of balance sheet accounts. An example of such deficiencies in accounting for revenue and expense transactions is failure to distinguish properly between capital and revenue expenditures.

Audit by comparison

The monthly totals of individual revenue and expense accounts should be compared with the corresponding monthly figures of the preceding year. This comparison may disclose variations caused by unusual items which warrant investigation. Comparison of budgeted amounts with actual revenue and expenses may also draw the auditors' attention to areas requiring detailed analysis. Significant variations should be fully explored with a view toward the development of suggestions to management of means of reducing expenses and expanding revenue. The relative profitability or unprofitability of particular products or territories, as well as the development of significant trends in certain types of revenue and expense, may be disclosed by this process of *auditing by comparison.* The value of auditing services is certain to be increased in the eyes of management if the auditors will expand this approach to include a thorough appraisal of the methods of controlling both revenue and expenses.

Conservatism in the measurement of income

Conservatism in the valuation of assets means that when two (or more) reasonable alternative values are indicated, the accountant will choose the lower of the two. Of course, the principles used in valuing assets, such as inventories and accounts receivable, also have an effect upon the measurement of income. The traditional policy of choosing the lower of two possible valuations for an asset has the supplementary effects of minimizing net income for the current period and of minimizing owners' equity. The doctrine of conservatism is a powerful force influencing distinctions between capital and revenue expenditures; this force always is exerted in favour of treating borderline cases as expenses of the period.

Another aspect of conservatism in the measurement of income is the policy of not recording revenue until the point of delivery of goods or services; at this point, the revenue is realized through the receipt of cash or the acquisition of a receivable or the equivalent. The other side of income measurement is the recognition of expenses; in this area, conservatism requires that all expenses associated with the revenue of the period be recognized, even though some of these expenses (as for pension plans or for the warranty of products sold) are not subject to precise measurement until a later date.

Most auditors have a considerable respect for the doctrine of conservatism. In part, this attitude springs from the concept of legal liability to third parties. Bankers, creditors, and investors who have sustained losses as a result of the failure of auditors to detect overstated assets and exaggerated earnings have time and again collected heavy damages from public accounting firms, and have damaged many a professional reputation. Financial statements which *understate* financial position and operating results almost never lead to legal action against the auditors who approve these statements. Nevertheless, leaders of the public accounting profession must recognize that overemphasis on conservatism in financial reporting is a narrow and shortsighted approach to meeting the needs of our society. To be of greatest value, financial statements should present fairly, rather than understate, financial position and operating results.

Time of examination

The audit of revenue and expense accounts stresses the review of internal control and the compliance testing of transactions, rather than the observation, inspection, and confirmation of year-end balances, as in the case of balance sheet accounts. Consequently, most of the audit work can be performed advantageously before the end of the year.

REVENUE

Audit objectives

In the examination of revenue, the principal objectives of the auditors are (a) to study and evaluate internal control, with particular emphasis upon the use of accrual accounting to record revenue; (b) to verify that all earned revenue has been recorded and all recorded revenue has been earned; and (c) to identify and interpret significant trends and variations in the dollar amounts of various categories of revenue.

Relationship of revenue to balance sheet accounts

The auditors' review of sales activities was considered in connection with accounts receivable in Chapter 13. As pointed out previously, most revenue accounts are verified by the auditors in conjunction with the audit of a related asset or liability. The following list summarizes the revenue verified in this manner:

Balance sheet item	*Revenue*
Accounts receivable	Sales
Notes receivable	Interest
Securities and other investments	Interest, dividends, gains on sales, share of investee's income
Property, plant, and equipment	Rent, gains on sale
Intangible assets	Royalties

A common characteristic of the revenue items listed above is that most, if not all, are accounted for on the accrual basis. Accrual basis accounting for revenue results in stronger internal control, because it requires the recording of a receivable when the revenue is earned. Once the receivable is recorded, some follow-up is inevitable. Additional assurance is provided that attention will be drawn to any delay in the receipt of cash, or any failure to record a cash receipt. For example, if dividends earned are recorded as receivables by an accrual entry at the date of record, any failure to receive or to record dividend cheques will be readily apparent.

Miscellaneous revenue

One category of revenue not included in the above listing but of interest to the auditors is miscellaneous revenue. Miscellaneous revenue, by its very nature, is a mixture of minor items, some non-recurring and others likely to be received at irregular intervals. Consequently, many companies do not accrue such revenue but merely debit Cash and credit Miscellaneous Revenue when cash is received. The weakness inherent in this procedure is not of particular significance if the amounts involved are minor and infrequent. However, the weakness can become serious if revenue of substantial amount is misclassified as Miscellaneous Revenue, a practice sometimes followed because of its convenience.

ILLUSTRATIVE CASE. An old story in public accounting circles concerns the auditors who enquired of a new client how extensive was the classification by the company of revenue and expenses. "Just two of each," was the reply, "general and miscellaneous."

For the reasons indicated above, the auditors should obtain an analysis of the Miscellaneous Revenue account. Among the items the auditors might find improperly included as miscellaneous revenue are the following:

1. Collections on previously written-off accounts or notes receivable. These collections should be credited to the allowance for doubtful accounts and notes receivable.
2. Write-offs of old outstanding cheques or unclaimed wages. If unclaimed properties revert to the government after statutory periods, these write-offs should be credited to a liability account rather than to miscellaneous revenue.
3. Proceeds from sales of scrap. Scrap sales proceeds should generally be applied to reduce cost of goods sold, under by-product cost accounting principles.
4. Rebates or refunds of insurance premiums. These refunds should be offset against the related expense or unexpired insurance.
5. Proceeds from sales of plant assets. These proceeds should be accounted for in the determination of the gain or loss on the assets sold.

The auditors should propose adjusting journal entries to classify correctly any material items of the types described above which have been included in miscellaneous revenue by the client. Before concluding the work on revenue, the auditors should perform the "audit by comparison" techniques described earlier in this chapter, and investigate unusual fluctuations. Material amounts of unrecorded revenue may be discovered by this procedure, as well as significant misclassifications affecting revenue accounts.

EXPENSES

The auditors' work relating to purchases and cost of goods sold was covered, along with inventories, in Chapter 14. We are now concerned with audit objectives and procedures for other types of expenses.

Audit objectives

In the examination of payrolls, selling expenses, and general and administrative expenses, the auditors study and evaluate the internal controls in force and try to determine whether expenses have been recognized in the proper accounting period. In other words, the auditors want evidence that expenses have been properly matched with revenue. They also consider whether expenses have been properly classified and are reasonable in amount, as compared with forecast estimates, with expenses of prior years, and with the sales of the current year.

The work required to attain these objectives has in large part already been performed in connection with the verification of balance sheet accounts. Let us consider for a moment the number of expense accounts for which we have already outlined verification procedures in the chapters dealing with balance sheet topics:

Relationship of expenses to balance sheet accounts

Balance sheet items	*Expenses (and costs)*
Accounts and notes receivable	Uncollectible account and notes expense
Inventories	Purchases and cost of goods sold
Property, plant, and equipment	Depreciation, repairs and maintenance, and depletion
Prepaid expenses and deferred charges	Various related expenses, such as rent, property taxes, advertising, postage, and others
Intangible assets	Amortization
Accrued liabilities	Commissions, fees, bonuses, product warranty expenses, and others
Interest-bearing debt	Interest

In the following sections, we shall complete our review of expenses by considering additional audit objectives and procedures for payrolls, and for selling, and general and administrative expenses, other than those listed above. The audit of payroll is presented as a unit without regard to the division of salaries and wages between manufacturing operations and other operations. Manufacturing salaries and wages are, of course, charged to inventories, either directly or by means of the allocation of factory overhead.

The forecast—a vital element in controlling costs and expenses

In approaching the examination of costs and expenses, perhaps the most important single question to raise is the following: "Does the client have a good forecasting program?" The existence of a good forecasting program means that department heads, foremen, and other supervisors who authorize expenditures have prepared a year in advance a statement of the expenses which must be incurred for a given volume of operations. These estimates of expenses to be incurred have been assembled and summarized by the accounting department, and reviewed and approved by top management. A definite plan of operations exists; standards of performance have been set; and, month by month, the costs and expenses actually incurred are compared carefully with the amounts shown by the forecast. Any significant discrepancy between estimated expenses and actual expenses immediately receives the attention of management, and the supervisor responsible for the expenses in question is called upon for an explanation. When a forecasting program of this type is in operation, the integrity of the accounts is greatly increased, the opportunities for misclassification of expenses, for omission of transactions, and for fraud are reduced to a minimum.

Much of the audit work on costs and expenses, therefore, may be devoted to a study of the client's forecasting program. If the auditors find that the client does not prepare a forecast, or merely makes a pretense of using forecasting techniques, the conduct of the audit must be modified accordingly. One of the most effective substitutes for comparison of actual expenses with forecasted expenses is to compare the expenses of each month with the expenses of the corresponding month for the preceding year. Other procedures to be stressed in the absence of forecasting controls include close review of variations in gross profit margins and extensive analysis of ledger accounts for expenses.

Payrolls

The payroll in many companies is by far the largest operating cost, and, therefore, deserves the close attention of the auditors. In the past, payroll frauds were common and often substantial. Today, however, payroll frauds are more difficult to conceal for several reasons: (a) extensive subdivision of duties relating to payroll, (b) use of computers for preparation of payrolls, and (c) necessity of frequent reports to government, listing employees' earnings and tax withholdings.

The principal objectives of the auditors in the examination of payrolls are:

1. To determine that the authorized records and procedures are so designed and operated as to provide adequate internal control.
2. To determine that the client has complied with government regulations concerning pension contribution, unemployment insurance, workmen's compensation insurance, wages and hours, income tax withholding, and other federal, provincial, and local requirements concerning employment.
3. To determine that the company is complying with terms of union agreements as to wage rates, vacation pay, and similar items.

4. To suggest methods of simplifying and improving payroll procedures.

Internal control

The establishment of strong internal control over payrolls is particularly important for several reasons. Although payroll frauds are infrequent today, compared to the past, the possibility of large-scale payroll fraud still exists. Such frauds may involve listing fictitious persons on the payroll, overpaying employees, and continuing employees on the payroll after their separation from the company. A second reason for emphasizing internal control over payrolls is that a great mass of detailed information concerning hours worked and rates of pay must be processed quickly and accurately if workers are to be paid promptly and without error. Good employee relations demand that paycheques be ready on time and be free from error. As pointed out in previous chapters, internal control is a means of securing accuracy and dependability in accounting data as well as a means of preventing fraud.

Still another reason for emphasizing the importance of internal control over payrolls is the existence of various payroll tax laws and income tax laws, which require that certain payroll records be maintained, and that payroll data be reported to the employee and to governmental agencies.

Methods of achieving internal control.

Budgetary control of labour costs. To control payroll costs means to avoid waste and to obtain the maximum production from the dollars expended for services of employees. As a means of establishing control over payroll costs, many companies delegate to department heads and other supervisors responsibility for the control of costs in their respective units of the business. The supervisor may be requested at the beginning of each year to submit for the forecast an estimate of departmental labour costs for the coming period. As the year progresses and actual labour costs are compiled, the controller submits monthly reports to top management comparing the forecasted labour costs and the actual labour costs for each department. The effectiveness of this control device will depend largely upon the extent to which top management utilizes these reports and takes action upon variances from the forecast.

Reports to governmental agencies. Another important internal control over payroll lies in the necessity of preparing reports to government agencies showing the earnings and tax deductions for all employees. This type of control is not concerned with holding labour costs to a minimum, but is an effective means of preventing and detecting payroll fraud. Now that every employee must have a social insurance number, and the employer must report earnings and deductions for each employee, the opportunities for payroll fraud are greatly reduced. In a few cases, falsified reports to government agencies have been prepared as part of a payroll fraud, but this involves such extensive scheming and falsification of records as to make fraud of this type rather unlikely.

Subdivision of duties.   Most important of all internal controls over payroll is the division of payroll work among several departments of the company. Payroll activities include the functions of employment, timekeeping, payroll preparation and record keeping, and the distribution of pay to employees. For strong internal control, each of these functions should be handled by a separate department of the company. Combination of these functions in a single department or under the authority of one person opens the door to payroll fraud. These several phases of payroll activities will now be considered individually.

The employment function

The first significant step in building a strong system of internal control over payrolls is taken by the personnel department when a new employee is hired. At this point, the authorized rate of pay should be entered on a pay rate record. The employee also should sign a payroll deduction authorization specifying any amounts to be withheld, and a tax deduction return form (TDI). These records should be kept in the personnel department; but a notice of the hiring of the new employee, the rate of pay, and the payroll deductions should be sent to the payroll department. Notice of employment and of the authorized pay rate also is sent to the head of the department in which the employee is to work.

Under no circumstances is the payroll department justified in adding a name to the payroll without having received the formal authorization notice from the personnel department. When an employee's rate of pay is changed, the new rate will be entered on the pay rate record that is maintained in the personnel department. An authorization for the new rate must be sent to the payroll department before the change can be made effective on the payroll. Upon the termination of an employee, notice of termination is sent from the personnel department to the payroll department. The work of the payroll department and the propriety of names and pay rates used in preparing the payroll, therefore, rest upon formal documents originating outside the payroll department.

An adequate system of internal control demands that the addition and removal of names from the company payroll, as well as rate changes and reclassification of employees, be evidenced by written approval of an executive in the personnel department and by the head of the operating department concerned. To permit the payroll department to initiate changes in pay rates, or to add names to the payroll without formal authorization from the personnel department, is to invite payroll fraud.

Timekeeping

The function of timekeeping consists of determining the number of hours (or units of production) for which each employee is to be paid. The use of electronic time-recording equipment is of considerable aid in establishing adequate internal control over the timekeeping function. Report prepared by timekeepers who travel through the plant and contact an employee only once or twice during the day may be less dependable than time reports prepared by foremen whose supervisory duties keep them in continuous contact with a small group of employees.

Internal control can be improved by the practice of regular comparison of the time reports prepared by timekeepers or foremen with time clock records showing arrival and departure times of employees. If pay is based on piecework, a comparison may be made between the reports of units produced and the quantities which are added to the perpetual inventory records.

Salaried employees receiving a fixed monthly or weekly salary may not be required to use time clocks. Some companies require salaried employees to fill out a weekly or semimonthly report indicating the time devoted to various activities. If a salaried employee is absent, the department head usually has authority to decide whether a pay reduction should be made.

Undesirable practices related to the timekeeping function include permitting employees to maintain their own records of time worked or units completed, and basing payment on these records without any independent verification. Combination of the timekeeping function with that of payroll preparation is also extremely dangerous from an internal control standpoint. If time clock records are to contribute significantly to internal control, it is imperative that all employees punch their own timecard and no others. Any overtime worked by employees paid on an hourly basis should be approved in writing by the appropriate supervisor.

Payroll records and payroll preparation

The payroll department has the responsibility of computing the amounts to be paid to employees, and of preparing all payroll records. It is imperative that the payroll department should **not** perform the related functions of timekeeping, employment, or distribution of pay to employees. The output of the payroll department may be thought of as (1) the payroll cheques (or pay envelopes, if wages are paid in cash); (2) individual employee statements of earnings and deductions;

(3) a payroll journal; (4) an employees' ledger, summarizing earnings and deductions for each employee; (5) a payroll distribution schedule, showing the allocation of payroll costs to direct labour, overhead, and various departmental expense accounts; and (6) quarterly and annual reports to the government showing employees' earnings and taxes withheld. If the client utilizes an electronic data processing installation, many of these functions may be delegated to the data processing department.

The computation of the payroll is made from the work hours reported by the timekeeping department, and from authorized pay rates and payroll deductions reported by the personnel department.

The auditors may find payroll records and procedures varying in complexity from a manual "write it once" system to the most sophisticated computerized techniques. However, they should expect the client's system to include such basic records as timecards, payroll journals, labour distributions, and employee earnings records.

Distributing paycheques or cash to employees

The distribution of paycheques or pay envelopes to employees is the task of the paymaster. If employees are paid in cash, a copy of the payroll register is forwarded from the payroll department, and the paymaster uses this record as a guide to filling the payroll envelopes. These envelopes preferably should be prepared by the payroll department. If employees are paid by cheque, the cheques may be made ready for signature in the payroll department and forwarded to the paymaster for signature.

The paymaster handles large amounts of cheques and cash; consequently, this employee's work usually comes under the treasurer's department. Under no circumstances should the signed payroll cheques or pay envelopes containing cash be returned to the payroll department. Neither is it acceptable to turn paycheques or pay envelopes over to supervisors in the operating departments for distribution to employees. The function of distributing paycheques should be lodged exclusively with an employee who should perform no other payroll activity. When delivering a cheque to an employee, the paymaster will require proof of identity by presentation of a badge or by signing of a receipt. A cheque or pay envelope for an absent employee should be retained and never turned over to another employee for delivery. When the absentees later pick up their pay, they should be required to sign a receipt for it.

Most companies which pay employees by cheque use a special payroll bank account. A voucher for the entire amount of the weekly payroll may be prepared in the general accounting department based on the payroll summary prepared in the payroll department. This voucher is sent to the treasurer who issues a cheque on the general bank account for the amount of the payroll. The cheque is deposited in the special payroll bank account, and cheques to individual employees are drawn on this bank account. It also is the practice of some companies to have printed on the cheque a statement that this type of cheque is not valid if issued for an amount in excess of a specified dollar amount, such as $500 or $1,000.

The payment of employees in cash is undesirable from the standpoint of internal control, but is a practice still followed by a significant number of companies. Reasons advanced to justify meeting a payroll in cash include inadequate banking facilities in the area, employee attitudes, and a desire on the part of management to eliminate the need for cheque signing and bank reconciliations. When employees are paid in cash, one cheque is written and cashed for the entire amount of the payroll. The paymaster fills the envelopes with cash and inserts a form listing the gross earnings, deductions, and net pay.

In small concerns it is not uncommon to find that the person compiling the payroll also fills the pay envelopes and distributes them to employees. This combination of duties affords no protection against payroll fraud. The functions of timekeeping, payroll preparation, and distribution of pay envelopes must be segregated if satisfactory control is to be exercised over wages paid in cash.

Another desirable control device is to obtain a receipt from each employee showing the pay period, gross earnings, deductions, cash payment, and signature of employee. To obtain an adequate receipt, some concerns prepare regular paycheques but pay employees in cash upon endorsement of the paycheque by the employee. The paycheques are then deposited by the company and serve as detailed support for the cash distributed.

If wages are paid in cash, any unclaimed wages should be deposited in the bank and credited to a special liability account. Subsequent disbursement of these funds to employees then will be controlled by the necessity of drawing a cheque and preparing supporting documents. The auditors should investigate thoroughly all debits to the Unclaimed Wages account. The dangers inherent in permitting unclaimed pay envelopes to be retained by the paymaster, returned to the payroll clerk, or intermingled with petty cash should be obvious.

Description of internal control for payroll

Typical of the questions to be answered by the auditors for the completion of a systems flowchart or other record of payroll internal controls are the following: Are employees paid by cheque? Is a payroll bank account maintained on an imprest basis? Are the activities of timekeeping, payroll compilation, payroll cheque signing, and paycheque distribution performed by separate departments or employees? Are all operations involved in the preparation of payrolls subjected to independent verification before the paycheques are distributed? Are employee time reports approved by supervisors? Is the payroll bank account reconciled monthly by an employee having no other payroll duties?

AUDIT PROGRAM FOR PAYROLLS

The following audit procedures are representative of the work generally completed to establish the propriety of payments for salaries, wages, bonuses, and commissions:

1. Obtain description of internal control for payrolls.
2. Make compliance tests of payroll transactions for one or more pay periods, including the following specific procedures:
   a. Trace names and wage or salary rates to records maintained by personnel department.
   b. Trace time shown on payroll to timecards and time reports approved by supervisors.
   c. If payroll is based on piecework rates rather than hourly rates, reconcile earnings with production records.
   d. Determine basis of deductions from payroll and compare with records of deductions authorized by employees.
   e. Test extensions and footings of payroll.
   f. Compare total of payroll with total of payroll cheques issued.
   g. Compare total of payroll with total of labour cost summary prepared by cost accounting department.
   h. If wages are paid in cash, compare receipts obtained from employees with payroll.
   i. If wages are paid by cheque, compare paid cheques with payroll and compare endorsements to signatures on withholding tax exemption certificates.
   j. Review subsequent payment of unclaimed wages, comparing receipts with payroll records, wage rates, and time reports.
3. If wages are paid in cash, appraise the control procedures applicable to the filling and distribution of pay envelopes.
4. Observe the use of time clocks by employees reporting for work, and investigate timecards not used.
5. Plan a surprise observation of one of the paycheque distributions, including control of payroll records and an accounting for all employees listed.
6. Determine that payrolls for the year do not exceed the number of weekly or monthly pay periods, and that all payrolls have been properly approved.

7. Obtain or prepare a summary of compensation of officers for the year and trace to contracts, minutes of directors' meetings, or other authorization.
8. Investigate any extraordinary fluctuations in salaries, wages, and commissions.
9. Test computation of compensation earned under profit-sharing plans.
10. Test commission earnings by examination of contracts and detailed supporting records.
11. Test pension payments by reference to authorized pension plans and to supporting records.

The fifth procedure in the above list, calling for the auditors to plan a surprise observation of a regular distribution of paycheques to employees, deserves special consideration. The auditors' objective in observing the distribution of cheques or cash to employees on a regular payday is to determine that every name on the company payroll is that of a bona fide employee presently on the job. This audit procedure is particularly desirable if the various phases of payroll work are not sufficiently segregated by departments to afford good internal control. The history of payroll frauds shows that permitting one person to have custody of employment records, timecards, paycheques, and employees' earnings records has often led to the entering of fictitious names on the payroll, and to other irregularities, such as use of excessive pay rates and continuance of pay after the termination of an employee.

The auditors' observation of a paycheque distribution should be on a surprise basis, and may conveniently be done at some time other than the peak of the audit work season. Efficient planning of the payroll observation requires that the auditors know in advance the general procedure and timing of payroll preparation and distribution. Without any prior announcement the auditors should appear on a regular payday and take control of the paycheques or pay envelopes. Before the distribution to employees is begun, the auditors will compare the name and amount on each cheque or envelope with the corresponding entry in the payroll register. The auditors must make sure that they have a cheque or envelope for every employee on the payroll register. The footings of the payroll register should also be verified so that there is no doubt that the auditors are accounting for the distribution of every dollar of the payroll. In a company so large that the auditors cannot conveniently observe the distribution of the entire payroll, the test may be limited to one or more selected departments.

The auditors first will determine that they have possession of all the cheques or envelopes comprising the payroll. They will then accompany representatives of the client around the plant as all the cheques or envelopes are distributed to employees. The whole procedure will be meaningless unless the auditors establish the identity of each employee receiving payment.

AUDIT PROGRAM FOR SELLING, GENERAL, AND ADMINISTRATIVE EXPENSES

For other expenses not verified in the audit of balance sheet accounts, the following substantive tests are appropriate. The extent to which the first four procedures are applied is dependent upon the auditors' evaluation of internal control for expenses.

1. Compare actual expenses and budgeted expenses.
2. Compare monthly operating expenses with those of the prior year, both in dollar amounts and expressed as a percentage of net sales.
3. Investigate all significant variations disclosed by comparison of expenses with the forecasts and with amounts of prior years.
4. Obtain or prepare analyses of expense accounts selected as a result of the above three procedures.
5. Obtain or prepare an analysis of professional fees expense.
6. Obtain or prepare analyses of critical expenses in income tax returns.

1. Compare actual expenses and budgeted expenses.

The effectiveness of a good forecasting program in controlling expenses was discussed earlier in this chapter. In the examination of companies which prepare forecasts, the auditors should compare actual and forecast expenses, and analyze variances from forecasts. Often management will have investigated thoroughly the variances from the forecast and will be able to provide logical explanations. The existence of a good forecasting program may reduce considerably the audit time which otherwise would be devoted to analysis of expense accounts.

2. Compare monthly operating expenses with those of the prior year, both in dollar amounts and expressed as a percentage of net sales.

Even though a forecast is not in use by the client, the auditors may still apply the principle of "audit by comparison" by obtaining or preparing analyses which compare the various operating expenses month by month with the figures for corresponding months of the preceding year. One of the previously mentioned audit objectives was determining whether expenses had been correctly classified. The issue of classification is most important as between factory overhead costs, on the one hand, and selling, general, and administrative expenses, on the other. Factory overhead costs may properly be carried forward as part of inventory cost, whereas the expenses of selling, general, and administrative functions usually are deducted from revenue in the period incurred. Consequently, an error in classification may cause an error in the net income of the period. The auditors' review of the propriety of classification of expenses can be linked conveniently with the comparison of monthly amounts of the various expenses. Comparison of yearly totals is accomplished by inclusion of amounts for the preceding year on the auditors' grouping sheets or working trial balance, but this procedure should be supplemented by comparison of expenses on a month-by-month basis.

3. *Investigate all significant variations disclosed by comparison of expenses with the forecasts and with amounts of prior years.*

The principal method of investigating significant variations in expenses is analysis of ledger accounts. Entries in the expense accounts are traced back to the voucher register, or to the cash disbursements journal if the company records expenses only at time of making payment. From these accounting records, reference may be made to invoices, receiving reports, purchase orders, or other supporting evidence.

4. *Obtain or prepare analyses of expense accounts selected as a result of the above three procedures.*

As a result of the above three procedures, the auditors will have chosen certain expense accounts for further verification. The client should be requested to furnish analyses of the accounts selected, together with related vouchers and other supporting documents, for the auditors' review. An illustration of an expense account analysis is presented in Figure 19–1.

Which expense accounts are most likely to contain errors, and are most important for the auditors to analyze? Generally, auditors have found that the accounts for traveling expense, entertainment, contributions, professional fees, officers' compensation, repairs and maintenance, and miscellaneous expense should be analyzed.

5. *Obtain or prepare an analysis of professional fees expense.*

As indicated in the preceding paragraph, the auditors should analyze professional fees expense. This analysis often will disclose legal and audit fees properly chargeable to costs of issuing stock or debt instruments, or to costs of business combinations. A study of professional fees expense for a new client will inform the auditors of fees charged by the predecessor CAs. Also, the analysis of professional fees expense furnishes the names of attorneys to whom letters should be sent requesting information as to pending litigation and other loss contingencies. Figure 19–1 illustrates an analysis of professional fees expense.

6. *Obtain or prepare analysis of critical expenses in income tax returns.*

Income tax returns in use at present generally require schedules for charitable donations, royalties and management fees, and registered pension plan contributions. Accordingly, the auditors should obtain or prepare analyses of any of these expenses which were not analyzed in connection with the audit of payrolls or the fourth procedure of this audit program. The auditors should bear in mind that details of these expenses will

FIGURE 19–1

Cheviot Corporation Limited

Acct. No. 547   Professional Fees Expense   R-3-7

Year Ended December 31, 1979

Date	Reference	Payee	Description	Amount	
Various	Various	Hale and Hale	Monthly retainer for legal services – 12 × $500 ч	6 000 –	
Mar. 5, 79	CD411	Gay & Wall, CAs	Fee for 1978 audit	7 500 –	ч
May 2, 79	CD602	Hale and Hale	Fee for legal services relating to acquisition of real property adjoining Vancouver plant	3 000 –	ч
Sept 18, 79	CD1018	Hale and Hale	Fee for legal services relating to modification of installment sales contract forms	400 –	ч
Dec. 31, 79			Balance per ledger	16 900 –	
Dec. 31, 79	A.J.E. 41	To capitalize May 2, 79, disbursement as part of cost of land		K-1 (3 000 –)	
Dec. 31, 79			Adjusted balance	13 900	∧
				R-3	

A.J.E. 41

Land	3 000 –	
Professional Fees		3 000 –
To capitalize legal fees re obtaining land.		

Prepared by client

∧ – Footed and agreed to general ledger balance.
ч – Examined billing and copy of client's cheque in payment thereof.

Conclusion:
  Professional fees expense is fairly presented in the adjusted amount of $13,900.

U. M. H.
Jan. 12, 80

probably be closely scrutinized when the Department of National Revenue examines the client's tax returns.

INCOME STATEMENT PRESENTATION

How much detail in the income statement?

One of the more interesting problems of statement presentation of revenue and expenses is the question of how much detailed operating information may be disclosed without causing the income statement to become unreasonably long and complex. As a minimum, the income statement should show the net sales revenue, income from investments, government assistance credited directly to income, depreciation, depletion, and amortization expenses, interest expense, cost of goods sold, selling expenses, general and administrative expenses, income taxes, extraordinary items, cumulative effects of changes in accounting principle, net income, and earnings per share. However, the auditors should ensure that the income statement is presented in accordance with the disclosure requirements of Section 1520 of the *CICA Handbook* and the relevant corporation laws.

Extraordinary items

To qualify for presentation as an extraordinary item, an event or transaction must be both unusual in nature and infrequent in occurrence, with reference to the environment in which a company operates. Thus, the auditors must examine carefully any extraordinary item reported in the client's income statement to determine whether it qualifies for such treatment. If so, the extraordinary item is reported, net of applicable income taxes, following income before extraordinary item.

Cumulative effects of changes in accounting principle

When a client has made a change in accounting principle during the year, the auditors must determine that the change is presented in the financial statements in accordance with the reporting requirements of the *CICA Handbook* and the relevant corporation laws. The SEC in the United States has taken the position that the auditors should state whether the accounting change represents a move to a preferable accounting principle.

Reporting earnings per share

After the net income figure, per share figures should be reported for income from continuing operations, income before extraordinary items, and net income. The computations should be based upon the weighted-average number of common shares outstanding during the year. In addition to these basic earnings per share, companies with a complex capital structure may be required to report *fully diluted* earnings per share. The auditors should ensure that earnings per share presentation is in accordance with Section 3500 of the *CICA Handbook*.

Reporting by diversified companies

The business combination movement in recent years has created many large "conglomerate" corporations by bringing together companies in quite unrelated industries. Although the word *conglomerate* is usually applied to a large family of corporations created by business combinations, other companies have achieved the same degree of diversification among unrelated industries through internal development and expansion. The term *diversified company* is therefore more appropriate for our use in considering the special financial reporting problems created by the emergence of this new type of business entity.

For the diversified company carrying on operations in several unrelated industries, we may well question whether the traditional form of income statement constitutes a fair presentation. Would the income statement be more useful to financial analysts and others if it showed separately the revenue and operating results of the various industry segments comprising the diversified company? In the past, an investor or financial analyst easily could associate a given corporation with a specific industry. Since this is hardly possible for many of the new, large, diversified companies, a worth-while analysis of the income statement may require disclosure of profitability of the several industry segments.

Accordingly, Section 47 of the Canada Business Corporation Act Regulations required that "each class [segment] of business the revenue from which is 10 percent or more of the corporation's total revenues for the period" should be separately reported. It also stipulates that a class or segment "shall be designated in accordance with the Statistics Canada Standard Industrial Classification Code." Similarly, Section 1700 of the *CICA Handbook* recommends that "the basis of segmentation should generally be the industries in which the enterprise operates. If segmentation is not based on industrial classification, the basis, together with the reason for its use, should be disclosed in the financial statements."

A study group of the Financial Executives Institute in the United States recommended that diversified companies report sales or other gross revenue and the relative percentage contribution to net income of any separate industry segment producing 15 percent or more of the company's gross revenue. The SEC in the United States accepted this proposal for companies with total sales and revenue of $50 million or less; for larger companies the SEC enacted a more stringent rule which requires them to report net sales and the contribution to net income of each product line contributing 10 percent or more to total net sales or net earnings.

The Financial Accounting Standards Board in the United States has recommended a more elaborate reporting format for segments of a diversified enterprise. The FASB proposal requires presentation of the following, either within the body of the financial statements, entirely in notes to the financial statements, or in a separate schedule included as an integral part of the financial statements:

Segment revenue
Segment profit or loss contribution, defined as segment revenue less directly traceable costs and expenses
Segment operating profit or loss, defined as segment profit or loss contribution minus a reasonably allocated share of nontraceable operating costs and expenses

Also, the FASB proposal requires disclosure of information about a multinational company's operations in different countries or groups of countries. The proposal also provides for disclosure of information about the identity and relative importance of a single customer or a few customers on whose business a company or a segment depends significantly.

KEY TERMS INTRODUCED OR EMPHASIZED IN CHAPTER 19

audit by comparison   A substantive test in which the auditors compare the current year's monthly revenue and expense account totals with the corresponding monthly amounts of the preceding year, or with budgeted amounts. Significant variations are investigated further by the auditors.

basic earnings per share   A presentation of earnings per share based on outstanding common shares.

conservatism   An accounting doctrine for asset valuation in which the lower of two alternative acceptable asset valuations is chosen.

extraordinary item   An event or transaction that is distinguished by its unusual nature and by the infrequency of its occurrence.

forecast   An estimate of the most probable financial position, results of operations, and changes in financial position for one or more future periods.

fully diluted earnings per share   A pro forma presentation which reflects the dilution of earnings per share that would have occurred if all contingent issuances of common stock that individually would reduce earnings per share had taken place at the beginning of the period.

segment   A component of an entity whose activities represent a separate industry or class of business.

GROUP I
REVIEW QUESTIONS

19–1.   Describe how the auditors use the *audit by comparison* technique in the examination of selling, general and administrative expenses.

19–2.   When you are first retained to examine the financial statements of Wabash Ltd., you enquire whether a forecast is used to control costs and expenses. The controller, James Lowe, replies that he personally prepares such a forecast each year, but that he regards it as a highly confidential document. He states that you may refer to it if necessary, but he wants you to make sure that no employee of the firm sees any of the forecast data. Comment on this use of a forecast.

19–3.   What influence does the existence of a good forecasting program in the client's business have on the conduct of an audit?

19–4.   During an initial audit, you observe that the client is not complying with the laws concerning wages and hours. Would you (a) report the violation to government authorities. (b) discuss the matter with the client, (c) ignore the matter completely, (d) withdraw from the engagement, or (e) follow some other course of action? Explain.

19–5.   What division of duties among independent departments is desirable to achieve maximum internal control over payrolls?

19–6.   What specific procedures are suggested by the phrase "compliance test of payroll transactions"?

19–7.   Identify three revenue accounts which are verified during the audit of balance sheet account; also, identify the related balance sheet accounts.

19–8.   Identify three items which are often misclassified as miscellaneous revenue and state how the misclassified items should be accounted for.

19–9.   How is the *audit by comparison* technique applied in the verification of revenue?

19–10.   Identify three expense accounts which are verified during the audit of balance sheet accounts; also, identify the related balance sheet accounts.

19–11.   For which expense accounts should the auditors obtain or prepare analysis to be used in preparation of the client's income tax returns?

19–12.   What safeguards should be employed when the inaccessibility of banking facilities makes it desirable to pay employees in cash?

19–13.   You are asked by a client to outline the procedures you would recommend for disposing of unclaimed wages.

19–14.   What auditing procedures can you suggest for determining the reasonableness of selling, general, and administrative expenses?

19–15.   What are *extraordinary items?*

19–16.   How do the independent auditors determine the propriety of extraordinary items in the client's income statement?

19–17.   What rule did the Canada Business Corporations Act and the SEC in the United States enact for disclosures of operating details on the income statements of diversified companies?

GROUP II
QUESTIONS REQUIRING ANALYSIS

19–18.   In a properly planned examination of financial statements, the auditors coordinate their reviews of specific balance sheet and income statement accounts.

Required:

Why should the auditors coordinate their examinations of balance sheet accounts and income statement accounts? Discuss and illustrate by examples. (AICPA, adapted)

19–19.   In your first examination of the financial statements Willman Ltd., you discover that the company has included in the Miscellaneous Revenue account a $10,000 commission from Bradley Realtors, Inc. Your investigation discloses that Bradley negotiated Willman's purchase for $500,000 of a tract of land from Payne Company, and that Payne had paid Bradley's commission of $50,000 on the sale.

Required:

Would you take exception to Willman Ltd.'s accounting for the commission received from Bradley Realtors, Inc.? Explain.

19–20.   Your new audit client, Coin-O-Mat Ltd., leases coin-operated laundry equipment to military bases. Usage of the equipment requires the insertion of coins into metered receptacles, which record expired time of equipment operation. How can you determine whether all revenue earned by Coin-O-Mat has been recorded in the accounting records?

19–21.   Bowden Ltd. owed property taxes of $5,972. Through error Morton Bryant, who served the company as office manager, cashier, and accountant, paid the tax bill twice. Realizing his error after having mailed the second cheque, he wrote to the county officials requesting a refund.

When the refund was received some weeks later, Bryant substituted the cheque from the city for cash receipts and abstracted $5,972 in currency.

Would this error and theft probably be discovered in an audit by independent public accountants? Indicate what auditing procedure, if any, would disclose the facts.

19–22.   The controller of Moorehead Ltd., a client, calls you on September 25 for advice on financial statement presentation of a gain on the sale of a 5 percent investment in stock of a principal supplier. The stock was acquired March 18, 1977, for $100,000 to strengthen relations with the supplier, and was sold September 24, 1979, for $150,000. No dividends were received by Moorehead on the investment. Exclusive of the gain on the stock, the controller estimates pretax income of $100,000 for the year ending December 31, 1979. Assume combined federal and provincial income tax rates of 55 percent on ordinary income and 35 percent on capital gains.

Required:

How would you advise the controller to present the gain in Moorehead's financial statements? Explain.

19–23. Barton Ltd. is highly diversified, with segments which manufacture and sell antibiotics, dairy products, hospital supplies, toiletries, and chemicals. In what form should the income statement of Barton Ltd. be prepared?

19–24. Select the best answer for each of the following, and explain fully the reason for your selection.

> *a.* In testing the payroll of a large company, the auditors want to establish that the individuals included in a sample actually were employees of the company during the period under review. What will be the best source to determine this?
>
> (1) Telephone contacts with the employees.
>
> (2) Tracing from the payroll register to the employees' earnings records.
>
> (3) Confirmation with the union or other independent organization.
>
> (4) Examination of personnel department records.
>
> *b.* The auditors generally give most emphasis to ratio and trend analysis in the examination of the statement of—
>
> (1) Retained earnings.
>
> (2) Income.
>
> (3) Financial position.
>
> (4) Changes in financial position.
>
> *c.* Operating control over the payroll cheque signature plate normally should be the responsibility of the—
>
> (1) Secretary.
>
> (2) Chief accountant.
>
> (3) Vice president of finance.
>
> (4) Treasurer.
>
> *d.* A factory foreman at Merton Ltd. discharged an employee but did not notify the payroll department. The foreman then forged the ex-employee's signature on timecards and work tickets and, when giving out the cheques, diverted the payroll cheques drawn for the discharged worker to his own use. The most effective procedure for preventing this activity is to—
>
> (1) Require written authorization for all employees added to or removed from the payroll.
>
> (2) Have a paymaster who has no other payroll responsibility distribute the payroll cheques.
>
> (3) Have someone other than persons who prepare or distribute the payroll obtain custody of unclaimed payroll cheques.
>
> (4) From time to time, rotate persons distributing the payroll cheques. (AICPA, adapted)

GROUP III
PROBLEMS

19–25. In connection with an examination of the financial statements of Olympia Ltd., the auditors are reviewing procedures for accumulating direct labour hours. They learn that all production is by job order and that all employees are paid hourly wages, with time and one half for overtime hours.

Olympia's direct labour hour input process for payroll and job-cost determination is summarized in the following flowchart:

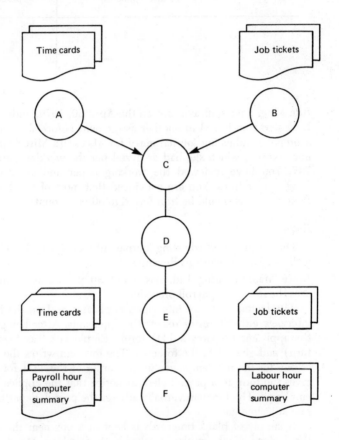

Steps A and C are performed in timekeeping, step B in the factory operating departments, step D in payroll audit and control, step E in data preparation (keypunch), and step F in computer operations.

Required:

For each input processing step A through F:

a. List the possible errors or discrepancies that may occur.

     b. Cite the corresponding control procedure that should be in effect for each error or discrepancy.

Note: Your discussion of Olympia's procedures should be limited to the input for direct labour hours, as shown in steps A through F in the flow chart. ***Do not discuss*** personnel procedures for hiring, promotion, termination, and pay rate authorization. ***In step F do not discuss*** equipment, computer program, and general computer operational controls.

Organize your answer for each input-processing step as follows:

Step	Possible errors or discrepancies	Control procedures

(AICPA, adapted)

19–26.   Rita King, your staff assistant on the April 30, 1979, audit of Maxwell Ltd., was transferred to another assignment before she could prepare a proposed adjusting journal entry for Maxwell's Miscellaneous Revenue account, which she had analyzed per the working paper on page 747. You have reviewed the working paper and are satisfied with King's procedures. You are convinced that most of the Miscellaneous Revenue items should be transferred to other accounts.

Required:

    Draft a proposed adjusting journal entry at April 30, 1979, for Maxwell Ltd.'s Miscellaneous Revenue account.

19–27.   Rowe Manufacturing Ltd. has about 50 production employees and uses the following payroll procedures.

    The factory foreman interviews applicants and on the basis of the interview either hires or rejects the applicants. After being employed, the applicant prepares a TD1 form (Employee's Tax Deduction Return) and gives it to the foreman. The foreman writes the hourly rate of pay for the new employee in the corner of the TD1 form and then gives the form to a payroll clerk as notice that the applicant has been employed. The foreman verbally advises the payroll department of pay rate adjustments.

    A supply of blank timecards is kept in a box near the entrance to the factory. Each employee takes a timecard on Monday morning, signs it, and notes in pencil on the timecard the daily arrival and departure times. At the end of the week the employees drop the timecards in a box near the door to the factory.

    The completed timecards are taken from the box on Monday morning by a payroll clerk. Two payroll clerks divide the cards alphabetically between them, one taking the A to L section of the payroll, and

Maxwell Ltd.

Acct. No. 430   Miscellaneous Revenue   G-2

Year Ended April 30, 1979

Date	Description	Reference	Amount	
May 8, 78 through Apr. 7, 79	Proceeds of sale of scrap from manu-facturing process (total of 12 monthly sales)	Various CR	5 843	ν
July 18, 78	Write-off of old outstanding cheques: nos. 118 – $500; 214 – $400; 407 – $200	GJ 7-4	1 100	ν
Sept. 22, 78	Recovery of previously written off account receivable from Wilson Company	CR 9-1	4 381	ν
Feb. 6, 79	Cash proceeds from sale of machine. Cost of $10,000 and accumulated depreciation of $8,000 as of Feb. 6, 79 not removed from accounts.	CR 2-1	3 500	ν
Apr. 28, 79	Refund of premium overcharge on fire insurance policy no. 1856, for period Apr. 1, 79 – Mar. 31, 80	CR 4-1	600	ν
Apr. 30, 79	Balance per ledger		15 424	

ν — Traced to cash receipts journal or general journal; vouched to appropriate supporting documents.

R. A. K.
May 18, 79

the other taking the M to Z section. Each clerk is fully responsible for one section of the payroll. The payroll clerks compute the gross pay, deductions, and net pay; post the details to the employee's earnings records; and prepare and number the payroll cheques. Employees are automatically removed from the payroll when they fail to turn in a timecard.

The payroll cheques are manually signed by the chief accountant and given to the foreman. The foreman distributes the cheques to the employees in the factory and arranges for the delivery of the cheques to the employees who are absent. The payroll bank account is reconciled by the chief accountant, who also prepares the various quarterly and annual payroll tax reports.

Required:

List your suggestions for improving Rowe Manufacturing Ltd.'s system of internal control for factory hiring practices *and* payroll procedures. (AICPA, adapted)

19-28.   Your client is a shopping centre with 30 store tenants. All leases with the store tenants provide for a fixed rent plus a percentage of sales, net of sales taxes, in excess of a fixed dollar amount computed on an annual basis. Each lease also provides that the lessor may engage a CA to audit all records of the tenant for assurance that sales are being properly reported to the lessor.

You have been requested by your client to audit the records of Traders Restaurant to determine that the sales totaling $390,000 for the year ended December 31, 1979, have been properly reported to the lessor. The restaurant and the shopping centre entered into a five-year lease on January 1, 1979. Traders Restaurant offers only table service; no liquor is served. During meal times there are four or five waitresses in attendance who prepare handwritten prenumbered restaurant cheques for the customers. Payment is made at a cash register, manned by the proprietor, as the customer leaves. All sales are for cash. The proprietor also is the accountant. Complete files are kept of restaurant cheques and cash register tapes. A daily sales journal and general ledger are also maintained.

Required:

List the auditing procedures that you would employ to verify the total annual sales of Traders Restaurant. (Disregard vending machine sales and counter sales of chewing gum, candy, and the like.) (AICPA, adapted)

19-29.   City Loan Ltd. has 100 branch loan offices. Each office has a manager and four or five employees who are hired by the manager. Branch managers prepare the weekly payroll, including their own salaries, and pay employees from cash on hand. The employees sign the payroll sheet signifying receipt of their salary. Hours worked by hourly personnel are inserted in the payroll sheet from time reports prepared by the employees and approved by the manager.

The weekly payroll sheets are sent to the home office, along with other accounting statements and reports. The home office compiles employee earnings records and prepares all federal payroll tax returns from the weekly payroll sheets.

Salaries are established by home office job-evaluation schedules. Salary adjustments, promotions, and transfers of full-time employees are approved by a home office salary committee based upon the recommendations of branch managers and area supervisors. Branch managers advise the salary committee of new full-time employees and terminations. Part-time and temporary employees are hired without referral to the salary committee.

Required:

a.   How might funds for payroll be diverted in the above system?

b.   Prepare a payroll internal audit program to be used in the home office to audit the branch office payrolls of City Loan Ltd. (AICPA, adapted)

19–30.   You are a senior accountant of the CA firm Jones & Paul, in charge of the April 30, 1979, audit of Windsor Ltd., a manufacturer of motors. Your staff assistant has prepared the analysis of Windsor's Miscellaneous Expense account, which appears on page 750. You have reviewed the working paper and are satisfied with your assistant's work. You are convinced that all items in the Miscellaneous Expense account belong in other accounts.

Required:

Draft an adjusting journal entry for Windsor Ltd.'s Miscellaneous Expense account as of April 30, 1979.

GROUP IV
CASE STUDIES IN AUDITING

19–31.   TIMBER PRODUCTS CORPORATION

During the first audit of Timber Products Corporation, the auditor, James Wills, CA, found the payroll activities to be concentrated in the hands of an experienced and trusted employee, Richard Cardiff. Cardiff prepares a payroll register from time reports. The register is presented for approval of the treasurer, who then issues a cheque for the total amount of the payroll. Cardiff cashes this cheque, fills pay envelopes for all of the company's 400 hourly employees, and distributes the pay envelopes to the employees.

In verifying the hourly payroll, the auditor selected two test periods, the first week in July and the second week in December. For these test periods, he proved the accuracy of the footings and the extensions on the payroll register. The totals shown by the payroll register corresponded with the cheques issued for the total payrolls. Employee names and rates of pay were traced to a file of employment records

Windsor Ltd.

Acct. No. 567

Miscellaneous Expense

Year Ended April 30, 1979

Date	Payee	Description	Amount	
June 26, 78	Ford Collection Agency	Fee for collecting $10,000 doubtful account receivable of Odds Company	1,000	✓
Aug. 14, 78	Wade Mfg. Co., Inc.	Cost of new motor to replace defective motor under product warranty. Defective motor has $1,500 net realizable value.	9,000	✓
Oct. 16, 78	Cain Printing Co. Ltd.	Printing of debenture certificates and registration statement for $1,000,000, 9% debentures issued Oct. 1, 78, to mature Oct. 1, 98	4,800	✓
Dec. 13, 78	Jones & Paul, CAs	Fee for management advisory services engagement to revise cost accounting system	3,800	✓
Mar. 2, 79	George & Arthur, Attorneys	Fee for legal advice in connection with 10% common stock dividend distributed Feb. 28, 79	1,500	✓
Apr. 30, 78		Balance per ledger	20,100	

✓ — Examined invoice or statement and related paid cheque.

U. M. H.
May 23, 79

maintained by Cardiff. These records indicated the date of employment, the job classification, and the hourly rate of pay. When an employee was reclassified to a higher pay classification, the date and nature of the reclassification were noted on these records. When employees terminated, their records were transferred to another file.

In support of the hours worked during the test period, the auditor found time reports on file for all employees, showing time of arrival and departure each day. Cardiff stated that he personally observed the punching in and out of employees and had custody of the time reports.

Cardiff produced for inspection by the auditor an envelope containing $97 in cash, which he stated to be the pay due a former employee who had left in the middle of November without claiming the fraction of a week's pay due him.

The auditor's examination of the payroll register, employment records, and cheques for the total payroll during the two periods selected for testing revealed no discrepancies. A comparison of the payroll during the year under audit with the payroll for the two preceding years on a month-to-month basis indicated no significant variation. The auditor also compared the number of employees in each job classification with the number employed in such jobs in the two preceding years, and compared the rates of pay for various jobs during the three-year period. He noted that the output of the company during these three years had been fairly stable. Enquiries made of officers substantiated this lack of trend and evoked the observation that profits were down slightly.

Officers and supervisory employees of the company were paid by cheque on a monthly basis. The auditor traced these payments to salary authorizations in the minutes of directors' meetings and found no exceptions. Although his tests had served to substantiate the accuracy of the payroll records, the auditor felt somewhat concerned over the lack of internal control caused by the delegation of so much responsibility to Cardiff. Consequently, the auditors decided to observe employees punching in and out of the plant on the time clock, and observe (on a surprise basis) the distribution of pay envelopes by Cardiff to the employees.

The auditor's observation of employees arriving at and leaving the plant disclosed no improper use of time reports. When the auditor appeared without warning on payday and informed Cardiff that he wished to observe the distribution of pay envelopes, Cardiff expressed some impatience with this procedure. Cardiff explained that he had a very busy day in prospect and proposed to distribute pay envelopes at intervals during the day as his other duties took him to various parts of the plant. The auditor insisted on carrying out this observation of the payoff and accompanied Cardiff until the last pay envelope had been delivered, although this process was interrupted a good many times while Cardiff attended to other matters. Cardiff knew all of the 400 employees personally and did not require any identification from them. The auditor enquired if the employees were required to carry identification badges, but was informed that this practice had been abandoned because the plant was so small that Cardiff knew each employee. Furthermore, when badges had been required in prior years, employees frequently came to work without them. When an employee reported for work without a badge, he was refused admission to the plant, but this practice led to so much lost time and employee resentment that the company had discontinued the use of badges. Cardiff added that since the use of badges had been discontinued, each employee was required to sign a receipt for his pay.

Since his surprise observation of the payoff and his other verification procedures had revealed no irregularities, the auditor concluded that the payroll records were dependable, despite the concentration of duties in the hands of Cardiff. Other phases of the audit were completed satisfactorily, and an unqualified audit report was issued by the auditor.

Several months later, a sudden illness of Richard Cardiff caused an officer of the company to take over the payroll work temporarily. The officer discovered that ten fictitious employees were on the payroll and had been on the payroll continuously for three years, with consequent loss to the company of approximately $300,000. The company sought to recover a part of its losses from the auditor on the grounds that he must have been guilty of gross negligence not to have discovered that approximately 2½ percent of the payroll was fictitious. The auditor attempted to defend himself against the charges by emphasizing his surprise observation of the payoff, which he stated was evidence of his having gone beyond normal auditing procedures in recognition of the weakness in internal control. The auditor contended that a "padded payroll" could not have avoided detection by this test, but Cardiff explained that during the payday in question, when accompanied by the auditor, he had delivered five extra pay envelopes to one employee and five more to another, both employees being good friends of his and willing to "help him out of a tight spot."

The pay envelopes delivered to these employees had been presented to them at various hours during the day at various locations in the plant, and the auditor had apparently not remembered having seen the employees previously.

Required:

a. Did the audit conform to generally accepted auditing standards? Explain.
b. Discuss the purpose and effectiveness of the auditor's observation of the distribution of pay to employees.
c. Do you believe Timber Products Corporation had a valid claim against the auditor? Explain.
d. Would this payroll fraud have been prevented if the company had paid its employees by cheque rather than in cash? Explain.

20

Audit reports

The expressing of an independent and expert opinion on the fairness of financial statements is the most important and valuable service rendered by the public accounting profession. This independent opinion may be expressed through either a standard or long-form report, or both types of reports may be issued for a single audit engagement. The standard audit report, consisting of a concise description of the scope of the examination and a statement of the auditors' opinion on the financial statements, was illustrated and discussed in Chapter 1. The long-form report, although popular for many years, is seldom issued today. Long-form reports, with their extensive supplementary details, are very expensive to draft and process. Besides, the supplementary details are available in the client's internal records; therefore, the long-form report, unless required by a bank or other outsider, is often considered nonessential and not the most efficient utilization of the auditors' time.

In this chapter we shall develop further some of the most important ideas concerning the standard audit report, and then turn our attention briefly to long-form audit reports and reports to the SEC in the United States. In addition to audit reports on financial statements, we shall consider other types of reports to clients, in which the customary wording of the standard audit report does not apply.

Financial statements

The reporting phase of an auditing engagement begins when the independent auditors have completed their field work and their proposed adjustments have been accepted and recorded by the client. Before writing their report, the auditors must review the client-prepared financial statements for form and content, or draft the financial statements on behalf of the client.

The financial statements on which the independent auditors customarily report are the balance sheet, the income statement, the statement of retained earnings, and the statement of changes in financial position. Often, the statement of retained earnings is combined with the income statement. In some cases, the retained earnings statement may be expanded to a statement of shareholders' equity. Financial statements generally are presented in comparative form for the current year and the preceding year and are accompanied by explanatory footnotes. The financial statements for a parent corporation usually are consolidated with those of the subsidiaries.

Notes to financial statements

As indicated previously, notes to financial statements are to achieve adequate disclosure when information in the financial statements is insufficient to attain this objective. Although the notes, like the financial statements themselves, are representations of the client, the independent auditors generally assist in drafting the notes. The writing of notes to financial statements is a challenging task because complex issues must be summarized in a clear and concise manner.

The types of information provided in notes to financial statements may be classified into the following broad categories.

1. Financial data. These data are included as notes either to simplify the structure of the financial statements or to clarify certain items in the financial statements due to uncertainty as to the amounts involved, for example, current expense for remuneration of directors and officers, and lawsuits or possible judgments against the company.
2. Accounting information. This area deals essentially with accounting matters such as explanations of accounting principles used and changes therein, and existence of commitments, for example, disclosure of accounting policies such as basis for consolidation, assets pledged or liabilities secured, and restrictions or declaration of dividends.
3. Extraneous matters. This category includes information and explanations not directly affecting the financial statements but which may be essential for a proper understanding of the future prospects of the company, for example, events subsequent to the balance sheet date.[1]

---

[1] CICA, *Financial Reporting in Canada,* 12th ed. (Toronto, 1977), pp. 233–34.

Much of the information included in notes to financial statements is required by the *CICA Handbook* recommendations and the various corporations and securities acts. The following listing represents a few of the most common requirements.

1. Significant accounting policies, such as principles of consolidation and the basis of valuation of assets.
2. Changes in accounting principle and practice.
3. Significant events between the date of the financial statements and the date of the auditors' report.

Similar disclosure is also required by the Financial Accounting Standards Board and the Securities and Exchange Commission in the United States. Listed below are a few of the many items for which footnotes are now mandatory because of an increasing emphasis on disclosure. For each of the sample items listed, reference is made to the FASB *Statement of Financial Accounting Standards* (SFAS), the AICPA *Accounting Principles Board Opinion* (APBO), and the SEC *Accounting Series Release* (ASR) which mandates the disclosure.

1. Significant accounting policies, such as principles of consolidation, and the basis of valuation and amortization of assets (APBO 22).
2. Accounting changes (APBO 20).
3. Business combinations completed during the period (APBO 16).
4. Replacement cost data for inventories, cost of goods sold, property and equipment, and depreciation (ASR 190).
5. Exchange gains and losses from foreign currency translation (SFAS 8).

The list of required disclosures in both Canada and the United States could easily be expanded to many times the number shown. The variety and extent of required footnote disclosure have perhaps gone beyond reasonable boundaries of effective communication in financial statements.

In drafting or revising proposed notes to financial statements, the auditors should consider two important guidelines. First, notes should not be utilized to *correct* improper financial statement presentations. Second, notes should be worded to *inform,* not *confuse,* the reader of the financial statements. A great deal of rewriting, editing, and polishing is required to finalize notes which are in accord with these guidelines.

The standard audit report

For convenient reference the standard audit report which was introduced and discussed in Chapter 1 is presented again:

We have examined the balance sheet of X Co. Ltd., as at December 31, 19XX and the statements of income, retained earnings and changes in

GAAS

financial position for the year then ended. Our examination was made in accordance with generally accepted auditing standards, and accordingly included such tests and other procedures as we considered necessary in the circumstances.

In our opinion, these financial statements present fairly the financial position of X Co. Ltd., as at December 31, 19XX and the results of its operations and the changes in its financial position for the year then ended in accordance with generally accepted accounting principles ap-

GAAP

consistent plied on a basis consistent with that of the preceding year.

The standard audit report illustrated above is appropriate for a *firm* of chartered accountants. A CA performing an audit as an individual practitioner should use "I" instead of "we" in the standard audit report.

Restatement of basic points concerning the standard report

Among the major points made in Chapter 1 concerning the standard audit report were the following:

1. The financial statements (including notes thereto) are the statements of the client, not of the auditors. The auditors' product is their report, in which they express their opinion about the client's financial statements.

2. The statement in the audit report that an examination has been made in accordance with "generally accepted auditing standards" refers to an official statement of standards of the Canadian Institute of Chartered Accountants. This official set of standards includes a general standard (such as objectivity), standards of field work (such as the gathering of sufficient evidence), and standards of reporting. In this chapter we are particularly concerned with standards of reporting. Four standards of reporting have been enunciated by the CICA and deserve careful attention. These four standards are:

   a. *The scope of the auditors' examination should be referred to in the report.*

   b. *The report should contain either an expression of opinion on the financial statements or an assertion that an opinion cannot be expressed. In the latter case, the reasons therefor should be stated.*

   c. *Where an opinion is expressed, it should indicate whether the financial statements present fairly the financial position, results of operations and changes in financial position in accordance with an appropriate disclosed basis of accounting, which except in special circumstances should be generally accepted accounting principles. The report should provide adequate explanation with respect to any reservation contained in such opinion.*

   d. *Where an opinion is expressed, the report should also indicate whether the application of the disclosed basis of accounting is consistent with that of the preceding period. Where the basis or its application is not consistent, the report should provide adequate explanation of the nature and effect of the inconsistency.*

3. The auditors' opinion indicates whether the financial statements "present fairly. . . ." In Section 5400, the *CICA Handbook* emphasizes that the auditors' judgment as to fairness of financial statement presentation should be applied within the framework of generally accepted accounting principles. In essence, the quality of *presenting fairly* may be equated with *not being misleading.*

4. The auditors' opinion that the financial statements were prepared in conformity with "generally accepted accounting principles applied on a basis consistent with that of the preceding year" gives assurance to bankers, shareholders, and other interested persons that these statements may reasonably be compared with the company's statements in prior years, and with statements of other companies in the industry. The banker or shareholder is thereby enabled to weigh the merits of one company against another.

In Canada, the recommendations of the *CICA Handbook* are recognized by the provincial securities commissions and the Canada Business Corporations Act as generally accepted accounting principles. In the United States, a compendium of generally accepted accounting principles may be found in the AICPA's loose-leaf service entitled *Professional Standards.* All currently effective *FASB Statements, APB Opinions,* and *Accounting Research Bulletins* are integrated in volumes 3 and 4 of *Professional Standards.*

Expression of an opinion by the auditors

The principal alternatives in reporting on financial statements may be summed up as follows:

1. An unqualified opinion;
2. A qualified opinion;
3. An adverse opinion;
4. A denial of opinion.

These alternatives are based on the second standard of reporting recommended by CICA. This standard does not prevent the auditors from expressing separate opinions on the balance sheet and the income statement. For example, they may express an unqualified opinion on the balance sheet and deny an opinion or express a qualified or adverse opinion on the income statement.

1. Unqualified opinions.

The unqualified opinion (illustrated on pages 755–56) is, of course, the most desirable opinion from the client's point of view. The auditors express an unqualified opinion on the client's financial statements when there has been no unresolvable restriction on the scope of the examination, and the auditors have no significant exceptions as to the fairness and applicability of the accounting principles reflected in the financial statements, the consistency of their application, and the adequacy of informative disclosures in the financial statements.

The unqualified opinion usually contains the precise wording illustrated in the standard report. However, circumstances such as reliance upon other auditors, statutory requirements, or emphasis on a special matter may justify a deviation from the standard wording.

Reliance upon other auditors.   On occasion it may be necessary for the principal auditors of a company to rely upon another CA firm to perform a portion of the audit work. The most common situation in which CAs rely upon the work of other auditors is in the audit of consolidated entities. If certain subsidiaries are audited by other CA firms, the auditors of the parent company may decide to rely upon the work of these other CAs. In other situations, the auditors of a multibranch client may retain another CA firm to perform audit procedures at a specific branch location. When more than one CA firm participates in an engagement, some modification of the conventional unqualified opinion may be necessary. The principal auditors must decide, according to the particular circumstances, how much responsibility they will assume for the engagement and whether to make reference to the other CA firm in their audit report. The principal auditors' decision should be guided by Section 5530 of the *CICA Handbook*, "Reliance on Other Auditors," which describes the principal auditors' responsibility in both the *agency relationship* and *no agency relationship* situations.

In an agency relationship, the principal auditors enter into an arrangement with other public accountants to carry out part of the examination, either for a branch or a subsidiary. The principal auditors are fully responsible for the audit as a whole and should not make any reference, in their audit report, to the work or report of the other auditors.

On the other hand, in the audit of consolidated entities when there is no agency relationship between the parent company (principal) auditors and the auditors of one or more subsidiaries, the parent company auditors may reasonably rely on the work and report of the subsidiary auditors. To justify such a reliance on the subsidiary auditors by the parent company auditors, Section 5530 of the *CICA Handbook* suggests that the following steps should be taken:

(a)   assurance that the subsidiary company auditors are independent practising public accountants, licensed where required or otherwise appropriately qualified;

(b)   direct communication with the subsidiary company auditors to ensure that they are aware

(i)   that the audited financial statements of the subsidiary are to be included in the consolidated financial statements, and that their work and opinion will be relied on by the parent company auditors for the purpose of forming an opinion on the consolidated financial statements;

(ii) of the financial reporting requirements relevant to the consolidated financial statements;

(c)   consideration of the content of the report of the subsidiary company auditors as supporting the credibility of the related financial statements;

(d)   enquiry into the extent to which the accounting policies reflected in the financial statements of the subsidiary company differ from those of the parent company or from those followed in the preceding year.

In addition, the parent company auditors may consider it necessary to enquire into the scope of the examination conducted by the subsidiary company auditors.

In addition, the parent company auditors should refer to the report of the other auditors in the scope paragraph of their report on the consolidated financial statements. Such a reference does not constitute a qualification of the opinion of the parent company auditors, it is designed to define the scope of the examination by stating clearly their reliance on the other auditors. The following report is suggested by the *CICA Handbook*.

> We have examined the consolidated balance sheet of X Co. Ltd., as at December 31, 19XX and the consolidated statements of income, retained earnings and changes in financial position for the year then ended. Our examination of the financial statements of X Co. Ltd. and those subsidiaries of which we are the auditors was made in accordance with generally accepted auditing standards, and accordingly included such tests and other procedures as we considered necessary in the circumstances. We have relied on the reports of the auditors who have examined the financial statements of the other subsidiaries.
>
> In our opinion, these consolidated financial statements present fairly the financial position of the company as at December 31, 19XX and the results of its operations and the changes in its financial position for the year then ended in accordance with generally accepted accounting principles on a basis consistent with that of the preceding year.

When other auditors are reporting, on a non-agency relationship situation, on non-consolidated subsidiaries and/or long-term intercorporate investments accounted for by the equity method or on consolidated effectively controlled companies, the same procedures that are applicable to the no agency relationship situation discussed earlier should be followed by the parent company auditors. The following report is suggested by the *CICA Handbook:*

We have examined the consolidated balance sheets of Y Co. Ltd., as at December 31, 19XX and the consolidated statements of income, retained earnings and changes in financial position for the year then ended. For Y Co. Ltd. and for those other companies of which we are the auditors and which are consolidated in these financial statements, our examination was made in accordance with generally accepted auditing standards, and accordingly included such tests and other procedures as we considered necessary in the circumstances. For other companies accounted for by the equity method we have relied on the reports of the auditors who have examined their financial statements.

In our opinion, these consolidated financial statements present fairly the financial position of the company as at December 31, 19XX and the results of its operations and the changes in its financial position for the year then ended in accordance with generally accepted accounting principles applied on a basis consistent with that of the preceding year.

Similarly, the Canada Business Corporations Act stipulates that the parent company auditors may reasonably rely upon the auditors' report of a subsidiary or effectively controlled corporation *if the fact of such reliance is disclosed* in the parent company auditors' report. Of course, the steps suggested by the *CICA Handbook* discussed earlier should be followed by the parent company auditors in order to justify such a reliance.

Statutory requirements. Governing statutes under which the audit is performed may require certain additional information to be provided by the auditors in their standard report. The auditors should modify the wording of their standard report in order to meet such statutory requirements. Where statutory information is lengthy, Section 5500 of the *CICA Handbook* suggests that such information "should be set out in a separate paragraph after the opinion paragraph, with a reference, if appropriate, to the particular governing statute which makes it necessary to provide the additional information."

Emphasis of a matter. Another modification of the standard audit report is the auditors' emphasis upon a matter regarding the client's financial statements. For example, the auditors may add a paragraph to their unqualified audit report calling attention to a significant subsequent event described in a note to the financial statements. If the conventional wording is used in the opinion paragraph, such an audit report is unqualified.

Conditions preventing issuance of an unqualified opinion. The auditors are not always able to give the "clean bill of health" indicated by the model report on pages 755–56. Among the reasons which may prevent the issuance of an unqualified opinion are the following:

1. The examination may not have been made in accordance with generally accepted auditing standards.
    a. Internal control may be so seriously inadequate that a satisfactory

examination cannot be performed within reasonable time limits.

b. The client may place restrictions on the scope of the auditors' examination, by, for example, not permitting the confirmation of accounts receivable, not taking a physical inventory, which the auditors must observe, or not permitting the auditors to examine a subsidiary company or to visit a distant branch location where an important portion of the company's assets are located.

Under the circumstances described above, the auditors will generally *deny* an opinion on the financial statements. In some situations where the exceptions as to the scope of the examination are not too significant, the auditors may *qualify* their opinion, using the words *"except for"* in their qualification.

2. For reasons beyond the control of the client or the auditors, it may not have been possible to perform certain necessary auditing procedures.

a. In a first audit, if inventory records are very poor, there may be no way to verify the beginning inventories; consequently, the cost of goods sold and net income for the year cannot be verified. If beginning inventories were substantial, the auditors must *deny* an opinion on the income statement and statements of retained earnings and changes in financial position. If the auditors have no other exceptions, they may express an *unqualified opinion* on the balance sheet.

b. Substantial uncertainties may prevent the auditors from determining or estimating the resolution of a significant contingency, such as a pending lawsuit. In this situation the auditors typically will issue a *qualified opinion* with the words *"subject to"* emphasizing the uncertainty. If the uncertainty is too significant, the auditors may *deny* an opinion on the financial statements.

3. The financial statements may not present fairly the client's financial position and operating results.

a. The financial statements may not have been prepared in accordance with generally accepted accounting principles. When the auditors find that assets have been improperly valued, that liabilities have been omitted or that other violations of generally accepted accounting principles exist, their first reaction will be to attempt to persuade management of the client company to revise the statements. In most cases, management will agree, and the deficiencies will be remedied; occasionally, however, management will not agree to the changes considered necessary by the auditors, and consequently an unqualified opinion cannot be issued. If the violations of generally accepted accounting principles are too significant, the auditors will issue an *adverse opinion* on the financial statements. A *qualified* opinion with the words *"except for"* will be issued if the violations are significant but not too significant to warrant an adverse opinion.

b. Accounting principles may not have been applied consistently as compared with the preceding year. An unqualified audit report cannot be issued if the client company has changed its method of inventory valuation, if it has adopted a new method of computing depreciation, or if it has made other material changes in accounting principle as compared with the preceding year. Usually, the auditors issue an *"except for"* *qualified opinion* to call attention to the change in accounting principle, its justification, and its effects on the financial statements.

c. Fairness in financial statements often hinges on the issue of what constitutes adequate informative disclosure. Assume, for example, that pending legislation indicates that a certain type of business, such as the operation of a race track, may soon be outlawed. Disclosure of this threat to continued existence of the business is essential to a fair presentation. A similar contingency requiring disclosure is the existence of lawsuits in the process of litigation. The client company's failure to disclose such significant matters in notes to the financial statements customarily necessitates the issuance of an *"except for"* *qualified opinion* by the auditors. Only in extreme cases of inadequate disclosure would the auditors have to issue an *adverse opinion*.

The types of audit reports which are appropriate under the preceding conditions are summarized in Figure 20–1.

2. Qualified opinions.

A qualified opinion is a modification of the unqualified opinion stating that *"except for"* the *effects* of some limitation on the scope of the examination, a change in accounting principle, or some unsatisfactory financial statement presentation, the financial statements are fairly presented. If a scope limitation resulted from the inability of the auditors to resolve some uncertainty, the words *"subject to"* are included in the opinion paragraph.

The materiality of the exception governs the use of the qualified opinion. The exception must be sufficiently significant to warrant mentioning in the auditors' report, but it must not be too significant as to necessitate a denial of opinion or an adverse opinion. Consequently, the propriety of a qualified opinion in the event of a significant exception is a matter for careful professional judgment by the auditors.

The audit reports for all qualified opinions, except those dealing with changes in accounting principle, should have a separate explanatory paragraph disclosing the reasons for the qualification. However, the reasons for scope limitations may be disclosed in the scope paragraph

FIGURE 20–1
Departures from an unqualified audit report

	Nature of auditors' exception			
		Inability to perform necessary auditing procedures		Financial statements not presented fairly
	Examination not in accordance with GAAS[1]	Beginning inventories in first audit	Major uncertainty	
Usual type of report	Denial of opinion	Denial on operations statements; unqualified opinion on balance sheet	"Subject to" qualified opinion	"Except for" qualified opinion
	or	or	or	or
Less frequent type of report	"Except for" qualified opinion (when departure from GAAS not too significant)	"Except for" qualified opinion on operations statements (when beginning inventories not too material)	Denial of opinion (when uncertainty is too significant)	Adverse opinion (when departures from GAAP[2] are too significant)

1 GAAS—generally accepted auditing standards
2 GAAP—generally accepted accounting principles

or in a separate paragraph. The opinion paragraph of a qualified report includes the appropriate qualifying language and a reference to the scope or explanatory paragraph.

Limitations on scope of examination. We have pointed out that limitations on the scope of the auditors' examination may result from failure to comply with generally accepted auditing standards (weak internal control or client-imposed restrictions), or from inability of the auditors to perform necessary auditing procedures (inability to verify beginning inventories of a new client or major uncertainties). If the scope limitations other than major uncertainties are not so material as to require a denial of opinion, the auditors would issue a qualified opinion such as the following:

We have examined the balance sheet of Y Co. Ltd., as at December 31, 19X2 and the statements of income, retained earnings and changes in financial position for the year then ended. Except as explained in the following paragraph, our examination was made in accordance with generally accepted auditing standards, and accordingly included such tests and other procedures as we considered necessary in the circumstances.

We did not observe the taking of the physical inventory at December 31, 19X1, since that date was prior to the time we were engaged initially as auditors for the company. Due to the nature of the company's records, we were unable to obtain evidence as to the inventory quantities by means of other auditing procedures.

In our opinion, *except for the effects of such adjustments, if any, as might have been determined to be necessary had we been able to observe the physical inventory at December 31, 19X1,* the accompanying statements of income, retained earnings, and changes in financial position present fairly the results of the company's operations and the changes in its financial position for the year ended December 31, 19X2, in accordance with generally accepted accounting principles applied on a basis consistent with that of the preceding year. Also in our opinion, the accompanying balance sheet presents fairly the financial position of the company as at December 31, 19X2 in accordance with generally accepted accounting principles applied on a basis consistent with that of the preceding year.

Major uncertainty affecting a client's business.   If substantial uncertainty exists as to the outcome of an important matter affecting the client's financial statements, the auditors are not able to accumulate sufficient appropriate audit evidence and hence must usually issue an opinion which is "*subject to*" the outcome of the pending uncertainties. The term *uncertainty* does not include matters whose outcome is merely *difficult* to estimate. As emphasized by the AICPA in *SAS No. 2:*

> Matters are not to be regarded as uncertainties . . . unless their outcome is not susceptible of reasonable estimation, . . .

Following is an example of an audit report qualified as to uncertainty. Since the wording of the standard scope paragraph is not affected, that paragraph is omitted from the illustration, and only the middle paragraph and opinion paragraph are shown.

(Standard scope paragraph)

> As disclosed in Note 8 to the financial statements, the company is defendant in a lawsuit alleging infringement of certain patent rights and claiming royalties and punitive damages. The company has filed a counter action, and preliminary hearings and discovery proceedings on both actions are in progress. Company officers and counsel believe the company has a good chance of prevailing, but the ultimate outcome of the lawsuits cannot be determined at this time, and no provision for any liability that may result has been made in the financial statements.
>
> In our opinion, *subject to the effects, if any, on the financial statements of the ultimate resolution of the matter discussed in the preceding paragraph,* these financial statements present fairly the financial position of the company as at December 31, 19XX and the results of its operations and the changes in its financial position for the year then ended in accordance with generally accepted accounting principles applied on a basis consistent with that of the preceding year.

Qualifications as to accounting principles or disclosure.   The auditors sometimes must qualify their opinion because they do not agree with the accounting principles used in preparing the statements, or they believe disclosures in the statements are inadequate. In most cases when the auditors' objections are carefully explained, the client will agree to change the statements in an acceptable manner. If the client does not agree to make the suggested changes, the auditors will be forced to qualify their opinion (or if the exception is sufficiently material, to issue an adverse opinion). An example of an audit report with the opinion paragraph qualified as to accounting principles follows:

(Standard scope paragraph)

As disclosed in Note 4 to the financial statements, the company has not recorded depreciation of its fixed assets for the year. In our opinion, generally accepted accounting principles required that the depreciation charges of $500,000 be recorded for the current year. Had the depreciation charges been made for the current year, the accumulated depreciation would have been increased by $500,000, net income, and retained earnings would have been less by $500,000, and net income per share would have been less by $1.

In our opinion, *except for the failure to provide for depreciation and to make related adjustments as set out in the preceding paragraph,* these financial statements present fairly the financial position of the company as at December 31, 19XX and the results of its operations and the changes in its financial position for the year then ended in accordance with generally accepted accounting principles applied on a basis consistent with that of the preceding year.

If the auditors consider disclosures in the client's financial statements or footnotes to be inadequate, they generally will issue a qualified audit report. For example, if the client fails to include a statement of changes in financial position when one is required, the auditors should word their report as follows after a standard scope paragraph:

The company declined to present a statement of changes in financial position for the year ended December 31, 19XX. Presentation of such statement summarizing the company's financing and investing activities and other changes in its financial position is required by generally accepted accounting principles.

In our opinion, *except for the omission of a statement of changes in financial position,* resulting in an incomplete presentation as explained in the preceding paragraph, these financial statements present fairly the financial position of the company as at December 31, 19XX and the results of its operations for the year then ended in accordance with generally accepted accounting principles applied on a basis consistent with that of the preceding year.

Consistency qualifications. If a client company makes a change in accounting principle (including a change in the reporting entity), the nature of, justification for, and effect of the change are reported in a note to the financial statements for the period in which the change was made.

Any such change having a material effect upon the financial statements will also require qualification of the auditors' report, even though they are in full agreement with the change. The auditors' qualification as to consistency appears in the *opinion paragraph* of their report, rather than in a *separate paragraph.*

Conditions surrounding a consistency qualification may be varied. For example, the accounting change may be one which requires retroactive restatement of preceding years' financial statements instead of inclusion of the cumulative effect of the change in the current year's income statement. Further, the auditors may be reporting on comparative financial statements for more than one year, rather than on the current year's statements only. The auditors' consistency qualifications must be tailored to fit these varied conditions.

An example of an audit report on financial statements for a single year which include the cumulative effects of an accounting change would read as follows, after the standard scope paragraph.

(Standard scope paragraph)

In our opinion, these financial statements present fairly the financial position of the company as at December 31, 19XX and the results of its operations and the changes in its financial position for the year then ended in accordance with generally accepted accounting principles which, *except for the change, with which we concur, in the method of computing depreciation as described in Note 1 to the financial statements,* have been applied on a basis consistent with that of the preceding year.

In the preceding example, Note 1 would describe fully the nature of and justification for the change in method of computing depreciation and the related effect upon net income. If the auditors did not concur with any aspects of the change or its disclosure, they would qualify their opinion or issue an adverse opinion, as appropriate.

A change in accounting estimate, such as the estimated service life of a patent, and a changed condition unrelated to accounting, such as the sale of a plant, do not require a consistency qualification by the auditors if they are properly disclosed in notes to the financial statements.

If the auditors are reporting on the financial statements for the first accounting period of a newly organized company, no previous accounting period exists. Accordingly, the auditors should not refer to consistency, unless there had been a change in accounting principle during the first accounting period which had not been retroactively applied for the entire period.

"Explained opinions."   Some audit reports have been issued containing a qualification worded in such a cautious manner that it could be interpreted as no qualification at all. Typically, the opinion paragraph following an ambiguous qualification might contain the expression "with the foregoing explanation as to inventories, the accompanying financial statements present fairly. . . ." Such indecisive or contradictory audit reports are not satisfactory. The acceptable alternatives in such cases are to issue an unqualified opinion or a qualified opinion which incorporates the words *"except for"* or *"subject to."*

3. Adverse opinions.

An adverse opinion is the opposite of an unqualified opinion; it is an opinion that the financial statements *do not* present fairly the financial position, results of operations, and changes in financial position of the client, in conformity with generally accepted accounting principles. When the auditors express an adverse opinion, they must have no unresolved scope qualifications; they must have accumulated sufficient evidence to support their unfavourable opinion.

The auditors should express an adverse opinion if the statements are so lacking in fairness that a qualified opinion would not be warning enough. If the auditors know the statements to be an unfair presentation, they cannot deny an opinion. Whenever the auditors issue an adverse opinion, they should disclose in a separate paragraph of their report the reasons for the adverse opinion and the principal effects of the adverse opinion on the client company's financial position and operating results.

Thus, an audit report which included an adverse opinion would include an unqualified scope paragraph, a middle paragraph describing the reasons for the adverse opinion and the principal effects of the subject matter of the adverse opinion, and an opinion paragraph such as the one following:

> In our opinion, because of the effects of the matters discussed in the preceding paragraph, these financial statements *do not present fairly* in accordance with generally accepted accounting principles the financial position of the company as at December 31, 19XX, or the results of its operations and changes in its financial position for the year then ended.

Unless the auditors have specific exceptions as to consistency, they should make no reference to consistency in an audit report containing an adverse opinion. An expression of opinion on consistency would imply the application of generally accepted accounting principles and thus soften the impact of the adverse opinion.

Adverse opinions are rare because most clients follow the recommendations of the independent auditors with respect to fair presentation in financial statements. In the United States, an important source of adverse opinions is the actions of regulatory agencies which prescribe accounting practices not in accordance with generally accepted accounting principles.

4. Denial of opinion.

A denial of opinion is no opinion. In an audit engagement, a denial is required when substantial restrictions upon the scope of the auditors' examination or other conditions preclude their compliance with generally accepted auditing standards.

Restrictions imposed by client. In some engagements, the client may impose restrictions limiting the auditors' compliance with generally accepted auditing standards. Common examples are the prohibition of inventory observation and receivables confirmation. Since inventories and receivables are usually important factors in determining both financial position and operating results, the auditors (if prohibited by the client from observing the physical inventory or confirming receivables) must qualify the scope paragraph of their report. Generally, failure to observe the physical inventory or to confirm receivables will represent such a material shortcoming in the scope of the examination that the auditors will not be able to express an opinion on the fairness of the statements taken as a whole.

Another example of a client-imposed restriction on the scope of the audit is the client's denial of permission for the auditors to examine the financial statements of a significant subsidiary company or branch, or to apply required auditing procedures to the financial statements of a significant investee company.

However, it may not be legally permissible for auditors to accept any statutory audit engagement containing limitations which infringe on their statutory duties. If significant limitations are imposed by the client during the audit, the auditors should seriously consider resigning from the audit engagement. In any event, auditors encountering client imposed limitations on the scope of their audit examination should seek legal advice on their course of action.

When the client imposes restrictions that limit significantly the scope of the audit, the CA firm generally must deny an opinion on the client's financial statements. In a separate paragraph of the audit report, the auditors should describe all substantive reasons for the denial of opinion and should disclose any reservations they have regarding fairness of the financial statements. In a denial of opinion, the auditors should not describe the auditing procedures actually performed, to avoid diluting the impact of the denial.

An example of a denial of opinion follows:

> The company did not take a physical inventory of merchandise, stated at $863,198, in the accompanying financial statements as at December 31, 19XX. The company's records do not permit the application of adequate alternative procedures regarding the inventories.
>
> Since the company did not take a physical inventory and we were unable to apply adequate alternative procedures regarding inventories, as noted in the preceding paragraph, the scope of our work was not sufficient for us to express, and *we do not express, an opinion on these financial statements.*

Denial because of uncertainty.[2]   In its *SAS No. 2*, the AICPA in the United States, took the position that a *qualified opinion* is generally appropriate for a material uncertainty which is described adequately in notes to the client's financial statements. However, it did not rule out the issuance of a *denial of opinion* because of major uncertainty. If a denial because of uncertainty is issued by the auditors, it should be in the same format as the denial of opinion illustrated above.

An audit report in which the CA firm denies an opinion of the fairness of the financial statements is not likely to be of much use to the client. Consequently, the auditors should consider at the beginning of the engagement what obstacles may exist to their expression of an opinion and should reach an understanding with the client as to any special problem that may prevent the endorsement of the statements.

Negative assurance clause in audit report

Statements of *negative assurance* have sometimes been included in audit reports to comfort or reassure a client when the auditors cannot express an unqualified opinion. For example:

> Our examination did not include confirmation of accounts receivable or observation of physical inventory. Consequently, we do not express an opinion on the fairness of the financial statements referred to above. However, nothing came to our attention which would lead us to question the fairness of the amounts shown for receivables and inventories.

The purpose of such a statement is to soften the denial of opinion and to avoid giving the impression of a blunt denial of responsibility by the auditors. Such statements of negative assurance are likely to be misleading; they encourage the reader to believe that the amounts shown for receivables and inventory are dependable. Furthermore, they are probably a violation of the CICA reporting standards which include a requirement that "either an expression of an opinion on the financial statements or an assertion that an opinion cannot be expressed." In the United States, statements of negative assurance are a violation of the AICPA reporting standards.

For the auditors to report that "nothing came to their attention" which would cause them to doubt the amounts shown for receivables or inventories creates confusion as to what responsibility, if any, the auditors are assuming. If the auditors made no investigation of these items, then there was little opportunity for anything unfavourable to come to their attention. The use of negative assurance in comfort letters for preliminary prospectuses in Canada and letters for underwriters in the United States will be discussed later in this chapter.

---

[2] In the United States, the term disclaimer is used instead of the term denial.

Piecemeal opinions

In the past, auditors who were forced to deny an opinion for reasons other than client-imposed restrictions, or to express an adverse opinion on the overall fairness of the financial statements, sometimes would express a *piecemeal opinion* indicating the fairness of certain items in the statements. For example, let us assume that the auditors had completed an examination unlimited in scope and had found all accounts satisfactory except those relating to inventories which were not properly valued. Because inventories were quite material and affected the income statement, balance sheet, and statement of changes in financial position, the auditors had to express an *adverse opinion* on the financial statements. The CAs, however, also expressed a *piecemeal opinion* naming other accounts such as Cash, Accounts Receivable, and Plant and Equipment which were fairly stated.

However, piecemeal opinions tend to overshadow or contradict the adverse opinion or denial of opinion. Consequently, piecemeal opinions, while permitted in Canada, are rarely used in practice. Section 5500 of the *CICA Handbook* recommends that piecemeal opinions should be used cautiously and under the following circumstances only—

1. In conjunction with adverse opinions or denials of opinion;
2. Where the effects of the reservations causing the adverse opinion or denial of opinion can be related to specific items;
3. With respect to items which are significant, either individually or as a group.

In the United States, however, in *SAS No. 2* the AICPA has prohibited the issuance of a piecemeal opinion in *any* situation.

Comparative financial statements in audit reports

The CICA has long supported the presentation of comparative financial statements for a series of accounting periods in annual or interim reports to shareholders. Comparative statements show changes and trends in the financial position and operating results of a company over an extended period, and thus are more useful to investors and creditors than are financial statements for a single period.

When comparative financial statements are presented by the client company, the auditors' report covers only the current period unless an extension to cover the statements of prior periods is specifically stated in their report. However, when the comparative financial statements were reported on by other auditors, this fact should be disclosed in the notes to the financial statements or in a separate paragraph of the auditors' report following the opinion paragraph. Similar disclosure should be made when comparative financial statements are unaudited and are not clearly identified as such.

If in the auditors' report for the prior period reservations were expressed which may impair the comparability with the current period, the auditors should refer to such reservations in their report for the current period.

In the United States, however, the auditors should report upon the comparative financial statements if the CPA firm has examined them. The scope paragraph would describe the periods for which the statements were examined, and the opinion paragraph of an unqualified audit report would be worded as follows:

> In our opinion, the financial statements referred to above present fairly the financial position of X Company as of December 31, 19X1, and December 31, 19X2, and the results of its operations and the changes in its financial position for the years then ended, in conformity with generally accepted accounting principles applied on a consistent basis.

Dating the audit report; dual dating

The audit report usually is dated as of the day the audit field work was completed, regardless of the date the report is actually issued. The completion of audit field work in most cases also signifies the completion of all important audit procedures. However, if an event subsequent to the date of field work completion, but prior to issuance of the audit report, requires disclosure in a note to the audited financial statements, the auditors have two options for dating their report. They may use *dual dating*, such as "February 10, 19—, except for Note 7 as to which the date is February 22, 19—"; or they may date the report as of the later date. If the auditors choose the second option, they should return to the client's premises and apply additional auditing procedures to disclose other subsequent events through the later date.

Auditors' responsibility for other data in the annual report

Audit reports on the financial statements of large companies usually are included in an annual report to shareholders. These documents include a multitude of information in addition to audited financial statements. In *SAS No. 8*, "Other Information in Documents Containing Audited Financial Statements," the AICPA in the United States set forth guidelines for the independent auditors with respect to such information. The auditors should read the other information and consider whether it, or its manner of presentation, is materially inconsistent with information appearing in the audited financial statements or footnotes. If the other information is inconsistent, and the auditors conclude that neither the audited financial statements nor the audit report requires revision, they should request the client to revise the other information. If the client refuses to do so, the auditors should consider such alternatives as: (1) revising the audit report to describe the inconsistency; (2) withholding use of their audit report by the client; or (3) withdrawing from the engagement. The auditors should also be alert for, and discuss with the client, any other types of material misstatements included in the other information. In Canada, however, there are no specific professional pronouncements in this area, even though the auditors usually follow practices similar to those recommended by the AICPA.

Long-form audit reports

Long-form audit reports contain information which supplements and analyzes the basic financial statements. Reporting standards require that the auditors indicate the responsibility they assume with respect to the supplementary information. If the auditors have examined the information, they should express an opinion on its fairness; otherwise, they must deny an opinion.

An opinion on supplementary information may be included as a preface to the supplementary information, in the following language:

> Our report on our examination of the financial statements of X Co. Ltd appears on page 1. This examination was made primarily for the purpose of expressing an opinion on the basic financial statements, taken as a whole, shown on pages 2 to 7 of this report. The data included in this report on pages 9 to 15, inclusive, although not considered necessary for a fair presentation of financial position, results of operations and changes in financial position, are presented primarily for supplemental analysis purposes. This supplementary information has been subjected to the audit procedures applied in the examination of the basic financial statements and, in our opinion, is fairly stated in all material respects in relation to the basic financial statements taken as a whole.

Content of supplementary information. Supplementary information presented in a long-form audit report customarily includes many of the following:

1. Comparative summary of operations, stressing changes in dollar amounts and in percentage relationships.
2. Operating ratios.
3. Comparative summary of financial position and measurement of changes.
4. Details of selected balance sheet items, such as receivables and inventories.
5. Supporting analyses of selling and administrative expenses and property and related depreciation accounts.

In addition, general price-level financial information may be included with supplementary information.

The inclusion of supplementary information in the long-form audit report should not be regarded as a satisfactory substitute for adequate informative disclosure in the basic financial statements or footnotes. Furthermore, nothing in the supplementary information should contradict data in the financial statements or in the auditors' opinion.

Reports to the SEC in the United States

Many audit clients in the United States and those Canadian companies listed on the stock exchanges there are subject to the financial reporting requirements of the federal laws administered by the SEC. Thus, it is important for Canadian auditors to be familiar with these reporting requirements. Two principal laws, the Securities Act of 1933 and the Securities Exchange Act of 1934, provide for a multitude of reports requiring audited financial statements. The most important of these reports, or *forms*, are the following:

1. Forms S–1, S–7, or S–16. These forms are the "registration statements" for clients planning to issue securities to the public.
2. Form 10. This is the principal device for registering securities for trading on a national securities exchange.
3. Form 10–K. This report is filed annually with the SEC by companies subject to the periodic reporting provisions of the Securities Acts.
4. Proxy Statement. Companies planning to solicit proxies for the election of directors at shareholders' meetings often are required to submit audited financial statements in the proxy statements mailed to shareholders.
5. Form 8–K. This is a "current report" filed for any month in which significant events occur for a company subject to the Securities Acts. If the significant event is a business combination, audited financial statements of the acquired company often are required in the current report.

The preceding points represent only a brief sumary of the complex reporting requirements of the SEC. The auditors dealing with these reports should be well versed in the requirements of each form, as well as in the provisions of the SEC's *Regulation S–X*, which governs the form and content of financial statements and supporting schedules required to be filed with the various forms.

Reporting on audits of unincorporated businesses

While minimum standards of disclosure recommended by the *CICA Handbook* are applicable to both incorporated and unincorporated businesses, certain special problems are unique to unincorporated businesses. Unincorporated businesses are not separate entities from their owners. Since income taxes on business profits are payable by the owners as individuals, they are usually not shown in the financial statements. Owners' salaries and interest on invested capital are determined by the owners at their discretion and may not necessarily reflect the economic costs of the business. Furthermore, the owners may have other business interests in addition to the concern being audited.

To ensure that these problems are properly disclosed, Section 1800 of the *CICA Handbook* recommends the following:

1. The financial statements of an unincorporated business should indicate clearly the name under which the business is conducted and, where practicable, the names of the owners.
2. It should also be made evident that the business is unincorporated and that the statements do not include all the assets, liabilities, revenues, and expenses of the owners.
3. Any salaries, interest, or similar items accruing to owners of an unincorporated business should be clearly indicated. If no such charges are made, this fact should be disclosed.
4. No provision for income taxes should be made in the financial statements of unincorporated businesses, and such omission should be noted specifically.

The standard audit report might be modified as follows to fit the needs of an unincorporated business:

> We have examined the balance sheet of William Kerr & Company (a proprietorship owned by William J. Kerr) as at December 31, 19XX and the statements of income, proprietary equity, and changes in financial position for the year then ended. Our examination was made in accordance with generally accepted auditing standards, and accordingly included such tests and other procedures as we considered necessary in the circumstances.
>
> As indicated in Note 1 to the financial statements, these financial statements do not include William J. Kerr's personal assets, liabilities, revenue, and expenses which are not shown in the accounting records of the proprietorship.
>
> In our opinion, these financial statements present fairly the financial position of William Kerr & Company as at December 31, 19XX and the results of its operations and the changes in its financial position for the year then ended in accordance with generally accepted accounting principles applied on a basis consistent with that of the preceding year.

Reporting on audits of personal financial statements

Financial statements for individuals have been audited and made public by a number of political candidates in recent years. Personal financial statements are also often required for credit applications and for income tax and estate tax planning. To provide guidelines for such statements, the AICPA in the United States has issued an Industry Audit Guide entitled *Audits of Personal Financial Statements*. The Guide states the basic financial statements for individuals or families—the statement of assets and liabilities and the statement of changes in net assets—should utilize dual money columns, one for *cost* and the other for *estimated value*. The statements should reflect the accrual basis of accounting, including income tax allocation for differences between cost and tax bases, and provide, in the *estimated value* column, for accrued income taxes on unrealized appreciation of assets.

An unqualified audit report for personal financial statements includes the two paragraphs of the standard report, expressing an opinion only on the *cost* column amounts in the financial statements. In a third paragraph, the auditors assert that they have determined that the *estimated value* column amounts are presented on the bases described in the statements or footnotes. The auditors do not express an opinion on the amounts shown as estimated values.

OTHER REPORTS BY AUDITORS

The standard audit report which we have considered in some detail is appropriate when the auditors make an examination of basic financial statements for a business concern operated for profit. These basic financial statements are designed to show financial position, results of operations, and changes in financial position. However, CAs issue a variety of reports other than reports on audited financial statements. Among these are disclaimers on unaudited financial statements, reports on limited review of interim financial information, reports covered by the *CICA Handbook* section on accounting and auditing guidelines, *comfort letters* to securities commissions and underwriters, reports on internal control, and numerous other *special reports*.

Disclaimers on unaudited financial statements

Chartered accountants are often engaged to prepare or review financial statements for clients without performing an examination of the statements in accordance with generally accepted auditing standards. When CAs are involved in these "non-audit" engagements, they should comply with the following *professional standards* set forth in Section 8100 of the *CICA Handbook:*

(a) ensure that the services are performed, and any accompanying communication is prepared, by a person or persons having **adequate technical training and proficiency in accounting,** and with due care; and

(b)   ensure that the work is adequately planned and properly executed and that, if assistants are employed, they are properly supervised. (Emphasis added.)

These are professional, not auditing, standards, and they refer to the CAs competence in accounting, not auditing. Also, there is no reference to the CAs objectivity. Thus, they should be distinguished from the generally accepted auditing standards which are inappropriate for non-audit engagements.

Non-audit engagements are classified into two types: *review* engagements and *non-review* engagements. The additional professional standards and the type of disclaimer associated with each of these two types of engagements are discussed below.

Review engagements.   In a review engagement, the CA's objective is to ensure that the client's financial statements are "plausible" in the circumstances. The term "plausible" means "appearing to be worthy of belief," based on the information obtained by the CA in connection with his review. The additional professional standards with which the CA must comply in a review engagement, as recommended by Section 8100 of the *CICA Handbook*, are:

(a)   possess or acquire the amount of knowledge of the business carried on by the enterprise that a public accountant should reasonably be expected to have so that he can make intelligent enquiry and assessment of information obtained;

(b)   perform a review, consisting primarily of enquiry, comparison and discussion, with the limited objective of considering whether the information provided to him relative to the financial statements and the statements themselves are plausible in the circumstances. Such a review does not require:

(i)   a study or evaluation of internal controls; or

(ii)   an examination of evidence as to representations made or information supplied to him, except where such representations or information are not plausible; and

(c)   determine, so far as he knows and based on information provided to him and the review carried out by him, whether the financial statements appear to be in accordance with generally accepted accounting principles (or in special circumstances the appropriate disclosed basis of accounting) consistently applied.

The same section of the *CICA Handbook* also recommends that the CA should clearly convey the limited nature of his involvement with the unaudited financial statements in his disclaimer which should:

(a)   identify the financial statements;

(b)   state who prepared the financial statements;

(c)   indicate the source of the information used in the preparation of the financial statements when these have been prepared by the public accountant;

(d) state that a review was performed and briefly describe its nature;

(e) state that an audit has not been performed and disclaim an opinion; and

(f) not express any form of negative assurance.

Where the CA has prepared unaudited financial statements, the following disclaimer should be used:

Accountant's Comments

I have prepared the accompanying balance sheet as at December 31, 19XX and the statements of income, retained earnings and changes in financial position for the year then ended from the records of XYZ Company and from other information supplied to me by the company. In order to prepare these financial statements I made a review, consisting primarily of enquiry, comparison and discussion, of such information. However, in accordance with the terms of my engagement, I have not performed an audit and consequently do not express an opinion on these financial statements.

However, if the unaudited financial statements were prepared by the client, the CA should modify the wording of the disclaimer to clearly disclose that fact. Another modification of the above disclaimer is required when the client's unaudited financial statements were not in accordance with generally accepted accounting principles. The CA should clearly disclose the nature and effect of such non-compliance in his disclaimer. If the client refuses to attach such a disclaimer to the unaudited financial statements, the CA should refuse to be further associated with the statements.

Non-review engagements. Chartered accountants should undertake non-review engagements under specified circumstances and the unaudited financial statements should contain a warning concerning the restricted purposes for which they are intended. Typical examples of these specified circumstances, as suggested by Section 8100 of the *CICA Handbook*, are:

(a) interim monthly statements for management purposes, prepared by computer or by other means;

(b) interim statements for a specific creditor such as a bank; and

(c) statements prepared as part of tax returns.

The additional professional standard with which the CA must comply in a non-review engagement, as recommended by Section 8100 of the *CICA Handbook*, is that he should, "based on the information provided to him, prepare financial statements which are, so far as he knows, suitable for the purpose intended."

The CA should convey, in his disclaimer, the nature of his involvement with the statements and the very limited responsibility he assumes. Accordingly, the *CICA Handbook* recommends that his disclaimer, entitled "Notice to Reader," should:

(a)   state the nature of the work done;

(b)   state the restriction in use;

(c)   state that the public accountant did not audit, review or otherwise attempt to verify the accuracy or completeness of the statement;

(d)   employ wording which is distinctly dissimilar to that in other forms of disclaimer or report; and

(e)   not express any form of opinion or negative assurance.

An example of such a disclaimer is presented below.

Notice to Reader

This statement has been compiled solely for (indicate specific use, for example, income tax) purposes. I have not audited, reviewed or otherwise attempted to verify its accuracy or completeness.

Also, the *CICA Handbook* recommends that if the CA is aware of specific accounting deficiencies which would cause the statements to be materially misstated for the purposes intended, he should request that appropriate amendments be made. If the client refuses to make such amendments, the CA should refuse to be further associated with the statements.

In both review and non-review engagements, the CA should ensure that each page of the financial statements is conspicuously marked unaudited and referenced to the appropriate disclaimer.

In the United States, unaudited financial statements are not differentiated into review and non-review types. The conclusions of the AICPA on unaudited financial statements included the following:

1.   CPAs have no responsibility to apply any auditing procedures to unaudited financial statements.

2.   A disclaimer of opinion should accompany unaudited financial statements prepared by a CPA firm, and each page of the financial statements should be clearly marked as **unaudited.** Suggested wording for the disclaimer is as follows:

The accompanying balance sheet of X Company as of December 31, 19XX, and the related statements of income, retained earnings and changes in financial position for the year then ended were not audited by us and accordingly we do not express an opinion on them.

3.   Financial statements drafted for a client's internal use may not include all notes or other disclosures necessary for adequate informative disclosure. In such cases, the CPA firm's disclaimer should include this fact.

4.   If the CPAs know that unaudited financial statements intended to be distributed to external users are not in accordance with generally accepted accounting principles, or do not contain adequate informative disclosures, they should insist upon appropriate revision or should

state their reservations in the disclaimer of opinion. If necessary, the CPAs should withdraw from the engagement.

In addition, when a CPA firm is not independent of its client, the firm must disclose this lack of independence in its disclaim accompanying the unaudited financial statements. Also, the AICPA has published, to assist its members, a *Guide for Engagements of CPA's to Prepare Unaudited Financial Statements*.

Reports on unaudited interim and quarterly financial data

Since many companies are required by statute or regulatory authority to issue unaudited interim financial data to their shareholders and these companies often ask their auditors to review these data, the CICA has issued an exposure draft on *The Auditor's Involvement with Interim Financial Reporting to Shareholders of Public Companies*. This exposure draft proposes certain professional standards and procedures to be followed by the auditors in a review of interim financial data. The professional standards include the auditors' (*a*) adequate technical training and proficiency in auditing, due care, and objectivity, (*b*) adequate planning, execution, and supervision, (*c*) adequate knowledge of the client's business and accounting systems, and (*d*) determination of the plausibility of interim financial data and the conformity with generally accepted accounting principles applied on a consistent basis. The principal procedures consist primarily of enquiry, comparison, and discussion. The main objective of the auditors' *review* is to ensure that the unaudited interim financial data are *plausible* in the circumstances and in accordance with generally accepted accounting principles applied on a consistent basis. The exposure draft suggests that the auditors report the results of their review to the *client's company's board of directors,* and when the results are to be distributed to the shareholders, the following format should be used.

Auditors' Comments on Interim Financial Information

To the Board of Directors of X Limited:

We have reviewed the accompanying unaudited interim financial information comprising the balance sheet of X Limited as at June 30, 19X2, and the statements of income, retained earnings and changes in financial position for the six-month period then ended. Our review was made in accordance with standards for such reviews established by the Canadian Institute of Chartered Accountants and consisted primarily of enquiry comparison, and discussion.

We have not performed an audit and consequently do not express an opinion on this interim financial information. The most recent audited financial statements issued to shareholders on which we have expressed an opinion were for the year ended December 31, 19X1.

In the United States, the SEC's *Accounting Series Release No. 177* required disclosure of selected quarterly financial data in a note to the annual financial statements of certain companies subject to its jurisdiction. The Commission permitted the required note to be labeled *unaudited,* even though independent auditors had examined the *annual* financial statements in accordance with generally accepted auditing standards.

Also in *ASR No. 177,* the SEC urged companies it supervises to have independent CPAs *review* the unaudited quarterly financial data reported in Form 10–Q, which is filed with the Commission within 45 days following the end of each of a company's first three fiscal quarters.

The AICPA in the United States has issued *SAS No. 10,* "Limited Review of Interim Financial Information," and *SAS No. 13,* "Reports on a Limited Review of Interim Financial Information," to provide guidance for CPAs engaged in a *review* of unaudited quarterly financial data. The principal procedures for a limited review established by *SAS No. 10* include enquiries of client company officers and other executives, analytical review of the quarterly financial data by reference to interim financial statements and other data, and reading minutes of meetings of shareholders, board of directors, and committees of the board. *SAS No. 10* provided the following format for reporting the results of the limited review to the *client company's board of directors:*

> We have performed a limited review of the balance sheet of X Company as of September 30, 19XX, and the related statements of income, retained earnings and changes in financial position for the three-month and nine-month periods then ended.
>
> Our limited review was performed in accordance with standards for such reviews promulgated by the American Institute of Certified Public Accountants and, accordingly, consisted principally of obtaining an understanding, by inquiries, of the accounting system for preparation of interim financial information; making an analytical review of pertinent financial data; and making inquiries of and evaluating responses from certain officials of the Company who have responsibility for financial and accounting matters.
>
> Because our limited review did not constitute an examination made in accordance with generally accepted auditing standards, we express no opinion on the financial statements referred to above.
>
> In connection with our limited review, no matters came to our attention that we believe should be reported to you. Had we performed additional procedures or had we made an examination of the financial statements referred to above in accordance with generally accepted auditing standards, matters might have come to our attention that would have been reported to you.

This report is solely for the information of the board of directors and management and is not to be quoted in documents setting forth the unaudited interim financial information or in any other document available to the public.

In *SAS No. 13*, the AICPA established guidelines for a CPA firm's report on a limited review to accompany unaudited quarterly financial data distributed to shareholders or filed with the SEC in Form 10–Q. An example of such a report, which should be addressed to the client company, its board of directors, or its shareholders, follows:

> We have made a limited review, in accordance with standards established by the American Institute of Certified Public Accountants, of the balance sheet of X Company as of September 30, 19XX, and the related statements of income, retained earnings and changes in financial position for the three-month and nine-month periods than ended. Since we did not make an audit, we express no opinion on the financial statements referred to above.

Reports governed by accounting and auditing guidelines

Accounting and auditing guidelines represent the opinions of the Accounting and Auditing Steering Committees of the CICA and do not have the authority of the recommendations issued by the Accounting Research Committee or the Auditing Standards Committee. Furthermore, these guidelines may be withdrawn due to changes in legislation or may be superseded by *CICA Handbook* recommendations. However, these guidelines, especially those in the auditing area, should be useful to auditors. Consequently, the auditors' reports on supplementary general price-level restatements and on political candidates under the Canada Election Act will be briefly discussed.

Independent auditors may be requested by their client to audit supplementary general price-level restatements in addition to the historical cost financial statements. In such a case, the independent auditors' opinion on these restatements should be included, *as a final paragraph*, in their report on the historical cost financial statements. The suggested form of the final paragraph in which the auditors are able to express an unqualified opinion on the general price-level restatements is as follows:

> We have also examined the supplementary general price-level restated data accompanying the above-mentioned historical cost financial statements. Uniform criteria for the preparation and presentation of such data have not yet been established and accordingly restatement procedures could vary from one enterprise to another. In our opinion the restatement procedures described in the note appended to the supplementary data have been applied in an appropriate manner in compiling such data from the above-mentioned historical cost financial statements.

When independent auditors are engaged to examine a political candidate's return on election expenses under the Canada Elections Act, the following suggested report should be used:

Auditors' Report
Pursuant to Section 62.1 of the Canada Elections Act

Mr. B,
Official Agent for Mr. A, a candidate at the election of a member to serve in the House of Commons of Canada, held on 6th day of April, 19XX, in the Electoral District of Y.
100 Victoria Street,
Anytown, Ontario

We have examined the Candidate's Return Respecting Election Expenses, which includes the Summary of the Return, in respect of the above candidacy of A. Our examination was designed solely to enable us to report as required under the Canada Elections Act; as explained below, it was not designed to determine the extent of omissions, if any, from the accounting records. Our examination included such tests and other procedures as we considered necessary in the circumstances to make this report. In our opinion the Return of A presents fairly the information contained in the accounting records on which the Return is based in accordance with the accounting treatment required by the Act and the Guidelines issued by the Chief Electoral Officer. Furthermore, I confirm that the amounts shown in the Summary of the Return are the same as the related totals in the Return.

The extent of omissions, if any, from the accounting records relating to a candidacy is not susceptible to practicable determination by audit procedures. Accordingly the Act does not require me to report, nor was it practicable for me to determine, that the accounting records include all transactions relating to the Candidacy of A.

As indicated earlier, these accounting and auditing guidelines may be withdrawn for various reasons. Thus, students should refer to the *CICA Handbook* for subsequent changes.

Comfort letters to securities commissions and underwriters

In Canada, the independent auditors who examine the financial statements included in a prospectus are often required by regulatory authorities such as the securities commissions to submit *comfort letters* and *letters of consent.*

The purpose of a comfort letter is to inform the regulatory authority of the status of the auditors' examination and to bring to the regulatory authority's attention any reservations the auditors may have on the financial statements before the auditors render an opinion on these statements. A comfort letter, filed with a preliminary prospectus, is addressed to the regulatory authority and should cover the following:

1. Identify the company involved, the security to be issued, and the relationship between the company and the independent auditors.
2. Specify the financial statements included in the preliminary prospectus.
3. State the status of the examination and the reason for not expressing an opinion on the financial statements.
4. Provide a negative assurance on the financial statements.
5. State that the letter is for the sole use of the regulatory authority.

Sometimes, unaudited interim financial statements, in addition to the audited statements, are included in a prospectus filed with regulatory authorities. In such a case, the authorities may require a comfort letter in respect of the unaudited statements from the independent auditors. This comfort letter should be addressed to the regulatory authority and should include the following:

1. State the relationship between the independent auditors and the company and describe the security to be issued.
2. Identify both the audited financial statements and unaudited interim financial statements.
3. Specify that no audit was performed and no opinion is expressed on the interim financial statements.
4. Provide a negative assurance on the unaudited interim financial statements, based on a limited review of those statements by the auditors.
5. State that the letter is solely for the use of the regulatory authority.

A letter signed by the independent auditors consenting to the use of their audit report on the financial statements included in a prospectus is called a letter of consent. Such a letter is required by most securities acts in Canada. In issuing a letter of consent, the independent auditors should perform the following procedures recommended by Section 7000 of the *CICA Handbook:*

1. The auditors should ascertain that the statements and information included in a prospectus conform with the requirements of the applicable corporations and securities acts and with the standards of financial statement disclosure of the *CICA Handbook.*
2. The auditors should review the entire prospectus in its final form to satisfy themselves that the contents, insofar as they relate to matters on which they might reasonably be expected to have knowledge as a result of their examination, are presented fairly. In addition, if there are qualifications in the auditors' report, the letter of consent should refer to such qualifications.

When auditors are involved in issuing comfort letters and letters of consent, they should be familiar with the provisions in Sections 4000 and 7000 of the *CICA Handbook.*

In the United States, investment banking firms which underwrite a securities issue often request the independent auditors who examined the financial statements and schedules included in the registration statement to issue a letter for the underwriters. This letter, commonly called a *comfort letter,* usually covers the following:

1. A statement as to the auditors' independence.
2. An opinion as to whether the audited financial statements and schedules included in the registration statement comply in all material respects with the applicable requirements of the Securities Act of 1933 and related rules and regulations of the SEC.
3. *Negative assurances* as to whether any unaudited financial statements and schedules included in the registration statement comply with the 1933 Act and SEC pronouncements, and are fairly presented on a basis consistent with the audited financial statements and schedules included in the registration statement.
4. *Negative assurances* as to whether during a specified period following the date of the latest financial statements in the registration statement there had been any change in long-term debt or capital stock, or any decrease in other specified financial statement items.

Letters for underwriters are highly specialized and require a great deal of skill and care in their writing. The independent auditors engaged in writing a letter for underwriters should consult the AICPA's *SAS No. 1* which contains detailed instructions for and illustrations of typical letters.

Reports to regulatory agencies on internal control

It was pointed out in earlier chapters that the auditors, following their study and evaluation of internal control, usually issue an *internal control letter* to the client describing weaknesses in the existing internal control and making recommendations for improvement. An internal control letter should not be confused with a report to regulatory agencies or other outside groups on a company's internal control. The internal control letter is an informal report intended only for management. Since it is an informal communication, no standard format has developed. The internal control letter is written for internal use by persons having a detailed knowledge of the company's operations and interested in making improvements in internal control. Such a letter need not carry the extensive warnings and precautions needed in a report to outsiders.

In recent years, groups outside the client company have become interested in obtaining internal control reports prepared by CA firms. Regulatory agencies may want such reports because of their relevance to regulatory purposes or to the agencies' examination functions. However, if a report on internal control similar to the internal control letter were sent to regulatory agencies or other outside groups, they might misinterpret it and reach many unwarranted conclusions. In summary, a report on internal control to be sent by a CA firm to regulatory agencies or other outsiders should include very carefully drafted precautionary language. The report should make clear that it relates to accounting controls only, that the extent of internal control is limited by cost factors, that weaknesses may exist which did not come to the auditors' attention, and that controls functioning at the time of the audit may no longer be in force.

In *SAS No. 1,* the AICPA in the United States set forth guidelines for reports on internal control issued to regulatory agencies. One of the objectives of the AICPA was to standardize the language of internal control reports issued by CPA firms for use by regulatory agencies so that these agencies would not misunderstand the reports. An illustration of an internal control report follows.

We have examined the financial statements of Midwest Corporation for the year ended December 31, 19X1, and have issued our report thereon dated February 23, 19X2. As a part of our examination, we reviewed and tested the company's system of internal accounting control to the extent we considered necessary to evaluate the system as required by generally accepted auditing standards. Under these standards the purpose of such evaluation is to establish a basis for reliance thereon in determining the nature, timing, and extent of other auditing procedures that are necessary for expressing an opinion on the financial statements.

The objective of internal accounting control is to provide reasonable, but not absolute, assurance as to the safeguarding of assets against loss from unauthorized use or disposition, and the reliability of financial records for preparing financial statements and maintaining accountability for assets. The concept of reasonable assurance recognizes that the cost of a system of internal accounting control should not exceed the benefits derived, and also recognizes that the evaluation of these factors necessarily requires estimates and judgments by management.

There are inherent limitations that should be recognized in considering the potential effectiveness of any system of internal accounting control. In the performance of most control procedures, errors can result from misunderstanding of instructions, mistakes of judgment, carelessness, or other personal factors. Control procedures whose effectiveness depends upon segregation of duties can be circumvented by collusion. Similarly, control procedures can be circumvented intentionally by management with respect either to the execution and recording of transactions or with respect to the estimates and judgments required in the preparation of financial statements. Further, projection of any evaluation of internal accounting control to future periods is subject to the risk that the procedures may become inadequate because of changes in conditions, and that the degree of compliance with the procedures may deteriorate.

Our study and evaluation of the company's system of internal accounting control for the year ended December 31, 19X1, which was made for the purpose set forth in the first paragraph above, was not designed for the purpose of expressing an opinion on internal accounting control and it would not necessarily disclose all weaknesses in the system. However, such study and evaluation disclosed the following conditions that we believe to be material weaknesses:

    ✻   ✻   ✻   ✻   ✻

(At this point any major internal control weaknesses would be listed and discussed, and recommendations for improvement would be presented.)

    ✻   ✻   ✻   ✻   ✻

We have discussed these recommendations with affected personnel in the company and have found general agreement on the desirability of studies and corrective action along the lines indicated. If the suggested studies are initated, we shall, of course, be glad to lend any desired assistance.

Special reports

Although the term *special report* might be applied to all the reports we have considered other than the standard report, it is usually applicable to reports on:[3]

1. Financial statements prepared on a basis other than generally accepted accounting principles, such as the cash basis, a basis prescribed by regulatory authorities, or a unique basis used by certain not-for-profit organizations for which generally accepted accounting principles have not been published.
2. Specific elements of financial statements, such as rentals, royalties, profit sharing, or income taxes.
3. Agreed-upon procedures on specified accounts or items.
4. Compliance with contractual arrangements such as bond indentures, or with requirements of governmental regulatory agencies.

In all special reports, the independent CAs must describe the scope of their engagement and report clearly on their findings. Because of the wide variety of special reports enumerated above, we shall limit our discussion to reports on cash basis financial statements and reports for not-for-profit entities with a unique accounting basis.

---

[3] The exposure draft on *Special Reports,* issued in December 1977, by the CICA Auditing Standards Committee, focuses essentially on financial information other than financial statements and on compliance with aspects of contractual agreements related to financial statements, as identified in items 2, 3, and 4 above.

Reports on cash basis statements

Is an independent CA firm justified in issuing the standard report for a small company which uses the cash basis of accounting? This question is a practical one, for many such organizations do retain CAs and request that all work necessary be done to permit issuance of an unqualified audit report.

It is sometimes argued that if a company does not have significant amounts of inventory, plant and equipment, or accrued revenue and expenses, financial statements prepared on the basis of cash receipts and disbursements will be approximately the same as if prepared on the accrual basis. Even if we grant that cash basis statements for *some* organizations in *some* years will not differ significantly from statements based on the accrual basis, this line of argument still appears to ignore the real issue. That issue may be stated as follows: are cash basis statements prepared in accordance with *generally accepted accounting principles* as that phrase is used in the standard audit report? The answer is *no*. However, this fact does not condemn the cash basis of accounting nor prevent the auditors from expressing an opinion on cash basis statements. It is important that cash basis financial statements disclose that the reporting is being done on the cash basis.

Financial statements prepared on the cash basis of accounting do not present fairly either financial position or changes therein or operating results for the period; such statements merely summarize the cash transactions for the period. The auditors' opinion attached to cash basis statements may serve a very useful purpose, but the opinion should omit any reference to conformity with generally accepted accounting principles and should recognize the statements for what they are.

The following wording is suggested for a report on cash basis financial statements:

> We have examined the statement of assets and liabilities arising from cash transactions of X Company as at December 31, 19XX, and the statement of revenue and expenses for the year then ended. Our examination was made in accordance with generally accepted auditing standards, and accordingly included such tests and other procedures as we considered necessary in the circumstances.
>
> As more fully described in Note 1, the company's policy is to prepare its financial statements on the basis of cash receipts and disbursements; consequently, the financial statements do not include certain assets, liabilities, revenue, and expenses. Accordingly, the financial statements are not intended to present financial position and results of operations in accordance with generally accepted accounting principles.
>
> In our opinion, these financial statements present fairly the assets and liabilities arising from cash transactions of X Company as at December

31, 19XX, and the revenue collected and expenses paid during the year then ended on the basis indicated in the preceding paragraph, which basis is consistent with that used in the preceding year.

The essence of the audit report is the expression of an opinion as to whether the statements fairly present what they purport to present. The wording of the footnote mentioned in the report will vary from case to case in order to give an accurate indication of the content of statements, because the cash basis or modified cash basis sometimes includes accounting records of various assets other than cash.

Reports on not-for-profit organizations

In the United States the AICPA has issued *Industry Audit Guides* which establish accounting standards for hospitals, universities and colleges, and voluntary health and welfare organizations. However, generally accepted accounting principles have not been codified for such other not-for-profit organizations as churches, private foundations, and community organizations, in both Canada and the United States. The following audit report should be appropriate:

> We have examined the statement of assets, liabilities and fund balances of X Church as at June 30, 19XX, and the related statements of revenue and expenses and changes in fund balance for the year then ended. Our examination was made in accordance with generally accepted auditing standards, and accordingly included such tests and other procedures as we considered necessary in the circumstances.
>
> In the absence of established generally accepted accounting principles for this type of organization, the church's policy is to prepare its financial statements on the basis described in Note 1.
>
> In our opinion, these financial statements present fairly the assets, liabilities and fund balances of X Church as at June 30, 19XX, and the revenue and expenses and the changes in fund balance for the year then ended on the basis referred to in the preceding paragraph, which basis is consistent with that used in the preceding year.

KEY TERMS INTRODUCED OR EMPHASIZED IN CHAPTER 20

accounting change   A change in an acounting principle, in an accounting estimate, or in the reporting entity. Changes in accounting principle and in the reporting entity result in *consistency qualifications* in the auditors' standard report.

adverse opinion   An opinion that the financial statements *do not* present fairly financial position, results of operations, and changes in financial position, in accordance with generally accepted accounting principles.

comfort letter   A letter issued by the independent auditors to the securities commissions in Canada and, in the United States to the underwriters of securities registered with the SEC under the Securities Act of 1933.

denial of opinion   A form of report in which the auditors state that they do not express an opinion on the financial statements.

dual dating   Dating of audit reports with two dates: the date of completion of field work, and the date of a significant subsequent event described in a note to the financial statements. The latter date is later than the former.

internal control letter   A letter issued only to the chief executive officer of the client company or the audit committee of the client company's board of directors following the auditors' study and evaluation of the client's existing internal control. In the letter, the auditors describe weaknesses in existing internal control, and recommendations for improvement.

letter of consent   A letter signed by independent auditors consenting to the use of their report upon the financial statements in the prospectus filed with the regulatory authority. This letter is required by most securities acts in Canada.

limited review   Procedures which *are not* equivalent to an audit in accordance with generally accepted auditing standards, performed by independent CPAs on unaudited quarterly financial data issued and filed with the SEC in the United States by an annual audit client. The objective of a limited review is to provide the CPAs with a basis for reporting to the board of directors on matters the CPAs believe should be brought to the board's attention.

long-form audit report   An audit report which attests to supplementary information issued by the client company, in addition to reporting on the basic financial statements.

negative assurance   An unacceptable statement in an audit report containing other than an unqualified opinion, stating that "nothing came to the attention of the independent auditors" with respect to the matter preventing an unqualified opinion. Negative assurances are permitted in *comfort letters.*

non-audit engagement   An engagement in which the public accountant provides accounting services rather than auditing services. Non-audit engagements are classified into two types: review and non-review.

non-review engagement   One of the two types of non-audit engagements in which the public accountant issues a "Notice to Reader" to clearly identify the nature and limitations of the unaudited financial statements.

plausible   This term means appearing to be worthy of belief. It generally applies to unaudited financial statements.

principal auditors   Auditors who use the work and reports of other independent CAs who have examined the financial statements of one or more subsidiaries, branches, or other segments of the principal auditors' client.

Professional Standards   A four-volume publication of the AICPA, of which volumes 3 and 4 represent a compendium of generally accepted accounting principles.

review engagement   One of the two types of non-audit engagements in which the public accountant should ensure that the unaudited financial statements are "plausible" in the circumstances.

special report   A report by independent CAs which includes different wording from the standard audit report on financial statements. The different wording is necessary to identify the basis on which the subject financial information is prepared, or to describe the character of the engagement.

unqualified opinion   An opinion that the financial statements present fairly financial position, results of operations, and changes in financial position, in accordance with generally accepted accounting principles.

GROUP I
REVIEW QUESTIONS

20–1.   Under what circumstances, if any, may a CA firm issue a *piecemeal opinion?* Would your answer be the same for a CPA firm in the United States?

20–2.   What standard for *fairness* has been established by the CICA and the AICPA?

20–3.   The auditors plan to add a separate paragraph to their standard audit report to call attention to a significant subsequent event described in a note to the financial statements. Will the auditors' action result in a *qualified opinion?* Explain.

20–4.   Under what circumstances do the auditors issue an *"except for"* qualified opinion?

20–5.   Under what circumstances, if any, does a qualified opinion audit report *not* include a separate paragraph?

20–6.   Identify the principal causes of a denial of opinion in an audit engagement.

20–7.   Why are comparative financial statements preferable in audit reports?

20–8.   What is the independent auditors' obligation with respect to information in annual reports to shareholders other than the audited financial statements?

20–9.   How does a *limited review* by CPAs in the United States differ from an audit?

20–10.   Compare the audit report issued on cash basis financial statements with the standard audit report.

20–11.   An non-audit engagement can be either a review or non-review engagement. Briefly distinguish a review engagement from a non-review engagement.

20–12.   What is the function of notes to financial statements?

20–13.   List five items generally covered in notes to financial statements.

20–14.   Your client refuses to include a statement of changes in financial position among the financial statements for the current year. Would this prevent you from issuing an unqualified audit report?

20–15.   Describe the reports containing audited financial statements customarily filed by a company subject to the reporting requirements of the SEC in the United States.

20–16. How do *special reports* differ from the standard audit report?

20–17. Wade Company has been your audit client for the last several years. At the beginning of 1979 the company changed its method of inventory valuation from average cost to Lifo. The change, which had been under consideration for some time, was in your opinion a logical and proper step for the company to take. What effect, if any, would this change have upon your standard audit report for the year ended December 31, 1979?

20–18. List several factors which would prevent the issuance of an unqualified audit report.

20–19. In the annual examination of Powell Co. Ltd. the auditors did not confirm accounts receivable from customers, at the client's request. During the course of the examination, virtually all the accounts receivable outstanding at the balance sheet date were collected and the auditors examined the cheques and remittance advices received from customers. Under these circumstances, can the auditors issue an unqualified audit report? Explain.

20–20. Describe the supplementary information generally included in long-form audit reports.

GROUP II
QUESTIONS REQUIRING ANALYSIS

20–21. An auditor of a public company is often required to issue his report very soon after the company's fiscal year-end in order to meet the client's deadline for publication of the annual report.

Required:

Explain briefly the audit problems caused by the deadline imposed by a client. What could the auditor do to minimize his problems? (CICA)

20–22. What type of audit report (unqualified opinion, qualified opinion, adverse opinion, denial of opinion) should the auditors *generally* issue in each of the following situations? Explain.
   a. Client-imposed restrictions limit significantly the scope of the auditors' procedures.
   b. The auditors decide to make reference to the report of another CA firm as a basis, in part, for the auditors' opinion.
   c. The auditors believe that the financial statements have been stated in accordance with generally accepted accounting principles in all respects other than those contingent on the outcome of a material uncertainty.

20–23. As part of your annual audit of Call Ltd., you have the responsibility for preparing a report on internal control to management. Your working papers include a completed internal-control questionnaire and documentation of other tests of the internal-control system which you have reviewed. This review identified a number of material weaknesses; for some of these corrective action by management is not practicable in the circumstances.

Required:

a. Discuss the form and content of the report on internal control to management based on your annual audit and the reasons or purposes for such a report. Do not write a report.
b. Discuss the differences in the form and content of the report if it were based on a special study for the purpose of reporting to a regulatory agency. (AICPA, adapted)

20–24. The following statement is representative of attitudes and opinions sometimes encountered by CAs in their professional practices:

"It is important to read the footnotes to financial statements, even though they often are presented in technical language and are incomprehensible. The auditors may reduce their exposure to third-party liability by stating something in the footnotes that contradicts completely what they have presented in the balance sheet or income statement."

Required:

Evaluate the above statement and indicate:

a. Areas of agreement with the statement, if any.
b. Areas of misconception, incompleteness or fallacious reasoning included in the statement, if any. (AICPA, adapted)

20–25. It has been proposed that public accountants should observe certain professional standards and carry out certain review procedures in the preparation of unaudited financial statements.

Required:

a. List the professional standards public accountants are being called upon to observe when undertaking a non-audit engagement.
b. List the procedures which may be followed and the matters which might be considered by a public accountant when preparing unaudited financial statements to which is attached a *Disclaimer of Opinion.* List major headings *only* and under these headings briefly indicate the review procedures which would be followed or the type of information that would be sought. (CICA)

20–26. During your examination of the financial statements of Raymond Ltd. for the current year, you discover that the company has included in its income statement the material cumulative effect, net of applicable income taxes, of a change in depreciation expense for prior years resulting from an increase during the current year in the estimated service lives of plant assets. Will you be able to express an unqualified opinion on Raymond's financial statements for the current year? Explain.

20–27. *Comment upon the following:* "The standard audit report was adopted substantially in its present form over 40 years ago. Considerable accounting literature has been devoted to the wording used in it, and its intended meaning is fairly well understood by the accounting profession and by the more sophisticated users of auditors' reports. However, despite continuous efforts on the part of the profession to educate the vast mass of less sophisticated users—those who consciously, but somewhat innocently, rely on the reports—the auditors' role still seems to be misunderstood. Most users think of the financial statements themselves, and probably even more so the notes, as comprising part of the auditors' report rather than being the representations of management. The report itself does little to dispel this notion or to make clear that the auditors are only expressing their opinion on management's report."

20–28.   Upon completion of the examination of the client's financial statements the CA firm, in its report, must either express an opinion or deny an opinion on the financial statements. The opinion may be unqualified, qualified, or adverse.

Required:

a. Under what general conditions may a CA firm express an unqualified opinion on the client's financial statements?

b. Define and distinguish among (1) a qualified opinion, (2) an adverse opinion, and (3) a denial of opinion on the statements. (AICPA, adapted)

20–29.   Presented below are three independent, unrelated audit or other reports. The corporation being reported on, in each case, is profit oriented and publishes general-purpose financial statements for distribution to owners, creditors, potential investors, and the general public. Each of the following reports contains deficiencies.

Report I

We have examined the consolidated balance sheet of Belasco Corporation Ltd. and subsidiaries as at December 31, 1979 and the consolidated statements of income, retained earnings and changes in financial position for the year then ended. Our examination was made in accordance with generally accepted auditing standards, and accordingly included such tests and other procedures as we considered necessary in the circumstances. We did not examine the financial statements of Seidel Ltd., a major consolidated subsidiary. These statements were examined by other auditors whose report thereon has been furnished to us, and our opinion expressed herein, insofar as it relates to Seidel Ltd., is based solely upon the report of the other auditors.

In our opinion, except for the report of the other auditors, these financial statements present fairly the financial position of Belasco Corporation Ltd. and subsidiaries as at December 31, 1979 and the results of its operations and the changes in its financial position for the year then ended in accordance with generally accepted accounting principles applied on a basis consistent with that of the preceding year.

Report II

The accompanying balance sheet of Jones Corporation Ltd. as at December 31, 1979 and the related statements of income, retained earnings and changes in financial position for the year than ended were not audited by us; however, we confirmed cash in the bank and performed a general review of the statements.

During our engagement, nothing came to our attention to indicate that the financial statements do not present fairly the financial position of Jones

Corporation Ltd. as at December 31, 1979 and the results of its operations and the changes in its financial position for the year then ended in accordance with generally accepted accounting principles applied on a basis consistent with that of the preceding year; however, we do not express an opinion on them.

Report III

I made my examination in accordance with generally accepted auditing standards. The accompanying balance sheet as of December 31, 1979 and the statements of income, retained earnings and changes in financial position for the year then ended were not audited by me; accordingly, I do not express an opinion on them.

Required:

For each report describe the reporting deficiencies, explain the reasons therefor, and briefly discuss how the report should be corrected. Each report should be considered separately. When discussing one report, ignore the other two. *Do not discuss the addressee, signatures, and date. Also do not rewrite any of the reports.* Organize your answer sheet as follows:

Report no.	Deficiency	Reason	Correction

(AICPA, adapted)

20–30. Marlene Rogers, CA, after several years' experience on the audit staff of a national firm of chartered accountants, opened her own public accounting office in partnership with another CA.

In a discussion with Ralph Jay, the president of one of the clients of the new firm, Rogers placed great emphasis upon the importance of a well-designed system of internal control. She pointed out the usefulness of internal control to management and also the importance of a careful evaluation of internal control by the auditors as a basis for determining the extent and nature of tests to be made.

Jay appeared to be quite favourably impressed with Roger's emphasis upon internal control, and explained that for years he had encouraged the development of strong internal controls in his company. On the following day, Jay requested that the standard report to be issued upon completion of the examination include a statement that the auditors had made a thorough review of the system of internal control. He also requested that the report contain a formal expression of opinion by the auditors as to the adequacy of the system of internal control.

What answer do you believe Rogers should make to Jay, and what special statement, if any, should be included in the wording of the audit report?

20–31. What type of audit report would be isued in each of the following cases? Justify your choice.

a. Bowles Ltd. is engaged in a hazardous trade and cannot obtain insurance coverage from any source. A material portion of the company's assets could be destroyed by a serious accident. The company has an excellent safety record and has never suffered a catastrophe.

b. Draves Ltd. owns substantial properties which have appreciated significantly in value since the date of purchase. The properties were appraised and are reported in the balance sheet at the appraised values with full disclosure. The CA firm believes that the values reported in the balance sheet are reasonable.

c. London Ltd. has material investments in stocks of subsidiary companies. Stocks of the subsidiary companies are not actively traded in the market, and the CA firm's engagement does not extend to any subsidiary company. The CA firm is able to determine that all investments are carried at original cost, and the auditors have no reason to suspect that the amounts are not stated fairly.

d. Slade Ltd. has material investments in stocks of subsidiary companies. Stocks of the subsidiary companies are actively traded in the market, but the CA firm's engagement does not extend to any subsidiary company. Management insists that all investments shall be carried at original costs, and the CA firm is satisfied that the original costs are fairly stated. The CA firm believes that the client will never ultimately realize a substantial portion of the investments, and the client has fully disclosed the facts in footnotes to financial statements. (AICPA, adapted)

20–32. Douglas McGraw, senior partner in a small public accounting firm, received a telephone call at eleven o'clock one morning from R. J. Dunn, owner of Dunn Ltd. Dunn stated that he needed a balance sheet of his company by two o'clock that afternoon to use in a meeting with a banker. He urged that McGraw come over at once and prepare the statement from the accounting records. McGraw had rendered a variety of accounting services for Dunn Ltd. over a period of 20 years. These services had included audits, preparation of tax returns, the design of accounting systems, and other management advisory services. An audit had not been performed for several years. Dunn was a widely known figure in the community and had recommended McGraw's firm to other business executives on several occasions.

What response do you think McGraw should have made to the request from Dunn?

20–33. Select the best answer for each of the following and explain fully the reason for your selection.

a. Even though an expression of opinion as to certain identified items in financial statements tends to overshadow or contradict a denial of opinion or adverse opinion, it is still appropriate for a CA firm to issue—

(1) A piecemeal opinion.
(2) An unqualified opinion.
(3) An "except for" opinion.
(4) A "subject to" opinion.

  b. It is less likely that a denial of opinion would be issued when the auditors have reservations arising from—

   (1) Inability to apply necessary auditing procedures.

   (2) Uncertainties.

   (3) Inadequate internal control.

   (4) Lack of independence.

  c. For which of the following accounting changes would the auditors' report normally *not* contain a consistency qualification?

   (1) A change in principle which does not result in non-comparable statements because the previous year's statements are not presented.

   (2) A change to a principle required by a new CICA pronouncement.

   (3) A change in principle properly reported by restating the financial statements of prior years.

   (4) A change in an accounting estimate. (AICPA, adapted)

20–34. Regarding the problem of deciding what type of auditors' report should be used in reporting on personal financial statements, a recent article stated that, "The difficulty (of choosing an appropriate type of report) arises because . . . the auditors have no way of knowing whether the financial statements they examine reflect all of the assets and liabilities of the individual for whom the financial statements were prepared."

Required:

  The *CICA Handbook* refers to several different types of auditors' reports, each reflecting a different method of expressing the auditors' reservation on the financial statements. Discuss the applicability of each of these types of reports for reporting on personal financial statements. (CICA)

20–35. Select the best answer for each of the following:

  a. The use of the phrase "subject to" in an auditors' opinion is appropriate when the qualification pertains to:

   (1) Non-adherence to generally accepted accounting principles.

   (2) Inability to perform an essential audit procedure.

   (3) Lack of consistency with the preceding year.

   (4) Uncertainty as to the outcome of a material event.

   (5) None of the above.

  b. When public accountants associate themselves with review engagements on unaudited financial statements, they should perform a review of such financial statements. The extent of the review should be sufficient to satisfy themselves that the financial statements:

   (1) Present fairly the financial position and results of operations.

   (2) Are prepared in comparative form.

   (3) Reflect plausible circumstances.

   (4) Include income as determined under the Income Tax Act (Canada).

   (5) None of the above.

c. A CA ethically may:
   (1) Perform an examination for a financially distressed client at less than his customary fees.
   (2) Advertise only as to his expertise in preparing income tax returns.
   (3) Base his audit fee on a percentage of the proceeds of his client's share issue.
   (4) Own preferred shares in a corporation which is an audit client.
   (5) None of the above. (CICA, adapted)

GROUP III
PROBLEMS

20–36. Upon completion of all field work on September 23, 1979, the following standard report was rendered by Timothy Ross to the directors of Rancho Corporation Ltd.

To the Directors of
Rancho Corporation Ltd.:

We have examined the balance sheet and the statement of income and retained earnings of Rancho Corporation as at July 31, 1979. In accordance with your instructions, a complete audit was conducted.

In many respects, this was an unusual year for Rancho Corporation Ltd. The weakening of the economy in the early part of the year and the strike of plant employees in the summer of 1979 led to a decline in sales and net income. After making several tests of sales records, nothing came to our attention that would indicate that sales have not been properly recorded.

In our opinion, with the explanation given above, and with the exception of some minor errors that are considered immaterial, these financial statements present fairly the financial position of Rancho Corporation Ltd. as at July 31, 1979 and the results of its operations for the year then ended in accordance with pronouncements of the Canadian Institutes of Chartered Accountants applied consistently throughout the period.

Timothy Ross, CA
September 23, 1979

Required:

List and explain deficiencies and omissions in the auditor's report. The type of opinion (unqualified, qualified, adverse, or denial) is of no consequence and need not be discussed.

Organize your answer sheet by paragraph (scope, explanatory, and opinion) of the auditor's report. (AICPA, adapted)

20–37. The financial statements of Tiber Ltd. have never been audited by an independent CA. Recently Tiber's management asked Anthony Burns, CA, to conduct a special study of Tiber's internal control; this management advisory services engagement will not include an examination of Tiber's financial statements.

Required:

a. Describe the inherent limitations that should be recognized in considering the potential effectiveness of any system of internal control.

b. Explain and contrast the review of internal control that Burns might make as part of an examination of financial statements with his special study of Tiber's internal control, covering each of the following:

1. Objectives of review or study.
2. Scope of review or study.
3. Nature and content of reports.

Organize your answer for part b as follows:

Examination of financial statements	Special study
1. Objective	1. Objective
2. Scope	2. Scope
3. Report	3. Report

c. In connection with a loan application, Tiber plans to submit the CA's report on his special study of internal control, together with its unaudited financial statements, to the Fourth Provincial Bank.

Discuss the propriety of this use of the CA's report on internal control. (AICPA, adapted)

20–38. Your client, Quaid Ltd., requests your assistance in rewriting the footnote presented below, to make it clearer and more concise.

Note 6. The indenture relating to the long-term debt contains certain provisions regarding the maintenance of working capital, the payment of dividends, and the purchase of the company's capital stock. The most restrictive of these provisions requires that (a) working capital will be maintained at not less than $4,500,000; (b) the company cannot pay cash dividends or purchase its capital stock, if after it has done so, working capital is less than $5,000,000; and (c) cash dividends paid since January 1, 1975, plus the excess of capital stock purchased over the proceeds of stock sold during the same period, cannot exceed 70 percent of net earnings (since January 1, 1975) plus $250,000. At December 31, 1979, $2,441,291 of retained earnings was available for the payment of dividends under this last provision, as follows:

Net earnings since January 1, 1975	$5,478,127
70 percent of above	$3,834,688
Additional amount available under indenture	250,000
	$4,084,688
Cash dividends paid since January 1, 1975	1,643,397
Retained earnings available	$2,441,291

Required:

Rewrite the footnote in accordance with your client's instructions.

20–39. "The accounting profession should encourage public companies to present budgeted financial statements for the forthcoming year in the same detail and following the same rules as those used in preparing historical financial statements. The auditor's report should be required to encompass both the historical and budgeted statements."

Required:

From the accounting and auditing points of view, what are the:

a. Advantages of the proposal.

b. Difficulties in implementing the proposal. (CICA)

20–40. Y Co. Ltd. manufactures, sells, and services heating equipment. Most of the manufacturing activity takes place during the summer months and the selling and servicing during the winter. Normally, therefore, the company generates a positive cash flow in the winter and a negative cash flow in the summer. Y Co. Ltd.'s fiscal year-end is April 30.

The president of the company, Mr. D, has stated that in recent years the company has been experiencing increasing financial difficulty, largely because of changes in heating equipment technology. He also maintains that the company could adapt to these changes if only it could raise the capital to cover the necessary product development costs. However, the company's shares have dropped from $5 to $1 in the past two years, making a share issue unrealistic in the foreseeable future. Moreover, the company has debentures outstanding of $1,000,-000 which are payable over the next twenty years, beginning in 1979.

The financial statements of Y Co. Ltd. for the year ended April 30, 1978, showed the following information:

	1978	1977
Loss for the year	$ 238,000	$ 115,000
Working capital deficiency	605,000	310,000
Share capital	1,000,000	1,000,000
Deficit	820,000	582,000

In addition, during the winter season of 1977/78, the company had for the first time experienced a negative cash flow.

The opinion paragraph of the auditors' report on the financial statements for the year ended April 30, 1978, was as follows:

In our opinion, subject to the ability of the company to continue as a going concern, these financial statements present fairly the financial position of the company as at April 30, 1978 and the results of its operations and the change in financial position for the year then ended, in accordance with generally accepted accounting principles applied on a basis consistent with that of the preceding year.

Required:

List the arguments for and against the above qualification in the auditors' report. (CICA, adapted)

20–41. Jiffy Clerical Services is a corporation which furnishes temporary office help to its customers. Billings are rendered monthly based on predetermined hourly rates. You have examined the company's financial statements for several years. Following is an abbreviated statement of assets and liabilities on the modified cash basis as of December 31, 1979:

Assets

Cash	$20,000
Advances to employees	1,000
Equipment and autos, less accumulated depreciation	25,000
Total Assets	$46,000

Liabilities

Employees' payroll taxes withheld	$ 8,000
Bank loan payable	10,000
Estimated income taxes on cash basis profits	10,000
Total Liabilities	$28,000
Net Assets	$18,000

Represented by

Common stock	$ 3,000
Cash profits retained in the business	15,000
	$18,000

Required:

a. Prepare the report you would issue covering the statement of assets and liabilities as of December 31, 1979, as summarized above, and the related statement of cash revenue and expenses for the year ended that date.

b. Briefly discuss and justify your modifications of the standard audit report on accrual basis statements.

20–42. Global Ltd., an audit client of your CA firm, has several wholly owned subsidiaries in foreign countries which are audited by other independent auditors in those countries. The financial statements of all subsidiaries were consolidated with the financial statements of the parent company and the foreign auditors' reports were furnished to your CA firm.

You are now preparing your firm's opinion on the consolidated balance sheet and statements of income, retained earnings, and changes in financial position for the year ended June 30, 1979. These statements were prepared on a comparative basis with those of last year.

Required:

a. How would you evaluate and accept the independence and professional reputations of the foreign auditors?

b. Under what circumstances may the principal auditors assume responsibility for the work of another CA firm to the same extent as if they had performed the work themselves?

c. Assume that both last year and this year you were willing to utilize the reports of the other independent auditors in expressing your opinion on the consolidated financial statements, but were unwilling to take full responsibility for performance of the work underlying their opinions. Assuming your examination of the parent company's financial statements would allow you to render an unqualified opinion, prepare (1) the necessary disclosure to be contained in the scope paragraph and (2) the complete opinion paragraph of your firm's audit report.

d. What modification(s), if any, would be necessary in your firm's report if the financial statements for the prior year were unaudited? (AICPA, adapted)

20–43. Various types of accounting changes can affect the consistency reporting standard of the generally accepted auditing standards.

Assume that the following list describes changes which have a material effect on a client's financial statements for the current year.

1. A change from the completed-contract method to the percentage-of-completion method of accounting for long-term construction-type contracts.
2. A change in the estimated service lives of previously recorded plant assets based on newly acquired information.
3. Correction of a mathematical error in inventory pricing made in a prior period.
4. A change from prime costing to full absorption costing for inventory valuation.
5. A change from presentation of financial statements of individual companies to presentation of consolidated financial statements.
6. A change from deferring and amortizing preproduction costs to recording such costs as an expense when incurred because future benefits of the costs have become doubtful. The new accounting method was adopted in recognition of the change in estimated future benefits.
7. A change from the Fifo method of inventory pricing to the Lifo method of inventory pricing.

Required:

Identify the type of change which is described in each item above, state whether any modification is required in the auditors' report *as it relates to the standard of reporting*, and state whether the prior years' financial statements should be restated when presented in comparative form with the current year's statement. Organize your answer sheet as shown below.

For example, a change from the Lifo method of inventory pricing to Fifo method of inventory pricing would appear as shown.

Item no.	Type of change	Should auditors' report be modified?	Should prior-year's statements be restated?
Example	An accounting change from one generally accepted accounting principle to another generally accepted accounting principle.	Yes	Yes

(AICPA, adapted)

20–44. Nancy Miller, CA, has completed field work for her examination of the financial statements of Nickles Ltd. for the year ended March 31, 1979, and now is preparing her audit report. Presented below are four independent and unrelated assumptions concerning this examination:

Assumption 1

The CA was engaged on April 15, 1979, to examine the financial statements for the year ended March 31, 1979, and was not present to observe the taking of the physical inventory of March 31, 1979. Her alternative procedures included examination of shipping and receiving documents with regard to transactions during the year under review as well as transactions since the year-end; extensive review of the inventory-count sheets; and discussion of the physical inventory procedures with responsible company personnel. She has also satisfied herself as to inventory valuation and consistency in valuation method. Inventory quantities are determined solely by means of physical count (*Note:* Assume that the CA properly is relying upon the examination of another auditor with respect to the beginning inventory.)

Assumption 2

During the year ended March 31, 1979, Nickles's new Pollution Control Systems Division incurred developmental costs which are material to the company's financial statements and are presented in the balance sheet as deferred research and development costs. The pollution-control equipment developed thus far has performed well in controlled laboratory simulations, but it has not been tested in a practical setting. Nickles cannot afford to proceed further with this project, but in management's opinion sufficient governmental funds can be obtained to fully develop functioning equipment that can be sold at a price that will permit recovery of these costs. There is support for management's optimism, but no commitment of governmental funds has been received to date. Nickles' board of directors refuses to write off development costs applicable to the Pollution Control Systems division.

Assumption 3

As of April 1, 1979, Nickles has an unused balance of $1,378,000 of federal income tax net operating loss carry-over that will expire at the end of the company's fiscal years as follows: $432,000 in 1980, $870,000 in 1981, and $76,000 in 1982. Nickles's management expects that the company will have enough taxable income to use the loss carry-over before it expires.

Assumption 4

On February 28, 1979, Nickles paid cash for all of the outstanding stock of Ashworth, Inc., a small manufacturer. The business combination was consummated as of that date and has been accounted for as a purchase.

Required:

For each assumption described above discuss:

a. In detail, the appropriate disclosures, if any, in the financial statements and accompanying footnotes.

b. The effect, if any, on the standard audit report. For this requirement assume that Nickles makes the appropriate disclosures, if any, recommended in "*a*."

Note: Complete your discussion of each assumption (both *"a"* and *"b"*) before beginning discussion of the next assumption. In considering each independent assumption, assume that the other three situations did not occur. Organize your answer sheet as follows:

Assumption number	a.	Financial statements and footnotes	b.	Audit report

(AICPA, adapted)

20–45. The complete set of financial statements for Kaye Ltd. for the year ended August 31, 1979, is presented below.

KAYE LTD.
Balance Sheet
(August 31, 1979)   (in thousands of dollars)

Assets

Cash		$ 103
Marketable securities, at cost which approximates market value		54
Trade accounts receivable (net of $65,000 allowance for doubtful accounts)		917
Inventories, at cost		775
Property, plant and equipment	$3,200	
Less: Accumulated depreciation	1,475	1,725
Prepayments and other assets		125
Total Assets		$3,699

Liabilities and Shareholders' Equity

Accounts payable	$ 221
Accrued taxes	62
Bank loans and long-term debt	1,580
Total Liabilities	$1,863
Capital stock, $10 par value (authorized 50,000 shares, issued and outstanding 42,400 shares) ...	424
Premium on capital stock	366
Retained earnings	1,046
Total Shareholders' Equity	$1,836
Total Liabilities and Shareholders' Equity	$3,699

KAYE LTD.
Statement of Income and Retained Earnings
(for the year ended August 31, 1979)

(in thousands of dollars)

Product sales (net of $850,000 sales returns and allowances)		$10,700
Cost of goods sold		8,700
Gross profit on sales		$ 2,000
Operating expenses:		
Selling expenses	$1,500	
General and administrative expenses	940	2,440
Operating loss		$ (440)
Interest expense		150
Net loss		$ (590)
Retained earnings, September 1, 1978		1,700
		$ 1,110
Dividends:		
Cash—$1 per share	$ 40	
Stock—6% of shares outstanding	24	64
Retained earnings, August 31, 1979		$ 1,046

Required:

List deficiencies and omissions in Kaye Ltd.'s financial statements and discuss the probable effect of the deficiency or omission on the auditors' report. Assume that Kaye Ltd. is unwilling to change the financial statements or make additional disclosures therein.

Consider each deficiency or omission separately, and do not consider the cumulative effect of the deficiencies and omissions on the auditors' report. There are no arithmetical errors in the statements.

Organize your answer sheet in two columns as indicated below and write your answer in the order of appearance within the general headings of Balance Sheet. Statement of Income and Retained Earnings, and Other.

Financial statement deficiency or omission	Discussion of effect on auditors' report

(AICPA, adapted)

Comprehensive case

D ENTERPRISES LIMITED

Nature of engagement

CA is employed by a firm of Chartered Accountants. His employer has accepted an engagement which involves assisting a firm of lawyers in a potential lawsuit. The lawyers' clients are the new shareholders of D Enterprises Limited (hereafter referred to as DEL or the company) and its subsidiary. The possible defendants in the potential lawsuit are (1) the former shareholders of DEL (none of whom were directors or officers); (2) some of the former directors or officers of DEL; (3) the two former auditors of DEL and its subsidiary; and (4) a firm of public accountants who were engaged by the new shareholders of DEL to perform a purchase investigation of DEL and its subsidiary.

A brief introduction to the parties involved in this action follows:

New shareholders of D Enterprises Limited (DEL) (Messrs. X, Y, and Z)

The group which purchased all the voting shares of DEL as of July 1, 1978, in accordance with a Purchase and Sale Agreement.

Former shareholders of D Enterprises Limited

The group which entered into the Purchase and Sale Agreement with the new shareholders.

A firm of lawyers, CA's client

The firm of lawyers hired by the new shareholders of DEL to assist in a potential lawsuit. These lawyers have engaged CA's firm to assist them.

R Manufacturing Limited (RML) (the subsidiary company)

DEL acquired 80 percent of the voting shares of RML effective July 1, 1975.

Former directors or officers of DEL

The former management group of DEL was largely replaced by the new shareholders. Of the seven-person board of directors, three were also senior officers of the company. These three were dismissed in August 1978, leaving only two of the five senior officers of DEL in the new management group.

New & Co.

Appointed auditors of DEL and its subsidiary effective July 1, 1978, the date of purchase of DEL.

Purchinvest & Co.

Firm of public accountants hired by the new shareholders to do a purchase investigation of DEL and its subsidiary prior to buying the shares.

Old & Co.

Former auditors of DEL.

Previous & Co.

Former auditors of RML. No agency relationship with Old & Co.

CA's employer was not anxious to accept this type of engagement whereby it might end up in court criticizing the work of another firm of public accountants. However, the lawyers pointed out the responsibility which public accountants in general have to society to ensure quality and fairness. CA's employer then checked with the ethics committee of its provincial institute/order which agreed that it would not be unethical to accept such an assignment.

CA has been asked by his employer to write the first draft of a report addressed to the firm of lawyers. The lawyers have asked CA's employer to focus on the following two broad matters:

1. The new shareholders of DEL have been told by their auditors, New & Co. (who were appointed auditors of DEL and its subsidiary effective the date of purchase of DEL's shares by the new shareholders), that the accounting and auditing principles and procedures used in the past were not the most appropriate for the company. The new shareholders were very concerned to learn this because a portion of the purchase price of DEL's shares was determined with the assumption that "generally accepted accounting principles and auditing standards" had been adhered to in respect of the financial statements and the audit examination. They thus hired the lawyers to investigate these matters and advise them whether there were grounds for possible out-of-court settlement or a court case. The new shareholders had specifically hired another firm of public accountants, Purchinvest & Co., to do a purchase investigation of DEL and its subsidiary prior to buying the shares.

The lawyers wish CA's firm to investigate the allegations made by New & Co. so that the lawyers (*not CA's firm*) can form a judgment on whether there are grounds for a lawsuit. That is, the lawyers wish to appraise the likelihood of being successful against some or all of the defendants in the potential lawsuit. Not being accountants, the lawyers wish a report using language and detail which will be informative to them in accomplishing their clients' wishes. They also wish to be in a position where they will have anticipated the validity of counter arguments which could be raised by lawyers for possible defendants.

The lawyers must prove that financial damages to the new shareholders have resulted. Hence, the lawyers wish a tabulation of *important* "errors" in accounting and auditing in DEL and its subsidiary. This tabulation must indicate, where possible, the approximate dollar effect of "errors." The tabulation must also indicate which so-called "errors" are clearly unacceptable from the point of view of generally accepted accounting principles and auditing standards and those which are debatable or disputable because (for example) more than one principle or practice exists in Canada or the industry.

2. The new management of DEL and its subsidiary have also encountered some former questionable or unusual business practices, which they reported to the new shareholders of DEL. The new management felt that further investigation was needed in order to ascertain whether these practices were reasonable, or intentional fraud, or simply due to incompetence and inefficiency by some members of the former management teams of the two companies.

CA's firm has been engaged by the same lawyers to investigate the list of "former business practices" and transactions (*see Appendix IV*). The firm is to give its opinion as to the wisdom of these practices and transactions and its calculations of their effect. Also, where possible, the firm should give recommendations on how it would have arranged the transaction or business practice so that the problem could have been avoided. CA's firm has clearly informed the lawyers that it is not undertaking to ascertain whether some members of the former management team were incompetent, or intended to commit fraud.

However, CA's firm is prepared to gather relevant data and give its opinion on the approximate dollar amounts involved (wherever ascertainable) and also to indicate possible counter arguments, if any. The lawyers wish to use this information to form an opinion on the extent of possible damages and on the likelihood of success of a potential lawsuit by either the new shareholders or the company against the various defendants.

Required:

Assume the role of CA and prepare the first draft of the report requested by the lawyers. Additional information is provided in the following Appendices. (CICA, adapted)

INDEX TO APPENDICES

APPENDIX I

Description of companies

DEL owns 80 percent of the voting shares of RML (the subsidiary). Both companies were incorporated some time ago under the *Canada Corporations Act,* which is still the governing legislation. (*Ignore the Canada Business Corporations Act.*) RML was acquired effective July 1, 1975, for $3,300,000. The remaining 20 percent of the subsidiary's voting shares are owned by the founders of the company. These minority shareholders have stated that they may wish to sell their shares to DEL sometime around June 1980. The selling price will have to be negotiated at that time.

DEL has two main operating divisions, the "Real Estate and Investment" division and the "Construction" division. All of its operations are in one Canadian province. The former division is engaged in buying and selling land, office and apartment buildings, and shopping centres, as well as in managing some of these investments. It will occasionally acquire undeveloped land, subdivide it and sell it, but generally tends to avoid single dwelling housing projects. The Construction division acts as a general contractor and builds many of the apartment and office buildings and shopping centres which are owned or managed by the Real Estate and Investment division. The Construction division also bids for other general building construction, and sometimes receives cost-plus contracts from federal, provincial, and municipal governments.

RML makes inexpensive furniture, kitchen cabinets, vanities and similar items which DEL uses in the apartments and other buildings which it constructs. The subsidiary must actively compete with several other companies for most of its sales because only 20 percent to 30 percent of recent sales are to DEL. RML has one manufacturing plant and does most of its business within a 100-mile radius of the plant.

APPENDIX II

Purchase and Sale Agreement

CA and his staff, some of whom are junior employees who require supervision, commence the task of assembling data which might be relevant for the report. One staff member has taken the following excerpts from the agreement between the former and new shareholders of DEL.

Clause 4: This agreement is effective July 1, 1978 . . . whereupon the purchasers will deliver in cash or certified cheque to the sellers the consideration as set out in Clause 5 in exchange for all of the issued and outstanding voting shares of D Enterprises Limited. . . .

Clause 5: The total purchase consideration referred to in Clause 4 is made up of the following sums:

(a) a lump sum of $8,000,000 which is entirely independent of the past and future profitability of D Enterprises Limited and its subsidiary, and

(b) a sum equal to the net income of D Enterprises Limited and its subsidiary for the two years ended June 30, 1978, as computed in accordance with generally accepted accounting principles and auditing standards. . . .

(c) a contingent consideration based on average annual profits of each of the three years ended June 30, 1981, computed as follows:

10 percent of any annual average profits for July 1, 1978, to June 30, 1981, in excess of 120 percent of the average annual profits of the two years ended June 30, 1978. This contingent consideration is payable on or before December 31, 1981.

APPENDIX III

Report of Purchinvest & Co.

To Messrs, X, Y, and Z (prospective shareholders of D Enterprises Limited):

You have engaged us, per your letter of May 3, 1978, and per our written agreement of May 7, 1978, to conduct a purchase investigation of D Enterprises Limited and its subsidiary.

You have asked us to investigate whether the financial statements of these two companies for the years ended June 30, 1977, and June 30, 1978, were prepared in accordance with generally accepted accounting principles and examined in accordance with generally accepted auditing standards. You have specifically asked us to review the working papers of the respective auditors of these companies to ascertain the appropriateness of accounting policies and procedures followed in these two years. You have also asked for a thorough investigation of business practices which might have an effect on future profitability of the companies. We understand that you intend to use our report to assist you in deciding whether or not to buy the voting shares of D Enterprises Limited and what price you should pay for the shares.

We have conducted an examination of the financial statements and audit working papers of the two companies for the two years ended June 30, 1978. We have also made such enquiries as we thought necessary in order to assess any possible negative impact of current business practices on future profitability of the companies. We report that nothing has come to our attention which would indicate that the financial statements of these two companies for the two years ended June 30, 1978, are not presented in accordance with generally accepted accounting principles or were not examined in accordance with generally accepted auditing standards. We also report that both of these businesses are subject to more than average risk, due to the nature of their operations, but that nothing out of the ordinary has come to our attention regarding future profitability of these companies.

Faithfully yours,
PURCHINVEST & CO.

APPENDIX IV

Former business practices and transactions

The lawyers furnished the following list, prepared by the new management of DEL, of business practices and transactions in DEL which they were asked to investigate in collaboration with CA's firm:

1. Payments had been made in calendar years 1975, 1976, and 1977 to a variety of persons and organizations. Although some of these payments were to political parties, several smaller sums seem to have been paid to individuals who were described as "lobbyists" for the company. As far as could be determined at the moment, the sums involved were $180,000, $75,000, and $55,000 respectively in the years ended June 30, 1976, 1977, and 1978.

2. In June 1976, the company sold for $5,000,000 to the brother of the vice president of the company at that time, under a sale-and-leaseback agreement, equipment with a net book value of $5,800,000. The terms of the non-cancellable lease required the company to pay the lessor the following annual sums:

July 1, 1976	$ 221,000
July 1, 1977	221,000
July 1, 1978	221,000
July 1, 1979	2,300,000
July 1, 1980	2,300,000
July 1, 1981	2,300,000

The company has use of the equipment until June 30, 1982, and must pay for all operating costs of it. Its resale value at June 30, 1982, is estimated at $400,000 and the lessor is willing to arrange a new lease at this future date.

3. Effective January 1, 1976, an executive pension plan was arranged for the five senior officers of DEL by the seven-person board of directors (three of whom were also the senior officers who might benefit from the plan). At this same date, each signed a five-year management contract. (Three of the five were dismissed in August 1978, and the company is negotiating a settlement of their contract with lawyers for each.) The terms of the plan called for a lump-sum payment of $1,000,000 to the independent trustee of the plan for past services plus current payments of 10 percent of annual salary. The past service lump sum of $1,000,000 was paid in June 1976 and expensed. Also a $1,000,000 payment on account for the five-year period from 1976 to 1980 was made to the trustee in June 1976 and expensed.

4. Effective January 1, 1978, for a period of three years and six months the same five senior officers (as in 3 above) agreed to a bonus plan. The plan was negotiated with the approval of the board of directors of DEL.

   The plan called for a bonus of 5 percent of income before income taxes in the "Real Estate and Investment" division of the company to be paid into a special fund which would then be allocated among the five at the discretion of the then president of DEL (who was one of the five). The only informative definitions set forth in the plan described the "Real Estate and Investment" division as one separate from DEL's other division, "Construction."

5. Commencing July 1, 1976, the company chose to capitalize all property taxes and interest on projects under construction until such time as they are 50 percent occupied. Interest was capitalized at 10 percent per annum of cost (or cost-to-date) of these projects. Management believed that the latter charge fairly reflected the cost needed to finance these assets.

6. An accrual of $200,000 was made in the accounts of DEL as of June 30, 1978, for supposed bonuses to executives. On further examination, the new manager learned that this was prepaid salary for the year

commencing July 1, 1978. The $200,000 was borrowed from RML and paid to three former executives of DEL in July 1978.

7. Neither Old & Co. nor Purchinvest & Co. obtained letters of representation from the executives of DEL because the executives "did not want to bother with such nonsense."

8. In 1972, DEL established a policy of using the "completed contract" basis of recognizing revenue from construction contracts expected to take less than one year to complete. Contract 74-002 was completed in August 1976 after a seven-month construction period. A profit of $620,000 resulted, but $600,000 of the profit was accrued in the year ended June 30, 1976, on orders from the former executives of DEL.

APPENDIX V

Review by CA's staff

CA's staff has not been allowed access to the working papers of the former auditors of DEL and its subsidiary (ie., Old & Co. and Previous & Co.). The latter two auditing firms are aware of the situation and are being very careful. However, some of the audit working papers were prepared by the client, who retained a copy, and others were photocopied by the auditors and given to the client to assist them in various reconciliations. Hence, for some aspects of the business, CA's staff has been able to piece together what work each auditor likely performed before expressing an opinion on the financial statements. CA's staff has noted the following, in some instances using information furnished by New & Co.:

1. The auditors' reports for each company for the years ended June 30, 1977, and 1978 were standard form *CICA Handbook* wording with no qualifications. However, the auditors' report for DEL added the following sentence after the opinion paragraph: "In verifying the Investment in R Manufacturing Limited, we have relied on the report of the auditors of that Company."

2. Contract 74-008 of DEL, completed in late August 1978 seems to have been recorded in the audited financial statements as follows:

	Years ended June 30		
	1978	*1977*	*1976*
Revenues	$1,800,000	$1,200,000	$ 400,000
Costs	1,500,000	900,000	850,000
Gross profit (loss)	$ 300,000	$ 300,000	$(450,000)

According to several employees of DEL, neither the old auditors (Old & Co.) nor Purchinvest & Co. discussed this contract with senior officials or engineers of the company. In late August 1978, the company had to record a further cost of $150,000, offset by no revenue. From what CA's staff was able to learn, both Purchinvest & Co. and Old & Co. performed the same audit tests, which were:

a. They read the contract between DEL and the customer.
b. They examined billings to the customer and checked subsequent receipt of cash.
c. They test-checked invoices in one week per year through from the placing of purchase requisitions to cash disbursements. This included some checking of payroll records for construction site employees.
d. The invoices checked in (c) were chosen using a statistical sample method.

CA's staff obtained the following figures from the company's engineering staff re Contract 74-008:

a. The planned costs, revenues and completion dates per the bidding schedule dated January, 1975, showed:

	Completion date	Costs	Revenue	Profit
Stage 1.............	March 1976	$ 350,000	$ 400,000	$ 50,000
Stage 2.............	April 1977	1,050,000	1,200,000	150,000
Stage 3.............	June 1978	1,600,000	1,800,000	200,000
		$3,000,000	$3,400,000	$400,000

b. Actual costs as of late August 1978 showed:

	Completion date	Costs	Revenue	Profit (loss)
Stage 1.............	May 1976	$ 850,000	$ 400,000	$(450,000)
Stage 2.............	June 1977	900,000	1,200,000	300,000
Stage 3.............	August 1978	1,650,000	1,800,000	150,000
		$3,400,000	$3,400,000	$ —

CA's staff also gathered the undernoted from a check of the company's accounting records, plus discussions with the company's senior engineering staff:

Status as of	Costs to date	Expected future costs to completion	Revenue on work completed to date (billed and unbilled revenue)
June 30, 1976	$1,100,000	$3,300,000	$ 500,000
June 30, 1977	2,400,000	1,200,000	1,700,000
June 30, 1978	3,200,000	200,000	3,400,000
August 31, 1978 (completion) ...	3,400,000	nil	3,400,000

The senior engineering staff stated that the contract was very unusual because they encountered serious foundation problems. To quote the senior engineer, "In the spring of 1976, we thought that we would lose our shirts; nothing went according to plan." The senior engineer reviewed CA's work sheets and asked several questions about the above cost and revenue tabulation, and concluded that it "seems as accurate as we'll ever get it."

3. RML employs job order costing in its manufacturing operations using actual costs of direct material and direct labour but predetermined overhead rates. The rate was set in September 1975, at 30 percent of direct labour cost and has not been revised since. The company's products are sometimes made in batches of 40 or 50 (e.g., tables, chairs and store display racks and counters) in which case the total manufacturing cost for the batch is divided by 40 or 50 to arrive at a unit cost.

A working paper prepared by Previous & Co. for the year ended June 30, 1977 shows:

Direct labour cost $1,300,000
Manufacturing overhead 310,000

RML uses its unit costs to bid on contracts for furniture required by shopping centres and apartment building owners. Also, a bonus system for manufacturing foremen is based on unit manufacturing costs.

4. RML uses a computer service to process its payroll, inventory and cost accounting reports. RML maintains hand-compiled general ledger control accounts for all of the subsidiary records and reports processed by the computer. The control accounts have not been balanced to the subsidiary ledgers for several years (since the computer has been used). Previous & Co. ignored the differences, using the general ledger accounts except for work in process and finished goods inventory balances.

5. The replacement value of RML's major assets and liabilities was as follows on July 1, 1975:

	Net book value	Replacement value
Finished goods inventory	$ 50,000	$ 54,500
Building	1,250,000	1,650,000
Equipment	1,600,000	1,740,000
Long-term investments	30,000	15,000
Land	250,000	550,000
Debenture payable	500,000	560,000

The company depreciates its building at a 3 percent rate and equipment at a 10 percent rate both on the straight-line basis. The remaining life of the building was 20 years and the equipment 7 years as of July 1, 1975.

6. RML's long-term investments consist of common shares of three Canadian companies listed on a major Canadian stock exchange. The shares were acquired many years ago; their market value at June 30, 1978, was $12,000.

7. RML's provision for warranty was set up in 1974. It represents a provision in case of unusual warranty costs incurred under the company's one year guarantee on most of its manufactured goods. The company expenses warranty expenditures as they are incurred. In the years ended June 30, 1978, 1977, and 1976, the respective expenditures were $20,100, $14,200, and $7,300.

8. RML's debenture is payable in a foreign currency unit. At the time of issue in 1960, $1 Canadian = Foreign Currency (F.C.) unit. The exchange rates for 1 F.C. were as follows in recent years:

June 30, 1978	$1.40 Canadian = 1 F.C. unit
June 30, 1977	1.35 Canadian = 1 F.C. unit
June 30, 1976	1.10 Canadian = 1 F.C. unit
June 30, 1975	1.00 Canadian = 1 F.C. unit

9. RML sold furniture and related products to DEL per orders from DEL's management, at 10 percent above RML's cost. These sales and their fair market values as estimated by CA's staff with the assistance of RML's staff were:

Year ended	Selling price to DEL	Fair market value
June 30, 1978	$650,000	$700,000
June 30, 1977	750,000	800,000
June 30, 1976	700,000	900,000

DEL had the following inventory acquisitions from RML in its year-end inventory, at cost to DEL:

Year ended June 30, 1978	$ 71,500
Year ended June 30, 1977	123,750
Year ended June 30, 1976	77,000

10. In March 1978, one of DEL's fully owned apartment buildings was totally destroyed by fire through the negligence of contractors work-

ing on a site nearby. By June 30, 1978, insurance companies admitted liability in writing and agreed to pay DEL $1,700,000 for the furniture, contents, and structure. Although most of DEL's buildings are now being depreciated on a sinking fund basis at 5 percent interest over 40 years, this particular one had been depreciated on the declining-balance method. Also, the contents had been fully depreciated. Hence, its overall carrying value at June 30, 1978, was $860,000 net of deferred taxes and accumulated depreciation. No entry has yet been made to record the fire loss and resulting claim.

11. DEL is 50 percent owner of a joint venture incorporated in July, 1977. The other 50 percent is held by another real estate development company. The principal asset of the joint venture is a 60-unit row-housing development under construction, which is fully sold. The unaudited financial statements to June 30, 1978, have recorded revenue based on the selling prices of the 60 units and have estimated costs for the 40 uncompleted units. The unaudited income statement shows a profit of $280,000, but DEL has not recorded any of this. The owner of the other 50 percent of the joint venture does not want to pay for the cost of an audit.

APPENDIX VI

D ENTERPRISES LIMITED (DEL)
Balance Sheets
(audited)

	June 30		
	1978	1977	1976
Assets			
Revenue-producing properties, at cost	$30,004,700	$28,900,300	$26,500,000
Accumulated depreciation	12,401,600	11,650,000	10,400,000
	17,603,100	17,250,300	16,100,000
Investment in joint venture, at cost	600,000	–	–
Investment in R Manufacturing Limited at cost	3,300,000	3,300,000	3,300,000
Land held for future development	1,960,000	1,960,000	1,300,200
Construction in progress	3,215,840	3,101,970	2,960,800
Cash	1,538,500	2,217,440	3,874,600
Accounts receivable	3,891,500	3,195,600	1,020,400
Inventories	160,500	212,400	187,300
Prepaid expenses	84,770	61,490	33,700
	5,675,270	5,686,930	5,116,000
Construction equipment	4,243,990	4,101,665	3,890,700
Accumulated depreciation	2,640,100	2,260,065	2,160,700
	1,603,890	1,841,600	1,730,000
	$33,958,100	$33,140,800	$30,507,000

Liabilities and Shareholders' Equity

Bank loan	$ 100,000	$ —	$ 120,000
Due to subsidiary company	360,000	220,000	100,000
Accounts payable and accrued charges	1,510,300	1,220,000	1,115,800
Income tax payable	110,100	160,500	49,600
Other liabilities	104,700	67,300	121,200
	2,185,100	1,667,800	1,506,600
Mortgages payable, 10%–14%, annually to 2000	13,987,600	13,492,700	12,300,400
Debenture payable, 10%, due 1994	5,000,000	5,000,000	5,000,000
Deferred income taxes	2,890,000	2,710,000	2,690,000
Deferred progress billings	2,001,400	2,610,300	2,510,000
Shareholders' equity:			
Common shares—authorized and issued 50,000 shares	1,000,000	1,000,000	1,000,000
Contributed surplus	1,200,000	1,200,000	1,200,000
Retained earnings	5,694,000	5,460,000	4,300,000
	7,894,000	7,660,000	6,500,000
	$33,958,100	$33,140,800	$30,507,000

Income Statements
(audited)

Year ended June 30

	1978	1977	1976
Revenue:			
Rentals	$ 4,445,650	$ 4,177,500	$ 4,026,450
Construction profit	3,101,700	1,960,350	2,455,000
Sale of revenue-producing assets and construction equipment	2,921,290	5,271,650	9,137,150
Other	390,600	490,900	964,400
	10,859,240	11,900,400	16,583,000
Expenses:			
Net cost of assets sold	1,004,760	643,080	7,047,950
Depreciation	1,365,340	1,354,100	1,234,600
Maintenance	1,003,770	988,315	963,400
Administration	2,355,400	2,001,620	4,101,250
Rental and other	330,100	363,200	210,000
Interest	2,265,870	2,190,085	2,620,800
	8,325,240	7,540,400	16,178,000
Income before income taxes	2,534,000	4,360,000	405,000
Taxes on income	1,300,000	2,200,000	200,000
Net Income	$ 1,234,000	$ 2,160,000	$ 205,000
Net income per share	$24.68	$43.20	$ 4.10

Statements of Retained Earnings
(audited)

	Year ended June 30		
	1978	1977	1976
Beginning of year	$ 5,460,000	$ 4,300,000	$ 4,195,000
Add net income	1,234,000	2,160,000	205,000
	6,694,000	6,460,000	4,400,000
Deduct dividends	1,000,000	1,000,000	100,000
End of year	$ 5,694,000	$ 5,460,000	$ 4,300,000

APPENDIX VII

R MANUFACTURING LIMITED (RML)
Balance Sheets
(audited)

	June 30		
	1978	1977	1976
Assets			
Current:			
Cash	$ 206,000	$ 161,000	$ 270,000
Refundable income tax	3,000	3,000	—
Accounts receivable	514,500	466,000	222,000
Inventories, at cost:			
Finished goods	162,400	120,500	78,000
Work in process	79,300	65,000	49,000
Materials	81,200	70,000	60,000
Prepaid expenses	34,600	26,000	21,000
	1,081,000	911,500	700,000
Long-term productive assets:			
Building	2,195,000	2,190,000	2,100,000
Equipment	3,065,000	2,810,000	2,700,000
	5,260,000	5,000,000	4,800,000
Less accumulated depreciation	2,545,000	2,190,000	1,850,000
	2,715,000	2,810,000	2,950,000
Land	350,000	240,000	250,000
	3,065,000	3,050,000	3,200,000
Long-term investments, at cost	30,000	30,000	30,000
	$4,176,000	$3,991,500	$3,930,000

Liabilities and Shareholders' Equity

Current liabilities:

Accounts payable	$ 162,000	$ 140,000	$ 280,000
Income tax payable	8,000	12,000	20,000
Bank loan payable	–	16,000	–
	170,000	168,000	300,000
Debenture payable, 12%, due June 30, 1980 (Note 1)	500,000	500,000	500,000
Deferred income taxes	31,000	32,000	30,000
Provision for warranty	100,000	100,000	100,000
Shareholders' equity:			
Common shares—authorized and issued 100,000 shares of no par value	1,000,000	1,000,000	1,000,000
Contributed surplus	100,000	100,000	200,000
Retained earnings	2,275,000	2,091,500	1,800,000
	3,375,000	3,191,500	3,000,000
	$4,176,000	$3,991,500	$3,930,000

Income Statements
(audited)

	Year ended June 30		
	1978	*1977*	*1976*
Revenue	$4,100,000	$4,350,000	$4,200,000
Cost of goods sold	3,098,000	3,200,000	3,000,000
Gross profit	1,002,000	1,150,000	1,200,000
Expenses:			
Depreciation	48,200	45,800	35,000
Interest expense	81,300	77,200	44,240
Selling	383,500	411,900	522,100
Administration	267,500	311,100	323,000
	780,500	846,000	924,340
Income before income taxes	221,500	304,000	275,660
Taxes on income	110,000	152,500	135,660
Income before extraordinary items	111,500	151,500	140,000
Extraordinary items, net of income tax:			
Gain on disposal of land	–	60,000	–
Gain on disposal of equipment	102,000	–	–
	102,000	60,000	–
Net income	$ 213,500	$ 211,500	$ 140,000
Net income per share	$2.14	$2.12	$1.40

Statements of Retained Earnings
(audited)

| | Year ended June 30 | | |
	1978	1977	1976
Balance, beginning of year	$2,091,500	$1,800,000	$1,890,000
Add:			
Net income	213,500	211,500	140,000
Transfer from contributed surplus	–	100,000	–
	213,500	311,500	140,000
Total	2,305,000	2,111,500	2,030,000
Deduct:			
Dividends	30,000	20,000	50,000
Investments written off	–	–	180,000
	30,000	20,000	230,000
Balance, end of year	$2,275,000	$2,091,500	$1,800,000

Notes to Financial Statements

1. Accounting Policy—The company follows the practice of recording debt payable in a foreign currency at the amount received in Canadian funds when the debt was issued. The debenture is payable in F.C. units. At the date of issuance of the debenture, $1 Canadian = 1 F.C. unit. At June 30, 1978, 1 F.C. unit = $1.40 Canadian. At June 30, 1977, 1 F.C. = $1.35 Canadian.

Index

A

This book has been set in 10 and 9 point Caledonia, leaded 2 points. Chapter numbers are 30 point Craw Modern and chapter titles are 18 point Helvetica. The size of the type page is 27 by 45½ picas.